THE BARBOUR COLLECTION OF CONNECTICUT TOWN VITAL RECORDS

THE BARBOUR COLLECTION OF CONNECTICUT TOWN VITAL RECORDS

ROCKY HILL 1765–1854

ROXBURY 1796–1835

SALEM 1836–1852

SALISBURY 1741–1846

Compiled by
Lillian Bentley Karlstrand

General Editor
Lorraine Cook White

Copyright © 2000
Genealogical Publishing Co., Inc.
Baltimore, Maryland
All Rights Reserved
Library of Congress Catalogue Card Number 94-76197
International Standard Book Number 0-8063-1652-7
Made in the United States of America

INTRODUCTION

As early as 1640 the Connecticut Court of Election ordered all magistrates to keep a record of the marriages they performed. In 1644 the registration of births and marriages became the official responsibility of town clerks and registrars, with deaths added to their duties in 1650. From 1660 until the close of the Revolutionary War these vital records of birth, marriage, and death were generally well kept, but then for a period of about two generations until the mid-nineteenth century, the faithful recording of vital records declined in some towns.

General Lucius Barnes Barbour was the Connecticut Examiner of Public Records from 1911 to 1934 and in that capacity directed a project in which the vital records kept by the towns up to about 1850 were copied and abstracted. Barbour previously had directed the publication of the Bolton and Vernon vital records for the Connecticut Historical Society. For this new project he hired several individuals who were experienced in copying old records and familiar with the old script.

Barbour presented the completed transcriptions of town vital records to the Connecticut State Library where the information was typed onto printed forms. The form sheets were then cut, producing twelve small slips from each sheet. The slips for most towns were then alphabetized and the information was then typed a second time on large sheets of rag paper, which were subsequently bound into separate volumes for each town. The slips for all towns were then interfiled, forming a statewide alphabetized slip index for most surviving town vital records.

The dates of coverage vary from town to town, and of course the records of some towns are more complete than others. There are many cases in which an entry may appear two or three times, apparently because that entry was entered by one or more persons. Altogether the entire Barbour Collection--one of the great genealogical manuscript collections and one of the last to be published--covers 137 towns and comprises 14,333 typed pages.

TABLE OF CONTENTS

ROCKY HILL	1
ROXBURY	111
SALEM	123
SALISBURY	141

ABBREVIATIONS

ae.---------age
b.----------born, both
bd.--------buried
B. G.------Burying Ground
bp.--------baptized
d.--------- died, day, or daughter
decd.------deceased
f.----------father
h.----------hour, husband
J. P.-------Justice of Peace
m.---------married or month
res.--------resident
s.----------son
st.---------stillborn
st.b.-------stillborn
w.---------wife
wid.-------widow
wk.--------week
y.----------year

THE BARBOUR COLLECTION OF CONNECTICUT TOWN VITAL RECORDS

ROCKY HILL VITAL RECORDS
1765 – 1854

	Page
ABBE, ABBY, George, of Chatham, m. Mary BROOKS, Feb. 5, 1784	62
Mary Stocking, bp. July 1, 1832	147
Mary Stocking*, m. Chauncey HOLDEN, of Colebrook, Jan. 6, 1833 *(Arnold Copy has "Mary Stocking ABBOT")	77
Reuben, of Glastonbury, m. wid. Mary TRYON, of Chatham, July 9, 1812, by [ ]	72
Sarah, m. Elisha WELLES, b. of 1st Society, [ ], 1805	69
ABBOT*, Mary Stocking, m. Chauncey HOLDEN, of Colebrook, Jan. 6, 1833 *("ABBY" in Church Rec.)	77
ACKINS, Reuben, s. Jos[ep]h, bp. [Dec.] 1765	117
ACKLEY, Michael, m. Anna HUNT, b. of Rocky Hill, Nov. 13, 1853, by Rev. L. Burton Rockwood	47
ADAMS, Amasa, m. Wid. Sarah GRISWOLD, Jan. 15, 1783	62
Augustus F., of Wethersfield, m. Martha Jane GRISWOLD, of Rocky Hill, Oct. 9, 1851, by Rev. L.B. Rockwood	37
Elizabeth P., of Wethersfield, m. Joseph H.B. BUTLER, of Rocky Hill, May 26, 1852, by Rev. L.B. Rockwood	40
Horace, of 1st Society, m. Emeline GOODALE, Nov. 25, 1829	76
James, m. Martha WRIGHT, [ ], [1788]	64
James, his w. [ ], d. May 18, 1791, ae 38	90
Levi, m. Nancy A. WHITFORD, of Wethersfield, Apr. 5, 1846, by Charles Bartlet	18
Lucy, m. Curtis CRANE, b. of 1st Society, [, 1800]	68
Rebecca, m. Humphrey WOODHOUSE, (Old Society), Jan. 1, 1795	66
Russel[l], of 1st Society, m. Mary* M. GRISWOLD, Nov. 26, 1829 *("Mercy" in Church Records)	76
Susanna, m. Nathaniel HURLBURT [Jr.], Apr. 27, 1772	61
[AKINS], [see under ACKINS]	
AMES, Abigail, d. John, bp. June 12, 1774	124
Abigail, wid., d. Feb. 23, 1800, ae 63	94
Benjamin, m. Lois WARNER, Sept. 8, 1785	63
Benj[amin], s. Benj[amin], bp. Aug. 17, 1794	134
Benjamin, d. Nov. 19, 1794, ae 32	92
Benjamin, 2nd, d. Oct. 22, 1795	92
Eunice, d. John, bp. Sept. 10, 1769	120
Eunice*, d. Oliver, bp. Aug. 26, 1787 *("Eunice, dau. of Philemon AMES" in Church Rec.)	130
Eunice, m. Frederick ROBBINS, Jr., Sept. 19, 1805	69
Ira, s. W[illia]m, bp. June 16, 1793	134
Jerusha, w. W[illia]m, d. Dec. 15, 1793, ae 27	91
John, had s. [ ] & two d. [ ], d. Sept. 2, 1775 to Sept 16, 1775	83

	Page
AMES, (cont.)	
John, Jr., d. July 12, 1776	84
John*, d. Daniel, d. Aug. 30, 1784 *(Arnold Copy has "John **LEWIS**")	87
John, d. July 16, 1790, ae 57	90
Lois, wid., d. Mar. 23, 1841, ae 78 ("from Glastonbury" in Church Rec.)	111
Lydia, wid., d. Dec. 3, 1828, ae 62	106
Mehetable, d. John, bp. Apr. 7, 1765	117
Nabby, m. Russel **MACKEE**, of East Hartford, Feb. 4, 1798	67
Philemon, d. June 9, 1797, ae 40	93
Polly, m. Rev. Saulmon* **KING**, of East Hartford, Nov. 19, 1807 *("Salmon" in Church Rec.)	70
Rhoda, d. Benjamin, bp. July 8, 1787	130
Rhoda, m. Jacob **GOODRICH**, of Glastonbury, Sept. 4, 1806, by Rev. Nathan Strong	69
Robert, d. Nov. 12, 1770	82
Robert, s. John, bp. Apr. 26, 1772	122
Robert Butler, s. Benjamin, bp. Mar. 1, 1789	131
Roger Warner, s. Benjamin, bp. Mar. 31, 1791	132
Ruth, wid., m. Ezekiel **SMITH**, Feb. 2, 1800	67
Sarah*, d. wid. Sarah, bp. [Apr. 28], 1771 *(Born after its father's death". See Church Rec.)	121
Sarah, m. Eli **DEMING**, Feb. 8, 1776	61
William, s. Robert, bp. Jan. 27, 1767	118
William,* s. Robert, d. Jan. 29, 1767 *("Infant" in Church Rec.)	81
William, s. John, bp. Aug. 2, 1767	118
William, s. Robert, bp. Aug. 14, 1768	119
W[illia]m, m. Jerusha **GOODRICH**, [Nov.] 4, [1790]	65
W[illia]m, m. Lydia **CALLENDER**, Apr. 14, 1796	66
William, d. July 3, 1811, ae 44	99
ANDREWS, ANDRUS, Desire, m. Solomon **BLYN**, Sept. 30, 1784	62
Lois, wid., d. [ ] 28*, 1825, ae 96 *("25" in Church Rec.)	104
Obed, m. Loretta **CASWELL**, b. of Glastonbury, May 1, 1832	77
Obed, of Glastonbury, m. Abigail A. **RUSSEL**, Mar. 10, 1836	78
Ruth, wid., d. [ ] 25, 1825, ae 97 *("from Berlin" in Church Rec.)	104
ARCHER, Benjamin, his w. [ ], d. Jan. 7, 1821, ae 44	102
Benjamin, m. Chloe **WILLIAMS**, July 18, 1822	75
Israel Williams, s. Benjamin, bp. May 5, 1826	146
ARNOLD, Aaron C., of Middletown, m. Eliza Ann **SMITH**, Nov. 17, 1830	77
Elizabeth W., m. Solomon **GRISWOLD**, Nov. 11, 1827	76
Harriet, d. Aug. 12, 1843, ae 21	113
Julius, d. Apr. 25, 1847, in Hartford, ae 63	115
Laura, d. Sept. 2, 1839, ae 10	110
Lydia C.*, of East Haddam, m. Thomas **HANDY**, of Chatham, Aug. 26, 1825 *(Arnold Copy has "Lydia C. **GRISWOLD**")	75
Sarah S., m. Ralph Wyllys **WILLIAMS**, Dec. 7, 1836	79
Sophia, d. Sept. 3, 1834, ae 15, [Hartford*] *(From Church Rec.)	108
Tallcott A., m. Caroline **HOLMES**, Mar. 5, 1834	78
ATWOOD, Ann S., of Rocky Hill, m. Oscar **FLETCHER**, of Kinderhook, Apr. 28, 1845, by Rev. John Lovejoy	11
AUROLT, Jane, m. Ashbel **RILEY**, July 27, 1773	61
AVERY, Edmund*, of Mansfield, m. Sophia **BULKLEY**, Apr. 13, 1806	

ROCKY HILL VITAL RECORDS 3

Page

AVERY, (cont.)
  *("Edmund **HOVEY**" in Church Rec.)   69
  Elisha P., of Breeksville, O., m. Betsey **GOODRICH**, May 27, 1841   80
BAILEY, BAYLEY, James, of Haddam, m. Nancy **BELDEN**, of Rocky Hill,
  Apr. 15, 1849, by Rev. Calvin Chapin   28
  John A*, of Middletown, m. Sarah Jane **KELSEY**, of Rocky Hill, Oct. 15,
    1854, by Rev. L.B. Rockwood   *("of N.Y.")   52
  Mary, Mrs. [wid.], m. Capt. Eleazer **GOODRICH**, b. of Rocky Hill, Aug.
    27, 1848, by Rev. T.M. Dwight   27
  Romanzo N., of St. Louis, Mo., m. Adeline C. **PULSIFER**, of Rocky Hill,
    Aug. 15, 1849, by Rev. Calvin Chapin   29
  Rosella Clark, d. Alfred, bp. Jan. 1, 1830   146
  W[illia]m, d. May 17, 1846, ae 65   114
BAKER, Ebenezer, of Boston, Mass., m. Prudence **BULKLEY**, Aug. 9, [1812]   72
BALDWIN, Hiram, his child, d. Oct. 8, 1844, ae 3   114
  Junius E., of Winchester, m. Mehetable S. **BELDEN**, of Rocky Hill, Mar.
    30, 1845, by Rev. C. Chapin   9
  Lydia P., of Winchester, m. Otis **PENHOLLOW**, of Rocky Hill, Aug. 31,
    1845, by Rev. C. Chapin   13
BARBER, George Washington, of Hebron, m. Martha Ann **JAGGER**, [ ]30,
  1831   77
  Washington*, Rev. his w. [   ], d. Oct. 21, 1836, ae 27
    *("Worthington" in Arnold Copy)   109
  Worthington*, Rev. his w. [   ], d. Oct. 21, 1836, ae 27
    *("Washington" in Church Rec.)   109
BARMAN*, Rebecca, m. Thomas **BROWN**, b. of 1st Society, Dec. 3, 1809
  *("**BARNUM**" in Church Rec.)   71
BARNES, Anson John, s. John, bp. May 7, 1775   124
  Aziel, s. John, bp. Sept. 27, 1767   119
  Edmond, s. John, bp. Apr. 1, 1770   120
  Hartwell, of Farmington, m. Hannah **CLARK**, May 27, 1783   62
  John, d. between May 7 & Aug. 17, 1782, at New York (Soldier)   85
  Jo[h]n Hazeltine, s. John, bp. Nov. 3, 1782   128
  Melvin, s. John, bp. July 26, 1772   122
  Otis*, s. Ephraim, bp. Apr. 20, 1806   *("Otis **BOWERS**" in Church Rec.)   140
  Reuben, of Middletown, m. Nancy **WEBB**, May 15, 1814   72
BARNUM*, Rebecca, m. Thomas **BROWN**, b. of 1st Society, Dec. 3, 1809
  *(Arnold Copy has "**BARMAN**")   71
BARRETT*, Lazarus, of New York, m. Sarah **DICKINSON**, of Rocky Hill,
  Jan. 24, 1853, by Rev. L.B. Rockwood   *(Perhaps "**BUNELL**")   43
BARROWS, Andrew Otis, s. Ashbel W.*, bp. Nov. 5, 1847   *("Ashbel
  Ward" in Church Rec.)   151
  Samuel Ward*, s. Ashbel W., bp. Sept. 14, 1844   *("s, of Ashbel Ward"
    in Church Rec.)   151
BATES, Benjamin Robinson, of Rocky Hill, m. Laura Ann **PETERS**, of
  Glastonbury, Jan. 2, 1852, by Rev. L.B. Rockwood   38
BEACHGOOD*, Edward, s. Hannah, bp. Apr. 15, 1781, by Rev. Mr. Lewis
  *("**BREATHGOOOD**" in Arnold Copy)   126
  Hannah, m. Jona[tha]n **HAND**, Feb. 7, 1790   64
[BEAMON], BEAMONT, [see also **BEAUMONT**], Ira, of East Hartford, m.
  Mabel **BULKLEY**, Oct. 10, 1811   71

	Page
BEARCE, Gideon N., m. wid. Lydia C. **SHAYLOR**, July 12, 1837 (Arnold Copy has "Gideon N. **BEARD** mar. Lydia G. **SHAILER**")	79
BEARD, Gideon N*., m. wid. Lydia G. **SHAILER**, July 12, 1837 (Church Rec. give "Gideon N. **BEARCE** m. Lydia C. **SHAYLOR**")	79
BEAUMONT, [see also **BEAMON**], Laura Mabel, d. Lucius M., bp. [June 6], 1847	151
Lucius M., m. Martha G. **BULKLEY**, of Rocky Hill, Nov. 27, 1845, by Rev. C. Chapin	17
BECKET, Jonas, of Brystol, m. Hannah **DEMING**, [ ] 30, 1787	64
BECKLEY, Amanda Amelia, m. Ellelar **BOTELL**, of Mereden, Feb. 9, 1834	78
Clarissa*, m. Reuben **SHIPMAN**, of Glastonbury, Dec. 3, 1818 *(Arnold Copy has "Clarissa **BUCKLEY**")	74
David, Jr., m. Eunice **WILLIAMS**, Mar. 31, 1785	63
Eliza, of Rocky Hill, m. Hiram **HUBBARD**, of Berlin, Nov. 16, 1845, by Goerge O. Chambers, J.P.	15
Elizabeth, m. Walter **BELDEN**, May 6, 1830	77
Emily, m. Simeon **BELDEN**, Feb. 13, 1817	73
Lotan, m. Lucy K. **BECKLEY**, b. of Berlin, [ ] 16, 1820	74
Lucy, m. Urbane **KELSEY**, b. of Berlin, May 22, 1812	72
Lucy K., m. Lotan **BECKLEY**, b. of Berlin, [ ] 16, 1820	74
Mariam*, m. Aaron **PORTER**, Jr., b. of 1st Society, Apr. 12, 1815 *("Mariam **BULKLEY**" in Arnold Copy)	73
Mary, of Worthington, m. L[ ] D[ ], Feb. 11, 1787	63
Nancy, m. Samuel **GOODRICH**, Dec. 8, 1814	73
Oliver, m. Lucinda **BELDEN**, Jan. 19, 1785	63
Ruth*, m. Silas **BELDEN**, Mar. 4, 1783 *("Ruth **BUCKLEY**" in Arnold Copy)	62
BELDEN, BELDING, Aaron, Jr., m. Rhoda **WRIGHT**, July 30, 1797	66
Aaron, his w. [ ], d. Dec. 28, 1807, ae 78	97
Aaron, Jr., d. July 18, 1814, ae 45	100
Aaron, s. Justus, bp. Aug. 14, 1814	143
Aaron, his w. [ ], d. Feb. 21, 1841, ae 25	111
Abigail, wid., d. Dec. 13, 1822, ae 50	102
Abner, m. Mary **STANDISH**, Oct. 24, 1771	61
Abraham, m. Mary **WRIGHT**, Nov. 13, 1785	63
Abraham, his wid. [ ], d. Sept. 14, 1840, ae 77	111
Abram, d. Aug. 22, 1814, ae 53	100
Albert, bp. July 4, 1841	149
Alfred, s. Jeremiah, bp. July 28, 1799	136
Allen, m. Achsah **DEMING**, May 9, 1811	71
Allen, his w. [ ], d. Jan. 13, 1845, ae 52	114
Amelia, m. Ira **CRAWFOOT**, of Middletown, [ ] 31, 1821	74
Amos, m. Comfort **BLYNN**, Oct. [ ], 1773	61
Amos*, s. Othniel, bp. Apr. 29, 1781 *("Arnol" in Arnold Copy)	127
Andrew, s. Jere[miah], bp. June 19, 1796	135
Arnol*, s. Othniel, bp. Apr. 29, 1781 *("Amos" in Church Rec.)	127
Asa*, s. David, bp. Feb. 8, 1789 *("Twin with Asahel" in Church Rec.)	131
Asa, d. Feb. 16, 1800, ae 80	94
Asa, s. Samuel Spencer, bp. Apr. 28, 1805	139
Asahel*, s. David, bp. Feb. 8, 1789 *("Twin with Asa" in Church Rec.)	131
Asenath, d. [ ], bp. July 12, 1795	134

BELDEN, BELDING, (cont.)

	Page
Ashbel, s. Aaron, Jr., bp. Oct. 14, 1798	136
Ashbel, m. Philia **BLINN**, Feb. 27, 1823	75
Austin, m. Sarah **WRIGHT**, May 3, 1843	80
Austin, his w. [ ], d. Dec. 22, 1843, ae 28	113
Aziel, s. Elisha, bp. Apr. 8, 1770	120
Aziel, of Berlin, m. wid. Abigail **MILLER**, Oct. 29, 1809	71
Barzillai, s. Elisha, [Jr.*], bp. Oct. 13, 1799 *(Church Rec.)	137
Betsey, d. Justin*, bp. Nov. 18, 1810 *("Justus" in Church Rec.)	142
Betsey, m. Russel **MORGAN**, of Middletown, Jan. 6, 1833	77
Bildad, m. Mary **RILEY**, Feb. 14, 1770	60
Bildad, his infant*, d. Sept. 16, 1770 *(named "Rosanna" in Church Rec.)	82
Bildad, his w. [ ]d, July 6, 1811, ae 62	99
Bildad Butler, s. Bildad, bp. Nov. 13, 1785	129
Burrage, s. David, bp. Feb. 2, 1783	128
Calvin, s. David, bp. Oct. 30, 1796	135
Chester, s. Abraham, bp. Feb. 10, 1805	139
Chloe, d. Abraham, bp. July 25, 1790	132
Chloe, m. Ozias **DICKINSON**, July 7, 1805	69
Clarissa, m. Joel **SPENCER**, of Berlin, Mar. 18, 1810	71
Clarissa, m. Seth **COLTON**, of West Springfield, Mass., Jan. 31, 1812	71
Clarissa M., m. Rockwell Goodrich **FRANKLIN**, Dec. 16, 1835	78
Clifford, s. Bildad, bp. Apr. 5, 1789	131
Comfort, wid., d. June 8, 1790, ae 41	90
Cynthia, d. Moses, bp. Jan. 18, 1789	131
Daniel, d. Mar. 31, 1774	83
Daniel*, s. David, bp. Apr. 29, 1781 *(Arnold Copy has "David")	127
David, m. Hepsibeth **GOODRICH**, Aug. 3, [1769]	60
David*, s. David, bp. Apr. 29, 1781 *("Daniel" in Church Rec.)	127
David, s. David, bp. Oct. 31, 1802	138
Delia, of Rocky Hill, m. Levi **DEMING**, of Berlin, Dec. 2, 1845, by Rev. Charles Bartlett	16
Dorothea, w. John, bp. Nov. 26, 1797	136
Edmond, s. Samuel S., bp. Dec. 19, 1808	141
Elisha, s. Elisha, bp. Dec. 8, 1771	122
Elisha, d. Sept. 29, 1813, ae 77	99
Elisha*, his wid. d. July 11, 1817, at Berlin, ae 78 *(Arnold Copy has "Elisha **BUTLER**")	100
Elisha*, d. Feb. 25, 1848, ae 77 *("Eliza" in Church Rec.)	115
Elisha, his wid. [ ] d. Mar. 26, 1848, ae 81	115
Eliza*, wid., d. Jan. 15, 1784, ae 88 *("Eliz." in Church Rec.)	86
Eliza, m. William **HOLMES**, Mar. 7, 1827	76
Eliza, d. May 14, 1838, ae 26	110
Eliza*, d. Feb. 25, 1848, ae 77 *("Elisha" in Church Rec.)	115
Elizabeth, d. Aaron, bp. Oct. 27, 1771	122
Elizabeth, d. Bildad, bp. [Oct. 15, 1775	125
Elizabeth, m. Levi **GOFF**, Jan. 27, 1791	65
Elizabeth*, of Glastonbury, m. Luther **GOODRICH**, Nov. 1, 1797 *("Elizabeth **BELL**?")	66
Elizabeth, wid., m. Hezekiah **WINCHELL**,of Berlin, Aug. 25, 1804	69

Page

BELDEN, BELDING, (cont.)
Elizabeth*, d. Aaron, Jr., bp. Aug. 14, 1814 *("dau. of the late Aaron, Jr." in Church Rec.)	143
Elizabeth, m. Ambrose **WOLCOTT**, Oct. 20, 1842	80
Ellen S., of Rocky Hill, m. Norman R. **FREEMAN**, of South Glastonbury, Dec. 28, 1851, by Rev. Philo Judson	39
Emily, d. Aaron, Jr., bp. [Oct. 5], 1806	140
Emily, d. Dec. 14, 1840, ae 35	111
Enos*, d. Jan. 23, 1775 *("Ezra in Church Rec.)	83
Eunice, d. John, bp. Oct. 7, 1792	133
Eunice, m. Edward **CONE**, of Middletown, Dec. 26, 1811	71
Eunice*, wid., from Middletown, d. Oct. 1, 1847, ae 93 *("Eunice **BUTLER**" in Church Rec.)	115
Ezekiel, s. Jeremiah, bp. [Sept.] 17, 1786	130
Ezekiel P., m. Mary **PARSONS**, of Amherst, Mass., Nov. 1, 1790	65
Florilla, m. Sylvester **WRIGHT**, Nov. 27, 1825	75
Frances, m. Nancy **BLINN**, b. of Rocky Hill, Dec. 7, 1854, by Mark Tucker	55
George, s. Elisha, bp. Dec. 3, 1797	136
George, [s. Norris & Anna], b. Feb. [ ], 1841	48
Hannah, d. Othniel, bp. Aug. 14, 1790	132
Hannah, d. Othniel, d. Aug. 23, 1790	90
Hannah, w. Albert, bp. July 4, 1841	149
Harriet, m. Jeremy **GOODRICH**, Dec. 23, 1832	77
Harriet Sage, d. Seth, bp. Nov. 23, 1806	140
Harry*, s. Daniel, bp. Nov. 13, 1791 *("Harvey" in Church Rec.)	133
Harry, d. Nov. 2, 1824, ae 35	104
Harvey*, s. Daniel, bp. Nov. 13, 1791 (Arnold Copy has "Harry")	133
Henry, m. Mabel **DICKINSON**, Sept. 24, 1812	72
Henry Butler, s. Jere[miah], bp. Oct. 18, 1801	138
Hezekiah, d. Oct. 20, 1793, ae 69	91
Honor, d. Elisha, bp. Nov. 29, 1767	119
Honor, m. Thomas **RILEY**, Mar. 5, 1789	64
Horace, s. Abraham, bp. Nov. 11, 1790	132
Horace, m. wid. Abigail **ROGERS**, May 15, 1823	75
Horace, [s. Nerris & Anna], b. May 3, 1838	48
Horace, his child, d. Nov. 29, 1843, ae 7	113
Horace, his w. [ ], d. Jan. 16, 1846, ae 45 ("Perhaps Jan. 16" in Church Rec.)	114
Isaac, s. Elisha, bp. Oct. 10, 1779, by Rev. Mr. Pitkin of Farmington	126
Isaac, s. Elisha, Jr., bp. May 22, 1803	138
Isaac, m. Marietta **HOLMES**, July 16, 1829	76
James, m. Dorcas **GOODRICH**, Nov. 5, 1772	61
Jerusha, d. Jeremiah, bp. Dec. 22, 1793	134
Joel, s. Elisha, bp. May 26, 1782	127
John, s. Elisha, bp. Feb. 2, 1766	118
John, m. Dorothy **HOLMES**, [, 1788]	64
John, s. Patty, bp. Sept. 17, 1797	136
John, s. John, bp. Nov. 10, 1800	137
John, his w. [ ] d. Jan. 10, 1807, ae 41	97
John, m. wid. Mehetabel **PRICE**, Mar. 9, 1807	70

	Page
BELDEN, BELDING, (cont.)	
John, d. Nov. 10, 1835, ae 70	109
John, bp. July 4, 1841	150
Joshua, d. Nov. or Dec. [ ], 1786, at sea	88
Joshua, s. Abraham, bp. Nov. 11, 1790	132
Joshua, m. Eleanor **NOTT**, of Berlin, Oct. 15, 1810	71
Joshua, his w. [ ], d. Apr. 19, 1825, ae 38	104
Josiah Wolcott, s. David, bp. May 3, 1801	137
Julia, m. Ambrose **WALCOTT**, of Winsted, Apr. 6, 1834	78
Juliana, d. Aaron, Jr., bp. Jan. 29, 1809	141
Justus, m. Mary **RILEY**, Apr. 17, 1792	65
Justus, his w. [ ], d. [ ], 1792	90
Justus, m. Hannah **MORTON**, Dec. 3, 1797	67
Justus, d. Oct. 19, 1846, ae 80	114
Laura, m. William **NOTT**, May 2, 1811	71
Laura, m. Elisha **NORTON**, of Berlin, [ ]28, 1830	76
Leonard, s. Aaron, Jr., bp. Oct. 12, 1800	137
Leonard, m. Lucretia **HOLMES**, Aug. 6, 1826	75
Leonard, m. Sarah A. **GOODRICH**, b. of Rocky Hill, July 31, 1853, by Rev. L. Burton Rockwood	46
Lois, d. Moses, bp. [May 6], 1781	127
Lois, d. David, bp. Feb. 18, 1798	136
Lotta, d. Jeremiah, bp. June 21, 1789	131
Louisa*, d. Seth, bp. Jan. 15, 1804 *("Twin infant with Lucy" in Church Rec.)	139
Lucinda, m. Oliver **BECKLEY**, Jan. 19, 1785	63
Lucy, m. Josiah **DICKEMON***, Dec. 6, 1781 *(Arnold Copy has "**DICKINSON**")	61
Lucy*, d. Seth, bp. Jan. 15, 1804 *("Twin infant with "Louisa" in Church Rec.)	139
Lucy, d. Justus, bp. May 4, 1806	140
Lydia, d. Elisha, bp. [Aug. 6], 1775	125
Lydia, m. Leonard **MILLER**, Aug. 7, 1796	66
Marilla, d. May 4, 1847, ae 35	115
Martha, m. John **WELLES**, Nov. 26, 1765	60
Martha, of Rocky Hill, m. Edgar B. **PRIOR**, of Middletown, Aug. 5, 1849, by Rev. Philo Judson	30
Mary, d. Jan. 23, 1772	82
Mary, d. Moses, bp. Jan. 4, 1795	134
Mary, d. Justus, bp. Nov. 29, 1799	137
Mary, d. Samuel Spencer, bp. Jan. 31, 1808	141
Mary, m. Jared **HALE**, of Chatham, June 2, 1818	74
Mary J., m. Henry J. **GRISWOLD**, b. of Rocky Hill, Jan. 13, 1850, by Rev. Calvin Chapin	32
Mary Jane, bp. July 4, 1841	150
Mary Jane, [d. Norris & Anna], b. Mar. 4, 1843	48
Mehetable, d. Abraham, bp. June 11, 1797	136
Mehetable, m. Seth **SPENCER**, of Middletown Upper Houses, Mar. 6, 1816	73
Mehetable S., of Rocky Hill, m. Junius E. **BALDWIN**, of Winchester, Mar. 30, 1845, by Rev. C. Chapin	9

BELDEN, BELDING, (cont.)

	Page
Mercy, d. Justus, bp. Sept. 18, 1808	141
Mercy, m. George **KIRTLAND**, of New Haven, Apr. 28, 1830	77
Mercy, m. James W. **GOODRICH**, Feb. 8, 1838	79
Milly, d. David, bp. Nov. 12, 1786	130
Molly, wid., d. Feb. 19, 1828, ae 80	105
Moses, d. June 14, 1824, ae 69	103
Mose, his wid., d. Sept. 17, 1846, ae 88	114
Nancy, d. Elisha, Jr., bp. May 24, 1801	137
Nancy, d. Jeremiah, bp. Apr. 13, 1806	140
Nancy, of Rocky Hill, m. James **BAILEY**, of Haddam, Apr. 15, 1849, by Rev. Calvin Chapin	28
Norris, m. Anna **HARLOW***, June 17, 1832 *("**HALLOW**" in Church Rec.)	77
Olive, d. Samuel, bp. Sept. 14, 1800 (Dau of Samuel Spencer" in Church Rec.)	137
Oliver, s. Moses, bp. [ ], 1783 ("bp. Jan. 26" in Church Rec.)	128
Oliver, d. Dec. 11, 1797, ae 37* *("ae 15 in Church Rec.)	93
Otis, s. Elisha, Jr., bp. [Oct. 11], 1807	141
Otis, d. Sept. 20, 1840, ae 34	111
Patty, bp. [Aug.] 20, 1797, an adult	136
Patty, had s. John, bp. [ ], 1797	136
Patty, m. Lyman **WRIGHT**, Aug. 13, 1801	68
Philip, s. Sam[uel] Spencer, bp. Apr. 11, 1802	138
Philip, d. Apr. 30, 1841, ae 40	112
Phelomela, d. Jeremiah, bp. [Nov. 6], 1791	133
Philomela, d. Jeremiah, d. June 28, 1794	91
Philomela, d. Jeremiah, bp. [Apr.] 15, 1804	139
Polly, d. Jeremiah, bp. Nov. 13, 1785	129
Polly, m. Benoni **THOMPSON**, of Bristol, Jan. 1, 1818	74
Prudence, d. Elisha, bp. May 29, 1774	124
Prudence, m. W[illia]m **HOLDEN**, of Granville, Mass., Feb. 21, 1795	66
Prudence, d. Abraham, bp. Sept. 27, 1795	135
Reuben, [s. Norris & Anna], b. Feb. 7, 1847	48
Rhoda, d. Martha **COLLINS**, bp. Oct. 30, 1791	133
Richard, m. Mercy **COLLINS**, Sept. 28, 1785	63
Richard, Jr., his infant d. Mar. 5, 1792	90
Ric[har]d, d. July 28, 1797, ae 69	93
Richard, his w. [ ], d. Feb. 22, 1844, ae [ ]	113
Richard, d. Jan. 31, 1848, ae 87	115
Richard, d. [ ], 1848, ae 45	115
Rosannah, d. Beldad, bp. Sept. 16, 1770	121
Rosanna, d. Bildad, bp. Sept. 8, 1782	128
Rosanna, d. David, bp. Nov. 14, 1793	134
Rosetta, m. Silas **WALTON**, [ ]27, 1787	64
Roswel[l], d. Dec. 16, 1815, ae 51	100
Roswell, his wid. [ ], d. Jan. 31, 1835, ae 58	108
Ruth, d. Othniel, bp. Apr. 14, 1782	127
Sally, d. Seth, bp. May 10, 1801	137
Salmon*, s. Othniel, bp. Feb. 19, 1792 *("Arnold Copy has "Solomon")	133
Samuel, d. July 31, 1771	82

	Page
BELDEN, BELDING, (cont.)	
Samuel, his w. [ ]d. [ ]23, 1775	83
Samuel, d. Jan. 10, 1782	85
Samuel Spencer, s. Richard, bp. Aug. 11, 1771	121
Sarah, d. Moses, bp. [May 6], 1781, by [ ]	127
Sarah, d. Othniel, bp. Oct. 3, 1790	132
Sarah, m. Daniel **HUBBARD**, of Berlin, Dec. 15, 1799	67
Sarah, m. Lowry **BLINN**, Oct. 23, 1836	79
Selah, s. David, bp. Apr. 29, 1781	127
Seth, m. Christian **DICKENSON**, Apr. 16, 1772	61
Seth, his w. [ ], d. Mar. 16, 1799, ae 21	94
Seth, bp. Apr. 14, 1799	136
Silas, m. Ruth **BECKLEY**, Mar. 4, 1783	62
Silas, d. Mar. 5, 1824, ae 63	103
Silas, his wid. [ ], d. Mar. 20, 1830, ae 70, [at U. H[house]s]	106
Simeon, m. Emily **BECKLEY**, Feb. 13, 1817	73
Solomon, m. Elizabeth **ROCKWELL**, June 27, 1768	60
Solomon*, s. Othniel, bp. Feb. 19, 1792 *("Salmon" in Church Rec.)	133
Solomon, s. Justus, bp. Dec. 6, 1801	138
Sophia, d. Elisha, Jr., bp. Sept. 25, 1805	140
Stephen*, of Lebanon, m. Dorothy **GOODRICH**, Jan. 16, 1787 *("Stephen **TILDEN**" in Church Rec.)	63
Stephen, bp. July 4, 1841	150
Susan, bp. July 4, 1841	150
Susanna, d. Bildad, bp. Jan. 5, 1772	122
Susanna*, d. Bildad, b**. Mar. 26, 1782, in 11th y. *("Susanna **DEMING**" in Arnold Copy) **(Probably should be "d.")	85
Sylvester, s. Othniel, bp. June 26, 1785	129
Sylvester, m. Abigail **WRIGHT**, July 29, 1804	69
Thomas, m. Mehitable **HARRIS**, Aug. 8, 1782	61
Thomas, d. Nov. 27, 1839, ae 25	111
Thomas Morton, s. Justus, bp. Aug. 5, 1804	139
Walter, m. Elizabeth **BECKLEY**, May 6, 1830	77
Willys, [s. Norris & Anna], b. Jan. 18, 1833	48
BELL (?)*, Elizabeth, of Glastonbury, m. Luther **GOODRICH**, Nov. 1, 1797 *(Written "**BELDEN**")	66
Elizabeth Prudence, m. Philo Chapell **GOODALE**, Dec. 1, 1833	78
Lucy Ann, m. Hiram **SMITH**, of East Windsor, June 17, 1833	78
Nancy, m. Jasper **GOODRICH**, [ ]6, 1823	75
BEMBOREA, Harry, d. Dec. 26, 1805, ae 61	97
BENTON, Esther, d. John, bp. [May] 27, 1781	127
Esther, wid., m. Benajah **BOWERS**, Nov. 27, 1791	65
Esther, m. Ephraim **BOWERS**, of Chatham, Mar. 5, 1801	68
Fanny M., of Rocky Hill, m. L. Wesley **SMITH**, of Hartford, Dec. 17, 1854, by Rev. L.B. Rockwood	55
James, of New Haven, m. Amanda A. **FLINT**, May 9, 1833	77
John, d. Feb. 6, 1783	86
John, m. Metty **WARNER**, Nov. 29, 1798	67
Sarah, d. John, bp. [May] 27, 1781	127
W[illia]m Tyler, s. John, bp. Sept. 22, 1782	128
BERRY, Mandus, m. Sally **WRIGHT**, Oct. 2, 1814	72

	Page
BERRY, (cont.)	
Sally, m. Jacob **GRISWOLD**, Oct. 26, 1824	75
BIDWELL, ----------, m. Betsey **STRONG**, b. of Glastonbury, Oct. 2, 1799	67
BIGELOW, Eben*, of Hartford, m. Hannah **CURTISS**, Oct. 24, [1782]	
*("Elvin" in Church Rec.)	62
Elvin*, of Hartford, m. Hannah **CURTISS**, Oct. 24, [1782] *(Arnold Copy has "Eben")	62
Jessie, of East Haddam, m. Roxy **ROBBINS**, Oct. 12, 1818	74
BILL, Isaac, of Glastonbury, m. Eunice **BULL**, Oct. 24, 1803	68
BISHOP, Amos, of Bethleham, m. Mrs. Mary G. **GUTHRIE**, late of Rocky Hill, Sept. 10, 1843, by Rev. Joseph Holdrich	2
BLAIR*, Fanny, m. Deuel **HIGGINS**, of East Glastonbury, Mar. 24, 1819 *(Church Rec. give "**BLIN**")	74
BLAKELEY, Joseph, of Willink (?), N.Y., m. Sally **WILLIAMS**, Feb. 7, 1816	73
Joseph*, his w. [ ], d. Aug. 8, 1842, in Aurora, N.Y., *(Arnold Copy has "Joseph **BULKLEY**")	113
BLINN, BLYN, BLYNN, Abigail, m. Charles **DeWOLF**, of Ashfield, Mass., Nov. 20, 1828	76
Abraham, d. [ ] 14, 1790, ae 49	89
Almira, d. Apr. 5, 1819, ae 17	101
Asahel, s. wid. Hannah, bp. Sept. 9, 1785	129
Betsey, m. Sylvester **NOTT**, of Berlin, Mar. 25, 1802	68
Betsey Deming, d. Theodore, bp. Oct. 6, 1799	137
Carrile W., m. Walter R. **RUSSELL**, b. of Rocky Hill, May 6, 1852, by Rev. L. Burton Rockwood	40
Christiana, m. Ethan **HOLMES**, Oct. 21, 1798	67
Comfort, m. Amos **BELDING**, Oct. [ ], 1773	61
Cornelia, m. Charles **FREEMAN**, June 5, 1836	78
Corra*, m. Ruth **SMITH**, Nov. 8, 1773 *("Hosea" in Church Rec.)	61
Daniel, s. wid. Hannah, bp. Sept. 9, 1785	129
Daniel, m. Sally **WELLES**, of Berlin, Jan. 17, 1802	68
Daniel, his w. [ ], d. June 7, 1802, ae 20	95
Daniel, d. Dec. 20, 1802, in Charleston, S.C. ("ae 26" in Church Rec.)	95
David, m. Prudence **GOODRICH**, Dec. 14, 1790	65
David, s. David, bp. Apr. 22, 1798	136
Emily, d. David, bp. June 28, 1795	134
Emily, of 1st Society, m. Charles **FRANCIS**, Oct. 5, 1825	75
Esther, d. Justus, d. Mar. 7, 1789	89
Ethan, d. [ ] 20, 1832, ae 11	107
Fanny, d. Theodore, bp. Oct. 6, 1799	137
Fanny*, m. Deuel **HIGGINS**, of East Glastonbury, Mar. 24, 1819 *(Arnold Copy has "Fanny **BLAIR**')	74
Frederic*, s. Theodore, bp. July 19, 1807 *(Arnold Copy has "Roderic")	140
Frederick, m. Lucinda **FRANKLIN**, Dec. 5, 1824	75
Frederic, 2nd, his w. [ ], d. Sept. 2, 1840, ae 28	111
Frederic*, 2nd, d. Feb. 16, 1847, ae 42 *("Treat" in Arnold Copy)	115
Hannah, d. wid. Hannah, bp. Sept. 19, 1785	129
Hannah, m. Joseph **BLINN**, Nov. 22, 1803	68
Hannah, wid., d. Feb. 27, 1812, ae 70	99
Hannah, wid., d. Feb. 27, 1812, ae 70	99

ROCKY HILL VITAL RECORDS   11

	Page
BLINN, BLYN, BLYNN, (cont.)	
Hezekiah, d. between May 7 & Aug. 17, 1782, at New York (Soldier)	85
Hezekiah, m. wid. Mary **RASH**, Oct. 16, 1814	72
Hezekiah, d. Jan. 2, 1820, ae 55	101
Horace, of Great Barrington, Mass., m. Charlotte **GRISWOLD**, June 2, 1824	75
Hosea*, m. Ruth **SMITH**, Nov. 8, 1773 *(Arnold Copy has "Corra")	61
Huldah, d. Samuel, bp. Oct. 1, 1773	123
John Selah, m. Elizabeth Maria **FRANKLIN**, Feb. 23, 1831	77
John Selah, bp. [Sept.] 5, 1841	150
Johney, s. Prudence, bp. Apr. 28, 1793	133
Joseph, m. Hannah **BLINN**, Nov. 22, 1803	68
Joseph, his w. [ ], d. Feb. 1, 1835, ae 57	108
Julia, d. David, bp. June 13, 1802	138
Justus, m. Margaret **CRAWFOOT**, [Sept. , 1772]	61
Justus, his w. [ ], d. July 2, 1798, ae 40	93
Justus, m. wid. Mary **STODDARD**, June 27, 1800	68
Justus, d. Apr. 19, 1834*, ae 86 *("1833" in Church Rec.)	107
Levi, s. Abraham, bp. May 22, 1785	129
Levi, d. Nov. 11, 1800, in West Indies	95
Lodovicia, d. Theodore, bp. Feb. 10, 1805	139
Lois, m. Eben **RANNY**, of Middletown, Nov. 30, 1769	60
Lois, d. wid. Hannah, bp. Sept. 9, 1785	129
Lois, m. Jonathan **PRICE**, Dec. 10, 1807	70
Lowry, m. Sarah **BELDEN**, Oct. 23, 1836	79
Lucretia, d. David, bp. [Apr.] 29, 1804	139
Lucy, m. Ashbel **HURLBURT**, b. of 1st Society, Mar. 19, 1810	71
Lydia, m. Amos **SANDFORD**, May 10, 1797	66
Martha, wid., d. June 18, 1812, ae 66	99
Mary, d. wid. Hannah, bp. Sept. 9, 1785	129
Mary, m. Levi **TREAT**, of Glastonbury, Apr. 30, 1804	69
Mary, of Old Society, m. Charles **DIX**, Nov. 22, 1804	69
Nabby, d. Theodore, bp. Apr. 2, 1801	137
Nabby, d. Theodore, bp. July 3, 1808	141
Nancy, m Frances **BELDEN**, b. of Rocky Hill, Dec. 7, 1854, by Mark Tucker	55
Nancy S., m. Calvin **WHAPLES**, of Newington, Dec. 28, 1842	80
Parmelia, d. David, bp. May 4, 1800	137
Peter, his w. [ ], d. Apr. 27, 1793, ae 30	91
Peter, d. Dec. 2, 1793, ae 80	91
Peter, his w. [ ], d. Sept. 7, 1796, ae 44	93
Peter, m. wid. Jane **TREAT**, of Glastonbury, Nov. 2, 1800	68
Peter, d. July 10, 1818, ae 68	101
Philia, m. Ashbel **BELDEN**, Feb. 27, 1823	75
Prudence, d. Daniel*, bp. Dec. 22, 1805 *("David" in Church Rec.)	140
Roderic*, s. Theodore, bp. July 19, 1807 *("Frederic" in Church Rec.)	140
Roxana, of Whitestown, N.Y., m. Selah **BLINN**, May 2, 1813	72
Roxy, d. Prudence, bp. [May 29], 1791	132
Sally, m. George **SMITH**, b. of 1st Society, Mar. 18, 1810	71
Samuel, of Wethersfield, m. Eliza **WHITMORE**, Aug. 31, 1842	80
Samuel, his w. [ ], d. July 11, 1848, ae 39 *("ae 29" in Church Rec.)	116

BARBOUR COLLECTION

	Page
BLINN, BLYN, BLYNN, (cont.)	
Selah, m. Roxana **BLINN**, of Whitestown, N.Y., May 2, 1813	72
Shingleton, s. Abraham, bp. May 22, 1785	129
Singleton, d. Mar. 21, 1808, ae 36	98
Solomon, m. Desire **ANDRUS**, Sept. 30, 1784	62
Sophia, d. David, bp. June 19, 1796	135
Theodore, m. Hannah **MISNER**, May 21, 1796	66
Theodore, d. Apr. 22, 1832, ae 59	107
Theodore, of R.H., m. Fanny B. * **REED**, of Durham, Aug. 23, 1840 *("Fanny F." in Church Rec.)	79
Treat, 2nd*, d. Feb. 16, 1847, ae 42 *("Frederic **BLIN**, 2nd," in Church Rec.)	115
Wardsworth F., m. Jane C. **TRYON**, June 21, 1853, by by Rev. L.B. Rockwood	45
William, m. Sally **TREAT**, of Glastonbury, May 10, 1797	66
Zerah, s. Hezekiah, d. between May 7 & Aug. 17, 1782, at New York (Soldier)	85
BLISS, Alfred, of Martinsburg, N.Y., m. Elizabeth **ROBBINS**, Dec. 25, 1839	79
BOARDMAN, Asahel, d. Nov. [ ], 1823, ae 34 (sailed for Martinique; not heard from)	103
Ashbel, s. John, bp. Sept. 20, 1767	119
Ashbel, s. Jason, bp. Sept. 19, 1790	132
Candace, d. El[ ], d. Dec. 24, 1767	81
Candace, d. Elnathan, bp. [Feb. 5], 1769	120
Candace, m. Thomas **STEELE**, Jr., of Lenox, Mass., May 13, 1798	67
Charles*, s. Esther, d. Sept. 18, 1803, ae 5 *("Charles **BURNHAM**" in Church Rec.)	96
Chauncey, s. Jonathan, Jr., bp. [Sept. 19], 1790	132
Chloe, wid., d. Jan. 28, 1825, ae 60	104
Daniel, s. John, bp. May 5, 1771	121
Daniel, d. Jan. 29, 1834, ae 65	108
Elijah, s. Elnathan, bp. Nov. 17, 1765	117
Elijah, m. Mercy **NOTT**, Sept. 16, 1781	61
Elijah, his infant d. Dec. 16, 1784	87
Elijah, his infant d. Nov. 24, 1786	88
Elijah, s. Elijah, bp. Dec. 30, 1787	131
Elijah, his infant d. Oct. 13, 1793	91
Elijah, of Hartford, d. Sept. 4, 1808, ae 52; bd. [in Rocky Hill]	98
Elisha, of Middletown, m. Mary **WRIGHT**, May 29, 1783	62
Eliza*, wid., d. Aug. 30, 1776 *("Eliz." in Church Rec.)	84
Eliza Jane, of Rocky Hill, m. Freeman **GRISWOLD**, of Wethersfield, Oct. 8, 1854, at the house of Rev. L.B. Rockwood, by Rev. Robert G. Williams, of Durham	54
Elizabeth, d. John, bp. Dec. 11, 1774	124
Elizabeth, m. James **PRICE**, Dec. 4, 1775	61
Elizabeth, m. Charles **MORGAN**, of Hartford, May 15, 1791	65
Elizabeth, wid., d. Mar. 17, 1825, ae 87	104
Elnathan, s. Elnathan, bp. Nov. 17, 1765	117
Elnathan, his w. [ ], d. Sept. 26, 1805, ae 73	96
Elnathan, d. May 9, 1811, ae 85	98
Esther*, had s. Charles, d. Sept. 18, 1803, ae 5 *("Esther **BURNHAM**"	

	Page
BOARDMAN, (cont.)	
in Church Rec.)	96
Frederick, s. John, bp. June 23, 1765	117
Frederick, m. Chloe **BULKLEY**, July 28, 1790	64
Frederick, d. Oct. 24, 1821, ae 57	102
Hannah, d. Elnathan, bp. Aug. 21, 1774	124
Hannah*, d. Jason, d. Dec. 17, 1795 *("Infant" in Church Rec.)	92
Hannah, d. Jason, bp. Dec. 17, 1795	135
Hannah, m. Elias **ROBBINS**, May 14, 1800	67
Henry, s. Elijah, bp. Nov. 10, 1786	130
James, s. Elijah, bp. Sept. 26, 1790	132
James*, s. wid. Abigail **GRISWOLD**, bp. Mar. 9, 1794 *(Church Rec. give "James, child of wid. Abigail **GRISWOLD**")	134
Jason, m. Hepsibeth **CURTIS**, July 7, 1784	62
Jason, s. Jason, bp. June 14, 1801	137
Jason, his w. [ ], d. Jan. 4, 1807, ae 50	97
Jason, his child d. Jan. 21, 1807, ae 7	97
Jason, m. Lydia **DEMING**, Jan. 3, 1808	70
Jason, s. Jason, bp. [June] 18, 1809	141
Jason, his w. [ ], d. Feb. 11, 1842, ae 65	112
Jason, d. Feb. 6, 1844, ae 83	113
John, s. Jason, bp. Mar. 29, 1789	131
John, s. Jason, d. Nov. 25, 1792, ae 4	90
John, s. Jason, bp. Sept. 3, 1793	134
John, m. Sally **COREY**, Apr. 27, 1828	76
John, d. Oct. 18, 1837, ae 45	110
Jonathan, d. Dec. 25, 1775	83
Jonathan, his w. [ ], d. Sept. 13, 1776	84
Jonathan, s. Jonathan, bp. [Oct.] 25, 1795	135
Julia, m. Richard **GILLET**, of Farmington, Mar. 17, 1835	78
Juliana, d. Jason, bp. Nov. 20, 1791	133
Levi, m. Rachel **RILEY**, [ ], 1789	64
Levi, m. Elizabeth **WARNER**, Sept. 2, 1790	65
Levi, d. Jan. 16, 1818, ae 59	101
Lucy, d. Elnathan, bp. Feb. 16, 1772	122
Lucy, m. Seth **HART**, Aug. 9, 1812	72
Luther, s. Jason, bp. Feb. 16, 1813	142
Mabel*, m. Justus **BULKLEY**, Mar. 22, 1781 *(Arnold Copy has "Mary")	61
Martha, d. Jona[than], bp. Sept. 2, 1792	133
Martha*, d. wid. Abigail **GRISWOLD**, bp. Mar. 9, 1794 *(Church Rec. give "Martha, child of wid. Abigail **GRISWOLD**")	134
Mary*, m. Justus **BULKLEY**, Mar. 22, 1781 *(Church Rec. give "Mabel")	61
Mary Jane, d. Jason, bp. July 2, 1820	145
Mary Jane, m. Thomas Danforth **WILLIAMS**, Apr. 6, 1842	80
Mehetabel, m. Pownal **DEMING**, of Hartford, May 29, 1791	65
Mercy, wid. of Elijah, d. Feb. 23, 1838, [in] Wallingford *("ae 85" Interred in Rocky Hill." From Church Rec.)	110
Nathaniel, d. May 12, 1776	84
Nathaniel P. Jr.*, d. May 4, 1776 *("Nath[anie]l **BOARDMAN**, Jr."	

	Page
BOARDMAN, (cont.)	
in Church Rec.	84
Norman, s. Jason, bp. Aug. 18, 1811	142
Rebecca, d. Frederick, bp. Aug. 4, 1799	136
Return, d. [ ], 1831, ae 88	107
Rhoda, d. Nathaniel C., Jr., bp. Mar. 31, 1776 *("Nathaniel, Jr." in Church Rec.)	125
Rhoda, d. Jason, bp. [Oct. 14], 1787	131
Rhoda, m. Sabin **COLTON**, of Long Meadow, Mass., Jan. 2, 1811	71
Roland, s. Frederick, bp. Apr. 18, 1804	139
Ruth, d. Nathaniel, Jr., bp. Dec. 18, 1768	120
Ruth, wid., d. May 7, 1790	89
Sarah, d. Elnathan, bp. Nov. 17, 1765	117
Sarah, d. Nathaniel*, bp. Apr. 17, 1774 *("Nathaniel, Jr." in Church Rec.)	124
Sarah, m. Samuel **STEBBINS**, Aug. 12, 1784	62
Sarah B[uell], of Rocky Hill, m. Samuel **COLES**, of Wethersfield, Apr. 27, 1848, by Rev. C. Chapin	25
Simeon, s. Nathaniel, Jr., bp. Aug. 31, 1766	118
Simeon, d. Nov. 23, 1815, ae 50	100
Thomas, Curtis, s. Jason, bp. July 22, 1798	136
William, s. Elnathan, bp. Sept. 3, 1765	117
William, s. Elnathan, d. Sept. 3, 1765	81
W[illia]m, s. Nathaniel, Jr., bp. Feb. 24, 1771	121
W[illia]m, s. Frederick, d. July [ ], 1793	91
William, bp. Mar. 7, 1819	144
W[illia]m Bulkley, s. Frederick, bp. June 5, 1791	132
W[illia]m Bulkley, s. Fred, bp. June 29, 1794	134
W[illia]m Elnathan, s. Elijah, bp. Dec. 15, 1784	129
W[illia]m Henry*, s. Elijah, bp. [July] 17, 1785 *("Only son of Elijah" in Church Rec.)	129
W[illia]m Henry, s. Elijah, d. Mar. 6, 1786	87
BOOTH, Salmon, of Berlin, m. Lois **WRIGHT**, Apr. 19, 1797	66
BOTELL, Ellelar, of Mereden, m. Amanda Amelia **BECKLEY**, Feb. 9, 1834	78
BOWEN*, Ephraim, bp. June 20, 1802 *("**BOWERS**?)	138
BOWERS, Benajah, m. wid. Esther **BENTON**, Nov. 27, 1791	65
Benajah, d. [ ] 24, 1823, ae 84	103
Burrell*, child of Ephraim, bp. Aug. 23, 1818 *(Arnold Copy has "Permula")	144
Ephraim, of Chatham, m. Esther **BENTON**, Mar. 5, 1801	68
Ephraim*, bp. [ ], 1802 *(Written "**BOWEN**")	138
Ephraim, s. Ephraim, bp. Aug. 2, 1818	144
Ephraim, Jr., d. [ ] 24, 1826, ae 12	104
Ephraim, his w. [ ], d. Dec. 17, 1834, ae 55	108
Ephraim, m. wid. Hannah **STEVENS**, of Glastonbury, Nov. 22, 1835	78
Ephraim, d. Apr. 1, 1840, ae 63	111
Esther Marie, d. Ephraim, bp. Aug. 2, 1818 *("Aug. 23" in Church Rec.)	144
Eunice, d. Ephraim, bp. [Sept.] 18, 1803	139
Eunice, d. Sept. 28, 1820, ae 18	101
Eunice, d. Ephraim, bp. Nov. 17, 1822	145

ROCKY HILL VITAL RECORDS 15

	Page
BOWERS, (cont.)	
Henry, s. Ephraim, bp. Aug. 2, 1818 ("Aug. 23" in Church Rec.)	144
Henry, d. Jan. 10, 1824, ae 15, at Heb[ ]	103
James, s. John, bp. June 12, 1808	141
Jane, of Cromwell, m. Chauncey **WHITMORE**, of Rocky Hill, Aug. 14, 1853, by Rev. L. Burton Rockwood	46
Jason, s. Ephraim, bp. Aug. 2, 1818 ("Aug. 23" in Church Rec.)	144
Jerusha, d. John, bp. [Nov.] 10, 1805	140
John, of Chatham, m. Hannah **WHITE**, Feb. 16, 1803	68
John, bp. Nov. 3, 1805, an adult	140
Lotta, d. Benajah, bp. Apr. 21, 1793	133
Lucinda, d. Benajah, bp. Apr. 21, 1793	133
Mary, d. Ephraim, bp. Aug. 2, 1818	144
Mari*, d. Ephraim, bp. Aug. 2, 1818 *("Esther Mari" bp. Aug. 23" in Church Rec.)	144
Mary, d. Ephraim, bp. Aug. 23, 1818	144
Otis*, s. Ephraim, bp. Apr. 20, 1806 *("Otis **BARNES**" in Arnold Copy)	140
Otis, d. Apr. 3, 1821, at New London, ae 17	102
Permula*, child of Ephraim, bp. Aug. 2, 1818 *("Burrell" in Church Rec.)	144
Rachel, d. Ephraim, bp. Aug. 1, 1819	144
Sarah, d. Ephraim, bp. Aug. 2, 1818 ("Aug. 23" in Church Rec.)	144
Sarah, m. Joel **HART**, of Burlington, Sept. 7, 1820	74
Walter, s. John, bp. [Nov.] 10, 1805	140
W[illia]m, d. [ ] 26, 1825, ae 24, drowned in New York	104
William Tyler, s. Ephraim, bp. Aug. 15, 1802	138
BOWLER*, Philip, of Middletown, m. Caroling Hart **BULKLEY**, Nov. 28, 1833 *(Church Rec. give "**BUTLER**")	78
BRADFORD, Betsey, m. Ralph **BULKLEY**, Jan. 21, 1808	70
Charlotte, m. Richard **GRIMES***, June 27, 1824 *(Arnold Copy has "**GRENNIS**")	75
Elizabeth, wid., d. Oct. 13, 1828, ae 71	105
Fanny, d. W[illia]m, bp. Nov. 8, 1795	135
George, s. W[illia]m, bp. Mar. 28, 1790	132
Horace, s. W[illia]m, bp. Oct. 27, 1793	134
Nancy, m. Sylvester **BULKLEY**, of Middletown, May 1, 1825	75
Sophia, d. W[illia]m, bp. [Oct.] 18, 1801	138
Sophia, m. Charles **HILL**, of New York, May 5, 1831	77
William, s. W[illia]m, bp. Sept. 26, 1784	129
W[illia]m, d. [Sept. 21], 1824, ae 65	104
BRADLEY, Charles, of Plymouth, m. Caroline **SMITH**, of Hartford, May 4, 1839	79
BRAINARD, Ezra, of East Hartford, m. Louisa **ROBBINS**, May 14, 1809	70
John H., m. Lucy **GRIMES**, Dec. 23, 1852, by Reb. A.B. Chapin, of Glastonbury	48
Mary A., m. Ethiel **SANGER**, of New Britain, Apr. 17, 1836	78
BREATHGOOD*, Edward, s. Hannah, bp. Apr. 15, 1781, by Rev. Mr. Lewis *("**BEACHGOOD**" in Church Rec.)	126
BREWER, ----------, Mrs., d. May 21, 1787	88
BROOKS, Joseph, m. Lucy **SMITH**, of Glastonbury, Jan. 17, 1786	63
Mary, m. George **ABBY**, of Chatham, Feb. 5, 1784	62

Page

BROWN, Roger, of Stamford, m. Mehetabel **NOTT**, Apr. 22, 1781   61
   Thomas, m. Rebecca **BARMAN***, b. of 1st Society, Dec. 3, 1809
      *("**BARNUM**" in Church Rec.)   71
BUCK, Isaac, m. [   ] **DEMING**, Apr. 16, 1771   61
   Sarah, wid., d. June 7, 1800, ae 89   94
BULKLEY, BUCKLEY, Abby Jane, d. Prescott, bp. July 3, 1846   151
   Abigail, d. Giles, bp. Oct. 22, 1769   120
   Abigail, wid., d. Sept. 8, 1782, ae 55   85
   Abigail, m. Jasper **LACY**, of Suffield, Sept. 9, 1789   64
   Abigail, d. Hosea, bp. Nov. 29, 1795   135
   Abigail, m. Davis **SMITH**, of Haddam, Mar. 18, 1819   74
   Abigail Stanley, d. Hosea, bp. Apr. 28, 1799   136
   Alan, s. Stephen, bp. Aug. 27, 1786   130
   Amelia, d. Hosea, bp. May 5, 1782   127
   Amelia, m. Allen **ROBBINS**, Oct. 17, 1804   69
   Amelia Ann, d. John G., bp. July 26, 1818   144
   Amelia Ann, m. Norman **BUTLER**, [July] 28, 1825   75
   Anna, wid., d. Aug. 20, 1828, ae 91   105
   Arthur*, s. Charles, bp. June 3, 1792   *("Ashur twin with Ashbel" in
      Church Rec.)   133
   Ashbel*, s. Charles, bp. June 3, 1792   *("twin with Ashur" in Church
      Rec.)   133
   Augusta, d. Charles, bp. [Apr. 8], 1787   130
   Belinda, d. Prescott, bp. Aug. 29. 1790   132
   Benjamin Griswold, s. John G., bp. July 26, 1818   144
   Betsey, d. Justus, bp. Aug. 1, 1793   134
   Betsey, m. Jedediah **NORTON**, 2nd, of Berlin, Mar. 10, 1813   72
   Burrage, s. Jon[atha]n, bp. Aug. 9, 1767   118
   Burrage, d. between May 7 & Aug. 17, 1782, at New York (Soldier)   85
   Burrage, his s. [   ], d. Aug. 16, 1845, ae 7   114
   Caroline Hart, d. John G., bp. July 26, 1818   144
   Caroline Hart, m. Philip **BUTLER***, of Middletown, Nov. 28, 1833
      (Arnold Copy has "**BOWLER**")   78
   Caty, m. Zenas **EDWARDS**, of Middletown, Dec. 7, 1800   68
   Charles, m. Eunice **ROBBINS**, Oct. 24, 1782   62
   Charles, of Williamstown, Mass., m. wid. Prudence **BULKLEY**, Aug. 27,
      1798   67
   Charles, d. [   ], 1798*, ae 38, in West Indies   *("1797" in Church
      Rec.)   93
   Charles, d. Jan. 12, 1824, at Granville, N. [   ], ae 72   103
   Charlotte, d. Edward, bp. [   ] 23, 1799   136
   Charlotte, m. Orin **LEWIS**, [, 1820]   74
   Chauncey, s. Jehiel, bp. Sept. 8, 1782   128
   Chauncey, m. Nancy **HART**, Aug. 27, 1805   69
   Chesterfield, s. Justus, bp. Nov. 7, 1784   129
   Chesterfield*, d. Nov. [   ], 1845, ae 52   *("Christopher" in Arnold
      Copy)   114
   Chloe, d. Gershom, d. June 20, 1765   81
   Chloe, d. Gershom, bp. Sept. 8, 1765   117
   Chloe, m. Frederick **BOARDMAN**, July 28, 1790   64

	Page
BULKLEY, BUCKLEY, (cont.)	
Christian, wid., d. [ ] 22, 1802, ae 77	95
Christopher*, d. Nov. [ ], 1845, ae 62 *("Chesterfield" in Church Rec.)	114
Clarissa, d. Justus, bp. May 1, 1791	132
Clarissa*, m. Reuben **SHIPMAN**, of Glastonbury, Dec. 3, 1818 *("Clarissa **BECKLEY**?)	74
Cyrus, s. Stephen, bp. [Sept. 1], 1799 *("**BUTLER**" in Church Rec.)	137
Daniel, s. Giles, bp. June 28, 1772	122
David, s. Giles, bp. Aug. 3, 1766	118
Dorothy, d. Jonathan, bp. June 17, 1770	121
Edmond, s. Joseph, bp. Feb. 3, 1788	131
Edmund, m. Nancy **ROBBINS**, Apr. 18, 1811	71
Edward, m. Rachel **POMEROY**, Oct. 27, 1771	61
Edward, m. Prudence **WILLIAMS**, Nov. 2, 1774	61
Edward, d. May 30, 1787, ae 46	88
Edward, his infant, d. Feb. 13, 1792	90
Edward, d. July 22, 1801, ae 23, in West Indies	95
Edward, d. June 20, 1806, ae 54	97
Edward Rodney, s. Edward, bp. July 5, 1789	131
Eleanor, m. Joseph **EDWARDS**, of Middletown, Feb. 10, 1768	60
Elizabeth, m. John **MYGATE**, Aug. 26, 1773	61
Ellen Louisa, d. Prescott, bp. June 29, 1838	149
Emeline, twin with Erastus, d. Charles, bp. May 21, 1797	136
Emeline, m. Samuel H.P. **HALL**, of Middletown, May 14, 1826	75
Erastus, twin with Emeline, s. Charles, bp. May 21, 1797	136
Eunice, wid., d. Mar. 29, 1835, ae 75	109
Fanny, d. Edward, Jr., bp. Apr. 29, 1781, by Rev. Mr. Lewis	126
Fanny, m. Elihu **FRISBIE**, of Albany, Oct. 29, 1813	72
Frances Amelia, d. of the late John G., bp. Aug. 31, 1832	147
Frederick, s. Stephen, bp. June 3, 1792	133
Frederic, m. Nancy **RILEY**, Oct. 6, 1814	72
George, d. July 1, 1805, in West Indies, ae 19	96
Gershom, s. Ho[sea], bp. [Apr. 19], 1789	131
Gershom, his w. [ ], d. Dec. 17, 1794, ae 71	92
Gershom, his w. [ ], d. Dec. 23, 1798, ae 57	94
Gershom, d. Aug. 21, 1800, ae 87	95
Gershom, m. Laura **GOODRICH**, July 4, 1816	73
Giles, d. Aug. 4, 1785, ae 57	87
Harriet, d. David, bp. Nov. 9, 1794	134
Harriet, d. Justin, bp. Oct. 11, 1801	138
Harriet, m. George **BUNCE**, Sept. 27, 1821	74
Harriet Griswold, d. Prescott, bp. May 1, 1840	149
Harry, s. Charles, bp. May 31, 1789	131
Henry, s. Joseph, bp. Aug. 1, 1793	134
Henry, of Rocky Hill, m. Martha **TUCKER**, of Wethersfield, May 16, 1847, by Rev. C. Chapin	23
Henry Williams, [s. Henry & Martha], b. June 30, 1847	23
Hetty, d. Giles, bp. Apr. 15, 1781, by Rev. Mr. Lewis	126
Honor, d. Stephen, bp. Sept. 25, 1774	124
Horace, s. Prescott, bp. Oct. 10, 1779, by Rev. Mr. Pitkin, of Farmington	126

BULKLEY, BUCKLEY, (cont.)

	Page
Horace, s. Prescott, bp. June 29, 1838	149
Horace, d. June 11, 1848, in So. Glastonbury, ae 18	116
Hosea, m. Abigail **GRISWOLD**, May 1, 1781	61
Hosea, his child d. June 5, 1798, ae 3	93
Hosea, s. John G., bp. July 26, 1818	144
Hosea, his w. [ ], d. Aug. 28, 1823, ae 63	103
Hosea, d. Nov. 4, 1838, ae 82	110
James, m. Hannah **MYEARS**, Feb. 14, 1805	69
Jehiel, m. Mary **ROBBINS**, Mar. 2, 1775	61
Jehiel, his child d. Apr. 29, 1781	84
John, s. Stephen*, bp. Dec. 11, 1785 *("Joseph" in Church Rec.)	130
John, d. June 2, 1806, ae [ ]	97
John, s. John G., bp. July 26, 1818	144
John, m. wid. Mary **HUBBARD**, Jan. 12, 1830	76
John, d. Sept. 22, 1832, ae 22	107
John, [s. Henry & Martha], b. Feb. 6, 1855	23
John G., m. Nabby **HART**, Nov. 25, 1804	69
John G., d. Nov. 14, 1829, ae 46	106
John Griswold, s. Hosea, bp. Apr. 17, 1785	129
John Henry, s. John, bp. July 6, 1834	148
Jonathan, his d. [ ], d. Aug. 18, 1766	81
Jonathan, m. Mary **EDWARDS**, Jan. 16, 1787	63
Jonathan, his w. [ ], d. Feb. 14, 1823, ae 62	103
Jonathan, d. [ ] 30, 1836, ae 77	109
Joseph, m. Mary **WILLIAMS**, May 3, 1776	61
Joseph, s. Joseph, bp. Feb. 21, 1790	132
Joseph, d. Mar. 31, 1821, ae 80	102
Joseph*, his w. [ ], d. Aug. 8, 1842, in Aurora, N.Y., *("Joseph **BLAKELY**" in Church Rec.)	113
Joseph, [s. Henry & Martha], b. Oct. 16, 1851	23
Joseph Edmond, s. Edmond, bp. May 23, 1819	144
Julius, s. Justus, bp. [Nov.] 13, 1803	139
Julius, [s. Henry & Martha], b. Nov. 13, 1857	23
Julius Huntington, s. Edmond, bp. May 23, 1819	144
Justus, m. Mary* **BOARDMAN**, Mar. 22, 1781 *("Mabel" in Church Rec.)	61
Justus, his child d. June 11, 1781	85
Justus, his infant d. Oct. 19, 1786	88
Justus, s. Justus, bp. Sept. 25, 1795	134
Justus, his w. [ ], d. Sept. 11, 1804, ae 47* *("ae 44" in Church Rec.)	96
Justus, m. [ ] **RILEY**, wid. of Ackley, June 19, 1805, by Rev. Dr. Marsh	69
Justus, his w. [ ], d. [ ] 12, 1826, ae 75	105
Justus, m. wid. Mehitable **CULVER**, Nov. 12, 1826	75
Justus, d. May 9, 1829, ae 77	106
Justus Robbins, s. Edmond, bp. May 23, 1819	144
Katy, d. Stephen, bp. Mar. 4, 1781, by Rev. Mr. Lewis	126
Laura, d. Prescott, bp. Mar. 21, 1784	128
Laura, d. Prescott, bp. June 29, 1838	149

	Page
BULKLEY, BUCKLEY, (cont.)	
Laura, [d. Henry & Martha], b. Nov. 22, 1858	23
Levi, s. Giles, bp. Sept. 30, 1764	117
Levi, d. [ ] 3, 1789, at Sea	89
Lois, wid., m. Isaac **HALL**, of Leyden, N.Y., Dec. 20, 1802	68
Lorey*, d. Justus, bp. Nov. 7, 1790 *(Arnold Copy has "Lucy")	132
Louisa, d. Prescott, bp. Apr. 9, 1786	130
Lucy*, d. Justus, bp. Nov. 7, 1790 *("Lorey" in Church Rec.)	132
Lucy*, d. Stephen, bp. June 3, 1792 *("Lucy **BUTLER**" in Church Rec.)	133
Lucy, d. Prescott, bp. June 29, 1838	149
Lucy, of Rocky Hill, m. Hamilton R. **HORTON**, of Glastonbury, Aug. 1, 1844, by Rev. C. Chapin	5
Lydia, m. Solomon **SAVAGE**, of Middletown, Nov. 27, 1783	62
Lydia, d. Prescott, bp. Feb. 27, 1788 ("Feb. 24" in Church Rec.)	131
Mabel, m. Wait **ROBBINS**, Nov. 9, 1789	64
Mabel, d. Hosea, bp. Feb. 26, 1792	133
Mabel, m. Ira **BEAMONT**, of East Hartford, Oct. 10, 1811	71
Maria [Wells*], d. May 12, 1835, ae 35 *(In Church Rec.)	109
Mariam*, m. Aaron **PORTER**, Jr., b. of 1st Soc., Apr. 12, 1815 *("Mariam **BECKLEY**" in Church Rec.)	73
Martha, wid., m. Elizur **GOODRICH**, Mar. 6, 1796	66
Martha, d. Prescott, bp. June 29, 1838	149
Martha G., m. Lucius M. **BEAUMONT**, Nov. 27, 1845, by Rev. C. Chapin	17
Martha Griswold, d. Gershom, bp. May 27, 1827	146
Martha Robbins, [d. Henry & Martha], b. Dec. 31, 1848	23
Mary, d. Joseph, bp. June 10, 1781	127
Mary, m. Elisha **WETHERELL**, Jan. 26, 1783	62
Mary, m. Joseph **BUTLER**, May 23, 1803	68
Mary, m. Thomas **SELDEN**, of Chatham, [May] 17, 1832	77
Mary, d. Prescott, bp. June 29, 1838	149
Mary, wid., d. Dec. 23, 1845, ae 90	114
Mary, [d. Henry & Martha], b. Apr. 23, 1850	23
Mary Sophia, d. John, bp. [Sept. 2], 1838	149
Mehetabel, m. George **LATIMER**, of 1st Society, May 15, 1803	68
Nabby, d. Joh[natha]n (?), bp. [Feb. 19], 1792	133
Nabby, m. Israel **STERMS***, of Glastonbury, Apr. 20, 1819 *("Isaac **STEVENS**" in Church Rec.)	74
Nancy, d. Prescott, bp. Nov. 11, 1781	127
Nancy, m. Joshua **GOODRICH**, July 25, 1800	68
Nancy, m. Nathan **NORTH**, of Exeter, N.H., Aug. 4, 1805	69
Noah Edwards, s. Prescott, bp. July 3, 1846	151
Olive, d. Hosea, bp. Nov. 2, 1793	134
Oliver, d. [, 1771], at Sea	82
Oliver Pomeroy, s. Edward, bp. Apr. 8, 1787	130
Onner, m. Daniel **EDWARDS**, Jr., of Middletown, Nov. 16, 1795	66
Pamela, d. Edward, bp. [June] 6, 1784	129
Parmela, d. Sept. 16, 1814, ae 31	100
Patty, d. Stephen, bp. May 2, 1790	132
Patty, d. Sept. 22, 1795, ae 8	92

	Page
BULKLEY, BUCKLEY, (cont.)	
Peter, m. Christian **SMITH**, [Jan. 26, 1769]	60
Peter, d. Apr. 4, 1776	84
Polly, d. Charles, bp. [Oct.] 30, 1785	129
Prescott, d. Sept. 10, 1791, ae 47	90
Prescott, s. Jonathan, bp. June 11, 1797	136
Prudence, d. Edward, Jr., bp. Apr. 1, 1787	130
Prudence, wid., m. Charles **BULKLEY**, of Williamstown, Mass., Aug. 27, 1798	67
Prudence, m. Ebenezer **BAKER**, of Boston, Mass., Aug. 9, [1812]	72
Prudence, wid., d. Jan. 26, 1825, ae 71	104
Prudence, wid., d. Feb. 5, 1837, ae 70* *("ae 79" in Church Rec.)	109
Rachel, w. Edward, d. Aug. 14, 1774	83
Rachel, d. Edward, bp. Feb. 16, 1783	128
Ralph, s. Joseph, bp. Oct. 26, 1783	128
Ralph, m. Betsey **BRADFORD**, Jan. 21, 1808	70
Rebecca, m. Samuel **DIMOCK**, July 4, 1782	61
Rhoda, d. Edward, Jr., bp. Aug. 11, 1776	126
Rhoda, d. Joseph, bp. June 10, 1781	127
Rhoda, m. Josiah **EDWARDS**, Apr. 14, 1796	66
Rhoda*, d. Stephen, bp. May 1, 1796 *("Rhoda **BUTLER**" in Church Rec.)	135
Rhoda, m. Willys **WILLIAMS**, June 19, 1799	67
Rodney, s. of Edward, Jr., bp. June 13, 1784 *("Rodney, s. of Fredk **ROBBINS**" in Arnold Copy)	129
Roxy, d. Edmund*, bp. Oct. 25, 1772 *("Edward" in Church Rec.)	122
Roxy, d. Stephen, bp. July 19, 1789	131
Ruth*, m. Silas **BELDEN**, Mar. 4, 1783 *("Ruth **BECKLEY**" in Church Rec.)	62
Sally, d. Jonathan, bp. Dec. 2, 1787	131
Sally, m. Elisha **GOODRICH**, of Glastonbury, [ ] 30, 1821	74
Simeon, s. Prescott, bp. Aug. 21, 1774	124
Simeon, d. [ ], 1793, ae 19	91
Solomon, m. Martha **WILLIAMS**, June 6, 1776, by Mr. Lewis	61
Solomon, d. Mar. 4, 1790, ae 43	89
Sophia, d. Justus, bp. Oct. 6, 1782	128
Sophia, m. Edmund **AVERY***, of Mansfield, Apr. 13, 1806 *(Church Rec. give "**HOVEY**")	69
Stephen, s. Stephen, bp. Apr. 28, 1776	125
Stephen, s. Stephen, bp. June 1, 1783	128
Stephen, his w. [ ], d. Apr. 6, 1804, ae [ ]	96
Stephen, d. May 6, 1813, ae 64	99
Susan Mansfield, d. Edmund, bp. Sept. 10, 1825	146
Sylvester, s. Hosea, bp. July 28*, 1787 *("July 22" in Church Rec.)	130
Sylvester, of Middletown, m. Nancy **BRADFORD**, May 1, 1825	75
Thankful, d. Oct. 1, 1839, ae 96	110
Thomas Goodrich, s. John, bp. July 6, 1834	148
Ursula, d. Hosea, bp. July 27, 1783	128
Ursula B., m. Josiah **BUTLER***, of East Haddam, Dec. 28, 1828 *("**BUTTON**" in Church Rec.)	76
Ursula Bull, d. John G., bp. July 26, 1818	144

	Page
BULKLEY, BUCKLEY, (cont.)	
Wait C., m. Charlotte **WHITMORE**, May 10, 1838	79
Walter, s. Prescott, bp. June 29, 1838	149
Walter, [s. Henry & Martha], bp. June 1, 1853	23
Walter W., d. Mar. 5, 1834, ae 37 ("d. in or near Philadelphia." See Church Rec.)	108
Walter Williams, s. Joseph, bp. Jan. 28, 1798	136
Walter Williams, m. Lucy **ROBBINS**, June 17, 1830	77
W[illia]m, m. Olive **WILLIAMS**, Jan. 31, 1776	61
William, s. W[illia]m, bp. Mar. 25, 1781, by Rev. Mr. Lewis	126
W[illia]m, d. July 23, 1788	89
W[illia]m, d. Feb. 14, 1790, ae 10	89
William, s. Justus, bp. Apr. 14, 1799	136
William, s. John G., bp. July 26, 1818	144
William, d. Mar. 13, 1840, ae 35	111
----------, of Somers, m. Anna **HOWARD**, [Feb.] 6, [1798]	67
BULL, Aaron, m. Lydia **WILLIAMS**, Aug. 9, 1786	63
Aaron, d. Apr. 17, 1797	93
Eunice, d. Roger, bp. [Dec. 25], 1768	120
Eunice, m. John **WILLIAMS**, May 6, 1784	62
Eunice, m. Isaac **BILL**, of Glastonbury, Oct. 24, 1803	68
Fanny W., m. Lyman **BURKE**, of East Haddam, Jan. 4, 1820	74
George Hayland, s. Aaron, bp. [May] 15, 1796	135
Lydia, wid., m. Seth **HART**, Nov. 10, 1799	67
Mary, d. Aaron, bp. [May] 15, 1796	135
Mary, m. Sylvester **CLARK**, Sept. 20, 1807	70
Roger, m. Ruth **RUSSELL**, Nov. 19, 1767	60
Roger, d. May 24, 1783, ae 41	86
Russell, s. Roger, bp. Mar. 1, 1772	122
Russel, m. Lucy **WARNER**, Dec. 17, 1795	66
Russel, his w. [ ], d. Nov.*, 14, 1808, ae 34 *("Dec." in Church Rec.)	98
Ruth, wid., m. Jacob **RILEY**, [, 1788]	64
Ursula, d. Roger, bp. June 9, 1782	127
Ursula, d. Roger, d. Dec. 9, 1782	85
BUNCE, Anna, d. Thomas, bp. Nov. 4, 1798	136
Anne, m. Joel **GOODRICH**, Oct. 17, 1805	69
Betsey, d. Thomas, bp. Nov. 4, 1798	136
Caty, d. Thomas, bp. Nov. 4, 1798	136
Caty, d. June 26, 1802, ae 9	95
Eunice, wid., d. [ ], 1835, ae 83	108
George, s. Thomas, bp. Nov. 4, 1798	136
George, m. Harriet **BULKLEY**, Sept. 27, 1821	74
James, s. Thomas, bp. Nov. 4, 1798	136
Joseph, m. Rhoda **PORTER**, Jan. 29, 1798	67
Joseph, d. Aug. 3, 1798, ae 19	93
Joseph, bp. Aug. 29, 1798 *(Church Rec. say "bp. Aug. 3, 1798, an adult")	136
Polly, m. Elizur **DICKINSON**, Mar. 11, 1798	67
Sarah*, m. Moses **LOCKWOOD**, Sept. 9, 1773 *(Arnold Copy has "Sarah **BURETT**")	61

BUNCE, (cont.)
    Thomas, m. Eunice* **DICKINSON**, Apr. 17, 1774   *("Eunnice" or
        Emmice?")   61
    Thomas*, d. Sept. 21, 1820, ae 72   *("Thomas **PRINCE**" in Arnold
        Copy)   101
    W[illia]m, s. Thomas, 2nd, d. Feb. 11, 1784   87
BUNNELL, BUNNEL, Lazarus*, of New York, m. Sarah **DICKINSON**, of
    Rocky Hill, Jan. 24, 1853, by Rev. L.B. Rockwood   *("Perhaps
    "Lazarus **BARRETT**")   43
    Sally, of Berlin, m. Levi **LEWIS**, of Southington, Aug.* 2, 1801
        *("July" written in a later hand)   68
    Zarr, m. Julia Ann **COOK**, b. of Middletown, Mar. 12, 1843   80
BURETT*, Sarah, m. Moses **LOCKWOOD**, Sept. 9, 1773   *("**BUNCE**"
    in Church Rec.)   61
BURKE, Lyman, of East Haddam, m. Fanny W. **BULL**, Jan. 4, 1820   74
BURKITT, BURKETT, BURKIT, Jane M., of Rocky Hill, m. Albert A.
    WARNER, of Wilmington, N.C., Oct. 12, 1845, by Rev. C. Chapin   14
    John, of Middletown, m. Polly **MARSH**, Nov. 7, 1816   73
    John, d. [   ] 9, 1841, ae 51   112
    Susan, of Rocky Hill, m. Hiram **DEWING**, of Charleston, S.C., Aug. 29,
        1850, by Rev. L.B. Rockwood   34
BURNHAM, Anthony, of East Hartford, m. Ann M[aria] **JAGGER**, of Rocky
    Hill, June 28, 1848, by Rev. Theodore M. Dwight   27
    Charles*, s. Esther, d. Sept. 18, 1803, ae 5   *(Arnold Copy has "Charles
    BOARDMAN")   96
    Esther*, had s. Charles, d. Sept. 18, 1803, ae 5   *(Arnold Copy has
    "Esther **BOARDMAN**")   96
    Lucy, m. Peter **CLOUD**, of New York, June 4, 1834   78
    Mary Ann, of Berlin, m. Julius **COLLINS**, of Rocky Hill, Feb. 9, 1851,
        by Rev. Calvin Chapin   35
BURR, Samuel, of Hartford, m. Rebecca **STILLMAN**, June 17, 1773   61
BUTLER, Abigail. d. Simeon, bp. Oct. 2, 1785   129
    Abigail, d. Aug. 13, 1824, ae 39   104
    Abigail, d. Norman, bp. Mar. 20, 1835   148
    Abigail Clarissa, d. Elisha, bp. [Nov. 3], 1843   150
    Allen, s. Benjamin, bp. Nov. 2, 1783   128
    Alvin, s. David, bp. Dec. 28, 1790   132
    Ann, m. Sylvester **BUTLER**, Dec. 28, 1814   73
    Anna, of Middletown, m. Levi **WARNER**, Sept. 1, 1782   61
    Anselm, s. Simeon, bp. Apr. 11, 1802   138
    Anselon, d. Oct. 15, 1825, ae 25   104
    Archibold*, s. Elisha, bp. Apr. 19, 1781, by Rev. Mr. Lewis   *("Church
        Rec. say "a child of Elisha **BUTLER**, bp. soon after birth, supposed
        of short life, without a name")   126
    Azubah, m. Eli **MARSH**, Jan. 25, 1787   63
    Barzillai, s. Elisha, bp. Mar. 19, 1775   124
    Benjamin, m. Eunice **ROBBINS**, Dec. 13, 1775   61
    Benj[amin], s. Benj[amin], bp. [Feb.] 28, 1795   134
    Calma, d. Richard, bp. Sept. 3, 1793   134
    Catharine Maria, d. Elisha, bp. Aug. 31, 1838   149
    Charles, d. Jan. 18, 1783, ae 50   85

ROCKY HILL VITAL RECORDS 23

	Page
BUTLER, (cont.)	
Charles, d. June 26, 1785, ae 71	87
Charles, s. Joel, bp. Apr. 4, 1790	132
Charles, s. David, bp. Dec. 28, 1790	132
Charles Churchill, s. Samuel, bp. June 24, 1821	145
Charles Churchill, m. Elizabeth **STEVENS**, b. of Rocky Hill, May 7, 1844, by Rev. Calvin Chapin	4
Cornelia, d. Joseph, bp. [Nov.] 15, 1812	142
Cornelia, m. Benjamin **SMITH**, May 17, 1837	79
Cyrus*, s. Stephen, bp. Sept. 1, 1799 *("Cyrus **BULKELEY**" in Arnold Copy)	137
Daniel, d. Mar. 17, 1766	81
David, s. David, bp. June 16, 1793	134
Desire, d. Charles, Jr., bp. Dec. 31, 1775	125
Dorothy, d. Charles, Jr., bp. Oct. 2, 1768	119
Elisha, m. Eunice **WILLIAMS**, Oct. 19, 1769	60
Elisha, his child d. [ ], 1781	84
Elisha, d. Feb. 5, 1783, ae 35	86
Elisha, d. Aug. 11, 1799, ae 22, in West Indies	94
Elisha, s. Elisha, decd., bp. Feb. 2, 1800	137
Elisha*, his wid., d. July 11, 1817, at Berlin, ae 78 *("Elisha **BELDEN**" in Church Rec.)	100
Elisha H., m. Catharine B. **WRIGHT**, of Ber[ ], July 7, 1833	78
Elisha Hurlburt, s. Samuel, bp. Sept. 20, 1818	144
Elizabeth, wid., d. Sept. 14, 1847, ae [ ]	115
Elizabeth B.*, m. Elisha L. **SAGE**, b. of Middletown, Jan. 28, 1829 *("Elizabeth B. **HUBBARD**" in Church Rec.)	76
Emeline E., m. Eli **GOODRICH**, [Oct.] 9, 1839	79
[Emera*], child of Sim[ ], d. Mar. 29, 1792 *(Supplied from Church Rec.)	90
Emma, d. Simeon, bp. Mar. 23, 1792	133
Emma*, Robbins, d. Joseph, bp. Sept. 11, 1814 *("Eunice" in Church Rec.)	143
Erastus, s. Alpheas, bp. June 15, 1794	134
Eunice, wid., m. Simeon **WILLIAMS**, Feb. 15, 1784	62
Eunice, d. Benjamin, bp. Mar. 31, 1793	133
Eunice*, wid., d. Oct. 1, 1847, ae 93, in Up. Middletown *("Eunice **BELDEN**, from Middletown" in Church Rec.)	115
Eunice R., of Rocky Hill, m. George H. **FAIRFIELD**, of Hartford, June 2, 1847, by Rev. C. Chapin	23
Eunice* Robbins, d. Joseph, bp. Sept. 11, 1814 *("Emma in Arnold Copy	143
Frederick, s. David, bp. Dec. 28, 1790	132
Frederick R., m. Elizabeth **GOODRICH**, Mar. 6, 1853, by Rev. L. Burton Rockwood	44
Frederick Robbins, s. Ullysses, bp. May 25, 1823	145
George, s. Benjamin, bp. Nov. 4, 1798	136
George Augustus, s. Samuel, bp. July 18, 1819	144
Hervey, s. Richard, bp. [Apr.] 12, 1789	131
Horace, of Middletown, m. Julia **BUTLER**, May 21, 1812	72
Jamin, d. May 30, 1813, at Middletown, ae 18	99

BUTLER, (cont.)
	Page
Jerome, s. Benjamin, bp. Aug. 21, 1796	135
Jerusha, d. Benjamin, bp. Apr. 15, 1781, by Rev. Mr. Lewis	126
John, s. Charles, Jr., bp. Mar. 30, 1766	118
John, d. Apr. 21, 1792	90
John Wadsworth, s. Elisha H., bp. July 3, 1835	148
Joseph, d. [, 1769], at Sea	81
Joseph, s. Benjamin, bp. [ ], 1776	126
Joseph, m. Mary **BULKLEY**, May 23, 1803	68
Joseph, d. [ ] 9, 1826, ae 50	104
Joseph H.B., of Rocky Hill, m. Elizabeth P. **ADAMS**, of Wethersfield, May 26, 1852, by Rev. L.B. Rockwood	40
Josiah, m. Martha **RILEY**, Oct. 16, 1769	60
Josiah, d. [, 1771], at Sea	82
Josiah, s. Elisha, bp. Nov. 8, 1772	122
Josiah, of Middletown, m. Elizabeth **RUSSELL**, [Nov.] 11, [1790]	65
Josiah, m. Mary **ROBBINS**, Dec. 24, [1797]	67
Josiah*, of East Haddam, m. Ursula B. **BULKLEY**, Dec. 28, 1828 *("Josiah **BUTTON**" in Church Rec.)	76
Josiah, 1st, d. Mar. 4, 1845, [at] Upper Middletown, ae 78	114
Julia, m. Horace **BUTLER**, of Middletown, May 21, 1812	72
Julia Ann, m. Jonathan F. **PENFIELD***, of Pittsfield, Mass., Nov. 12, 1840 *("**FAIRFIELD**" in Church Rec.)	80
Juliana, d. Joseph, bp. May 21, 1809	141
Leonard, s. David, bp. Dec. 28, 1790	132
Levi*, d. June 14, 1790, ae 7 *("Lois" in Church Rec.)	90
Levi, s. David, bp. Apr. 17, 1791	132
Lois, d. Ric[hard], bp. May 4, 1784	128
Lois, d. Richard, bp. Feb. 6, 1791	132
Lucy*, d. Stephen, bp. June 3, 1792 *("Lucy **BULKLEY**" in Arnold Copy)	133
Manley, of Ephiatah, N.Y., m. Prudence **BUTLER**, of Rocky Hill, July 31, 1851, by Rev. L.B. Rockwood	36
Mary, wid., d. Feb. 27, 1787, ae 82	88
Mary, d. Benjamin, bp. June 7, 1789	131
Mary, d. Benjamin, d. May 24, 1790	90
Mary, wid., m. Ichabod **GOODRICH**, Oct. 11, 1815	73
Mary Ann, d. Elisha, bp. Nov. 1, 1839	149
Mary E., of Rocky Hill, m. Charles H. **KIMBALL**, of Exeter, N.H., Nov. 22, 1853, by Rev. L.B. Rockwood	47
Mary Williams, d. Joseph, bp. May 4, 1806	140
May (?), s. Benjamin, bp. Apr. 17, 1791	132
Nancy, d. Simeon, bp. May 27, 1788	131
Nancy, d. Joseph, bp. June 18, 1820	145
Nancy, m. Albert Gallatin **PORTER***, May 15, 1843 *("**PARKER**" in Church Rec.)	80
Norman, s. Simeon, bp. Dec. 15, 1798	136
Norman, m. Amelia Ann **BULKLEY**, [July] 28, 1825	75
Philip*, of Middletown, m. Caroline Hart **BULKLEY**, Nov. 28, 1833 *("Philip **BOWLER**" in Arnold Copy)	78
Philip, his child d. July 16, 1841, ae 3	112

	Page
BUTLER, (cont.)	
Polly, d. Joel, bp. Feb. 26, 1792	133
Prudence, d. Samuel, bp. Sept. 20, 1818	144
Prudence, m. Frances **CASWELL**, of Bristol, Aug. 26, 1836	78
Prudence, wid., d. Feb. 23, 1842, ae 97	112
Prudence, of Rocky Hill, m. Manley **BUTLER**, of Ephiatah, N.Y., July 31, 1851, by Rev. L.B. Rockwood	36
Prudence Ellen, d. Elisha, bp. Sept. 3, 1841	150
Rhoda*, d. Stephen, bp. May 1, 1796 *("Rhoda **BULKLEY**" in Arnold Copy)	135
Richard, m. Lois **GOODRICH**, Feb. 5, 1784	62
Richard, his w. [ ], d. Apr. 23, 1784, ae 19	87
Russel, d. May 19, 1821, at sea, ae 29	102
Samuel, d. Aug. 27, 1810, ae 65	98
Samuel, had grand son Myron **FRANCIS**, bp. Sept. 3, 1841	150
Samuel, d. May 19, 1848, ae 64	116
Samuel Bidwell, s. Samuel, bp. Sept. 20, 1818	144
Samuel Bidwell, m. Charlotte Kirkham **PRICE**, Nov. 5, 1833	78
Sarah, wid., d. Dec. 22, 1767	81
Sarah, d. Charles, Jr., bp. June 16, 1771	121
Sarah, m. James **STANLEY**, Jan. 21, 1773	61
Sarah, d. Dec. 23, 1783, ae 49	86
Sarah, wid., d. May 10, 1795, ae 98 or 99	92
Sena, d. David, bp. Dec. 28, 1790	132
Sim, his infant*, d. Mar. 29, 1792 *(Named "Emera" in Church Rec.)	90
Simeon, m. Anna **MARSH**, Sept. 18, 1783	62
Simeon, d. Dec. 29, 1831, ae 77	107
Sophia, m. Jared G. **DIMOCK**, Dec. 17, 1823	75
Sophronia, d. Benjamin, bp. Jan. 17, 1802	138
Stephen, s. Charles, bp. Oct. 21, 1764	117
Stephen, m. Ruth **RUSSELL**, [ ], 1788	64
Stephen, d. Dec. [ ], 1803, ae 41, at Sea	96
Sylvanus, s. David, bp. Aug. 23, 1795	134
Sylvester, s. Benjamin, bp. [Nov.] 20, 1785	129
Sylvester, m. Ann BUTLER, Dec. 28, 1814	73
Ullyses, s. Simeon, bp. June 7, 1795	134
Ulysses, m. Orpah **ROBBINS**, Mar. 29, 1820	74
Ulysses, d. Sept. 1, 1823, at Chatham, ae 29	103
W[illia]m, s. Simeon, bp. Aug. 22, 1790	132
W[illia]m Henry, s. Elisha, decd., bp. Feb. 2, 1800	137
W[illia]m S.*, d. Nov. [ ], 1823, ae 36 (sailed for Martinique, not heard from) *("William Sage **BUTLER**" in Church Rec.)	103
W[illia]m Sage, s. Gideon, bp. May 20, 1792	133
BUTTON, Abigail Butler, d. Josiah, bp. [July 1], 1836	148
Catharine Amelia, d. Josiah, bp. [July 1], 1836	148
Hosea Bulkley, s. Josiah, bp. [July 1], 1836	148
John Griswold, s. Josiah, bp. [July 1], 1836	148
Josiah*, of East Haddam, m. Ursula B. **BULKLEY**, Dec. 28, 1828 *(Arnold Copy has "Josiah **BUTLER**")	76
CADWELL, Chester, of Springfield, Mass., m. Mary **HURLBURT**, Sept. 19, 1809	70

	Page
CADWELL, (cont.)	
Elisha C., of Torrington, m. Sophia **HOLMES**, Apr. 30, 1833	77
CALLENDER, Charlotte, wid., m. Erastus **DEMING**, Feb. 1, 1829	76
Elisha, m. Sarah **CRANE**, Sept. 25, 1766	60
Elisha, his servant Newport, m. Rose, servant of Elisha **WOLCOTT**, Oct. 10, 1782	62
Elisha, his w. [ ], d. Feb. 7, 1820, ae 41	101
Fanny, bp. Oct. 19, 1794, an adult	134
Fanny, m. Daniel **DEMING**, Oct. 11, 1795	66
Horace, m. Betsey **ROBBINS**, Oct. 23, 1817	73
Horace, d. Mar. 2, 1846, in Wethersfield, ae 57	114
Lucy, w. W[illia]m, bp. May 17, 1823	145
Lydia, bp. Oct. 19, 1794, adult	134
Lydia, m. W[illia]m **AMES**, Apr. 14, 1796	66
Nancy, bp. Nov. 22, 1796, an adult	135
Nancy, d. Jan. 30, 1797, ae 25	93
Polly, bp. Mar. 19, 1797, an adult	135
Polly, m. Timothy **COE**, of Durham, Jan. 10, 1803	68
Sarah, m. Nathan **FIELD**, of East Guilford, Nov. 29, 1801	68
Sarah, wid., d. Feb. 5, 1823, ae 80	103
Sarah, bp. July 4, 1841	150
Sarah, m. Alfred M. **FISH**, of Hartford, May 1, 1843	80
William, m. Lucy **DICKINSON**, Oct. 29, 1807	70
W[illia]m, his w. [ ], d. May 22, 1823, ae 39	103
William, 2nd, m. Charlotte **KELSEY**, July 14, 1825	75
W[illia]m, d. [Mar.] 21, 1826, ae 22	104
CANDEE, Justus, of Oxford, m. Delia **MERRIAM**, Oct. 15, 1833	78
CARROLL*, Lucy Ann, of Glastonbury, m. Josiah **THAYER**, Nov. 16, 1826	
*("**CASWELL**" in Church Rec.)	75
CARTER, Alfred H., m. Cynthia C. **CHAPMAN**, b. of East Haddam, Sept. 3, 1829	76
CASE, Pheneas S., of Berlin, m. Lucy **COLLINS**, of Rocky Hill, Aug. 24, 1846, by Rev. C. Chapin	20
CASSIDY, Caroline, bp. Mar. 3, 1843	150
CASWELL, Caroline Amelia, of Glastonbury, m. Charles **WILLIAMS**, Nov. 29, 1827	76
Frances, of Bristol, m. Prudence **BUTLER**, Aug. 26, 1836	78
Francis, his w. [ ], d. [ ] 21, 1837, ae 21	109
John, Jr., of Glastonbury, m. Sally **DICKINSON**, Oct. 12, 1803	68
Loretta, m. Obed **ANDRUS**, b. of Glastonbury, May 1, 1832	77
Lucy Ann, of Glastonbury, m. Josiah **THAYER**, Nov. 16, 1826	75
CHAMBERS, Francis, [s. George O. & Martha], b. May 7, 1828	10
Francis, s. George D., bp. Oct. 31, 1828	146
George O., of Middletown, m. Martha **ROBBINS**, Dec. 14, 1825	75
George O., m. Martha **ROBBINS**, Dec. 16, 1825	10
Henry Richardson, [s. George O. & Martha], b. Apr. 28, 1832	10
Henry Richardson, s. George O., bp. Nov. 2, 1832	147
John, s. Phebe **CHAMBERS**, bp. Nov. 17, 1768	119
Martha A., of Rocky Hill, m. Henry S. **GEAR**, of Cromwell, Oct. 29, 1854, by Rev. L.B. Rockwood	53
Martha Augusta, [d. George O. & Martha], b. Oct. 29, 1826	10

	Page
CHAMBERS, (cont.)	
Martha Augusta, d. George O., bp. [Apr.] 6, 1827	146
Phebe, had s. John & d. Polly, bp. Nov. 17, 1768 (Also "dau. Deborah" in Church Rec.)	119
Phebe, m. John **TAYLOR**, of Glastonbury, Sept. 25, 1773	61
Polly, d. with John, s. of Phebe **CHAMBERS**, bp. Nov. 17, 1768	119
Ruth, wid., d. Oct. 13, 1833, ae 56	108
CHAPIN, Aaron, of Hartford, d. Dec. 25, 1838, in Hartford	110
Alpheas, d. Mar. 18, 1826, at Springfield, ae 61	104
Amzi, d. Feb. 19, 1835, ae 67, [Northfield, Ohio]	108
Calvin, Rev., m. Jerusha **EDWARDS**, of New Haven, Feb. 2, 1795, by Dr. Edwards	66
Calvin, his w. [ ], d. Dec. 5, 1847, ae 72	115
Edward, Jr., d. June 22, 1795, ae 40, at Springfield	92
Edward, s. Rev. C[ ], bp. Feb. 19, 1799	136
Edward, Dea., d. Jan. 6, 1800, ae 76, in Springfield, Mass. ("Of and at Springfield" in Church Rec.)	94
Eliza, d. Calvin, bp. [ ], 1797 ("bp. May 14" in Church Rec.)	135
Eliza, m. Asher **ROBBINS**, Jan. 14, 1819	74
Eunice, wid., d. Apr. 8, 1806, at Springfield, Mass., ae 78	97
Eunice L., w. Rev. Joel, d. Apr. 16, 1837, ae 66, [Bainbridge*] *(from Church Rec.)	109
Jerusha, d. Calvin, bp. Feb. 28, 1796 *("Infant dau. of Rev. Calvin **CHAPIN**" in Church Rec.)	135
Jerusha, d. Rev. Calvin, d. Mar. 1, 1796, ae 18 d.	92
Jerusha, d. Rev. Calvin, bp. June 20, 1802	138
Joel, Rev., late of New York, d. Aug. 8, 1845, at Bainbridge, N.Y., ae 84	114
Lautes*, d. Oct. 30, 1847, in New York; bd. in Hartford *("Lacates" in Church Rec.)	115
CHAPMAN, Amelia Maria, d. Revele, bp. July 29, 1827	146
Anna*, wid., d. June 6, 1829, ae 79 *("Amy, d. in Hartford, bd. here" Church Rec.)	106
Cynthia C., m. Alfred H. **CARTER**, b. of East Haddam, Sept. 3, 1829	76
David, d. Nov. 19, 1820, ae 73	102
Edna, of Glastonbury, m. Asahel **TENNANT**, of Chatham, Nov. 1, 1797	66
Esther, m. William B. **MAY**, of Hartford, Nov. 29, 1807	70
Gilbert, m. Sabra **WINCHELL**, May 23, 1806, by Rev. Mr. Brace	69
Henry B., d. [ ], 1842, in Rochester, Ms., ae 19	112
Ira, of Glastonbury, m. Sally **GLASSENGER**, Dec. 31, 1811	71
Julius, of East Hartford, m. Fanny **ROBBINS**, Dec. 9, 1818	74
Laura, of Glastonbury, m. Leverett **WRIGHT**, July 17, 1821	74
Sarah Jane, d. Revilo, bp. July 3, 1829	146
CHAPPELL, Solomon, d. Dec. 23, 1829, ae 70	106
CHAUNCEY, CHAUNCY, Eunice, d. Oliver, bp. May 26, 1765	117
Eunice, d. May 1, 1814, ae 46	100
Eunice, d. July 14, 1825, ae 28	104
Huldah*, d. May 1, 1798, ae 70 *("wid. about 70" in Church Rec.)	93
CHESTER, Sarah, m. Thomas **COIT**, of Norwich, Oct. 16, 1782	62
CHURCH, Ann, d. Jan. 26, 1832, ae 92	107
Anne, wid., d. [ ] 3, 1790	90
Christian, d. May 26, 1821, ae 79	102

CHURCH, (cont.)
Elisha, d. Feb. 18, 1800, ae 53	94
Hepsibah, d. Jan. 3*, 1782 *("Jan. 5" in Church Rec.)	85
John, d. Apr. 1, 1811, ae 75	98

CHURCHILL, Eunice, wid., d. June 17, 1798, ae 73 or 74 — 93
Josiah d. Feb. 28, 1791, ae 71	90
Marquis, m. Rebecca **WARD**, of Glastonbury, May 14, 1807	70
Marquiss, colored, d. Mar. 4, 1835, ae 51	108
Rebecca, w. of Marquis, colored, d. Jan. 18, 1835, ae 61 (Surname omitted in Arnold Copy)	108

CLARK, CLARKE, Aaron, 2nd, of Middletown, m. Tryphena **GOODRICH**, Mar. 25, 1805 — 69
Aaron, d. Dec. 25, 1836, ae 53	109
Ann M., of Guilford, m. Hezekiah **TUTTLE**, of Rocky Hill, Aug. 7, 1852, by Rev. L. Burton Rockwood	41
Barnum*, d. Sept. 19, 1847, ae 28 *("Wm. Barnum **CLARK**" in Church Rec.)	115
Eliza Jane, m. Oliver **PALMER**, Nov. 18, 1845, by Warren G. Jones, of Glastonbury	17
Hannah, w. Daniel, of Middletown, d. Aug. 21, 1765, ae 70	81
Hannah, m. Hartwell **BARNES**, of Farmington, May 27, 1783	62
Henry LaFayette, m. Elizabeth Juliaette **HENRY**, Mar. 19, 1848, by Rev. Calvin Chapin	25
Jonathan, of Berlin, m. Mehetabel **CULVER**, Feb. 8, 1801	68
Lafayette, s. Barnum, d. Oct. 30, 1838, ae 15	110
Maria Elizabeth Stanton, bp. July 4, 1841	149
Mercy, m. Martin **HUMPHREY**, of Simsbury, Sept. 25, 1811	71
Moses, of Old Society, m. [ ] **COLLINS**, [ ] 10, [1801]	68
Samuel, d. May 27, 1813, ae 59	99
Susan, wid. of Samuel, d. Jan. 23, 1838, ae 82	110
Sylvester, m. Mary **BULL**, Sept. 20, 1807	70
William, of Colchester, m. Eunice **MILLER**, June 1, 1826	75
William, his w. [ ], d., Aug. 19, 1828, ae 25	105
W[illia]m Barnum*, d. Sept. 19, 1847, ae 28 *(Arnold Copy has "Barnum **CLARK**")	115
----------, of Berlin, m. Asenath **MILLER**, Apr. 16, 1799	67

CLEVELAND, CLEAVELAND, David, s. Joseph, bp. Aug. 19, 1798 — 136
Freeman, s. Joseph, bp. Apr. 14, 1793	133
Freeman, his w. [ ], d. Sept. 15, 1842, ae 49	113
Joseph, of Freetown, Mass., m. Rebecca **COLLINS**, Feb. 23, 1787	64
Joseph, d. Feb. 7, 1813, ae 47	99
Joseph, bp. [ ], 1818	144
Nancy, d. Joseph, bp. Oct. 31, 1790	132
Nancy, m. John **DARRELL**, Apr. 9, 1809	70
Sally, m. Asa **DOW**, of Weston, N.Y., June 27, 1811	71
Sarah, d. Joseph, bp Nov. 8, 1789	132

CLOUD, Peter, of New York, m. Lucy **BURNHAM**, June 4, 1834 — 78

CLOUGH, Joseph, of Springfield, Mass., m. Fanny **GOODRICH**, Sept. 10, 1798 — 67

COE, Timothy, of Durham, m. Polly **CALLENDER**, Jan. 10, 1803 — 68

COIT, Thomas, of Norwich, m. Sarah **CHESTER**, Oct. 16, 1782 — 62

ROCKY HILL VITAL RECORDS 29

	Page
COLEMAN, Chauncey, of Wethersfield, m. Sarah R. **WILLARD**, of Rocky Hill, Oct. 30, 1844, by Rev. C. Chapin	6
Elisha, m. Hannah **LOVELAND**, [, 1788]	64
COLES, Samuel, of Wethersfield, m. Sarah B[uell] **BOARDMAN**, of Rocky Hill, Apr. 27, 1848, by Rev. C. Chapin	25
COLLINS, Abial, m. Thomas **MATSON**, of Glastonbury, Dec. 21, 1794	66
Abigail, her d. Lois, bp. [ ], 1782	128
Abigail*, d. Aug. 7, 1783, ae 36 *("Abijah" in Church Rec.)	86
Abijah, s. Abijah, bp. May 5, 1776	125
Abijah*, d. Aug. 7, 1783, ae 36 *("Arnold Copy has "Abigail")	86
Abijah, m. Patty **WARNER**, Jan. 9, 1812	71
Abijah, his w. [ ], d. Apr. 20, 1820, ae 40	101
Allen, s. Isaac, bp. May 26, 1771	121
Alpheas*, his s. [ ], bp. Jan. 15, 1775 *("Appleton **HOLMES**"in Church Rec.)	124
Alvin, s. Jonathan, bp. Sept. 5, 1802	138
Amanda, m. Samuel **COLLINS**, b. of Rocky Hill, Oct. 15, 1854, by Rev. L.B. Rockwood	52
Anna, m. Jeremiah **RASH**, Jan. 22, 1784	62
Burrage, s. Levi, bp. June 23, 1785	129
Charles, d. [ ], 1826, ae 80	104
Curtiss, of Rocky Hill, m. Martha R. **CURTISS**, of Mereden, June 22, 1846, by Rev. C. Chapin	19
David, d. June 28, 1795, ae 84	92
Eleanor, m. Jessie **SANDFORD**, Dec. 25, 1783	62
Elisha, s. Martha, bp. Nov. 4, 1798	136
Elizabeth Eunice, d. Abijah, bp. Oct. 13, 1774	124
Esther, d. Isaac, bp. Nov. 29, 1767	119
Esther, wid., d. Nov. 23, 1810, ae 77	98
Isaac, his child d. Feb. 23, 1775	83
Isaac, d. Apr. 27, 1776	84
Isaac, s. Jonathan, bp. Sept. 5, 1802	138
James, his w. [ ], d. Oct. 14, 1803, ae 75	96
James, d. Apr. 3, 1805, ae 78	96
Jane R. of Rocky Hill, m. Douglas **WOODWORTH**, of Middletown Apr. 10, 1845, by Rev. J. Goodwin	10
Jonathan, m. Chloe **CURTIS**, Jan. 25, 1787	63
Jonathan, his infant, d. Aug. 22, 1787	88
Jonathan, s. Jonathan, bp. Sept. 5, 1802	138
Jonathan, Jr., m. Eunice **GOODRICH**, Dec. 28, 1815	73
Jonathan, his w. [ ], d. July 26, 1831, ae 58 *("ae about 58. Bapt. funeral" in Church Rec.)	106
Jonathan, Jr., his w. [ ], d. July 17, 1839, ae 43	110
Jonathan, d. Mar. 29, 1843, ae 82	113
Josiah, d. [ ] 25, 1825, ae 76	104
Julia, bp. July 4, 1841	150
Julius, of Rocky Hill, m. Mary Ann **BURNHAM**, of Berlin, Feb. 9, 1851, by Rev. Calvin Chapin	35
Levi, his w. [ ], d. Dec. 25, 1804, ae 44	96
Levi, d. June 9, 1828, ae 76	105
Levi, m. Margaret **MAGUIER**, b. of Rocky Hill, Apr. 9, 1854, by Rev.	

	Page
COLLINS, (cont.)	
L.B. Rockwood	50
Lois, m. Jesse **WILLIAMS**, Sept. 19, 1771	61
Lois, d. Abigail, bp. Sept. 22, 1782	128
Lucy, of Rocky Hill, m. Pheneas S. **CASE**, of Berlin, Aug. 24, 1846, by Rev. C. Chapin	20
Mabel, of Glastonbury, m. Samuel **WHEAT**, of Chatham, July 5, 1797	66
Margaret S., of Rocky Hill, m. Barzillai G. **NEFF**, of Wilmington, N.C., Oct. 17, 1854, by Rev. L.B. Rockwood	53
Margaret Simpson, d. Abijah, bp. July 1, 1831	147
Martha, d. James, bp. Mar. 31, 1766	118
Martha, had d. Rhoda **BELDING**, bp. Oct. 30, 1791	133
Martha, had s. Elisha, bp. [ ], 1798	136
Martha Williams, d. Abijah, bp. July 1, 1825	146
Mehetabel, m. Robert **HURLBURT**, July 5, 1781	61
Mercy, d. Isaac, bp. Oct. 13, 1765	117
Mercy, m. Richard **BELDEN**, Sept. 28, 1785	63
Olive, m. Eben **WELTON**, of Farmington, Nov. [ ], 1767	60
Patience, m. Jona[tha]n **PRICE**, Dec. 11, 1775	61
Prudence*, d. Isaac, bp. June 23, 1776 *("dau. of the wid. of Isaac, lately deceased" in Church Rec.)	125
Prudence, d. Jonathan, bp. Sept. 5, 1802	138
Prudence, m. Sylvester **DORE**, of Winchester, Apr. 10, 1825	75
Rachel*, d. May 26, 1795, ae 46 *("The first that died of 3 twins at a birth" in Church Rec.)	92
Rebecca, m. Joseph **CLEAVELAND**, of Freetown, Mass., Feb. 23, 1787	64
Rebena, wid., d. Apr. 28, 1776	84
Rhoda, d. David, d. May 26*, 1772 *("May 16" in Church Rec.)	82
Rhoda, d. Levi, bp. Oct. 10, 1784	129
Robert, d. June 28, 1802, ae 69	95
Roger, s. James, bp. May 6, 1770	121
Samuel, d. Nov. 6, 1784, ae 80	87
Samuel, m. Amanda **COLLINS**, b. of Rocky Hill, Oct. 15, 1854, by Rev. L.B. Rockwood	52
Sarah, m. Levi **SMITH**, Jan. 29, 1784	62
Sarah, wid., d. Feb. 9, 1800, ae 83	94
Sarah, m. George **WRIGHT**, Nov. 25, 1839	79
Silas, s. Jonathan, bp. Sept. 5, 1802	138
Simeon, s. Jonathan, bp. Sept. 5, 1802	138
Simeon, d. [ ], 1826, ae 72	105
Ursula, d. Levi, bp. Oct. 10, 1784	129
Zebulon, d. Mar. 25, 1800, ae 45	94
----------, Miss, d. Sept. 13, 1765	81
----------, m. Moses **CLARK**, of Old Society, [ ] 10, [1801]	68
COLTON, Luther, of Long Meadow, Mass., m. wid. Mehetable **DEMING**, Apr. 2, 1799	67
Sabin, of Long Meadow, Mass., m. Rhoda **BOARDMAN**, Jan. 2, 1811	71
Seth, of West Springfield, Mass., m. Clarissa **BELDEN**, Jan. 31, 1812	71
CONE, Edward, of Middletown, m. Eunice **BELDEN**, Dec. 26, 1811	71
COOK, George, of St.Armand, in Lower Canada, m. Sarah **HOOKER**, of Farmington, Sept. 23, 1810	71

	Page
COOK, (cont.)	
Julia Ann, m. Zarr **BUNNEL**, b. of Middletown, Mar. 12, 1843	80
Maria*, wid., d. Oct. 8, 1832, ae 33 *("of Hartford" in Church Rec.)	107
COOLEY*, Cynthia M., m. William **PORTER**, Jr., of Lee, Mass., Nov. 5, 1837 *("**CODEY**"?)	79
COPLEY, Nathaniell, d. Mar. 26, 1773	82
Noah, d. Aug. 5, 1765	81
COREY, Calvin F., m. Martha E. **GOODRICH**, Nov. 9, 1836	79
Calvin Francis, s. Oliver, bp. [Oct.] 30, 1808	141
Eliza Ame, d. Oliver, bp. Aug. 30, 1812	142
Elizabeth, d. Oliver, bp. Sept. 27, 1795	135
Elizabeth, m. William A. **WORTHINGTON**, of Colchester, Oct. 29, 1815	73
Emily, d. Oliver, bp. May 6, 1798	136
Emily, m. John S.R. **HENDERSON**, of Queensbury, N.Y., Sept. 14, 1817	73
James Hervey*, s. Oliver, bp. Jan. 10, 1815 *("James Henry **COREY**" in Church Rec.)	143
Martha, d. Oliver, bp. Sept. 16, 1792	133
Martha, m. Nathan **LEE**, of Salem, N.Y., Sept. 26, 1813	72
Molly, d. W[illia]m, bp. Apr. 14, 1765	117
Molly, m. Levi **HOLMES**, [ ], 1788	64
Oliver, s. Oliver*, bp. Aug. 10, 1766 *("William" in Church Rec.)	118
Oliver, s. Oliver, bp. [Aug.] 23, 1801	137
Oliver, s. Oliver, bp. Apr. 24, 1803	138
Oliver, Jr., d. Nov. [ ], 1823 sailed for Martinique, not heard from)	103
Oliver, his w. [ ], d. Jan. 11, 1835, ae 67	108
Oliver, d. Feb. 26, 1847, ae 81	115
Patience, wid., d. Feb. 18, 1806, ae 68	97
Ruth, d. William, bp. Mar. 6, 1768	119
Ruth, d. W[illia]m, d. Apr. 11, 1769	81
Ruth, d. W[illia]m, bp. Dec. 11*, 1769 *("Dec. 10" in Church Rec.)	120
Ruth, of Wethersfield, m. Noah **SHEPHERD**, of Chatham, Aug. 30, 1795	66
Sally, d. Oliver, bp. Nov. 9, 1799	137
Sally, d. Oliver, bp. Oct. 12, 1806	140
Sally, m. John **BOARDMAN**, Apr. 27, 1828	76
CORNING, Shubael, of Hartford, m. Anna **SMITH**, Oct. 26, 1809	71
CORNWALL, Harvey B., of Portland, m. Jennette L. **GOODRICH**, of Rocky Hill, Feb. 24, 1850, by Rev. Calvin Chapin	33
COVEL, Ephraim, of Glastonbury, m. Abigail **RILEY**, Oct. 19, 1785	63
COWIN, COWAN, COWING, Israel, m. Lois **STANDISH**, May 27, 1773	61
Isaac*, his child d. [ ], 1775 *("Israel" in Church Rec.)	83
Israel*, his child d. [ ], 1775 *(Arnold Copy has "Isaac")	83
Lois, d. Feb. 2, 1815, ae 77	100
COY, Amasa, of Hartford, m. Harriet **MYEARS**, Apr. 26, 1809	70
CRAIG, Peregrine, s. [ ], bp. June 14, 1789	131
CRAMPTON, Stephen P., of Hartford, m. Mary **WRIGHT**, [ ] 28, 1829	76
CRANE, Curtis, m. Lucy **ADAMS**, b. of the 1st Society, [, 1800]	68
Lydia, m. Simon **GIFFIN**, Dec. 12, 1772	61
Rebecca, of the 1st Society, m. William **ROBBINS**, May 19, 1808	70
Sarah, m. Elisha **CALLENDER**, Sept. 25, 1766	60

BARBOUR COLLECTION

	Page
CROCKER, Z----------, Rev., d. Nov. 14, 1847, in Upper Houses Middletown, ae 46	115
CROFOOT, CRAWFOOT, Betsey E., of Rocky Hill, m. Willard **HOADLEY**, of Waterbury, June 1, 1845, by Rev. Charles Bartlet	12
Charlotte A., of Rocky Hill, m. Julius S. **KNOWLTON**, of Middletown, Apr. 28, 1844, by Rev. William Bentley	4
Ira, of Middletown, m. Amelia **BELDEN**, [ ] 31, 1821	74
Ira, d. Nov. 2, 1846, ae 67	114
Joseph, of Berlin, m. Olive **MONTAGUE**, Mar. 29, 1810	71
Margaret, m. Justus **BLYN**, Sept. [, 1772]	61
CULVER, Abigail, d. W[illia]m, d. Apr. [6], 1782	85
Clarinda*, d. Edward, bp. Apr. 16, 1786 *("Clarissa" in Arnold Copy)	130
Clarinda, d. Edward, d. Sept. 13, 1787	88
Clarinda, d. Edward, bp. [Oct. 26], 1788	131
Clarissa*, d. Edward, bp. Apr. 16, 1786 *("Clarinda" in Church Rec.)	130
Clarissa*, d. Edward, d. Feb. 7, 1789, in 1st y. *("Clarinda" in Church Rec.)	89
Edward, his w. [ ], d. Jan. 13, 1789, ae 35	89
Edward, m. Hetty **WILLIAMS**, Jan. 21, 1796	66
Edward, d. Feb. 28, 1823, ae 73	103
Jemimah, d. Edward, bp. May 9, 1784	129
Jemima, m. James **DEMING**, [of Newington*], Apr. 18, 1810 *(From Church Rec.)	71
Jeremiah, his wid. [ ], d. Feb. 10, 1792, at Long Island	90
John, s. Edward, bp. Sept. 2, 1781	127
Lucy Caroline, m. James Robinson **PORTER**, b. of Rocky Hill, July 3, 1843, by Rev. C. Chapin	1
Lucy Caroline, see Lucy Caroline **PORTER**	80
Mehetable, d. Edward, bp. Aug. 25, 1782	127
Mehetabel, m. Jonathan **CLARK**, of Berlin, Feb. 8, 1801	68
Mehitable, wid., m. Justus **BULKLEY**, Nov. 12, 1826	75
Sarah, of Bristol, m. John **WRIGHT**, Mar. 24, 1791	65
W[illia]m, his w. [ ], d. Feb. 9, 1782	85
CURTIS, CURTISS, Chloe, m. Jonathan **COLLINS**, Jan. 25, 1787	63
Dorothy, d. Mar. 8, 1772	82
Dorothy, wid., d. Dec. 7, 1801, ae 86	95
Eben, m. Rebecca **LATTIMORE**, Apr. 4, 1781	61
Eliazer, s. Josiah, bp. June 19, 1785	129
Eleazer, s. Josiah, d. Sept. 29, 1785	87
Fanny, d. Sept. 28, 1821, ae 23	102
Hannah, m. Eben* **BIGELOW**, of Hartford, Oct. 24, [1782] *("Elvin" in Church Rec.)	62
Hannah, m. Reuben **ROBINSON**, of Berlin, Oct. 5, 1791	65
Hepsibeth, m. Jason **BOARDMAN**, July 7, 1784	62
John, d. Sept. 6, 1785, ae 65	87
Jonathan, s. Jonathan, bp. June 8, 1766	118
Jonathan, d. June 20, 1783, ae 69	86
Jona[tha]n, m. Hannah **WRIGHT**, Aug. 5, 1789	64
Josiah, his w. [ ], d. Dec. 24, 1788	89
Josiah, d. May 12, 1832, ae 88	107
Josiah, his wid. [ ], d. Sept. 22, 1834, ae 79	108

	Page
CURTIS, CURTISS, (cont.)	
Lucy, d. Josiah, bp. Apr. 22, 1781, by Rev. Mr. Lewis	126
Mabel, d. Josiah, bp. Sept. 9, 1787	130
Martha R., of Mereden, m. Curtiss **COLLINS**, of Rocky Hill, June 22, 1846, by Rev. C. Chapin	19
Mary, wid., d. June 30, 1790, ae 69	90
Mary, d. Jan. 20, 1807, ae 52	97
Mellecent, wid., d. [ ], 1826, ae 71	104
Rachel, m. David **RILEY**, Apr. 12, 1770	60
Rachel, d. Josiah, bp. [Nov.] 22, 1795	135
Rachel, m. Joseph **GOODRICH**, of Weth'd, Ill., June 17, 1841	80
Thomas, Dea., d. Nov. 6, 1789, ae 80	89
Wait, m. Millecent **GOODRICH**, Mar. 16, 1786	63
Wait, d. Mar. 11, 1808, ae 58	98
William, d. between May 7 & Aug. 17, 1782, at New York (Soldier)	85
----------, wid., d. [Apr. ?] 23, 1770, ae 90	82
D----------, L----------, m. Mary **BECKLEY**, of Worthington, Feb. 11, 1787	63
DANFORTH, Almira, d. Tho[ma]s, bp. Nov. 9, 1794	134
Almira, d. Dec. 12, 1801, ae 8	95
Betsey, m. Merriam **WILLIAMS**, Mar. 25, 1819	74
Elizabeth, d. Thomas, bp. Aug. 30, 1789	132
Ellen Cornelia, d. Thomas, Jr., bp. July 5, 1833	147
Hannah, m. Richard **WILLIAMS**, Sept. 28, 1794, by Rev. Mr. Fenn. Int. Pub.	65
Henry Palmer*, s. Thomas, bp. Dec. 31, 1830 *("Henry Talman **DANFORTH**" in Church Rec.)	146
Martha, m. Simeon **ROBBINS**, Jr., July 7, 1796	66
Mary Bulkley, d. Thomas, bp. Dec. 31, 1830	146
Sally, m. Luther **GOODRICH**, of East Haddam, Nov. 16, 1797	67
Thomas, s. Thomas, bp. July 8, 1792	133
Thomas, his w. [ ], d. [ ] 30, 1826, ae [ ]	105
Thomas, Jr., d. Mar. 23, 1836, ae 44	109
Thomas, d. Jan. 15, 1840, ae 84	111
Walter Williams, s. Thomas, Jr., bp. Sept. 4, 1835	148
DANIELS, M., of New London, m. Asa **ROBBINS**, of the Old Society, June 21, 1798	67
DARRELL, John, m. Nancy **CLEAVELAND**, Apr. 9, 1809	70
Nancy, wid., d. Dec. 28, 1833, ae 42 or 43	108
DARROW*, ----------, wid., d. Jan. 2, 1828, ae 59 *("**DURREN**, from Southington" in Church Rec.)	105
DAVENPORT, John G., of New Haven, m. Roxana S. **WILCOX**, of Rocky Hill, Dec. 29, 1844, by Rev. John Lovejoy	8
DEMING, Abigail, d. Jonathan, bp. Nov. 23, 1766	118
Abigail, m. Asahel **SAVAGE**, Mar. 22, 1792	65
Abraham, his child d. Feb. 24, 1775	83
Abraham, d. Sept. 26, 1776	84
Abraham, s. Justus, bp. July 22, 1787	130
Achsah, child of Luman, bp. July 19, 1801	137
Achsah, m. Allen **BELDEN**, May 9, 1811	71
Alfred Augustus, s. Erastus, bp. July 5, 1844	151
Ann Maria, d. Linus, bp. Mar. 2, 1837	149

	Page
DEMING, (cont.)	
Asahel*, s. Giles, bp. July 7, 1765 *("Arnold Copy has "Ashbel")	117
Ashbel*, s. Giles, bp. July 7, 1765 *(Asahel" in Church Rec.)	117
Betsey, d. Mehetabel, bp. Apr. 30, 1797	135
Burrage Goodrich, s. Simeon*, bp. [July 6], 1834 *("Linus" in Church Rec.)	148
Charles Thomas, s. Linus, bp. Oct. 31, 1845	151
Dan[ie]ll, s. Jonathan, bp. Mar. 3, 1765	117
Daniel, m. Fanny **CALLENDER**, Oct. 11, 1795	66
Ebenezer, d. Feb. 24, 1824, ae 83	103
Edward Sherman, s. Erastus, bp. July 4, 1845	151
Eli, m. Sarah **AMES**, Feb. 8, 1776	61
Elijah, s. W[illia]m*, bp. Sept. 10, 1769 *("Abra[ha]m" in Church Rec.)	120
Elijah*, his wid., d. Oct. 11, 1788, ae 68 *("Widow Elizabeth **DEMING**" in Church Rec.)	89
Elizabeth, d. John, bp. Apr. 14, 1765	117
Elizabeth, m. Nathaniell **ROBBINS**, Oct. 29, 1767	60
Elizabeth*, wid., d. Oct. 11, 1788, ae 68 *("Elijah" in Arnold Copy)	89
Emily, d. Daniel, bp. Nov. 13, 1796	135
Emily W., m. Alexander N. **WRIGHT**, of Berlin, Nov. 22, 1835	78
Ephraim, d. Mar. 2, 1817, ae 58	100
Erastus, s. Luman, bp. July 19, 1801	137
Erastus, m. wid. Charlotte **CALLENDER**, Feb. 1, 1829	76
Erastus, his s. [ ], d. Oct. 25, 1846, ae 13 (Church Rec. say "Burned to death in Suffield)	114
Eunice, wid., d. Oct. 6, 1768	81
Eunice, d. Abraham, bp. Apr. 5, 1772	122
Eunice, d. Mehetable, bp. Sept. 3, 1786	130
Eunice, d. Justus, bp. Feb. 3, 1799	136
Frederick, s. Abraham, bp. July 31, 1774	124
Frederick, s. Abraham, bp. June 23, 1776	125
Frederic, s. Justus, bp. Aug. 24, 1794	134
Giles, his w., [ ], d. Feb. 9, 1799, ae 72	94
Giles, d. Oct. 19, 1824, ae 89	104
Hamlin, s. Jonathan, bp. July 8, 1770	121
Hamlin, s. Jonathan, d. [ ], 10, 1776	84
Hannah, d. Giles, bp. Nov. 15, 1767	119
Hannah, m. Jonas **BECKET**, of Brystol, [ ] 30, 1787	64
Hannah, d. Luman, bp. Oct. 26, 1800	137
Harriet, d. Jonathan, bp. May 22, 1774	124
Harriet, m. Lemuel **GOODRICH**, Aug. 20, 1797	66
James, [of Newington*], m. Jemima **CULVER**, Apr. 18, 1810 *(From Church Rec.)	71
Jared, m. Charlotte **PORTER**, Jan. 25, 1807	70
Jerusha, wid., d. Jan. 21, 1815, ae 79	100
John, m. Hannah **WRIGHT**, Nov. 11, 1817	73
John, d. Feb. 26, 1842, ae 52	112
John Beckley, s. Luman, bp. July 19, 1801	137
John Harvey, s. Erastus, bp. July 5, 1844	151
Jona[than], d. Mar. 31, 1799, ae 69	94
Jonathan Hamlin, s. Daniel, bp. Oct. 3, 1802	138

	Page
DEMING, (cont.)	
Josephine Emma, d. Linus, bp. [Nov. 1], 1839	149
Josiah, d. Oct. 22, 1826, ae 48	105
Lardner, of Berlin, m. wid. Sally **WILLIAMS**, May 2, 1816	73
Leonard, s. Justus, bp. July 19, 1789	131
Levi, of Berlin, m. Delia **BELDEN**, of Rocky Hill, Dec. 2, 1845, by Rev. Charles Bartlett	16
Linus, s. Simeon*, bp. [Nov.] 25, 1804 *(In pencil "Luman")	139
Linus, m. Sophia **GOODRICH**, Dec. 11, 1828	76
Lucy, d. Luman, bp. July 19, 1801	137
Lucy, m. Benjamin **WRIGHT**, Nov. 2, 1809	71
Luman, s. Giles, bp. [Aug. 31], 1766	118
Luman*, d. May 30, 1821, ae 55 *("Simeon" in Arnold Copy)	102
Luther, s. Abraham, bp. Mar. 8, 1767	118
Luther, s. Luman, bp. [May] 26, 1811	142
Luther, m. Celista **HOLMES**, Nov. 27, 1833	78
Lydia, d. Giles, bp. Nov. 27, 1768	120
Lydia, m. Jason **BOARDMAN**, Jan. 3, 1808	70
Lydia, d. Apr. 25, 1841, ae 73	111
Mabel, d. Sept. 23, 1840, ae 77	111
Mary, d. Luman, bp. Sept. 18, 1808	141
Mary, d. Feb. 8, 1820, ae 17	101
Mary, m. Warren **TAYLER**, of Glastonbury, Dec. 2, 1829	76
Mehetable, d. Elijah, bp. Oct. 14, 1764	117
Mehetabelle, wid., d. Jan. 6, 1784, ae 80	86
Mehetable, had d. Eunice, bp. Sept. 3, 1786	130
Mehetabel, her d. Betsey, bp. [ ], 1797	135
Mehetabel, wid., m. Luther **COLTON**, of Long Meadow, Mass., Apr. 2, 1799	67
Mercy, d. Giles, bp. June 26, 1774	124
Nancy, d. Daniel, bp. May 27, 1798	136
Pownal, his w. [ ], d. Feb. 23, 1785, ae 19	87
Pownal, of Hartford, m. Mehetabel **BOARDMAN**, May 29, 1791	65
Sarah, m. Solomon **GRISWOLD**, Feb. 2, 1775	61
Sarah J., of Rocky Hill, m. Hiram N. **LULL**, of Middletown, June 25, 1848, by Rev. Theodore M. Dwight	26
Sarah Jane, d. Simeon*, bp. [July 6], 1834 *("Linus" in Church Rec.)	148
Silence, d. Giles, bp. June 7, 1772	122
Silence, d. Oct. 4, 1839, ae 68	111
Simeon*, d. May 30, 1821, ae 55 *("Luman" in Church Rec.)	102
Sophia, d. Justus, bp. Aug. 28, 1791	133
Sophronia, d. Daniel, bp. Aug. 31, 1800	137
Susan Sophia, d. Linus, bp. [July] 19, 1835	148
Susanna*, d. Beldad, d. Mar. 26, 1782 *("Susanna **BELDING**" in "11th" y. in Church Rec.)	85
William Henry, s. Daniel, bp. [Feb.] 17, 1805	139
William Henry, s. Erastus, bp. July 5, 1844	151
----------, m. Isaac **BUCK**, Apr. 16, 1771	61
DERRICK, Lucy [wid.], of Rocky Hill, m. Charles **McLAREN**, of Perth, in Scotland, Oct. 30, 1845, by Rev. C. Chapin	14
Thomas, of St. Croix, Ill,*, m. Lucy **GOODRICH**, Sept. 15, 1839	

	Page
DERRICK, (cont.)	
*("Isl." in Church Rec.)	79
DEWING, Hiram, of Charleston, S.C., m. Susan **BURKETT**, of Rocky Hill, Aug. 29, 1850, by Rev. L.B. Rockwood	34
DeWOLF, Charles, of Ashfield, Mass., m. Abigail **BLINN**, Nov. 20, 1828	76
DICKEMON*, Josiah, m. Lucy **BELDING**, Dec. 6, 1781 *(Arnold Copy has "**DICKINSON**")	61
DICKINSON, Abiah, m. Giles **WRIGHT**, Apr. 12, 1781	61
Abigail, w. Wait, formerly (Abigail **RUSSELL**), d. [ ] 24, 1827, ae 78	105
Barzillai, m. Mehetable **WRIGHT**, Sept. 22, 1805	69
Bethman*, s. Ozias, bp. June 16, 1782 *("Bethun" in Church Rec.)	127
Burrage, s. Elias, bp. Oct. 10, 1779, by Rev. Mr. Pitkin, of Farmington	126
Burrage*, d. Aug. 22, 1786 *("son of Elias" in Church Rec. "ae 8")	87
Burrage, s. Seth, bp. [July] 11, 1807	140
Celesta, child of Eleazer*, bp. Feb. 15, 1801 *("Elizur")	137
Charles, s. Wait, bp. Oct. 26, 1774	124
Charles, m. Eleanor **LIBY**, Jan. 13, 1805	69
Christian, m. Seth **BELDING**, Apr. 16, 1772	61
Doran, s. Moses, bp. Oct. 29, 1797	136
Dorcas, d. Ozias, bp. Nov. 14, 1773	123
Edwin, s. Seth, bp. Aug. 28, 1808	141
Eleanor*, d. July 24, 1768 *("Eleazer" in Church Rec.)	81
Elias, s. Elias, bp. Aug. 25, 1782	127
Elias*, d. Aug. 26, 1786 *("son of Elias" in Church Rec. ae 4)	87
Elias, d. Nov. 29, 1822, ae 81	102
Elias, his wid., d. Dec. 7, 1834, ae 92 *("d. in Glastonbury". See Church Rec.)	108
Elizabeth, bp. July 5, 1818, an adult	144
Elizur, s. Wait, bp. Apr. 4, 1773	123
Elizur, m.Polly **BUNCE**, Mar. 11, 1798	67
Elizur, of Rocky Hill, m. Harriet **LOCKROW**, of Wethersfield, Oct. 15, 1843, by Rev. C. Chapin	1
Elizur, of Rocky Hill, m. Harriet **LOCKROW**, of Wethersfield, Oct. 15, 1843	80
Elizur, d. May 8, 1848, ae 77	115
Elva*, d. Wait, bp. Nov. 6, 1785 *(Arnold Copy has "Elvira")	129
Elva, m. Ansel **RICE**, of Berlin, July 30, 1807	70
Elvira*, d. Wait, bp. Nov. 6, 1785 *("Elva" in Church Rec.)	129
Eunice*, m. Thomas **BUNCE**, Apr. 17, 1774 *("Eunnice" or "Emmice?")	61
Eunice, d. Ozias, bp. Mar. 3, 1776	125
Hannah, w. Obadiah & d. of [ ] **ROCKWELL**, d. May 23, 1781	85
Hannah, d. Sept. 26, 1810, ae 66	98
Hannah, wid., d. Sept. 1, 1831, ae 63	106
Harley, s. Ozias, bp. Oct. 4, 1795	135
Harley, his wid. d. Feb. 26, 1848, ae 53 *(His wife or wid. ae 52 or 53" in Church Rec.)	115
Harvey, s. Elias, bp. Apr. 1, 1770	120
Huldah, m. Elisha **STILLMAN**, Jr., of 1st Society, Apr. 7, 1800	67
Jalon*, child of Elizur, bp. Feb. 15, 1801 *(Arnold Copy has "Julian, s.	

	Page
DICKINSON, (cont.)	
Eleazer")	137
Jemima, wid., d. June 6, 1776	84
Jerusha, d. Seth, bp. June 16, 1799	136
Julian*, child of Eleazer*, bp. Feb. 15, 1801 *("Jalon child of Elizur" in Church Rec.)	137
Lester, s. Seth, bp. Sept. 2, 1810	142
Lois, d. Elias, bp. Aug. 7, 1768	119
Lois, d. Jan. 20, 1802, ae 34	95
Lucy, d. Elias, bp. Apr. 24, 1785	129
Lucy, m. William **CALLENDER**, Oct. 29, 1807	70
Lucy, m. Samuel W. **RUSSEL**, of Middletown, Oct. 14, 1819	74
Mabel, d. Ozias, bp. Apr. 13, 1788	131
Mabel, m. Henry **BELDEN**, Sept. 24, 1812	72
Mary, d. [ ] 25, 1830, ae 22	106
Mercy, w. Seth (formerly Mercy **GOODRICH**), d. Mar. 5, 1799, ae 24	94
Moses, s. Ozias, bp. May 2, 1773	123
Moses, m. Sarah **WRIGHT**, Aug. 13, 1794, by Mr. Chapin	65
Moses, d. July 19, 1802, ae 31; his w. [ ], d. July 19, 1802, ae 36, both drowned at Middletown	95
Nabby, d. Wait, bp. Oct. 25, 1789	132
Nabby, m. Zachariah **NORTON**, of Berlin, May 7, 1812	72
Norris, s. Eleazer*, bp. July 11, 1802 *("Elizur" in Church Rec.)	138
Norris, s. Elizur, bp. [Oct.] 25, 1807	141
Obadiah, h. (of Hannah **ROCKWELL**), d. Apr. 23, 1782, ae 81	85
Obadiah, his w. [ ], d. Sept. 25, 1794, ae 75	91
Olive, m. Thomas **MORTON**, Apr. 14, 1796	66
Olly, d. Wait, bp. Apr. 14, 1776	125
Orrin, m. Merriam **WRIGHT**, Dec. 13, 1807	70
Ozias, m. [ ] **GOODRICH**, Oct. [ ], 1772	61
Ozias, s. Ozias, bp. Mar. 6, 1785	129
Ozias, m. Chloe **BELDEN**, July 7, 1805	69
Polly, d. Ozias, bp. [Apr. 8], 1781, by Rev. Mr. Lewis	126
Polly, w. Eleazer, bp. Feb. 15, 1801 *("Polly, w. of Elizur" in Arnold Copy)	137
Polly Bunce, d. Elizur, bp. [ ] 30, 1812	142
Ransom, s. Elizur, bp. Aug. 5, 1804	139
Ransom, his w. [ ], d. Feb. 2, 1835, ae 27	108
Ransom, d. [ ], 1835, ae 32	108
Raphael, s. Moses, bp. Oct. 29, 1797	136
Rockwell, s. Elias, bp. Nov. 27*, 1771 *("Nov. 24" in Church Rec.)	122
Rockwell, d. June 9, 1794, ae 22	91
Ruhamah, m. Sylvester **WILCOX**, of Berlin, Apr. 27, 1812	72
Russel, s. Wait, bp. Nov. 2, 1794	134
Russel, his w. [ ], d. July 3, 1826, ae 31	105
Sally, m. John **CASWELL**, Jr., of Glastonbury, Oct. 12, 1803	68
Sarah*, m. Daniel **WRIGHT**, of Farmington, June 24, 1784 *("Sarah **WILKINSON**" in Church Rec.)	62
Sarah, of Rocky Hill, m. Lazarus **BARRETT***, of New York, Jan. 24, 1853, by Rev. L.B. Rockwood *(Perhaps "BUN[N]ELL")	43
Seth, s. Elias, bp. June 19, 1774	124

	Page
DICKINSON, (cont.)	
Seth, m. Jerusha **GOODRICH**, May 20, 1798	67
Seth, his w. [ ], d. May 29, 1810, ae 27	98
Seth, m. Mary **GRIMES**, Jan. 24, 1813	72
Seth, d. Oct. 26, 1836, ae 63	109
Sophia, m. John **LEWIS**, of Chapel Hill, N.C., Oct. 2, 1825	75
Susan, d. Aug. 8, 1826, ae 13	105
Susannah, d. Apr. 3, 1828, ae 83	105
Truman, s. Ozias, bp. Aug. 21, 1791	133
Wait, m. Abigail **RUSSELL**, Mar. 19, 1772	61
Wait, d. Apr. 1, 1835, ae 84	109
W[illia]m, d. Sept. [ ], 1823 (sailed for West Indies, not heard from)	103
DILLINGS, Lucetta, of Rocky Hill, m. Allis L. **WEBSTER**, of Mansfield, O., Nov. 10, 1844, by Rev. C. Chapin	7
DIMOCK, Abigail M., m. Phineas B. **WHITMORE**, of New Haven, Jan. 23, 1828	76
Abigail Maria, d. Joseph, Jr., bp. Aug. 21, 1803	139
Andrew, s. Samuel, bp. Jan. 28, 1787	130
Andrew, s. Samuel, d. June 5, 1796, ae 9	93
Andrew, s. Samuel, bp. Jan. 14, 1800	137
Andrew, s. Samuel, bp. June 28, 1801	137
Andrew, s. Jared G., bp. July 6, 1834	148
Burrage Bulkley, s. Samuel, bp. Oct. 3, 1784	129
David, his child, d. Oct. 13, 1775	83
David, his child d. [ ], 1775	83
Davis, s. Joseph, bp. June 28, 1772	122
Davis, m. Eleanor **WILLIAMS**, July 8, 1798	67
Davis, d. Aug. 30, 1798, ae 27 [at Haddam*] *(From Church Rec.)	94
Eleanor, wid., m. Jason **ROBBINS**, Aug. 30, 1801	68
Elizabeth, d. Joseph, d. Mar. 17, 1773	82
Elizabeth, d. Joseph, Jr., bp. May 5, 1816	143
Elizabeth, m. Elizur **WILLARD***, of Greenville, N.Y., [May] 12, 1816 *("**KIRTLAND**" in Church Rec.)	73
Eunice*, d. Samuel, bp. Feb. 24, 1771 *("Eunice **DUNN**" in Church Rec.)	121
Frederick Warner, s. Samuel, bp. Oct. 5, 1806	140
Hannah, d. Joseph, bp. Dec. 6, 1767	119
Jared G., his w. [ ], bp. July 6, 1834, adult	148
Jared G., m. Sophia **BUTLER**, Dec. 17, 1823	75
Jared Goodrich, s. Samuel, bp. June 5, 1803	138
Joseph, his child d. May 3, 1768	81
Joseph, s. Joseph, bp. May 14, 1769	120
Joseph, his child d. [ ], 1776	84
Joseph, Jr., m. Sarah **WARNER**, Aug. 12, 1789	64
Joseph, s. Joseph, Jr., bp. Aug. 23, 1801	137
Joseph, his w. [ ], d. Apr. 11, 1807, ae 71	97
Joseph, Jr., his child d. Oct. 4, 1808, ae 4; his child d. Oct. 8, 1808, ae 1	98
Joseph, Jr., d. Mar. 1, 1819, in Bermuda, ae 50	101
Joseph, Jr., his w. [ ], d. Mar. 7, 1819, ae 47	101
Lucy*, m. Wait **WILLIAMS**, June 25, 1818 *(Church Rec. give "Sally")	74
Lucy Robbins, d. Samuel, bp. May 27, 1810	142

	Page
DIMOCK, (cont.)	
Marianne, d. Joseph, bp. May 26, 1799	136
Mary, d. Joseph, bp. Jan. 3, 1765	117
Mary, m. Elias **WILLIAMS**, Feb. 19, 1787	64
Mary Jane, d. Joseph, Jr., bp. Aug. 18, 1811	142
Mary Olivia, d. Jared G., bp. Apr. 29, 1836	148
Mary Olivia, d. Jared G., d. Feb. 27, 1840, ae 5	111
Moses, s. Samuel, bp. July 31, 1774	124
Moses, s. Joseph, Jr., bp. Mar. 18, 1792	133
Moses, d. Sept. [ ], 1823, (sailed for West Indies, not heard from)	103
Rachel, d. Joseph, Jr., bp. Dec. 28, 1794	134
Rachal, m. Horace **WILLIAMS**, Nov. 6, 1816	73
Sally, d. Joseph, bp. May 7, 1797	135
Sally*, m. Wait **WILLIAMS**, June 25, 1818 (Arnold Copy has "Lucy")	74
Samuel, m. Rebecca **BULKLEY**, July 4, 1782	61
Samuel, his w. [ ], d. Oct. 14, 1798, ae 39	94
Samuel, m. Mary **GOODRICH**, Mar. 25, 1799	67
Samuel, his infant d. Jan. 18, 1800	94
Samuel, his w. [ ], d. Nov. 3, 1803, ae 39	96
Samuel, m. Eunice **WARNER**, Oct. 8, 1804	69
Samuel*, d. Dec. 27, 1820, ae 61 *(Arnold Copy has "**DIMOND**")	102
Samuel, his wid. [ ], d. [ ], 1827, in Hartford, ae 59	105
Samuel, s. Jared G., bp. July 6, 1834	148
Samuel, m. Mary S. **SMITH**, Oct. 14, 1846, by Rev. Warren G. Jones	20
Samuel, town clerk, certified on Oct. 20, 1879, it was voted, at the annual meeting of the legal voters of the town of Rocky Hill held by adjournment, that such portions of the Cong. Ch. and society records from 1765 to the year 1848 as refer to marriages, baptisms and deaths be copied on the town records by the town clerk for preservation	60
Selina **HARPER**, d. Jared G., bp. Aug. 31, 1838	149
Wait Warner, s. Joseph, Jr., bp. [Dec. 22], 1805	140
Wait Warner, s. Joseph, Jr., bp. June 4, 1809	141
W[illia]m Davis, s. Joseph, Jr., bp. Dec. 30, 1792	133
DIMOND*, Samuel, d. Dec. 27, 1820, ae 61 *("**DIMOCK**" in Church Rec.)	102
DIX, Benjamin, his child d. Sept. 27, 1782	85
Charles, m. Mary **BLINN**, of Old Society, Nov. 22, 1804	69
George, m. Olive **HUBBARD**, b. of 1st Society, Sept. 19, [1805]	69
Mary Goodrich, of 1st Society, m. Abner **SQUIRES**, Oct. 13, 1814	72
Rosa, wid., of 1st Society, m. Appleton **HOLMES**, of Glastonbury, Apr. 26, 1812	72
DORE, Sylvester, of Winchester, m. Prudence **COLLINS**, Apr. 10, 1825	75
DORRANCE, William, of Andover, Conn., m. Hepsey Penfield **GOODRICH**, of Rocky Hill, May 6, 1846, by Rev. Calvin Chapin	19
DORRELL, Thomas Gibbs, s. John, bp. July 12, 1818	144
DOW, Asa, of Weston, N.Y., m. Sally **CLEAVELAND**, June 27, 1811	71
DUGGAN, Dannis, d. Dec. 13, 1813, ae 88* *("ae about 85" in Church Rec.)	100
DUNHAM, Solomon, d. July or Aug. [ ], 1786, in West Indies	88
DUNN*, Eunice, d. Samuel, bp. Feb. 24, 1771 *(**DIMOCK**" in Arnold Copy)	121
Mabel, d. Samuel, bp. [May 29], 1768	119
Mary, m. Alexander **GRIMES**, Aug. 17, 1769	60

	Page
DUNN, (cont.)	
Richard, his w. [ ], d. Aug. 15, 1789, ae 65	89
Richard, d. May 17, 1790, ae 69 or 70	90
Samuel, bp. May 29, 1768	119
DURREN*, ----------, wid., d. Jan. 2, 1828, ae 59 *(Arnold Copy has "**DARROW**")	105
EASTMAN, John R., of Pawling, N.Y., m. Adeline* **GIBBS**, Nov. 24, 1833 *("Arnold Copy has "Adalaide")	78
EBRO, Margaret, m. George **STOMER**, [Nov. 19], 1767	60
EDWARDS, Abel, of Middletown, m. Betsey **MARSH**, July 12, 1804	69
Daniel, Jr., of Middletown, m. Onner **BULKLEY**, Nov. 16, 1795	66
Elisha, s. John, bp. Nov. 4, 1781	127
Honor, d. John, bp. Nov. 4, 1781	127
Honor, m. Jonathan **THAYER**, Sept. 1, 1796	66
Jerusha, of New Haven, m. Rev. Calvin **CHAPIN**, Feb. 2, 1795, by Dr. Edwards	66
John, his w. [ ], d. Mar. 6, 1770	82
John, s. John, bp. [Oct. 16], 1785	129
John*, d. July 11, 1794 (Church Rec. say "John, s. of John")	91
John, d. Apr. 25, 1796, ae 81	93
John, d. Mar. 17, 1801, ae 56	95
John, his w. [ ], d. June 16, 1813, ae 63	99
John, m. Mary Bulkley **WILLIAMS**, Dec. 11, 1836	79
Jonathan, Rev., D.D., d. Aug. 1, 1801, at Schenectady, N.Y. ("Of and at Schenectady, N.Y., ae 5[ ]" in Church Rec.)	95
Jonathan N*, d. Apr. 3, 1831, ae 60 *("Jonathan W., of and in Hartford" in Church Rec.)	106
Joseph, of Middletown, m. Eleanor **BULKLEY**, Feb. 10, 1768	60
Joseph, d. Jan. [ ]*, 1812, ae 69 *("Jan. 6" in Church Rec.)	99
Josiah, s. John, bp. Aug. 3, 1783	128
Josiah, m. Rhoda **BULKLEY**, Apr. 14, 1796	66
Josiah, d. Aug. 21, 1807, ae 25	97
Levi, s. John, bp. July 7, 1765	117
Levi, his infant s. [ ], d. June 25, 1796	93
Levi, d. Mar. 6, 1811, ae 46	98
Levi, his wid., d. Nov. 28, 1843, ae 75	113
Lewis, s. Josiah, bp. Aug. 6, 1797	136
Lucy, bp. Nov. 1, 1818, adult	144
Martha, d. Sept. 17, 1835, ae 80	109
Mary, m. Jonathan **BULKLEY**, Jan. 16, 1787	63
Mercy, wid., d. [ ] 23, 1823, at Lewis*, Mass., *("Lenox, ae 65" in Church Rec.)	103
Nancy, d. John, bp. [Apr. 1], 1793	133
Nancy, d. Aug. 13, 1799, ae 8	94
Onner, wid., m. Frederick **TAILER***, of Berlin, July 28, 1800 *("**FAILS**" in Church Rec.)	68
Patience, d. John, Jr., bp. June 7, 1789	131
Rebecca, d. Dec. 31, 1842, ae 90	113
Sarah, d. Mar. 4, 1836, ae 87	109
Sarah, m. Edward W. **RASH**, Mar. 14, 1836	78
Zenas, of Middletown, m. Caty **BULKLEY**, Dec. 7, 1800	68

	Page
ELDREDGE, Benjamin, of Chatham, Mass., d. Nov. 13, 1790	90
ELMER, Edward, of Hartford, m. Jerusha H. **GOODRICH**, of Rocky Hill, Dec. 18, 1844, by Rev. Calvin Chapin	7
ELY, Margaret, d. Dolphin, d. [ ] 27, 1768	81
FAILS*, Frederick, of Berlin, m. wid. Onner **EDWARDS**, July 28, 1800 *(Arnold Copy has "**TAILER**")	68
FAIRFIELD, George H., of Hartford, m. Eunice R. **BUTLER**, of Rocky Hill, June 2, 1847, by Rev. C. Chapin	23
Joseph Butler, s. Jona T., bp. Apr. 30, 1847	151
FIELD, Nathan, of East Guilford, m. Sarah **CALLENDER**, Nov. 29, 1801	68
Sally, w. Nathan, bp. June 20, 1802	138
FILBY*, John, his child d. Mar. 19, 1774 *("**TILLEY**" in Church Rec.)	83
FISH, Alfred M., of Hartford, m. Sarah **CALLENDER**, May 1, 1843	80
FLETCHER, Oscar, of Kinderhook, m. Ann S. **ATWOOD**, of Rocky Hill, Apr. 28, 1845, by Rev. John Lovejoy	11
FLINT, Amanda A., m. James **BENTON**, of New Haven, May 9, 1833	77
Hiram, d. Apr. 14, 1840, ae 24	111
Jane A., m. William F. **WHITNEY**, of Harvard, Mass., Jan. 1, 1840	79
Jared, d. Dec. 31, 1841, ae 37	112
John, his w. [ ], d. Aug. 30, 1847, ae 65	115
Maria Webb, m. William Wait **WARNER**, Mar. 19, 1829	76
Mary E., m. Asaph U. **THOMAS**, of New Britain, Nov. 29, 1835	78
Sarah, of Rocky Hill, m. Everett L. **STANLEY**, of New Britain, June 11, 1848, by Rev. T.M. Dwight	26
FORBES, Caroline, d. Jotham, bp. [May] 21, 1809	141
Joseph, s. Betsey **MILLER**, bp. Apr. 14, 1765 (Perhaps "Joseph Forbes **MILLER**")	117
Jotham, of Waterbury, m. Nancy **OLMSTEAD**, Jan. 8, 1805	69
Mary Ames*, d. Jotham, bp. Sept. 20, 1807 *("Mary Ann" in Church Rec.)	140
Sarah, m. James **HALE**, Dec. 30, 1770	60
FORDHAM, Appollos, s. Gideon, of Long Island, bp. [Apr.]16, 1781, by Rev. Mr. Lewis	126
John, s. Gideon, bp. Mar. 8, 1782	127
John, s. Gideon, d. Mar. 12, 1782	85
John*, s. Gideon, bp. Mar. 3, 1783 *(s. of Gideon, of L.I., bp. Mar. 30" in Church Rec.)	128
Polly, d. Gideon, bp. June 4, 1786	130
Silas, s. Gideon, of Long Island, bp. [Apr.] 16, 1781, by Rev. Mr. Lewis	126
FOSTER, Betsey, d. Samuel, d. Oct. 6, 1775	83
Catharine Webb, d. Samuel, bp. June 29, 1783	128
Elizabeth, d. Samuel, bp. June 9, 1776	125
Mary, d. Samuel, bp. Feb. 16, 1772	122
Mehetable, d. July 9, 1786	130
Mehetable*, m. George **PRICE**, Aug. 8, 1790 *(Arnold Copy has "Mehetable **PORTER**")	65
Samuel, m. Elizabeth **WEBB**, Sept. 4, 1769	60
Samuel, s. Samuel, bp. Sept. 5, 1773	123
Samuel, his servant Frank, d. Apr. 12, 1781	84
Samuel, had 2 negro infants d. [ ], 1788	89
Samuel, Jr., d. Jan. [ ], 1793, at Sea	91

	Page
FOSTER, (cont.)	
Samuel, d. Nov. 13, 1797, ae 59	93
FRANCIS, FRANCES, Albert, of Wethersfield, m. Sarah Ann **ROBBINS**, [ ] 15, 1837	79
Albert, bp. Sept. 2, 1838	149
Albert, d. June 14 or 15, 1844, at Hartford, ae 34	113
Charles, m. Emily **BLINN**, of 1st Society, Oct. 5, 1825	75
Josiah, Jr., m. Abigail **GOODRICH**, Jan. 17, 1771 *(Church Rec. give "Josiah **GRIMES**, Jr.")	60
Mary Lyman, d. Selah, bp. Sept. 7, 1794	134
Myron, grand son of Samuel **BUTLER**, bp. Sept. 3, 1841	150
Roxy Butler*, d. Selah, bp. Oct. 9, 1796 *("Bulkley" in Church Rec.)	135
Sarah Ann, of Rocky Hill, m. Edwin H. **HEMINWAY**, of Hartford, May 29, 1845, by Rev. C. Chapin	12
Susan Kirby, d. Albert, bp. Feb. 28, 1840	149
FRANKLIN, Elizabeth, d. Moses, bp. Nov. 10, 1816	143
Elizabeth Maria, m. John Selah **BLINN**, Feb. 23, 1831	77
Lucinda, m. Frederick **BLINN**, Dec. 5, 1824	75
Maria, d. Moses, bp. Nov. 10, 1816	143
Moses E., m. Lucinda **GOODRICH**, Apr. 7, 1808	70
Rockwell G., d. Feb. 5, 1848, ae 34	115
Rockwell Goodrich, s. Moses, bp. Nov. 10, 1816	143
Rockwell Goodrich, m. Clarissa M. **BELDEN**, Dec. 16, 1835	78
FREDERICK*, Edwin, d. May 3, 1842, ae 44 *("**GOODRICH**" in Church Rec.)	112
FREEMAN, Ceaser, his w. [ ], d. Aug. 1, 1810, ae 48	98
Cesar, m. Lemon **HARRISON**, Nov. 15, 1810	71
Charles, m. Cornelia **BLINN**, June 5, 1836	78
Norman R., of South Glastonbury, m. Ellen S. **BELDEN**, of Rocky Hill, Dec. 28, 1851, by Rev. Philo Judson	39
FRISBIE, Elihu, of Albany, m. Fanny **BULKLEY**, Oct. 29, 1813	72
FRY, William, his w. [ ], d. July 24, 1840, ae 29	111
FULLER, Amanda, d. Daniel, bp. July 26, 1818	144
Daniel, m. Mabel **ROBBINS**, Oct. 15, 1806	70
Daniel, his w. [ ], d. Oct. 21, 1835, ae 54	109
Daniel, M.D., d. Dec. 16, 1843, ae 69	113
Edward, s. Daniel, bp. July 26, 1818	144
Jonathan*, d. Sept. [ ], 1833, at New Orleans, ae 22 *("Josiah Butler **FULLER**" in Church Rec.)	108
Josiah Butler, s. Daniel, bp. July 26, 1818	144
Josiah Butler*, d. Sept. [ ], 1833, at New Orleans, ae 22 *(Arnold Copy has "Jonn")	108
Walter, s. Daniel, bp. July 26, 1818	144
GARDNER, GARDINER, Lucy S., m. John G. **MERROW**, b. of Hartford, Apr. 11, 1847, by Rev. C. Chapin	21
Martha, of Rocky Hill, m. James **WARNER**, of Wethersfield, June 17, 1849, by Rev. Philo Judson	29
Martha J., of Rocky Hill, m. Aden E. **HASKELL**, of Hartford, May 25, 1854, by Rev. L.B. Rockwood	51
Melzar, of Hartford, m. Martha G. **WARNER**, Dec. 31, 1832	77
GAYNARD, Lewis, of New York, m. Huldah **PARSONS**, May 22, 1803	68

	Page
GEAR, Henry S., of Cromwell, m. Martha A. **CHAMBERS**, of Rocky Hill, Oct. 29, 1854, by Rev. L.B. Rockwood	53
GIBBS, Adalaide*, m. John R. **EASTMAN**, of Pawling, N.Y., Nov. 24, 1833 *("Adeline" in Church Rec.)	78
Adeline*, m. John R. **EASTMAN**, of Pawling, N.Y., Nov. 24, 1833 *(Arnold Copy has "Adalaide")	78
Betsey, d. John, bp. May 22, 1785	129
Betsey, m. Levi **SMITH**, May 7, 1806	69
Harriet, m. Bennet **HICKOX**, of Watertown, Apr. 30, 1832	77
Jacob, his w. [ ], d. Mar. 22, 1830, ae 52	106
Jacob, d. Apr. 1, 1848, ae 73	115
Jerusha, m. Daniel **GRISWOLD**, Nov. 23, 1769	60
Jerusha, d. John, bp. Oct. 14, 1781	127
Jerusha, m. Abner **NORTHRUP**, of Saulsbury, Oct. 16, 1803	68
John, m. Elizabeth **WEED**, May 13, 1773	61
John, s. John, bp. July 28, 1776	126
John, Jr., d. Sept. 3, 1795, ae 22	92
John, his w. [ ], d. Mar. 20, 1820, ae 67	101
John, d. Dec. 9, 1835, ae 89	109
Julia Ann, m. William **GRISWOLD**, Mar. 16, 1834	78
Mary, d. John, bp. Oct. 10, 1779, by Rev. Mr. Pitkin, of Farmington	126
Mary, m. Farrand **HARTWELL**, of Charlotteville, N.Y., Nov. 27, 1834	78
Milly, d. John, bp. [Nov.] 15, 1795	135
Milly, d. John, d. Dec. 23, 1795	92
GIFFIN, [see under **GRIFFIN**]	
GILBERT, Abigail, d. John, bp. Apr. 13, 1788	131
Elisha, of West Hartford, m. Martha **SMITH**, Sept. 7, 1842	80
Joseph*, d. Sept. 13, 1820, in Delaware, ae 40 *("Joseph Gilbert **MERROW**" in Church Rec.)	102
Josiah, of Berlin, m. Hannah **TRYON**, Nov. 11, 1790	65
GILLET, Richard, of Farmington, m. Julia **BOARDMAN**, Mar. 17, 1835	78
GLADDEN, John, d. Aug. 6, 1814, ae 45* *("42" in Church Rec.)	100
Rhoda, wid., d. Feb. 6, 1823, ae 48	103
GLASSENGER, Sally, m. Ira **CHAPMAN**, of Glastonbury, Dec. 31, 1811	71
GOFF, Abigail, d. Gideon, bp. [Nov. 11], 1787	131
Abigail, m. Benjamin L. **HAMLIN**, of Hartford, May 12, 1817	73
Ambrose, d. May 5, 1783, ae 24	86
Ambrose, s. Silas, bp. Nov. 20, 1791	133
Anna Deming, d. Gedeon, bp. May 20, 1792	133
Elishabah*, d. Dec. 22, 1802, ae 76 or 77 *(Arnold Copy has "Elizabeth")	95
Elizabeth*, d. Dec. 22, 1802, ae 76 ir 77 *("Elishabah" in Church Rec.)	95
Gideon, m Anne **NOTT**, Aug. 21, 1786	63
Gideon, s. Gideon, bp. Oct. 14, 1798	136
Gideon, his w. [ ], d. Feb. 7, 1809, ae 54	98
Gideon, d. Nov. [ ], 1823, ae 26 (sailed for Martinique, not heard from)	103
Gideon, his w. [ ], d. [ ], 1838, ae 65	110
Hezekiah, s. Gideon, bp. [Oct. 4], 1789	132
Hezekiah, s. Gideon, d. Apr. 27, 1790	89
John Robbins, s. Josiah, bp. May 23, 1773	123

	Page
GOFF, (cont.)	
Jona*, d. Oct. [ ], 1793, in West Indies *("Josiah **GOFF**, Jr." in Church Rec.)	91
Josiah, s. Josiah, bp. Mar. 12, 1775	124
Josiah, his child d. June 1, 1776	84
Josiah, Jr., d. Oct. [ ], 1793, in West Indies *(Arnold Copy has "Jona **GOFF**")	91
Levi, s. Josiah, bp. [July 7], 1765	117
Levi, m. Elizabeth **BELDEN**, Jan. 27, 1791	65
Lois, d. Josiah, d. Dec. 9, 1781	85
Lois, d. Josiah, bp. [Dec*] 22, 1782 *(Church Rec.)	128
Lydia, d. Gideon, bp. [Aug.] 24, 1794	134
Lydia, d. Geo*, d. Jan. 12, 1795 *("Gid[eon]" in Church Rec.)	92
Mehetable, w. Gideon, bp. July 5, 1818	144
Nancy, m. Jason **GOODRICH**, Apr. 10, 1811	71
Samuel, d. Sept. 12, 1781	85
Sarah, d. Josiah, bp. June 21, 1767	118
Sarah, m. Luman **SAVAGE**, of Berlin, Nov. 24, 1791	65
Silas, s. Josiah, bp. May 23, 1773	123
Silas, m. Rosanna **GOODRICH**, Jan. 13, 1791	65
Silas, his d. [ ], bp. Apr. 28, 1793	133
GOODALE, Almira, m. Charles **SELDEN**, of Chatham, May 5, 1833	77
Ebenezer, his w. [ ], d. [ ] 29, 1832, ae 48	107
Ebenezer, d. Feb. 18, 1847, ae 67	115
Emeline, m. Horace **ADAMS**, of 1st Society, Nov. 25, 1829	76
Fanny, d. Feb. 24, 1823, ae 11	103
Nelson, his w. [ ], d. Jan. 14, 1840, ae 35	111
Philo Chapell, m. Elizabeth Prudence **BELL**, Dec. 1, 1833	78
GOODRICH, Aaron Hosford, s. Barzillai, bp. June 2, 1805	139
Abby Ann, bp. [ ], 1831	147
Abby Ann, m. Allen Austin **ROBBINS**, Oct. 29, 1840	80
Abigail, m. Jacob **WEBSTER**, of Glastonbury, May 13, 1770	60
Abigail, m. Josiah **FRANCIS***, Jr., Jan. 17, 1771 *("**GRIMES**" in Church Rec.)	60
Abigail, d. Joshua, bp. [Mar. 7], 1773	123
Abigail, d. Gurdon, Jr., bp. Aug. 22, 1773	123
Abigail, w. Gurdon, d. Feb. 2, 1787	88
Abigail, m. Amos **MILLER**, Dec. 7, 1794	66
Abigail, d. Eph[rai]m, bp. June 26, 1796	135
Adaline, d. Barzillai, bp. June 7, 1807	140
Admiral Ichabod*, s. Ichabod, bp. Apr. 23, 1797 *(Church Rec. say "Admiral, afterward by the parents named Ichabod")	135
Albert*, s. Israel, bp. Oct. 4, 1809 *("Albert, s. of Isaac, bp. Oct. 1" in Church Rec.)	141
Alfred, s. Israel, bp. Dec. 31, 1797	136
Alfred Bailey, s. Levi, bp. Sept. 4, 1835	148
Allen, s. Roger, bp. Jan. 24, 1768	119
Allen*, s. Roger, bp. Jan. 28, 1781, by Rev. Mr. Lewis *("twin with Asahel" in Church Rec.)	126
Allen, brother of Asahel, sailed for Lisbon, [ ], 1802, not heard from	95
Almira, m. Eleazer **GOODRICH**, May 28, 1815	73

GOODRICH, (cont.)

	Page
Alpheas, s. Alpheas, bp. Apr. 13, 1766	118
Alpheas, his w. [ ], d. Aug. 17, 1793, ae 59	91
Alpheas, d. June 14*, 1803, ae 77 *("June 24" in Church Rec.)	95
Alpheas, his w. [ ], d. Apr. 22, 1813	99
Alpheas, his w. [ ], d. Mar. 22, 1837, ae 58	109
Alvin, s. Micah, bp. Apr. 28, 1776	125
Amelia, of Glastonbury, m. Samuel **SMITH**, of Middlebury, Sept. 28, 1797	66
Amelia Bulkley, d. W[illia]m, bp. Nov. 14, 1802	138
Anna, d. Gideon, bp. July 29, 1804	139
Arch[ibal]d, s. Oliver, bp. Oct. 25, 1789	132
Archibald, d. Apr. 6, 1819, at Havanna, ae 29	101
Asahel, s. Roger, bp. May 31, 1776	125
Asahel*, s. Roger, bp. Jan. 28, 1781, by Rev. Mr. Lewis *("twin with Allen" in Church Rec.)	126
Asahel, d. Aug. [ ], 1802, ae 23, in Wilmington, N.C.	95
Ashbel*, s. Roger, d. June 11, 1776 *("Asahel" in Church Rec.)	84
Austin, s. Philer, bp. Nov. 6, 1791	133
Barnabus, d. Apr. 10, 1800, ae 22	94
Barzillai, s. Oliver, Jr., bp. July 7, 1776	126
Barzillai, his infant bp. Jan. 2, 1800	137
Belinda, wid., m. Jason **GOODRICH**, of East Hartford, Apr. 10, 1837	79
Benjamin, [s. Chauncey & Mary Louisa], b. Feb. 10, 1845	44
Beria*, m. Ichabod **GOODRICH**, [, 1788] *(Church Rec. have "Bina")	64
Betsey, d. Joel, bp. May 30, 1819	144
Betsey, m. Elisha P. **AVERY**, of Breeksville, O., May 27, 1841	80
Betsey, [d. Chauncey & Mary Louisa], b. May 2, 1843	44
Bina*, m. Ichabod **GOODRICH**, [, 1788] *(Arnold Copy has "Beria")	64
Burrage, s. Isaac, bp. May 20, 1798	136
Burrage, d. Sept. [ ], 1823 (sailed for West Indies, not heard from)	103
Burret, [s. Chauncey & Mary Louisa], b. Sept. 1, 1840	44
Caroline, d. Philer, bp. June 14, 1801	137
Caroline Cassidy, d. Jason, bp. Mar. 3, 1843	150
Caroline Louisa, d. William, bp. July 5, 1839	149
Caroline Louisa, of Rocky Hill, m. Albert C. **GRISWOLD**, of Wethersfield, Jan. 13, 1853, by Rev. L.B. Rockwood	43
Caroline Sophia, d. Barzillai, bp. July 1, 1821	145
Catharine, her d. Hannah, bp. [ ], 1782	128
Caty, d. Sept. 5, 1799, ae 45	94
Caty, d. Alpheas, d. Sept. 26, 1806, ae 5	97
Celestia Chappell, d. Harvey, bp. July 26, 1818	144
Charles Sage, [s. William, 2nd], b. Sept. 22, 1843	18
Charlotte, d. Isaac, bp. Sept. 28, 1788	131
Charlotte, d. Eleazer, bp. [May 3], 1835	148
Charlotte Griswold, d. Jason, bp. May 3, 1844	151
Chauncey, s. Gideon, bp. Dec. 15, 1823	145
Chauncey, m. Mary Louisa **PEN HALLOW**, May 7, 1840	79
Chauncey Butler, [s. Chauncey & Mary Louisa], b. Aug. 25, 1849	44

GOODRICH, (cont.)

	Page
Chauncey Welles, s. Oliver, bp. Aug. 18, 1816	143
Chancey William, [s. William, 2nd], b. May 16, 1837	18
Chester, brother of Asahel, sailed for Lisbon, [ ], 1802, not heard from	95
Chester Bridger, s. Lemuel, bp. Jan. 16, 1803	138
Chester Bridger, his w. [ ], d. Nov. 25, 1838, ae 29	110
Chloe, d. Oliver, bp. [Sept. 8], 1765	117
Chloe, m. Calvin **WINCHEL**, of Berlin, [, probably 1787]	64
Clarissa, d. Oliver, bp. Oct. 10, 1779, by Rev. Mr. Pitkin, of Farmington	126
Clarissa Maria, d. Barzillai, bp. [June] 12, 1803	138
Cynthia, d. Wait, bp. Jan. 9, 1801	137
David, Dea., his w. [ ], d. Dec. 8, 1783, ae 82	86
David, Dea., d. July 24*, 1785, ae 91 *("July 14" in Church Rec.)	87
David Lindsley, s. Israel, bp. [Apr.] 18, 1804	139
Deborah, wid., d. [June] 27, 1841, ae 73	112
Deborah, wid., d. Dec. 17, 1842, ae 74	113
Delia, m. John C. **SMITH***, Nov. 14, 1838 *("John H. **SMITH**" in Church Rec.)	79
Dorcas, m. James, **BELDING**, Nov. 5, 1772	61
Dorothy, m. Stephen **BELDEN***, of Lebanon, Jan. 16, 1787 *(Church Rec. have '**TILDEN**")	63
Ebenezer, s. Ebenezer, bp. Sept. 25, 1774	124
Ebenezer, s. Gideon, d. Aug. 7, 1796	93
Ebenezer, s. Gideon, bp. Aug. 7, 1796	135
Ebenezer, d. Sept. 19, 1813, ae 81	99
Ebenezer, s. Gideon, bp. Mar. 7, 1814	143
Edwin, s. Wait, bp. Oct. 27, 1799	137
Edwin*, d. May 3, 1842, ae 44 *(Arnold Copy has "Edwin **FREDERICK**")	112
Eleazer, s. Gurdon, Jr., bp. June 3, 1781	127
Eleazer, m. Almira **GOODRICH**, May 28, 1815	73
Eleazer, his w. [ ], d. May 20, 1843, ae 53	113
Eleazer, Capt., m. Mrs. Mary **BAILEY**, [wid.], b. of Rocky Hill, Aug. 27, 1848, by Rev. T.M. Dwight	27
Eli, m. Rhoda **WILLIAMS**, Nov. 11, 1784	62
Eli, s. Joshua, bp. Sept. 22, 1811	142
Eli, his w. [ ], d. Apr. 1, 1815, ae 51	100
Eli, m. Sally **ROBBINS**, June 4, 1817	73
Eli, d. Jan. 26, 1821, ae 59	102
Eli, m. Emeline E. **BUTLER**, [Oct.] 9, 1839	79
Eli, his wid. [ ], d. Feb. 12, 1840, ae 61	111
Elijah, s. Elijah, bp. Apr. 29, 1770	121
Elijah, s. Elijah, d. [, 1772]	82
Elijah*, his w. [ ], d. Oct. 11, 1795, ae 38 *("Elizur" in Church Rec.)	92
Elijah, d. Mar. 3, 1803, ae 77	95
Elisha, of Glastonbury, m. Sally **BULKLEY**, [ ] 30, 1821	74
Eliza, d. Ephraim, bp. Feb. 17, 1817	143
Elizabeth, m. Thomas **RUSSELL**, [winter], 1766	60
Elizabeth, d. Abial*, bp. June 12, 1774 *("Micah" in Church Rec.)	124

	Page
GOODRICH, (cont.)	
Elizabeth, m. William **NOTT**, Nov. 28, 1784	63
Elizabeth*, d. Jason, bp. [May] 26, 1833 *("14 y. of age" in Church Rec.)	147
Elizabeth, m. Frederick R. **BUTLER**, Mar. 6, 1853, by Rev. L. Burton Rockwood	44
Elizabeth Brainard, d. [Levi], bp. Sept. 4, 1835	148
Elizabeth M., of Rocky Hill, m. Horace D. **STOW**, of Cromwell, Aug. 27, [probably 1854], by Rev. L.B. Rockwood	51
Elizur, s. Gurdon, Jr., bp. Nov. 15, 1789	132
Elizur*, his w. [ ], d. Oct. 11, 1795, ae 38 *(Arnold Copy has "Elijah")	92
Elizur, m. wid. Martha **BULKLEY**, Mar. 6, 1796	66
Elizur, m. Fanny L. **SCRANTON**, of Durham, [ ] 26, 1820	74
Ellen Sophia, d. William, bp. July 5, 1839	149
Elmira, d. Ephraim, bp. [May 1], 1791	132
Elnora Deming, d. Isaac, bp. Oct. 11, 1801	138
Emelina, d. Philo, bp. May 20, 1798	136
Emeline, d. Joel, bp. May 30, 1819	144
Emeline, m. John **HALLOW**, Apr. 22, 1832	77
Emeline, m. Henry **SMITH**, b. of Rocky Hill, Jan. 29, 1845, by Rev. C. Chapin	8
Ephraim, d. Apr. 28, 1826, ae 75	104
Ephraim, s. Eleazer, bp. [May 3], 1835	148
Ephraim, m. Laura C. **RASH**, b. of Rocky Hill, Jan. 19, 1848, by Rev. Philo Judson	24
Erastus, s. Tyler, bp. Mar. 16, 1788	131
Esther, d. Ebenezer, bp. Aug. 19, 1770	121
Esther, m. James **RILEY**, Jan. 8, 1792	65
Eunice, d. Seth, bp. June 19, 1774	124
Eunice, d. Ezekiel, bp. Apr. 29, 1781, by Rev. Mr. Lewis	126
Eunice, m. Jeremiah **PARKER**, of Long Island, July 4, 1782	61
Eunice, d. Ezekiel, d. [ ] 13, 1783, ae 3	86
Eunice, m. Joel* **MORGAN**, of West Springfield, Dec. 3, 1797 *(Arnold Copy has "Jere")	67
Eunice, d. Gideon, bp. Sept. 16, 1798	136
Eunice, m. Jonathan **COLLINS**, Jr., Dec. 28, 1815	73
Eunice, wid. of Seth, d. Jan. 10, 1838, ae 87	110
Eveline, d. Isaac, bp. July 31, 1803	138
Ezekiel, m. Elizabeth **WARNER**, Jan. 1, 1783	62
Ezekiel, d. Sept. 19, 1783, ae 25	86
Ezekiel, s. wid. Elizabeth, bp. June 13, 1784	129
Ezekiel, d. Sept. 8, 1806, lost at Dominie, ae 23	97
Ezra, s. Joshua, bp. July 6, 1766	118
Fanny, m. Joseph **CLOUGH**, of Springfield, Mass., Sept. 10, 1798	67
Filer, m. Lucretia **WILLIAMS**, Oct. 9, 1783	62
Filer, his infant d. Oct. 17, 1793	91
Frances, m. Edward Franklin **ROBBINS**, b. of Rocky Hill, Nov. 12, 1845, by Rev. C. Chapin	15
Francis, s. Jason, bp. Aug. 31, 1832	147
Francis Curtis, s. Levi, bp. Sept. 4, 1835	148

GOODRICH, (cont.)

	Page
Frederick, bp. [May 6], 1838, adult	149
Garranter*, s. Ichabod, bp. Jan. 15, 1804 *("Son of Israel" in Church Rec.)	139
George, s. Isaac, bp. Oct. 4, 1794	134
George, m. Abigail **PRICE**, Aug. 27, 1818	74
George, s. Luther, bp. Sept. 20, 1818	144
George, d. May 6, 1844, ae 52 ("from Cheraw, S.C." See Church Rec.)	113
George W., d. [ ] 16, 1834*, in Hartford, ae 28 *("1833" in Church Rec.)	107
George Williams, s. Joshua, bp. [Apr. 27], 1806	140
Gideon, d. Aug. 8, 1769	81
Gideon, s. Seth, bp. June 27, 1773	123
Gideon, m. Eunice **WARNER**, Feb. 22, 1787	64
Gideon, s. Gideon, bp. Mar. 7, 1814	143
Gideon Franklin, s. Jason, bp. Aug. 31, 1832	147
Gurdon, his child d. Nov. 2*, 1783 *("Nov. 21" in Church Rec.)	86
Gurdon, s. Ephraim, bp. Oct. 7, 1792	133
Gurdon, d. Jan. 24, 1794, ae 77	91
Gurdon, 2nd, m. Mary **WADSWORTH**, of East Hartford, Nov. 6, 1814	72
Gurdon, d. Dec. 2, 1815, ae 70	100
Gurdon, s. Eleazer, bp. [May 3], 1834	148
Hannah, d. Hezekiah, bp. Oct. 6, 1765	117
Hannah, d. Catharine, bp. Nov. 3, 1782	128
Hannah, d. Michael, bp. May 11, 1783	128
Hannah, d. Michael, bp. June 7, 1783	128
Hannah, d. Michael, d. June 8, 1783	86
Hannah, m. Thomas **HOLMES**, May 3, 1786	63
Hannah, d. Catharine, d. Oct. 9, 1786	88
Harriet, d. Isaac, bp. July 8, 1808	141
Harriet, m. Salmon **GOODRICH**, Apr. 2, 1828	76
Harriet, wid., d. Nov. 27, 1838, ae 64	110
Harriet Augusta, d. Lemuel, bp. Nov. 4, 1804	139
Harriet Augusta, d. Oct. 24, 1838, ae 35	110
Harvey, m. Sally **LEWIS**, Sept. 6, 1809	70
Henry, s. Philer, bp. July 24, 1796	135
Henry Deming, s. Lemuel, bp. Mar. 7, 1801	137
Henry Lawson, s. Harvey, bp. July 26, 1818	144
Hepsey Penfield, d. Luther, bp. Sept. 20, 1818	144
Hepsey Penfield, of Rocky Hill, m. William **DORRANCE**, of Andover, Conn., May 6, 1846, by Rev. Calvin Chapin	19
Hepsibeth, m. David **BELDING**, Aug. 3, [1769]	60
Hepsibeth, m. Eben Mitchell **HOLDEN**, of Granville, Nov. 3, 1785	63
Hezekiah, s. Hezekiah, bp. Apr. 2, 1769	120
Hezekiah, d. Nov. 21, 1788	89
Honor, d. Ebenezer, bp. Dec. 11, 1768	120
Honor, m. Isaac **GOODRICH**, [ ] 16, 1787	64
Horace, s. Gurdon, bp. Sept. 30, 1787	131
Hubbard, m. Susannah **GRAVES**, of Granville, Mass., [ ] 26, 1787	64
Hugh Malcom, s. Jason, bp. Nov. 3, 1848	152
Ichabod, m. Bina* **GOODRICH**, [, 1788] *(Arnold Copy has	

	Page
GOODRICH, (cont.)	
"Beria")	64
Ichabod*, s. Ichabod, bp. Apr. 23, 1797 *(First named "Admiral." See Church Rec.)	135
Ichabod, his w. [ ], d. June 10, 1813, ae 43	99
Ichabod, m. wid. Mary **BUTLER**, Oct. 11, 1815	73
Ichabod, his w. [ ], d. Apr. 17, 1826	104
Ichabod, d. Sept. 3, 1844, ae 88	114
Ira, s. Ichabod, bp. May 26, 1799	136
Isaac, s. Gurdon, bp. Nov. 11, 1764	117
Isaac, m. Honor **GOODRICH**, [ ] 16, 1787	64
Isaac, d. [ ] 11, 1831, ae 68	107
Isaac Thomas, s. Ephraim, bp. May 5, 1799	136
Israel, m. Mercy **WHITE**, Jan. 4, 1785	63
Israel, s. Israel, bp. Mar. 10, 1793	133
Israel, his w. [ ], d. Apr. 15, 1804	96
Israel, d. July 19, 1806, ae 55	97
Jacob, of Glastonbury, m. Rhoda **AMES**, Sept. 4, 1806, by Rev. Nathan Strong	69
James, s. Ichabod, bp. Oct. 15, 1806	140
James Henry, s. Joel, bp. Nov. 9, 1823	145
James Hubbard, bp. July 4, 1841	150
James W., m. Mercy **BELDEN**, Feb. 8, 1838	79
James Wright, s. Oliver, bp. June 21, 1812	142
Jared, d. Nov. 24, 1833, ae 73	108
Jason, s. Joshua, bp. Oct. 21, 1770	121
Jason, s. Ephraim, bp. July 4, 1790	132
Jason, m. Nancy **GOFF**, Apr. 10, 1811	71
Jason, his w. [ ], d. June 5, 1832, ae 41	107
Jason, of East Hartford, m. wid. Belinda **GOODRICH**, Apr. 10, 1837	79
Jason, bp. [ ], 1843	150
Jason Lewis, s. Jason, bp. Aug. 31, 1832	147
Jason Lewis, d. Apr. 1, 1843, ae 27	113
Jasper, s. Ichabod, bp. Apr. 15, 1791	132
Jasper, his w. [ ], d. Sept. 12. 1822, ae 31	102
Jasper, m. Nancy **BELL**, [ ] 6, 1823	75
Jasper, his twins d. Aug. [ ], 1832, ae [ ]	107
Jasper, Jr., d. Apr. 14, 1842, ae 14	112
Jemima, had s. Putnam, bp. [ ], 1782	127
Jemima, m. Jonathan **PRICE**, Apr. 17, 1783	62
Jennette L., of Rocky Hill, m. Harvey B. **CORNWALL**, of Portland, Feb. 24, 1850, by Rev. Calvin Chapin	33
Jeremy, s. Stephen*, bp. Oct. 9, 1768 *("Alpheus" in Church Rec.)	119
Jeremy, m. Harriet **BELDEN**, Dec. 23, 1832	77
Jeremy, his w. [ ], d. Apr. 24, 1840, ae 32	111
Jeremy, m. Mary **SHAILER**, Jan. 21, 1841	80
Jerusha, m. Ebenezer **MILLER**, of Middletown, June 18, 1767	60
Jerusha, d. Elisha, bp. Dec. 13, 1767	119
Jerusha, d. Gurdon, bp. Oct. 1, 1775	125
Jerusha, m. W[illia]m **AMES**, [Nov.] 14, [1790]	65
Jerusha, wid., d. Apr. [ ], 1794	91

GOODRICH, (cont.)

	Page
Jerusha, d. Israel, bp. June 7, 1795	134
Jerusha, m. Seth **DICKINSON**, May 20, 1798	67
Jerusha, d. Joshua, bp. Aug. 27, 1815	143
Jerusha H., of Rocky Hill, m. Edward **ELMER**, of Hartford, Dec. 18, 1844, by Rev. Calvin Chapin	7
Joel, s. Seth, bp. July 13, 1783	128
Joel, m. Anne **BUNCE**, Oct. 17, 1805	69
Joel Edward, s. Joel, bp. May 4, 1832	147
John, sailed for Lisbon, [ ], 1802, not heard from	95
John, s. Gideon, bp. Mar. 7, 1814	143
John Chester, s. Harvey, bp. July 26, 1818	144
Jonathan Welles, s. Ichabod, bp. May 31, 1801	137
Joseph, of Weth'd, Ill., m. Rachel **CURTIS**, June 17, 1841	80
Joseph B., of Mereden, m. Lucretia* **SMITH**, of Rocky Hill, May 6, 1847, by Rev. C. Chapin *("Jerusha" in Church Rec.)	22
Joseph Bunce, s. Joel, bp. May 30, 1819	144
Joseph Butler, s. Hezekiah, bp. Dec. 20, 1772	123
Joshua, s. Hezekiah, bp. Sept. 10, 1775	125
Joshua, m. Nancy **BUCKLEY**, July 25, 1800	68
Joshua, d. Apr. 11, 1839, ae 64	110
Julia Etta, d. Barzillai, bp. May 7, 1809	141
Laura, d. Tyler*, bp. June 20, 1784 *("Filer" in Church Rec.)	129
Laura, m. Roderick **RUSSEL**, Jan. 31, 1803	68
Laura, m. Gershom **BULKLEY**, July 4, 1816	73
Lawrence, child of Jason, bp. Aug. 31, 1832	147
Lemuel, s. Roger, bp. Feb. 24, 1771	121
Lemuel, m. Harriet **DEMING**, Aug. 20, 1797	66
Lemuel, d. May 3, 1806, ae [ ]	97
Lemuel*, Henry, s. wid. Harriet, bp. June 20, 1806 *("Samuel" in Arnold Copy)	140
Levi, s. Ephraim, bp. [June] 29, 1794	134
Levi, s. W[illia]m, bp. Apr. 5, 1795	134
Levi, 2nd, m. Cynthia **WHITMORE**, Sept. 12, 1816	73
Leui, his d. [ ], d. July 31, 1823, ae 9	103
Levi Hildress, s. Levi, bp. Sept. 4, 1835	148
Lewis, s. Wait, bp. [Nov. 9], 1806	140
Lewis Butler, s. Harvey, bp. Aug. 29, 1819	144
Lois, d. Ebenezer, bp. Jan. 5, 1766	118
Lois, m. Richard **BUTLER**, Feb. 5, 1784	62
Lois, d. Isaac, bp. Mar. 10, 1793	133
Lois, d. Wait, bp. June 28, 1795	134
Lorin, s. Gideon, bp. Dec. 15, 1823	145
Lorin, m. Mary Louisa **GOODRICH**, b. of Rocky Hill, Jan. 16, 1854, by Rev. L.B. Rockwood	50
Lorin Henry, [s. William, 2nd], b. May 17, 1841	18
Lucinda, d. Ichabod, bp. Sept. 13, 1789	132
Lucinda, m. Moses E. **FRANKLIN**, Apr. 7, 1808	70
Lucinda, [d. Chauncey & Mary Louisa], b. Dec. 15, 1847	44
Lucretia, d. Oliver, bp. [Aug. 14], 1791	133
Lucretia, m. Frederic **WARNER**, Nov. 14, 1809	71

	Page
GOODRICH, (cont.)	
Lucy, d. Tyler, bp. Mar. 19, 1786	130
Lucy, m. Thomas **DERRICK**, of St. Croix, Ill.*, Sept. 15, 1839 *("Isl." in Church Rec.)	79
Luther, m. Elizabeth **BELDEN***, of Glastonbury, Nov. 1, 1797 (**BELL**?)	66
Luther, of East Haddam, m. Sally **DANFORTH**, Nov. 16, 1797	67
Luther, s. Ichabod, bp. July 31, 1803	138
Luther, d. Nov. 12, 1832, ae 57	107
Lydia, m. Appleton **HOLMES**, Nov. 14, 1771	61
Lydia, d. Israel, bp. Sept. 21, 1788	131
Lydia, wid., d. Jan. 10, 1804, at Eastbury, ae 75	96
Lydia, m. Asa **SHAYLER**, Sept. 10, 1806, by Rev. Mr. Bulkley	70
Lydia, wid., d. Apr. 8, 1824, ae 86	103
Mabel, d. Isaac, bp. Aug. 14, 1791	133
Manus*, s. Wait, bp. Dec. 9, 1770 *("Marvin" in Church Rec.)	121
Manas*, of Anadelia, N.Y., m. Ruth **GOODRICH**, Oct. 7, 1804 *("Manus")	69
Maria, d. Barzillai, bp. [Nov.] 22, 1801	138
Marinda, bp. Sept. 6, 1818 *("Adult, dau. of Luther **GOODRICH**" in Church Rec.)	144
Martha E., m. Calvin F. **COREY**, Nov. 9, 1836	79
Martha Elizabeth, of Rocky Hill, m. George Warren **SLATER**, of Hartford, May 8, 1850, by Rev. Calvin Chapin	33
Martha Elvira, d. Joshua, bp. Apr. 16, 1809	141
Marvin*, s. Wait, bp. Dec. 9, 1770 *("Manus" in Church Rec.)	121
Marvin, his d. [ ], d. Mar. 15, 1847, ae 23* *("ae 13" in Church Rec.)	115
Marvin W., m. Amelia **WRIGHT**, July 10, 1828	76
Marvin Wait, s. Gideon, bp. Nov. 9, 1800	137
Mary, d. Levi, bp. [July], 1765	117
Mary, d. Elijah, bp. [July 7], 1765	117
Mary, m. Holmes **GRISWOLD***, Nov. 11, 1794 *("**GREENWOOD**" in Church Rec.)	66
Mary, m. Samuel **DIMOCK**, Mar. 25, 1799	67
Mary, d. Ephraim, bp. [July] 12, 1807	140
Mary, m. James H. **HUBBARD**, of Middletown, Oct. 23, 1825	75
Mary Louisa, m. Lorin **GOODRICH**, b. of Rocky Hill, Jan. 16, 1854, by Rev. L.B. Rockwood	50
Mehetable, m. Asbel **RILEY**, Feb. 23, 1786	63
Mehetable, wid., d. June 7, 1841, ae 80	112
Mercy, d. Joshua, bp. Aug. 7, 1768	119
Mercy, d. Gurdon, bp. July 3, 1785	129
Mercy, d. Gideon, bp. Apr. 25, 1805	139
Mercy, m. William **WARNER**, of 1st Society, Nov. 27, 1808	70
Mercy, see Mercy **DICKINSON**	94
Micah, m. Elizabeth **HILL**, Mar. 17, 1774	61
Millecent, m. Wait **CURTIS**, Mar. 16, 1786	63
Miranda, d. Feb. 25, 1828, ae 25	105
Nancy, d. Roger, bp. May 18, 1766	118
Norman Whitmore, s. Levi, bp. Sept. 4, 1835	148

GOODRICH, (cont.)

	Page
Olive, wid., d. Aug. 4, 1842, ae 65	112
Oliver, his twin, d. [ ], d. Feb. 25, 1781	84
Oliver, s. Oliver, bp. Aug. [1], 1784	129
Oliver, his infant d. June 29, 1793	91
Oliver, his w. [ ], d. July 17, 1810, ae 58	98
Oliver, m. Sarah **WARNER**, [ ]	60
Oliver Butler, s. Joshua, bp. May 27, 1804	139
Olivia Mallory, d. Harvey, bp. July 26, 1818	144
Olney, s. Isaac, bp. Aug. 23, 1789	132
Orinda, d. Wait, bp. July 5, 1810	142
Orinda, m. Franklin **KELLOGG**, of Newington, Nov. 18, 1830	77
Orinia*, d. Oliver, Jr., bp. Feb. 6, 1774 *("Oxinia" in Church Rec.)	123
Orren Gilbert, s. Isaac, bp. Oct. 20, 1799	137
Otis, s. Wait, bp. May 2, 1802	138
Otis, s. Wait, d. Aug. 22, 1808, ae 7	98
Otis H., of Middletown, m. Marietta **HOLMES**, of Rocky Hill, May 13, 1847, by Rev. C. Chapin	22
Oxinia*, d. Oliver, Jr., bp. Feb. 6, 1774 *("Orinia" in Church Rec.)	123
Ozia, s. Israel, bp. Oct. 6, 1799	137
Parmelia, d. Oliver, bp. [Aug.] 26, 1787	130
Patty, m. Chester **WILLIAMS**, Aug. 16, 1795	66
Prudence, d. Roger, bp. Dec. 6, 1772	123
Prudence, m. David **BLYN**, Dec. 14, 1790	65
Purnam, s. Jemima, bp. Mar. 24, 1782	127
Rachel, d. Seth, bp. Apr. 5*, 1781, by Rev. Mr. Lewis *("Apr. 8" in Church Rec.)	126
Rachel, d. Seth, d. [ ] 30, 1783, ae 46 ("d. Oct. 30, [ae] 4th" in Church Rec.)	86
Rachel, d. Gideon, bp. Apr. 30, 1797	135
Rachel, m. Chauncey **STEELE**, of Berlin, Mar. 8, 1820	74
Rachel Sophia, [d. William, 2nd], b. Mar. 30, 1839	18
Ralph, s. Isaac, bp. Sept. 29, 1805	140
Ralph Warner, s. Oliver, bp. Aug. 28, 1785	129
Ralph Warner, s. Barzillai, bp. June 18, 1815	143
Rebecca, d. Gurdon, bp. May 10, 1767	118
Rebecca, m. Andrew **M'COMB**, of Salem, Mass., May 28, 1786	63
Rebecca, wid., d. Apr. 8, 1805, ae 78	96
Rhoda, m. Theodore **WOLCOTT**, Apr. 11, 1785	63
Rockwell, s. Ichabod, bp. July 13, 1794	134
Rockwell, d. Dec. 23, 1814, ae 21	100
Roger, his child d. June 14, 1776	84
Roger, his w. [ ], d. May 25, 1819, ae 78	101
Roger, d. Nov. 1, 1828, ae 88	106
Rosanna, d. Roger, bp. Feb. 5, 1769	120
Rosanna, m. Silas **GOFF**, Jan. 13, 1791	65
Roxy, m. Aaron **HOSFORD**, Jr., Nov. 8, 1795	66
Roxy, d. Isaac, bp. Feb. 9, 1797	135
Roxy, m. Samuel **STILLMAN**, of Sheffield, Mass., June 13, 1820	74
Russel, s. Wait, bp. July 3, 1808	141
Ruth, d. Ebenezer, bp. Feb. 14, 1773	123

	Page
GOODRICH, (cont.)	
Ruth, m. Manas **GOODRICH**, of Anadelia, N.Y., Oct. 7, 1804	69
Sally*, m. Silas **WILLIAMS**, Dec. 24, 1797 *("Sally **GRISWOLD**" in Church Rec.)	67
Sally, m. Elias **WILLARD**, of Trenton, N.Y., Feb. 8, 1807	70
Sally Thomas, d. Ephraim, bp. [ ], 24, 1802	138
Salmon, m. Harriet **GOODRICH**, Apr. 2, 1828	76
Samuel, s. Seth, bp. May 18, 1794	134
Samuel, m. Nancy **BECKLEY**, Dec. 8, 1814	73
Samuel, his child d. July 28, 1842, ae 6	112
Samuel* Henry, s. wid. Harriet, bp. June 20, 1806 *("Lemuel" in Church Rec.)	140
Sarah, m. David **RILEY**, May 17, 1773	61
Sarah, wid., d. May 10, 1781, ae 84 (Left 65 grandchildren and 69 great grandchildren)	85
Sarah, d. Oliver, bp. May 29, 1814	143
Sarah, bp. Sept. 6, 1818 *("Adult, dau. of Luther **GOODRICH**" in Church Rec.)	144
Sarah A., m. Leonard **BELDEN**, b. of Rocky Hill, July 31, 1853, by Rev. L. Burton Rockwood	46
Sarah Jane, d. William, bp. July 5, 1839	149
Seth, his child d. June 12, 1776	84
Seth, d. Oct. 20, 1834, ae 88	108
Silas, d. Sept. 1, 1800, at Newport, R.I., ae 24	95
Solomon, d. [ ], 1834, ae 17	108
Sophia, d. Isaac, bp. Nov. 9, 1806	140
Sophia, m. Linus **DEMING**, Dec. 11, 1828	76
Stephen Taylor, bp. July 4, 1841	149
Susan Amelia, d. Levi, bp. Sept. 4, 1835	148
Susannah, d. Wait, bp. Jan. 12, 1766	118
Sylvester, s. Tyler, bp. Oct. 4, 1789	132
Temperance, m. David **SMITH**, Sept. 25, 1766	60
Temperance, wid., d. Oct. 24, 1803, ae 80	96
Thomas, m. Belinda **WEBB**, Feb. 27, 1828	76
Thomas Russel, s. Eleazer, bp. [May 3], 1835	148
Triphena, d. Alpheas, bp. Jan. 20, 1771	121
Tryphena, m. Aaron **CLARK**, 2nd, of Middletown, Mar. 25, 1805	69
Wait, s. Ebenezer, bp. Apr. 7, 1776	125
Wait, m. Olive **WILLIAMS**, June 26, 1798	67
Walter, s. Lemuel, bp. Oct. 14, 1798	136
Walter, d. [ ] 7, 1821, in Norfolk, Va., ae 24	102
Walter Bulkley, s. Joshua, bp. May 22, 1803	138
Warren, s. James*, bp. Aug. 15, 1790 *("s. Israel" in Church Rec.)	132
Wealthy, d. Oliver, Jr., bp. Oct. 13, 1771	122
Wealthy, m. James **RICARD**, of Boston, [, 1788]	64
W[illia]m, m. Mehetabel [ ], Aug. 20, 1783	62
W[illia]m, s. W[illia]m, bp. Sept. 11, 1791	133
William, Jr., m. Sally **WHITMORE**, May 5, 1813	72
William, s. Gideon, bp. Mar. 7, 1814	143
W[illia]m, his w. [ ], d. Feb. 8, 1819, ae 54	101
William, d. July 4, 1837, ae 77	109

	Page
GOODRICH, (cont.)	
William, d. Mar. 6, 1845, ae 39	114
William Henry, s. Ichabod, bp. Oct. 23, 1808	141
William Henry, s. William, bp. July 5, 1839	149
----------, m. Ozias **DICKINSON**, Oct. [ ], 1772	61
GOODWIN, Lucy, of 1st Society, m. John **ROBBINS**, of Rochester, N.Y., May 7, 1828	76
GORHAM, Henry, d. Feb. 9, 1824, ae 8	103
GRAHAM, Eliza Jane, m. Norman **WHITMORE**, July 28, 1830	77
Elizabeth, of Stockbridge, Mass., m. Winthrop **ROBBINS**, Feb. 3, 1828	76
Jasper, m. Lois **WILLIAMS**, [ ] 28, 1823	75
Jasper*, d. Mar. 10, 1841, ae 69 *(Arnold Copy has "Joseph")	111
Joseph*, d. Mar. 10, 1841, ae 69 *("Jasper" in Church Rec.)	111
GRANNIS, Anson, his w. [ ], d. Sept. 25, 1830, ae 31	106
Richard*, m. Charlotte **BRADFORD**, June 27, 1824 *("Richard **GRIMES**" in Church Rec.)	75
GRANT, Prudence, wid., m. Joel **SANDERSON**, of Petersham, Mass., Mar. 10, 1824	75
GRAVES, Susannah, of Granville, Mass., m. Hubbard **GOODRICH**, [ ] 26, 1787	64
GRAY, Jerry W., of Manchester, m. Sarah **SHAYLOR**, of Rocky Hill, Aug. 20, 1845, by Rev. John Lovejoy	13
GREENWOOD*, Holmes, m. Mary **GOODRICH**, Nov. 11, 1794 *(Arnold Copy has "**GRISWOLD**")	66
Rodney, s. Holmes, bp. Sept. 16, 1798	136
GRENNIS*, Richard, m. Charlotte **BRADFORD**, June 27, 1824 *("**GRIMES**" in Church Rec.)	75
[**GRIFFIN**], **GIFFIN**, Simon, m. Lydia **CRANE**, Dec. 12, 1772	61
GRIMES, Abigail, m. Benjamin J. **GRISWOLD**, Jan. 13, 1791	65
Abigail, wid., d. Mar. 25, 1792, ae 90	90
Agnes, bp. July 4, 1841	150
Agnes, m. Frances W. **SHIPMAN**, b. of Rocky Hill, Nov. 19, 1845, Rev. C. Chapin	16
Alexander, m. Mary **DUNN**, Aug. 17, 1769	60
Alexander, his child, d. Apr. 21, 1771	82
Alexander, his w. [ ], d. Feb. 26, 1823, ae 76	103
Alexander, d. Mar. 25, 1840, ae 95	111
Hezekiah, d. Sept. 24, 1775	83
Hezekiah, his w. [ ], d. Dec. 12, 1822, ae 46	102
Hezekiah, d. Dec. 19, 1833, ae 59	108
John, his w. [ ], d. Mar. 4, 1767	81
John, m. Bena **SMITH**, Oct. [ ], 1768	60
John, d. May 21, 1790, ae 66	89
Jonathan, d. [ ] 29, 1792, ae 32	90
Josiah, Jr.*, m. Abigail **GOODRICH**, Jan. 17, 1771 *(Arnold Copy has "Josiah **FRANCIS**, Jr.")	60
Josiah, Jr., his w. [ ], d. Nov. 22*, 1771 *("Nov. 12" in Church Rec.)	82
Josiah, Jr., m. Mehetable **WARNER**, June 14, 1773	61
Josiah, d. Jan. 27 or 28, 1781, ae 86* (single) *("ae 84" in Church Rec.)	84
Josiah, d. Jan. 13, 1797, ae 54	93

ROCKY HILL VITAL RECORDS 55

	Page
GRIMES, (cont.)	
Lois, bp. Sept. 7, 1794, adult	134
Lois, m. Charles **LYON**, Mar. 13, 1796	66
Lucy, m. John H. **BRAINARD**, Dec. 23, 1852, by Rev. A.B. Chapin, of Glastonbury	48
Lydia, bp. July 1, 1796, an adult	135
Lydia, d. Oct. 17, 1796, "supposed about" ae 24	93
Margaret, d. W[illia]m, bp. Oct. 3, 1819	145
Marshall*, bp. [May 6], 1838, adult *("Marhal" in Church Rec.)	149
Mary, m. Seth **DICKINSON**, Jan. 24, 1813	72
Mary, wid., d. Apr. 18, 1845, ae 59, [at Tariff[ ]]	114
Mary Ann, m. F.W. **SHIPMAN**, Aug. 6, 1851, by Rev. L.Burton Rockwood	37
Mehetabel, wid., d. Sept. 27, 1802, ae 53	95
Nathaniel, d. [ ], 1796, ae 24, in West Indies	93
Polly, bp. Sept. 7, 1794, adult	134
Richard*, m. Charlotte **BRADFORD**, June 27, 1824 *(Arnold Copy has "Richard **GRENNIS**")	75
Sabina, d. Aug. 31, 1793, ae [ ]	91
Samuel, d. Sept. 12, 1794, ae 17, in West Indies	92
William, m. Mary **JAGGER**, Apr. 23, 1809	70
William Johnson, s. Marshall, bp. Sept. 4, 1846	151
GRISWOLD, Abigail, m. Hosea **BULKLEY**, May 1, 1781	61
Abigail, wid. of Benj[amin] Ja[me]s, bp. Mar. 2, 1794	134
Abigail, wid., d. June 6, 1795, ae 66	92
Abigail, wid., m. Frederic **ROBBINS**, Jan. 13, 1811	71
Albert C., of Wethersfield, m. Caroline Louisa **GOODRICH**, of Rocky Hill, Jan. 13, 1853, by Rev. L.B. Rockwood	43
Alfred, s. Jacob, bp. Sept. 8, 1816	143
Alfred, m. Louisa Mariah **RASH**, b. of Rocky Hill, July 17, 1843, by Rev. C. Chapin	1
Alfred, m. Louisa Maria **RASH**, [ ] 17, 1843	80
Almira, w. Henry, d. Sept. 16, 1848, in Worcester, Mass., ae 45 *("Almira, once w. of Henry **GRISWOLD**, but divorced". See Church Rec.)	116
Alonzo, s. Jacob, bp. Sept. 22, 1811	142
Alonzo, s. Jacob, bp. June 5, 1814	143
Ashbel Boardman, s. Con[stan]t, bp. [Oct.] 10, 1784	129
Augusta, m. Roger **RILEY**, Oct. 24, 1791	65
Benjamin J., m. Abigail **GRIMES**, Jan. 13, 1791	65
Benjamin J., d. Dec. 19, 1793, coming from West Indies, ae 25	91
Charlotte, d. W[illia]m, bp. Aug. 29, 1773	123
Charlotte, m. W[illia]m **WEBB**, Jr., Apr. 10, 1791	65
Charlotte, d. Josiah, bp. [May 5], 1816	143
Charlotte, m. Horace **BLINN**, of Great Barrington, Mass., June 2, 1824	75
Charlotte, wid., d. Sept. 3, 1847, ae 73	115
Chauncey Jerome, s. Jacob, bp. July 4, 1834	148
Chloe, m. Joseph **RILEY**, Sept. [, 1772]	61
Constant, his s. [ ], bp. Feb. 2, 1797 *(His s. "Frederic"in Church Rec.)	135
Constant, his w. [ ], d. Mar. 20, 1825, ae 65	104

	Page
GRISWOLD, (cont.)	
Constant, d. [ ], 1839, ae 87	110
Cornelius, s. Jacob, bp. July 2, 1826	146
Daniel, m. Jerusha **GIBBS**, Nov. 23, 1769	60
Daniel, s. Daniel, bp. Aug. 15, 1773	123
Deborah, d. Josiah, bp. Apr. 10, 1768	119
Deborah, d. Constant, bp. July 6, 1794	134
Deborah, wid., d. Apr. 28, 1825	104
Ebenezer Grimes, s. Jehiel, bp. July 22, 1781	127
Eliza Ann, d. Jacob, bp. Oct. 4, 1831	147
[Frederic*], s. Constant, bp. Feb. 2, 1797 *(Supplied from Church Rec.)	135
Frederick, his child d. Feb. 10, 1830, ae 7	106
Freeman, of Wethersfield, m. Eliza Jane **BOARDMAN**, of Rocky Hill, Oct. 8, 1854, at the house of Rev. L.B. Rockwood, by Rev. Robert G. Williams, of Durham	54
Henry J., m. Mary J. **BELDEN**, b. of Rocky Hill, Jan. 13, 1850, by Rev. Calvin Chapin	32
Holmes*, m. Mary **GOODRICH**, Nov. 11, 1794 *("Holmes **GREENWOOD**" in Church Rec.)	66
Jacob, d. Sept. 2, 1768	81
Jacob, m. Rachel **WARNER**, Dec. 25, 1785	63
Jacob, s. Jacob, bp. [Oct. 29], 1786	130
Jacob, his w. [ ], d. Nov. 23, 1789, ae 23	89
Jacob, m. Lydia **WRIGHT**, Nov. 12, 1807	70
Jacob, his w. [ ], d. Jan. 19, 1823, ae 37	102
Jacob, m. Sally **BERRY**, Oct. 26, 1824	75
Jacob, his w. [ ], d. [July] 24, 1841, ae 45	112
Jacob, d. Feb. 2, 1848, in Taunton (?), Mass., ae 62	115
James*, s. wid. Abigail, bp. Mar. 9, 1794 *(Arnold Copy has "James, child of wid. Abigail Griswold **BOARDMAN**")	134
James, of 1st Society, m. Lucy **ROBBINS**, Jan. 22, 1812	71
Jehiel, his w. [ ], d. Oct. 16, 1770	82
John, d. Nov. 19, 1765	81
Joseph, d. Dec. 3, 1841, at Bristol, ae 30* *("ae 39" in Church Rec.)	112
Josiah, d. Oct. 20, 1774	83
Josiah, s. Solomon, bp. Jan. 7, 1776	125
Josiah, s. Constant, bp. Oct. 24, 1790	132
Josiah, s. Josiah, bp. [May 5], 1816	143
Josiah, d. Dec. 19, 1832, ae 58	107
Lester, s. Josiah, bp. Feb. 3, 1816	143
Lester, d. William, bp. Feb. 16, 1841	149
Lester*, d. Feb. 17, 1841, ae 5 *("s. of William" in Church Rec.)	111
Lydia C.*, of East Haddam, m. Thomas **HANDY**, of Chatham, Aug. 26, 1825 *("Lydia C. **ARNOLD**" in Church Rec.)	75
Lydia Wright, d. Jacob, bp. July 13, 1823	145
Martha, m. Elijah **ROBBINS**, [, [1788]	64
Martha, w. William, d. [ ] 8, 1789	89
Martha *, d. wid. Abigail, bp. Mar. 9, 1794 *(Arnold Copy has Martha, child of wid. Abigail Griswold **BOARDMAN**")	134
Martha, m. Asher **ROBBINS**, Oct. 23, 1815	73
Martha, d. Josiah, bp. [May 15], 1816	143

	Page
GRISWOLD, (cont.)	
Martha, d. Jan. 25, 1834*, ae 20 *("1833" in Church Rec.)	107
Martha, of 1st Society, d. Nov. 17, 1834, ae 18	108
Martha, d. Jacob, bp. Sept. 2, 1836	148
Martha A., of Rocky Hill, m. Charles F. **SMITH**, of Cromwell, Dec. 13, 1853, by Rev. L.B. Rockwood	49
Martha Ann, bp. [Nov.] 21, 1847	151
Martha Jane, of Rocky Hill, m. Augustus F. **ADAMS**, of Wethersfield, Oct. 9, 1851, by Rev. L.B. Rockwood	37
Mary, d. Josiah, bp. Aug. 14, 1817	143
Mary, m. James W. **REILLY**, of Bristol, Jan. 16, 1837	79
Melissa, [d. Josiah], bp. [May 5], 1816	143
Melissa, m. Walter **WARNER**, Mar. 10, 1831	77
Mercy, wid., d. Nov. 3, 1819, ae 82	101
Mercy M., m. Russel **ADAMS**, of 1st Society, Nov. 26, 1829	76
Mercy Miller, d. Josiah, bp. [May 5], 1816	143
Moses, m. Nancy **ROBBINS**, b. of 1st Society, Oct. 11, 1804	69
Nancy, d. Josiah, bp. Nov. 17, 1765	117
Nancy, d. Oct. 1, 1781	85
Nancy, d. Constant, bp. June 24, 1787	130
Ozias, s. Ozias, bp. Aug. 8, 1773	123
Rachel Warner, d. Jacob, bp. [Oct.] 20, 1811	142
Ralph H., of Wethersfield, m. Harriet A. **ROBBINS**, of Rocky Hill, July 4, 1852, by Rev. Theodore M. Dwight	42
Sally*, m. Silas **WILLIAMS**, Dec. 24, 1797 *("Sally **GOODRICH**" in Arnold Copy)	67
Sally, d. Jacob, bp. Oct. 27, 1818	144
Sarah, wid., m. Daniel **WARNER**, Apr. 24, 1766	60
Sarah, d. W[illia]m, bp. Oct. 10, 1779, by Rev. Mr. Pitkin, of Farmington	126
Sarah, wid., m. Amasa **ADAMS**, Jan. 15, 1783	62
Sarah D., m. Chester **WILCOX**, of Bristol, Sept. 3, 1823	75
Sarah Deming, d. Josiah, bp. [May 5], 1816	143
Sarah Wilkinson, d. Jacob, bp. May 1, 1829	146
Solomon, m. Sarah **DEMING**, Feb. 2, 1775	61
Solomon, s. Constant, bp. May 26, 1782	127
Solomon, s. Josiah, bp. [May 5], 1816	143
Solomon, m. Elizabeth W. **ARNOLD**, Nov. 11, 1827	76
Solomon, d. Jan. 20*, 1830, ae 49 *("Jan. 2" in Church Rec.)	106
Sylvester, s. Constant, bp. Dec. 11, 1791	133
Wait, s. Jacob, bp. Apr. 6, 1788	131
Wait R., his w. [ ], d. Aug. 4, 1848, bd. in Wethersfield	116
William, d. Sept. 7, 1806, ae 75	97
William, s. Josiah, bp. [May 5], 1816	143
William, m. Julia Ann **GIBBS**, Mar. 16, 1834	78
Willis W., m. Roxana **RASH**, b. of Rocky Hill, Mar. 20, 1845, by Rev. John Lovejoy	9
Wyllis Williams, s. Jacob, bp. Nov. 4, 1821	145
GUSTIAN*, Lydia, d. Feb. 18, 1782, ae 64 y. *("**JUSTAIN**" in Arnold Copy)	85
GUTHRIE, Mary G., Mrs., late of Rocky Hill, m. Amos **BISHOP**, of Bethleham, Sept. 10, 1843, by Rev. Joseph Holdrich	2

	Page
HALE, [see also HALL], David, m. Amelia KINNE, b. of Glastonbury, Dec. 29, 1819	74
James, m. Sarah FORBES, Dec. 30, 1770	60
Jared, of Chatham, m. Mary BELDEN, June 2, 1818	74
HALL, [see also HALE], Isaac, of Leyden, N.Y., m. wid. Lois BULKLEY, Dec. 20, 1802	68
Josephine Mehetable Emeline, d. Samuel H.P., bp. Feb. 8, 1832	147
Samuel H.P., of Middletown, m. Emeline BULKLEY, May 14, 1826	75
Theodore Parson, s. Samuel H.P., bp. [Sept. 2], 1836	148
HALLOW, [see also PENHOLLOW], Anna*, m. Norris BELDEN, June 17, 1832 *(Arnold Copy has "Anna HARLOW")	77
John, m. Emeline GOODRICH, Apr. 22, 1832	77
HAMLIN, Benjamin L., of Hartford, m. Abigail GOFF, May 12, 1817	73
HAMMOND, James, of Hartford, m. Rebecca WILKINSON, [ ] 25, 1787	64
HAND, Abigail, d. Jonathan, bp. [Nov.] 29, 1795 *("d. Jonathan's wife" in Church Rec.)	135
Daniel, s. Jonathan, bp. Aug. 26, 1795	134
Daniel, d. Aug. 31, 1795	92
Hannah, d. Jonathan, bp. Nov. 29, 1795	135
Harriet, d. Jonathan, bp. Nov. 29, 1795	135
Jonathan, of Long Island, m. Abigail WEED, Feb. 17, 1781	61
Jonathan, his w. [ ], d. Oct. 23, 1789, ae 33	89
Jona[tha]n, m. Hannah BEACHGOOD, Feb. 7, 1790	64
Sylvanus, s. Jonathan, bp. Nov. 8, 1795	135
HANDY, Thomas, of Chatham, m. Lydia C. ARNOLD, of East Haddam, Aug. 26, 1825	75
HANMORE, Prudence, m. John TREAT, Oct. 16, 1782	62
HARLOW*, Anna, m. Norris BELDEN, June 17, 1832 *("HALLOW" in Church Rec.)	77
HARRIS, Betsey, m. Ezekiel TRYON, b. of Glastonbury, Aug. 11, 1799	67
Lucy, m. Henry SMITH, b. of Middletown, May 19, 1811	71
Mehitable, m. Thomas BELDING, Aug. 8, 1782	61
HARRISON, Lemon, m. Cesar FREEMAN, Nov. 15, 1810	71
HART, Caroline, d. Seth, bp. Oct. 11, 1801	138
Caroline, d. [ ], 1812, ae 11	99
Caroline, d. [ ], 1812, ae 11	99
Joel, of Burlington, m. Sarah BOWERS, Sept. 7, 1820	74
Lucius, s. Seth, bp. July 31, 1803	138
Nabby*, d. Seth, bp. Nov. 12, 1786 *(Arnold Copy has "Nabby HUNT")	130
Nabby, m. John G. BULKLEY, Nov. 25, 1804	69
Nancy, m. Chauncey BULKLEY, Aug. 27, 1805	69
Norman, s. Seth, bp. Aug. 14, 1794	134
Norman, s. Seth, bp. Dec. 22, 1805	140
Roxy, d. Seth, bp. [Nov. 6], 1791	133
Roxey, m. Nathan JAGGER, May 11, 1808	70
Selah, twin with Seth, s. Seth, bp. Oct. 1, 1796	135
Seth, twin with Selah, s. Seth, bp. Oct. 1, 1796	135
Seth, his w. [ ], d. June 27, 1799, ae 36	94
Seth, m. wid. Lydia BULL, Nov. 10, 1799	67

	Page
HART, (cont.)	
Seth, his infant, bp. [ ] 26, 1799	136
Seth, his w. [ ], d. Mar. 5, 1812, ae 50	99
Seth, m. Lucy **BOARDMAN**, Aug. 9, 1812	72
Seth, d. Dec. 12, 1813, ae 53	99
HARTWELL, Farrand, of Charlotteville, N.Y., m. Mary **GIBBS**, Nov. 27, 1834	78
HASKELL, Aden E., of Hartford, m. Martha J. **GARDINER**, of Rocky Hill, May 25, 1854, by Rev. L.B. Rockwood	51
Timothy, of Middletown, m. Roxy **RASH**, Apr. 11, 1815	73
HASTINGS, Charles H., m. Nancy **WHITMORE**, Sept. 3, 1834	78
William, his child d. Sept. 16, 1802, ae 4	95
----------, wid., d. Aug. 10, 1848, ae 76	116
HATCH, Esther, wid., d. Jan. 9, 1822, ae 91	102
HAVENS, Joseph Thomas, bp. July 4, 1841	150
HEMINWAY, Edwin H., of Hartford, m. Sarah Ann **FRANCES**, of Rocky Hill, May 29, 1845, by Rev. C. Chapin	12
HENDERSON, John S.R., of Queensbury, N.Y., m. Emily **COREY**, Sept. 14, 1817	73
HENRY, Elizabeth Juliaette, m. Henry LaFayette **CLARK**, Mar. 19, 1848, by Rev. Calvin Chapin	25
HICKOX, Bennet, of Watertown, m. Harriet **GIBBS**, Apr. 30, 1832	77
George Myron, s. Jeremiah, bp. [ ], 1818	144
Horace, s. Jeremiah, bp. Oct. 22, 1820	145
Horace, d. July 19, 1822, ae 3	102
Horace Frances, s. Jeremiah, bp. Nov. 3, 1822	145
Jeremiah, d. Oct. 4, 1827, ae 49	105
Laura O., m. Henry R. **TAYLOR**, of Glastonbury, [ ] 20, 1840	79
Laura Olive, d. Jeremiah, bp. July 26, 1818	144
Mary Caroline, d. Jeremiah, bp. July 26, 1818	144
Mary Caroline, m. Andrew **WILLIAMS**, Feb. 24, 1835	78
Sidney Norton, s. Jeremiah, bp. July 26, 1818	144
HIGGINS, Deuel, of East Glastonbury, m. Fanny **BLAIR***, Mar. 24, 1819 *("**BLIN**" in Church Rec.)	74
Edwin, s. [Joseph], bp. June 6, 1796	135
Joseph, m. Nancy **WILLIAMS**, Dec. 18, 1785	63
Joseph, s. [Joseph], bp. June 6, 1796	135
Joseph, Dr., d. July 18, 1797, ae 38	93
Mary, d. Joseph, bp. Aug. 6, 1797 *("d. Joseph, decd" in Church Rec.)	136
Nancy, d. Joseph, bp. June 6, 1796	135
Nancy, wid., m. Josiah **WOOLCOTT**, of Bristol, Feb. 16, 1806	69
Silas, s. Joseph, bp. June 6, 1796	135
Wait W., d. Sept. 12, 1796, ae 9	93
Wait Williams, s. Joseph, bp. July 19, 1796	135
W[illia]m Henry, s. [Joseph], bp. June 6, 1796	135
HILL, Charles, of New York, m. Sophia **BRADFORD**, May 5, 1831	77
Elizabeth, m. Micah **GOODRICH**, Mar. 17, 1774	61
Noble*, d. Oct. 2, 1810, ae 19 *("Apprentice to Samuel Bull" in Church Rec.)	98
HINE, Daniel S., of Humphreyville, m. Abigail **MILLER**, Nov. 27, 1831	77
Daniel S., his w. [ ]d. Oct. 24, 1832, ae 25	107

	Page
HINSDALE, Elijah, his child d. Apr. [ ], 1772	82
Elijah, his child d. Nov. 5, 1772	82
Elizabeth, had d. Ruth, bp. Dec. 30, 1770	121
Elizabeth, d. Elijah, bp. Feb. 12, 1775	124
Ruth, d. Elizabeth*, bp. Dec. 30, 1770 *("Elijah" in Church Rec.)	121
HOADLEY, Willard, of Waterbury, m. Betsey E. **CRAWFOOT**, of Rocky Hill, June 1, 1845, by Rev. Charles Bartlet	12
HOLDEN, Austin, s. W[illia]m, bp. Dec. 3, 1797	136
Chauncey, of Colebrook, m. Mary Stocking **ABBY**, Jan. 6, 1833	77
Eben Mitchell, of Granville, m. Hepsibeth **GOODRICH**, Nov. 3, 1785	63
Edmond, s. W[illia]m, bp. Mar. 8, 1807	140
Isaac, s. W[illia]m, bp. Oct. 13, 1799	137
Marilla, d. Jan. 29, 1838, ae 18	110
Sylvester, s. William, bp. Oct. 11, 1801	138
W[illia]m, of Granville, Mass., m. Prudence **BELDEN**, Feb. 21, 1795	66
W[illia]m, his child d, Mar. 17, 1807, ae 2	97
HOLLISTER, Samuel*, his wid. [ ], d. Mar. 6, 1765 *("Wid. Susanna HOLLISTER" in Church Rec.)	81
Susanna*, wid., d. Mar. 6, 1765 *(Arnold Copy has "Samuel")	81
HOLMES, Aaron Hale, twin with Annis, s. Charles, bp. Oct. 2, 1785	129
Abigail, d. John, d. Feb. 22, 1776	83
Allen, m. Patty **WRIGHT**, July 17, 1804	69
Allen, d. [ ], 1841, ae 58	112
Allen, his w. [ ], d. Oct. 6, 1848, ae 28	116
Allen B., d. Oct. 5, 1843, ae 45	113
Allen Boardman, s. Daniel, bp. Sept. 1, 1799	137
Allen E., of Rocky Hill, m. Maria **PENFIELD**, of Glastonbury, May 19, 1844, by Rev. John Lovejoy	5
Alma, d. Levi, bp. Oct. 14, 1798	136
Alma, m. Nathan **LEE**, Feb. 21, 1821	74
Annis, twin with Aaron Hale, d. Charles, bp. Oct. 2, 1785	129
Appleton, m. Lydia **GOODRICH**, Nov. 14, 1771	61
Appleton*, had s. bp. Jan. 15, 1775 *("Alpheas **COLLINS**" in Church Rec.)	124
Appleton, of Glastonbury, m. wid. Rosa **DIX**, of the 1st Society, Apr. 26, 1812	72
Boardman, his d. [ ], d. Apr. 26, 1838, ae 6	110
Caroline, m. Tallcott A. **ARNOLD**, Mar. 5, 1834	78
Celista, m. Luther **DEMING**, Nov. 27, 1833	78
Charles, his s. [ ], bp. Oct. 10, 1779, by Rev. Mr. Pitkin, of Farmington	126
Chester, s. Thomas, bp. Oct. 14, 1787	131
Chester, d. Sept. 1, 1830, ae 44 [N. Orleans]	106
Christian, w. Etha[ ], bp. June 20, 1802	138
Daniel, his s. [ ], d. Jan. 23, 1797, ae 4	93
Daniel, d. Jan. 12, 1812, ae 50	99
Daniel, m. Julia M. **TREAT**, of Norfolk, Dec. 26, 1833	78
Dorothy, m. John **BELDEN**, [, 1788]	64
Electa B., d. W[illia]m, bp. Jan. 1, 1844	151
Eliza, w. W[illia]m, bp. July 4, 1841	149
Eliza Al.*, d. W[illia]m, bp. Jan. 1, 1844 *(Perhaps Elizabeth")	151

	Page
HOLMES, (cont.)	
Elizabeth, w. Phineas, d. Oct. 7, 1783	86
Elizabeth, d. Samuel*, bp. [Sept. 26], 1790 *("Lemuel" in Church Rec.)	132
Ellen Boardman, d. Daniel, bp. July 27, 1794	134
Epaphras*, s. Thomas, bp. Aug. 22, 1790 *(Arnold Copy has "Ephraim")	132
Ephraim*, s. Thomas, bp. Aug. 22, 1790 *("Epaphras" in Church Rec.)	132
Esther, d. Apr. 22, 1812, ae 32	99
Ethan, m. Christiana **BLINN**, Oct. 21, 1798	67
Ethan, d. Jan. 22, 1812, ae 32	99
Florinda, d. Appleton, bp. July 12, 1772	122
Florinda, wid., m. Edward **NEFF**, Oct. 29, 1837	79
Francis, of Rocky Hill, m. Louisa **SMITH**, of Berlin, Feb. 5, 1852, by Rev. L.B. Rockwood	39
Frances Boardman, s. Boardman, bp. Oct. 4, 1831	147
George, s. Ethan, bp. Aug. 15, 1802	138
Henry Chauncey, s. Boardman, bp. June 30, 1827	146
Jerusha, bp. July 5, 1818, an adult	144
Jerusha, d. Aug. 10, 1823, ae 24	103
John, his w. [ ], d. Apr. 19, 1807, ae 67	97
John, d. Dec. 11, 1821, ae 84	102
Jonas, d. May 22, 1815, ae 79	100
Joseph T., s. W[illia]m, bp. Jan. 1, 1844	151
Josiah, s. Charles, bp. Sept. 7, 1783	128
Laura, d. Samuel*, bp. [Sept. 26], 1790 *("Lemuel" in Church Rec.)	132
Levi, m. Molly **COREY**, [, 1788]	64
Levi, s. Levi, bp. July 26, 1795	134
Levi, d. Apr. 10, 1819, ae 68	101
Lucretia, d. Ethan, bp. July 3, 1808	141
Lucretia, m. Leonard **BELDEN**, Aug. 6, 1826	75
Mabel, d. Daniel, bp. Oct. 12, 1788	131
Maria, d. Daniel, bp. Oct. 2, 1803	139
Maria, d. Jan. 21, 1848, ae 46	115
Marietta, m. Isaac **BELDEN**, July 16, 1829	76
Marietta, of Rocky Hill, m. Otis H. **GOODRICH**, of Middletown, May 13, 1847, by Rev. C. Chapin	22
Martha, w. Allen, bp. May 4, 1832	147
Mary, d. Levi, bp. May 4, 1800 *("Mary, infant of Levi, bp. Mar. 31" in Church Rec.)	137
Mary, d. Boardman, bp. Nov. 28, 1826	146
Mary, wid., d. Jan. 7, 1828, ae 64	105
Mary, d. Mar. 4, 1842, ae 45	112
Molly, d. [ ], 1827, ae 86* *("ae 80" in Church Rec.)	105
Nancy, d. Ethan, bp. Aug. 15, 1802	138
Nancy, m. Joseph **TREAT**, of Middletown, Oct. 5, 1820	74
Patty, d. Charles, bp. Jan. 20, 1782	127
Phineas, d. July 5, 1785, ae 73	87
Phineas, s. Levi, bp. July 8, 1792	133
Phinehas, d. Aug. 22, 1796, ae 5	93
Phinehas, s. Levi, bp. June 25, 1797	136
Polly, d. Thomas, bp. Sept. 24, 1797	136

BARBOUR COLLECTION

Page

HOLMES, (cont.)
Ralph, s. Levi, bp. Oct. 17, 1790	132
Ralph, d. Sept. 11, 1820, ae 34	102
Richard, s. Appleton, bp. Aug. 22, 1773	123
Ruth, d. Charles, bp. July 27, 1774	124
Samuel*, his child, d. Mar. 31, 1789; born dead *("Lem[ue]l" in Church Rec.)	89
Sarah, d. Sept. 29, 1793	91
Sarah, d. Daniel, bp. Sept. 25, 1796	135
Sarah, d. Dec. 1, 1834, ae 39	108
Sophia, m. Elisha C. **CADWELL**, of Torrington, Apr. 30, 1833	77
Thomas, m. Hannah **GOODRICH**, May 3, 1786	63
Thomas, s. Thomas, bp. Sept. 20, 1795	134
Thomas*, d. Feb. 6, 1816, ae 73 *("Thomas **HORNER**" in Church Rec.)	100
Thomas, his w. [ ], d. Oct. 26, 1838, ae 74	110
Thomas, d. Sept. 13, 1841, ae 85	112
Walter, m. Florinda **PORTER**, Nov. 30, 1828	76
Walter, d. July 20, 1835, ae 29	109
W[illia]m, of Eastbury, his w. [ ], d. Aug. 5, 1794, ae 79	91
William, s. Ethan, bp. June 12, 1803	138
William, m. Eliza **BELDEN**, Mar. 7, 1827	76

HOMISS, John, of Middletown, m. Mary E. **THAYER**, of Rocky Hill, May 15, 1851, by Rev. F.W. Bill — 36

HOOKER, Bryan E., of Bristol, m. Maria R. **WILLIAMS**, Mar. 27, 1833 — 77
Sarah, of Farmington, m. George **COOK**, of St. Armand, in Lower Canada, Sept. 23, 1810 — 71

HOPKINS, Ira, s. Caleb, bp. [May] 29, 1796 — 135
Joseph, s. Caleb, bp. [May] 29, 1796 — 135
Susan M., of Middletown, m. Moss* **KNEASS**, of Philadelphia, Pa., May 15, 1843 *("Mars" in Church Rec.) — 80

HORKINS*, Mingo, of Simsbury, m. Violet **LONDON**, July 3, 1796 *(Perhaps "HOSKINS") — 66

HORNER*, Thomas, d. Feb. 6, 1816, ae 73 *("**HOLMES**" in Arnold Copy) — 100

HORTON, Hamilton R., of Glastenbury, , m. Lucy **BULKLEY**, of Rocky Hill, Aug. 1, 1844, by Rev. C. Chapin — 5
Russell, his w. [   ], d. [Dec. 3*], 1803, ae 27 *(From Church Rec.) — 96

HOSFORD, HORSFORD, Aaron, Jr., m. Roxy Goodrich, Nov. 8, 1795 — 66
Aaron, Dr., d. Apr. 7, 1804, ae 57	96
Aaron, d. Feb. 6, 1805, at Hartford, ae 33	96
Aaron Adams, s. Harley, bp. Nov. 8, 1818	144
Aaron Adams, d. Nov. 5, 1840, ae 28	111
Charlotte*, d. Othniel, bp. July 7, 1782 *("twin with Lauretta" in Church Rec.)	127
Esther, wid., d. July 18, 1828, ae 78	105
Etty, d. May 8, 1840, ae 62	111
Harley, s. Aaron, bp. Mar. 14, 1791	132
Joel Hall, s. Aaron, bp. Feb. 17, 1784	128
Joel Hall, s. Aaron, d. Sept. 3, 1786	87
Lauretta*, d. Othniel, bp. July 7, 1782 *("twin with Charlotte" in Church Rec.)	127

ROCKY HILL VITAL RECORDS 63

	Page
HOSFORD, HORSFORD, (cont.)	
Lydia, d. Othniel, bp. Oct. 28, 1781	127
Othniel, s. Aaron, bp. July 29, 1787	130
Roxy Goodrich, d. Aaron, Jr., bp. Feb. 9, 1797 ("Feb. 7" in Church Rec.)	135
Sally, d. Othniel, bp. Oct. 28, 1781	127
HOSKINS*, Mingo, of Simsbury, m. Violet **LONDON**, July 3, 1796 *(Perhaps "**HORKINS**")	66
HOUGH, Horace, of Wallingford, m. Polly **WHITMORE**, [June] 7, [1801]	68
John, s. John, bp. Sept. 27, 1767, [of Meriden*] *(From Church Rec.)	119
HOVEY*, Edmund, of Mansfield, m. Sophia **BULKLEY**, Apr. 13, 1806 *(Arnold Copy has "**AVERY**")	69
HOW, Solomon, s. Ebenezer, bp. Nov. 2, 1793	134
HOWARD, Anna, m. [ ] **BULKLEY**, of Somers, [Feb.] 6, [1798]	67
HOYT, James J., d. Sept. 30, 1812, at Colebrook, ae 43	99
James J., d. May 3, 1819, ae 17	101
HUBBARD, Catharine, m. Edwin **PORTER**, b. of Berlin, June 30, 1822	75
Daniel, of Berlin, m. Sarah **BELDEN**, Dec. 15, 1799	67
Elizabeth B., m. Elisha L. **SAGE**, b. of Middletown, Jan. 28, 1829 *(Arnold Copy has "Elizabeth B. **BUTLER**")	76
Elvira Jane, bp. [May 7], 1837, adult	149
Hiram, of Berlin, m. Eliza **BECKLEY**, of Rocky Hill, Nov. 16, 1845, by George O. Chambers, J.P.	15
James H., of Middletown, m. Mary **GOODRICH**, Oct. 23, 1825	75
Mary, wid., m. John **BULKLEY**, Jan. 12, 1830	76
Olive, m. George **DIX**, b. of 1st Society, Sept. 19, [1805]	69
Zenas, of Berlin, m. Roxy **STOW**, June 13, 1814	72
HUMPHREY, Martin, of Simsbury, m. Mercy **CLARK**, Sept. 25, 1811	71
HUNKEY, ----------, his w. [ ], d. [ ], 1842, ae 46 [Interred at Chatham*] *(From Church Rec.)	113
HUNT, Anna, m. Michael **ACKLEY**, b. of Rocky Hill, Nov. 13, 1853, by Rev. L. Burton Rockwood	47
Nabby, d. Seth, bp. Nov. 12, 1786 *("Nabby **HART**" in Church Rec.)	130
Robert, of Glastonbury, m. Keturah **SHIPMAN**, Mar. 31, 1819	74
HUNTER, Caty, d. Oct. 10, 1825, ae 21	104
HUNTINGTON, Abigail, d. Jos[ia]h, bp. Sept. 5, 1784	129
Clarinda, m. Justus **ROBBINS**, Mar. 31, 1790	64
Eleazer, s. Josiah, bp. May 10, 1789	131
Josiah, s. Josiah, bp. June 24, 1787	130
Nathaniel Gilbert, s. Josiah, bp. Nov. 6, 1785	129
Wealthy, d. Josiah, bp. Sept. 15, 1782	128
HUNTLEY, Gurdon, of Farmington, m. Jemima **PRICE**, [ ] 22, 1820	74
HURLBURT, Ashbel, m. Lucy **BLINN**, b. of 1st Society, Mar. 19, 1810	71
Daniel*, d. Jan. 17, 1800, in West Indies *("David, ae 40" in Church Rec.)	94
David*, d. Jan. 17, 1800, [ae 40], in West Indies *(Arnold Copy has "Daniel")	94
Hiram H., of New Britain, m. Emily F. **WORTHINGTON**, Oct. 12, 1836	79
Lemuel*, m. Tabitha **NOTT**, Dec. 22, 1774 *(Arnold Copy has "Samuel")	61
Mary, m. Chester **CADWELL**, of Springfield, Mass., Sept. 19, 1809	70

	Page
HURLBURT, (cont.)	
Nathaniel, Jr., m. Susanna Adams, Apr. 27, 1772	61
Robert, m. Mehetable **COLLINS**, July 5, 1781	61
Sally, wid., m. William **REED**, of Hartford, July 25, 1802	68
Samuel*, m. Tabitha **NOTT**, Dec. 22, 1774 *("Lemuel" in Church Rec.)	61
Sarah*, wid., d. Sept. 12, 1828, ae 86 *("of Chatham" in Church Rec.)	105
HYDE, Acshah, wid., m. Aaron **McKEE**, of Middletown, July 23, 1815	73
Thomas, of Labonon, m. Achsa **MARSH**, Nov. 26, 1806	70
JAGGAR, JAGGER, JAGGERS, Abr[aha]m, his child, d. Jan. 8, 1786	87
Abraham, d. Oct. 17, 1833, ae 80	108
Ann M[aria], of Rocky Hill, m. Anthony **BURNHAM**, of East Hartford, June 28, 1848, by Rev. Theodore M. Dwight	27
Daniel, s. Stephen*, bp. Sept. 17, 1797 *("Abraham" in Church Rec.)	136
Daniel, d. May 18, 1827, ae 31	105
Lucy, d. Abraham, bp. [ ], 1803	139
Lucy Sizer, bp. [July] 3, 1842	150
Martha Ann, m. George Washington **BARBER**, of Hebron, [ ] 30, 1831	77
Mary, d. Stephen*, bp. [Sept.] 17, 1797 *("Abraham" in Church Rec.)	136
Mary, m. William **GRIMES**, Apr. 23, 1809	70
Nathan, [s. Stephen*], bp. Sept. 17, 1798 *("Abraham" in Church Rec.)	136
Nathan, m. Roxey **HART**, May 11, 1808	70
Nathan, his d. [ ], d. Mar. 22, 1829, ae 8	106
Nathan, his w. [ ], d. Mar. 22, 1842, ae 51	112
Rachel, d. Stephen*, bp. Sept. 17, 1797 *("Abraham" in Church Rec.)	136
Rhoda, d. Abraham, bp. June 24, 1797	136
Sylvanus, s. Abraham, bp. Oct. 2, 1803	139
JAMES, Benjamin*, bp. Apr. 9, 1797 *(Should be "Benj[amin] James **RILEY**, s. of Roger." See Church Rec.)	135
JOHNSON, Abigail, of Berlin, m. William **WEBSTER**, of West Hartford, July 25, 1800	68
Sylva, w. W[illia]m, d. June 8, 1814, ae 43	100
JOREY, William, d. Apr. 24, 1845, ae 68	114
JUDD, Lydia, m. Isaac **LEWIS**, b. of Southington, June 25, 1785	63
JUSTAIN*, Lydia, d. Feb. 18, 1782, ae 64 y. *("**GUSTAIN**" in Church Rec.)	85
KELLOGG, Franklin, of Newington, m. Orinda **GOODRICH**, Nov. 18, 1830	77
KELLY, Eliza, m. James **SHERIDEN**, b. of Rocky Hill, Sept. 4, 1849, by Rev. Philo Judson	30
KELSEY, Charlotte, m. William **CALLENDER**, 2nd, July 14, 1825	75
Moses, of Newington, m. wid. Marcy **MILLER**, Nov. 6, 1808	70
Moses, his w. [ ], d. Mar. 20, 1840, ae 73	111
Sarah Jane, of Rocky Hill, m. John A. **BAILEY***, of Middletown, Oct. 15, 1854, by Rev. L.B. Rockwood *(of N.Y.)	52
Urbane, m. Lucy **BECKLEY**, b. of Berlin, May 22, 1812	72
KILBOURNE, Ashbel, of Hartford, m. Louisa **PRICE**, Apr. 24, 1833	77
KILBY*, Abby Menerva, m. Richard **RALPH**, of Middletown, Mar. 12, 1833, by Dr. Calvin Chapin *(Arnold Copy has '**TRILBY**")	77
Diantha, m. Lorin B*. **WHITFORD**, b. of Wethersfield, [ ] 18, 1843 *("Loren R." in Church Rec.)	80
George W., m. Sarah **RALPH**, of Middletwon, Sept. 8, 1833	78
KIMBALL, Charles H., of Exeter, N.H., m. Mary E. **BUTLER**, of Rocky Hill,	

	Page
KIMBALL, (cont.)	
Nov. 22, 1853, by Rev. L.B. Rockwood	47
KING, Saulmon, Rev., of East Hartford, m. Polly **AMES**, Nov. 19, 1807	70
KINNE, Amelia, m. David **HALE**, b. of Glastonbury, Dec. 29, 1819	74
KIRKHAM, Henry, of Newington, m. Charlotte **PRICE**, Aug. 25, 1807	70
KIRTLAND*, Elizur, of Greenville, N.Y., m. Elizabeth **DIMOCK**, [May] 12, 1816 *(Arnold Copy has "**WILLARD**")	73
George, of New Haven, m. Mercy **BELDEN**, Apr. 28, 1830	77
KNEASS, Moss*, of Philadelphia, Pa., m. Susan M. **HOPKINS**, of Middletown, May 15, 1843 *("Mars" in Church Rec.)	80
KNOWLTON, Julius S., of Middletown, m. Charlotte A. **CROFOOT**, of Rocky Hill, Apr. 28, 1844, by Rev. William Bentley	4
LACY, Jasper, of Suffield, m. Abigail **BULKLEY**, Sept. 9, 1789	64
LANA, Molly, d. Mar. 9, 1827, ae 56	105
LANCEY, Lydia, m. Moses **WILCOX**, of Colebrook, [ ] 22, 1787	64
Lydia*, w. of Michael, had d. Mary, bp. Sept. 25, 1774 *("Lydia **LOOCEY**" in Arnold Copy)	124
Mary*, d. Lydia, the w. of Michael, bp. Sept. 25, 1774 *("Mary **LOOCEY**" in Arnold Copy)	124
LATHAM, Isaac, of Hebron, m. Nancy **NEFF**, Apr. 20, 1820	74
LATHROP, James, his w. [ ], d. Nov. 28, 1836, ae 19	109
LATIMER, LATIMORE, LATTIMORE, George, of 1st Society, m. Mehetabel **BULKLEY**, May 15, 1803	68
Olive, d. Mar. 20, 1828, ae 68	105
Rebecca, m. Eben **CURTIS**, Apr. 4, 1781	61
Rhoda, m. Abijah **MARKS**, Apr. 21, 1768	60
LEACH, Sarah K., of Winchester, m. Elias **WRIGHT**, Oct. 9, 1814	72
LEE, Caroline, d. Nathan, bp. [Aug.] 19, 1827	146
Eliza Mary, d. Nathan, bp. July 1, 1831	147
Ira Spencer, s. Nathan, bp. June 29, 1832	147
Julius Adolphus, s. Nathan, bp. [May] 15, 1836	148
Martha, d. Nathan, bp. Aug. 4, 1822	145
Nathan, of Salem, N.Y., m. Martha **COREY**, Sept. 26, 1813	72
Nathan, his w. [ ], d. Mar. 26, 1820, ae 29 (Church Rec. say "Mr. **LEE** belongs to Royalton, Holla. Purch. St. of N.")	101
Nathan, m. Alma **HOLMES**, Feb. 21, 1821	74
Ralph Holmes, s. Nathan, bp. June 6, 1824	145
Samuell, of New Hartford, m. Mehetable **ROBBINS**, May 22, 1783	62
LEEDS, John, of Stamford, m. Honor **WILLIAMS**, Dec. 5, 1796	66
LEONARD, Asa, his w. [ ], d. July 10, 1786	87
Moses, of Orwell, Vt.*, m. Amelia **RILEY**, Jan. 30, 1800 *(Arnold Copy has "Cromwell")	67
LeVAUGHN, William, m. Abigail **THAYER**, May 19, 1829	76
LEWIS, Benony, bp. [Mar.], 1792	133
Caroline Elizabeth*, d. Elias, bp. Mar. 19, 1820 *("Twin with Cornelia Riccard, dau. of the late Eldad **LEWIS**" in Church Rec.)	145
Cornelia Riccard*, d. Elias, bp. Mar. 19, 1820 *("Twin with Caroline Elizabeth, daus. of the late Eldad **LEWIS**" in Church Rec.)	145
Edward Bulkley, s. Orrin, bp. Oct. 20, 1822	145
Edwin Elisha, s. Rev. John, bp. Feb. 15, 1791	132
Eldad, father of Rev. John, d. June 22, 1784, ae 77*, at Southington	

	Page
LEWIS, (cont.)	
*("74th" in Church Rec.)	87
Eldad, m. Betsey **RICORD**, Nov. 20, 1811	71
Eldad, his w. [ ], d. Mar. 29, 1816, ae 26	100
Hart, his w. [ ], d. Aug. 20, 1804, ae 40	96
Isaac, m. Lydia **JUDD**, b. of Southington, June 25, 1785	63
James, his w. [ ], d. Feb. 12, 1828, ae 35	105
John*, s. Daniel, d. Aug. 30, 1784 *("John, s. of Daniel **AMES**" in Church Rec. ae 4)	87
John, Rev., his w. [ ], d. Aug. 11, 1786, ae 35	87
John, Rev., d. [ ] 29, 1792, ae 47	90
John, of Chapel Hill, N.C., m. Sophia **DICKINSON**, Oct. 2, 1825	75
Levi, of Southington, m. Sally **BUNNELL**, of Berlin, Aug.* 2, 1801 *("July" written in a later hand)	68
Olevia, m. James **MALLORY**, of Troy, N.Y., Nov. 2, 1813	72
Orin, m. Charlotte **BULKLEY**, [, 1820]	74
Rachel, bp. Nov. 1, 1818, adult	144
Rachel, d. [ ], 1819	101
Sally, m. Harvey **GOODRICH**, Sept. 6, 1809	70
Sarah Jerusha, d. Rev. John, bp. [July] 31, 1785	129
W[illia]m Fabin*, s. Rev. John, bp. Jan. 23, 1783 *("Wm. Fabius bp. Jan. 26" in Church Rec.)	128
LIBY, Eleanor, m. Charles **DICKINSON**, Jan. 13, 1805	69
LINDSEY, LINDLEY, LINSLEY, LINDSLEY, David, s. David, bp. Jan. 12, 1766	118
David, his infant, d. [Apr. (?)], 21, 1770	82
David, his infant, d. Sept. 22, 1771	82
David, his child d. May 10, 1776	84
Hannah, wid., d. Aug. 23, 1805, ae 65 or 66	96
Samuel, s. David, bp. Sept. 22, 1771	122
LOCKROW, Harriet, of Wethersfield, m. Elizur **DICKINSON**, of Rocky Hill, Oct. 15, 1843, by Rev. C. Chapin	1
Harriet, of Wethersfield, m. Elizur **DICKINSON**, of Rocky Hill, Oct. 15, 1843	80
LOCKWOOD, Moses, m. Sarah **BUNCE***, Sept. 9, 1773 *(Arnold Copy has "**BURETT**")	61
LONDON, Violet, m. Mingo **HOSKINS***, of Simsbury, July 3, 1796 *(Perhaps "**HORKINS**")	66
LOOCEY, Lydia*, had d. Mary, bp. Sept. 25, 1774 *("w. of Michael **LANCEY**" in Church Rec.)	124
Mary*, d. Lydia, bp. Sept. 25, 1774 *("Mary **LANCEY**, dau. of Lydia, the w. of Michael **LANCEY**" in Church Rec.)	124
LOVEJOY, Frances C., m. Jerusha M. **WHITMORE**, Dec. 8, 1844, by Rev. Joseph L. Morse	6
LOVELAND, Hannah, m. Elisha **COLEMAN**, [, 1788]	64
LULL, Hiram N., of Middletown, m. Sarah J. **DEMING**, of Rocky Hill, June 25, 1848, by Rev. Theodore M. Dwight	26
LYON, Charles, m. Lois **GRIMES**, Mar. 13, 1796	66
McCOMB, M'COMB, McCOMBES, McCOMBE, Andrew, of Salem, Mass., m. Rebecca **GOODRICH**, May 28, 1786	63
Andrew, s. Andrew, bp. [Oct.] 16, 1803	139

	Page
McCOMB, M'COMB, McCOMBES, McCOMBE, (cont.)	
Charlotte, d. Andrew, bp. Apr. 10, 1796	135
Clarissa, d. Andrew, bp. Mar. 2, 1794	134
James, s. Andrew, bp. Aug. 17, 1788	131
James, d. Nov. 24, 1810, ae 24	98
Nancy, d. And[re]w, bp. [Oct. 24], 1790	132
Nancy, m. Daniel **PHELPS**, Jr., of Hartford, Mar. 2, 1809	70
Sally, d. Andrew, bp. Sept. 16, 1792	133
McKEE, MACKEE, Aaron, of Middletown, m. Acshah **HYDE**, wid. July 23, 1815	73
Achsa, wid., d. Feb. 20, 1848, in Hartford, ae 62	115
Russel, of East Hartford, m. Nabby **AMES**, Feb. 4, 1798	67
McLAREN, Charles, of Perth, in Scotland, m. wid. Lucy **DERRICK**, of Rocky Hill, Oct. 30, 1845, by Rev. C. Chapin	14
MAGUIER, Margaret, m. Levi **COLLINS**, b. of Rocky Hill, Apr. 9, 1854, by Rev. L.B. Rockwood	50
MALLORY, James, of Troy, N.Y., m. Olevia **LEWES**, Nov. 2, 1813	72
MARKS, Abijah, m. Rhoda **LATTIMORE**, Apr. 21, 1768	60
MARSH, Achsa, m. Thomas **HYDE**, of Labonon, Nov. 26, 1806	70
Anna, m. Simeon **BUTLER**, Sept. 18, 1783	62
Anna, d. Eli, bp. Jan. 17, 1796	135
Betsey, d. John, Jr., bp. July 29, 1781	127
Betsey, m. Abel **EDWARDS**, of Middletown, July 12, 1804	69
Daniel, d. between May 7 & Aug. 17, 1782, at New York (Soldier)	85
Daniel, s. John, bp. [Dec.*] 29, 1782 *(Church Rec.)	128
Daniel, d. Jan. 6, 1801, at Surinam ("ae 19" in Church Rec.)	95
Eli, s. John, bp. Apr. 28, 1765	117
Eli, m. Azubah **BUTLER**, Jan. 25, 1787	63
Frederick, of Montpelier, Vt., m. Chloe W. **ROBBINS**, Oct. 7, 1839	79
John, Jr., his infant d. Dec. 15, 1784	87
John, his w. [ ], d. [June] 13 or 14, 1790, ae 69	90
John, d. Sept. 20, 1799, ae 73	94
John, his w. [ ], d. Mar. 2, 1834*, ae 75 *("1833" in Church Rec.)	107
John, d. Dec. 8, 1836, ae 84	109
Lathrop, s. Eli, bp. Aug. 22, 1790	132
Marilla, d. Eli, bp. Dec. 2, 1792	133
Mary, m. John **MORTON**, Mar. 26, 1766	60
Norman, s. Eli, bp. Sept. 28, 1788	131
Polly, d. John, Jr., bp. Mar. 8, 1795	134
Polly, m. John **BURKETT**, of Middletown, Nov. 7, 1816	73
MASON, Benijah King, bp. July 4, 1841	150
MATSON, Thomas, of Glastonbury, m. Abial **COLLINS**, Dec. 21, 1794	66
MAY, William B., of Hartford, m. Esther **CHAPMAN**, Nov. 29, 1807	70
MAYNARD, Joshua L., of Cornwall, m. Abigail Ursula Bulkly **ROBBINS**, Oct. 14, 1840	79
MERRIAM, Asahel, s. Rev. Burrage, bp. Nov. 10, 1771	122
Asahel, m. Hannah **ROBBINS**, Oct. 1, 1794, by Rev. Mr. Fenn	65
Asahel, Dea., d. June 18, 1808, ae 37	98
Burrage, s. Rev. Burrage, bp. Sept. 26, 1773	123
Burrage, m. Harriet **WILLIAMS**, [Feb.] 11, 1829	76
Burrage, d. Dec. 14, 1848, ae 52	116

68 BARBOUR COLLECTION

	Page
MERRIAM, (cont.)	
Delia, d. Asahel, bp. Oct. 27, 1799	137
Delia, m. Justus **CANDEE**, of Oxford, Oct. 15, 1833	78
Edmond, s. Asahel, bp. July 5, 1807	140
Edmund, m. Caroline Tracy **ROBBINS**, Mar. 27, 1834	78
Edmund, d. Feb. 27, 1846, at Goldsborough, N.C., Justus Candee, Adm.	21
Edmund, d. Feb. 27, 1846, in [North Carolina]*, ae 39 *("Gouldsborough, N.C." in Church Rec.)	114
Hannah, d. Ashbel*, bp. Aug. 14, 1796 *("Asahel" in Church Rec.)	135
Hannah, wid., d. Aug. 1, 1845, ae 74	114
Horace, s. Asahel, bp. [ ] 24, 1804	139
Horace, d. Oct. 16, 1834, ae 31, [in Monte[ ]ma, Indiana*] *(Church Rec.)	108
Lucy, d. Asahel, bp. [ ] 25, 1802	138
Lucy, d. Jan. 14, 1819, ae 18	101
MERROW, John G., m. Lucy S. **GARDNER**, b. of Hartford, Apr. 11, 1847, by Rev. C. Chapin	21
Joseph G., of Middletown, m. Betsey **PRICE**, Mar. 20, 1805	69
Joseph Gilbert*, d. Sept. 13, 1820, in Delaware, ae 40 *(Arnold Copy has "Joseph **GILBERT**")	102
MILDRUM, John, d. Feb. 25, 1776	83
Lydia, d. John, bp. June 18, 1769	120
Lydia, had child Serea Raphel, bp. Sept. 5, 1790	132
Lydia, wid., d. Apr. 7, 1791, ae 56	90
Lydia, d. Oct. 11, 1841, [at Hartford], ae 73	112
Mercy, d. John, bp. Oct. 5, 1766	118
Mercy, m. David **MILLER**, Feb. 15, 1787	63
Serea Raphel*, child of Lydia, bp. Sept. 5, 1790 *("Servee Raphael" in Church Rec.)	132
William, d. between May 7 & Aug. 17, 1782, at New York (Soldier)	85
MILLER, Abigail, d. Eb[enezer], bp. Apr. 19, 1772 *("Dau. of Ebenezer's wife" in Church Rec.)	122
Abigail, had d. Betsey, bp. Nov. 14, 1790	132
Abigail, m. Luther **PATERSON**, of Berlin, Apr. 28, 1791	65
Abigail, wid., m. Aziel **BELDEN**, of Berlin, Oct. 29, 1809	71
Abigail, d. Leonard, bp. June 25, 1809	141
Abigail, m. Daniel S. **HINE**, of Humphreyville, Nov. 27, 1831	77
Allen Williams, s. Leonard, bp. [Apr. 20], 1806	140
Allen William, m. Emeline **SMITH**, Apr. 14, 1830	76
Amos, s. Nathaniel, bp. Feb. 19, 1769	120
Amos, m. Abigail **GOODRICH**, Dec. 7, 1794	66
Andrew, s. Leonard, bp. May 10, 1812	142
Andrew, m. Mary Maria **PORTER**, Sept. 26, 1833	78
Asenath*, d. Eben[eze]r, bp. Oct. 10, 1779, by Rev. Mr. Pitkin, of Farmington *(Arnold Copy has "Henah")	126
Asenath, m. [ ] **CLARK**, of Berlin, Apr. 16, 1799	67
Betsey, d. Abigail, bp. Nov. 14, 1790	132
Betsey*, d. Apr. 25, 1803, ae 66 *("Betty" in Church Rec.)	95
Caleb, s. Nathaniel, bp. Apr. 5, 1767	118
Daniel, s. Joseph, bp. [ ], 1764	117
David, s. of w. of Eben[eze]r, bp. Apr. 30, 1769	120

ROCKY HILL VITAL RECORDS 69

	Page
MILLER, (cont.)	
David, m. Mercy **MILDRAM**, Feb. 15, 1787	63
Diana, d. Joseph, bp. Nov. 14, 1773	123
Dianna, d. Joseph, d. [ ], 1783 ("d. Oct. 7" in Church Rec.)	86
Ebenezer, of Middletown, m. Jerusha **GOODRICH**, June 18, 1767	60
Elijah, s. Nathaniel, bp. Sept. 29, 1782	128
Eunice, d. Leonard, bp. June 6, 1802	138
Eunice, m. William **CLARK**, of Colchester, June 1, 1826	75
Henah*, d. Eben[eze]r, bp. Oct. 10, 1779, by Rev. Mr. Pitkin, of	
Farmington *("Asenath" in Church Rec.)	126
Huldah, of Middletown, m. Samuel **READING**, Oct. 2, 1785	63
Jason, s. Eph[raim]*, bp. Oct. 22, 1769 *("s. of Eb[eneze]r's wife" in	
Church Rec.)	120
Jason, d. May 1, 1812, ae 22, drowned in West Indies	99
Jerusha, d. Leonard, bp. Dec. 13, 1798	136
Jerusha, d. Mar. 23, 1825, ae 27	104
Joseph, his w. [ ], d. Mar. 15, 1812, ae 78	99
Joseph, d. Feb. 21, 1813, ae 81	99
Joseph Forbes, s. Betsey, bp. Apr. 14, 1765 (Perhaps 'Joseph **FORBES**,	
son of Betsey **MILLER**")	117
Joshua, s. Joseph, bp. July 16, 1769	120
Leonard, m. Lydia **BELDEN**, Aug. 7, 1796	66
Lydia, d. Oct. 4, 1804, ae 10* *("ae 18" in Church Rec.)	96
Marcy, wid., m. Moses **KELSEY**, of Newington, Nov. 6, 1808	70
Maria, d. Leonard, bp. [Aug. 18], 1816	143
Maria, d. May 2, 1834*, ae 18 *("1833" in Church Rec.)	107
Martha, m. W[illia]m **WEARE**, Oct. 11, 1784	62
Mary, m. Moses **WILCOX**, b. of Middletown, Apr. 16, 1801	68
Mercy, d. Mar. 15, 1791, ae 28	90
Nancy, d. Joseph, bp. June 15, 1766	118
Nancy, m. Zadock **SELAH**, of Stamford, Feb. 23, 1786	63
Nancy, d. Amos, bp. May 29, 1796	135
Nathan Bulkley, s. Amos, bp. Oct. 20, 1799	137
Nathaniel, s. Nathaniel, bp. June 16, 1771	121
Oliver, s. Amos, bp. Dec. 10, 1797	136
Onor, d. Leonard, bp. Sept. 10, 1797	136
Oner, m. Sylvester **WHITMORE**, Sept. 28, 1815	73
Phebe, bp. Apr. 22, 1798, an adult	136
Phineas T., of Westville, m. Elvira **WHITMORE**, Aug. 31, 1836	79
Rebecca, d. Nathaniel, bp. Jan. 7, 1776	125
Stephen, s. Eben, d. Apr. 29, 1783, ae 2	86
William, m. Anne **WEBSTER**, of Berlin, Oct. 6, 1812	72
MILLS, Daniel A., of Hartford, m. Martha G. **ROBBINS**, Mar. 9, 1837	79
Ellen Augusta, d. Daniel, bp. [Nov. 4], 1842	150
James Robbins, s. Daniel, bp. Jan. 1, 1841	149
MISNER, Elizabeth, m. Alpha **TUCKER**, of Bolton, [Feb.] 12, [1798]	67
Hannah, m. Theodore **BLYN**, May 21, 1796	66
MITCHELL, James, m. Hannah **WARNER**, Mar. 30, 1772	61
MONTAGUE, John, of 1st Society, m. Lucy **WRIGHT**, Nov. 20, 1833	78
Julia, d. [ ], bp. July 10, 1794	134
Olive, m. Joseph **CRAWFOOT**, of Berlin, Mar. 29, 1810	71

	Page
MONTAGUE, (cont.)	
Samuel, of 1st Society, m. wid. Olive **MORTON**, Feb. 13, 1800	67
MORGAN, Amasa, of 1st Society, m. Polly **WITHERELL**, Apr. 22, 1813	72
Charles, of Hartford, m. Elizabeth **BOARDMAN**, May 15, 1791	65
James Henry, [of New Britain], m. Martha A. **WHITMORE**, Nov. 14, 1847, by Rev. Calvin Chapin	24
Joel*, of West Springfield, m. Eunice **GOODRICH**, Dec. 3, 1797	67
*(Arnold Copy has "Jere")	
Russel[l], of Middletown, m. Betsey **BELDEN**, Jan. 6, 1833	77
MORLEY, Anna, wid., d. Jan. 24, 1819, ae 63	101
Sally, d. Nov. 22, 1815, ae 17	100
MORRELL, Emma*, wid., d. Feb. 20, 1798, ae 76 *("Eunice **MORRICE**" in Church Rec.)	93
MORRIS, Abram*, d. Nov. 6, 1765 *(Abra[ha]m)	81
MORTON, Benjamin, s. Benjamin, bp. May 2, 1790	132
Benjamin, d. Oct. 12, 1808, ae 64	98
Comfort, m. Eliel **WILLIAMS**, Jan. 26, 1769	60
Eldredge Williams, s. George, bp. Aug. 31, 1832	147
Elizabeth, d. Jan. 22, 1775	83
Elizabeth, d. Benjamin, bp. Jan. 9, 1785	129
Frederick, s. Benjamin, bp. June 3, 1792	133
George, s. Benjamin, bp. Aug. 12, 1787	130
George, m. Lauretta **WARNER**, Dec. 5, 1830	77
George, d. [ ] 25, 1835, ae 49	109
George Wallace, s. George, bp. Nov. 2, 1834	148
Hannah, wid., d. Sept. 7, 1791, ae 78	90
Hannah, m. Justus **BELDEN**, Dec. 3, 1797	67
John, m. Mary **MARSH**, Mar. 26, 1766	60
John, d. Nov. 5, 1773	82
John, s. John, bp. July 31, 1774	124
John, his child d. [ ], 1776	84
John, s. Benjamin, bp. [ ], 1781	127
John, d. July 7, 1804, ae 64	96
John, his wid. [ ], d. Sept. 3, 1804, ae 55	96
Lucy, d. John, Jr., bp. Oct. 4, 1772	122
Lucy, d. Benjamin, bp. May 18, 1783	128
Lucy, wid., d. Mar. 26, 1838, ae 92	110
Lucy, d. [6, 1848], ae 66	116
Olive, wid., m. Samuel **MONTAGUE**, of 1st Society, Feb. 13, 1800	67
Ruth, d. July 19, 1817, ae 69	101
Sarah, d. John, bp. Sept. 25, 1768	119
Thomas, s. John, Jr., bp. Oct. 21, 1770	121
Thomas, m. Olive **DICKINSON**, Apr. 14, 1796	66
Thomas, d. June [ ], 1796, in West Indies	93
MOSES*, John M., s. Rev. J.L.W., d. Dec. 30, 1832, ae [ ] *("Wms." in Church Rec.)	107
MURRY, Sollomon, m. Caty **PELL**, of Ch[ ], June 8, 1817	73
MYERS, MYEARS, Denis, m. Reny **ROBINSON**, Sept. 13, 1789	64
Hannah, d. John, bp. Aug. 12, 1787	130
Hannah, m. James **BULKLEY**, Feb. 14, 1805	69
Harriet, d. John, bp. Sept. 6, 1789	132

	Page
MYERS, MYEARS, (cont.)	
Harriet, m. Amasa **COY**, of Hartford, Apr. 26, 1809	70
Henry, s. John, bp. Dec. 17, 1786	130
Henry, m. Elizabeth **WELLES**, of 1st Society, Newington, Apr. 5, 1810	71
John, of Penn., m. Mehetable **RILEY**, Jan. 5, 1786	63
Mehetable, d. Jan. 23 or 24, 1846, ae 82* *("ae 81" in Church Rec.)	114
MYGATT, MYGATE, Austin, of Berlin, m. Rhoda **RUSSEL**, July 22, 1799	67
John, m. Elizabeth **BULKLEY**, Aug. 26, 1773	61
NEFF, Abiel, wid., d. Jan. 30, 1830, ae 59	106
Barzillai G., of Wilmington, N.C., m. Margaret I. **COLLINS**, of Rocky Hill, Oct. 17, 1854, by Rev. L.B. Rockwood	53
Caroline, d. Joseph, bp. Nov. 9, 1817	143
Cynthia, d. [ ], 1829, ae 20	106
Cynthia Amelia, d. Joseph, bp. June 2, 1811	142
Edward, twin with Edwin, s. Joseph, bp. Sept. 27, 1812	142
Edward, m. wid. Florinda **HOLMES**, Oct. 29, 1837	79
Edwin, twin with Edward, s. Joseph, bp. Sept. 27, 1812	142
Eliza, d. Joseph, bp. Oct. 6, 1805	140
Eliza, m. James S. **WHITNEY**, of Pittsfield, Mass., Feb. 15, 1830	76
Esther, d. Joseph, bp. Oct. 15, 1797	136
Esther, m. Benjamin **ROBBINS**, [May] 30, 1816	73
Joseph, m. Esther **WEBB**, Nov. 5, 1772	61
Joseph, d. Apr. 8, 1774	83
Joseph, bp. Oct. 15, 1797	136
Joseph, d. Jan. 4, 1829, ae 54	106
Joseph Henry, s. Joseph, bp. [June] 25, 1809	141
Joseph Henry, d. July 20, 1831, ae 23, [New Jersey*] *(Church Rec.)	106
Lucy, d. Joseph, bp. Apr. 26, 1807	140
Lucy, d. [ ] 28, 1831, ae 25	107
Mary, d. Joseph, bp. June 20, 1804	139
Mary, m. Isaac **WARD**, of Pittsfield, Mass., [ ] 17, 1836	78
Nancy, d. Joseph, bp. May 11, 1800	137
Nancy, m. Isaac **LATHAM**, of Hebron, Apr. 20, 1820	74
William, s. Joseph, bp. Oct. 14, 1798	136
W[illia]m, his s. [ ], d. Aug. 1, 1838, ae 6	110
NICHOLS, Martha Jane, bp. July 4, 1841	150
NORTH, Mary, m. Moses **WILLIAMS**, July 2, 1789	64
Nathan, of Exeter, N.H., m. Nancy **BULKLEY**, Aug. 4, 1805	69
NORTHRUP, Abner, of Saulsbury, m. Jerusha **GIBBS**, Oct. 16, 1803	68
NORTON, Elisha, of Berlin, m. Laura **BELDEN**, [ ] 28, 1830	76
Jedediah, 2nd, of Berlin, m. Betsey **BULKLEY**, Mar. 10, 1813	72
Zachariah, of Berlin, m. Nabby **DICKINSON**, May 7, 1812	72
NOTT, Abigail, d. May 2, 1782, ae 22	85
Abraham, his w. [ ], d. Dec. 27, 1787, ae 65	88
Abraham, d. July 29, 1794, ae 76	91
Anne, m. Gideon **GOFFE**, Aug. 21, 1786	63
Eleanor, of Berlin, m. Joshua **BELDEN**, Oct. 15, 1810	71
Elizabeth, m. George **WOLCOTT**, Mar. [ ], 1774	61
Elizabeth, d. W[illia]m, bp. Apr. 16, 1786	130
Jabez Dimock, d. Jan. 15, 1771	82
John, s. W[illia]m, bp. Mar. 10, 1793	133

	Page
NOTT, (cont.)	
John, his w. [ ], d. Aug. 27, 1844, ae 52	114
Lydia, d. Sept. 3, 1814, ae 64	100
Marshall, of Rocky Hill, m. Mary Ann **WHITMAN**, of East Hartford, Dec. 15, 1850, by Rev. L.B. Rockwood	34
Mehetabel, m. Roger **BROWN**, of Stamford, Apr. 22, 1781	61
Mercy, m. Elijah **BOARDMAN**, Sept. 16, 1781	61
Oliver, s. W[illia]m, bp. [Sept.] 23, 1798	136
Sylvester, of Berlin, m. Betsey **BLINN**, Mar. 25, 1802	68
Tabitha, m. Samuel* **HURLBURT**, Dec. 22, 1774 *("Lemuel" in Church Rec.)	61
W[illia]m, his w. [ ], d. Sept. 16, 1781	85
William, m. Elizabeth **GOODRICH**, Nov. 28, 1784	63
William, s. William, bp. May 4, 1788	131
W[illia]m, d. May 11, 1790, ae 67 ("ae 66 or 67" in Church Rec.)	89
William, d. Apr. 16, 1801, ae 58	95
William, m. Laura **BELDEN**, May 2, 1811	71
OCKRY, Eliza, of Hartford, m. Oliver **RUSSEL**, of Marlboro, Jan. 17, 1837	79
OLMSTEAD, Nancy, m. Jotham **FORBES**, of Waterbury, Jan. 8, 1805	69
PACKARD, Leonard, of Williamsburg, Mass., m. [wid.] Lucy Ann **THAYER**, of Rocky Hill, Dec. 2, 1849, by Rev. C. Chapin	31
PAGE, Eliza, d. Jeremiah, bp. Oct. 7, 1804	139
Eunice, d. Jeremiah, bp. Aug. 1, 1802	138
Eunice, w. Jeremiah, bp. June 20, 1802	138
Fanny, d. Jeremiah, bp. Aug. 1, 1802	138
Martha, d. Jeremiah, bp. Aug. 1, 1802	138
PALMER, Oliver, m. Eliza Jane **CLARK**, Nov. 18, 1845, by Warren G. Jones, of Glastonbury	17
Thomas, negro, m. Jenny, servant of John Robbins, Nov. 23, 1786	63
PARDEE, Philo, d. May 27, 1821	102
PARKER, A.G., his child d. June 24, 1847, ae 2	115
Albert Gallatin, his w. [ ], d. [ ] 24, 1842, ae 41	112
Gertrude Amelia, d. Albert G., bp. [ ], 1844	151
Huldah, d. Jeremiah, bp. Sept. 30, 1787	131
Jeremiah, of Long Island, m. Eunice **GOODRICH**, July 4, 1782	61
Mary Elizabeth*, d. Albert G., bp. Sept. 1, 1848 *("dau. of Albert Gallatin **PARKER**" in Church Rec.)	152
Mary Matilda, d. Albert Gallatin, bp. Oct. 30, 1846	151
Matilda, d. Jeremiah, bp. Aug. 28, 1785	129
PARLIN, ----------, wid., d. Nov. 6, 1828, ae 80	106
PARSONS, Henry L., of Lenox, Mass., m. Fanny **WETHERELL**, Nov. 24, 1825	75
Huldah, bp. Nov. 4, 1798, an adult	136
Huldah, m. Lewis **GAYNARD**, of New York, May 22, 1803	68
Mary, of Amherst, Mass., m. Ezekiel P. **BELDEN**, Nov. 1, 1790	65
PATERSON, Luther, of Berlin, m. Abigail **MILLER**, Apr. 28, 1791	65
PELL, Caty, of Ch[ ], m. Sollomon **MURRY**, June 8, 1817	73
PENFIELD, Eldridge Huntington, s. Asahel, bp. June 17, 1821	145
Eliza E., b. Aug. 3, 1823	45
Eliza Eveline, bp. [May 7], 1837, adult	149
Eliza Eveline, d. Mar. 24, 1842, ae 19	112

	Page
PENFIELD, (cont.)	
Jonathan F*., of Pittsfield, Mass., m. Julia Ann **BUTLER**, Nov. 12, 1840 *("Jonathan F. **FAIRFIELD**" in Church Rec.)	80
Mariah, of Glastonbury, m. Allen E. **HOLMES**, of Rocky Hill, May 19, 1844, by Rev. John Lovejoy	5
PEN HOLLOW, Mary Louisa, m. Chauncey **GOODRICH**, May 7, 1840	79
Otis, of Rocky Hill, m. Lydia P. **BALDWIN**, of Winchester, Aug. 31, 1845, by Rev. C. Chapin	13
PETERS, Laura Ann, of Glastonbury, m. Benjamin Robinson **BATES**, of Rocky Hill, Jan. 2, 1852, by Rev. L.B. Rockwood	38
Paulina, m. Roswell **RUSSELL**, [colored], b. of of Glastonbury, Jan. 9, 1851, by Rev. Calvin Chapin	35
PHELPS, Bishop, m. Patty **STORRS**, Oct. 2, 1791	65
Daniel, Jr., of Hartford, m. Nancy **McCOMBE**, Mar. 2, 1809	70
Emily R., m. Luther **WHITE**, of Middletown, Oct. 9, 1831	77
POMEROY, Oliver, d. Oct. 1, 1776	84
Rachel, m. Edward **BULKLEY**, Oct. 27, 1771	61
PORTER, Aaron, Jr., m. Mariam **BULKLEY***, Apr. 12, 1815 *("**BECKLEY**, b. of 1st Soc." in Church Rec.)	73
Albert Gallatin*, m. Nancy **BUTLER**, May 15, 1843 *("Albert Gallatin **PARKER**" in Church Rec.)	80
Charlotte, m. Jared **DEMING**, Jan. 25, 1807	70
Edwin, m. Catharine **HUBBARD**, b. of Berlin, June 30, 1822	75
Florinda, m. Walter **HOLMES**, Nov. 30, 1828	76
James Robinson, m. Lucy Caroline **CULVER**, b. of Rocky Hill, July 3, 1843, by Rev. C. Chapin	1
James Robinson, m. Lucy Caroline **PORTER***, July 3, 1843 *(In pencil "**CULVER**")	80
Leeman, of 1st Society, m. Harriet **STEELE**, of Berlin, Feb. 4, 1810	71
Lucy Caroline*, m. James Robinson **PORTER**, July 3, 1843 *(In pencil "Lucy Caroline **CULVER**")	80
Mary Maria, m. Andrew **MILLER**, Sept. 26, 1833	78
Mehetable*, m. George **PRICE**, Aug. 8, 1790 *("Mehetable **FOSTER**" in Church Rec.)	65
Rhoda, m. Joseph **BUNCE**, Jan. 29, 1798	67
William, Jr., of Lee, Mass., m. wid. Cynthia M **COOLEY***, Nov. 5, 1837 *(**CODEY**?)	79
POST*, Samuel, of "Putty Paug," d. June 12, 1800, ae 24 *(Arnold Copy has "**POTT**")	94
POTT*, Samuel, of "Putty Paug," d. June 12, 1800, ae 24 *("**POST**" in Church Rec.)	94
PRICE, Abigail, d. Richard, bp. June 7, 1795	134
Abigail, m. George **GOODRICH**, Aug. 27, 1818	74
Abigail, wid., d. Apr. 2, 1832, ae 78	107
Anna, d. James, bp. July 22, 1781	127
Anna, d. Richard, bp. Aug. 8, 1790	132
Betsey, m. Joseph G. **MEROW**, of Middletown, Mar. 20, 1805	69
Charlotte, d. Rich[ar]d, bp. [Nov.] 26, 1786	130
Charlotte, m. Henry **KIRKHAM**, of Newington, Aug. 25, 1807	70
Charlotte Kirkham, m. Samuel Bidwell **BUTLER**, Nov. 5, 1833	78
Ebenezer, his w. [ ], d. Aug. 28, 1789, ae 66	89

	Page
PRICE, (cont.)	
Ebenezer, d. Apr. 17, 1791, ae 67	90
Elizabeth, d. James, bp. July 22, 1781	127
Elizabeth, d. John*, bp. Sept. 10, 1786 *("Jona[than]" in Church Rec.)	130
Eunice, d. Benj[amin], bp. [Apr. 8], 1781, by Rev. Mr. Lewis	126
George, m. Mehetable **PORTER***, Aug. 8, 1790 *("FOSTER" in Church Rec.)	65
George, bp. Feb. 26, 1792	133
George, s. George, bp. May 20, 1798	136
George, d. Feb. 24, 1800, ae 36	94
Hannah, d. James, bp. Apr. 10, 1785	129
Harriet, m. Ackley **WILLIAMS**, Jan. 26, 1825	75
Harriet Boardman, d. John, bp. Oct. 7, 1810	142
Hetty, d. John[atha]n, bp. July 22, 1781	127
Hetty, d. May 16, 1804, ae 26	96
Jacob, s. Jonathan, bp. Oct. 26, 1788	131
Jacob, d. Mar. 30, 1823, ae 35	103
James, m. Elizabeth **BOARDMAN**, Dec. 4, 1775	61
Jemima, d. Benjamin, bp. Apr. 20, 1783	128
Jemima, d. Jonathan, bp. May 20, 1798	136
Jemima, m. Gurdon **HUNTLEY**, of Farmington, [ ] 22, 1820	74
John, d. between May 7 & Aug. 17, 1782, on his return at Saybrook (Soldier)	85
John, s. Ebenezer, bp. Apr. 10, 1768	119
John, s. Richard, bp. [Sept. 5], 1784	129
John, s. John, bp. Aug. 23, 1812	142
John, d. Sept. 3, 1815, ae 33, lost at sea	100
Jona[tha]n, m. Patience **COLLINS**, Dec. 11, 1775	61
Jonathan, his child d. Apr. 16, 1781	84
Jonathan, his w. [ ], d. Apr. 30, 1781	85
Jon[atha]n, s. John[atha]n, bp. July 22, 1781	127
Jonathan, m. Jemima **GOODRICH**, Apr. 17, 1783	62
Jonathan, bp. Feb. 26, 1792	133
Jonathan, d. Aug. 7, 1807, at Sea, ae 56	97
Jonathan, m. Lois **BLINN**, Dec. 10, 1807	70
Josiah, d. July 15, 1831, ae 41	106
Laura, d. Richard, bp. [Oct. 26], 1788	131
Laura, m. Levi Ely **TAYLOR**, of Long Meadow, Mass., Dec. 25, 1816	73
Louisa, d. Joh[natha]n, bp. [ ] 29, 1809	141
Louisa, m. Ashbel **KILBOURNE**, of Hartford, Apr. 24, 1833	77
Lucy, d. George, d. Dec. 26, 1794, ae 2	92
Lucy, d. Richard, bp. July 20, 1794	134
Martha, d. Richard, bp. Sept. 9, 1781	127
Mary, d. James, bp. July 22, 1781	127
Mary Ann, d. John, bp. May 20, 1814	143
Mehetabel, wid., m. John **BELDEN**, Mar. 9, 1807	70
Nancy, m. Oliver **WAIT***, of Chatham, July 22, 1832 *("WEST" in Church Rec.)	77
Nancy Maria, d. John, bp. Nov. 19, 1809	142
Patience, d. John*, bp. Sept. 10, 1786 *("Jona[than]" in Church Rec.)	130
Patience, d. Nov. 13, 1801	95

ROCKY HILL VITAL RECORDS 75

	Page
PRICE, (cont.)	
Richard, s. Richard, bp. Aug. 26, 1792	133
Richard, Jr., d. Sept. 3, 1815, lost at sea	100
Richard, d. [ ] 23, 1826, ae 69, [in New York*] *(From Church Rec.)	105
Roger, s. James, d. Aug. 13, 1783	86
Roger, s. James, bp. Aug. 13, 1783	128
Roger, d. Sept. 8, 1783* (Prisoner in Jamaica) *("Sept. '82" in Church Rec.)	86
Sally, d. Jonathan, bp. Jan. 22, 1792	133
Sally, d. Jonathan, d. Jan. 25, 1792	90
Sally, d. Jonathan, bp. June 23, 1793	134
William, s. Joh[natha]n, bp. [ ] 29, 1809	141
PRINCE*, Thomas, d. Sept. 21, 1820, ae 72 *("BUNCE" in Church Rec.)	101
PRIOR, Edgar B., of Middletown, m. Martha **BELDEN**, of Rocky Hill, Aug. 5, 1849, by Rev. Philo Judson	30
PULSIFER, PILSIFER, Adeline C., of Rocky Hill, m. Romanzo N. **BAYLEY**, of St. Louis, Mo., Aug. 15, 1849, by Rev. Calvin Chapin	29
Huldah, of Glastonbury, m. Luther **WILCOX**, of Middletown, Oct. 1, 1794, by Rev. Mr. Fenn	65
Nancy R., d. [Oct.] 18, 1848, ae 23	116
RALPH, Richard, of Middletown, m. Abby Menerva **TRILBY***, Mar. 12, 1833, by Dr. Calvin Chapin *("KILBY" in Church Rec.)	77
Sarah, of Middletown, m. George W. **KILBY**, Sept. 8, 1833	78
RANNY, RANNEY, Eben, of Middletown, m. Lois **BLINN**, Nov. 30, 1769	60
Esther, d. Jan. 18, 1817, ae 87	100
Hope, [sister of Esther*], d. Jan. 22, 1817, ae 80 *(Church Rec.)	100
RASH, Burrage, s. Jeremiah, bp. May 17, 1786	130
Burrage, d. Nov. 22, 1842, ae 57	113
Edward, s. Jeremiah, bp. Apr. 10, 1785	129
Edward, bp. [ ] 5, 1848, his w. [ ], bp. [ ] 5, 1848	152
Edward W., m. Sarah **EDWARDS**, Mar. 14, 1836	78
Jeremiah, m. Anna **COLLINS**, Jan. 22, 1784	62
Jeremiah, d. Sept. 23, 1795, ae 38	92
Laura C., m. Ephraim **GOODRICH**, b. of Rocky Hill, Jan. 19, 1848, by Rev. Philo Judson	24
Louisa Mariah, m. Alfred **GRISWOLD**, b. of Rocky Hill, July 17, 1843, by Rev. C. Chapin	1
Louisa Maria, m. Alfred **GRISWOLD**, [ ] 17, 1843	80
Manus*, s. Jeremiah, bp. June 8, 1788 *(Arnold Copy has "Warner")	131
Mary, wid., m. Hezekiah **BLINN**, Oct. 16, 1814	72
Polly*, d. Sept. 26, 1795, ae 12 *("Polly RILEY" in Church Rec.)	92
Roxana, m. Willis W. **GRISWOLD**, b. of Rocky Hill, Mar. 20, 1845, by Rev. John Lovejoy	9
Roxy, d. Jeremiah, bp. July 18, 1790	132
Roxy, m. Timothy **HASKELL**, of Middletown, Apr. 11, 1815	73
Selah, s. Jeremiah, bp. Apr. 14, 1793	133
Selley, d. Sept. 25, 1795, ae 3	92
Warner*, s. Jeremiah, bp. June 8, 1788 *("Manus" in Church Rec.)	131
READING, Samuel, m. Huldah **MILLER**, [of] Middletown, Oct. 2, 1785	63
RECCORD, [see under **RICCARD**]	

	Page
REED, Fanny B*., of Durham, m. Theodore **BLINN**, of R.H., Aug. 23, 1840 *("Fanny F." in Church Rec.)	79
William, of Hartford, m. wid. Sally **HURLBURT**, July 25, 1802	68
REYNOLDS, Anna, m. John **SUTLER**, of Clarerack, Sept. 13, 1784	62
Susan, wid., d. Oct. [ ], 1772	82
RICE, Ansel, of Berlin, m. Elva **DICKINSON**, July 30, 1807	70
RICHARDS, Elizabeth, d. James, bp. [Sept.] 19, 1790	132
Simeon, m. Anna **WRIGHT**, Feb. 6, 1772	61
William, s. James, bp. May 31, 1789	131
RICHARDSON, Harry*, d. Jan. 25, 1841, ae 35 *("Harvey" in Church Rec.)	111
Har[r]y*, of Hartford, m. Parmelia **SHAYLOR**, May 12, 1830 *("Harvey" in Church Rec.)	77
Harvey*, of Hartford, m. Parmelia **SHAYLOR**, May 12, 1830 *("Har[r]ey" in Arnold Copy)	77
Harvey*, d. Jan. 25, 1841, ae 35 *(Arnold Copy has "Harry")	111
RICCARD, RICARD, RICORD, RECCORD, Betsey, m. Eldad **LEWIS**, Nov. 20, 1811	71
James, of Boston, m. Wealthy **GOODRICH**, [, 1788]	64
James, d. Nov. 29, 1805, ae 43	97
Sally, d. James, bp. May 26, 1799	136
RILEY, REILLY, REILLEY, Abigail, d. Stephen, bp. Feb. 17, 1765	117
Abigail, d. Jacob, bp. Nov. 19, 1769	120
Abigail, d. Jabez, bp. Feb. 28, 1773	123
Abigail, m. Ephraim **COVEL**, of Glastonbury, Oct. 19, 1785	63
Abigail, m. Rufus **RUSSEL**, Jan. 15, 1798	67
Abigail Newell, d. Allen, bp. Nov. 14, 1802	138
Ackley, d. Jan. 23, 1804, ae 59	96
Ackley, his wid. [ ], m. Justus **BULKLEY**, June 19, 1805, by Rev. Dr. Marsh	69
Alfred, s. Roger, bp. Jan. 5, 1800	137
Allen, s. Stephen, bp. June 14, 1772	122
Allen, his w. [ ], d. Nov. 24, 1808, ae 31	98
Amelia, d. Jacob, bp. May 8, 1768	119
Amelia, d. Jacob, bp. June 26, 1774	124
Amelia, d. Roger, bp. Mar. 22, 1795	134
Amelia, m. Moses **LEONARD**, of Orwell, Vt.*, Jan. 30, 1800 *(Arnold Copy has "Cromwell")	67
Amelia, m. Levi **ROBBINS**, May 3, 1801	68
Ashbel, m. Jane **AUROLT**, July 27, 1773	61
As[h]bel, m. Mehetable **GOODRICH**, Feb. 23, 1786	63
Ashbel, his w. [ ], d. Feb. 14, 1790, ae 28	89
Ashbel, s. wid. Lovinia, bp. Sept. 22, 1799	137
Asher, s. Stephen, bp. Apr. 22, 1770	121
Asher, d. May 2, 1800, ae 31	94
Asher Tolman, s. Allen, bp. Nov. 1, 1801	138
Austin, s. James, bp. Mar. 2, 1794	134
Austin, s. James, d. Sept. 17, 1795, ae 2	92
Austin, s. James, bp. Oct. 3, 1795	135
Austin, s. James, d. Feb. 8, 1796	92
Benj[amin] James*, s. Roger, bp. Apr. 9, 1797 *(Written "Benjamin James" in Arnold Copy)	135

	Page
RILEY, REILLY, REILLEY, (cont.)	
Caroline, d. Frederick, bp. Oct. 29, 1797	136
Chloe, d. Joseph, bp. Oct. 10, 1779, by Rev. Mr. Pitkin, of Farmington	126
Chloe, d. Joseph, d. May 23, 1785	87
Constant, s. Joseph, bp. Oct. 15, 1775	125
Daniel, d. Mar. 7, 1782, ae 50* *("58th" in Church Rec.)	85
David, his w. [ ], d. [ ]*, [1767] *("d. Mar. 4" in Church Rec.)	81
David, m. Rachel **CURTIS**, Apr. 12, 1770	60
David, s. David, bp. Jan. 20, 1771	121
David, his w. [ ], d. Feb. 11, 1772	82
David, m. Sarah **GOODRICH**, May 17, 1773	61
Deborah, d. Joseph, bp. May 2, 1773	123
Deborah, d. Roger, bp. Dec. 29, 1793	134
Eliza*, wid., d. [ ] 29, 1783 *("wid. Eliza **RILEY**, d. Oct. 22" in Church Rec.)	86
Eliza, d. Allen, bp. Nov. 17, 1808	141
Elizabeth Emeline, d. Allen, bp. July 11, 1807	140
Emory, s. Asahel, bp. July 12, 1789	131
Frederick, s. Jacob, bp. Apr. 14, 1771	121
Frederick, m. Rachel **WILLIAMS**, Apr. 23, 1794, by Mr. Marsh	65
Halsey, [s. John], bp. Oct. 21, 1792	133
Halsey, s. John, Jr., d. Sept. 13, 1795	92
Halsey, s. John, Jr., b. Apr. 17, 1796	135
Hannah, d. Jabez, bp. Sept. 9, 1770	121
Hannah, d. Jabez, d. Oct. [ ], 1773	82
Hannah*, d. Jabez, bp. May 16, 1776 *("twin with Mille" in Church Rec.)	125
Hannah, twin d. of Jabez, d. May 17, 1776	84
Hannah, wid., d. Apr. 5, 1825, ae 82	104
Honor, d. Jabez, bp. Aug. 23, 1767	119
Honor, m. Jason **ROBBINS**, Apr. 1, 1790	64
Horace, s. James, bp. Mar. 3, 1799	136
Isaac*, his w. [ ], d. Aug. 8, 1788, ae 41 *("Jacob" in Church Rec.)	89
Jabez, d. Mar. 14, 1824, ae 87	103
Jacob, his infant, d. Sept. 13, 1786	87
Jacob, m. wid. Ruth **BULL**, [, 1788]	64
Jacob, his w. [ ], d. Aug. 16, 1803, ae 61	95
Jacob, d. Apr. 14, 1807, ae 66	97
James, m. Esther **GOODRICH**, Jan. 8, 1792	65
James, an adult, bp. June 23, 1793	134
James, his w. [ ], d. Oct. 2, 1842, ae 73	113
James, d. Feb. 11, 1847, ae 82	115
James W., of Bristol, m. Mary **GRISWOLD**, Jan. 16, 1837	79
John, his child d. Sept. 15, 1775	83
John, his child d. Sept. 3, 1784	87
John, Jr., m. Huldah **ROBBINS**, Oct. 31, 1790	65
John, bp. Oct. 21, 1792	133
John, s. James, bp. June 28, 1801	137
John, d. Aug. 24, 1803, ae 63 or 64	96
John, of Thetford, Vt., m. wid. Rachel **RILEY**, Aug. 26, 1810	71

Page

RILEY, REILLY, REILLEY, (cont.)
Joseph*, his infant, d. Nov. 19, 1769 *("Jacob" in Church Rec.)	81
Joseph, m. Chloe **GRISWOLD**, Sept. [, 1772]	61
Joseph, his child d. Apr. 29, 1781	84
Justin, s. wid. Lovinia, bp. Sept. 22, 1799	137
Laura, d. John, Jr., bp. Dec. 29, 1793	134
Lois, d. David, bp. Jan. 20, 1771	121
Loviniah, w. Ashbel, bp. July 24, 1796	135
Lucy, d. James, bp. Apr. 2, 1797	135
Lucy, d. July 6, 1824, ae 28	104
Lydia, d. James, bp. May 14, 1804	139
Maria, d. Frederick, bp. Jan. 17, 1796	135
Martha, m. Josiah **BUTLER**, Oct. 16, 1769	60
Mary, m. Bildad **BELDING**, Feb. 14, 1770	60
Mary, d. Joseph, bp. Apr. 10, 1774	124
Mary, m. Justus **BELDEN**, Apr. 17, 1792	65
Mary, wid., d. Oct. 24, 1847, in New York, ae 31	115
Mehetable, d. Jabez, bp. Sept. 29, 1765	117
Mehetable, d. Jacob, bp. June 30, 1776	125
Mehetable, m. John **MYEARS**, of Penn., Jan. 5, 1786	63
Mille*, d. Jabez, bp. May 16, 1776 *("Twin with Hannah" in Church Rec.)	125
Nancy, d. James, bp. June 23, 1793	134
Nancy, m. Frederic **BULKLEY**, Oct. 6, 1814	72
Oner, bp. Aug. 4, 1805	139
Polly, d. Jacob, bp. May 26, 1782	127
Polly, d. Jacob, d. July 30, 1783	86
Polly, d. Jacob, bp. June 5, 1784	129
Polly*, d. Sept. 26, 1795, ae 12 *(Arnold Copy has "Polly **RASH**")	92
Rachel, d. David, bp. Feb. 16, 1772	122
Rachel, m. Levi **BOARDMAN**, [ ], [1789]	64
Rachel, wid., m. John **RILEY**, of Thetford, Vt., Aug. 26, 1810	71
Ralph, s. Jacob, bp. Oct. 10, 1779, by Rev. Mr. Pitkin, of Farmington	126
Ralph, s. Jacob, d. Sept. 24, 1782	85
Roger, m. Augusta **GRISWOLD**, Oct. 24, 1791	65
Roger, his s. [ ], bp. Apr. 22, 1797	135
Roger, s. James, bp. [Oct.] 11, 1802	138
Ruth, wid., d. May 23, 1806, ae 64	97
Sally, d. John, Jr., bp. June 3, 1798	136
Sally Orizatia, d. Allen, bp. [Oct.] 28, 1804	139
Selah, s. Stephen, bp. Oct. 10, 1779, by Rev. Mr. Pitkin, of Farmington	126
Selah*, d. July 22, 1786 *("s. of Stephen" in Church Rec.)	87
Selah, s. Ashbel, bp. July 29, 1787	130
Stephen, his w. [ ], d. Feb. 27, 1805, ae 66 or 67	96
Stephen, d. Feb. 22, 1813, ae 84	99
Thomas, m. Honor **BELDING**, Mar. 5, 1789	64
Thomas Hastings, s. David, bp. Jan. 20, 1771	121
William, s. Jabez, bp. July 2, 1769	120
W[illia]m, d. [ ], 1794, in St. Martins	91

RISLEY, RISLY, George, m. Jennie **SCOVILLE**, Oct. 22, 1794, by Rev. Mr. Fenn — 65

	Page
RISLEY, RISLY, (cont.)	
George, m. wid. Martha **WILLIAMS**, [ ] 23, 1820	74
George, his w. [ ], d. Sept. 11, 1822, ae 46	102
George, d. [ ] 27, 1825, ae 58	104
RITTER, Hannah, d. Thomas, bp. Aug. 17, 1834	148
ROBBINS, ROBINS, Abby Ann Amelia, d. W[illia]m H., bp. Aug. 31, 1832	147
Abigail, d. Richard, bp. Oct. 17, 1773	123
Abigail, wid., d. [ ] 18, 1819, ae [ ]	101
Abigail, d. Aug. 12, 1836, ae 62	109
Abigail Ursula Bulkley, d. Allen, bp. June 6, 1819	144
Abigail Ursula Bulkly, m. Joshua L. **MAYNARD**, of Cornwall, Oct. 14, 1840	79
Adalaide Amelia, d. Benjamin, bp. Oct. 7, 1832	147
Allen, s. Jacob, bp. Oct. 10, 1779, by Rev. Mr. Pitkin, of Farmington	126
Allen, m. Amelia **BULKLEY**, Oct. 17, 1804	69
Allen, his w. [ ], d. Oct. 5, 1847, ae 66	115
Allen Austin, s. Allen, bp. [Aug. 18], 1816	143
Allen Austin, m. Abby Ann **GOODRICH**, Oct. 29, 1840	80
Allen Williams, s. W[illia]m H., bp. [July 1], 1836	148
Almira, d. Sim, Jr., bp. Aug. 28, 1808	141
Amelia, wid., d. Jan. 12, 1823, ae 89	102
Anna Amelia*, d. Allen A., bp. May 3, 1846 *("d. Allen Austin **ROBBINS**" in Church Rec.)	151
Archibald, s. Jason, bp. Apr. 14, 1793	133
Archibald, m. Almira **WILLIAMS**, June 18, 1823	75
Archibald, m. Elizabeth Tolman **WILLIAMS**, May 3, 1836	78
Asa, of the Old Society, m. M. **DANIELS**, of New London, June 21, 1798	67
Ashbel, s. Fred, bp. June 20*, 1790 *("June 22" in Church Rec.)	132
Asher, s. Nathaniel, Jr., bp. Sept. 6, 1767	119
Asher, s. Wait, bp. May 20, 1787	130
Asher, m. Martha **GRISWOLD**, Oct. 23, 1815	73
Asher, his w. [ ], d. July 1, 1817, ae 24 (1st Society)	100
Asher, m. Eliza **CHAPIN**, Jan. 14, 1819	74
Asher, d. Feb. 3, 1846, in New York City, ae 59	114
Augusta, m. James **ROBBINS**, Jan. 1, 1817	73
Augusta, w. James, bp. [ ] 14, 1825	146
Augusta B., of Rocky Hill, m. William H. **WEBB**, of Rockingham, N.C., Feb. 13, 1850, by Rev. Calvin Chapin	32
Augusta Butler, d. James, bp. [ ], 1830	146
Augustin, s. Jason, bp. July 20, 1794	134
Augustus, s. Jason, d. Nov. 1, 1795	92
Augustus, s. Jason, bp. Oct. 30, 1796	135
Austin*, s. Jacob, bp. Sept. 2, 1787 *(Arnold Copy has "Fortin")	130
Austin, s. Wait, d. Aug. 15, 1787, ae 11	88
Austin A., his w. [ ], d. Aug. 4, 1846, ae 32	114
Benjamin, m. Esther **NEFF**, [May] 30, 1816	73
Benjamin, his w. [ ], d. Oct. 19, 1832, ae 37	107
Benjamin Griswold, s. Frederick, bp. July 20, 1817	143
Benjamin James, s. Benjamin, bp. Oct. 7, 1832	147
Benj[amin] James, d. June 8, 1846, ae 24	114
Betsey, m. Horace **CALLENDER**, Oct. 23, 1817	73

ROBBINS, ROBINS, (cont.)

	Page
Caroline, d. Fred[eric]k, bp. June 27, 1813	142
Caroline Amelia, d. Thomas S., bp. [Nov. 1], 1833	147
Caroline Tracy, m. Edmund **MERRIAM**, Mar. 27, 1834	78
Charles Elijah, s. Benjamin, bp. Oct. 7, 1832	147
Charles Hale, s. Jehiel, bp. Sept. 4, 1829	146
Charlotte Fuller, d. Jehiel, bp. Oct. 14, 1821	145
Chester H., of Matayorda, Texas, m. Chloe M.T. **ROBBINS**, of Rocky Hill, Nov. 13, 1854, by Rev. L.B. Rockwood	54
Chloe, d. Jacob, bp. July 12, 1789	131
Chloe, m. Richard **ROBBINS**, [Apr.] 29, 1819	74
Chloe Maria Serena*, d. Thomas S., bp. [May] 8, 1836 *("Chloe Maria Theresa, dau. Thomas Stanley" in Church Rec.)	148
Chloe M.T., of Rocky Hill, m. Chester H. **ROBBINS**, of Matayorda, Texas, Nov. 13, 1854, by Rev. L.B. Rockwood	54
Chloe W., m. Frederick **MARSH**, of Montpelier, Vt., Oct. 7, 1839	79
Chloe Williams, d. Allen, bp. Apr. 24, 1808	141
Christian, s. Enos, bp. Oct. 4, 1795	135
Clarinda, d. Justus, bp. Nov. 8, 1795	135
Cornelia, d. Jason, bp. Aug. 4, 1805	139
Cornelia, d. Jehiel, bp. [June] 27, 1824	145
Edward, s. Elijah, bp. Mar. 17, 1808	141
Edward, d. Mar. 18, 1808, ae 8	98
Edward, s. Elias, bp. Nov. 21, 1819	145
Edward Franklin, bp. May 6, 1838	149
Edward Franklin, m. Frances **GOODRICH**, b. of Rocky Hill, Nov. 12, 1845, by Rev. C. Chapin	15
Edward Griswold, s. Benjamin, bp. Oct. 7, 1832	147
Elias, s. Jacob, bp. Dec. 5, 1773	123
Elias, m. Hannah **BOARDMAN**, May 14, 1800	67
Elias, d. July 20, 1828, ae 55	105
Elias Williams, s. Elias, bp. Nov. 21, 1819	145
Elijah, m. Martha **GRISWOLD**, [, 1788]	64
Elijah, his w. [ ], d. Nov. 13, 1810, ae 40	98
Elijah, d. Sept. 30, 1815, ae 53	100
Eliza, d. Enos, bp. [ ], 1797	136
Eliza, d. Sim, Jr., d. Dec. 10, 1802, ae 5	95
Eliza, d. Simeon, Jr., bp. Sept. 11, 1803	139
Eliza, bp. [May 7], 1837, adult	149
Eliza, m. Roswell R. **ROBBINS**, [ ] 10, 1840	79
Elizabeth, d. Jehiel, bp. July 2, 1820	145
Elizabeth, m. Alfred **BLISS**, of Martinsburg, N.Y., Dec. 25, 1839	79
Elmoral, d. Simeon, Jr., bp. May 5, 1811	142
Elnora*, d. Simeon, Jr., bp. [Apr.] 20, 1806 *("Elnorael" in Church Rec.)	140
Emily Webster*, d. Allen, bp. June 15, 1823 *("Webster" supplied from Church Rec.)	145
Emily Webster, m. Robert **SUGDEN**, Jr., b. of Rocky Hill, Feb. 6, 1844, by Rev. C. Chapin	3
Emma Goff, d. Edward F., bp. June 6, 1847	151
Enos, s. Ric[hard], bp. July 7, 1765	117

	Page
ROBBINS, ROBINS, (cont.)	
Enos, m. Dorothy **WILLIAMS**, May 27, 1794, by Mr. Chapin	65
Eunice, m. Benjamin **BUTLER**, Dec. 13, 1775	61
Eunice, m. Charles **BULKLEY**, Oct. 24, 1782	62
Eunice, d. Jacob, bp. Nov. 24, 1793	134
Eunice, wid., d. Jan. 2, 1835, ae 79	108
Fanny, d. Robert, bp. July 13, 1788 *("dau. of Fred[eric]k" in Church Rec.)	131
Fanny, m. Julius **CHAPMAN**, of East Hartford, Dec. 9, 1818	74
Fortin*, s. Jacob, bp. Sept. 2, 1787 *("Austin" in Church Rec.)	130
Frances Bull, s. George, bp. June 16, 1822	145
Frances Bull, s. George, bp. Nov. 15, 1824	146
Franklin, s. Fred, bp. Sept. 23, 1792	133
Frederick, s. Frederick, bp. [June 6], 1784	129
Frederick, Jr., m. Eunice **AMES**, Sept. 19, 1805	69
Frederick, his w. [ ], d. May 31, 1806, ae 47	97
Frederick, his w. [ ], d. Dec. 2, 1809, ae 39	98
Frederic, m. wid. Abigail **GRISWOLD**, Jan. 13, 1811	71
Frederick, d. Nov. 1, 1821, ae 66	102
Frederick, d. Sept. 27, 1841, ae 58	112
Frederick Oliver Stephen, s. Jehiel, bp. May 4, 1838	149
Frederick Walter, s. Walter, bp. [Nov. 1], 1844	151
George, s. Simeon, bp. Aug. 23, 1789	132
George, m. Eunice **WILLIAMS**, Sept. 14, 1815	73
George, d. Jan. 22, 1836, ae 47	109
George Williams, s. George, bp. Sept. 20, 1818	144
Hannah, d. Wait, bp. [Mar. 7], 1773	123
Hannah, m. Asahel **MERNAIR***, Oct. 1, 1794, by Rev. Mr. Fenn *("**MERRIAM**" in Church Rec.)	65
Hannah, d. Zebulon, bp. May 10, 1795	134
Hannah, d. Feb. 23, 1820, ae 26	101
Harriet A., of Rocky Hill, m. Ralph H. **GRISWOLD**, of Wethersfield, July 4, 1852, by Rev. Theodore M. Dwight	42
Harriet Amelia, d. Horatio, bp. May 2, 1834	148
Henry Francis, s. Roswell R., bp. Nov. 1, 1844	151
Hetty, m. Washington **WILLIAMS**, Oct. 18, 1804	69
Hezekiah, d. [, 1785], in West Indies	87
Horace W., bp. [ ], 1834	148
Horace Wolcott, s. Fred, bp. Sept. 10, 1786	130
Horatio, s. Elias, bp. Nov. 21, 1819	145
Horatio, m. Amelia **RUSSELL**, Nov. 15, 1832	77
Huldah, d. John, bp. Dec. 15, 1771	122
Huldah, m. John **RILEY**, Jr., Oct. 31, 1790	65
Ira, s. Justus, bp. June 16, 1799	136
J. Archibald, his w. [ ], d. [Feb.] 18, 1835, ae 32	108
Jacob, m. Chloe **WILLIAMS**, Dec. 10, 1772	61
Jacob, his w. [ ], d. Oct. 10, 1783, ae 35* *("33rd" in Church Rec.)	86
Jacob, d. Aug. 9, 1823, ae 77	103
James, m. Augusta **ROBBINS**, Jan. 1, 1817	73
James, his w. [ ], d. Sept. 3, 1825, ae 34	104
James, m. Sarah **ROBBINS**, Feb. 28, 1827	76

ROBBINS, ROBINS, (cont.)

	Page
James Stanley, s. wid. Lucy*, bp. May 12, 1808 *("wid. Sally" in Church Rec.)	141
James Stanley, d. Dec. 26, 1821, in Cuba*, ae 20 *("St. Jago de Cuba" in Church Rec.)	102
Jason, m. Honor **RILEY**, Apr. 1, 1790	64
Jason, his w. [ ], d. Apr. 10, 1800, ae 33	94
Jason, m. wid. Eleanor **DIMOCK**, Aug. 30, 1801	68
Jason Augustus, s. W[illia]m H., bp. [ ], 1829	146
Jehiel, s. Zebulon, bp. Aug. 1, 1793	134
Jehiel, his w. [ ], d. Dec. 19, 1835, ae 40	109
Jemmin, s. Nathaniel, Jr., bp. Oct. 15, 1769	120
Jemmy*, s. Simeon, bp. Apr. 29, 1787 *(Arnold Copy has "Jeremy")	130
Jeremy*, s. Simeon, bp. Apr. 29, 1787 *("Jemmy" in Church Rec.)	130
Jeremy, s. Sim[eo]n, bp. Apr. 1, 1793	133
Jerusha, d. Elias, bp. Nov. 21, 1819	145
Jerusha W., m. Riley O. **SMITH**, of Bristol, May 1, 1845, by Rev. C. Chapin	11
Jerusha Williams, bp. [May 7], 1837, adult	149
John, his child d. Jan. 5, 1767	81
John, d. Mar. 1, 1768	81
John, his w. [ ], d. June 10, 1770	82
John, m. Sarah **WRIGHT**, Jan. 10, 1771	60
John, s. Zebulon, bp. Nov. 4, 1781	127
John, his w. [ ], d. Feb. 10, 1784, ae 58* *("53rd" in Church Rec.)	86
John, m. Mary **RUSSEL**, d. of the late Mr. Russell, Nov. 25, 1784	62
John, his servant Jenny, m. Thomas **PALMER**, negro, Nov. 23, 1786	63
John, Jr., his w. [ ], d. Nov. 28, 1792 *("in 53rd y." in Church Rec.)	90
John, Jr., d. Nov. 11, 1794, ae 57	92
John, d. May 31, 1797, ae 82	93
John, s. Frederick, bp. May 18, 1800	137
John, of Rochester, N.Y., m. Lucy **GOODWIN**, of 1st Society, May 7, 1828	76
Joseph Neff, s. Benjamin, bp. Oct. 7, 1832	147
Justus, s. John, 2nd*, bp. [Jan. 24], 1768 *("3rd" in Church Rec.)	119
Justus, m. Clarinda **HUNTINGTON**, Mar. 31, 1790	64
Justus, s. Justus, bp. [Nov.] 1803	139
Laura Sophia, d. Walter, bp. [Nov. 1], 1844	151
Leonora, d. Jason, bp. July 22, 1798	136
Leonora*, d. Mar. 16, 1824, ae 27 *("Leonard" in Arnold Copy)	103
Leonard*, d. Mar. 16, 1824, ae 27 *("Leonora" in Church Rec.)	103
Levi, s. Levi, bp. [Apr. 19], 1772	122
Levi, s. Wait, bp. Mar. 5, 1775	124
Levi, m. Amelia **RILEY**, May 3, 1801	68
Lorin Henry, s. Benjamin, bp. Oct. 7, 1832	147
Louisa*, d. Zebulon, bp. Nov. 1, 1789 *("Lovisa" in Church Rec.)	132
Louisa, m. Ezra **BRAINARD**, of East Hartford, May 14, 1809	70
Louisa Melissa, bp. July 4, 1841	150
Lucretia, d. Zebulon, bp. June 5, 1788	131
Lucy, d. Wait, bp. Mar. 24, 1782	127

	Page
ROBBINS, ROBINS, (cont.)	
Lucy, m. James **GRISWOLD**, of 1st Society, Jan. 22, 1812	71
Lucy, m. Walter Williams **BULKLEY**, June 17, 1830	77
Mabel, d. John, 2nd, bp. May 13, 1769	120
Mabel, d. John, d. [ ] 13, 1769	81
Mabel, d. Simeon, bp. June 16, 1782	127
Mabel, m. Daniel **FULLER**, Oct. 15, 1806	70
Mabel, wid., d. [ ] 30, 1834, ae 79	108
Maria, d. Frederick, bp. May 8, 1796	135
Maria, d. Jason, bp. May 20, 1810	142
Martha, m. John **WRIGHT**, Apr. 16, 1772	61
Martha, d. Simeon, bp. Jan. 31, 1773	123
Martha, bp. Nov. 1, 1818, adult	144
Martha, d. Asher, bp. June 10, 1821	145
Martha, m. George O. **CHAMBERS**, of Middletown, Dec. 14, 1825	75
Martha, m. George O. **CHAMBERS**, Dec. 16, 1825	10
Martha G., m. Daniel A. **MILLS**, of Hartford, Mar. 9, 1837	79
Martha Griswold, d. James, bp. [ ], 1825	146
Mary, m. Jehiel **BULKLEY**, Mar. 2, 1775	61
Mary, d. Richard, bp. Apr. 28, 1782	127
Mary, d. Zebulon, bp. May 7, 1797	135
Mary, m. Josiah **BUTLER**, Dec. 24, [1797]	67
Mary, wid., d. June 13, 1799, ae 83	94
Mary, d. May 29, 1842, ae 46	112
Mary Amelia, d. Allen, bp. Sept. 2, 1810	142
Mehetable, d. Fred[eric]k, bp. Mar. 2, 1783	128
Mehetable, m. Samuell **LEE**, of New Hartford, May 22, 1783	62
Meriam, d. Nathaniel, of Pittsfield, Mass., bp. Jan. 21, 1776	125
Moses, s. Jacob, bp. Aug. 14, 1791	133
Nancy, d. John, 2nd, bp. July 22, 1770	121
Nancy, d. John, Jr., d. Aug. 31, 1775	83
Nancy, d. Justus, bp. Dec. 25, 1791	133
Nancy, m. Moses **GRISWOLD**, b. of 1st Society, Oct. 11, 1804	69
Nancy, m. Edmund **BULKLEY**, Apr. 18, 1811	71
Nancy, w. Jehiel, bp. Sept. 6, 1818	144
Nathaniell, m. Elizabeth **DEMING**, Oct. 29, 1767	60
Nathaniel, Dea., his w. [ ], d. Nov. 7, 1781	85
Nathaniel, Dea., d. Oct. 6, 1783, ae 76	86
Nathaniel Warner, s. Roswell R., bp. Mar. 5, 1847	151
Oliver, s. Nathaniel, Jr., bp. May 10, 1772	122
Oliver, s. Zeb[ulon], bp. Feb. 22, 1784	128
Orpah, d. Fred, bp. Aug. 19, 1798	136
Orpah, m. Ulysses **BUTLER**, Mar. 29, 1820	74
Pamela, d. Justus, bp. Oct. 29, 1797	136
Patty, d. Simeon, Jr., bp. Aug. 2, 1801	137
Rhoda, d. Richard, bp. Oct. 11, 1767	119
Richard, d. [ ] 28, 1783, ae 46	86
Richard, m. Chloe **ROBBINS**, [Apr.] 29, 1819	74
Roderic, s. Zebulon, bp. May 20, 1787	130
Roderick, s. Zebulon, d. Jan. 29, 1788	88
Roderick, s. Zebulon, bp. May 20, 1792	133

ROBBINS, ROBINS, (cont.)

	Page
Roderick H., his w. [ ], d. Oct. 12, 1838, ae 53	110
Rodney*, s. [Frederick], bp. [June] 13, 1784 *(Should be "Rodney, s. of Edward Bulkley, Jr." See Church Rec.)	129
Roger, s. Richard, bp. Sept. 13, 1772	122
Roger, sailed for Lisbon, [ ], 1802, not heard from	95
Roswell R., m. Eliza **ROBBINS**, [ ] 10, 1840	79
Roswell Rose, s. George, bp. Sept. 20, 1818	144
Roxy, d. Fred, bp. Mar. 9, 1794	134
Roxy, m. Jessie **BIGELOW**, of East Haddam, Oct. 12, 1818	74
Russel, s. Horatio, bp. Oct. 30, 1835	148
Sally, d. Frederick, bp. Apr. 5, 1812	142
Sally, m. Eli **GOODRICH**, June 4, 1817	73
Sally, w. James, bp. Apr. 29, 1830	146
Samuel, s. John, 3rd, bp. July 21, 1765	117
Samuel, s. John, Jr., d. May 12, 1775	83
Samuel, s. Wait, bp. June 12, 1785	129
Samuel, s. Wait, d. Oct. 23, 1787	88
Samuel, s. Justus, d. Apr. 10, 1796	93
Samuel Huntington, s. Justus, bp. Mar. 31, 1793	133
Sarah*, d. Wait, bp. Oct. 10, 1779, by Rev. Mr. Pitkin, of Farmington *("Warner" in Church Rec.)	126
Sarah, d. Wait, d. Mar. 29, 1783, ae 4	86
Sarah, d. May 3, 1794, ae 24	91
Sarah, m. James **ROBBINS**, Feb. 28, 1827	76
Sarah, wid.Simeon, d. Sept. 6, 1843, ae 89	113
Sarah Ann, d. James, bp. [ ], 1825	146
Sarah Ann, d. Jehiel, bp. Aug. 30, 1833	147
Sarah Ann, m. Albert **FRANCIS**, of Wethersfield, [ ] 15, 1837	79
Silas, s. Jacob, bp. Oct. 15, 1775	125
Silas, s. Jacob, bp. Dec. 18, 1785	130
Simeon, m. Sarah **ROSE**, Apr. 8, 1772	61
Simeon, his child d. [ ] 13, 1774	83
Simeon, s. Simeon, bp. Apr. 13, 1774	124
Simeon, Jr., m. Martha **DANFORTH**, July 7, 1796	66
Simeon, d. May 15, 1819, ae 68	101
Sophia, d. Jason, bp. May 20, 1810	142
Susan Caroline, d. George, bp. July 2, 1830	146
Thomas Hamlin*, s. Allen A., bp. [Apr.] 10, 1842 *("s. of Allen Austin **ROBBINS**" in Church Rec.)	150
Thomas Stanley, s. Allen, bp. Jan. 5, 1806	140
Wait, s. Walter*, bp. Oct. 13, 1771 *("Wait" in Church Rec.)	122
Wait, his w. [ ], d. Aug. 15, 1787	88
Wait, m. Mabel **BULKLEY**, Nov. 9, 1789	64
Wait, Jr., m. Sally **STANLEY**, June 4, 1801	68
Wait, Jr., d. Jan. 22, 1806, at Kingston, J.[ ], ae 35	97
Wait, s. wid. Sally, bp. July 10, 1808	141
Wait, d. May 15, 1826, ae 83	104
Walter, s. Frederick, bp. [ ] 21, 1809	141
Walter, s. Frederic, bp. Oct. 30, 1814	143
Walter, m. Abigail Sophia **WILDER**, Nov. 3, 1839	79

	Page
ROBBINS, ROBINS, (cont.)	
Warner, s. Richard, bp. Mar. 4, 1770	120
William, m. Rebecca **CRANE**, of the 1st Society, May 19, 1808	70
William, 2nd, m. Ruth **WILLIAMS**, Mar. 26, 1817	73
W[illia]m, his w. [ ], d. Apr. 28, 1824, ae 35	103
William George, s. Roswell R., bp. [Mar. 3], 1843	150
W[illia]m H., his w. [ ], d. Dec. 12, 1841, ae 44	112
W[illia]m Hubbard, s. Jason, bp. Sept. 11, 1791	133
William Hubbard, m. Abigail **WILLIAMS**, [ ] 14, 1828	76
William Riley, s. W[illia]m H., bp. [Nov. 5], 1841	150
Wilson Fuller, s. Jehiel, bp. May 2, 1828	146
Winthrop, m. Elizabeth **GRAHAM**, of Stockbridge, Mass., Feb. 3, 1828	76
Zeb, his w. [ ], d. Apr. 17, 1785 *("ae 24" in Church Rec.)	87
Zebulon, d. [ ] 30, 1840, ae 81	111
Zebulon, his wid. [ ], d. Feb. 27, 1842, ae 87	112
ROBERTS, Benjamin, d. Oct. 16*, 1775 *("Oct. 10" in Church Rec.)	83
ROBERTSON, John Clark, s. Clark, bp. [ ], 1806	140
Warner*, s. Clark, bp. Nov. 23, 1806 *("Warren" in Church Rec.)	140
Warren*, s. Clark, bp. Nov. 23, 1806 *(Arnold Copy has "Warner")	140
ROBINSON, Alfred, s. Ashbel, bp. Nov. 3, 1843	150
Ashbel, Jr., m. Susannah **SHAYLOR**, Mar. 4, 1830	76
Ashbel, his w. [ ], d. Nov. 9, 1835, ae 50	109
Ashbel, d. Oct. 29, 1843, ae 37	113
Benjamin, s. Ashbel, bp. Nov. 3, 1843	150
Caroline, d. Ashbel, bp. Nov. 3, 1843	150
Charles Shaylor, s. Ashbel, bp. Nov. 3, 1843	150
Francis Henry, d. May 28, 1848, ae 14 ("Henry Francis **ROBINSON**" in Church Rec.)	116
Henry, m. Ruth **STOW***, Aug. 28, 1831 *(Arnold Copy has "ROBINSON")	77
Henry, bp. [July 4], 1841	149
Henry Francis, s. Henry, bp. Sept. 3, 1841	150
Henry Francis, d. May 28, 1848, ae 14 *(Arnold Copy has "Francis Henry **ROBINSON**")	116
Luadiah, d. [ ], 1793, coming form West Indies, ae 23	91
Reny, m. Denis **MYERS**, Sept. 13, 1789	64
Reuben, of Berlin, m. Hannah **CURTIS**, Oct. 5, 1791	65
Reuben, his infant d. Dec. 15, 1791	90
Ruth*, m. Henry **ROBINSON**, Aug. 28, 1831 *(Church Rec. give "Ruth **STOW**")	77
Sophronia Tryon, d. Ashbel, bp. Nov. 3, 1843	150
Susanna, w. Ashbel, bp. July 2, 1843	150
ROCKWELL, Elizabeth, m. Solomon **BELDEN**, June 27, 1768	60
Hannah, see Hannah **DICKINSON**	85
Thomas, s. wid. Elizabeth, bp. Nov. 17, 1765	117
ROGERS, Abigail, wid., m. Horace **BELDEN**, May 15, 1823	75
Abigail Louisa, d. Theodore B., bp. [Nov. 4], 1842	150
Martha Helen, d. Theodore B., bp. Nov. 8, 1846	151
T.B., his w. [ ], d. Oct. 26, 1846, ae 37	114
ROSE, John, his w. [ ], d. May 30, 1832, ae 75	107
John, d. Apr. 1, 1838, ae 80	110

	Page
ROSE, (cont.)	
Sarah, m. Simeon **ROBBINS**, Apr. 8, 1772	61
RUSSELL, RUSSEL, Abigail, m. Wait **DICKINSON**, Mar. 19, 1772	61
Abigail, wid., d. Oct. 4, 1805, ae 87	96
Abigail, see Abigail **DICKINSON**	105
Abigail A., m. Obed **ANDRUS**, of Glastonbury, Mar. 10, 1836	78
Abigail Amanda, d. Rufus, bp. July 5, 1812	142
Abigail Amanda, d. Rufus, bp. June 19, 1814	143
Alice Lucilla, d. Horace, bp. [Oct. 31], 1845	151
Amelia, d. Rufus, bp. [Oct.] 21, 1810	142
Amelia, m. Horatio **ROBBINS**, Nov. 15, 1832	77
Ann Elizabeth, d. Horace, bp. [Nov. 4], 1842	150
Asher, his child d. Nov. 10, 1781	85
Asher, his w. [ ], d. July 10*, 1787, ae 44 *("July 18" in Church Rec.)	88
Austin, s. Rufus, bp. July 5, 1807	140
Austin, s. Rufus, bp. Oct. 15, 1815	143
Austin, d. [ ] 16, 1826, ae 12	105
Benjamin, s. Nathaniel, bp. Nov. 29, 1772	122
Caroline, d. Roderick, bp. Jan. 30, 1814	143
Catharine, d. Jonathan, bp. Feb. 22, 1784	128
Charles Augustus, s. W[illia]m R., bp. July 2, 1847	151
Daniel, s. Nathaniel, bp. [Jan. 24], 1768	119
Eliza, d. Rufus, bp. Sept. 4, 1803	139
Eliza, d. Rufus, bp. July 30, 1808	141
Elizabeth, d. Thomas, bp. June 10, 1770	121
Elizabeth, m. Josiah **BUTLER**, of Middletown, [Nov.] 11, [1790]	65
Elizabeth, wid., d. [ ], 1832, ae 86	107
Ellen Eliza, d. Horace, bp. [Nov. 4], 1842	150
Erastus, s. Roderick, bp. Mar. 2, 1809	141
Francis Godrich, s. Horace, bp. [Nov. 4], 1842	150
George Stillman, s. Nathaniel, bp. [Jan.] 25, 1784	128
Giles, s. Nathaniel, bp. Aug. 6, 1775	125
Hamlin, s. Nathaniel, bp. [Apr. 8], 1781, by Rev. Mr. Lewis	126
Horace, s. Rufus, bp. [June] 30, 1805	139
James, s. Rufus, bp. Aug. 31, 1800	137
James, s. Rufus, bp. May 16, 1802	138
James, d. [Dec.] 24, 1828, ae 27	106
James, s. William R., bp. Nov. 4, 1842	150
Jerusha, d. Thomas, bp. Apr. 12, 1801	137
Jerusha, m. Samuel W. **RUSSEL**, of Middletown, July 11, 1814	72
John Willard, s. Nathaniel, bp. Apr. 15, 1770	120
Laura Ann, d. Rod[eric]k, bp. July 14, 1811	142
Lucretia Williams, d. Roderic, bp. Oct. 28, 1804	139
Lucy Wilcox, d. William R., bp. July 3, 1840	149
Martha, m. John **SAUNDERS**, of Litchfield, Mar. 17, 1774	61
Mary, had s. Solomon, bp. Oct. 6, 1771	122
Mary, d. of late Mr. Russell, m. John **ROBBINS**, Nov. 25, 1784	62
Mary Ann, d. W[illia]m, bp. Aug. 30, 1833	147
Mary Eliza, d. W[illia]m R., bp. May 2, 1845	151
Mat[t]hew*, s. Jonathan, bp. May 1, 1774 *(Arnold Copy has "Nathan")	124

	Page
RUSSELL, RUSSEL, (cont.)	
Matthew, s. Jonathan, d. Oct. 26, 1787, ae 14	88
Mehetabel, d. Tho[ma]s, bp. July 25, 1767	118
Nathan*, s. Jonathan, bp. May 1, 1774 *("Mathew" in Church Rec.)	124
Oliver, of Marlboro, m. Eliza **OCKRY**, of Hartford, Jan. 17, 1837	79
Philip, s. Thomas, bp. Aug. 9, 1772	122
Philip, d. about [Sept.] 18, 1799, ae 28, in West Indies	94
Rachel, d. Jonathan, bp. June 30, 1776	125
Ralph, s. Roderick, bp. Sept. 1, 1805	140
Rhoda, d. Thomas, bp. Oct. 10, 1779, by Rev. Mr. Pitkin, of Farmington	126
Rhoda, m. Austin **MYGATT**, of Berlin, July 22, 1799	67
Roderick, m. Laura **GOODRICH**, Jan. 31, 1803	68
Rosama, d. Jon[atha]n, bp. Apr. 1, 1781, by Rev. Mr. Lewis	126
Roswell, m. Paulina **PETERS**, [colored], b. of Glastonbury, Jan. 9, 1851, by Rev. Calvin Chapin	35
Rufus, s. Thomas, bp. May 14, 1775	125
Rufus, m. Abigail **RILEY**, Jan. 15, 1798	67
Rufus, d. Apr. 9, 1846, ae 72	114
Rufus Austin, s. Horace, bp. [Nov. 4], 1842	150
Ruth, m. Roger **BULL**, Nov. 19, 1767	60
Ruth, d. Thomas, bp. May 1, 1768	119
Ruth, m. Stephen **BUTLER**, [ ], 1788	64
Samuel W., of Middletown, m. Jerusha **RUSSELL**, July 11, 1814	72
Samuel W., his w. [ ], d. Feb. 2, 1818, in Middletown, ae 27; bd. in Rocky Hill	101
Samuel W., of Middletown, m. Lucy **DICKINSON**, Oct. 14, 1819	74
Sarah Jane, d. Horace, bp. [Nov. 4], 1842	150
Shubael, s. Thomas, bp. Apr. 12, 1801	137
Solomon, s. Mary, bp. Oct. 6, 1771	122
Sophia Dimock, d. Horace, bp. [Nov. 4], 1842	150
Stephen, s. John *, bp. Oct. 10, 1779, by Rev. Mr. Pitkin, of Farmington ("Jonathan" in Church Rec.)	126
Thomas, m. Elizabeth **GOODRICH**, [winter] 1766	60
Thomas, s. Roderick, bp. Sept. 20, 1807	140
Thomas, d. [ ] 21, 1827, ae 87	105
Walter, s. W[illia]m R., bp. July 1, 1831	147
Walter R., m. Carrile W. **BLINN**, b. of Rocky Hill, May 6, 1852, by Rev. L. Burton Rockwood	40
William, s. Thomas, bp. [Jan.] 29, 1784	128
William, s. Thomas, bp. Mar. 17, 1787	130
W[illia]m, s. Tho[ma]s, d. Apr. 4, 1787	88
W[illia]m, his child d. Mar. 12, 1837, ae 4	109
William Henry*, s. William R., bp. June 30, 1837 *("s. of William Riley **RUSSELL**" in Church Rec.)	149
W[illia]m Riley, s. Rufus, bp. Mar. 10, 1799	136
SAGE, Charles P., m. Elizabeth C. **THAYER**, b. of Cromwell, Nov. 24, 1852, by Rev. L.B. Rockwood	42
Elisha L., m. Elizabeth B. **HUBBARD**, b. of Middletown, Jan. 28, 1829	76
Linus, s. Calvin, bp. May 13, 1789	131
Linus, s. Calvin, d. May 14, 1789	89
Lucy, d. Calvin, bp. Nov. 23, 1788	131

	Page
SAGE, (cont.)	
Orrin, d. Calvin, bp. Nov. 23, 1788	131
SAMBUN, Jed, d. Apr. 21, 1810, ae 49	98
SANDERSON, Joel, of Petersham, Mass., m. wid. Prudence **GRANT**, Mar. 10, 1824	75
SANFORD, SANDFORD, Amos, m. Lydia **BLINN**, May 10, 1797	66
Ceslesty, d. Nov. 7, 1821, ae 14	102
Daniel, [s. Urben K. & Jane], b. June 10, 1843	49
Daniel, d. Oct. 27, 1844, ae 23	114
Jessie, m. Eleanor **COLLINS**, Dec. 25, 1783	62
Oliver H., [s. Urben K. & Jane], b. Sept. 5, 1845	49
Stephen E., [s. Urben K. & Jane], b. June 16, 1840	49
SANGER, Ethiel, of New Britain, m. Mary A. **BRAINARD**, Apr. 17, 1836	78
SAUNDERS, John, of Litchfield, m. Martha **RUSSEL**, Mar. 17, 1774	61
SAVAGE, Abigail, d. Asahel, bp. July 17, 1803	138
Asahel, m. Abigail **DEMING**, Mar. 22, 1792	65
Asahel, s. Asahel, bp. [ ] 27, 1806	140
Charlotte, d. Lemuel, bp. [Sept.]18, 1796	135
Clarissa, d. Lemuel, bp. [Sept.] 18, 1796	135
Giles, of Middletown, m. Olive **SMITH**, Mar. 14, 1790	64
Hamlin, s. Asahel, bp. Feb. 22, 1795	134
Liman*, s. Asahel, bp. May 7, 1797 *("Simeon" in Arnold Copy)	135
Luman, of Berlin, m. Sarah **GOFF**, Nov. 24, 1791	65
Marietta, d. Ashbel*, bp. May 5, 1799 *("Asahel" in Church Rec.)	136
Norman, s. Asahel, bp. Apr. 14, 1793	133
Sarah Jerusha, d. Asahel, bp. Aug. 16, 1801	137
Simeon*, s. Asahel, bp. May 7, 1797 *("Liman" in Church Rec.)	135
Solomon, of Middletown, m. Lydia **BULKLEY**, Nov. 27, 1783	62
SCOVILLE, Jennie, m. Goerge **RISLEY**, Oct. 22, 1794, by Rev. Mr. Fenn	65
SCRANTON, Fanny L., of Durham, m. Elizur **GOODRICH**, [ ] 26, 1820	74
SELAH, Zadock, of Stamford, m. Nancy **MILLER**, Feb. 23, 1786	63
SELDEN, Charles, of Chatham, m. Almira **GOODALE**, May 5, 1833	77
Charles Elliot, of Middle Haddam, d. Aug. 31, 1833, ae 23	108
Charles Elliott*, s. Charles Elliott, bp. July 4, 1834 *("s. of the late Charles Elliott **SELDEN**, of Middle Haddam" in Church Rec.)	148
Hannah, wid., d. Jan. 10, 1816, ae 73	100
Thomas, his w. [ ], d. Feb. 25, 1831, ae 50, [of Middle Haddam*] *(Chuech Rec.)	106
Thomas, of Chatham, m. Mary **BULKLEY**, [May] 17, 1832	77
SEZER, Anthony, m. Lucretia **WARD**, of Middletown, Jan. 4, 1785	63
SHAILER, SHAYLER, SHAYLOR, Abigail, m. Isaac **TRYON**, 3rd, of Glastonbury, Sept. 9, 1813	72
Asa, m. Lydia **GOODRICH**, Sept. 10, 1806, by Rev. Mr. Bulkley	70
Asa, d. July 26, 1834*, ae 48 *("1833" in Church Rec.)	107
Charles, d. Sept. [ ], 1823 (sailed for West Indies, not heard from)	103
Edward, d. Jan. 13, 1846, ae 34	114
James*, d. May 11, 1830, ae 12 *("Jared, son of Asa" in Church Rec.)	106
Lydia G., wid., m. Gideon N. **BEARD**, July 12, 1837	79
Mary, m. Jeremy **GOODRICH**, Jan. 21, 1841	80
Parmelia, m. Harvey* **RICHARDSON**, of Hartford, May 12, 1830 (Arnold Copy has "Har[r]y")	77

	Page
SHAILER, SHAYLER, SHAYLOR, (cont.)	
Roeweny, m. William **TRYON**, Jr., Sept. 8, 1808	70
Samuel, d. May 25, 1807, ae 49	97
Samuel, his wid. [ ], d. Dec. 24, 1838, ae 78	110
Sarah, of Rocky Hill, m. Jerry W. **GRAY**, of Manchester, Aug. 20, 1845, by Rev. John Lovejoy	13
Susannah, m. Ashbel **ROBINSON**, Jr., Mar. 4, 1830	76
Weltha, m. Jessie **TRYON**, of Glastonbury, July 15, 1804	69
SHEPHERD, Noah, of Chatham, m. Ruth **COREY**, of Wethersfield, Aug. 30, 1795	66
SHERIDEN, James, m. Eliza **KELLY**, b. of Rocky Hill, Sept. 4, 1849, by Rev. Philo Judson	30
SHIPMAN, Alfred, s. Reuben, bp. May 3, 1833	147
F.W., m. Mary Ann **GRIMES**, Aug. 6, 1851, by Rev. L. Burton Rockwood	37
Francis, his w. [ ], d. Feb. 6, 1847, ae 23	115
Frances W., m. Agnes **GRIMES**, b. of Rocky Hill, Nov. 19, 1845, by Rev. C. Chapin	16
James Henry, s. Reuben, bp. Apr. 4, 1827	146
John, d. Jan. 20, 1842, ae 90 *("Interred in Glastonbury." See Church Rec.)	112
Keturah, m. Robert **HUNT**, of Glastonbury, Mar. 31, 1819	74
Mary Jane, d. Reuben, bp. [ ] 13, 1829	146
Reuben, of Glastonbury, m. Clarissa **BUCKLEY**, Dec. 3, 1818	74
William Cornelius, s. Reuben, bp. Oct. 31, 1824	146
SKINNER*, Elizabeth, d. Enos, bp. Nov. 24, 1805 *(Arnold Copy has "**WARNER**")	140
Eunice*, d. Enos, bp. Nov. 24, 1805 *(Arnold Copy has "**WARNER**")	140
SLATER, George Warren, of Hartford, m. Martha Elizabeth **GOODRICH**, of Rocky Hill, May 8, 1850, by Rev. Calvin Chapin	33
SLOPER, Betsey, b. July 27, 1807, in Middletown; m. John L. **THAYER**, Jan. 4, 1826	45
SMITH, Abigail, twin with Elizabeth, d. Jona[h], Jr., bp. Apr. 1, 1773	123
Abigail B., m. Moses W. **WILLIAMS**, Oct. 26, 1841	80
Adalaide Williams, d. Benjamin, bp. Aug. 31, 1838	149
Adelia, d. Levi, bp. Dec. 8, 1816	143
Almira Amelia, d. of the late Edmond, bp. Nov. 3, 1843	150
Ann, wid., d. Mar. 29, 1774	83
Anna, d. Eunice, bp. Aug. 27, 1786 *("dau. of Ezek[iel]" in Church Rec.)	130
Anna, m. Shubael **CORNING**, of Hartford, Oct. 26, 1809	71
Anna, wid., d. June 14, 1832, ae 72	107
Bena, m. John **GRIMES**, Oct. [ ], 1768	60
Benjamin, s. Eliakim, bp. Aug. 31, 1817	143
Benjamin, m. Cornelia **BUTLER**, May 17, 1837	79
Billy, s. Horvillah, bp. [Apr.] 24, 1796	135
Caroline, of Hartford, m. Charles **BRADLEY**, of Plymouth, May 4, 1839	79
Caroline Eliza, d. Davis, bp. Nov. 2, 1838	149
Charles F., of Cromwell, m. Martha A. **GRISWOLD**, of Rocky Hill, Dec. 13, 1853, by Rev. L.B. Rockwood	49
Christian, m. Peter **BUCKLEY**, [Jan. 26, 1769]	60

SMITH, (cont.)

	Page
Clarissa, d. Ezekiel, bp. Apr. 14, 1782	127
Clarissa, d. Feb. 9, 1840, ae 61	111
David, m. Temperance **GOODRICH**, Sept. 25, 1766	60
David, s. David, bp. Nov. 3, 1782	128
David, d. [ ], 1794, in West Indies	92
David, his w. [ ], d. Sept. 6, 1831, ae 72	107
David, d. July 14, 1844, ae 88	113
Davis, of Haddam, m. Abigail **BULKLEY**, Mar. 18, 1819	74
Edmond, s. Eliakim, bp. May 28, 1815	143
Edmund, d. Mar. 20, 1843, ae 29	113
Edmund, his wid., d. Dec. 3, 1846, ae 29	115
Eliakim, m. wid. Abigail **WILLIAMS**, June 2, 1813	72
Eliakim, d. Jan. 26, 1846, ae 88	114
Eliza Ann, d. Levi, bp. Sept. 10, 1809	141
Eliza Ann, m. Aaron C. **ARNOLD**, of Middletown, Nov. 17, 1830	77
Eliza Jane, d. Apr. 4, 1843, ae 21	113
Elizabeth, twin with Abigail, d. Jona[h], Jr., bp. Apr. 1, 1773	123
Elizabeth, d. Havilla, bp. Sept. 15, 1795	134
Elizabeth, d. Havilah, d. Sept. 17, 1795, ae 2	92
Ellen Cornelia, d. Benjamin, bp. Sept. 3, 1841	150
Emeline, d. Levi, bp. Oct. 4, 1807	141
Emeline, m. Allen William **MILLER**, Apr. 14, 1830	76
Eunice, had d. Anna, bp. [ ], 1786	130
Ezekiel, his w. [ ], d. Oct. 26, 1797, ae 40* *("ae 48" in Church Rec.)	93
Ezekiel, m. wid. Ruth **AMES**, Feb. 2, 1800	67
Ezekiel, his w. [ ], d. Mar. 11, 1842, ae 83	112
Ezekiel, d. Feb. 9, 1847, ae 91	115
George, m. Sally **BLINN**, of 1st Society, Mar. 18, 1810	71
Henry, m. Lucy **HARRIS**, b. of Middletown, May 19, 1811	71
Henry, s. Levi, bp. [June] 12, 1814	143
Henry, his w. [ ], d. Oct. 12, 1843, ae 31	113
Henry, m. Emeline **GOODRICH**, b. of Rocky Hill, Jan. 29, 1845, by Rev. C. Chapin	8
Hiram, of East Windsor, m. Lucy Ann **BELL**, June 17, 1833	78
Honor, d. David, bp. Sept. 5, 1773	123
Jerusha, d. Mar. 7, 1776 (Church Rec. say 'died in same house with wid. Mary Smith")	84
Jerusha, d. Jonathan, bp. Mar. 24, 1782	127
Jerusha, d. Levi, bp. July 11, 1819	144
John, d. Aug. 5, 1836, ae 17 (Church Rec. say "orphan fr. O. Engl.")	109
John C.*, m. Delia **GOODRICH**, Nov. 14, 1838 *(Church Rec. give "John H.")	79
John Henry, bp. July 4, 1841	149
John Lorin, s. Levi, bp. Nov. 5, 1830	146
Jonathan, his infant, d. Apr. 3, 1773	82
Jonathan, d. June [ ], 1775	83
Jona[than], his child d. Oct. 22, 1775	83
Justus, s. Jonathan*, bp. Aug. 28, 1768 (Jonathan, Jr." in Church Rec.)	119
L. Wesley, of Hartford, m. Fanny M. **BENTON**, of Rocky Hill, Dec. 17,	

	Page
SMITH, (cont.)	
1854, by Rev. L.B. Rockwood	55
Larry*, s. Ezekiel, bp. May 24, 1789 *("Lorey" in Church Rec.)	131
Levi, s. Ezekiel, bp. Apr. 14, 1782	127
Levi, m. Sarah **COLLINS**, Jan. 29, 1784	62
Levi, m. Betsey **GIBBS**, May 7, 1806	69
Levi Horatio, s. Levi, bp. Oct. 3, 1824	145
Lorey*, s. Ezekiel, bp. May 24, 1789 *("Larry" in Arnold Copy)	131
Louisa, of Berlin, m. Francis **HOLMES**, of Rocky Hill, Feb. 5, 1852, by Rev. L.B. Rockwood	39
Lucretia*, of Rocky Hill, m. Joseph B. **GOODRICH**, of Mereden, May 6, 1847, by Rev. C. Chapin *(Church Rec. give "Jerusha")	22
Lucy, of Glastonbury, m. Joseph **BROOKS**, Jan. 17, 1786	63
Lucy Ann, d. Henry, bp. Oct. 22, 1843	150
Margaret Ursula, d. Davis, bp. May 1, 1836	148
Mariah D., of Rocky Hill, m. Chatfield **SPENCER**, of Haddam, Nov. 28, 1849, by Rev. Calvin Chapin	31
Martha, d. Levi, bp. Oct. 17, 1821	145
Martha, m. Elisha **GILBERT**, of West Hartford, Sept. 7, 1842	80
Martha Amelia, d. Davis*, bp. July 29, 1832 *("Here from N.Y." in Church Rec.)	147
Martin, s. Havilla, bp. Sept. 12, 1795	134
Martin, s. Havilah, d. [ ], 1795	92
Martin, s. Horvilla, bp. [Apr.] 24, 1796	135
Mary, d. Jonathan, Jr., bp. June 9, 1771	121
Mary, wid., d. Feb. 27, 1776 (Church Rec. say "d. in same house with Jerusha Smith"	84
Mary, m. William **WRIGHT**, Jan. 1, 1834	78
Mary, bp. July 4, 1841	150
Mary Buckley, d. Benj[amin], bp. [Aug. 30], 1844	151
Mary Johnson, bp. July 4, 1841	150
Mary S., m. Samuel **DIMOCK**, Oct. 14, 1846, by Rev. Warren G. Jones	20
Mary Sophia, d. Levi, bp. Aug. 5, 1827	146
Milly, d. David, bp. Sept. 14, 1788	131
Moses, d. Oct. 12, 1783, ae 40	86
Nathan, s. Samuel, bp. Jan. 3, 1765	117
Norman, s. Levi, bp. May 10, 1812	142
Olive, d. David, bp. Sept. 11, 1768	119
Olive, m. Giles **SAVAGE**, of Middletown, Mar. 14, 1790	64
Percy, s. David, bp. Dec. 23, 1770	121
Rhoda, d. Ezekiel, bp. June 20, 1784	129
Richard, his w. [ ], d. June 9, 1835, ae 32	109
Riley O., of Bristol, m. Jerusha W. **ROBBINS**, of [ ], May 1, 1845, by Rev. C. Chapin	11
Ruth, m. Hosea* **BLINN**, Nov. 8, 1773 *(Arnold Copy has "Corra")	61
Samuel, of Middlebury, m. Amelia **GOODRICH**, of Glastonbury, Sept. 28, 1797	66
Sarah, d. Mar. 24, 1837, ae [ ]	109
Sarah Maria, d. Henry, bp. [July 5], 1839	149
Solomon*, his wid. [ ], d. May 22, 1784 *("wid. "Susanna" in Church Rec.)	87

	Page
SMITH, (cont.)	
Sophia, d. Ezekiel, bp. May 29, 1791	132
Susan, wid., d. May 1, 1806, ae 75	97
W[illia]m, his wid., d. Apr. 15, 1843, ae [ ]	113
SPENCER, Chatfield, of Haddam, m. Mariah D. **SMITH**, of Rocky Hill, Nov. 28, 1849, by Rev. Calvin Chapin	31
Joel, of Berlin, m. Clarissa **BELDEN**, Mar. 18, 1810	71
Seth, of Middletown, Upper Houses, m. Mehetable **BELDEN**, Mar. 6, 1816	73
SQUIRES, Abner, m. Mary Goodrich **DIX**, of the 1st Society, Oct. 13, 1814	72
STADICK*, Hannah, d. Jeremiah, Jr., bp. Oct. 30, 1768 *("STADISH" in Church Rec.)	119
STANDISH, STADISH, Hannah*, d. Jeremiah, Jr., bp. Oct. 30, 1768 *("Hannah **STADICK**" in Arnold Copy)	119
Jeremiah, d. May 11, 1769	81
Jeremiah, s. Jeremiah, bp. Feb. 5, 1774	123
Josiah, s. Jeremiah, bp. Sept. 2, 1770	121
Lois, d. Jeremiah, bp. Oct. 18, 1772	122
Lois, m. Israel **COWING**, May 27, 1773	61
Mary, m. Abner **BELDEN**, Oct. 24, 1771	61
Rachel, d. Jeremiah, bp. Oct. 10, 1779, by Rev. Mr. Pitkin, of Farmington	126
Simeon, s. Jeremiah, bp. [Aug. 6], 1775	125
STANLEY, Everett L., of New Britain, m. Sarah **FLINT**, of Rocky Hill, June 11, 1848, by Rev. T.M. Dwight	26
James, m. Sarah **BUTLER**, Jan. 21, 1773	61
James, d. Mar. 30, 1816, ae 69	100
James, his wid., d. Oct. 25, 1829, ae 84	106
Sally, m. Wait **ROBBINS**, Jr., June 4, 1801	68
Sarah, d. James, bp. Mar. 20, 1774	124
STEBBINS, Harlow, s. Samuel, bp. July 17, 1791	133
Samuel, m. Sarah **BOARDMAN**, Aug. 12, 1784	62
STEELE, Chauncey, of Berlin, m. Rachel **GOODRICH**, Mar. 8, 1820	74
Harriet, of Berlin, m. Leeman **PORTER**, of 1st Society, Feb. 4, 1810	71
Thomas, Jr., of Lenox, Mass., m. Candace **BOARDMAN**, May 13, 1798	67
STEPHENSON, John, s. Thomas, bp. Apr. 26, 1767	118
STERMS, Israel*, of Glastonbury, m. Nabby **BULKLEY**, Apr. 20, 1819 *("Isaac **STEVENS**" in Church Rec.)	74
STEVENS, Elizabeth, m. Charles Churchill **BUTLER**, b. of Rocky Hill, May 7, 1844, by Rev. Calvin Chapin	4
Hannah, wid., of Glastonbury, m. Ephraim **BOWERS**, Nov. 22, 1835	78
Isaac*, of Glastonbury, m. Nabby **BULKLEY**, Apr. 20, 1819 *(Arnold Copy has "Israel **STERMS**")	74
STILLMAN, Elisha, Jr., of 1st Society, m. Huldah **DICKINSON**, Apr. 7, 1800	67
Hope, d. W[illia]m, bp. Feb. 19, 1792	133
Jared Allen, s. W[illia]m, bp. [May] 16, 1790	132
Lois Goodrich, d. W[illia]m, bp. June 2, 1805	139
Mary, d. Samuel, bp. May 21, 1797	135
Mary Amelia, d. Samuel, bp. Oct. 3, 1802	138
Rebecca, m. Samuel **BURR**, of Hartford, June 17, 1773	61
Samuel, s. Samuel, bp. July 5, 1795	134

	Page
STILLMAN, (cont.)	
Samuel, of Sheffield, Mass., m. Roxy **GOODRICH**, June 13, 1820	74
Southmit Russel, s. W[illia]m, bp. Apr. 6, 1788	131
William, s. Samuel, bp. Sept. 7, 1800	137
----------, wid., d. May 16, 1843, ae 81	113
STODDARD, Eben, m. Deborah **WILLIAMS**, Oct. [ ], 1767	60
Elizabeth Williams, d. Edward, bp. Jan. 12, 1784 *("dau. of Eben[eze]r" in Church Rec.)	128
Mary, wid., m. Justus **BLINN**, June 27, 1800	68
Samuel, s. Eb, bp. July 18, 1773	123
STOMER, George, m. Margaret **EBRO**, [Nov. 19], 1767	60
STORRS, Patty, m. Bishop **PHELPS**, Oct. 2, 1791	65
STOW, STOWS, Cornelia, d. Solomon, bp. July 26, 1818	144
Ebenezer, his child d. June 4, 1781	85
Ebenezer, his w. [ ], d. [ ] 15, 1825, ae 74	104
Ebenezer, d. Jan. 14, 1830, ae 77	106
Eleazer, his d. [ ], d. Oct. 3, 1776	84
Emila*, d. Eben[eze]r, bp. Apr. 27, 1783 *("Ursula" in Church Rec.)	128
Emily, d. Ebenezer, bp. May 5, 1776	125
Enos, s. Eben, bp. Aug. 29, 1790	132
Enos, m. Mary Ann **WRIGHT**, May 16, 1814	72
Enos, d. [ ] 19, 1822, ae 33	102
Eunice, w. Solomon, bp. July 5, 1818	144
Horace D., of Cromwell, m. Elizabeth M. **GOODRICH**, of Rocky Hill, Aug. 27, [probably 1854], by Rev. L.B. Rockwood	51
Orson William, s. Solomon, bp. Sept. 24, 1820	145
Roxy, s. Ebenezer, bp. June 10, 1787	130
Roxy, m. Zenas **HUBBARD**, of Berlin, June 13, 1814	72
Ruth, d. Ebenezer, bp. Sept. 10, 1797	136
Ruth*, m. Henry **ROBINSON**, Aug. 28, 1831 *("Ruth **ROBINSON**" in Arnold Copy)	77
Ursula*, d. Eben[eze]r, bp. Apr. 27, 1783 *(Arnold Copy has "Emila")	128
William, s. Sol, bp. Dec. 12, 1818	144
STRONG, Betsey, m. [ ] **BIDWELL**, b. of Glastonbury, Oct. 2, 1799	67
SUGDEN, Eunice Ann, of Middletown, m. John T. **WRIGHT**, of Rocky Hill, Oct. 5, 1848, by Rev. Theodore M. Dwight	28
Robert, Jr., m. Emily Webster **ROBBINS**, b. of Rocky Hill, Feb. 6, 1844, by Rev. C. Chapin	3
Robert A., s. Robert, Jr., bp. [May] 7, 1848	152
SUTLER, John, of Clarerack, m. Anna **REYNOLDS**, Sept. 13, 1784	62
TAYLOR, TAILER, TAYLER, Abigail, d. Timothy, bp. [Apr. 2], 1769	120
Elizabeth, d. Timothy, bp. [Apr. 2], 1769	120
Elizur, s. Stephen, bp. Dec. [ ], 1765	117
Eunice, d. Stephen, bp. Aug. 26, 1770	121
Frederick*, of Berlin, m. wid. On[n]er **EDWARDS**, July 28, 1800 *("Frederick **FAILS**" in Church Rec.)	68
George, of Kent, m. Caroline D. **WILLIAMS**, Mar. 26, 1832	77
Henry R., of Glastonbury, m. Laura O. **HICKOK**, [ ] 20, 1840	79
John, of Glastonbury, m. Phebe **CHAMBERS**, Sept. 25, 1773	61
Justus, s. Timothy, bp. [Apr. 2], 1769	120
Levi, s. Timothy, bp. Dec. 24, 1769	120

BARBOUR COLLECTION

Page

TAYLOR, TAILER, TAYLER, (cont.)
Levi Ely, of Long Meadow, Mass., m. Laura **PRICE**, Dec. 25, 1816	73
Lois, d. Stephen, bp. [Apr. 10], 1768	119
Lucy, d. Stephen, bp. Aug. 16, 1772	122
Lydia, had s. Thomas, bp. Feb. 1, 1767	118
Lydia, m. Michael [ ], Jan. 23, 1771	60
Lydia, wid., d. Jan. 12, 1791, ae 87	90
Molly, d. Stephen, bp. Apr. 28, 1776	125
Simeon, s. Timothy, bp. [Apr. 2], 1769	120
Stephen, s. Stephen, bp. Aug. 28, 1774	124
Thomas, s. Lydia **TAYLOR**, bp. Feb. 1, 1767	118
Warren, of Glastonbury, m. Mary **DEMING**, Dec. 2, 1829	76

TENNANT, Asahel, of Chatham, m. Edna **CHAPMAN**, of Glastonbury, Nov. 1, 1797 — 66

THATCHER, Amy, d. Amos, bp. Oct. 8, 1811 — 142
Charles, s. Amos, bp. Oct. 8, 1811 — 142
George, s. Amos, bp. Oct. 8, 1811 — 142
Polly, d. Amos, bp. Oct. 8, 1811 — 142

THAYER, THEYER, Abigail, wid., d. May 8, 1800, ae 59 — 94
Abigail, d. Jona[than], bp. [Apr. 20], 1806 — 140
Abigail, m. William **LeVAUGHN**, May 19, 1829 — 76
Agnes, d. Jonathan, bp. Sept. 3, 1841 — 150
Chapin, [s. John L. & Betsey], b. Aug. 4, 1828 — 45
Chapin, 2nd, [s. John L. & Betsey], b. Mar. 26, 1831 — 45
Chapin, s. John L., d. Apr. 23, 1842, ae 12 — 112
Cynthia Elizabeth, d. Jonathan, bp. [Sept. 4], 1835 — 148
Edward*, s. Jonathan, bp. [ ], 1835 *("Jonathan Edwards **THAYER**" in Church Rec.) — 148
Elizabeth C., m. Charles P. **SAGE**, b. of Cromwell, Nov. 24, 1852, by Rev. L.B. Rockwood — 42
Ellis, s. Jonathan, bp. [June 29], 1838 — 149
James, [s. John L. & Betsey], b. Dec. 7, 1835 — 45
James, s. John Lewis, bp. Apr. 2, 1842 — 150
John L., b. Feb. 6, 1803, in Rocky Hill, m. Betsey **SLOPER**, Jan. 4, 1826 — 45
John L., m. Lucy B. **WARNER**, b. of Rocky Hill, Jan. 7, 1844, by Rev. John Lovejoy — 3
John Lewis, s. Jonathan, bp. June 12, 1803 — 138
John Lewis, his w. [ ], d. Apr. 13, 1843, ae 36 — 113
Jonathan, m. Honor **EDWARDS**, Sept. 1, 1796 — 66
Jonathan, d. Sept. 13, 1809 — 98
Jonathan, s. wid. of Jonathan, bp. Oct. 1, 1809 — 141
Jonathan, m. wid. Laura **WRIGHT**, [ ] 7, 1828 — 76
Jonathan Edwards, s. Jonathan, bp. Sept. 4, 1835 — 148
Josiah, s. Jonathan, bp. Sept. 7, 1800 — 137
Josiah, m. Lucy Ann **CASWELL***, of Glastonbury, Nov. 16, 1826 *(Arnold Copy has "**CARROLL**") — 75
Josiah, d. Aug. 14, 1839, ae 40 — 110
Laura, w. Jonathan, bp. May 3, 1835 — 148
Lewis, [s. John L. & Betsey], b. Sept. 15, 1826 — 45
Lewis, d. Mar. 3, 1842, ae 16 — 112
Lucy Ann, [wid.], of Rocky Hill, m. Leonard **PACKARD**, of

THAYER, THEYER, (cont.)
 Williamsburg, Mass., Dec. 2, 1849, by Rev. C. Chapin   31
 Lydia, d. Jonathan, bp. Oct. 27, 1798   136
 Margaret, d. Jonathan, bp. July 1, 1836   148
 Maria, d. Jonathan, bp. Sept. 4, 1835   148
 Maria, d. Mar. 25, 1843, ae 15   113
 Mary Chapin, d. John Lewis, bp. Apr. 2, 1842   150
 Mary E., [d. John L. & Betsey], b. Dec. 20, 1829   45
 Mary E., of Rocky Hill, m. John **HOMISS**, of Middletown, May 15,
  1851, by Rev. F.W. Bill   36
 Welthy, [d. John L. & Betsey], b. July 25, 1834   45
 Wealthy, d. John Lewis, bp. Apr. 2, 1842   150
THOMAS, Asaph U., of New Britain, m. Mary E. **FLINT**, Nov. 29, 1835   78
THOMPSON, Benoni, of Bristol, m. Polly **BELDEN**, Jan. 1, 1818   74
 Cyrus, of Hartford, m. Ursula **WILLIAMS**, July 28, 1823   75
TILDEN*, Stephen, of Lebanon, m. Dorothy **GOODRICH**, Jan. 16, 1787
 *(Arnold Copy has "**BELDEN**")   63
TREAT, Jane, wid., of Glastonbury, m. Peter **BLINN**, Nov. 2, 1800   68
 John, m. Prudence **HANMORE**, Oct. 16, 1782   62
 Joseph, of Middletown, m. Nancy **HOLMES**, Oct. 5, 1820   74
 Julia M., of Norfolk, m. Daniel **HOLMES**, Dec. 26, 1833   78
 Levi, of Glastonbury, m. Mary **BLINN**, Apr. 30, 1804   69
 Levi, d. Nov. 28, 1805, in New York   96
 M[ ], wid., d. Oct. 2, 1839, at Hartford, ae 66   110
 Sally, of Glastonbury, m. William **BLYN**, May 10, 1797   66
TRILBY*, Abby Menerva, m. Richard **RALPH**, of Middletown, Mar. 12,
  1833, by Dr. Calvin Chapin   *("**KILBY**" in Church Rec.)   77
TRYON, Ezekiel, m. Betsey **HARRIS**, b. of Glastonbury, Aug. 11, 1799   67
 Hannah, m. Josiah **GILBERT**, of Berlin, Nov. 11, 1790   65
 Isaac, 3rd, of Glastonbury, m. Abigail **SHAYLOR**, Sept. 9, 1813   72
 Jane C., m. Wardsworth F. **BLINN**, June 21, 1853, by Rev. L.B.
  Rockwood   45
 Jessie, of Glastonbury, m. Weltha **SHAYLOR**, July 15, 1804   69
 Mary, wid., of Chatham, m. Reuben **ABBE**, of Glastonbury, July 9, 1812   72
 William, Jr., of Glastonbury, m. Roeweny **SHAYLOR**, Sept. 8, 1808   70
TUCKER, Alpha, of Bolton, m. Elizabeth **MISNER**, [Feb.] 12, [1798]   67
 Martha, of Wethersfield, m. Henry **BULKLEY**, of Rocky Hill, May 16,
  1847, by Rev. C. Chapin   23
 Mary, m. Josiah **WELLES**, May 11, 1786   63
 Zabor, of "Putty Paug," d. July 19, 1795, ae 66   92
TUTTLE, Hezekiah, of Rocky Hill, m. Ann M. **CLARK**, of Guilford, Aug. 7,
  1852, by Rev. L. Burton Rockwood   41
WADSWORTH, Mary, of East Hartford, m. Gurdon **GOODRICH**, 2nd, Nov.
  6, 1814   72
WAIT*, Oliver, m. Nancy **PRICE**, of Chatham, July 22, 1832   *("**WEST**" in
  Church Rec.)   77
WALCOTT, Ambrose, of Winsted, m. Julia **BELDEN**, Apr. 6, 1834   78
WALTON, Almira, d. Silas, bp. [Oct. 3], 1790   132
 Lemuel Hurlburt, s. John, bp. July 8, 1792   133
 Richard Belding, s. John, bp. July 8, 1792   133
 Silas, m. Rosetta **BELDING**, [ ] 27, 1787   64

WARD, Isaac, of Pittsfield, Mass., m. Mary **NEFF**, [　　] 17, 1836   78
  Lucretia, of Middletown, m. Anthony **SEZER**, Jan. 4, 1785   63
  Rebecca, of Glastonbury, m. Marquis **CHURCHILL**, May 14, 1807   70
WARNER, Abigail, d. Wait, d. [　　] 13, 1776   84
  Abigail, m. Daniel **WILLIAMS**, Mar. 24, 1807   70
  Abigail, wid., d. Apr. 19, 1841, ae 73   111
  Albert A., of Wilmington, N.C., m. Jane M. **BURKITT**, of Rocky Hill, Oct. 12, 1845, by Rev. C. Chapin   14
  Albert A., his w. [　　], d. Dec. 6, 1848, ae 26   116
  Allen, s. Daniel, bp. Mar. 24, 1771   121
  Andrew, d. Sept. 27, 1811, lost at sea   99
  Anna Butler, d. Levi, bp. Aug. 9, 1789   132
  Aurelia*, d. Daniel, Jr., bp. Sept. 4, 1796   *(Arnold Copy has "Marilia")   135
  Caroline, d. Daniel, bp. Sept. 21, 1815   143
  Daniel, m. wid. Sarah **GRISWOLD**, Apr. 24, 1766   60
  Daniel, s. Daniel, bp. Feb. 1, 1767   118
  Daniel, his servant Doyglas, d. June 5, 1788   88
  Dan[ie]l, d. July 16, 1798, ae 56   93
  Daniel, d. June 16, 1822, ae 56   102
  Elias*, his wid., d. Aug. 16, 1789   *("wid. Eliz. **WARNER**, ae 83" in Church Rec.)   89
  Elizabeth, m. Ezekiel **GOODRICH**, Jan. 1, 1783   62
  Elizabeth, m. Levi **BOARDMAN**, Sept. 2, 1790   65
  Elizabeth, d. Levi, bp. Oct. 23, 1791   133
  Elizabeth*, d. Enos, bp. [Nov.] 24, 1805   *("Elizabeth **SKINNER**" in Church Rec.)   140
  Enos, s. Roger, bp. Mar. 5, 1769   120
  Eunice, d. Roger, bp. Oct. 20, 1765   117
  Eunice, d. Daniel, bp. Dec. 25, 1768   120
  Eunice, m. Gideon **GOODRICH**, Feb. 22, 1787   64
  Eunice, m. Samuel **DIMOCK**, Oct. 8, 1804   69
  Eunice*, d. Enos, bp. [Nov.] 24, 1805   *("Eunice **SKINNER**" in Church Rec.)   140
  Frederick, s. Daniel, bp. Mar. 7, 1773   123
  Frederic, m. Lucretia **GOODRICH**, Nov. 14, 1809   71
  Frederick, d. July 22, 1813, ae 41   99
  Hannah, d. Roger, bp. [Aug.　　], 1767   118
  Hannah, m. James **MITCHELL**, Mar. 30, 1772   61
  Harriet, d. Enos, bp. [June] 26, 1808   141
  Harriet, wid., bp. Jan. 6, 1839   149
  Hope, d. Wait, bp. Dec. 24, 1769   120
  Hope, d. Wait, d. Sept. 25, 1773   82
  Hope, d. Wait, bp. Aug. 28, 1774   124
  Huldah Welles, d. Levi, bp. June 22, 1794   134
  James, of Wethersfield, m. Martha **GARDNER**, of Rocky Hill, June 17, 1849, by Rev. Philo Judson   29
  Jane, d. Wait, bp. Aug. 25, 1765   117
  Jane, d. Wait, d. Dec. 2, 1786, ae 22   88
  John, d. Oct. 26, 1786, ae 82   88
  Jon[atha]n, d. Oct. 4, 1786, ae 74   88

	Page
WARNER, (cont.)	
Lauretta, d. Daniel, bp. May 25, 1800	137
Lauretta, m. George **MORTON**, Dec. 5, 1830	77
Levi, m. Anna **BUTLER**, of Middletown, Sept. 1, 1782	61
Levi, his w. [ ], d. Dec. 13, 1782, ae 20	85
Levi, his infant, d. Apr. 23, 1787	88
Levi, s. Levi, bp. June 26, 1796	135
Levi, d. Jan. 26, 1803, ae 48	95
Lois, m. Benjamin **AMES**, Sept. 8, 1785	63
Lucy, d. Daniel, bp. Apr. 2, 1775	124
Lucy, m. Russel **BULL**, Dec. 17, 1795	66
Lucy B., m. John L. **THEYER**, b. of Rocky Hill, Jan. 7, 1844, by Rev. John Lovejoy	3
Lucy Bull, d. Daniel, bp. [Nov. 3], 1805	140
Marilia*, d. Daniel, bp. Sept. 4, 1796 *("Aurelia, da. Daniel, Jr." in Church Rec.)	135
Martha, adopted d. Roger, bp. Nov. 21, 1819	145
Martha G., m. Melzar **GARDNER**, of Hartford, Dec. 31, 1832	77
Martha Honora, d. Daniel, bp. Nov. 19, 1809	142
Mary, d. Jonathan, d. [ ] 23, 1783, ae 49	86
Mary, wid., d. Nov. 3*, 1811, ae 98 *("Nov. 23" in Church Rec.)	99
Mehetable, m. Josiah **GRIMES**, Jr., June 14, 1773	61
Metty, m. John **BENTON**, Nov. 29, 1798	67
Patty, d. Daniel, bp. Feb. 10*, 1781, by Rev. Mr. Lewis *("Feb. 18" in Church Rec.)	126
Patty, m. Abijah **COLLINS**, Jan. 9, 1812	71
Prudence, m. Josiah **WOLCOTT**, Mar. 25, 1772	61
Rachel, d. Wait, bp. Jan. 24, 1768	119
Rachel, m. Jacob **GRISWOLD**, Dec. 25, 1785	63
Rhoda Butler, d. Enos, bp. [July] 22, 1810	142
Robbins, d. Nov. 7, 1805, ae 36	96
Roger, d. Dec. 12, 1770	82
Roger, s. Wait, bp. May 26, 1776	125
Roger, m. Nancy **WETHERELL**, Nov. 2, 1803	68
Roger, his w. [ ], d. Oct. 15, 1807, ae 25, at Troy, N.Y.	97
Roger, d. Feb. 17, 1839, ae 62	110
Sally, m. John **WILLIAMS**, Apr. 17, 1806	69
Sarah, d. Wait, bp. Jan. 3, 1773	123
Sarah*, d. Wait, bp. Oct. 10, 1779, by Rev. Mr. Pitkin, of Farmington *("Sarah **ROBBINS**" in Church Rec.)	126
Sarah, m. Joseph **DIMOCK**, Jr., Aug. 12, 1789	64
Sarah, wid., d. Apr. 15, 1808, ae 69	98
Sarah, m. Oliver **GOODRICH** [ ]	60
Wait, his w. [ ], d. Dec. 19, 1795, ae 59	92
Wait, d. [ ] 19, 1804, ae 72	96
Wait, s. Roger, bp. Nov. 1, 1812	142
Walter, s. Roger, bp. Feb. 2, 1806	140
Walter, m. Melissa **GRISWOLD**, Mar. 10, 1831	77
Walter, his child d. Aug. 30, 1838, ae 2	110
Warren, s. Dan[ie]l, Jr., bp. Sept. 10, 1797	136
Watson W., m. Harriet **WHEAT**, Dec. 25, 1817	73

	Page
WARNER, (cont.)	
Watson Williams, s. Daniel, bp. Sept. 4, 1796	135
Wells, s. Levi, bp. Aug. 17, 1800	137
William, of 1st Society, m. Mercy **GOODRICH**, Nov. 27, 1808	70
W[illia]m Wait, s. Wait, bp. Apr. 15, 1781, by Rev. Mr. Lewis	126
William Wait, s. Roger, bp. Nov. 4, 1804	139
William Wait, m. Maria Webb **FLINT**, Mar. 19, 1829	76
WARREN*, Levi, his child d. Apr. 19, 1783, ae 1 *("WARNER" in Church Rec.)	86
WEAR, WEARE, Diana, d. W[illia]m, bp. Aug. 14, 1785	129
W[illia]m, m. Martha **MILLER**, Oct. 11, 1784	62
WEBB, Abigail, d. David, bp. Dec. 21, 1766	118
Abigail, d. wid. [ ], d. Sept. 29, 1775	83
Abigail, d. W[illia]m, bp. Sept. 18, 1795	134
Abigail, d. W[illia]m, d. Sept. 19, 1795	92
Belinda, d. W[illia]m, bp. Aug. 30, 1807	140
Belinda, m. Thomas **GOODRICH**, Feb. 27, 1828	76
Benjamin G., m. Elizabeth B. **WHITMORE**, [May] 31, 1837	79
Catharine Bryan, bp. Nov. 5, 1841	150
Charlotte, d. W[illia]m, bp. May 11, 1800	137
Charlotte, d. Apr. 23, 1824, ae 26	103
David, his servant Rose, m. May **DICK**, servant of Elias **WILLIAMS**, [ ], 1768	60
David, d. Oct. 9, 1770	82
Elizabeth, m. Samuel **FOSTER**, Sept. 4, 1769	60
Esther, m. Joseph **NEFF**, Nov. 5, 1772	61
Henry, s. W[illia]m, bp. Nov. 11, 1803	139
Henry, s. W[illia]m, bp. Apr. 14, 1805	139
John, d. Sept. 9, 1769	81
Katy, d. Oct. 8, 1775	83
Martha, d. David, bp. Mar. 5, 1769	120
Martha, d. wid., d. Feb. 14, 1776	83
Mary, m. Joshua **WILLIAMS**, A.B., Oct. 24, 1781	61
Mary, wid., d. Aug. 6, 1808, ae 81	98
Nancy, m. Reuben **BARNES**, of Middletown, May 15, 1814	72
Polly, d. W[illia]m, bp. Apr. 9, 1797	135
Rodolphus L., bp. July 2, 1848	152
Rodolphus L., m. Harriet M. **WILLIAMS**, Nov. 26, 1851, by Rev. L.B. Rockwood	38
Susan, bp. Jan. 1, 1837	149
Susan, m. Edward **WHITMORE**, [ ] 20, 1838	79
W[illia]m, s. David, bp. Feb. 17, 1765	117
W[illia]m, m. Charlotte **GRISWOLD**, Apr. 10, 1791	65
W[illia]m, his child d. Oct. 22, 1793	91
William, s. William, bp. June 6, 1802	138
William, d. Apr. 2, 1843, ae 80	113
William H., of Rockingham, N.C., m. Augusta B. **ROBBINS**, of Rocky Hill, Feb. 3, 1850, by Rev. Calvin Chapin	32
WEBSTER, Allis L., of Mansfield, O., m. Lucetta **DILLINGS**, of Rocky Hill, Nov. 10, 1844, by Rev. C. Chapin	7
Anne, of Berlin, m. William **MILLER**, Oct. 6, 1812	72

	Page
WEBSTER, (cont.)	
Jacob, of Glastonbury, m. Abigail **GOODRICH**, May 13, 1770	60
William, of West Hartford, m. Abigail **JOHNSON**, of Berlin, July 25, 1800	68
WEED, Abigail, m. Jonathan **HAND**, of Long Island, Feb. 17, 1781	61
Elizabeth, m. John **GIBBS**, May 13, 1773	61
Jacob, s. James, bp. July 12, 1772	122
James, his w. [ ], d. July 25, 1787, ae 59	88
James, d. Jan. 17, 1789, ae 63	89
Mary, d. Belding, bp. Apr. 29, 1781, by Rev. Mr. Lewis	126
WELLES, Elisha, m. Sarah **ABBE**, b. of 1st Society, [ ], 1805	69
Elizabeth, of 1st Society, Newington, m. Henry **MYEARS**, of [ ], Apr. 5, 1810	71
Gideon, d. Feb. 11, 1795, on passage from West Indies, ae 38	92
John, m. Martha **BELDEN**, Nov. 26, 1765	60
Josiah, m. Mary **TUCKER**, May 11, 1786	63
Sally, of Berlin, m. Daniel **BLINN**, Jan. 17, 1802	68
WELTON, Eben, of Farmington, m. Olive **COLLINS**, Nov. [ ], 1767	60
WEST*, Oliver, of Chatham, m. Nancy **PRICE**, July 22, 1832 *(Arnold Copy has "**WAIT**")	77
WESTOVER, Noah, d. [ ], 1834, ae 57	108
WETHERELL, WITHERELL, Daniel Bulkley, s. Elisha, bp. Aug. 14, 1785	129
Dan[ie]l Bulkley, s. Elis. d. Dec. 27, 1785	87
Elisha, m. Mary **BULKLEY**, Jan. 26, 1783	62
Elisha, d. May 12, 1818, ae 58	101
Fanny, d. Elisha, bp. Apr. 26, 1801	137
Fanny, m. Henry L. **PARSONS**, of Lenox, Mass., Nov. 24, 1825	75
Nancy, m. Roger **WARNER**, Nov. 2, 1803	68
Nany*, d. Elisha, bp. Oct. 3, 1784 *("Nancy" in Church Rec.)	129
Polly, d. Elisha, bp. Sept. 6, 1789	132
Polly, m. Amasa **MORGAN**, of 1st Society, Apr. 22, 1813	72
WHAPLES, Calvin, of Newington, m. Nancy S. **BLINN**, Dec. 28, 1842	80
Calvin*, his w. d. Nov. 21, 1844, ae 25 *("Calvin **WHAPLEY**" in Arnold Copy)	114
WHEAT, Harriet, m. Watson W. **WARNER**, Dec. 25, 1817	73
Mabel, d. Jan. 17, 1823, ae 20	102
Samuel, of Chatham, m. Mabel **COLLINS**, of Glastonbury, July 5, 1797	66
WHITE, Alice Ann, d. Henry A*, bp. July 1, 1842 *("d. of Henry Augustus **WHITE**" in Church Rec.)	150
Hannah, d. James, bp. Oct. 21, 1781	127
Hannah, m. John **BOWERS**, of Chatham, Feb 16, 1803	68
Henry Augustus, bp. July 4, 1841	149
James, d. between May 7 & Aug. 17, 1782, at New York (Soldier)	85
Luther, of Middletown, m. Emily R. **PHELPS**, Oct. 9, 1831	77
Mercy, m. Israel **GOODRICH**, Jan. 4, 1785	63
Sarah Jane, d. Henry A., bp. Aug. 10, 1848	152
WHITFORD, Lorin B*., m. Diantha **KILBY**, of Wethersfield, [ ] 18, 1843 *("Lorin R." in Church Rec.)	80
WHITMAN, Mary Ann, of East Hartford, m. Marshall **NOTT**, of Rocky Hill, Dec. 15, 1850, by Rev. L.B. Rockwood	34
Sally, d. Hezekiah, bp. Aug. 5, 1792 *(Arnold Copy has "Sally	

WHITMAN, (cont.)

	Page
WHITMORE")	133
WHITMORE, Asa, s. Hezekiah, bp. June 22, 1789	131
Asa, s. Hezekiah, d. June 29*, 1789 *("22" in Church Rec.)	89
Betsey, d. Oct. 1, 1843, ae 54	113
Celestia Madorah, d. Edward, bp. May 26, 1839	149
Celia Ann, d. Edward, bp. July 2, 1841	149
Charles, s. Henry, bp. Aug. 4, 1822	145
Charlotte, m. Wait C. **BULKLEY**, May 10, 1838	79
Chauncey, of Rocky Hill, m. Jane **BOWERS**, of Cromwell, Aug. 14, 1853, by Rev. L.Burton Rockwood	46
Cynthia, d. Hezekiah, bp. [Sept. 4], 1796	135
Cynthia, m. Levi **GOODRICH**, 2nd, Sept. 12, 1816	73
Cynthia Higgins*, d. Dorothy **WHITMORE**, bp. Oct. 1, 1786 *("Cynthia Higgins **WILLIAMS**" in Church Rec.)	130
Dorothy*, had d. Cynthia Higgins, bp. Oct. 1, 1786 *("Dorothy **WILLIAMS**" in Church Rec.)	130
Edward, s. Henry. bp. [Nov. 10], 1816	143
Edward, m. Susan **WEBB**, [ ] 20, 1838	79
Eliza, m. Samuel **BLINN**, of Wethersfield, Aug. 31, 1842	80
Elizabeth, d. Hezekiah, bp. Aug. 1, 1790	132
Elizabeth, d. Henry, bp. [Nov. 10], 1816	143
Elizabeth B., m. Benjamin G. **WEBB**, [May] 31, 1837	79
Elvira, d. Henry, bp. [Nov. 10], 1816	143
Elvira, m. Phineas T. **MILLER**, of Westville, Aug. 31, 1836	79
Henry, s. Hezekiah, bp. May 21, 1786	130
Henry, s. Henry, bp. [Nov. 10], 1816	143
Hezekiah, s. Hezekiah, bp. Sept. 16, 1798	136
Hezekiah, his w. [ ], d. Dec. 16, 1831, ae 69	107
Hezekiah, Jr., d. Aug. 28, 1835, ae 38	109
Hezekiah, d. [ ], 1842, ae 86	112
Jerusha M., m. Frances C. **LOVEJOY**, Dec. 8, 1844, by Rev. Joseph L. Morse	6
Martha A., m. James Henry **MORGAN**, [of New Britain], Nov. 14, 1847, by Rev. Calvin Chapin	24
Mehetable, d. Hezekiah, bp. Mar. 30, 1788	131
Mehetable, d. Hezekiah, d. July 22, 1788	88
Nancy, twin with Norman, d. Hezekiah, bp. Sept. 26, 1802	138
Nancy, m. Charles H. **HASTINGS**, Sept. 3, 1834	78
Nancy A., of Wethersfield, m. Levi **ADAMS**, Apr. 5, 1846, by Charles Bartlet	18
Norman, twin with Nancy, s. Hezekiah, bp. Sept. 26, 1802	138
Norman, m. Eliza Jane **GRAHAM**, July 28, 1830	77
Norman, his w. [ ], d. Sept. 23, 1845, ae 43	114
Phineas B., of New Haven, m. Abigail M. **DIMOCK**, Jan. 23, 1828	76
Phinehas Brainard, s. Hezekiah, bp. Apr. 8, 1804	139
Polly, d. Hezekiah, bp. Apr. 24, 1785	129
Polly, m. Horace **HOUGH**, of Wallingford, [June] 7, [1801]	68
Richard Graham, s. Norman, bp. Sept. 3, 1841	150
Sally*, d. Hezekiah, bp. Aug. 5, 1792 *("Sally **WHITMAN**" in Church Rec.)	133

	Page
WHITMORE, (cont.)	
Sally, m. William **GOODRICH**, Jr., May 5, 1813	72
Sally Goodrich, d. Henry, bp. [Nov. 10], 1816	143
Sally Goodrich, d. Apr. 15, 1834*, ae 17 *("1833" in Church Rec.)	107
Sylvester, s. Hezekiah, bp. July 13, 1794	134
Sylvester, m. Oner **MILLER**, Sept. 28, 1815	73
William, m. Delia A. **WRIGHT**, Aug. 25, 1852, by Rev. L.Burton Rockwood	41
WHITNEY, James S., of Pittsfield, Mass., m. Eliza **NEFF**, Feb. 15, 1830	76
William F., of Harvard, Mass., m. Jane A. **FLINT**, Jan. 1, 1840	79
WILCOX, Chester, of Bristol, m. Sarah D. **GRISWOLD**, Sept. 3, 1823	75
Luther, of Middletown, m. Huldah **PILSIFER**, of Glastonbury, Oct. 1, 1794, by Rev. Mr. Fenn	65
Moses, of Colebrook, m. Lydia **LANCEY**, [ ] 22, 1787	64
Moses, m. Mary **MILLER**, b. of Middletown, Apr. 16, 1801	68
Roxana S., of Rocky Hill, m. John G. **DAVENPORT**, of New Haven, Dec. 29, 1844, by Rev. John Lovejoy	8
Sylvester, of Berlin, m. Ruhamah **DICKINSON**, Apr. 27, 1812	72
WILDER, Abigail Sophia, d. Naham, bp. [ ], 1830	146
Abigail Sophia, m. Walter **ROBBINS**, Nov. 3, 1839	79
John Lyman, s. Naham, bp. [ ], 1830	146
Laura Parsons, d. Naham, bp. [ ], 1830	146
Nahum, d. Aug. 22, 1839, ae 49	110
Naham Cornelius, s. Naham, bp. July 1, 1831	147
William Smith, s. Naham, bp. [July 4], 1834	148
WILKINSON*, J[oh]n, his child d. Nov. 4, 1775 *(Arnold Copy has "**WILLIAMS**")	83
John*, d. May 5, 1807, ae 78 *("John **WILLIAMS**" in Arnold Copy)	97
Mehitabel, wid., d. Mar. 4, 1820, ae 87	101
Rebecca, m. James **HAMMOND**, of Hartford, [ ] 25, 1787	64
Sarah*, m. Daniel **WRIGHT**, of Farmington, June 24, 1784 *(Arnold Copy has "Sarah **DICKINSON**")	62
W[illia]m, d. Nov. or Dec. [ ], 1786, at Sea	88
WILLARD, Elias, of Trenton, N.Y., m. Sally **GOODRICH**, Feb. 8, 1807	70
Elizur*, of Greenville, N.Y., m. Elizabeth **DIMOCK**, [May] 12, 1816 *("Elizur **KIRTLAND**" in Church Rec.)	73
Sarah R., of Rocky Hill, m. Chauncey **COLEMAN**, of Wethersfield, Oct. 30, 1844, by Rev. C. Chapin	6
WILLIAMS, Abigail, d. Daniel, bp. May 22, 1768	119
Abigail, wid., m. Eliakim **SMITH**, June 2, 1813	72
Abigail, bp. Sept. 6, 1818 *(Church Rec. say "adult dau. of Luther **GOODRICH**)	144
Abigail, m. William Hubbard **ROBBINS**, [ ] 14, 1828	76
Ackley, s. Eliel, bp. [Apr.] 19, 1789	131
Ackley, his w. [ ], d. May 27, 1824, ae 35	103
Ackley, m. Harriet **PRICE**, Jan. 26, 1825	75
Aenus*, s. Eph[raim], bp. Oct. 29, 1786 *("Nenus" in Church Rec.)	130
Alan, s. Ephraim, bp. Apr. 29, 1781, by Rev. Mr. Lewis	126
Albert Irwin, twin with Alfred Henry, s. Wait, bp. [May 4], 1832	147
Alfred Henry, twin with Albert Irwin, s. Wait, bp. [May 4], 1832	147
Allen, d. July 14, 1817, ae 37	101

WILLIAMS, (cont.)

Entry	Page
Almira, d. Richard, bp. Sept. 11, 1803	139
Almira, m. Archibald **ROBBINS**, June 18, 1823	75
Amos, s. Jesse, bp. Sept. 23, 1781	127
Andrew, s. W[illia]m, bp. Sept. 4, 1785	129
Andrew, m. Mary Caroline **HICKOK**, Feb. 24, 1835	78
Andrew, d. Dec. 12, 1839, ae 55	111
Asa, s. Jesse, bp. June 3, 1781	127
Asahel, s. Jesse, bp. June 3, 1781	127
Asher, s. Jesse, d. Apr. 9 or 19, 1781	84
Bemis*, s. Eph[raim], d. Aug. 26, 1790 *("Venus or Nenus" in Church Rec.)	90
Betsey, d. Sept. 28, 1807, ae 28	97
Caroline, d. Jesse, bp. June 3, 1781	127
Caroline D., m. George **TAYLOR**, of Kent, Mar. 26, 1832	77
Caroline Danforth, d. Richard, bp. Oct. 11, 1801	138
Caroline Elizabeth, d. Tho[ma]s D., bp. May 5, 1848	152
Caroline Maria, d. Wait, bp. May 16, 1830	146
Catharine, d. Washington, bp. Oct. 11, 1807	141
Catharine, d. Dec. 10, 1846, ae 40	115
Catharine Louisa, d. Moses W., bp. [July 2], 1847	151
Charles, s. John, bp. [Sept.] 27, 1807	140
Charles, m. Caroline Amelia **CASWELL**, of Glastonbury, Nov. 29, 1827	76
Charles, his infant twin d. Sept. 27, 1833, ae [ ]	108
Charles Watson, s. Charles, bp. [Jan.] 5, 1844	151
Chester, s. Ephraim, bp. July 23, 1775	125
Chester, m. Patty **GOODRICH**, Aug. 16, 1795	66
Chester, d. Dec. 22, 1819, ae 45	101
Chloe, m. Jacob **ROBBINS**, Dec. 10, 1772	61
Chloe*, d. W[illia]m, bp. Oct. 26, 1783 *("Chlora" in Church Rec.)	128
Chloe, m. Benjamin **ARCHER**, July 18, 1822	75
Chlora*, d. W[illia]m, bp. Oct. 26, 1783 *("Chloe" in Arnold Copy)	128
Christian, d. Daniel, bp. Dec. 9, 1770	121
Comfort, s. Eliel, bp. Apr. 27, 1783	128
Comfort, m. Lucy **WILLIAMS**, May 20, 1811	71
Comfort, Rev., his w. [ ], d. Sept. 21, 1824, ae 42	104
Cornelius, s. Washington, bp. [May 4], 1806	140
Cynthia, d. Daniel, bp. June 25, 1809	141
Cynthia Higgins*, d. Dorothy, bp. Oct. 1, 1786 *("Cynthia Higgins **WHITMORE**" in Arnold Copy)	130
Daniel, s. Daniel, bp. Sept. 24, 1775	125
Daniel, d. Apr. 12, 1797, ae 59	93
Daniel, m. Abigail **WARNER**, Mar. 24, 1807	70
Daniel, d. Aug. 30, 1810, ae 36	98
Daniel, s. Daniel, bp. June 2, 1811	142
Deborah, s. Eben Stoddard, Oct. [ ], 1767	60
Diah, s. Elias, d. [, 1785]	87
Dorothy, m. Enos **ROBBINS**, May 27, 1794, by Mr. Chapin	65
Eleanor, d. Daniel, bp. Sept. 5, 1773	123
Eleanor, m. Davis **DIMOCK**, July 8, 1798	67
Elias, his servant May **DICK**, m. Rose, servant of David Webb, [ ],	

	Page
WILLIAMS, (cont.)	
1768	60
Elias, m. Mary **DIMOCK**, Feb. 19, 1787	64
Elias, his servant Lettace, d. Feb. 24, 1787	88
Elias, 2nd his w. [ ], d. Dec. 3, 1788	89
Elias, his w. [ ], d. [ ], 1794, ae 24	91
Elias, d. Dec. 5, 1798, ae 81	94
Elias, d. Mar. 15, 1801, ae 33	95
Eliel, m. Comfort **MORTON**, Jan. 26, 1769	60
Eliel, his w. [ ], d. Aug. 17, 1811, ae 65	99
Eliel, d. May 2, 1819, ae 77	101
Elizabeth, d. Eliel, bp. Oct. 15, 1775	125
Elizabeth, d. Silas, bp. [Oct.] 26, 1806	140
Elizabeth Morton, d. Merriam, bp. May 1, 1831	147
Elizabeth Tolman, m. Archibald **ROBBINS**, May 3, 1836	78
Ellen, d. Horace, bp. [ ], 1830	146
Ellen Augusta, d. Charles, bp. [Jan.] 5, 1844	151
Ephraim, his infant d. May 14, 1787	88
Ephraim, d. Apr. 22, 1793, ae 30	91
Ephraim, s. John, bp. Apr. 28, 1793	133
Ephraim, his wid. [ ], d. Aug. 6, 1794, ae 52	91
Esther, d. Daniel, bp. May 26, 1765	117
Eunice, m. Elisha **BUTLER**, Oct. 19, 1769	60
Eunice, wid., d. Apr. 14, 1770	82
Eunice, m. David **BECKLEY**, Jr., Mar. 31, 1785	63
Eunice, d. John, bp. Jan. 17, 1790	132
Eunice, m. George **ROBBINS**, Sept. 14, 1815	73
Eunice, wid., d. Jan. 7, 1821, ae 73	102
Fanny Eliza, d. Achley, bp. May 12, 1822	145
Fanny Eliza, d. July 5, 1834*, ae 12 *("1833" in Church Rec.)	107
Francis, s. Horace, bp. [ ], 1830	146
Francis Louisa, d. Washington, bp. June 2, 1816	143
Frances Louisa, of Rocky Hill, m. Rev. Richard **WOODRUFF**, of Unionville, Dec. 12, 1843, by Rev. C. Chapin	2
Frances Louisa, m. Rev. Richard **WOODRUFF**, of Unionville, Dec. 12, 1843	80
George, d. Feb. 5, 1824	103
George Lewis, s. Ephraim, bp. May 4, 1783	128
George Lewis, d. [ ], 1799, ae 17, in West Indies	94
George Lewis, s. Wyllis, bp. Aug. 16, 1801	137
Hannah, wid., d. Jan. 3, 1815, ae 40	100
Harriet, m. Burrage **MERRIAM**, [Feb.] 11, 1829	76
Harriet M., m. Rodolphus L. **WEBB**, Nov. 26, 1851, by Rev. L.B. Rockwood	38
Harriet Maria, d. William, bp. Oct. 3, 1802	138
Harriet Maria, d. Horace, bp. July 1, 1831	147
Henry Chapman, s. Moses N., bp. [July 5], 1844	151
Henry Davis*, s. Horace, bp. [ ], 1830 *(Arnold Copy has "Sidney Davis **WILLIAMS**")	146
Henry Dewitt, s. Charles, bp. June 8, 1843	150
Hetty, m. Edward **CULVER**, Jan. 21, 1796	66

	Page
WILLIAMS, (cont.)	
Honor, d. Moses, bp. Aug. 17, 1766	118
Honor, m. John **LEEDS**, of Stamford, Dec. 5, 1796	66
Horace, s. W[illia]m, bp. Dec. 29, 1793	134
Horace, m. Rachal **DIMOCK**, Nov. 6, 1816	73
Horace, s. Horace, bp. [ ], 1830	146
Horace, his w. [ ], d. July 21, 1844, ae 50	114
Irene* Elvira, d. Achley, bp. Aug. 23, 1818 *("Jane Elvira" in Church Rec.)	144
Isaac*, s. W[illia]m, bp. Oct. 30, 1791 *("Israel" in Church Rec.)	133
Israel, his child d. Nov. 6, 1775	83
Israel, s. W[illia]m, bp. July 31, 1788	131
Israel, d. Aug. 19, 1811, ae 68	99
J.L., Rev., (of Upper Houses), d. [ ], 1832, ae 48	107
Jacob, his s*.[ ], d. May 29, 1783 *("Infant child" in Church Rec.)	86
Jacob, his infant d. Jan. 6, 1788	88
Jacob, his child d. Apr. 1, 1796	93
Jacob, his w. [ ], d. July 6, 1798	93
Jacob, s. Silas, bp. Jan. 12, 1800	137
Jacob, d. Oct. 30, 1813, ae 59	99
James Andrew, s. Horace, bp. Aug. 30, 1833	147
Jane* Elvira, d. Achley, bp. Aug. 23, 1818 *("Irene Elvira" in Arnold Copy)	144
Jerusha, m. Levi **WILLIAMS**, Apr. 13, 1786	63
Jesse, m. Lois **COLLINS**, Sept. 19, 1771	61
Jesse, his child d. Oct. 21, 1775	83
J[oh]n*, his child d. Nov. 4, 1775 *("J[oh]n **WILKINSON**" in Church Rec.)	83
John, m. Eunice **BULL**, May 6, 1784	62
John, his w. [ ], d. Sept. 1, 1805, ae 37	96
John, m. Sally **WARNER**, Apr. 17, 1806	69
John *, d. May 5, 1807, ae 78 *("John **WILKINSON**" in Church Rec.)	97
John, his servant Phebe, d. July 12, 1809, ae 87 or 88	98
John, s. John, bp. [ ] 22, 1809	141
John, d. Aug. 13, 1827, ae 65	105
John Hinman, s. Charles, bp. [Jan. 5], 1844	151
John M*, s. Rev. J.L.W., d. Dec. 30, 1832 *(Arnold Copy has "John M. **MOSES**")	107
Joseph Dimock, s. Horace, bp. [ ], 1830	146
Joshua, A.B., m. Mary **WEBB**, Oct. 24, 1781	61
Joshua, Rev., d. Feb. 8, 1836, at Up. Middletown, ae 76	109
Joshua Lewis*, s. Joshua, bp. Mar. 6, 1785 *("son of Joshua **WILLIAMS**, A.M., Pastor elect, of S. Hampton, L.I." Church Rec.)	129
Julia Marinda, d. Achley, bp. Aug. 23, 1818	144
Levi, s. Ephraim, bp. Apr. 7, 1765	117
Levi, m. Jerusha **WILLIAMS**, Apr. 13, 1786	63
Levi, his w. [ ], d. Aug. 18, 1801	95
Levi, d. Oct. 26, 1803, ae [ ]	96
Lois, m. Jasper **GRAHAM**, [ ] 28, 1823	75
Lorenzo Lewis, s. Wyllis, bp. Apr. 24, 1808	141
Lucretia, m. Filer **GOODRICH**, Oct. 9, 1783	62

	Page
WILLIAMS, (cont.)	
Lucy, bp. Jan. 3, 1802, adult	138
Lucy, m. Comfort **WILLIAMS**, May 20, 1811	71
Luther Boardman, s. Thomas D., bp. Aug. 30, 1844	151
Lydia, m. Aaron **BULL**, Aug. 9, 1786	63
Lydia, his wid. [ ], d. [ ] 23, 1819	101
Maria* Ann, d. Jacob, bp. Oct. 30, 1803 *("Mary" in Church Rec.)	139
Maria R., m. Bryan E. **HOOKER**, of Bristol, Mar. 27, 1833	77
Maria Robbins, d. Washington, bp. Nov. 15, 1812	142
Marshal Thompson, s. Charles, bp. [Jan.] 5, 1844	151
Martha, m. Solomon **BULKLEY**, June 6, 1776, by Mr. Lewis	61
Martha, wid., m. George **RISLY**, [ ] 23, 1820	74
Martha Griswold, d. Charles, bp. [Jan. 5], 1844	151
Martha Palmer*, d. Merriam, bp. May 12, 1822 *("Martha Talman **WILLIAMS**" in Church Rec.)	145
Mary, m. Joseph **BULKLEY**, May 3, 1776	61
Mary, d. Elias, bp. Dec. 2, 1788 *("d. of Elias, 2nd" in Church Rec.)	131
Mary, d. John, bp. [Mar.] 29, 1795	134
Mary, d. Apr. 25, 1809, ae 22	98
Mary, wid., d. June 11, 1815, ae 57	100
Mary, d. Merriam, d. Dec. 12, 1829, ae 4	106
Mary Bulkley, d. Wyllis, bp. [June] 16, 1805	139
Mary Bulkley, m. John **EDWARDS**, Dec. 11, 1836	79
Mary Elizabeth, d. Marriam, bp. May 5, 1826	146
Mary Rose, d. Andrew, bp. [Aug. 31], 1838	149
Mehetabel, d. Eliel, bp. Jan. 21, 1770	120
Mehetable, wid., d. Jan. 20, 1840, ae 75	111
Merriam, s. Eliel, bp. Sept. 4, 1785	129
Merriam, m. Betsey **DANFORTH**, Mar. 25, 1819	74
Moses, s. Moses, bp. July 17, 1768	119
Moses, s. Moses, d. July 26, 1768	81
Moses, s. Eliel, bp. Apr. 28, 1771	121
Moses, his w. [ ], d. Feb. 9, 1788, ae 56	88
Moses, his servant Lucy d. Dec. 13, 1788	89
Moses, m. Mary **NORTH**, July 2, 1789	64
Moses, d. Jan. 17, 1794, ae 23, [at Port au Prince*] *(From Church Rec.)	91
Moses, d. Feb. 7, 1810, ae 81	98
Moses, s. Washington, bp. Aug. 18, 1810	142
Moses W., m. Abigail B. **SMITH**, Oct. 26, 1841	80
Moses Warner, s. Horace, bp. [ ], 1830	146
Moses Wolcott, s. Washington, bp. May 23, 1819	144
Nancy, d. Israel, bp. Aug. 30, 1767	118
Nancy, m. Joseph **HIGGINS**, Dec. 18, 1785	63
Nancy, d. Silas, bp. Apr. 29, 1804	139
Nenus*, s. Eph[raim], bp. Oct. 29, 1786 *(Arnold Copy has "Aenus")	130
Olive, m. W[illia]m **BULKLEY**, Jan. 31, 1776	61
Olive, m. Wait **GOODRICH**, June 26, 1798	67
Oliver Butler, s. Simeon, bp. Jan. 27, 1786	130
Oliver Butler, s. Sim, d. Jan. 31, 1786	87
Orinda, d. Jos[hu]a, bp. Mar. 23, 1783 *("Mar. 2" in Church Rec.)	128
Otis, s. Richard, bp. May 26, 1799	136

WILLIAMS, (cont.)

	Page
Prudence, d. Eliel, bp. Dec. 5, 1773	123
Prudence, m. Edward **BULKLEY**, Nov. 2, 1774	61
Prudence, d. Eliel, d. [ ] 11, 1783, ae 10	86
Prudence, wid., d. Jan. 12, 1799, ae 76	94
Rachel, d. Israel, bp. Dec. 2, 1770	121
Rachel, m. Frederick **RILEY**, Apr. 23, 1794, by Mr. Marsh	65
Ralph Henry, s. Wyllis, bp. Apr. 24, 1803	138
Ralph Wyllis, s. Wyllis, bp. Nov. 10, 1811	142
Ralph Wyllis, m. Sarah S. **ARNOLD**, Dec. 7, 1836	79
Rhoda, m. Eli **GOODRICH**, Nov. 11, 1784	62
Richard, m. Hannah **DANFORTH**, Sept. 28, 1794, by Rev. Mr. Fenn. Int. Pub.	65
Richard, s. Richard, bp. Feb. 4, 1797	135
Richard, s. Richard, bp. Jan. 12, 1798	136
Richard, d. Nov. 1, 1812, ae 41	99
Roger, s. John, bp. [Feb. 3], 1788	131
Ruth, d. Levi, bp. May 2, 1790	132
Ruth, m. William **ROBBINS**, 2nd, Mar. 26, 1817	73
Sally, m. Joseph **BLAKELEY**, of Willink, N.Y., Feb. 7, 1816	73
Sally, wid., m. Lardner **DEMING**, of Berlin, May 2, 1816	73
Sally, wid., d. Dec. 19, 1837, ae 61	110
Sarah, m. William **WILLIAMS**, Mar. 20, 1783	62
Sarah, wid., d. Nov. 29*, 1785, ae 71 *("Nov. 19" in Church Rec.)	87
Sarah, d. W[illia]m, bp. [Nov.] 12, 1786	130
Sarah Dimock, d. Wait, bp. May 16, 1830	146
Sarah Goodrich, d. Marriam, bp. Nov. 2, 1834	148
Sarah Sophronia, w. Ralph Wyllis, bp. May 7, 1837	149
Sidney Davis*, s. Horace, bp. [ ], 1830 *("Henry Davis **WILLIAMS**" in Church Rec.)	146
Silas, s. Israel, bp. Jan. 16, 1774	123
Silas, m. Sally **GOODRICH***, Dec. 24, 1797 *(Church Rec. give "**GRISWOLD**")	67
Silas, bp. Jan. 3, 1802, an adult	138
Silas, d. Feb. 20, 1807, ae 30	97
Simeon, m. wid. Eunice **BUTLER**, Feb. 15, 1784	62
Simeon, his infant d. Nov. 30, 1786	88
Simeon, d. Mar. 12, 1800, ae 40	94
Stephen, of Middletown, d. May 18, 1781 (Church Rec. give "24th y.")	85
Susan, d. Horace, bp. [ ], 1830	146
Thankful, wid., d. Apr. 8, 1817, ae 84	100
Thomas, d. May 21, 1821, ae 17	102
Thomas Butler, s. Jacob, bp. June 16, 1805	139
Thomas Danforth, s. Merriam, bp. Dec. 15, 1819	145
Thomas Danforth, m. Mary Jane **BOARDMAN**, Apr. 6, 1842	80
Ursula, d. John, bp. June [12], 1785	129
Ursula*, d. Sept. 19, 1786 *("dau. of John" in Church Rec. ae 2)	87
Ursula, d. John, bp. Oct. 4, 1801	137
Ursula, m. Cyrus **THOMPSON**, of Hartford, July 28, 1823	75
Wait, s. Isaac*, bp. Dec. 23, 1764 *("Israel" in Church Rec.)	117
Wait, d. Mar. 22, 1787, at New York, ae 23	88

	Page
WILLIAMS, (cont.)	
Wait, s. W[illia]m, bp. Nov. 8, 1789	132
Wait, m. Lucy* **DIMOCK**, June 25, 1818 *("Sally" in Church Rec.)	74
Walter, s. Silas, bp. Jan. 17, 1802	138
Walter Sage, s. Achley, bp. Aug. 23, 1818	144
Washington, m. Hetty **ROBBINS**, Oct. 18, 1804	69
William, m. Sarah **WILLIAMS**, Mar. 20, 1783	62
W[illia]m, his infant d. Aug. 1, 1788	88
W[illia]m, d. [ ], 1793, coming from West Indies, ae 21	91
William, s. W[illia]m, bp. Nov. 8, 1795	135
William, s. W[illia]m, d. Jan. 9, 1796	92
William, s. W[illia]m, bp. Dec. 11, 1796	135
William, d. Apr. 6, 1831, ae 73	106
W[illia]m, his wid. [ ], d. Sept. 8, 1834, ae 76	108
William Cooley, s. Andrew, bp. [Sept. 2], 1836	148
William W., d. Dec. 27, 1839, at New Orleans, ae 47* *("ae 44" in Church Rec.)	111
William Wait, s. Wait, bp. May 16, 1830	146
Willys, m. Rhoda **BULKLEY**, June 19, 1799	67
Wyllis, d. Mar. 9, 1813, ae 35	99
WILSON, Lucinda, d. John, bp. Feb. 6, 1774	123
Sylvester*, of Berlin, m. Ruhamah **DICKINSON**, Apr. 27, 1812 *(In pencil "Sylvester **WILCOX**")	72
WINCHELL, WINCHEL, Amelia*, d. Calvin, bp. Oct. 12, 1800 *("Aurelia" in Church Rec.)	137
Asa, s. Calvin, bp. July 8, 1792	133
Aurelia*, d. Calvin, bp. Oct. 12, 1800 *(Arnold Copy has "Amelia").	137
Calvin, of Berlin, m. Chloe **GOODRICH**, [ ] [probably 1787]	64
Calvin, s. Calvin, bp. Oct. 2, 1803	139
Eliza, d. Calvin, bp. [Aug.] 25, 1805	139
Elizabeth, wid., d. Jan. 28, 1817, ae 93	100
Hezekiah, of Berlin, m. wid. Elizabeth **BELDEN**, Aug. 25, 1804	69
Lucretia, d. Calvin, bp. Nov. 8, 1795	135
Lucy, d. Calvin, bp. May 27, 1798	136
Orrin, s. Calvin, bp. May 31, 1789	131
Sebra, d. Calvin, bp. July 18, 1790	132
Sabra, m. Gilbert **CHAPMAN**, May 23, 1806, by Rev. Mr. Brace	69
WOLCOTT, WOOLCOTT, Ambrose, his w. [ ], d. Aug. 9, 1840, ae 32	111
Ambrose, m. Elizabeth **BELDEN**, Oct. 20, 1842	80
Catharine, d. Josiah, bp. Mar. 20, 1781, by Rev. Mr. Lewis	126
Daniel Russel, s. Josiah, bp. Apr. 28, 1782	127
Elisha, his servant Rose, m. Newport, servant of Elisha **CALLENDER**, Oct. 10, 1782	62
George, m. Elizabeth **NOTT**, Mar. [ ], 1774	61
Horace, s. Josiah, bp. Jan. 9, 1785	129
Josiah, m. Prudence **WARNER**, Mar. 25, 1772	61
Josiah, d. Mar. 28, 1773	82
Josiah, had servant Hind*, d. May 31, 1776 *("Windsor" in Church Rec.)	84
Josiah, s. Thomas, bp. Nov. 11, 1787 *("son of Theod" in Church Rec.)	131
Josiah, of Bristol, m. wid. Nancy **HIGGINS**, Feb. 16, 1806	69

	Page
WOLCOTT, WOOLCOTT, (cont.)	
Lewis*, s. Thomas, bp. Dec. 31, 1786 *("s. of Theod." in Church Rec.)	130
Mary, d. Josiah, bp. Nov. 15, 1789	132
Susannah, d. Josiah, bp. May 6, 1787	130
Theodore, m. Rhoda **GOODRICH**, Apr. 11, 1785	63
WOODHOUSE, Humphrey, m. Rebecca **ADAMS** (Old Society), Jan. 1, 1795	66
WOODRUFF, Richard, Rev., of Unionville, m. Frances Louisa **WILLIAMS**, of Rocky Hill, Dec. 12, 1843, by Rev. C. Chapin	2
Richard, Rev., of Unionville, m. Frances Louisa **WILLIAMS**, Dec. 12, 1843	80
Richard, Rev., his w. [ ], d. Sept. 14, 1846, ae 31	114
WOODWORTH, Douglas, of Middletown, m. Jane R. **COLLINS**, of Rocky Hill, Apr. 10, 1845, by Rev. J. Goodwin	10
WORTHINGTON, Emily F., m. Hiram H. **HURLBURT**, of New Britain, Oct. 12, 1836	79
William A., of Colchester, m. Elizabeth **COREY**, Oct. 29, 1815	73
W[illia]m R., his w. [ ], d. Apr. 27, 1830, ae 36	106
W[illia]m R., d. July 11, 1831, ae 41	106
WRIGHT, Abiah, wid. Giles, d. Feb. 13, 1838, ae 77	110
Abigail, m. Sylvester **BELDEN**, July 29, 1804	69
Alexander N., of Berlin, m. Emily W. **DEMING**, Nov. 22, 1835	78
Amelia, m. Marvin W. **GOODRICH**, July 10, 1828	76
Anna, m. Simeon **RICHARDS**, Feb. 6, 1772	61
Benjamin, d. between May 7 & Aug. 17, 1782, at New York (Soldier)	85
Benjamin, m. Lucy **DEMING**, Nov. 2, 1809	71
Catharine B., of Ber[ ], m. Elisha H. **BUTLER**, July 7, 1833	78
Charles, d. June 25, 1828, ae 77	105
Daniel, of Farmington, m. Sarah **WILKINSON***, June 24, 1784 *(Arnold Copy has "DICKINSON")	62
Daniel, s. Daniel, bp. May 22, 1791	132
Daniel, s. Daniel, d. May 28, 1793, ae 4	91
Daniel, s. Daniel, bp. June 9, 1793	134
Daniel, his w. [ ], d. [Dec.] 8, 1828, ae 66	106
Daniel, d. Apr. 25, 1838, ae 76	110
Delia A., m. William **WHITMORE**, Aug. 25, 1852, by Rev. L. Burton Rockwood	41
Eben, Dea., d. Sept. 2, 1766	81
Electa, d. Charles, bp. July 14, 1800	137
Elias, m. Sarah K. **LEACH**, of Winchester, Oct. 9, 1814	72
Elias, his d. [ ], d. Dec. 13*, 1843, ae 14 *("Dec. 3" in Church Rec.)	113
Elijah, d. Feb. 13, 1815, ae 46	100
George, m. Sarah **COLLINS**, Nov. 25, 1839	79
Giles, m. Abiah **DICKINSON**, Apr. 12, 1781	61
Giles, his child d. Dec. 15, 1789	89
Giles, d. [ ] 27, 1836, ae 82	109
Hannah, d. Justus, bp. July 16, 1769	120
Hannah, wid., d. Sept. 30*, 1776 *("Sept. 18" in Church Rec.)	84
Hannah, m. Jonas* **CURTIS**, Aug. 5, 1789 *("Jona[tha]n" in Church Rec.)	64
Hannah, m. John **DEMING**, Nov. 11, 1817	73

WRIGHT, (cont.)

	Page
Henry*, s. Charles, bp. Jan. 18, 1795 *("Hervey" in Church Rec.)	134
Hervey*, s. Charles, bp. Jan. 18, 1795 *(Arnold Copy has "Henry")	134
Hetty, d. Charles, bp. Aug. 29, 1784	129
John, m. Martha **ROBBINS**, Apr. 16, 1772	61
John, m. Sarah **CULVER**, of Bristol, Mar. 24, 1791	65
John T., of Rocky Hill, m. Eunice Ann **SUGDEN**, of Middletown, Oct. 5, 1848, by Rev. Theodore M. Dwight	28
John Treby, s. Daniel, bp. June 26, 1785	129
John Treby, d. Apr. 11, 1806, ae 21	97
Joseph, s. Benj[amin], bp. Sept. 23, 1781	127
Justus, his w. [ ], d. July 12, 1802, ae 81	95
Justus, d. Mar. 28, 1804, ae 21	96
Laura, wid., m. Jonathan **THAYER**, [ ] 7, 1828	76
Leveret, s. Daniel, bp. Nov. 1, 1801	138
Leverett, m. Laura **CHAPMAN**, of Glastonbury, July 17, 1821	74
Lois, d. Charles, bp. May 6, 1781	127
Lois, m. Salmon **BOOTH**, of Berlin, Apr. 19, 1797	66
Lucy, d. Charles, bp. Sept. 30, 1792	133
Lucy, d. Daniel, bp. May 26, 1799	136
Lucy, m. John **MONTAGUE**, of 1st Society, Nov. 20, 1833	78
Lydia, d. Daniel, bp. Nov. 12, 1786	130
Lydia, m. Jacob **GRISWOLD**, Nov. 12, 1807	70
Lyman, m. Patty **BELDEN**, Aug. 13, 1801	68
Lyman, his w. [ ], d. Apr. 9, 1842, ae 68	112
Maria, d. Charles, bp. Oct. 29, 1797	136
Martha, m. James **ADAMS**, [, 1788]	64
Mary, m. Elisha **BOARDMAN**, of Middletown, May 29, 1783	62
Mary, m. Abraham **BELDING**, Nov. 13, 1785	63
Mary, m. Stephen P. **CRAMPTON**, of Hartford, [ ] 28, 1829	76
Mary Ann, m. Enos **STOW**, May 16, 1814	72
Mehetabel, d. Daniel, bp. Apr. 5, 1789	131
Mehetable, m. Barzillai **DICKINSON**, Sept. 22, 1805	69
Mehetable, d. Apr. 15, 1812, ae 21	99
Mehetable, d. Apr. 15, 1812, ae 21	99
Merian, d. Charles, bp. June 28, 1789	131
Merriam, m. Orrin **DICKINSON**, Dec. 13, 1807	70
Nabby, d. Charles, bp. [Dec. 31], 1786	130
Patty, m. Allen **HOLMES**, July 17, 1804	69
Rhoda, d. Charles, bp. May 6, 1781	127
Rhoda, m. Aaron **BELDEN**, Jr., July 30, 1797	66
Ruhamah, d. Benj[amin], bp. Sept. 23, 1781	127
Ruhamah, d. Benjamin, d. Aug. 1, 1782, ae 21 *("ae 2nd" in Church Rec.)	85
Ruhamah, d. Benjamin, bp. June 4, 1786	130
Sally, d. Daniel, bp. Jan. 8, 1797	135
Sally, m. Mandus **BERRY**, Oct. 2, 1814	72
Sarah, d. Justus, bp. Oct. 12, 1766	118
Sarah, m. John **ROBBINS**, Jan. 10, 1771	60
Sarah, m. Moses **DICKINSON**, Aug. 13, 1794, by Mr. Chapin	65
Sarah, m. Austin **BELDEN**, May 3, 1843	80

	Page
WRIGHT, (cont.)	
Sheldon, s. Charles, bp. July 14, 1782	127
Sylvester, s. Daniel, bp. [May] 27, 1804	139
Sylvester, m. Florilla **BELDEN**, Nov. 27, 1825	75
Sylvester, d. [ ] 9, 1826, ae 23	105
William, m. Mary **SMITH**, Jan. 1, 1834	78
YOUNG, Robert, d. [ ] 31, 1772	82
NO SURNAME, Eunice, bp. Nov. 8, 1795	135
Mehetabel, m. W[illia]m **GOODRICH**, Aug. 20, 1783	62
Michael, m. Lydia **TAYLOR**, Jan. 23, 1771	60
Rebecca*, colored, d. Jan. 18, 1835, ae 61 *("w. of Marquis **CHURCHILL**" in Church Rec.)	108

ROXBURY VITAL RECORDS
1796 - 1835

	Page
ALLEN, Treat, of South Britain, m. Sarah **BLACKMAN**, of Roxbury, Dec. 23, 1824, by Rev. Fosdic Harrison	263
ANDRUS, Elijah, of Woodbury, m. Lavina **JUDSON**, of Roxbury, Mar. 15, 1830, by Josiah R. Eastman, J.P.	269
BALDWIN, Betsey, of Roxbury, m. Henry **STRICKLIN**, of New Haven, June 2, 1822, at the house of Andrew Erwin, by Seth Higby	261-2
Harmon, of Bristol, m. Susan **HODGE**, of Roxbury, Feb. 6, 1833, by Rev. Fosdic Harrison	271
Herman, m. Anna Caroline **TROWBRIDGE**, Dec. 25, 1820, by Rev. Fosdic Harrison	258
Hiram, of Bristol, m. Susan **HODGE**, of Roxbury, Feb. 6, 1833, by Rev. Fosdic Harrison	349
BARNS, Polly, of Roxbury, m. Reuben S. **CASTLE**, of Woodbury, Nov. 29, 1829, by Rev. Fosdic Harrison	269
BARRITT, Daniel, m. Ann Maria **SEWARD**, b. of Roxbury, Oct. 23, 1825, by Rev. Fosdic Harrison	264
BARTRAM, Darius, of Danbury, m. Polly **HODGE**, of Roxbury, Nov. 26, 1828, by Rev. Fosdic Harrison	268
BATES, Elias A., of Roxbury, m. Sally **ROSWELL**, of Southbury, June 12, 1820, by Rev. Fosdic Harrison	257
Polly, m. Abel **VOSE**, Sept. 5, 1830, by William Pierce, J.P.	269
Truman, m. Polly **BOOTH**, b. of Roxbury, Sept. 15, 1826, by Josiah R. Eastman, J.P.	268
BEACH, Benjamin B., of Bridgewater, m. Rhody **MALLORY**, of Roxbury, June 17, 1829, by Rev. Fosdic Harrison	268
BEARDSLEE, Anna, m. Glover **FAIRCHILD**, b. of Roxbury, Dec. 27, 1820, by Fosdic Harrison, V.D.M.	258
Begardus, of Bridgewater, m. Statia **HODGE**, of Roxbury, Aug. 16, 1831, by Gordon Hayes	348
Charles, m. Jerusha A. **BOOTH**, b. of Roxbury, Jan. 26, 1831, by Rev. Fosdic Harrison	270
Julia A., of Roxbury, m. Chauncey **LEWIS**, of Monroe, Dec. 19, 1830, by Rev. Fosdic Harrison	270
Manerva A., m. Calvin H. **DOWNS**, b. of Roxbury, Mar. 23, 1835, by Rev. Fosdic Harrison	350
BEARDWELL, Ceaser, m. Diantha **HARDENBURG**, of New Milford, Oct. 5, 1825, by Rev. Fosdic Harrison	264
BEERS, Woster, of New Milford, m. Elcey **SQUIER**, of Roxbury, Dec. 27, 1820, by Rev. Fosdic Harrison	258
BELLAMY, David, of Bethleham, m. Betsey **SPAULDING**, of Roxbury, Nov. 24, 1825, by Rev. Fosdic Harrison	264
BENEDICT, Benjamin B., of Patterson, N.Y., m. Julia M. **PAINTER**, of Roxbury, Jan. 26, 1830, by Rev. Fosdic Harrison	269

	Page
[BENNETT], BENIT, Philo, m. Caroline **DOWNS**, b. of Roxbury, May 14, 1823, by Rev. Sturgis Gilbert	261
BLACKMAN, Avaline, m. Homer **FENN**, b. of Roxbury, Mar. 17, 1834, by Fosdic Harrison	350
Nancy, m. Orrin **SEWARD**, b. of Roxbury, Aug. 22, 1824, by Rev. Sturgis Gilbert	263
Sarah, of Roxbury, m. Treat **ALLEN**, of South Britain, Dec. 23, 1824, by Rev. Fosdic Harrison	263
BOGERT, Mary V.D., of Southbury, m. Almond W. **WARNER**, of Roxbury, Jan. 28, [1839], by Rev. Thomas Ellis, of South Britain	338
BOOTH, Ely, m. Abigail **MINOR**, Dec. 24, 1801	344
Jerusha, w. Samuel, d. May 19, 1806	344
Jerusha A., m. Charles **BEARDSLEE**, b. of Roxbury, Jan. 26, 1831, by Rev. Fosdic Harrison	270
Jerusha Ann, d. Ely & Abigail, b. Mar. 25, 1806	344
Judson, m. Rachal **HARRISON**, b. of Bridgewater, Jan. 8, 1827, by Rev. Fosdic Harrison	265
Lemira, d. Ely & Abigail, b. Oct. 23, 1802	344
Nancy, m. Joseph Thompson **LEWIS**, b. of Roxbury, June 13, 1820, by Rev. Sturges Gilbert, of Woodbury	257
Polly, m. Truman **BATES**, b. of Roxbury, Sept. 15, 1826, by Josiah R. Eastman, J.P.	268
Richard, s. Ely & Abigail, b. July 4, 1804	344
BRISCOE, Charles, m. Mary **DAVIDSON**, b. of Roxbury, July [ ], 1826, by Rev. Fosdic Harrison	265
BRONSON. BROWNSON, Abel, Jr., m. Eunice **JUDSON**, b. of Southbury, now of Roxbury, Apr. 25, 1824, by Josiah R. Eastman, J.P.	263
Butler, m. Lydia Ann **WARD**, of Roxbury, Mar. 14, 1821, by Rev. Sturgis Gilbert, of Woodbury	260
Hannah, m. John **SQUIER**, b. of Roxbury, May 9, 1824, by Josiah R. Eastman, J.P.	263
James Martin, s. Josiah & Laura, b. Oct. 18, 1823	346
Jeremiah, s. Josiah & Laura, b. Aug. 18, 1812	346
John Thomas, s. Josiah & Laura, b. Oct. 2, 1810	346
Josiah Gulielmus, s. Josiah & Laura, b. Oct. 13, 1815	346
Maria Parnel, d. Josiah & Laura, b. Nov. 25, 1818	346
BUCKINGHAM, Eliza, m. Morris **BUNNELL**, b. of Roxbury, June 22, 1825, by Rev. Fosdic Harrison	264
BUNNELL, BUNNEL, Chauncey, of Oxford, m. Mary Maria **WARNER**, of Roxbury, Jan. 27, 1839, by Rev. Thomas Ellis, of South Britain	338
Morris, m. Eliza **BUCKINGHAM**, b. of Roxbury, June 22, 1825, by Rev. Fosdic Harrison	264
BURDITT, Joseph, of Newtown, m. Dorcas **LUCAS**, of Roxbury, Dec. 29, 1823, by Josiah R. Eastman, J.P.	261
CANFIELD, Augustine, [s. Elihu & Sarah], b. May 15, 1786	341
Betsey, d. Elihu & Sarah, b. Mar. 11, 1784	341
Betsey, m. Thomas **HURD**, Mar. 30, 1806, by Rev. [ ] Mills	345
Caroline, [d. Elihu & Sarah], b. Mar. 30, 1799	341
Caroline, d. Elihu & Sarah, d. Sept. 2, 1816, ae 17 y. 5 m.	343
Elihu, m. Sarah **FRISBIE**, Jan. 23, 1783	341
Mary, w. Rev. Thomas, d. Oct. 14, 1790	341

	Page
CANFIELD, (cont.)	
Polly, [d. Elihu & Sarah], b. Feb. 15, 1801	341
Russell, [s. Elihu & Sarah], b. Aug. 28, 1789	341
Sally, [d. Elihu & Sarah], b. Oct. 9, 1791	341
Sally, m. Alson **LEAVENWORTH**, Oct. 17, 1811, by Rev. Zeph[ania]h Swift	345
Thomas, Rev., d. Jan. 16, 1795	341
Thomas Sterling, [s. Elihu & Sarah], b. Jan. 8, 1804	341
CASTLE, Abigail R., m. Heman **PATTERSON**, of New Milford, Mar. 28, 1824, by Rev. Fosdic Harrison	262
John M., Jr., m. Adaline **WELLER**, b. of Roxbury, Apr. 14, 1825, by Rev. Sturgis Gilbert	264
Laura, m. Sela **LUCAS**, b. of Roxbury, Sept. 4, 1820, by Josiah R. Eastman, J.P.	258
Reuben S., of Woodbury, m. Polly **BARNS**, of Roxbury, Nov. 29, 1829, by Rev. Fosdic Harrison	269
CHATFIELD, Betsey, m. Moses **MEAKER**, of Reading, June 17, 1821, by Rev. Fosdic Harrison	259
Philemon, m. Ann **COGSWELL**, b. of Roxbury, Oct. 31, 1825, by Rev. Fosdic Harrison	264
Yarmouth, of Woodbury, m. Charlotte **GAYLORD**, of Oxford, Oct. 17, 1830, by Rev. Fosdic Harrison	270
CHURCHIL, Mary Emily, of Litchfield, m. David Towsey **TAYLOR**, of Newtown, Mar. 25, 1828, by Rev. Fosdic Harrison	267
COGSWELL, Ann, m. Philemon **CHATFIELD**, b. of Roxbury, Oct. 31, 1825, by Rev. Fosdic Harrison	264
Polly, m. Levy **WARD**, b. of Roxbury, Dec. 22, 1822, by Rev. Sturgis Gilbert, of Woodbury	260-3
COLVIN, Isaac, m. Julia **WILLIAMS**, now b. of Roxbury, Dec. 2, 1819, by Josiah R. Eastman, J.P.	258
COON, Albert, m. Sarah Ann **THOMAS**, Dec. 6, 1824, by Daniel B. Brinsmade, J.P.	263
CURTIS, CURTISS, Abel, of Washington, m. Lucy **ERWINS**, of Roxbury, Oct. 9, 1821, by Rev. Fosdic Harrison	260
Lucretia, m. Robert **SMITH**, Jan. 23, 1812, by Elihu Canfield, J.P.	345
Rachel, of Washington, m. Peter **FAIRCHILD**, of Newtown, Nov. 12, 1826, by Rev. Stephen Mason, of Washington	265
DASCOM, Salina, m. Benjamin **NORMAN**, of Southbury, May 27, 1821, by Rev. Fosdic Harrison	259
DAVIDSON, Mary, m. Charles **BRISCOE**, b. of Roxbury, July [ ], 1826, by Rev. Fosdic Harrison	265
DAVIS, Henry, of New Milford, m. Mary O. **ERWIN**, of Roxbury, Dec. 15, 1822, by Rev. Fosdic Harrison	260-3
DAYTON, Tuttle, m. Caroline **HURD**, of Roxbury, Feb. 1, 1832, by Rev. Fosdic Harrison	348
DENNIE, Solomon, of Washington, m. Harriet **WARNER**, of Roxbury, Jan. 30, 1821, by Daniel B. Brinsmade, J.P.	258
DOWNS, Calvin H., m. Manerva A. **BEARDSLEE**, b. of Roxbury, Mar. 23, 1835, by Rev. Fosdic Harrison	350
Caroline, m. Philo **BENIT**, b. of Roxbury, May 14, 1823, by Rev. Sturgis Gilbert	261

	Page
DUFF, Joseph, of Dublin, Ireland, m. Anna **WARNER**, Nov. 23, 1820, by Fosdic Harrison, V.D.M.	258
EASTMAN, Richard H., m. Eunice **TYRELL**, Mar. 21, 1821, by Rev. Fosdic Harrison	259
EDWARDS, Eliza A., of Roxbury, m. John **FOSTER**, of Cheshire, Mar. 26, 1826, by Rev. Fosdic Harrison	265
Mary A., m. Truman **SHEPARD**, Dec. 25, 1839, by Rev. A. Isham	272
Sally M., of Roxbury, m. William H. **LIVINGSTONE**, of Woodbury, May 2, 1827, by Rev. Stephen Mason, of Washington	265
ELDERKIN, Susan, of Roxbury, m. Benjamin **HULL**, of Weston, June 2, 1825, by Josiah R. Eastman, J.P.	267
ELTON, Joseph T., of Sharon, m. Sarah **OSBORN**, of Roxbury, June 3, 1832, by Daniel B. Brinsmade, J.P.	348
ERWIN, ERWINS, Lucy, of Roxbury, m. Abel **CURTIS**, of Washington, Oct. 9, 1821, by Rev. Fosdic Harrison	260
Mary O., of Roxbury, m. Henry **DAVIS**, of New Milford, Dec. 15, 1822, by Rev. Fosdic Harrison	260-3
FAIRCHILD, Beartis, of Newtown, m. Hannah **WAKELEY**, of Roxbury, Oct. 25, 1825, by Rev. Sturgis Gilbert	264
Betsey, m. Lewis **FAIRCHILD**, May 30, 1821, by Rev. Fosdic Harrison	259
Beulah, of Roxbury, m. Homer **TREAT**, of Bridgewater, Mar. 19, 1823, by Rev. Fosdic Harrison	260-3
Glover, m. Anna **BEARDSLEE**, b. of Roxbury, Dec. 27, 1820, by Fosdic Harrison, V.D.M.	258
Lewis, m. Betsey **FAIRCHILD**, May 30, 1821, by Rev. Fosdic Harrison	259
Olive, m. Zachariah T. **PATTERSON**, Oct. 17, 1822, by Rev. Sturgis Gilbert	261-2
Peter, of Newtown, m. Rachel **CURTIS**, of Washington, Nov. 12, 1826, by Rev. Stephen Mason, of Washington	265
FENN, Chloe Pamela, d. Lyman & Fanny, b. Jan. 24, 1827	346
Homer, m. Avaline **BLACKMAN**, b. of Roxbury, Mar. 17, 1834, by Fosdic Harrison	350
Lyman, m. Fanny P. **LIVINGSTONE**, b. of Roxbury, Mar. 9, 1826, by Rev. Fosdic Harrison	265
FLOWER, Susan, of Roxbury, m. Horace B. **HAWLEY**, of Hamden, N.Y., May 7, 1829, by Rev. Fosdic Harrison	268
FOSTER, John, of Cheshire, m. Eliza A. **EDWARDS**, of Roxbury, Mar. 26, 1826, by Rev. Fosdic Harrison	265
FOWLER, Edward H., of Guilford, m. Martha L. **STRONG**, of Roxbury, Apr. 3, 1834, by Rev. Fosdic Harrison	350
Ellieser Bartlett, of Guilford, m. Catharine **THOMAS**, of Roxbury, Oct. 15, 1820, by Fosdic Harrison	257
FRENCH, Thomas C., of New Milford, m. Mahettabal **MALLORY**, Mar. 3, 1824, by Fosdic Harrison, V.D.M.	262
FRISBIE, Elizabeth, w. Dea. Ezekiel, d. Apr. 20, 1805	341
Ezekiel, Dea., d. Oct. 26, 1810	341
Sarah, m. Elihu **CANFIELD**, Jan. 23, 1783	341
Sherman, of Washington, m. Lucy **WARNER**, of Roxbury, Nov. 19, 1824, by Fosdic Harrison	263
GALPIN, Polly Maria, of Washington, m. Joel **HULL**, of Plymouth, Mar. 4, 1827, by Rev. Fosdic Harrison	265

	Page
GARLICK, Edmund E., m. Elizabeth A. **HAWLEY**, b. of Roxbury, Feb. 20, 1831, by Rev. Daniel Burhans	270
Samuel D., m. Harriet A. **THOMAS**, b. of Roxbury, Mar. 7, 1833, by Rev. Fosdic Harrison	271
Samuel D., m. Harriet A. **THOMAS**, b. of Roxbury, Mar. 7, 1833, by Rev. Fosdic Harrison	349
Tarissa, of Roxbury, m. William C. **PHELPS**, of New Milford, Jan. 20, 1828, by Fosdic Harrison, V.D.M.	265
GAYLORD, Charlotte, of Oxford, m. Yarmouth **CHATFIELD**, of Woodbury, Oct. 17, 1830, by Rev. Fosdic Harrison	270
GENNINGS, [see under **JENNINGS**]	
GILLET, David, m. Mrs. Ruth Ann **JONES**, Jan. 11, 1824, at the house of Andrew Hunt, by Seth Higby	262
GOODWIN, John J. Starks, m. Sebra **JOHNSON**, Aug. 6, 1827, by Royal R. Hinman, J.P.	265
GORAM (?), Hiram, m. Hannah **PECK**, Feb. 19, 1818, by Joel Sanford, J.P.	262
GOULD, Daniel, of Greenfield, m. Elizabeth **THOMSON**, of Roxbury, Dec. 30, 1821, by Fosdic Harrison, V.D.M.	260
GRAVES, Huldah Minerva, d. Ezra, b. July 8, 1799	342
GREGORY, Charry Ann, of Danbury, m. Henry **WARNER**, of Roxbury, Oct. 5, 1820, by Fosdic Harrison	257
GRIFFIN, Elizabeth, m. Nehemiah **PATTERSON**, b. of Roxbury, Dec. 24, 1823, by Rev. Sturgis Gilbert	261
GRISWOULD, Garry, m. Sarah **SMITH**, Feb. 17, 1823, by Maltby Gelston	260-3
HALL, Zillah, m. Leman D. **HOUGH**, Jan. 5, 1823, by Rev. Fosdic Harrison	260-3
HAMMOND, Harriet, [d. David & Elizabeth], b. May 4, 1798	342
Lorena, b. Dec. 13, 1790	342
Lorena, [d. David & Elizabeth], b. Dec. 13, 1790	342
Maria, [d. David & Elizabeth], b. Mar. 21, 1793	342
Nathan, [s. David & Elizabeth], b. Feb. 26, 1795	342
HARDENBURG, Diantha, of New Milford, m. Ceaser **BEARDWELL**, Oct. 5, 1825, by Rev. Fosdic Harrison	264
HARRISON, Rachal, m. Judson **BOOTH**, b. of Bridgewater, Jan. 8, 1827, by Rev. Fosdic Harrison	265
HARTWELL, William D., of Washington, m. Sarah S. **LEAVENWORTH**, of Roxbury, Jan. 17, 1828, by Fosdic Harrison, V.D.M.	265
HAWLEY, Elizabeth A., m. Edmund E. **GARLICK**, b. of Roxbury, Feb. 20, 1831, by Rev. Daniel Burhans	270
Horace B., of Hamden, N.Y., m. Susan **FLOWER**, of Roxbury, May 7, 1829, by Rev. Fosdic Harrison	268
HIBBOURNE, Harry, of Litchfield, m. Mary C. **JUDSON**, alias **SANDERSON**, Apr. 3, 1822, by Rev. Fosdic Harrison	261-2
HODGE, Amanda, of Roxbury, m. Lampson P. **MITCHELL**, of Woodbury, May 21, 1829, by Rev. Fosdic Harrison	268
Polly, of Roxbury, m. Darius **BARTRAM**, of Danbury, Nov. 26, 1828, by Rev. Fosdic Harrison	268
Statia, of Roxbury, m. Begardus **BEARDSLEE**, of Bridgewater, Aug. 16, 1831, by Gordon Hayes	348
Susan, of Roxbury, m. Harmon **BALDWIN**, of Bristol, Feb. 6, 1833, by Rev. Fosdic Harrison	271

	Page
HODGE, (cont.)	
Susan, of Roxbury, m. Hiram **BALDWIN**, of Bristol, Feb. 6, 1833, by Rev. Fosdic Harrison	349
HOUGH, Leman D., m. Zillah **HALL**, Jan. 5, 1823, by Rev. Fosdic Harrison	260-3
HOYT, Lucy C., of Washington, m. Silas **WARNER**, of Roxbury, Apr. 18, 1824, by Rev. Fosdic Harrison	262
HULL, Benjamin, of Weston, m. Susan **ELDERKIN**, of Roxbury, June 2, 1825, by Josiah R. Eastman, J.P.	267
Bradford J., of Weston, m. Catharine **TEEPLE**, of Roxbury, Jan. 26, 1823, by Daniel B. Brinsmade, J.P.	260-3
Joel, of Plymouth, m. Polly Maria **GALPIN**, of Washington, Mar. 4, 1827, by Rev. Fosdic Harrison	265
HUNGERFORD, Thomas, of Watertown, m. Abigail **MINOR**, of Roxbury, Dec. 13, 1832, by Rev. Fosdic Harrison	349
Thomas, of Watertown, m. Abigail **MINOR**, of Roxbury, Dec. 11, 1833, by Rev. Fosdic Harrison	271
HUNT, Lucy, of Roxbury, m. David **MERWIN**, of Brookfield, Oct. 19, 1828, by Josiah R. Eastman, J.P.	267
Sally, of Roxbury, m. Sterling **PIERCE**, of South Britain, Jan. 25, 1825, by Rev. Fosdic Harrison	263
HURD, Caroline, m. Tuttle **DAYTON**, Feb. 1, 1832, by Rev. Fosdic Harrison	348
Marinda, m. Stephen **SANFORD**, Jr., b. of Roxbury, Nov. 5, 1828, by Rev. Fosdic Harrison	269
Thomas, m. Betsey **CANFIELD**, Mar. 30, 1806, by Rev. [ ] Mills	345
HURLBURT, Abigail, of Roxbury, m. Asahel **TOWNER**, of Oxford, Oct. 2, 1821, by Rev. Fosdic Harrison	260
Amanda, d. Henry & Mariah, b. Mar. 1, 1801	343
Levi, s. Gideon & Martha, b. Oct. 5, 1787	343
Nancy, m. Eleazer **WELTON**, Feb. 11, 1835, by Rev. B.Y. Messenger	350
Philana, m. Levi **WARD**, Feb. 25, 1821, by Rev. Fosdic Harrison	259
Simeon, s. Gideon & Martha, b. Nov. 29, 1785	343
Warner, s. Henry & Mariah, b. Dec. 8, 1805	343
JENNINGS, GENNINGS, Harvey, of New Milford, m. Jane **WELLER**, of Roxbury, June 4, 1832, by Rev. Fosdic Harrison	349
Hervey, of New Milford, m. Jane **WELLER**, of Roxbury, June 4, 1832, by Rev. Fosdic Harrison	271
JOHNSON, Sebra, m. John J. Starks **GOODWIN**, Aug. 6, 1827, by Royal R. Hinman, J.P.	265
JONES, Ruth Ann, Mrs., m. David **GILLET**, Jan. 11, 1824, at the house of Andrew Hunt, by Seth Higby	262
JUDSON, Cloe, m. Rufus **THOMPSON**, Sept. 20, 1803	342
Eunice, m. Abel **BRONSON**, Jr., b. of Southbury, now of Roxbury, Apr. 25, 1824, by Josiah R. Eastman, J.P.	263
Jennett, m. Moses **WARNER**, b. of Roxbury, Nov. 12, 1826, by Rev. Fosdic Harrison	265
Lavina, of Roxbury, m. Elijah **ANDRUS**, of Woodbury, Mar. 15, 1830, by Josiah R. Eastman, J.P.	269
Mary, m. William **SMITH**, b. of New Milford, Sept. 18, 1830, by William Pierce, J.P.	270
Mary C., alias **SANDERSON**, m. Harry **HIBBOURNE**, of Litchfield, Apr. 3, 1822, by Rev. Fosdic Harrison	261-2

	Page
JUDSON, (cont.)	
Sarah, of New Milford, m. James **ROSWELL**, of Southbury, Aug. 14, 1826, by Josiah R. Eastman, J.P.	267
KING, Nancy, m. Abraham **WARD**, Sept. 7, [1833], by William Pierce, J.P.	350
LAMBERT, Henry, of Woodbury, m. Jennet **LEAVENWORTH**, of Roxbury, Oct. 28, 1829, by Rev. Fosdic Harrison	269
LAMPHERE, Jane, m. Nathan **SQUIER**, Oct. 28, 1796, by Rev. Truman Marsh	344
LAW, Sally, m. James **WAKELY**, Aug. 10, 1823, by Rev. Sturgis Gilbert	261
LEAVENWORTH, Alson, m. Sally **CANFIELD**, Oct. 17, 1811, by Rev. Zeph[aniah] Swift	345
Jennet, of Roxbury, m. Henry **LAMBERT**, of Woodbury, Oct. 28, 1829, by Rev. Fosdic Harrison	269
Sarah S., of Roxbury, m. William D. **HARTWELL**, of Washington, Jan. 17, 1828, by Fosdic Harrison, V.D.M.	265
LEWIS, Chauncey, of Monroe, m. Julia A. **BEARDSLEE**, of Roxbury, Dec. 19, 1830, by Rev. Fosdic Harrison	270
Joseph Thompson, m. Nancy **BOOTH**, b. of Roxbury, June 13, 1820, by Rev. Sturges Gilbert, of Woodbury	257
LIVINGSTONE, Fanny P., m. Lyman **FENN**, b. of Roxbury, Mar. 9, 1826, by Rev. Fosdic Harrison	265
Loudon B., m. Louis **YOUNG**, Oct. 26, 1823, by Fosdic Harrison,V.D.M.	261
William M., of Woodbury, m. Sally M. **EDWARDS**, of Roxbury, May 2, 1827, by Rev. Stephen Mason, of Washington	265
LOGAN, Eliza E., [d. Sheldon & Eunicy], b. Dec. 29, 1827	347
Samuel S., [s. Sheldon & Eunicy], b. Apr. 25, 1819	347
Sheldon, m. Eunicy **WELLER**, Jan. 1, 1818	347
LUCAS, Dorcas, of Roxbury, m. Joseph **BURDITT**, of Newtown, Dec. 29, 1823, by Josiah R. Eastman, J.P.	261
Sela, m. Laura **CASTLE**, b. of Roxbury, Sept. 4, 1820, by Josiah R. Eastman, J.P.	258
MALLORY, MALLERY, Ann, [d. John], b. June 20, 1780	342
Butler, [s. John], b. Mar. 12, 1779	342
Daniel, [s. John], b. Dec. 23, 1774	342
Eben, m. Rhodah **YOUNG**, b. of Roxbury, Nov. 29, 1821, by Josiah B. Eastman, J.P.	260
Elizabeth, [d. John], b. June 12, 1773	342
Esther, [d. John], b. July 10, 1782	342
John G., [s. John], b. June 5, 1772	342
Mahettabal, m. Thomas C. **FRENCH**, of New Milford, Mar. 3, 1824, by Fosdic Harrison, V.D.M.	262
Rhody, of Roxbury, m. Benjamin B. **BEACH**, of Bridgewater, June 17, 1829, by Rev. Fosdic Harrison	268
Sarah, [d. John], b. Mar. 5, 1777	342
MEAKER, Moses, of Reading, m. Betsey **CHATFIELD**, June 17, 1821, by Rev. Fosdic Harrison	259
MERIMBLE, Bronson, of Woodbury, m. Lois E. **PERKINS**, of Roxbury, Apr. 25, 1825, by Rev. Fosdic Harrison	264
MERWIN, David, of Brookfield, m. Lucy **HUNT**, of Roxbury, Oct. 19, 1828, by Josiah R. Eastman, J.P.	267
MILLER, Jane, m. Charles **THOMAS**, Jr., b. of Roxbury, Mar. 9, 1828, by	

	Page
MILLER, (cont.)	
Fosdic Harrison	267
MINOR, Abigail, m. Ely **BOOTH**, Dec. 24, 1801	344
Abigail, of Roxbury, m. Thomas **HUNGERFORD**, of Watertown, Dec. 11, 1833, by Rev. Fosdic Harrison	271
Abigail, of Roxbury, m. Thomas **HUNGERFORD**, of Watertown, Dec. 13, 1832, by Rev. Fosdic Harrison	349
Charles Perry, s. Silas & Sally, b. May 1, 1812	347
Shove, of Roxbury, m. Eunice Jerusha **NORTEN**, d. Issacher, of Washington, Jan. 29, 1807	345
Silas, Jr., s. Silas & Sally, b. Jan. 1, 1809; d. Mar. 10, 1809	347
William Peters, s. Silas & Sally, b. Apr. 1, 1806	347
MITCHELL, Lampson P., of Woodbury, m. Amanda **HODGE**, of Roxbury, May 21, 1829, by Rev. Fosdic Harrison	268
MOREHOUSE, Deman, of Washington, m. Phebe **SANFORD**, of Roxbury, May 18, 1823, by Rev. Sturgis Gilbert	261
MT. CALM (?), John, m. Alla **WARNER**, June 13, 1830, by Rev. Fosdic Harrison	270
MUNGER, Lucy Ann, had s. John **REYNOLDS**, b. June 28, 1801	343
Maria, m. Garry H. **WHEELER**, Mar. 24, 1824, by Rev. Fosdic Harrison	262
NORMAN, Benjamin, of Southbury, m. Salina **DASCOM**, May 27, 1821, by Rev. Fosdic Harrison	259
NORTEN, Eunice Jerusha, d. Issacher, of Washington, m. Shove **MINOR**, of Roxbury, Jan. 29, 1807	345
[**OSBORN**], **ORSBORN**, Sarah, of Roxbury, m. Joseph T. **ELTON**, of Sharon, June 3, 1832, by Daniel B. Brinsmade, J.P.	348
PAINTER, Henry N., m. Catharine A. **SMITH**, b. of Roxbury, Nov. 13, 1838, by Rev. F. Harrison	345
Julia M., of Roxbury, m. Benjamin B. **BENEDICT**, of Patterson, N.Y., Jan. 26, 1830, by Rev. Fosdic Harrison	269
PATTERSON, Abigail, m. John T.J.W. **SANFORD**, Dec. 18, 1839, by Rev. A. Isham	272
Betsey, of Roxbury, m. Enos **STODDARD**, of Litchfield, Feb. 26, 1833, by Josiah R. Eastman, J.P.	271
Betsey, of Roxbury, m. Enos **STODDARD**, of Litchfield, Feb. 26, 1833, by Josiah R. Eastman, J.P.	349
Heman, of New Milford, m. Abigail R. **CASTLE**, Mar. 28, 1824, by Rev. Fosdic Harrison	262
Jennet, of Roxbury, m. Samuel **TOMLINSON**, of Woodbury, Nov. 28, 1827, by Grove L. Brownell	265
Nehemiah, m. Elizabeth **GRIFFIN**, b. of Roxbury, Dec. 24, 1823, by Rev. Sturgis Gilbert	261
Susan A., m. Henry **POPE**, Dec. 8, 1839, by Rev. A. Isham	272
Zachariah T., m. Olive **FAIRCHILD**, Oct. 17, 1822, by Rev. Sturgis Gilbert	261-2
PECK, Hannah, m. Hiram **GORAM** (?), Feb. 19, 1818, by Joel Sanford, J.P.	262
PERKINS, Lois E., of Roxbury, m. Bronson **MERIMBLE**, of Woodbury, Apr. 25, 1825, by Rev. Fosdic Harrison	264
PHELPS, William C., of New Milford, m. Tarissa **GARLICK**, of Roxbury, Jan. 20, 1828, by Fosdic Harrison, V.D.M.	265
PIERCE, Sterling, of South Britain, m. Sally **HUNT**, of Roxbury, Jan. 25,	

	Page
PIERCE, (cont.)	
1825, by Rev. Fosdic Harrison	263
POPE, Henry, m. Susan A. **PATTERSON**, Dec. 8, 1839, by Rev. A. Isham	272
PRINDLE, Charlotte A., of Roxbury, m. Daniel **RIDER**, of Reading, Nov. 16, 1838, by Rev. F. Harrison, of Bethleham	345
Frances, of Woodbury, m. Debbe Ann **WHEATON**, of Roxbury, Sept. 23, 1832, by Rev. Fosdic Harrison	349
Francis, of Woodbury, m. Debbe Ann **WHEDON**, of Roxbury, Sept. 25, 1832, by Rev. Fosdic Harrison	271
REYNOLDS, John, s. Lucy Ann **MUNGER**, b. June 28, 1801	343
RIDER, Daniel, of Reading, m. Charlotte A. **PRINDLE**, of Roxbury, Nov. 16, 1838, by Rev. F. Harrison, of Bethleham	345
ROSWELL, James, of Southbury, m. Sarah **JUDSON**, of New Milford, Aug. 14, 1826, by Josiah R. Eastman, J.P.	267
Sally, of Southbury, m. Elias A. **BATES**, of Roxbury, June 12, 1820, by Rev. Fosdic Harrison	257
SANDERSON, Mary C., see Mary C. **JUDSON**	261-2
SANFORD, John T.J.W., m. Abigail **PATTERSON**, Dec. 18, 1839, by Rev. A. Isham	272
Joseph, of New Milford, m. Maria **YOUNG**, of Roxbury, Mar. 24, 1830, by Fosdic Harrison	269
Phebe, of Roxbury, m. Deman **MOREHOUSE**, of Washington, May 18, 1823, by Rev. Sturgis Gilbert	261
Stephen, Jr., m. Marinda **HURD**, b. of Roxbury, Nov. 5, 1828, by Rev. Fosdic Harrison	269
SCUDDER, John B., of Washington, m. Helena **THOMAS**, of Roxbury, Oct. 3, 1832, by Thomas J. Fenn, J.P.	349
SEWARD, Ann Maria, m. Daniel **BARRITT**, b. of Roxbury, Oct. 23, 1825, by Rev. Fosdic Harrison	264
Orrin, m. Nancy **BLACKMAN**, b. of Roxbury, Aug. 22, 1824, by Rev. Sturgis Gilbert	263
SHEPARD, Truman, m. Mary A. **EDWARDS**, Dec. 25, 1839, by Rev. A. Isham	272
SHIPMAN, Temperance, m. Daniel **WARNER**, b. of Woodbury, May 9, 1822, by Josiah R. Eastman, J.P.	261-2
SMITH, Catharine A., m. Henry N. **PAINTER**, b. of Roxbury, Nov. 13, 1838, by Rev. F. Harrison	345
Mansfield, of Washington, m. Eliza **WHEELER**, of Roxbury, Dec. 5, 1821, by Fosdic Harrison, V.D.M.	260
Robert, m. Lucretia **CURTISS**, Jan. 23, 1812, by Elihu Canfield, J.P.	345
Sarah, m. Garry **GRISWOULD**, Feb. 17, 1823, by Maltby Gelston	260-3
William, m. Mary **JUDSON**, b. of New Milford, Sept. 18, 1830, by William Pierce, J.P.	270
William, of Roxbury, m. Eliza Ann **WEBSTER**, of Oxford, Nov. 20, 1831, by Rev. Fosdic Harrison	348
SPAULDING, Betsey, of Roxbury, m. David **BELLAMY**, of Bethleham, Nov. 24, 1825, by Rev. Fosdic Harrison	264
[**SQUIRE**], **SQUIER**, Anna, d. Nathan & Jane, b. Feb. 8, 1797	342
Elcey, of Roxbury, m. Woster **BEERS**, of New Milford, Dec. 27, 1820, by Rev. Fosdic Harrison	258
John, m. Hannah **BRONSON**, b. of Roxbury, May 9, 1824, by Josiah R.	

	Page
[SQUIRE], SQUIER, (cont.)	
Eastman, J.P.	263
Nathan, m. Jane **LAMPHERE**, Oct. 23, 1796, by Rev. Truman Marsh	344
Nathan, d. Jan. 18, 1812	345
STODDARD, Enos, of Litchfield, m. Betsey **PATTERSON**, of Roxbury, Feb. 26, 1833, by Josiah R. Eastman, J.P.	271
Enos, of Litchfield, m. Betsey **PATTERSON**, of Roxbury, Feb. 26, 1833, by Josiah R. Eastman, J.P.	349
STRICKLIN, Henry, of New Haven, m. Betsey **BALDWIN**, of Roxbury, June 2, 1822, at the house of Andrew Erwin, by Seth Higby	261-2
STRONG, Martha L., of Roxbury, m. Edward H. **FOWLER**, of Guilford, Apr. 3, 1834, by Rev. Fosdic Harrison	350
TAYLOR, David Towsey, of Newtown, m. Mary Emily **CHURCHIL**, of Litchfield, Mar. 25, 1828, by Rev. Fosdic Harrison	267
TEEPLE, Catharine, of Roxbury, m. Bradford J. **HULL**, of Weston, Jan. 26, 1823, by Daniel B. Brinsmade. J.P.	260-3
TERRELL, TUREL, TYRELL, Eunice, m. Richard H. **EASTMAN**, Mar. 21, 1821, by Rev. Fosdic Harrison	259
Hiram, m. Laura **THOMAS**, Apr. 25, 1821, by Fosdic Harrison	259
Thomas, m. Elizabeth **WARD**, Feb. 2, 1834, by William Pierce, J.P.	350
THOMAS, Caroline, of Roxbury, m. John **WHITCOMB**, of Cornwall, Apr. 15, 1831, by Josiah R. Eastman, J.P.	270
Catharine, of Roxbury, m. Ellieser Bartlett **FOWLER**, of Guilford, Oct. 15, 1820, by Fosdic Harrison	257
Charles, Jr., m. Jane **MILLER**, b. of Roxbury, Mar. 9, 1828, by Fosdic Harrison	267
Harriet A., m. Samuel D. **GARLICK**, b. of Roxbury, Mar. 7, 1833, by Rev. Fosdic Harrison	271
Harriet A., m. Samuel D. **GARLICK**, b. of Roxbury, Mar. 7, 1833, by Rev. Fosdic Harrison	349
Helena, of Roxbury, m. John B. **SCUDDER**, of Washington, Oct. 3, 1832, by Thomas J. Fenn, J.P.	349
Laura, m. Hiram **TERRELL**, Apr. 25, 1821, by Fosdic Harrison	259
Sarah Ann, m. Albert **COON**, Dec. 6, 1824, by Daniel B. Brinsmade, J.P.	263
THOMPSON, THOMSON, Anna, d. Rufus [& Cloe], b. July 24, 1804	342
Cloe, w. Rufus, d. Feb. 20, 1815, ae 38 y. 4 m.	346
Elizabeth, of Roxbury, m. Daniel **GOULD**, of Greenfield, Dec. 30, 1821, by Fosdic Harrison, V.D.M.	260
Olive, d. Rufus, [& Cloe], b. Oct. 22, 1806	342
Olive, m. Alvin **TUTTLE**, Nov. 9, 1828, at Middlebury (Entered by request of Rufus Thompson, Feb. 2, 1829	268
Rufus, m. Cloe **JUDSON**, Sept. 20, 1803	342
TOMLINSON, Samuel, of Woodbury, m. Jennet **PATTERSON**, of Roxbury, Nov. 28, 1827, by Grove L. Brownell	265
TOWNER, Asahel, of Oxford, m. Abigail **HURLBURT**, of Roxbury, Oct. 2, 1821, by Rev. Fosdic Harrison	260
TREAT, Homer, of Bridgewater, m. Beulah **FAIRCHILD**, of Roxbury, Mar. 19, 1823, by Fosdic Harrison	260-3
TROWBRIDGE, Anna Caroline, m. Herman **BALDWIN**, Dec. 25, 1820, by Rev. Fosdic Harrison	258
TUREL, [see under **TERRELL**}	

	Page
TUTTLE, Alvin, m. Olive **THOMPSON**, Nov. 9, 1828, at Middlebury (Entered by request of Rufus Thompson, Feb. 2, 1829)	268
TYRELL, [see under **TERRELL**}	
VOSE, Abel, m. Polly **BATES**, Sept. 5, 1830, by William Pierce, J.P.	269
WAKELEY, WAKELY, Hannah, of Roxbury, m. Beartis **FAIRCHILD**, of Newtown, Oct. 25, 1825, by Rev. Sturgis Gilbert	264
James, m. Sally **LAW**, Aug. 10, 1823, by Rev. Sturgis Gilbert	261
WARD, Abraham, m. Nancy **KING**, Sept. 7, [1833], by William Pierce, J.P.	350
Elizabeth, m. Thomas **TUREL**, Feb. 2, 1834, by William Pierce, J.P.	350
Laura, of Roxbury, m. Horace **WHEELER**, of Southbury, May 1, 1831, by Rev. Fosdic Harrison	271
Laura, of Roxbury, m. Horace **WHEELER**, of Southbury, May 1, 1831, by Rev. Fosdic Harrison	348
Levi, m. Philana **HURLBURT**, Feb. 25, 1821, by Rev. Fosdic Harrison	259
Levy, m. Polly **COGSWELL**, b. of Roxbury, Dec. 22, 1822, by Rev. Sturgis Gilbert, of Woodbury	260-3
Lydia Ann, m. Butler **BRONSON**, Mar. 14, 1821, by Rev. Sturgis Gilbert, of Woodbury	260
Peter, m. Susan L. **WHEELER**, b. of Roxbury, Sept. 11, 1833, by Rev. Fosdic Harrison	350
WARNER, Alla, m. John Mt. **CALM** (?), June 13, 1830, by Rev. Fosdic Harrison	270
Almond W., of Roxbury, m. Mary V.D. **BOGERT**, of Southbury, Jan. 28, [1839], by Rev. Thomas Ellis, of South Britain	338
Amos E., [s. Zaccheas & Laura], b. Aug. 4, 1820	347
Anna, m. Joseph **DUFF**, of Dublin, Ireland, Nov. 23, 1820, by Fosdic Harrison, V.D.M.	258
Daniel, m. Temperance **SHIPMAN**, b. of Woodbury, May 9, 1822, by Josiah R. Eastman, J.P.	261-2
Ebenezer C., [s. Curtiss & Harriet], b. Apr. 29, 1819	347
Eunice Ann, [d. Curtiss & Harriet], b. Jan. 25, 1825	347
George Welton, [s. Curtiss & Harriet], b. May 8, 1821	347
Harriet, [d. Curtiss & Harriet], b. Nov. 12, 1816	347
Harriet, of Roxbury, m. Solomon **DENNIE**, of Washington, Jan. 30, 1821, by Daniel B. Brinsmade, J.P.	258
Henry, of Roxbury, m. Charry Ann **GREGORY**, of Danbury, Oct. 5, 1820, by Fosdic Harrison	257
Lucy, of Roxbury, m. Sherman **FRISBIE**, of Washington, Nov. 19, 1824, by Fosdic Harrison	263
Lyman F., [s. Zaccheas & Laura}, b. Feb. 19, 1825	347
Mary Maria, of Roxbury, m. Chauncey **BUNNEL**, of Oxford, Jan. 27, 1839, by Rev. Thomas Ellis, of South Britain	338
Moses, m. Jennett **JUDSON**, b. of Roxbury, Nov. 12, 1826, by Rev. Fosdic Harrison	265
Olive Ann Frances, [d. Curtiss & Harriet], b. Mar. 17, 1827	347
Sally, of Roxbury, m. Daniel Couch **WHITLOCK**, of Southbury, Aug. 18, 1822, by Rev. Fosdic Harrison	261-2
Silas, of Roxbury, m. Lucy C. **HOYT**, of Washington, Apr. 18, 1824, by Rev. Fosdic Harrison	262
Zillah, of Roxbury, m. Elijah **WOODRUFF**, of Washington, Mar. 9, 1828, by Rev. Stephen Mason, of Washington	267

	Page
WEBSTER, Eliza Ann, of Oxford, m. William **SMITH**, of Roxbury, Nov. 20, 1831, by Rev. Fosdic Harrison	348
WELLER, Adaline, m. John M. **CASTLE**, Jr., b. of Roxbury, Apr. 14, 1825, by Rev. Sturgis Gilbert	264
Charles Frederick, [s. Samuel S. & Sophia A.], b. May 12, 1825	348
Charlotte Betsey, [d. Samuel S. & Sophia A.], b. Jan. 8, 1829	348
Eleanor, wid., d. Feb. 17, 1828, in the 86th y. of her age	343
Eunicy, m. Sheldon **LOGAN**, Jan. 1, 1818	347
Eunice Sophia, [d. Samuel S. & Sophia A.], b. Mar. 1, 1827	348
Jane, of Roxbury, m. Hervey **JENNINGS**, of New Milford, June 4, 1832, by Rev. Fosdic Harrison	271
Jane, of Roxbury, m. Harvey **GENNINGS**, of New Milford, June 4, 1832, by Rev. Fosdic Harrison	349
Samuel Wyllys, [s. Samuel S. & Sophia A.], b. Nov. 6, 1821	348
William Wallace, [s. Samuel S. & Sophia A.], b. Sept. 17, 1823	348
Zacheus Sherman, [s. Samuel S. & Sophia A.], b. May 3, 1820	348
WELTON, Eleazer, m. Nancy **HURLBURT**, Feb. 11, 1835, by Rev. B.Y. Messenger	350
WHEATON, WHEDON, Debbe Ann, of Roxbury, m. Francis **PRINDLE**, of Woodbury, Sept. 23, 1832, by Rev. Fosdic Harrison	349
Debbe Ann, of Roxbury, m. Francis **PRINDLE**, of Woodbury, Sept. 25, 1832, by Rev. Fosdic Harrison	271
WHEELER, Eliza, of Roxbury, m. Mansfield **SMITH**, of Washington, Dec. 5, 1821, by Fosdic Harrison, V.D.M.	260
Garry H., m. Maria **MUNGER**, Mar. 24, 1824, by Rev. Fosdic Harrison	262
Horace, of Southbury, m. Laura **WARD**, of Roxbury, May 1, 1831, by Rev. Fosdic Harrison	271
Horace, of Southbury, m. Laura **WARD**, of Roxbury, May 1, 1831, by Rev. Fosdic Harrison	348
Susan L., m. Peter **WARD**, b. of Roxbury, Sept. 11, 1833, by Rev. Fosdic Harrison	350
WHITCOMB, John, of Cornwall, m. Caroline **THOMAS**, of Roxbury, Apr. 15, 1831, by Josiah R. Eastman, J.P.	270
WHITLOCK, Daniel Couch, of Southbury, m. Sally **WARNER**, of Roxbury, Aug. 18, 1822, by Rev. Fosdic Harrison	261-2
WILLIAMS, Julia, m. Isaac **COLVIN**, now b. of Roxbury, Dec. 2, 1819, by Josiah R. Eastman, J.P.	258
WOODRUFF, Elijah, of Washington, m. Zillah **WARNER**, of Roxbury, Mar. 9, 1828, by Rev. Stephen Mason, of Washington	267
YOUNG, Louis, m. Loudon B. **LIVINGSTONE**, Oct. 26, 1823, by Fosdic Harrison, V.D.M.	261
Maria, of Roxbury, m. Joseph **SANFORD**, of New Milford, Mar. 24, 1830, by Fosdic Harrison	269
Rhodah, m. Eben **MALLERY**, b. of Roxbury, Nov. 29, 1821, by Josiah B. Eastman, J.P.	260

SALEM VITAL RECORDS
1836 - 1852

	Page
ALLYN, James, of Montville, m. Martha A. **WILLIAMS**, of Salem, [ ], by Cha[rle]s Thompson, at the house of Henry Williams in Salem	50
Theophilus, of Salem, Mass., m. Elizabeth A. **TREADWAY**, of East Haddam, May 4, 1847, by Charles Thompson, at the house of Russell Treadway, East Haddam	46
APIS, William, of Cold Rain, Mass., m. Mary **WOOD**, of Salem, Dec. 16, 1821, by Rev. John Whittlesey	9
ARAM, Philenia, m. Caleb **MINNARD**, b. of Salem, Jan. 4, 1826, by Rev. Oliver Willson	17
ASHBY, Edward, of Groton, m. Eunice A. **HEWITT**, of Salem, May 22, 1836, by Charles Thompson	32
ATKINS, Lucy, m. Benjamin **HURLBUTT**, b. of Salem, Sept. 21, 1835, by Rev. Cha[rle]s Thompson	31
AVERY, Elizabeth E., of Montville, m. Nehemiah B. **PAYNE**, of Salem, Sept. 9, 1838, by Rev. Charles Thompson	22
Lucy C., m. Samuel A. **RAY**, b. of Bozrah, Nov. 26, 1845, by Rev. J.B. Denison	40
BAILEY, Susan E., m. Charles **TIFFANY**, b. of Salem, Mar. 16, 1851, by Rev. W.W. Meach	49
BAKER, Lemuel, of Montville, m. Rhoda **POWERS**, of Salem, Sept. 16, 1821, by Joseph Morgan, J.P.	7
Nancy, m. Nathan **SMITH**, of Lyme, Nov. 5, 1848, by Rev. C.H. Gates	47
Rhoda, of Salem, m. Christopher L. **LITTLEFIELD**, of Lyme, Aug. 2, 1835, by Cha[rle]s Thompson	31
BALCH, Ahimaar, m. Sarah K. **WAY**, Sept. 13, 1829, by Asa Wilcox, Elder, in Colchester	10
BARBER, Abigail G., m. Roswell **MORGAN**, b. of Salem, Feb. 28, 1830, by Rev. Ash[a]bel Steel	26
BARTHOLOMEW, Demis, of New London, m. Albert **WATERMAN**, of Bozrah, Nov. 24, 1847, by Charles Thompson, at the house of Mr. Thompson	46
BECKWITH, Butler, of East Haddam, m. Ann Maria **WOODBRIDGE**, of Groton, Feb. 24, 1846, by Cha[rle]s Thompson	44
Eliphalet B., m. Sarah Ann **RATHBONE**, b. of Salem, Mar. 23, 1845, by Levi Meech, Elder	43
Jesse, Jr., of Lyme, m. Mabel **HARRIS**, of Salem, Feb. 27, 1823, by Rev. Eli Hyde	13
Joseph C., of Colchester, m. Polly **WILLIAMS**, of Salem, Jan. 1, 1822, by Salmon Cone, V.D.M.	8
Lydia S., m. Joseph N. **TAYLOR**, Aug. 16, 1851, by Seth E. Lathrop, J.P.	51
Mabel, of Salem, m. Selden **FULLER**, of East Haddam, Sept. 11, 1831, by Salmon Cone, V.D.M.	28
Samuel, of East Lyme, m. Clarissa R. **CHAPMAN**, of Salem, Oct. 18,	

	Page
BECKWITH, (cont.)	
1846, by Charles Thompson, at the house of Wid. DeWolf	46
BERKA, Joseph George, of New London, m. Jerusha **MOODY**, of East Haddam, (colored persons), May 6, 1844, by Rev. Charles Thompson, at his dwelling house (Perhaps "**BERHA**")	23
BIGALOW, Erastus, of Albany, N.Y., m. Statira **RANSOM**, of Salem, Jan. 31, 1819, at the house of Asahel Ransom, by Royal Tyler	3
BILLINGS, Francis, m. George **RANSOM**, b. of Salem, Nov. 2, 1819, at the house of Anna Dennis, by Royal Tyler	3
BLAIR, [see under **BLAN**]	
BLAN, David R., of Salem, m. Ann **MINARD**, of Montville, Oct. 22, 1821, by Joseph Morgan, J.P. (Perhaps "**BLAIR**")	7
BLISH, Aaron F., of Marlborough, m. Emma P. **CLARK**, of Salem, Mar. 8, 1840, by Rev. Charles Thompson	36
BOGUE, Edwin H., of Salem, m. Samantha **RAUN**, of Lyme, July 30, 1848, by Charles Thompson, at the house of James S. Tew, in Salem	48
Jerusha J., m. Henry W. **YERRINGTON**, May 13, 1851, by Rev. Benjamin G. Goff	49
Sila E., of Salem, m. Nathan P. **WILLIAMS**, of Montville, Feb. 28, 1847, by Rev. E. Loomis	43
BRAINARD, David, of East Haddam, m. Elizabeth C. **GRIFFIN**, of Salem, Dec. 7, 1834, by Rev. Charles Thompson	29
Nancy A., m. Samuel **BUCKINGHAM**, of East Haddam, May 10, 1835, by Erastus Ripley, at the house of Rev. Mr. Thompson, in Salem	31
BROWN, Edwin J., m. Hannah M. **ROBBINS**, Apr. 30, 1840, by Rev. E. Loomis	7
Frances B., of Montville, m. William **TINKER**, of New London, Jan. 27, 1822, by Rev. John Whittlesey	9
Hannah A., m. Joshua **PRATT**, b. of Salem, Apr. 9, 1829, by John Whittlesey, Elder	26
Loiza, of Montville, m. Samuel **JENNINGS**, of Bozrah, June 28, 1821, in Salem, by John Whittlesey	6
Lucy, of Montville, m. Charles W. **BUTLER**, Aug. 27, 1837, by Rev. John Whittlesey	32
Lydia, of Preston, m. Christopher P. **RATHBONE**, of Salem, Nov. 1, 1823, by Rev. John Whittlesy	14
William B., m. Mary E. **ROGERS**, b. of Salem, Mar. 4, 1832, by Asa Wilcox, Elder	6
BUCK, William, of Montville, m. Sarah B. **FARGO**, of Salem, Jan. 22, 1819, at the house of Robert Fargo, by Royal Tyler	2
BUCKINGHAM, Samuel, of East Haddam, m. Nancy A. **BRAINARD**, May 10, 1835, by Erastus Ripley, at the house of Rev. Mr. Thompson, in Salem	31
BURCH, ----------, m. William **TINKER**, b. of East Lyme, Nov. 28, 1839, by Rev. Charles Thompson	35
BURDICK, Evan, of Norwich, m. Nancy A. **CHAPMAN**, of Salem, Nov. 26, 1843, by Levi Meech, Elder	42
BUTLER, Charles W., m. Lucy **BROWN**, of Montville, Aug. 27, 1837, by Rev. John Whittlesy	32
CARROLL, Ann, of Essex, m. Royal **PHELPS**, May 2, 1847, by Alfred Gallup, J.P.	45

	Page
CHAPMAN, Alfred Hamilton, of East Haddam, m. Sophia E. **LOOMIS**, of Salem, Nov. 13, 1842, by Cha[rle]s Thompson	39
Clarissa R., of Salem, m. Samuel **BECKWITH**, of East Lyme, Oct. 18, 1846, by Charles Thompson, at the House of Wid. DeWolf	46
Elijah, of East Haddam, m. Patty **WOODWORTH**, of Salem, Feb. 28, 1821, at the house of Royal Tyler, by Royal Tyler	6
Nancy A., of Salem, m. Evan **BURDICK**, of Norwich, Nov. 26, 1843, by Levi Meech, Elder	42
Sophronia, of Salem, m. John **JOHNSON**, of Montville, Jan. 9, 1844, by Cha[rle]s Thompson	42
William H., m. Tabatha **STODDER**, b. of Salem, Oct. 22, 1843, by Levi Meech, Elder	42
CHAPPELL, CHAPPEL, CHAPELL, Ann, of Montville, m. Benjamin **THOMPSON**, of Lebanon, Oct. 31, 1827, by Joseph Morgan, J.P.	19
Hannah, of Montville, m. Thomas **JONES**, of Lebanon, Oct. 22, 1826, by Shubael Park, J.P.	18
Japhet, of Salem, m. Mary **LEWIS**, of Montville, Dec. 6, 1821, by Joseph Morgan, J.P.	8
Laura, of Salem, m. John L. **LATIMER**, Jr., of Montville, Nov. 23, 1841, by Rev. Erastus Benton	23
CHURCH, George, of Montville, m. Maria **FARGO**, of Salem, Dec. 29, 1850, by Charles Thompson, at the house of Charles Thompson	50
Truman F., m. Eunice O. **WEBSTER**, b. of East Haddam, Oct. 7, 1849, by Charles Thompson	48
CLARK, CLARKE, Charlotte, of Salem, m. George H. **CLARKE**, of Lebanon, Jan. 14, 1844, by Cha[rle]s Thompson	42
Dudley, m. Keturah **CLARK**, b. of Salem, Sept. 30, 1842, by Cha[rle]s Thompson	38
Emma P., of Salem, m. Aaron F. **BLISH**, of Marlborough, Mar. 8, 1840, by Rev. Charles Thompson	36
George H., of Lebanon, m. Charlotte **CLARKE**, of Salem, Jan. 14, 1844, by Cha[rle]s Thompson	42
Keturah, m. Dudley **CLARK**, b. of Salem, Sept. 30, 1842, by Cha[rle]s Thompson	38
COLEMAN, Jesse O., of Colchester, m. Salina M. **GATES**, of Salem, Oct. 24, 1842, by Rev. Edmund A. Standish	37
COMSTOCK, Anson Lord, b. Dec. 31, 1802	16
Belinda, b. Sept. 4, 1793	16
Caleb, b. Jan. 27, 1790	16
Ebenezer Williams, b. Nov. 7, 1807	16
Fitch Bradford, b. Jan. 1, 1804	16
John Scott, b. Feb. 20, 1801	16
Joshua B., m. Hannah **RATHBUN**, b. of Salem, Apr. 28, 1822, by Shubael Park, J.P.	11
Joshua Bartlett, b. May 10, 1799	16
Mary Haynes, b. Mar. 15, 1795	16
Matilda, b. Jan. 31, 1799; m. Ebenezer **ROGERS**, Jr., Oct. 2, 1823	15
Matilda, m. Ebenezer **ROGERS**, Jr., b. of Salem, Oct. 2, [ ], by Joseph Morgan, J.P.	14
Samuel, b. Nov. 14, 1791	16
Sarah Harris, b. Mar. 1, 1797	16

	Page
COMSTOCK, (cont.)	
William Pitt, b. June 16, 1810	16
CONGDON, Abby N., [d. David & Lucretia], b. Dec. 28, 1825; d. Nov. 30, 1826, ae 11 m. 2 d.	33
David, b. Feb. 17, 1798, m. Lucretia **ROGERS**, Jan. 21, 1824	33
David, of Salem, m. Lucretia **ROGERS**, of East Haddam, Jan. 18, 1824, by Joseph Morgan, J.P.	17
Elisha, of Montville, m. Eleanor **FORSYTH**, of Salem, Nov. 21, 1821, by Nehemiah Dodge	8
Francis D., [s. David & Lucretia], b. July 18, 1829	33
Frederick C., [s. David & Lucretia], b. Sept. 28, 1834	33
George N., [s. David & Lucretia], b. Apr. 12, 1827	33
Harriet N., [d. David & Lucretia], b. Jan. 21, 1826	33
John H., [s. David & Lucretia], b. Nov. 28, 1830	33
Lorenzo, m. Elizabeth B. **MOORE**, b. of East Lyme, Oct. 9, 1842, by Cha[rle]s Thompson	39
Louisa Jane, [d. David & Lucretia], b. Feb. 2, 1833	33
Sarah Elizabeth, [d. David & Lucretia], b. July 26, 1836	33
COOK, Julia S., of Hartford, m. Cha[rle]s R. **COPELAND**, July 19, 1835, by Cha[rle]s Thompson	31
COON, Lois, of Hopkintown, R.I., m. Thomas **WAY**, of New London, Apr. 15, 1838, by Rev. Charles Thompson	22
COPELAND, Cha[rle]s R., m. Julia S. **COOK**, of Hartford, July 19, 1835, by Cha[rle]s Thompson	31
CROCKER, Emaline, m. Manning **FARGO**, b. of Salem, Dec. 13, 1827, by Rev. Robert Fargo	24
Sarah L., m. John **PAYN[E]**, b. of Salem, Aug. 13, 1829, by Rev. Oliver Wilson, of Montville,	25
CUSHING, John, of Bergen, N.Y., m. Elizabeth **LOOMIS**, of Salem, Nov. 6, 1820, at the house of Jacob Lo[o]mis, by William Palmer	1
DANIELS, Mary A., m. Henry P. **WHITTLESY**, b. of Salem, Aug. 17, 1835, by Rev. Charles Thompson	23
Mary A., m. Henry P. **WHITTLESY**, b. of Salem, Aug. 17, 1835, by Rev. Charles Thompson	31
DESHIE, Loiza, of Norwich, m. David **MOSELEY**, of East Haddam, Sept. 30, 1845, by Cha[rle]s Thompson, in Salem, (colored persons)	44
DeWOLF, Edward, of Salem, m. Sophia J. **LATIMER**, of Montville, Oct. 2, 1836, by Charles Thompson	32
Maria, m. William F. **TIFFANY**, b. of Salem, May 29, 1842, by Cha[rle]s Thompson	38
Mary Ann, of Salem, m. Ezra **WHALEY**, of Lyme, Feb. 18, 1833, by Rev. Alvin Ackley, at the house of wid. E. DeWolf	29
Orin, m. Mary L. **LATIMER**, b. of Salem, Mar. 15, 1846, by Cha[rle]s Thompson	44
DOLBEARE, ----------, of Montville, m. Mary **FARGO**, of Montville, May 25, 1851, by C. Thompson, at the house of C. Thompson	50
DOUBLEDEE, Phebe, of Salem, m. Solomon **GOODWIN**, of Lebanon, Nov. 30, 1837, by Rev. Cha[rle]s Thompson	34
DOUGLASS, John, of Waterford, m. Ann Elizabeth **RAYMOND**, of Salem, Dec. 12, 1838, by Rev. Nathaniel Miner, East Haddam	23
DOWNER, Uriah, m. Pamelia **PARKER**, Nov. 5, 1826, by Rev. Tubal	

DOWNER, (cont.)	Page
Wakefield	19
EDWARDS, Fordam, m. Aseneth **PHELPS**, b. of Lyme, Sept. 1, 1850, by Rev. W.W. Meach	49
Maria, of Lyme, m. Frederick **PHELPS**, of Saybrook, Feb. 17, 1850, by Rev. W[illia]m W. Meach	48
FAIRMAN, David, m. Mary **GARDNER**, b. of Salem, Apr. 25, 1830, by Asa Wilcox, Elder	27
FARGO, Manning, m. Emaline **CROCKER**, b. of Salem, Dec. 13, 1827, by Rev. Robert Fargo	24
Maria, of Salem, m. George **CHURCH**, of Montville, Dec. 29, 1850, by Charles Thompson, at the home of Charles Thompson	50
Mary, m. [ ] **DOLBEARE**, b. of Montville, May 25, 1851, by C. Thompson, at the house of C. Thompson	50
Sally, m. Nathaniel P. **RANSOM**, b. of Salem, Nov. 12, 1826, by John Billings, J.P.	18
Sarah B., of Salem, m. William **BUCK**, of Montville, Jan. 22, 1819, at the house of Robert Fargo, by Royal Tyler	2
FARNSWORTH, John, m. Mary **MINER**, b. of Salem, Mar. 17, 1839, by Rev. Charles Thompson	35
FISH, Caroline, m. Ebenezer A. **PACKER**, b. of Salem, May 2, 1830, by Asa Wilcox, Elder	27
Eunice, of Salem, m. Elisha J. **STODDARD**, of Groton, Dec. 28, 1819, at the house of Thomas Fish, by Royal Tyler	4
Eunice Elizabeth, m. Israel N. **JONES**, b. of Salem, [Jan.] 20, 1833, by John W. Salter	3
FITCH, John, of Montville, m. Fanny **TREADWAY**, of Salem, Apr. 27, 1836, by Charles Thompson	32
[FLORENCE], Julia Ann, b. Mar. 5, 1819, at Rahway, N.J.; m. David P. **OTIS**, [of East Haddam], Dec. 4, 1837, at Rahway, N.J.	47
FORSYTH, Ele[a]nor, of Salem, m. Elisha **CONGDON**, of Montville, Nov. 21, 1821, by Nehemiah Dodge	8
Jane, m. Col. Russell **HINCKLEY**, b. of Salem, Aug. 1, 1840, by Cha[rle]s Thompson	38
Latham, m. Abigail **LEE**, Aug. 27, 1804, by Rev. Reuben Palmer	7
Latham, d. Oct. 3, 1835	15
FOX, George W., m. Hannah **WAY**, b. of Salem, Feb. 25, 1835, by Charles Thompson	30
FULLER, Amos J., m. Sallinda **MILLER**, b. of Salem, Feb. 6, 1821, at the house of Thomas Miller, by Royal Tyler	5
Emily, of Colchester, m. Joseph **WOOD**, of Salem, Oct. 16, 1831, by Salmon Cone, V.D.M.	28
Selden, of East Haddam, m. Mabel **BECKWITH**, of Salem, Sept. 11, 1831, by Salmon Cone, V.D.M.	28
Warren, of Salem, m. Ann H. **MINARD**, of Salem, Aug. 7, 1849, by Charles Thompson, at the house of Nathan Minard	48
GARDINER, [see also **GARDNER**], Andrew J., of Colchester, m. Fanny R. **RANDALL**, of Salem, Apr. 19, 1840, by Rev. Charles Thompson	36
Asenath, of Bozrah, m. Ichabod **STODDAR**, of Salem, June 4, 1820, by Eben[eze]r A. Barker, J.P.	1
GARDNER, [see also **GARDINER**], Jedediah J., of East Haddam, m. Lucretia	

	Page
GARDNER, (cont.)	
THOMPSON, of Salem, Mar. 30, 1828, by John Whittlesy, Elder	25
Mary, m. David **FAIRMAN**, b. of Salem, Apr. 25, 1830, by Asa Wilcox, Elder	27
GATES, Abel, Capt., m. Eunice **HUNTLEY**, Jan. 6, 1825, by Rev. David Austin at Bozrah	17
David G., s. John & Anstrus G., b. Dec. 13, 1814	41
Gilbert, s. John & Anstrus G., b. July 29, 1819	41
Jemima J., d. John & Anstrus G., b. Sept. 29, 1816	41
Mary E., d. John & Anstrus G., b. Mar. 8, 1829	41
Mary J., m. Oliver M. **RATHBONE**, Dec. 16, 1849, by Rev. Benjamin G. Goff	48
Rhoda Ann, d. John & Anstrus G., b. Jan. 5, 1823	41
Salina H., d. John & Anstrus G., b. Mar. 9, 1821	41
Salina M., of Salem, m. Jesse O. **COLEMAN**, of Colchester, Oct. 24, 1842, by Rev. Edmund A. Standish	37
William A., s. John & Anstrus G., b. Apr. 26, 1825	41
GEER, John A., formerly of Akron, Ohio, m. Lucretia E. **ROGERS**, of Salem, Jan. 24, 1843, by James Lamb, J.P.	38
GOODWIN, Solomon, of Lebanon, m. Phebe **DOUBLEDEE**, of Salem, Nov. 30, 1837, by Rev. Cha[rle]s Thompson	34
GRANT, Eliza, of Salem, m. David **MITCHELL**, of East Haddam, Apr. 13, 1834, by Rev. Charles Thompson	29
GREEN, Temah, of Franklin, m. Amos **JONES**, of Hancock, Mar. 2, 1834, by Rev. Charles Thompson	29
GRIFFIN, Elizabeth C., of Salem, m. David **BRAINARD**, of East Haddam, Dec. 7, 1834, by Rev. Charles Thompson	29
GUILD, Joel D., of Colchester, m. Lucy Jane **PATTON**, of Salem, Apr. 7, 1835, by Charles Thompson	30
HAMLIN, Butler, of Salem, Penn., m. Sallinda **RATHBONE**, of Salem, Conn., Oct. 21, 1838, by Rev. Charles Thompson	22
HARRIS, Grace, m. Hardin **MINARD**, b. of Salem, Dec. 2, 1821, by Royal Tyler, at the house of Joseph Harris	11
Louisa M., of Salem, m. Richard S. **LEWIS**, of Hopkintown, R.I., Dec. 17, 1838, by Rev. John Whittlesy	22
Lydia, m. Asa **RATHBURN**, b. of Salem, Apr. 18, 1825, by Artemus Worthington, J.P.	24
Mabel, of Salem, m. Jesse **BECKWITH**, Jr., of Lyme, Feb. 27, 1823, by Rev. Eli Hyde	13
Mary A., m. Augustus S. **HOLMES**, b. of Salem, Nov. 9, 1845, by Rev. J. B. Denison	34
Sophia, m. Russell **WILLIAMS**, b. of Salem, Dec. 2, 1821, by Royall Tyler, at the house of Joseph Harris	10
HARRISON, John, Cpat., of Lyme, m. Francis **PATTEN**, of Salem, Oct. 25, 1837, by Cha[rle]s Thompson	34
HARVEY, Charles B., b. July 28, 1838	51
Elijah B., s. Levi & Lucy, b. Aug. 3, 1812, in Norwich	28
Elijah B., m. Sarah **HILLIARD**, b. of Conn., Sept. 21, 1837, by Rev. Joseph G. Price, of St. Stephen's Church, New York. Witnesses: Mrs. C.M. Lerret, Mr. J. Acholan. Recorded Oct. 19, 1851	51
Jerusha, d. Levi & Lucy, b. Dec. 25, 1809, in Bozrah	28

SALEM VITAL RECORDS 129

Page

HARVEY, (cont.)
Jerusha, m. Russell B. **RATHBUN**, b. of Salem, July 4, 1830, by Asa
 Wilcox, Elder   27
Levi, s. Levi & Lucy, b. Apr. 8, 1805, in Bozrah   28
Levinia, d. Levi & Lucy, b. June 4, 1807, in Bozrah   28
Lucy, d. Levy & Lucy, b. Mar. 29, 1803, in Bozrah   28
Olivia, d. Levi & Lucy, b. Apr. 10, 1819, in Colchester   28
Park Benjamin, s. Levi & Lucy, b. Oct. 28, 1822, in Colchester   28
Paul, s. Levi & Lucy, b. Jan. 13, 1816, in Stafford   28
HAYS, Seth, of East Haddam, m. Mary L. **LYON**, of Salem, Mar. 20, 1842,
 by Rev. James Hepburn, Montville   36
HAZARD, Henry, m. Hannah **SMITH**, b. of Salem, Feb. 4, 1840, by Artemus
 Worthington, J.P.   33
HERRICK, Elias B., of Windham, m. Mary L. **MAYNARD**, of Salem,
 [ ], by Rev. John Whittlesy   29
Elijah, of Norwich, m. Lucy **WISONBAKER**, of Salem, May 11, 1823,
 by Rev. John Whittlesey   14
Sarah A., m. Lafayette **LATIMER**, Dec. 20, 1846, by Alfred Gallup, J.P.,
 at the house of Matthias W. Baker, in Salem   45
HEWITT, Eunice A., of Salem, m. Edward **ASHBY**, of Groton, May 22, 1836,
 by Charles Thompson   32
HILLIARD, Henry Oscar, b. May 28, 1810   51
Joseph, b. Oct. 7, 1780   51
Joseph, Capt., m. Sarah **TREDWAY**, Aug. 30, 1809, by Joel
 Worthington, J.P. Recorded 1852   1
Julia A., m. Richard C. **TIFFANY**, b. of Salem, Sept. 14, 1842, by Rev.
 Tho[ma]s Dowling   37
Margaret A., of Salem, m. Richard **RANGER**, of Lyme, Jan. 26, 1845, by
 Rev. Thomas Dowling, of North Lyme   43
Sarah, m. Elijah B. **HARVEY**, b. of Conn., Sept. 21, 1837, by Rev.
 Joseph G. Price, of St. Stephen's Church, New York. Witnesses:
 Mrs. C.M. Lerret, Mr. J. Acholan. Recorded Oct. 19, 1851   51
Sarah, mother of W[illia]m Albert, d. Dec. 15, 1849   51
Sarah Amanda, b. Sept. 12, 1814   51
William Albert, b. Feb. 10, 1817; d. Oct. 24, 1817   51
HINCKLEY, Russell, Col., m. Jane **FORSYTH**, b. of Salem, Aug. 1, 1840, by
 Cha[rle]s Thompson   38
HOLMES, Augustus S., m. Mary A. **HARRIS**, b. of Salem, Nov. 9, 1845, by
 Rev. J.B. Denison   34
Dimmis, b. Dec. 13, 1786; m. Nathan **MINARD**, Nov. 4, 1813, by Rev.
 William Witter   15
Fanny A., m. Royal W. **TYLER**, b. of Salem, Jan. 29, 1827, by Rev.
 Nathaniel Miner, of Chesterfield Society   19
HOPKINS, Nancy, of Salem, m. David **WALDEN**, of Montville, Oct. 21,
 1823, by Joseph Morgan, J.P.   14
HOUSE, Lavinia, of Salem, m. Erastus **THACHMAN**, of Glastenbury, June
 16, 1850, by Rev. W[illia]m Harrison, of Franklin, at the house of
 Charles Thompson   48
HOYT, James F., of Norwich, m. Sarah P. **ROGERS**, Jan. 1, 1834, by Rev.
 Cha[rle]s Thompson   30
HUNTLEY, Demeris, m. Amos **OTIS**, b. of Colchester, May 11, 1842, by Rev.

	Page
HUNTLEY, (cont.)	
John Whittlesy	36
Eunice, m. Capt. Abel **GATES**, Jan. 6, 1825, by Rev. David Austin, at Bozrah	17
HURLBUTT, Benjamin, m. Lucy **ATKINS**, b. of Salem, Sept. 21, 1835, by Rev. Cha[rle]s Thompson	31
JENNINGS, Samuel, of Bozrah, m. Loiza **BROWN**, of Montville, June 28, 1821, in Salem, by John Whittlesey	6
JEROME, Jesse, of Waterford, m. Harriet **LOOMIS**, of Salem, Nov. 24, 1831, by Rev. Nathan E. Shailer	29
JOHNSON, John, of Montville, m. Sophronia **CHAPMAN**, of Salem, Jan. 9, 1844, by Cha[rle]s Thompson	42
Samuel C., of Colchester, m. Sophia **MILLER**, of Salem, Mar. 18, 1839, by Rev. Charles Thompson	35
JONES, Amos, of Hancock, m. Temah **GREEN**, of Franklin, Mar. 2, 1834, by Rev. Charles Thompson	29
Eliza B., m. Horace **MILLER**, Mar. 10, 1821, at the house of Sala Jones, by Royal Tyler	10
Fanny L., of Salem, m. Benjamin **LATHROP**, of Susqueehannah County, Penn., Aug. 30, 1831, by Salmon Cone, V.D.M.	28
Frances, m. Abby **LOOMIS**, b. of Salem, Jan. 13, 1820, at the house of Guy Loomis, by Royal Tyler	5
Henry Augustus, s. Frances & Abby, b. Oct. 5, 1823	5
Israel N., m. Eunice Elizabeth **FISH**, b. of Salem, [Jan.] 20, 1833, by John W. Salter	3
Thomas, of Lebanon, m. Hannah **CHAPPEL**, of Montville, Oct. 22, 1826, by Shubael Park, J.P.	18
KEITH, W[illia]m E., of Oxford, Mass., m. Harriet **TREADWAY**, of Salem, Aug. 20, 1846, by Cha[rle]s Thompson, Minister	44
KELLEY, Henry M., m. Mary A. **PRATT**, b. of Salem, Aug. 11, 1845, by Rev. Jesse B. Denison	43
LAMB, Albert, of Bozrah, m. Lydia Watson **WOODWARD**, May 28, 1821, by Royall Tyler, at his house in Salem	10
Celia Ann, of Salem, m. George **STRICKLAND**, of Salem, [ ], by Charles Thompson, at the house of Capt. Henry Bailey, in Salem	46
LAMBFUR, James, of Bozrah, m. Angelina **MORGAN**, of Salem, Jan. 6, 1822, by Joseph Morgan, J.P. **(LAMPHEAR?)**	9
LAPIER, Arnard, Jr., of Norwich, m. Sarah Ann **RATHBONE**, of Salem, May 28, 1843, by Levi Meech, Elder	41
LATHAM, Jeremiah S., of Lyme, m. Nancy A. **MORGAN**, of Salem, Aug. 8, 1847, by Charles Thompson, in Salem	46
LATHROP, Benjamin, of Susqueehannah County, Penn., m. Fanny L. **JONES**, of Salem, Aug. 30, 1831, by Salmon Cone, V.D.M.	28
LATIMER, LATTIMER, John L., Jr., of Montville, m. Laura **CHAPPELL**, of Salem, Nov. 23, 1841, by Rev. Erastus Benton	23
Lafayette, m. Sarah A. **HERRICK**, Dec. 20, 1846, by Alfred Gallup, J.P., at the house of Matthias W. Baker, in Salem	45
Lucy, of Lyme, m. Isaac **SPENCER**, of Montville, Dec. 27, 1812, by Henry Perkins, J.P., at Lyme	24
Mary L., m. Orin **DeWOLF**, b. of Salem, Mar. 15, 1846, by Cha[rle]s Thompson	44

SALEM VITAL RECORDS 131

Page

LATIMER, LATTIMER, (cont.)
Sophia J., of Montville, m. Edward **DeWOLF**, of Salem, Oct. 2, 1836, by
 Charles Thompson ... 32
LEE, Abigail, m. Latham **FORSYTH**, Aug. 27, 1804, by Reuben Palmer,
 Minister ... 7
Christopher H., of Lyme, m. Betsey **TIFFANY**, of Salem, Dec. 19, 1822,
 by Rev. William Palmer, at Ebenezer Tiffany's ... 12
LEWIS, Mary, of Montville, m. Japhet **CHAPELL**, of Salem, Dec. 6, 1821, by
 Joseph Morgan, J.P. ... 8
Richard S., of Hopkinton, R.I., m. Louisa M. **HARRIS**, of Salem, Dec.
 17, 1838, by Rev. John Whittlesy ... 22
LITTLEFIELD, Christopher L., of Lyme, m. Rhoda **BAKER**, of Salem, Aug.
 2, 1835, by Cha[rle]s Thompson ... 31
LOOMIS, Abby, m. Frances **JONES**, b. of Salem, Jan. 13, 1820, at the house
 of Guy Loomis, by Royal Tyler ... 5
Elijah, of Salem, m. Lucretia D. **WILLOUGHBY**, of Salem, Dec. 30,
 1838, by Rev. Charles Thompson ... 35
Elizabeth, of Salem, m. John **CUSHING**, of Bergen, N.Y., Nov. 6, 1820,
 at the house of Jacob Lo[o]mis, by William Palmer ... 1
Harriet, of Salem, m. Jesse **JEROME**, of Waterford, Nov. 24, 1831, by
 Rev. Nathan E. Shailer ... 29
Lucretia, m. John W. **MORGAN**, Feb. 23, 1851, by Charles Thompson, at
 the house of Hubbell Loomis, Salem ... 50
Sarah, m. Alpheas H. **TREADWAY**, b. of Salem, Mar. 18, 1840, by Rev.
 Charles Thompson ... 36
Sophia E., of Salem, m. Alfred Hamilton **CHAPMAN**, of East Haddam,
 Nov. 13, 1842, by Cha[rle]s Thompson ... 39
LYON, Frances, of Salem, m. Joseph **STRICKLAND**, of Lyme, Mar. 22,
 1847, by Rev. Jacob Gardiner, of Montville, ... 45
Mary L., of Salem, m. Seth **HAYS**, of East Haddam, Mar. 20, 1842, by
 Rev. James Hepburn, Montville ... 36
MAGINNIS, John T., of New London, m. Eliza **TULLY**, eldest d. of Cromel
 Whittlesy, of Salem, Dec. 18, 1851, by Rev. Edwin R. Warren, at the
 Normal Academy of Music in Salem ... 51
MANN, Cyrus, of Hebron, m. Elizabeth E. **WORTHINGTON**, of Colchester,
 Apr. 19, 1843, by Rev. Alpheas Geer, in Christ's Church, Salem ... 39
MAYNARD, Mary L., of Salem, m. Elias B. **HERRICK**, of Windham,
 [ ], by Rev. John Whittlesy ... 29
Zebdiah, m. Nancy **STRICKLAND**, b. of Montville, Oct. 11, 1846, by
 Alfred Gallup, J.P. ... 41
MILLER, Horace, m. Eliza B. **JONES**, Mar. 10, 1821, at the house of Sala
 Jones, by Royal Tyler ... 10
Sallinda, m. Amos J. **FULLER**, b. of Salem, Feb. 6, 1821, at the house of
 Thomas Miller, by Royal Tyler ... 5
Sarah, of Salem, m. William **WARREN**, of Ridgefield, N.Y., Sept. 21,
 1835, by Rev. Cha[rle]s Thompson ... 31
Sophia, of Salem, m. Samuel C. **JOHNSON**, of Colchester, Mar. 18,
 1839, by Rev. Charles Thompson ... 35
MILLS, Robert C., Rev., of Colchester, m. Mary S. **TIFFANY**, of Salem, June
 14, 1843, by Rev. Tho[ma]s Dowling ... 39
MINARD, MINNARD, Ann, of Montville, m. David R. **BLAN**, of Salem, Oct.

	Page
MINARD, MINNARD, (cont.)	
22, 1821, by Joseph Morgan, J.P.	7
Ann H., of Salem, m. Warren **FULLER**, of Salem, Aug. 7, 1849, by Charles Thompson, at the house of Nathan Minard	48
Anna Holmes, d. Nathan & Dimmis, b. Dec. 15, 1815	15
Caleb, m. Philenia **ARAM**, b. of Salem, Jan. 4, 1826, by Rev. Oliver Willson	17
Dimmis, w. Nathan, d. Apr. 6, 1824	73
Frances, m. Thomas **SMITH**, b. of Salem, Sept. 24, 1843, by Cha[rle]s Thompson	42
Hardin, m. Grace **HARRIS**, b. of Salem, Dec. 2, 1821, by Royal Tyler, at the house of Joseph Harris	11
Mary Ann*, of Salem, m. Enoch F. **TREADWAY**, of New London, Dec. 25, 1839, by Rev. Charles Thompson *(Handwritten correction in original says "**MINOR**")	35
Nathan, b. Aug. 18, 1788; m. Dimmis **HOLMES**, Nov. 4, 1813, by Rev. William Witter	15
Sally, m. Peter **WICKWIRE**, Mar. 23, 1831, by Asa Wilcox, Elder	27
Sarah Amelia, d. Nathan & Nancy, b. Jan. 25, 1835	15
Sarah Isham, d. Nathan & Dimmis, b. Apr. 8, 1819	15
Sarah Isham, d. Nathan & Dimmis, d. July 24, 1821	73
MINER, Abba M., of Salem, m. Gardner **WICKWIRE**, of Montville, Mar. 30, 1828, by Rev. Benjamin G. Goff	25
Joel, m. Minerva **MORGAN**, b. of Salem, Mar. 8, 1824, by Joseph Morgan, J.P.	17
Mary, m. John **FARNSWORTH**, b. of Salem, Mar. 17, 1839, by Rev. Charles Thompson	35
MITCHELL, David, of East Haddam, m. Eliza **GRANT**, of Salem, Apr. 13, 1834, by Rev. Charles Thompson	29
MONTALL, Tereasa, of Salem, m. Oliver **OLMSTED**, of East Haddam, Nov. 19, 1829, by Joseph Morgan, J.P.	6
MOODY, Jerusha, of East Haddam, m. Joseph George **BERKA**, of New London, (colored persons), May 6, 1844, by Rev. Charles Thompson, at his dwelling house	23
MOORE, Elizabeth B., m. Lorenzo **CONGDON**, b. of East Lyme, Oct. 9, 1842, by Cha[rle]s Thompson	39
MORGAN, Angelina, of Salem, m. James **LAMBFUR**, of Bozrah, Jan. 6, 1822, by Joseph Morgan, J.P.	9
Aran, of Montville, m. Charlotte **STAPLES**, of Waterford, May 4, 1823, by Rev. John Whittlesey	13
Charlotte, m. Oliver **WILLIAMS**, Mar. 5, 1848, by David P. Otis, J.P.	47
Charlotte Maconda, m. Daniel **WHITTLESY**, b. of Salem, Jan. 2, 1826, by Rev. Amasa Taylor	18
John W., m. Lucretia **LOOMIS**, Feb. 23, 1851, by Charles Thompson, at the house of Hubbell Loomis, Salem	50
Minerva, m. Joel **MINER**, b. of Salem, Mar. 8, 1824, by Joseph Morgan, J.P.	17
Nancy A., of Salem, m. Jeremiah S. **LATHAM**, of Lyme, Aug. 8, 1847, by Charles Thompson, in Salem	46
Nathan D., s. Amos & Elizabeth, b. Aug. 17, 1821	15
Roswell, m. Abigail G. **BARBER**, b. of Salem, Feb. 28, 1830, by Rev.	

	Page
MORGAN, (cont.)	
Ash[a]bel Steel	26
Sidney, m. Harriet **STODDARD**, b. of Salem, Feb. 23, 1823, by Joseph Morgan, J.P.	12
MORRIS, John, of Salem, m. Sarah A. **RANSOM**, of Colchester, Jan. 14, 1844, by Cha[rle]s Thompson	42
MOSELEY, David, of East Haddam, m. Loiza **DESHIE**, of Norwich, Sept. 30, 1845, by Cha[rle]s Thompson, in Salem (colored persons)	44
Jerusha, of East Haddam, m. George **RESHA**, of New London, (colored persons), May 6, 1844, by Cha[rle]s Thompson, at his dwelling house	44
NEWTON, Israel, of Colchester, m. Harriet **TURNER**, of Montville, Jan. 15, 1819, at the house of Matthew Turner, by Royal Tyler	2
NILES, Celia A.K., of Salem, m. Hezekiah H. **WILLIAMS**, of Pontiac, Mich., Sept. 8, 1850, by Charles Thompson, in the Congregational Church	50
NOYES, Abby B., of Westerly, R.I., m. Henry **PERKINS**, of Salem, Mar. 19, 1820, by Rev. Ira Hart, in Stonington	13
OLMSTED, Oliver, of East Haddam, m. Tereasa **MONTALL**, of Salem, Nov. 19, 1829, by Joseph Morgan, J.P.	6
OTIS, Amos, m. Demeris **HUNTLEY**, b. of Colchester, May 11, 1842, by Rev. John Whittlesy	36
Anna Matilda, [d. David P. & Julia Ann], b. June 4, 1847	47
David P., b. Feb. 28, 1809, at East Haddam,; m. Julia Ann **FLORENCE**, Dec. 4, 1837, at Rahway, N.J.	47
Dwight P., s. David P. & Julia Ann, b. Oct. 8, 1838, at Waterford	47
Harriet Elizabeth, d. David P. & Julia Ann, b. Sept. 11, 1844	47
Julia Florence, d. David P. & Julia Ann, b. May 23, 1841, at Salem	47
Richard, of Lyme, m. Nancy **PALMER**, of Salem, Sept. 30, 1829, by Thomas Fitch, J.P.	7
PACKER, Ebenezer A., m. Caroline **FISH**, b. of Salem, May 2, 1830, by Asa Wilcox, Elder	27
PAGE, Mary, m. William **TEW**, May 20, 1830, by Amhurst D. Scoville, J.P.	26
PAINE, [see under **PAYNE**]	
PALMER, Abigail, of Colchester, m. John **SMITH**, of Salem, Mar. 27, 1839, by Rev. Benjamin G. Goff, in Salem	34
Nancy, of Salem, m. Richard **OTIS**, of Lyme, Sept. 30, 1829, by Thomas Fitch, J.P.	7
Simeon, m. Caroline **TIFFANY**, Aug. 5, 1828, by Tubal Wakefield	25
PARK, Abigail, w. of Shubael, d. Dec. 2, 1833, ae 58 y.	37
Abigail, w. of Shubael, d. Dec. 2, 1833, ae 58 y.	73
Anna W., d. Shubael, d. Oct. 15, 1842, ae 24	37
Erasmus D., s. of Shubael, d. May 23, 1842, ae 27 y.	37
Paul S., s. of Shubael, d. July 28, 1844, at Adrian, Mich., ae 38 y.	37
Polly B., d. Shubael, d. Sept. 4, 1833, ae 22 y.	37
Polly B., d. Shubael, d. Sept. 4, 1833, ae 22 y.	73
Shubael W., s. Shubael, d. July 12, 1842, near Schenecktady, N.Y., ae 30 y.	37
PARKER, Pamelia, m. Uriah **DOWNER**, Nov. 5, 1826, by Rev. Tubal Wakefield	19
PATTEN, PATTON, Francis, of Salem, m. John **HARRISON**, of Lyme, Oct. 25, 1837, by Cha[rle]s Thompson	34

	Page
PATTEN, PATTON, (cont.)	
John, m. Elizabeth M. **WILLIAMS**, b. of Salem, Feb. 3, 1846, by Cha[rle]s Thompson	44
Lucy Jane, of Salem, m. Joel D. **GUILD**, of Colchester, Apr. 7, 1835, by Charles Thompson	30
Sarah, of Salem, m. Dea. Shubael **SMITH**, of Colchester, Dec. 23, 1847, by Charles Thompson, at the house of David Patten, in Salem	46
PAYNE, PAYN, Henrietta, m. Adams **RATHBONE**, Aug. 6, 1837, by Rev. John Whittlesy	32
John, m. Sarah L. **CROCKER**, b. of Salem, Aug. 13, 1829, by Rev. Oliver Wilson, of Montville,	25
Nehemiah B., of Salem, m. Elizabeth E. **AVERY**, of Montville, Sept. 9, 1838, by Rev. Charles Thompson	22
PERKINS, Henry, of Salem, m. Abby B. **NOYES**, of Westerly, R.I., Mar. 19, 1820, by Rev. Ira Hart, in Stonington	13
PHELPS, Aseneth, m. Fordam **EDWARDS**, b. of Lyme, Sept. 1, 1850, by Rev. W. W. Meach	49
Frederick, of Saybrook, m. Maria **EDWARDS**, of Lyme, Feb. 17, 1850, by Rev. W[illia]m W. Meach	48
Royal, m. Ann **CARROLL**, of Essex, May 2, 1847, by Alfred Gallup, J.P.	45
POWERS, Rhoda, of Salem, m. Lemuel **BAKER**, of Montville, Sept. 16, 1821, by Joseph Morgan, J.P.	7
PRATT, Joshua, m. Hannah A. **BROWN**, b. of Salem, Apr. 9, 1829, by John Whittlesy, Elder	26
Mary A., m. Henry M. **KELLEY**, b. of Salem, Aug. 11, 1845, by Rev. Jesse B. Denison	43
PURPLE, Hezekiah, of Salem, m. Lucinda **ROGERS**, of Salem, Jan. 5, 1834, by Rev. Cha[rle]s Thompson	30
RANDALL, Augustus Carlton, s. Laban & Ruth, b. Feb. 11, 1822	1
Cordelia Augusta, d. Laban & Ruth, b. Apr. 16, 1827	1
Fanny Mariah, [d Laban & Ruth], b. Sept. 28, 1820	1
Fanny R., of Salem, m. Andrew J. **GARDINER**, of Colchester, Apr. 19, 1840, by Rev. Charles Thompson	36
George Gates, [s. Laban & Ruth], b. Oct. 15, 1818	1
Laban, of Montville, m. Ruth **RATHBUN**, of Colchester, Nov. 5, 1817, at the house of Asa Rathbun, by Rev. W[illia]m Witter	1
Nehemiah G., of Colchester, m. Harriet E. **RATHBONE**, of Salem, Mar. 20, 1836, by Charles Thompson	32
RANGER, Richard, of Lyme, m. Margaret A. **HILLIARD**, of Salem, Jan. 26, 1845, by Rev. Thomas Dowling, of North Lyme	43
RANSOM, Clarissa, d. June 30, 1820	73
Elias, d. Dec. 30, 1799	73
Elizabeth, d. July 20, 1820	73
George, m. Francis **BILLINGS**, b. of Salem, Nov. 2, 1819, at the house of Anna Dennis, by Royal Tyler	3
Henry, d. Sept. 15, 1818	73
James, Capt., d. Aug. 12, 1823	73
Laura, of Salem, m. Harris **TINKER**, of Montville, Jan. 13, 1823, by Rev. Eli Hyde	12
Nathaniel P., m. Sally **FARGO**, b. of Salem, Nov. 12, 1826, by John Billings, J.P.	18

	Page
RANSOM, (cont.)	
Oran, d. Aug. 11, 1820	73
Sarah A., of Colchester, m. John **MORRIS**, of Salem, Jan. 14, 1844, by Cha[rle]s Thompson	42
Statira, of Salem, m. Erastus **BIGALOW**, of Albany, N.Y., Jan. 31, 1819, at the house of Asahel Ransom, by Royal Tyler	3
RATHBONE, RATHBURN, RATHBUN, Adams, m. Henrietta **PAYNE**, Aug. 6, 1837, by Rev. John Whittlesy	32
Asa, m. Lydia **HARRIS**, b. of Salem, Apr. 18, 1825, by Artemus Worthington, J.P.	24
Christopher P., of Salem, m. Lydia **BROWN**, of Preston, Nov. 1, 1823, by Rev. John Whittlesy	14
Hannah, m. Joshua B. **COMSTOCK**, b. of Salem, Apr. 28, 1822, by Shubael Park, J.P.	11
Harriet E., of Salem, m. Nehemiah G. **RANDALL**, of Colchester, Mar. 20, 1836, by Charles Thompson	32
Lucy Ann, d. Russell B. & Jerusha, b. Sept. 15, 1831	15
Lydia, m. William **REED**, b. of Salem, Nov. 17, 1819, at the house of Samuel Rathbone, by Royal Tyler	4
Oliver M., m. Mary J. **GATES**, Dec. 16, 1849, by Rev. Benjamin G. Goff	48
Russell, m. Lucy Ann **WELSH**, Dec. 19, 1847, by Rev. Benjamin G. Goff	45
Russell B., m. Jerusha **HARVEY**, b. of Salem, July 4, 1830, by Asa Wilcox, Elder	27
Ruth, of Colchester, m. Laban **RANDALL**, of Montville, Nov. 5, 1817, at the house of Asa Rathbun, by Rev. W[illia]m Witter	1
Ruth, m. Joshua **STARK**, July 18, 1831, by Asa Wilcox, Elder	27
Sallinda, of Salem, Conn., m. Butler **HAMLIN**, of Salem, Penn., Oct. 21, 1838, by Rev. Charles Thompson	22
Samuel, of Salem, m. Ruth **STARK**, of Colchester, Oct. 9, 1828, by Asa Wilcox, Elder	25
Sarah Ann, of Salem, m. Arnard **LAPIER**, Jr., of Norwich, May 28, 1843, by Levi Meech, Elder	41
Sarah Ann, m. Eliphalet B. **BECKWITH**, b. of Salem, Mar. 23, 1845, by Levi Meech, Elder	43
RAUN, Samantha, of Lyme, m. Edwin H. **BOGUE**, of Salem, July 30, 1848, by Charles Thompson, at the house of James S. Tew, in Salem	48
RAY, Samuel A., m. Lucy C. **AVERY**, b. of Bozrah, Nov. 26, 1845, by Rev. J.B. Denison	40
RAYMOND, Ann Elizabeth, of Salem, m. John **DOUGLASS**, of Waterford, Dec. 12, 1838, by Rev. Nathaniel Miner, East Haddam	23
RAYNSFORD, Joshua W., of Bridgewater Township of Susquehannah County, Pa., m. Lydia **TREADWAY**, of Salem, Sept. 29, 1833, by Rev. Cha[rle]s Thompson	30
REED, Sterling, of Salem, m. Phebe Ann **TAYLOR**, of East Haddam, Sept. 8, 1844, by Charles Thompson	40
William, m. Lydia **RATHBONE**, b. of Salem, Nov. 17, 1819, at the house of Samuel Rathbone, by Royal Tyler	4
ROBBINS, Hannah M., m. Edwin J. **BROWN**, Apr. 30, 1840, by Rev. E. Loomis	7
ROCKWELL, Alonzo, Dr., of Montville, m. Isabella T. **WOODWARD**, of Providence, R.I., Jan. 29, 1827, by Rev. Nathaniel Miner, of	

	Page
ROCKWELL, (cont.)	
Chesterfield Society	19
ROGERS, Ebenezer, Jr., b. Dec. 27, 1792; m. Matilda **COMSTOCK**, Oct. 2, 1823	15
Ebenezer, Jr., m. Matilda **COMSTOCK**, b. of Salem, Oct. 2, [ ], by Joseph Morgan, J.P.	14
John Beebe, s. William P. & Lucy C., b. Feb. 23, 1823	16
Lucinda, m. Hezekiah **PURPLE**, b. of Salem, Jan. 5, 1834, by Rev. Cha[rle]s Thompson	30
Lucretia, b. July 28, 1798; m. David **CONGDON**, Jan. 21, 1824	33
Lucretia, of East Haddam, m. David **CONGDON**, of Salem, Jan. 18, 1824, by Joseph Morgan, J.P.	17
Lucretia E., of Salem, m. John A. **GEER**, formerly of Akron, Ohio, Jan. 24, 1843, by James Lamb, J.P.	38
Mary E., m. William B. **BROWN**, b. of Salem, Mar. 4, 1832, by Asa Wilcox, Elder	6
Sarah P., m. James F. **HOYT**, of Norwich, Jan. 1, 1834, by Cha[rle]s Thompson	30
William Denison, s. William P. & Lucy C., b. Feb. 15, 1831	16
ROSHA, George, of New London, m. Jerusha **MOSELEY**, of East Haddam, (colored persons), May 6, 1844, by Cha[rle]s Thompson, at his dwelling house (Perhaps "**RESHA**")	44
ROTH, Marian, of Montville, m. George P. **STARK**, of Lyme, Feb. 7, 1826, by Rev. John Whittlesy	18
SMITH, Edwin Bailey, b. Aug. 19, 1823	16
Hannah, m. Henry **HAZARD**, b. of Salem, Feb. 4, 1840, by Artemus Worthington, J.P.	33
John, of Salem, m. Abigail **PALMER**, of Colchester, Mar. 27, 1839, by Rev. Benjamin G. Goff, in Salem	34
Nathan, of Lyme, m. Nancy **BAKER**, Nov. 5, 1848, by Rev. C.H. Gates	47
Shubael, Dea., of Colchester, m. Sarah **PATTEN**, of Salem, Dec. 23, 1847, by Charles Thompson, at the house of David Patten, in Salem	46
Thomas, m. Frances **MINARD**, b. of Salem, Sept. 24, 1843, by Cha[rle]s Thompson	42
[**SPENCER**], Francis Elizabeth, [d. Isaac], b. July 6, 1819, in Salem	24
Isaac, of Montville, m. Lucy **LATTIMER**, of Lyme, Dec. 27, 1812, by Henry Perkins, J.P., at Lyme	24
Isaac Hallam, s. [Isaac], b. Dec. 26, 1813, at Lyme	24
Lucy L., [d. Isaac], b. Nov. 2, 1821	24
Mary Ann, [d. Isaac], b. Nov. 21, 1816	24
Nancy Jane, [d. Isaac], b. July 3, 1824	24
STAPLES, Charlotte, of Waterford, m. Aran **MORGAN**, of Montville, May 4, 1823, by Rev. John Whittlesey	13
STARK, George P., of Lyme, m. Marian **ROTH**, of Montville, Feb. 7, 1826, by Rev. John Whittlesy	18
Joshua, m. Rath **RATHBUN**, July 18, 1831, by Asa Wilcox, Elder	27
Ruth, of Colchester, m. Samuel **RATHBURN**, of Salem, Oct. 9, 1828, by Asa Wilcox, Elder	25
STERLING, William, s. John & Jane, b. Mar. 5, 1804	15
STODDARD, STODDER, STODDAR, Elisha J., of Groton, m. Eunice **FISH**,	

	Page
STODDARD, STODDER, STODDAR, (cont.)	
of Salem, Dec. 28, 1819, at the house of Thomas Fish, by Royal Tyler	4
Harriet, m. Sidney **MORGAN**, b. of Salem, Feb. 23, 1823, by Joseph Morgan, J.P.	12
Ichabod, of Salem, m. Asenath **GARDINER**, of Bozrah, June 4, 1820, by Eben[eze]r A. Barker, J.P.	1
Ichabod, Jr., [s. Ichabod & Asenath], b. Jan. 19, 1825	15
Sophia, d. Ichabod & Asenath, b. Aug. 24, 1820	15
Tabatha, [d. Ichabod & Asenath], b. Sept. 22, 1822	15
Tabatha, m. William H. **CHAPMAN**, b. of Salem, Oct. 22, 1843, by Levi Meech, Elder	42
STRICKLAND, George, of Salem, m. Celia Ann **LAMB**, of Salem, [ ], by Charles Thompson, at the house of Capt. Henry Bailey, in Salem	46
Joseph, of Lyme, m. Frances **LYON**, of Salem, Mar. 22, 1847, by Rev. Jacob Gardiner, of Montville,	45
Nancy, m. Zebediah **MAYNARD**, b. of Montville, Oct. 11, 1846, by Alfred Gallup, J.P.	41
TAYLOR, Joseph N., m. Lydia S. **BECKWITH**, Aug. 16, 1851, by Seth E. Lathrop, J.P.	51
Phebe Ann, of East Haddam, m. Sterling **REED**, of Salem, Sept. 8, 1844, by Charles Thompson	40
TEW, William, m. Mary **PAGE**, May 20, 1830, by Amhurst D. Scoville, J.P.	26
THACHMAN, Erastus, of Glastenbury, m. Lavinia **HOUSE**, of Salem, June 16, 1850, by Rev. W[illia]m Harrison, of Franklin, at the house of Charles Thompson	48
THOMPSON, Benjamin, of Lebanon, m. Ann **CHAPPELL**, of Montville, Oct. 31, 1827, by Joseph Morgan, J.P.	19
Elias, Jr., m. Sarah **WILLIAMS**, b. of Salem, Mar. 24, 1822, by Rev. John Whittlesey	11
Lucretia, of Salem, m. Jedediah J. **GARDNER**, of East Haddam, Mar. 30, 1828, by John Whittlesy, Elder	25
TIFFANY, Betsey, of Salem, m. Christopher H. **LEE**, of Lyme, Dec. 19, 1822, by Rev. William Palmer, at Ebenezer Tiffany's	12
Caroline, m. Simeon **PALMER**, Aug. 5, 1828, by Tubal Wakefield	25
Charles, m. Susan E. **BAILEY**, b. of Salem, Mar. 16, 1851, by Rev. W.W. Meach	49
Ebenezer, Jr., m. Lucy **WHITING**, b. of Salem, Nov. 7, 1841, by Cha[rle]s Thompson	38
Mary S., of Salem, m. Rev. Robert C. **MILLS**, of Colchester, June 14, 1843, by Rev. Tho[ma]s Dowling	39
Richard C., m. Julia A. **HILLIARD**, b. of Salem, Sept. 14, 1842, by Rev. Tho[ma]s Dowling	37
William F., m. Maria **DeWOLF**, b. of Salem, May 29, 1842, by Cha[rle]s Thompson	38
TINKER, Harris, of Montville, m. Laura **RANSOM**, of Salem, Jan. 13, 1823, by Rev. Eli Hyde	12
William, of New London, m. Frances B. **BROWN**, of Montville, Jan. 27, 1822, by Rev. John Whittlesey	9
William, of East Lyme, m. [ ] **BURCH**, of East Lyme, Nov. 28, 1839, by Rev. Charles Thompson	35

	Page
TREADWAY, TREDWAY, Alpheas H., m. Sarah **LOOMIS**, b. of Salem, Mar. 18, 1840, by Rev. Charles Thompson	36
Amanda Prudence, b. Oct. 18, 1802	51
Elizabeth A., of East Haddam, m. Theophilus **ALLYN**, of Salem, Mass., May 4, 1847, by Charles Thompson, at the house of Russell Treadway, East Haddam	46
Enoch F., of New London, m. Mary Ann **MINARD***, of Salem, Dec. 25, 1839, by Rev. Charles Thompson *(handwritten correction in original says "**MINOR**")	35
Fanny, of Salem, m. John **FITCH**, of Montville, Apr. 27, 1836, by Charles Thompson	32
Harriet, of Salem, m. W[illia]m E. **KEITH**, of Oxford, Mass., Aug. 20, 1846, by Rev. Cha[rle]s Thompson	44
L.S., of East Haddam, m. N.L. **WEBSTER**, of Lebanon, Apr. 8, 1850, by C. Thompson	49
Lydia, of Salem, m. Joshua W. **RAYNSFORD**, of Bridgewater Township of Susquehannah County, Pa., Sept. 29, 1833, by Rev. Cha[rle]s Thompson	30
Oliver W., of Salem, m. Fanny A. **BEEBE**, of East Haddam, Nov. 22, 1836, by Cha[rle]s Thompson	33
Sarah, m. Capt. Joseph **HILLARD**, Aug. 30, 1809, by Joel Worthington, J.P. Recorded 1852	1
TURNER, Harriet, of Montville, m. Israel **NEWTON**, of Colchester, Jan. 15, 1819, at the house of Matthew Turner, by Royal Tyler	2
TYLER, Royal W., m. Fanny A. **HOLMES**, b. of Salem, Jan. 29, 1827, by Rev. Nathaniel Miner, of Chesterfield Society	19
WALDEN, David, of Montville, m. Nancy **HOPKINS**, of Salem, Oct. 21, 1823, by Joseph Morgan, J.P.	14
WARREN, William, of Ridgefield, N.Y., m. Sarah **MILLER**, of Salem, Sept. 21, 1835, by Rev. Cha[rle]s Thompson	31
WATERMAN, Albert, of Bozrah, m. Demis **BARTHOLOMEW**, of New London, Nov. 24, 1847, by Charles Thompson, at the house of Mr. Thompson	46
Sarah, b. Oct. 11, 1799	51
WAY, Hannah, m. George W. **FOX**, b. of Salem, Feb. 25, 1835, by Charles Thompson	30
Sarah K., m. Ahimaar **BALCH**, Sept. 13, 1829, by Asa Wilcox, Elder, in Colchester	10
Thomas, of New London, m. Lois **COON**, of Hopkintown, R.I., Apr. 15, 1838, by Rev. Charles Thompson	22
WEBSTER, Eunice O., m. Truman F. **CHURCH**, b. of East Haddam, Oct. 7, 1849, by Charles Thompson	48
N.L., of Lebanon, m. L.S. **TREADWAY**, of East Haddam, Apr. 8, 1850, by C. Thompson	49
WELSH, Lucy Ann, m. Russell **RATHBONE**, Dec. 19, 1847, by Rev. Benjamin G. Goff	45
WHALEY, Ezra, of Lyme, m. Mary Ann **DeWOLF**, of Salem, Feb. 18, 1833, by Rev. Alvin Ackley, at the house of Wid. E. DeWolf	29
WHITING, Lucy, m. Ebenezer **TIFFANY**, Jr., b. of Salem, Nov. 7, 1841, by Cha[rle]s Thompson	38
WHITTLESY, Alice Tredway, d. Henry Pond & Mary A., b. June 21, 1842	23

	Page
WHITTLESY, (cont.)	
Daniel, m. Charlotte Maconda **MORGAN**, b. of Salem, Jan. 2, 1826, by Rev. Amasa Taylor	18
Eliza Tully, eldest d. of Cromel, of Salem, m. John T. **MAGINNIS**, of New London, Dec. 18, 1851, by Rev. Edwin R. Warren, at the Normal Academy of Music in Salem	51
Henry P., m. Mary A. **DANIELS**, b. of Salem, Aug. 17, 1835, by Rev. Charles Thompson	23
Henry P., m. Mary A. **DANIELS**, b. of Salem, Aug. 17, 1835, by Rev. Charles Thompson	31
WICKWIRE, Gardner, of Montville, m. Abba M. **MINER**, of Salem, Mar. 30, 1828, by Benjamin G. Goff	25
Peter, m. Sally **MINARD**, Mar. 23, 1831, by Asa Wilcox, Elder	27
WILLIAMS, Elizabeth M., m. John **PATTEN**, b. of Salem, Feb. 3, 1846, by Cha[rle]s Thompson	44
Hezekiah H., of Pontiac, Mich., m. Celia A.K. **NILES**, of Salem, Sept. 8, 1850, by Charles Thompson, in the Congregational Church	50
Martha A., of Salem, m. James **ALLYN**, of Montville, [ ], by Cha[rle]s Thompson, at the house of Henry Williams, in Salem	50
Nathan P., of Montville, m. Sila E. **BOGUE**, of Salem, Feb. 28, 1847, by Rev. E. Loomis	43
Oliver, m. Charlotte **MORGAN**, Mar. 5, 1848, by David P. Otis, J.P.	47
Polly, of Salem, m. Joseph C. **BECKWITH**, of Colchester, Jan. 1, 1822, by Salmon Cone, V.D.M.	8
Russell, m. Sophia **HARRIS**, b. of Salem, Dec. 2, 1821, by Royall Tyler, at the house of Joseph Harris	10
Sarah, m. Elias **THOMPSON**, Jr., b. of Salem, Mar. 24, 1822, by Rev. John Whittlesey	11
WILLOUGHBY, Lucretia D., of Salem, m. Elijah **LOOMIS**, of Salem, Dec. 30, 1838, by Rev. Charles Thompson	35
WISONBAKER, Lucy, of Salem, m. Elijah **HERRICK**, of Norwich, May 11, 1823, by Rev. John Whittlesey	14
WOOD, Joseph, of Salem, m. Emily **FULLER**, of Colchester, Oct. 16, 1831, by Salmon Cone, V.D.M.	28
Mary, of Salem, m. William **APIS**, of Cold Rain, Mass., Dec. 16, 1821, by Rev. John Whittlesey	9
WOODBRIDGE, Ann Maria, of Groton, m. Butler **BECKWITH**, of East Haddam, Feb. 24, 1846, by Cha[rle]s Thompson	44
WOODWARD, Isabella T., of Providence, R.I., m. Dr. Alonzo **ROCKWELL**, of Montville, Jan. 29, 1827, by Rev. Nathaniel Miner, of Chesterfield Society	19
Lydia Watson, m. Albert **LAMB**, of Bozrah, May 28, 1821, by Royall Tyler, at his house in Salem	10
WOODWORTH, Patty, of Salem, m. Elijah **CHAPMAN**, of East Haddam, Feb. 28, 1821, at the house of Royal Tyler, by Royal Tyler	6
WORTHINGTON, Elizabeth E., of Colchester, m. Cyrus **MANN**, of Hebron, Apr. 19, 1843, by Rev. Alpheas Geer, in Christ's Church, Salem	39
YERRINGTON, Henry W., m. Jerusha J. **BOGUE**, May 13, 1851, by Rev. Benjamin G. Goff	49

SALISBURY VITAL RECORDS
1741 - 1846

	Vol.	Page

ABBOT, Bette, d. John & Sarah, b. Oct. 1, 1758; d. Oct. 31, 1758 — 1, 160
Bette, d. John & Sarah, b. Oct. 26, 1759 — 1, 160
Eunice, d. John & Sarah, b. Sept. 30, 1756 — 1, 160
Joel, s. John & Sarah, b. July 6, 1754 — 1, 160
John, s. John & Sarah, b. July 17, 1748, at Colchester — 1, 160
Samuel, s. John & Sarah, b. Aug. 28, 1752 — 1, 160
Sarah, d. John & Sarah, b. Jan. 14, 1749/50, at Colchester — 1, 160
ABEL, ABELLS, Julia, m. Halsey **TIBBELLS**, Oct. 16, 1822, by David L. Perry — 3, 117
Olivia, of Salisbury, m. Morris **GOODSELL**, of Kent, Oct. 14, 1835, by Leonard E. Lathrop — 3, 150
ACKLEY, Calvin, m. Phebe **SELLECK**, b. of Salisbury, Dec. 24, 1795, by Samuel Lee, J.P. — 3, 109
Clarissa, d. Calvin & Phebe, b. Aug. 1, 1796 — 3, 22
Levi, s. Calvin & Phebe, b. Jan. 21, 1798 — 3, 22
ACTON, Thomas, d. June 29, 1799, ae 49 — 3, 164
ADAMS, ADAM, Alice, d. Jeremiah & Rhoda, b. Sept. 6, 1772 — 2, 33
Anthony, s. Phinehas & Elizabeth, b. Aug. 15, 1768 — 2, 16
Benjamin, s. Hephzabah, b. Mar. 26, 1798 — 3, 5
Cynthia, d. Russel & Rachel, b. Sept. 14, 1796; d. Oct. [ ], 1798 — 3, 13
Daniel, s. Jeremiah & Rhoda, b. July 20, 1776 — 2, 33
Hephzabah, had s. Benjamin, b. Mar. 26, 1798 — 3, 5
Hiram, s. Selleck & Anna, b. June 22, 1796 — 3, 1
Ira, s. Russel & Rachel, b. Feb. 9, 1798 — 3, 13
Ira, m. Sally Sophronia **JONES**, b. of Salisbury, Apr. 27, 1823, by Rev. Charles Prentice, of Canaan — 3, 119
Isaac, d. Nov. 26, 1763 — 1, 238
Isaac, s. Jeremiah & Rhoda, b. Nov. 28, 1763 — 1, 148
Jason, s. Selleck & Anna, b. Feb. 18, 1792 — 3, 1
Jeremiah, s. Jeremiah & Rhoda, b. [ ] 10, 1768 — 2, 33
Jeremiah, s. Selleck & Anna, b. Jan. 15, 1794 — 3, 1
John, s. Phineas & Elizabeth, b. Feb. 27, 1763 — 1, 160
John, d. Apr. 17, 1802, in the 88th y. of his age — 3, 165
John, of Sandisfield, Mass., m. Alice **WALKER**, of Salisbury, Nov. 5, 1833, by Leonard E. Lathrop — 3, 145
John Timman, s. Selleck & Anna, b. Nov. 15, 1798 — 3, 1
Joshua, s. Phineas & Elizabeth, b. Mar. 28, 1760 — 1, 160
Levina, s. Russel & Rachel, b. Apr. 2, 1795 — 3, 13
Luman, s. Selleck & Anna, b. May 12, 1790 — 3, 1
Mary, m. Asa **HUTCHINSON**, b. of Salisbury, Apr. 17, 1804, by Rev. Joseph W. Crossman — 3, 112
Mary, of Salisbury, m. George W. **PEET**, of Canaan, Feb. 29,

	Vol.	Page
ADAMS, ADAM, (cont.)		
1848, by Rev. Adam Reed	3	103
Plinne, s. Jeremiah & Rhoda, b. Jan. 18, 1766	1	148
Robert, d. Aug. 26, 1796, in the 35th y. of his age	3	165
Selleck, s. Phineas & Elizabeth, b. Feb. 11, 1765	1	160
Selleck, m. Anne **CRANE**, b. of Salisbury, Jan. 1, 1789, by Adonijah Strong, J.P.	2	50
Totten, s. Selleck & Anna, b. Apr. 5, 1801	3	1
Zeruiah, d. Jeremiah & Rhoda, b. Dec. 5, 1774	2	33
ADEE (?)*, Samuel H., of Pleasant Valley, N.Y., m. Caroline B. **HARRISON**, [ ] 20, [1834?], by Leonard E. Lathrop *(Perhaps "**ALLEE**")	3	149
ALEXANDER, Amand[a], of Sheffield, m. Stewart M. G. **FULLERTON**, of Colebrook, Sept. 20, 1838, by Rev. Thomas Bainbridge	3	156
ALLEE (?)*, Samuel H., of Pleasant Valley, N.Y., m. Caroline B. **HARRISON**, [ ] 20, [1834?], by Leonard E. Lathrop *(Perhaps "**ADEE**")	3	149
ALLEN, [see also **ALLING**], Abigail, d. David & Mary, b. Jan. 1, 1737	LR1	351
Heber, m. Sarah **OWEN**, b. of Salisbury, Mar. 17, 1768, by Rev. Jonathan Lee	2	44
Heber, s. Heber & Sarah, b. June 16, 1769	2	23
Heman, m. Abigail **BEEBE**, b. of Salisbury, Feb. 18, 1773, by Rev. Jonathan Lee	2	45
Heman & Abigail, had s. [ ], b. July 8, 1773	2	33
Joseph, s. David & Mary, b. Apr. 27, 1738	LR1	351
Joseph, s. Ethan & Mary, b. Nov. 25, 1765	1	139
Lorain, d. Ethan & Mary, b. Apr. 20, 1763, in Cornwall	1	139
Sari, d. David & Mary, b. Feb. 23, 1739/40	LR1	351
ALLING, [see also **ALLEN**], Albert, of Sharon, m. Betsey **HINE**, of Salisbury, Mar. 12, 1840, by Rev. Thomas Bainbridge	3	159
ALTHOUSE, Almira, m. Ambrose **DECKER**, Nov. 9, 1846, by Rev. Jonathan Lee	3	99
Harriet, m. Jno **DECKER**, Nov. 21, 1847, by W.H. Ferris	3	103
ALWORTH, Alice, d. James & Mary, b. Dec. [ ], 1747	1	218
Elizabeth, d. James & Mary, b. July 22, 1746	1	218
Elizabeth, d. James, d. Mar. [ ], 1750	1	225
Mary, d. James & Mary, b. Oct. 2, 1744	1	218
William, s. James & Mary, b. Dec. 5, 1749	1	218
ANDREWS, Lyman Y., of Winchester, m. Mehitable **WRIGHT**, of Salisbury, Aug. 24, 1840, by Rev. Jacob Shaw	3	160
Orville A., of Sheffield, Mass., m. Mary A. **WINTERS**, of Salisbury, Oct. 26, 1846, by Rev. Jonathan Lee	3	99
ASHLEY, Ann, of Sheffield, m. Joshua **WHITNEY**, of Salisbury, Jan. 9, 1770, by John Ashley, J.P.	2	44
Thankfull, of Sheffield, m. Ens. John **DEAN**, of Salisbury, Nov. 6, 1753, by Rev. Jonathan Lee	1	241
ASHMAN, ASHMOND, Alexander, s. Ruth, b. Dec. 19, 1764, in Canaan	2	10
John, s. Amasiah & Ruth, b. Dec. 26, 1758	1	109

	Vol.	Page
ASHMAN, ASHMOND, (cont.)		
Ruth, had s. Alexander, b. Dec. 19, 1764, in Canaan	2	10
Ruth, of Canaan, m. William **WHITE**, of Salisbury, Dec. 28, 1766, by John Beebe, J.P.	2	44
AUSTIN, Abiel, s. Seth & Hannah, b. Oct. 15, 1774	2	27
Abigail, d. Seth & Hannah, b. Nov. 25, 1770	2	27
Dan, s. Thomas & Hannah, b. Jan. 18, 1738/9	LR1	352
Dan, s. Thomas & Hannah, b. Jan. 18, 1738/9	1	205
Eli, s. Seth & Hannah, b. Sept. 28, 1778	2	27
Hannah, [twin with Mary], d. Thomas & Hannah, b. June 9, 1757	1	191
Joel, s. Thomas & Hannah, b. Feb. 6, 1743/4	LR1	350
Joel, s. Thomas & Hannah, b. Feb. 6, 1743/4	1	205
Mary, [twin with Hannah], d. Thomas & Hannah, b. June 9, 1757	1	191
Mary Ann, of Sheffield, m. Joel **EVARTS**, of Salisbury, Feb. 15, 1786, in Dutchess Co., N.Y., by Uriah Lawrence, J.P.	2	43
Nathaniell, s. Thomas & Hannah, b. Apr. 24, 1752	1	205
Nathaniell, s. Thomas & Hannah, b. Mar. 3, 1754	1	205
Samuel, s. Thomas & Hannah, b. May 3, 1746	1	205
Samuel, s. Seth & Hannah, b. Feb. 7, 1773	2	27
Sarah, d. Thomas & Hannah, b. Sept. 9, 1750	1	205
Seth, s. Thomas & Hannah, b. Sept. 13, 1748	1	205
Seth, m. Hannah **SMITH**, b. of Salisbury, Apr. 26, 1770, by Rev. Jonathan Lee	2	45
Thomas, s. Thomas & Hannah, b. Feb. 16, 1741/2	LR1	352
Thomas, s. Thomas & Hannah, b. Feb. 16, 1741/2	1	205
Thomas, s. Seth & Hannah, b. Sept. 28, 1776	2	27
Thomas M., of Erie, Penn., m. Clarissa M. **HARRIS**, of Salisbury, Sept. 14, 1842, by Rev. Adam Reid	3	162
AVERILL, Garra, s. Nath[anie]ll P. & Mary, b. Mar. 15, 1796, in Washington, Conn.	3	50
Garra, m. Mary **BENTON**, b. of Salisbury, Apr. 12, 1827, by Leonard E. Lathrop	3	127
Harriet, d. Nath[anie]l P. & Mary, b. Dec. 9, 1793, in Washington, Conn.	3	50
Harriet, m. Daniel **BREWSTER**, b. of Salisbury, [Oct.] 18, 1831, Leonard E. Lathrop	3	139
Mary Beal, d. Nath[anie]ll P. & Mary, b. July 29, 1806	3	50
Matilda, of Salisbury, m. Daniel P. **NICHOLS**, of Danbury, June 9, 1846, by G.S. Brownell	3	98
May B., of Salisbury, m. William **WILLIAMS**, of Stockbridge, July 5, 1843, by Rev. Adam Reid	3	163
Nathaniel Charles, s. Nath[anie]ll P. & Mary, b. Mar. 16, 1803, in Washington, Conn.	3	50
Roger, s. Nath[anie]ll P. & Mary, b. Aug. 14, 1808	3	50
Roger, of Salisbury, m. Maria D. **WHITE**, of Danbury, Oct. 16, 1844, in Danbury, by Rev. Rollin S. Stone, of the Cong. Ch.	3	97
Sarah, d. Nath[anie]ll P. & Mary, b. Feb. 2, 1801, in Washington	3	50
Sarah, of Salisbury, m. Richard M. **HAIT**, of Edinburgh, Portage Cty., O., Sept. 1, 1840, by Rev. Adam Reid	3	159
AXTILL, Betsey, m. Benjamin **EVEREST**, of Salisbury, May 31, 1786, by Rev. Jonathan Lee	2	43

	Vol.	Page
BABCOCK, Bridget B., of Salisbury, m. Asa D. **PRATT**, of Sherbourne, Mass., Nov. 27, 1834, by Leonard E. Lathrop	3	147
Esther, of Canaan, m. Daniel **HUTCHINSON**, of Salisbury, July 18, 1782, at Canaan, by Rev. Daniel Farrand	2	42
Jane Maria, m. George W. **LINCOLN**, Oct. 3, 1833, by L.E. Lathrop	3	144
Mary, m. John **TOZER**, b. of Salisbury, Sept. 16, 1750, by Rev. Jonathan Lee	1	223
Stephen, of Stonington, m. Mary **BURTON**, of Salisbury, Mar. 20, 1831, by Rev. Stephen Beach, of St. Johns Ch.	3	138
BACON, Abigail, d. John Flavel & Sarah, b. Aug. 28, 1796	3	28
Alma, d. John F. & Sarah, b. July 29, 1800	3	28
Asa, s. Abner & Katharine, b. Oct. 30, 1796	3	23
Betsey, d. William & Polly, b. Jan. 2, 1797	3	7
John Flavel, m. Sarah **GALUSHA**, Sept. 13, 1795, by Samuel Lee, J.P.	3	109
Josepha, m. Eben[eze]r **CUTLER**, Aug. 24, 1794, by Samuel Lee, J.P.	3	109
Lucy, d. Jacob & Priscilla, b. May 3, 1749	1	212
Mary, d. John F. & Sarah, b. Jan. 21, 1803	3	28
Nancy, d. William & Polly, b. Dec. 25, 1798	3	7
Ruth, m. Ethelbert **BAKER**, July 6, 1794, by Samuel Lee, J.P.	3	110
Sarah, d. John Flavel & Sarah, b. Apr. 23, 1798	3	28
William, m. Polly **THURBER**, May 15, 1796, by Samuel Lee, J.P.	3	109
BAGROUGH, BAGBROUGH, BEGROUGH, BOGROUGH, Cary, s. Sarah Jacob (d. of Hyman Jacob Bograh), b. Sept. 27, 1787	2	14
Charity, d. Hyman Jacob & Jane, b. Feb. 13, 1762	1	165
Claudias, m. Martha **OWEN**, b. of Salisbury, Mar. 19, 1760, by Rev. Jonathan Lee	1	249
Hannah, w. Hyman Jacob, d. Sept. 23, 1771, in the 32nd y. of her age	2	48
Hyman Jacobs, s. Hyman Jacobs & Jane, Aug. 20, 1764	1	165
Hyman Jacob, of Salisbury, m. Mary **SEYMORE**, of Hartford, May 30, 1773, by Rev. Jonathan Lee	2	45
Hyman Jacob, his w. [ ], d. Mar. 30, 1778, in the 42nd y. of her age; his servant man [ ], d. Apr. 3, 1778	2	49
Hyman Jacobs, s. Hyman Jacobs, Jr. & Lucretia, b. Oct. 29, 1794	3	19
Jacob, m. Hannah **SIRDAM**, b. of Salisbury, Mar. 30, 1769, by Rev. Jonathan Lee	2	44
Jane, w. Hyman Jacob, d. June 13, 1767	1	230
Jane, d. Hyman Jacob & Hannah, b. Sept. 15, 1771	1	165
Jane, d. Hyman Jacobs & Hannah, b. Sept. 15, 1771	2	11
Samuel, s. Hyman Jacob & Hannah, b. Feb. 25, 1770	1	165
Samuel Hyman, s. Hyman Jacobs & Hannah, b. Feb. 25, 1770	2	11
Sarah, d. Hyman Jacob & Jane, b. Dec. 27, 1759	1	165
Sarah Jacob, d. Hyman Jacob, had s. Cary, b. Sept. 27, 1787	2	14
BAKER, Daniel, s. Rebeckah, b. Mar. 20, 1776	2	24
Ethelbert, m. Ruth **BACON**, July 6, 1794, by Samuel Lee, J.P.	3	110
John Adams, s. Ethelbert & Ruth, b. June 17, 1796	3	18

	Vol.	Page
BAKER, (cont.)		
John F., m. Clarissa **BENJAMIN**, b. of Salisbury, Apr. 19, 1847, by D.W. Clark	3	100
Josephe, d. Ethelbert & Ruth, b. Jan. 17, 1795	3	18
Phinehas Martin, s. Ethelbert & Ruth, b. July 28, 1798	3	18
Rebeckah, had s. Daniel, b. Mar. 20, 1776	2	24
Samuel Abbot, s. Ephraim & Phebe, b. Feb. 21, 1793	3	22
BALDWIN, BAULDWIN, BAWLDIN, Abel, s. Matthew & Abigail, b. Julu 9, 1758	1	158
Abigail, d. Matthew & Abigail, b. June 26, 1753, in Cornwell	1	158
Alexander, of Canaan, m. Margaret **DUTCHER**, of Salisbury, Mar. 31, 1755, by Rev. Jonathan Lee	1	247
Ame, d. Matthew & Abigail, b. Dec. 15, 1760	1	158
Anna, d. Matthew & Abigail, b. June 2, 1756, in Nine Partners	1	158
Cornelius, s. Alexander & Margaret, b. Nov. 11, 1755	1	191
[Elisabeth*], of Oblong, m. George **EDWARDS**, of Salisbury, Jan. 18, 1758, by Rev. Jonathan Lee *(Supplied from Rudd's book)	1	247
Harriet Clark, d. Noah & Sally, b. Apr. 25, 1808	3	27
Hiram Gilbert, s. Noah & Sally, b. July 19, 1805	3	27
Mary, d. Alexander & Margaret, b. Nov. 18, 1757, in Oblong	1	191
Sally, d. Noah & Sally, b. Oct. 16, 1798	3	27
Sally, d. Noah & Sally, d. Aug. 9, 1802, at Genessee, ae 3	3	165
Sally, d. Noah & Sally, b. Aug. 30, 1803	3	10
Sarah, d. Matthew & Abigail, b. Feb. 3, 1763	1	158
Semelda Adams, d. Noah & Sally, b. Jan. 9, 1797	3	27
BALL, Betsey, m. George **HOLMES**, Oct. 16, 1788, by Philip Spencer. Witnesses Thomas Mix & Lucy Mix	3	108
Caroline S., d. Robert & Sophia B. , b. [ ], 1835	3	69
Catharine, m. Martin **BATES**, b. of Salisbury, June 15, 1774, by Elder Dakins	2	46
Daniel, s. Daniel, b. July 25, 1780	2	25
Erastus, s. Erastus & Sarah, b. June 8, 1791	3	6
Frances, d. Robert & Sophia, b. [ ], 1837	3	69
Lois C., d. Robert & Sophia B. , b. Mar. 27, 1829	3	69
Lois C., see Lois C. **TICKNOR**	3	102
Luther T., s. Robert & Sophia, b. Mar. 28, 1833	3	69
Robert U., s. Robert & Sophia B., b. May 9, 1831	3	69
Sylvester, s. Daniel, b. Oct. 19, 1784	2	25
BALLARD, Hannah, d. Jesse & Roxana, b. Nov. 14, 1788	2	19
BALLOU, Anna Eliza, m. John **HOUSON**, b. of Salisbury, May 28, 1848, by Rev. Jonathan Lee	3	103
BANCROFT, Emily, of Salisbury, m. Rev. Wells **WOLCOTT**, of Salisbury, Oct. 11, 1832, by Rev. Thomas Sparks	3	141
BANKS, John, m. Hannah **BIRDSELL**, Feb. 6, 1766, by Rev. Jeremiah Leming	2	41
BARBER, Lucy, of Torrington, m. James **HOLMES**, 3rd, of Salisbury, June 21, 1780, by Rev. Mr. Marvin, of Torrington	2	41
Phebe, m. Martin **DUCKER***, Nov. 11, 1848, by W.H. Ferris *("DUTCHER" or "DECKER"?)	3	103
Uri, s. Nathaniel, of Torrington & Marcy, b. June 1, 1769	2	18

	Vol.	Page
BARD, Mary Ann, of Sharon, m. Ensign **PECK**, of Salisbury, Sept. 29, 1836, by Rev. Oliver V. Amerman, of M.E. Ch.	3	153
Norton J., m. Silence S. **PEET**, Sept. 6, 1836, by Leonard E. Lathrop	3	152
BARDON, Wealthy W., m. Lucius G. **SEELEY**, b. of Salisbury, Jan. 29, 1838, by Rev. O.V. Amerman	3	155
[**BARNES**], **BARNS**, Huldah, m. Isaac H. **JACOBS**, b. of Salisbury, Feb. 10, 1822, by Lavius Hyde	3	116
BARNETT, Frederick, m. Maria **KILMER**, b. of Salisbury, Feb. 21, 1847, by D.W. Clark	3	100
Mary S., m. Daniel **JOHNSON**, b. of Salisbury, May 2, 1841, by Rev. J. Shaw	3	161
BARNEY, William, s. Thomas & Mabel, b. July 17, 1766	1	135
BARNUM, Alanson, s. Levi & Mary, b. Nov. 5, 1799	3	21
Alanson, s. Levi & Mary, d. Oct. 19, 1803, ae 4	3	165
Betsey, of Salisbury, m. Hiram **BARTHOLOMEW**, of Sheffield, Mass., Feb. 5, 1827, by Leonard E. Lathrop	3	126
David, s. Levi & Mary, b. July 11, 1802	3	21
Esther, d. John & Esther, b. June 28, 1749	1	219
Horace, s. Levi & Mary, b. Jan. 18, 1798	3	21
Horace P., of Sheffield, Mass., m. Emily A. **BLODGET**, of Salisbury, Dec. 31, 1846, by D.W. Clark	3	100
Julia, d. Levi & Mary, b. Apr. 21, 1796	3	21
Loiza, of Salisbury, m. Sylvanus A. **WILBER**, of Hyde Park, N.Y., Oct. 16, 1833, by Leonard E. Lathrop	3	144
Lucy Ann, m. Leonard **RICHARDSON**, Apr. 16, 1832, by Rev. Stephen Beach, of St. Johns Ch.	3	140
Mary Ann, of Salisbury, m. Benjamin J. **VAN KEAVEN**, of Pleasant Valley, Feb. 13, 1833, by Leonard E. Lathrop	3	142
Seth, s. John & Esther, b. Dec. 8, 1751	1	219
BARRETT, BARET, BARRET, Abigail, m. John **NICHOLS**, Jr., b. of Salisbury, May 24, 1756, by Rev. Jonathan Lee. Witnesses Phineas Adams & Dorothy Cobb	1	243
Bartholomew, m. Mehettabel **REED***, b. of Salisbury, Mar. 6, 1755, by Rev. Jonathan Lee *("**ROOD**" in Rudd's book)	1	242
Bartholomew, s. Bartholomew & Mehettabel, b. Dec. 22, 1755	1	206
Ephraim, s. Bartholomew & Mahittable, b. Nov. 20, 1757	1	173
Heldrick, of Salisbury, m. Rebeckah **STEVENS**, of Killingworth, Nov. 29, 1763, by John Hutchinson, J.P.	1	251
Jannet, m. Ambrose **GRANT**, b. of Salisbury, Nov. 22, 1838, by Rev. Thomas Bainbridge	3	156
Polly, d. Hildrick & Rebeckah, b. Nov. 25, 1767	2	16
Rodger, s. Heldrick & Rebeckah, b. Mar. 11, 1766	1	140
Sarah, d. Heldrick & Rebeckah, b. Aug. 20, 1764	1	140
BARTHOLOMEW, Hiram, of Sheffield, m. Betsey **BARNUM**, of Salisbury, Feb. 5, 1827, by Leonard E. Lathrop	3	126
Jesse, of Sheffield, Mass., m. Lorinda Maria **DEMING**, of Salisbury, Sept. 15, 1841, by Rev. Adam Reid	3	161
BARTLETT, Alexander, s. Isaiah & Meriam, b. Feb. 5, 1826	3	74
Dorcas M., of Salisbury, m. Robert S. **BARTLETT**, of Binghamton, Nov. 8, 1834, by Leonard E. Lathrop	3	147

	Vol.	Page
BARTLETT, (cont.)		
Dorcas Maria, d. Loring & Phebe, b. Apr. 14, 1812	3	58
Ellen, of Salisbury, m. James **WOODWORTH**, of Great Barrington, Mass., May 31, 1848, by Rev. Adam Smith	3	103
Harriet Luthervia, d. Isaiah & Meriam, b. July 9, 1830	3	74
Hiram Everest, s. Loring & Phebe, b. Dec. 28, 1814	3	58
Jerusha, d. Isaiah & Merian, b. Feb. 20, 1822	3	74
Loring & Phebe, had child b. Apr. 13, 1811; d. July 12, 1811	3	58
Loring & Phebe, had child b. Sept. 17, 1813; d. same day	3	58
Lucius, s. Isaiah & Meriam, b. Feb. 11, 1824	3	74
Mary Elirhaba, d. Isaiah & Meriam, b. Feb. 2, 1828	3	74
Peter Mason, s. Isaiah & Meriam, b. Feb. 6, 1820	3	74
Robert S., of Binghamton, m. Dorcas M. **BARTLETT**, of Salisbury, Nov. 8, 1834, by Leonard E. Lathrop	3	147
Thankfull, of Guilford, m. Cotton **FLETCHER**, of Salisbury, Sept. 9, 1756, by Rev. Jonathan Lee	1	245
BARTON, Andrew, m. Desia **REED**, b. of Salisbury, Dec. 11, 1760, by James Landon, J.P.	1	248
Andrew, s. Andrew & Desia, b. Sept. 24, 1761	1	112
Anthony, s. Andrew & Desia, b. Jan. 3, 1764	1	112
Asher, s. Joseph & Elizabeth, b. June 2, 1800	3	3
Daniel, s. Joseph & Elizabeth, b. Nov. 27, 1789	3	3
Elias, s. Andrew & Disea, b. May 27, 1768	2	21
Joseph, s. Joseph & Elizabeth, b. Feb. 8, 1795	3	3
Mary, d. Andrew & Disea, b. June 20, 1770	2	21
Nathan, s. Andrew & Desia, b. Jan. 19, 1766	1	112
BATES, Abigail, of Hanover, Morris Cty., N.J., m. Adonijah **STRONG**, of Salisbury, July 28, 1777, by Rev. Joseph Grover	2	47
Catharine, d. Martin & Catharine, b. Dec. 6, 1781	2	37
Daniel, s. Martin & Catharine, b. Apr. 5, 1779	2	37
Eliza Ann, m. Henry W. **COOK**, b. of Salisbury, Jan. 12, 1835, by Rev. Julius Field	3	148
Elizabeth, d. Martin & Catharine, b. Nov. 3, 1776	2	37
Flora, m. Thomas **ELWELL**, Jan. 29, 1834, by Leonard E. Lathrop	3	146
Martin, m. Catharine **BALL**, b. of Salisbury, June 15, 1774, by Elder Dakins	2	46
Rebecca, m. John M. **SMITH**, b. of Salisbury, Nov. 3, 1830, by Rev. Aaron Pearce	3	137
BAYLIS, BALIS, George, s. Thomas, b. Jan. 22, 1738	LR1	354
George, m. Rebeckah **NICKERSON**, Jan. 5, 1791, by Lot Norton, J.P.	JC	152
John, s. Thomas, b. Dec. 21, 1741	LR1	354
Margit, d. Thomas, b. Dec. 1, 1739	LR1	354
Richard, s. Thomas, b. Mar. 13, 1736	LR1	354
Sarah, d. Thomas & Sarah, b. Nov. 30, 1743	LR1	354
BAYMONT, Clarissa, of Sheffield, m. Rufus **EDDY**, of Salisbury, June 27, 1802, by Rev. Joseph W. Crossman	3	111
BEACH, BEECH, Jemima, of Sheffield, m. Elijah **STANTON**, of Salisbury, Oct. 1, 1772, by John Hutchinson, J.P.	2	45

	Vol.	Page
BEACH, BEECH, (cont.)		
Layda*, d. Zerah* & Lucy, b. Oct. 20, 1769 *("Zayda"?)	2	24
Michael, s. Michael & Elizabeth, b. June 16, 1787	2	19
Philip, of Litchfield, m. Lucy B. **ROBBINS**, of Salisbury, Sept. 29, 1847, by Rev. Adam Reed	3	102
Zerah, m. Lucy **STEEVENS**, b. of Salisbury, Nov. 27, 1768, by Rev. Jonathan Lee	2	44
[BEAMAN], BEMAN, BEMENT, BEMONT, BEEMENT,		
Bingham, s. Samuel & Martha, b. Feb. 1, 1786	2	18
Cloe, had d, Clarissa, b. July 15, 1775	2	8
Clarissa, d. Cloe, b. July 15, 1775	2	8
Edith, d. Samuel & Martha, b. Aug. 4, 1770	2	23
Freelove, d. William, Jr., & Sarah, b. June 7, 1764	1	141
Hannah, d. Samuel & Martha, b. Feb. 20, 1766	1	150
Olive, m. Elijah **OWEN**, b. of Salisbury, Nov. 10, 1756, by James Landon, J.P.	1	244
Polly, d. Samuel & Martha, b. Feb. 21, 1784	2	18
Samuel, s. Samuel & Martha, b. Feb. 9, 1768	2	18
BEARD, Alfrost, s. Aaron & Lucy, b. Aug. 11, 1777	2	18
Lovisa, d. Aaron & Lucy, b. June 8, 1774	2	18
Sarah, of Sharon, m. Miles **HOTCHKISS**, of Cheshire, Jan. 31, 1841, by Rev. Andrew M. Smith, of North East, N.Y.	3	160
BECKWITH, Richard, of Bavaria, N.Y., m. Jane **POST**, of Sheffield, Oct. 11, 1841, by Rev. Adam Reid	3	161
BEEBE, Abigail, m. Heman **ALLEN**, b. of Salisbury, Feb. 18, 1773, by Rev. Jonathan Lee	2	45
Alice, m. Stephen **WILCOCKS**, b. of Salisbury, June 25, 1777, by Rev. Jonathan Lee	2	41
David, s. Samuel, Jr. & Abigail, b. May 13, 1764	1	142
David, s. Samuel, Jr. & Abigail, b. May 13, 1764	2	30
Ebenezer, s. Samuel, Jr. & Abigail, b. Aug. 8, 1777	2	30
Elizabeth, m. Simeon **LYMAN**, Jan. 5, 1748/9, by Rev. Jonathan Lee	1	222
Elizabeth, m. Solomon **DIMMICK**, b. of Salisbury, Apr. 5, 1770, by Rev. Jonathan Lee	2	45
Elizabeth, d. David & Abigail, b. Apr. 6, 1774	2	35
Hannah, of Canaan, m. Samuel **MOORE**, Jr., of Salisbury, Mar. 7, 1763, by Rev. Daniel Farrand, of Canaan	1	251
Hannah, d. Samuel, Jr., & Abigail, b. June 25, 1766	1	142
Hannah, d. Samuel, Jr., & Abigail, b. June 25, 1766	2	30
Jerusha, d. Joseph & Christian, b. Apr. 16, 1778	2	14
John, s. David & Abigail, b. June 20, 1764	1	117
John, s. Samuel, Jr. & Abigail, b. Apr. 21, 1771	2	30
Katharine, wid. Capt. Samuell, d. Mar. 18, 1784, in the 78th y. of her age	2	50
Lucy, d. David & Abigail, b. Apr. 11, 1766	1	117
Martha, d. David & Abigail, b. Sept. 25, 1762	1	117
Mary, d. David & Abigail, b. Oct. 13, 1758	1	117
Samuel, s. Samuel, Jr. & Abigail, b. Oct. 4, 1768	1	142
Samuel, s. Samuel, Jr. & Abigail, b. Oct. 4, 1768	2	30
Sarah, d. David & Abigail, b. Nov. 2, 1760	1	117

	Vol.	Page
BEEBE, (cont.)		
Solomon, s. Samuel, Jr. & Abigail, b. Mar. 14, 1774	2	30
----------, d. Dec. 17, 1779, in the 78th y. of his age	2	49
BEEMENT, [see under **BEAMAN**]		
BEGROUGH, [see under **BAGROUGH**]		
BELCHER, Adaline, d. Alexander & Harriet, b. Mar. 9, 1827	3	86
Alexander, m. Harriet **KELSEY**, b. of Salisbury, July 3, 1823, by Senica Petter, J.P.	3	119
John Alexander, s. Alexander & Harriet, b. May 25, 1831	3	86
Mary Ann, d. Alexander & Harriet, b. May 19, 1825	3	86
BELLOWS, Clarissa, see Clarry **BELLOWS**	2	7
Clarry, d. Samuel & Charity, b. Sept. 22, 1792	2	7
Esther, d. Samuel & Charity, b. July 26, 1785	2	7
Samuel, Capt., d. Apr. 11, 1759	1	229
Samuel, s. Samuel & Charity, b. Aug. 24, 1787	2	7
Samuel, on July 16, 1811, desired his d. Clarry to be recorded as "Clarissa"	2	7
Sarah, d. Samuell & Elizabeth, b. Jan. 26, 1740	1	204
BEMAS, [see also **BEMIS**], Jotham, of Oblong, m. Elizabeth **BICKNAL**, of Salisbury, Oct. 5, 1755, by Rev. Jonathan Lee	1	242
BEMIS, [see also **BEMAS**], William P., m. Sally **BLODGETT**, b. of Salisbury, Nov. 6, 1836, by Rev. O.V. Amerman	3	153
BEMONT, [see under **BEAMAN**]		
BENEDICT, Julius, of Canaan, m. Maria **CAMFIELD**, of Salisbury, Jan. 5, 1846, by Rev. Albert Nash	3	98
Olive, of Salisbury, m. Horace **WHEELER**, of Montecello, N.Y., Apr. 24, 1825, by Rev. Stephen Beach	3	121
BENJAMIN, Clarissa, m. John F. **BAKER**, b. of Salisbury, Apr. 19, 1847, by D.W. Clark	3	100
BENNETT, BENNET, Catharine, of the Co. of Albany, m. Robart **WARNE**, of Salisbury, Dec. 30, 1751, by Rev. Jonathan Lee	1	224
Katharine, of Salisbury, m. Robert H. **WRIGHT**, of Torrington, Jan. 1, 1847, by Robert N. Fuller, J.P.	3	100
BENNIS, William, m. Samantha **BLODGET**, Jan. 1, 1835, by Rev. Julius Field	3	148
BENSON, Benjamin, of Sharon, m. Chloe **NODINE**, of Salisbury, Dec. 5, 1847, by Rev. Jonathan Lee	3	102
[**BENTLEY**], **BENTLE,** Abisha, s. Samuel & Bethiah, b. Feb. 15, 1767, in Ankeburn	2	26
Anna, d. Samuel & Bethiah, b. Sept. 25, 1769	2	26
Charles, s. James & Mary, b. Apr. 11, 1756; d. Oct. 12, 1757	1	172
James, s. James & Mary, b. Mar. 20, 1753	1	172
Margaret, d. Samuel & Bethiah, b. Apr. 8, 1765	2	26
Nancy, d. James & Mary, b. Dec. 24, 1757	1	172
Paga, d. Samuel & Bethiah, b. Apr. 8, 1765	1	131
Samuel, s. James & Mary, b. Oct. 27, 1744, in East Haddam	1	172
Thomas, s. James & Mary, b. Jan. 25, 1754	1	172
BENTON, Abigail, d. John & Tamor, b. Aug. 3, 1767	2	10
Adah, d. Samuel & Lydia, b. Oct. 18, 1761	1	109
Andrew, s. John Jr. & Tamor, b. July 22, 1764	1	130

	Vol.	Page
BENTON, (cont.)		
Anna, d. Isaac, Jr. & Jemima, b. Sept. 14, 1756	1	177
Anna, m. Victory Sikes **TOUSLEY**, b. of Salisbury, Feb. 3, 1773, by Rev. Mr. Hall	2	45
Anne, d. Nathan & Esther, b. Aug. 9, 1773	2	19
Azubah, d. John, Jr. & Tamor, b. Apr. 27, 1758	1	181
Bette, d. Nathan & Esther, b. Dec. 22, 1768	2	19
Caleb, s. David & Sarah, b. Jan. 2, 1759	1	168
Charles, m. Sylvia P. **BREWSTER**, b. of Salisbury, Oct. 16, 1838, by Rev. Adam Reid	3	156
David, s. David & Sarah, b. Dec. 2, 1763	1	168
Didamia, d. Samuel & Lydia, b. Nov. 3, 1765	1	109
Eli, s. John & Tamer, b. Apr. 5, 1772	2	10
Esther, d. Nathan & Esther, b. Nov. 13, 1766	2	19
Felix, s. John, Jr. & Tamar, b. Apr. 3, 1762	1	130
Isaac, of Salisbury, m. Jemima **St JOHN**, of Sharon, Oct. 30, 1755, by Rev. Cotton Mather Smith	1	243
Isaac, d. Sept. 17, 1757	1	229
Isaac, s. Isaac & Jemima, b. Dec. 28, 1758	1	177
Jehiel, s. Isaac & Ruth, b. Aug. 9, 1752	1	216
Jeh[i]el, s. Isaac & Ruth, d. June 1, 1753	1	226
John, Jr. & Tamer, had d. [ ], b. Dec. 31, 1753; d. same day	1	227
John, Jr. & Tamer, had d. [ ], b. Nov. 14, 1754; d. same day	1	227
John & Tamor, had s. [ ], b. Aug. 7, 1766; d. Aug. 8, 1766	1	230
John, s. John & Tamer, b. Aug. 20, 1770	2	10
Jonathan, s. John, Jr. & Tamor, b. May 19, 1760	1	181
Levi, m. Mary **WOODWORTH**, b. of Salisbury, Oct. 30, 1769, by Rev. Mr. Lee	2	45
Levi, s. Levi & Mary, b. Feb. 26, 1774	2	25
Lucy, d. Nathan & Esther, b. Feb. 2, 1771	2	19
Lydia, d. Stephen & Prudence, b. June 19, 1760	1	115
Lydia, d. David & Sarah, b. Mar. 26, 1761	1	168
Maria J., m. Moses L. **GRAHAM**, June 19, 1845, by Rev. Jonathan Lee	3	97
Mary, d. John, Jr. & Tamor, b. Apr. 7, 1756	1	181
Mary, d. David & Sarah, b. Nov. 1, 1765	1	168
Mary, d. Levi & Mary, b. July 14, 1770	2	25
Mary, m. Garra **AVERILL**, b. of Salisbury, Apr. 12, 1827, by Leonard E. Lathrop	3	127
Nathan, s. Nathan & Esther, b. Apr. 13, 1776	2	19
Olive, d. Levi & Mary, b. Jan. 29, 1772	2	25
Polly, m. Ebenezer **BIRD**, June 12, 1783, by Peter Bishop, J.P.	2	42
Ruth, d. Isaac & Ruth, b. July 23, 1748, in Oblong	1	216
Ruth, d. David & Sarah, b. Feb. 29, 1776	2	18
Samuel, m. Lydia **STRONG**, b. of Salisbury, Dec. 17, 1760, by James Landon, J.P.	1	248
Sarah, d. Samuel & Lydia, b. Mar. 4, 1764	1	109
Sarah, d. David & Sarah, b. Mar. 22, 1768	2	18
Sarah, d. David & Sarah, d. Apr. 4, 1772, in the 5th y. of her age	2	49
Sarah, d. David & Sarah, b. Apr. 30, 1773	2	18
Stephen, of Salisbury, m. Prudence **RENALLS**, of Oblong,		

SALISBURY VITAL RECORDS 151

	Vol.	Page
BENTON, (cont.)		
May 4, 1759, by Rev. Jonathan Lee	1	248
Stephen, s. David & Sarah, b. July 22, 1770	2	18
BERNET, Tryphenia, m. Peter P. **EVERTS**, Dec. 28, 1834, by Rev. Julius Field	3	148
BERRY, Elizabeth, d. James & Hannah, b. May 19, 1762	1	189
Elizabeth, d. James & Hannah, d. May 9, 1764	1	238
John, s. James & Hannah, b. Feb. 10, 1767	1	189
Phebe, m. William **LANDON**, b. of Salisbury, Feb. 18, 1828, by Rev. Stephen Beach, of St. Johns Ch.	3	129
Seth, s. James & Hannah, b. Aug. 29, 1764	1	189
BETTS, Anna, d. John & Anna, b. June 8, 1793	2	29
Arthur, s. John & Ruth, b. Sept. 27, 1776	2	29
Hannah, d. John & Ruth, b. July 3, 1785	2	29
Hiram, s. John & Anna, b. Nov. 6, 1788	2	29
John, d. June 9, 1795, ae 68	3	164
Olivia, d. John & Anna, b. Nov. 27, 1787	2	29
Philomela, d. Arthur & Hannah, b. Feb. 22, 1806	3	32
Ruth, d. John & Ruth, b. Apr. 24, 1780	2	29
William, s. Arthur & Hannah, b. Oct. 7, 1804	3	32
BICKNELL, BICKNAL, BIGNALL, BIGNAL, Alta, d. Richard & Hannah, b. July 5, 1772	2	27
Anmaranda, d. Ruluff & Sabra, b. June 20, 1793	2	36
Betsey, d. Ruluff & Sabra, b. Apr. 25, 1789	2	36
Elizabeth, of Salisbury, m. Jotham **BEMAS**, of Oblong, Oct. 5, 1755, by Rev. Jonathan Lee	1	242
Elizabeth, d. Richard & Hannah, b. May 12, 1762	1	127
Elizabeth, d. Richard & Hannah, b. July 14, 1775	2	27
Henry, s. Richard & Hannah, b. Feb. 23, 1783	2	27
Horace, s. Ruluff & Sabra, b. July 20, 1791	2	36
Joel Thompson, s. Ruluff & Sabra, b. June 20, 1787	2	36
Lydia, d. Richard & Hannah, b. Nov. 24, 1763	1	127
Nathaniell Buell, s. Richard & Hannah, b. July [ ], 1780	2	27
Richard, m. Hannah **WHITE**, Apr. 16, 1761, by John Hutchinson, J.P.	1	248
Richard, s. Richard & Hannah, b. Sept. 23, 1777	2	27
Richard, Capt., d. June 4, 1809, ae 71	3	167
Ruluff, s. Richard & Hannah, b. Nov. 20, 1765	1	127
Ruluff, m. Sabra **THOMPSON**, b. of Salisbury, Aug. 20, 1786, by [ ]	2	43
Senath, d. Richard & Hannah, b. Mar. 9, 1770	2	27
BIDWELL, Laura E., m. Frederick C. **LANDON**, b. of Salisbury, Mar. 3, 1846, by Roger Averill, J.P.	3	98
BIGELOW, Samuel A., of Norfolk, m. Minerva **HOLMES**, of Salisbury, Sept. 16, 1823, by Rev. Charles Printice, of Canaan	3	119
BIGNALL, BIGNAL, [see under **BICKNELL**]		
BINGHAM, Abel, s. Benajah & Dolley, b. July 24, 1771	2	48
Abi, d. Daniel & Hannah, b. June 6, 1766	1	142
Abi, m. Truman **KELLOGG**, Dec. 3, 1789, by Rev. Daniel Farrand. Witnesses Benajah [ ] & Eunice [ ]	2	50

	Vol.	Page
BINGHAM, (cont.)		
Achsah, d. Jabez & Mary, b. Dec. 18, 1760	1	186
Agnes, d. Benjamin & Sarah, b. Oct. 2, 1773	2	31
Alice, d. Benajah & Dorothy, b. Oct. 24, 1766	1	139
Alice, m. Elisha **LANDON**, b. of Salisbury, Apr. 16, 1789, by Adonijah Strong, J.P.	2	50
Alvan, s. Jabez & Mary, b. Dec. 20, 1754	1	213
Bede, d. Benajah & Dolley, b. Nov. 20, 1775	2	24
Bede, m. William **BURROUGHS**, b. of Salisbury, Apr. 16, 1799, by Samuel Lee, J.P.	3	110
Benajah & Dolly, had d. [ ], d. Aug. 28, 17[ ]	2	49
Benajah, s. Benajah & Dorothy, b. July 15, 1764	1	139
Benajah, m. Lois **BINGHAM**, July 10, 1787, by Elisha Fitch, J.P.	2	43
Bethiah, d. Daniel & Hannah, b. Sept. 1, 1761	1	111
Bethiah, d. Daniel & Hannah, d. Sept. 2, 1763, on the 1st day in the 3rd y. of her age	1	238
Bethiah, d. Daniel & Hannah, b. Mar. 26, 1764	1	142
Bethiah, m. Benajah **TICKNOR**, b. of Salisbury, Feb. 9, 1786, by Rev. Jonathan Lee	2	43
Betsey, d. Shubael Conant & Elizabeth, b. Mar. 28, 1799	3	19
Betty, d. Benjamin & Sarah, b. Jan. 17, 1770	2	31
Caleb, s. Daniel & Hannah, b. Apr. 18, 1757	1	215
Caleb, s. Daniel, Jr. & Esther, b. Mar. 14, 1784	2	24
Daniel, s. Daniel & Hannah, b. Oct. 12, 1750; d. Oct. 15, 1750	1	215
Daniel, Jr., m. Esther **WILLARD**, b. of Salisbury, Jan. 12, 1775, by Rev. Jonathan Lee	2	46
Daniel, s. Daniel, Jr. & Esther, b. Jan. 23, 1791	2	24
Daniel, s. Caleb & Polly, b. July 29, 1811	3	52
Dolley, [twin with John], d. Benajah & Dolley, b. July 28, 1769	2	24
Dolly, d. Benajah & Dolly, d. Aug. 9, 1771	2	48
Dolley, d. Benajah & Dolly, b. Nov. 11, 1777	2	24
Dolly, m. Lewis **WEED**, June 4, 1797, by Samuel Lee, J.P.	3	110
Edward, s. Benajah & Lois, b. Aug. 20, 1801	3	23
Elizabeth, d. Alvan & Elizabeth, b. Jan. 11, 1782	2	38
Elizabeth, m. Job Spencer, July 17, 1822, by Lavius Hyde	3	117
Esther, d. Benajah & Lois, b. Sept. 21, 1793	2	33
Eunice, d. Daniel & Hannah, b. July 13, 1754	1	215
Eunice, d. Benajah & Dolley, b. Jan. 22, 1773	2	24
Eunice, d. Daniel, Jr. & Esther, b. July 24, 1788	2	24
Eunice, d. Benajah & Lois, b. Feb. 17, 1791	2	33
Frederic, m. Hannah **DREW**, b. of Salisbury, June 6, 1769, by Rev. Jonathan Lee	2	44
Hannah, d. Daniel & Hannah, b. Nov. 8, 1748, in Windham	1	215
Jabez, s. Jabez & Mary, b. Feb. 13, 1749, in Windham	1	213
Jabez, d. Aug. 30, 1785, in the 85th y. of his age	2	50
John, [twin with Dolley], s. Benajah & Dolley, b. July 28, 1769	2	24
John, s. Benajah & Dolly, b. Aug. 10, 1771	2	48
John, s. Benajah & Lois, b. Apr. 19, 1789	2	33
Laura, d. Daniel, Jr. & Esther, b. June 28, 1786	2	24
Levi, s. Solomon & Rachel, b. Nov. 30, 1771	2	23
Lois, d. Daniel & Hannah, b. May 16, 1759	1	215

	Vol.	Page
BINGHAM, (cont.)		
Lois, m. Benajah **BINGHAM,** July 10, 1787, by Elisha Fitch, J.P.	2	43
Lois, d. Benajah & Lois, b. Sept. 24, 1795	3	23
Louisa, m. John **LANDON,** 3rd, b. of Salisbury, Nov. 17, 1785, by Rev. Jonathan Lee	2	43
Lovisa, d. Jabez, Jr. & Mary, b. Feb. 18, 1763	1	186
Lovisia, d. Daniel, Jr. & Esther, b. Nov. 6, 1780	2	24
Lucy, d. Solomon & Rachel, b. Aug. 15, 1769	2	23
Luther, s. Daniel, Jr. & Esther, b. May 17, 1782	2	24
Marcy, d. Jabez, Jr. & Mary, b. June 17, 1767	1	186
Mary, d. Jabez & Mary, b. July 3, 1752	1	213
Mary, m. John **MOORE,** b. of Salisbury, Dec. 15, 1762, by Rev. Jonathan Lee	1	250
Mary, Jr., m. Samuel **LEE,** 3rd, b. of Salisbury, Sept. 29, 1774, by Rev. Jonathan Lee	2	46
Phebe, d. Solomon & Rachel, b. Aug. 24, 1764	1	122
Rachel, d. Solomon & Rachel, b. Dec. 30, 1761	1	122
Ralph, or Rodolphus Wheelock, s. Jabez & Mary, b. Feb. 17, 1750/1	1	213
Ralph, or Rodolphus Wheelock, d. Sept. 15, 1751	1	225
Ruth, d. Daniel, Jr. & Esther, b. Mar. 30, 1777	2	24
Samantha, d. Benajah & Lois, b. Aug. 17, 1787	2	33
Sarah, w. Benjamin, d. Dec. 5, 1773, in the 39th y. of her age	2	48
Shubael Conant, s. Daniel, Jr. & Esther, b. July 24, 1775	2	24
Silas, s. Jabez & Mary, b. July 29, 1758	1	186
Silas, late of Salisbury, now of Great Barrington, m. Anne **ORTON,** of Great Barrington, Feb. 28, 1773, by John Hutchinson, J.P.	2	45
Solomon, m. Rachel **MOER*,** b. of Salisbury, June 4, 1761, by Rev. Jonathan Lee *(**MOORE**")	1	249
Solomon, s. Solomon & Rachel, b. Apr. 13, 1767	1	122
Stuart, s. Benjamin & Sarah, b. Apr. 14, 1772	2	48
Stuartdale*, s. Benjamin & Sarah, b. Jan. 12, 1772 *(Probably "Stuart")	2	31
Sibal*, d. Benajah & Dolley, b. June 12, 1771 *("Sybil")	2	24
Zerruiah, of Windham, m. Joel **CAMP,** of Salisbury, Mar. 9, 1757, by Jedediah Elderkin, in Windham	1	245
BIRCH, John T., m. Fidelia **RACE,** b. of Salisbury, Mar. 12, 1828, by Rev. Stephen Beach, of St. Johns Ch.	3	129
BIRD, Abigail, d. James & Abigail, b. Mar. 7, 1761	1	153
Abigail, d. Isaac & Rhoda, b. June 9, 1787	2	13
Amos, s. Joseph & Huldah, b. Oct. 31, 1764, in Oblong	2	28
Annis, m. Elijah **LEACH,** b. of Salisbury, Nov. 16, 1841, by J. Shaw	3	161
Asenath, d. More & Rebekah, b. Dec. 5, 1752	1	182
Asenath, d. Thomas & Elizabeth, b. Sept. 28, 1778	2	31
Betsey, d. Thomas & Elizabeth, b. Feb. 9, 1781	2	31
Dorcas, w. Joseph, d. Oct. 28, 1750	1	225
Dorcas, d. James & Abigail, b. Nov. 4, 1751 O.S., in Litchfield	1	195
Ebenezer, m. Polly **BENTON,** June 12, 1783, by Peter Bishop, J.P.	2	42

BIRD, (cont.)

	Vol.	Page
Electe, d. More & Rebekah, b. June 1, 1754	1	182
Electe, m. Giles **HULL**, b. of Salisbury, Mar. 16, 1775, by John Hutchinson, J.P.	2	46
Eunice, d. Capt. James & Abigail, b. Aug. 26, 1769	2	23
Henry, s. Isaac & Rhoda, b. May 21, 1796	3	8
Huldah, d. Joseph & Huldah, b. Jan. 3, 1762	2	28
Isaac, s. James & Abigail, b. May 5, 1757	1	195
Isaac, m. Rhoda **SELLECK**, b. of Salisbury, Feb. 28, 1782, by Rev. Jonathan Lee	2	42
Isaac, s. Isaac & Rhoda, b. June 19, 1793	2	13
James, m. Abigail **GRIDLEY**, Aug. 23, 1750, by Rev. Mr. Barnum, of Kensington	1	244
James, s. Isaac & Rhoda, b. Jan. 27, 1785	2	13
Joseph, m. Sary **ELDREG**, b. of Salisbury, May 11, 1752, by Rev. Jonathan Lee	1	224
Joseph, Jr., m. Hulda **SPRAGUE**, b. of Salisbury, May 23, 1753, by Rev. Jonathan Lee	1	240
Joseph, d. Sept. 9, 1754, in the 58th y. of his age	1	227
Joseph, s. Joseph & Huldah, b. Aug. 4, 1764, in Oblong	2	28
Levina, d. Joseph & Huldah, b. Oct. 17, 1766	2	28
Maria, twin with William, d. John & Eunice, b. Mar. 29, 1797 *("Mar. 23"?)	3	8
Mary, d. Joseph & Huldah, b. May 31, 1769; d. June 23, 1769	2	28
Mary, d. Joseph & Huldah, b. May 8, 1770	2	28
Moore, m. Rebeckah J. **KINNON***, b. of Salisbury, Nov. 9, 1752, by Rev. Jonathan Lee *("Rebeckah **SKINNER**" in Rudd's book)	1	240
Moore, d. Sept. 3, 1756, in the 28th y. of his age	1	227
Moore, s. Joseph & Huldah, b. Oct. 22, 1756	1	185
Nathaniell, s. Moore & Rebekah, b. Mar. 25, 1756; d. next day	1	227
Nathaniell, d. Sept. 15, 1760	1	236
Nathaniel, s. Joseph & Huldah, b. May 18, 1763	2	28
Rachel, d. Joseph & Huldah, b. Apr. 19, 1758	1	185
Ruth, d. Oct. 3, 1754	1	227
Ruth, d. Joseph & Huldah, b. Oct. 22, 1754	1	185
Salome, d. Isaac & Rhoda, b. Nov. 1*, 1782 *("Nov. 10" in Rudd's book)	2	13
Samantha E., m. Charles G. **REED**, b. of Salisbury, Dec. 25, 1822, by Charles Prentice	3	118
Semantha Eliza, d. Isaac & Rhoda, b. Dec. 13, 1799	3	8
Sarah, d. Capt. Joseph & Sarah, b. Sept. 13, 1753	1	192
Sophia, d. Thomas & Elizabeth, b. June 14, 1784	2	31
Thomas, s. James & Abigail, b. Apr. 22, 1754 N.S.	1	195
Thomas, d. Oct. 4, 1754	1	227
Tho[ma]s, m. Elizabeth **CHAMBERLAIN**, b. of Salisbury, Feb. 14, 1776, by Rev. Jonathan Lee	2	41
William, s. Isaac & Rhoda, b. Sept. 19, 1790	2	13
William, twin with Maria, s. John & Eunice, b. Mar. 29*, 1797 *("Mar. 23"?)	3	8

BIRDSELL, Hannah, m. John **BANKS**, Feb. 6, 1766, by Rev.

	Vol.	Page
BIRDSELL, (cont.)		
Jeremiah Leming	2	41
BISHOP, Alonzo R., of Winsted, m. Mary **WEAVER**, of Salisbury, Oct. 10, 1833, by L.E. Lathrop	3	144
BISSELL, Asail, s. George & Lydia, b. Dec. 7, 1757	1	217
Bettee, d. David & Sarah, b. Feb.* 17, 1775 *("Jan." in Rudd's book)	2	7
Charles, s. John & Hannah, b. Nov. 8, 1782	2	40
Cynthia H., of Salisbury, m. Rev. Daniel P. **KIDDER**, of Rochester, Nov. 9, 1836, by Rev. O.V.Amerman	3	153
David, of Salisbury, m. Sarah **GOODRICH**, of Sharon, Feb. 14, 1767, by Rev. Cotton M. Smith	2	44
David, s. David & Sarah, b. Aug. 4, 1770	2	7
Edward, s. David & Sarah, b. June 21, 1776	2	7
Elisha, s. David & Sarah, b. Sept. 8, 1768	2	7
Esther, d. Samuel & Mary, b. Nov. 29, 1789	2	10
Esther, d. Samuel & Mary, d. Aug. 2, 1808, ae 19	3	166
George, s. George & Leddia, b. Jan. 4, 1749/50	1	217
Harriet, d. Samuel & Mary, b. Dec. 6, 1782	2	10
Ira, s. David & Sarah, b. Jan. 5, 1772	2	7
Jehiel, s. George, d. Oct. 2, 1760, at Oswego	1	237
Jehiel, s. David & Sarah, b. Oct. 13, 1767	2	7
Jesse, s. George & Lydia, b. Feb. 20, 1752	1	217
John, s. George & Lydia, b. Jan. 12, 1761	1	217
Joseph, s. George & Lydia, b. Jan. 12, 1759	1	217
Laura, twin with Polly, d. Samuel & Mary, b. Oct. 11, 1786	2	10
Lydia, d. George & Lydia, b. Sept. 20, 1754	1	217
Marian E., m. Alexander S. **HARRISON**, b. of Salisbury, Sept. 28, 1842, by Rev. Adam Reid	3	162
Milton, s. Samuel & Mary, b. Nov. 2, 1784	2	10
Mylo, s. John & Hannah, b. May 18, 1785	2	40
Polly, twin with Laura, d. Samuel & Mary, b. Oct. 11, 1786	2	10
Polly, d. Samuel & Mary, d. May 10, 1787, ae 7 m.	2	50
Sarah, d. David & Sarah, b. Sept. 14, 1773	2	7
William, m. Eliza Ann **LOVELAND**, b. of Salisbury, Mar. 8, 1822, by David L. Perry	3	117
BLACK, John, m. Sally **BRENTON**, b. of Salisbury, Dec. 26, 1822, by David L. Perry	3	118
William Duncan, m. Harriet Abigail **NOTT**, b. of Salisbury, Dec. 11, 1823, by Lot Norton, J.P.	3	120
[BLAKESLEE], BLACKESLEY, George W., m. Nancy M. **REED**, June 22, 1845, by Rev. D.W. Clark	3	97
BLODGETT, BLOGGET, BLODGET, BLOGET, Archepas, s. Asa & Irena, b. Dec. 29, 1755	1	198
Artemus, s. Asa & Irena, b. Dec. 31, 1752	1	198
Artemus, m. Rebeckah **TORNER**, b. of Salisbury, Aug. 4, 1774, by Elder Dakins	2	46
Asa, m. Irene **OWEN**, b. of Salisbury, Dec. 7, 1750, by Rev. Jonathan Lee	1	223
Asa, s. Asa & Irene, b. Jan. 11, 1765	1	114
Elijah, s. Asa & Irene, b. Apr. 19, 1761	1	114

	Vol.	Page
BLODGETT, BLOGGET, BLODGET, BLOGET, (cont.)		
Elijah, s. Asa & Irena, d. June 19, 1761	1	237
Elijah, s. Artemus & Rebecca, b. Oct. 29, 1780	2	39
Elijah, s. Solomon & Rebeckah, d. May 24, 1782	2	50
Emily A., of Salisbury, m. Horace P. **BARNUM**, of Sheffield, Mass., Dec. 31, 1846, by D.W. Clark	3	100
Irena, d. Asa & Irena, b. Aug. 9, 1757	1	198
Isaac, s. Artemus & Rebeckah, b. Dec. 26, 1774	2	35
Isaac, s. Artemus & Rebecca, b. Dec. 26, 1774	2	39
Sally, m. William P. **BEMIS**, b. of Salisbury, Nov. 6, 1836, by Rev. O.V. Amerman	3	153
Samantha, m. William **BENNIS**, Jan. 1, 1835, by Julius Field	3	148
Samuel, s. Asa & Irena, b. May 26, 1761	1	198
Samuel, m. Caroline **SAUNDERS**, b. of Salisbury, Dec. 9, 1824, by Rev. David Miller, of the M.E. Ch.	3	121
Sarah, d. Asa & Irena, b. Apr. 7, 1759	1	198
Sardias, s. Asa & Irena, b. May 25, 1754	1	198
Silvia, d. Asa & Irene, b. Nov. 5, 1762	1	114
Silva, d. Artemus & Rebecca, b. Jan. 6, 1778	2	39
BLOSS, Polly, d. Davis & Abigail, b. Aug. 20, 1796	3	14
Samuel, s. Easton Davis & Abigail, b. May 22, 1794	3	14
BOGROUGH, [see under **BAGROUGH**]		
BOROUGH, [see under **BAGROUGH**]		
BOSTWICK, Ansel, s. Edward & Ann, b. Dec. 27, 1770	2	30
Chloe, d. Edward & Ann, b. May 16, 1763	1	121
Daniel, s. Gilbert & Mary, b. Oct. 2, 1762	1	124
Hubbort, d. Aug. 26, 1773, in the 30th y. of his age	2	49
Jesse, m. Sarah **TICKNOR**, b. of Salisbury, July 25, 1762, by Rev. Jonathan Lee	1	250
John, s. John & Jemima, d. Aug. 23, 1760, in the Army	1	238
John, s. Jesse & Mary, b. Jan. 14, 1762	1	157
John, s. Gilbert & Mary, b. Apr. 27, 1772	1	124
Mary, w. Jesse, d. Jan. 26, 1762	1	237
Mary, d. Gilbert & Mary, b. Oct. 17, 1766	1	124
Merendah, d. Edward & Ann, b. Feb. 22, 1768	2	30
Milo, s. Jesse & Sarah, b. Mar. 8, 1763	1	157
Newell, s. Edward & Ann, b. Jan. 15, 1762	1	121
Phebe, d. Edward & Ann, b. June 22, 1769	2	30
Philomela, d. Jesse & Mary, b. July 16, 1760	1	157
Phillomele, d. Edward & Ann, b. Nov. 22, 1764	1	121
Rebecca F., m. John H. **COFFING**, b. of Salisbury, Feb. 27, 1833, by L.E. Lathrop	3	142
Rhoda, d. Edward & Ann, b. July 11, 1772	2	30
Robert, m. Eliza J. **PETTEE**, b. of Salisbury, June 2, 1835, by Leonard E. Lathrop	3	149
Sarah, d. Gilbert & Mary, b. Apr. 24, 1770	1	124
Trueman, s. Edward & Ann, b. July 22, 1766	1	121
William E., m. Clarissa **COFFING**, May 1, 1834, by Leonard E. Lathrop	3	146
BOSWORTH, Mary, m. William B. **WITHERELL**, b. of Salisbury, Sept. 22, 1839, by Rev. Thomas Bainbridge	3	158

SALISBURY VITAL RECORDS 157

	Vol.	Page
BOSWORTH, (cont.)		
Simeon, of Sandisfield, m. Abigail **PRINCE**, of Salisbury, Dec. 16, 1838, by Rev. Thomas Bainbridge	3	157
BOTCHFORD, [see under **BOTSFORD**]		
BOTSFORD, BOTCHFORD, Betsey, m. Abijah C. **PEET**, Dec. 8, 1822, by Samuel Church, J.P.	3	117
Eunice M., of Salisbury, m. William **REED**, of Canaan, Jan. 2, 1832, by L.E. Lathrop	3	139
Eunice Maria, d. Niram & Patience, b. Sept. 6, 1800	3	23
Mary, of Darby, m. Abiel **CAMP**, of Salisbury, Dec. 5, 1750, by Rev. Mr. Humphrey	1	223
Polly, m. Jacob D. **CROSSMAN**, Mar. 23, 1834, by Leonard E. Lathrop	3	146
Polly Anne, d. Niram & Patience, b. July 25, 1797	3	23
Rachel, Mrs., m. John **HOLMES**, Oct. 5, 1796, by Samuel Lee, J.P.	3	111
Samuel S., m. Emily **ENSIGN**, b. of Salisbury, Mar. 27, 1829, by L.E. Lathrop	3	133
Samuel Strong, s. Niram & Patience, b. Mar. 19, 1799	3	23
BRADLEY, Abigail, d. Daniel & Rebekah, b. May 17, 1770	2	18
Albert, of Torrington, m. Minerva L. **HUNT**, of Canaan, Sept. 21, 1828, by Rev. Stephen Beach, of St. Johns Ch.	3	131
Ame, d. Ansel & Mary, b. Nov. 9, 1763	1	144
Anna, d. Ariel & Ame, b. June 10, 1754, in York Gov.	1	175
An[n]e, d. Daniel & Rebekah, b. Sept. 8, 1774	2	18
Anne, m. Elisha **WOODWORTH**, b. of Salisbury, Jan. 11, 1776, by Rev. Jonathan Lee	2	47
Betsey, d. Deman, b. Dec. 22, 1805	3	67
Daniel, s. Daniel & Rebeckah, b. Feb. 20, 1768	2	18
Daniel & Rebekah, had d. [ ], d. Sept. 15, 1776, ae 2 y., & s. [ ], d. Oct. 9, 1776, ae 9 y.	2	49
Deman W[illia]m, s. Deman, b. Mar. 6, 1820	3	67
Electa, d. Daniel & Rebekah, b. Apr. 28, 1785	2	18
Electa, see Electa **PAGE**	3	166
Esther, d. Milton & Esther, b. Oct. 7, 1823	3	68
Harriet, d. Milton & Esther, b. June 28, 1827	3	68
James, s. Ariel & Ame, b. June 17, 1756	1	175
James Lane, s. Ariel, Jr. & Chloe, b. Nov. 25, 1793	3	24
John Anson, s. Ariel, Jr. & Chloe, b. Jan. 3, 1796	3	24
Martha, d. Daniel & Rebekah, b. Oct. 18, 1778	2	18
Mary, d. Daniel & Rebekah, b. Aug. 25, 1776	2	18
Mary, d. Deman, b. Dec. 10, 1814	3	67
Mary, d. Milton & Esther, b. Mar. 24, 1832	3	67
Miles, m. Jane **HOGABOOM**, of Canaan, Oct. 17, 1770, by John Hutchinson, J.P.	2	45
Milton, s. Milton & Esther, b. Apr. 11, 1822	3	68
Milton, Jr., m. Caroline **CONKLIN**, b. of Salisbury, Oct. 3, 1841, by J. Shaw	3	161
Nathaniel Everts, s. Deman, b. May 5, 1812	3	67
Orra, d. Deman, b. Feb. 8, 1810	3	67
Orville, s. Milton & Esther, b. Oct. 26, 1834	3	67

	Vol.	Page
BRADLEY, (cont.)		
Phebe, d. Milton & Esther, b. Aug. 21, 1825	3	68
Rebeckah, d. Daniel & Rebeckah, b. Apr. 21, 1766	1	130
Rebecca, m. Azariah **NEWCOMB**, b. of Salisbury, Jan. 17, 1782, by Rev. Jonathan Lee	2	41
Rebekah, m. Azariah **NEWCOMB**, b. of Salisbury, Jan. 17, 1782, by Rev. Jonathan Lee	2	42
Sarah, d. Daniel & Rebekah, b. Nov. 11, 1772	2	18
Susan, d. Milton & Esther, b. July 12, 1814	3	68
Thaddeus, s. Ariel & Ame, b. June 8, 1752, in York Gov.	1	175
Thomas Berry, s. Daniel & Rebekah, b. Mar. 9, 1781	2	18
Wesley, s. Milton & Esther, b. Feb. 16, 1830	3	68
BRASIE, BRASIA, BRASSIE, Almira, m. Allen **CHAPMAN**, b. of Salisbury, Jan. 8, 1840, by Thomas Bainbridge	3	159
Esther J., m. Hercules **THORP**, Mar. 20, 1848, by W.H. Ferris	3	103
Laura Ann, m. Orson B. **ELDRIDGE**, b. of Salisbury, Dec. 31, 1834, by Leonard E. Lathrop	3	147
BRENTON, Sally, m. John **BLACK**, b. of Salisbury, Dec. 26, 1822, by David L. Perry	3	118
BRERTHRONG, Horatio Gates, s. Abraham & Hannah, b. [ ]	2	33
Sarah, d. Abraham & Hannah, b. Apr. 6, 1779	2	33
BREWSTER, Ame, had d. Parmela, b. Jan. 29, 1769	2	22
Asenath Canfield, d. Daniel & Asenath, b. Jan. 8, 1820	3	29
Charles, s. Charles & Kesiah, b. June 8, 1755	1	215
Daniel, m. Asenath **CANFIELD**, b. of Salisbury, Oct. 2, 1811, by Charles Printice	3	114
Daniel, d. Mar. 31, 1814, ae 83	3	168
Daniel, m. Harriet **AVERILL**, b. of Salisbury, [Oct.] 18, 1831, by Leonard E. Lathrop	3	139
Daniel Hiram, s. Dan[ie]ll & Asenath, b. Feb. 29, 1812	3	29
Eliphaz, m. Elizabeth **GREEN***, b. of Salisbury, Feb. 15, 1770, by J. Hutchinson, J.P. *("**GRAVES**"?)	2	44
Elizabeth, twin with John, d. Charles & Kezia, b. Apr. 28, 1760	1	174
Elizabeth, d. Charles & Keziah, d. Aug. 16, 1761	1	237
Elizabeth, d. Charles & Keziah, b. June 20, 1762	1	174
John, twin with Elizabeth, s. Charles & Kezia, b. Apr. 28, 1760	1	174
John, s. Charles & Keziah, d. July 8, 1760	1	237
Kezia, d. Charles & Kezia, b. Sept. 3, 1757	1	174
Lewis, s. Eliphaz & Elizabeth, b. Dec. 21, 1774	2	31
Marvel, m. Silas **MOORE**, b. of Salisbury, June 24, 1798, by Samuel Lee, J.P.	3	110
Mary, d. Prudence, b. Apr. 16, 1768	2	8
Ozem, s. Charles & Keziah, b. Mar. 13, 1750/1	1	215
Parmela, d. Ame, b. Jan. 29, 1769	2	22
Persis, d. Charles & Keziah, b. May 31, 1753	1	215
Prudence, d. Charles & Kesiah, b. June 16, 1749	1	215
Prudence, had d. Mary, b. Apr. 16, 1768	2	8
Prudence, m. John **CAMMARON**, b. of Salisbury, Jan. 25, 1769, by Rev. Jonathan Lee	2	44
Sylvia P., m. Charles **BENTON**, b. of Salisbury, Oct. 16, 1838, by Rev. Adam Reid	3	156

	Vol.	Page
BREWSTER, (cont.)		
Sylvia Phebe, d. Dan[ie]ll & Asenath, b. Nov. 13, 1813	3	29
BRIGGS, BRIGS, Abigail, m. Joseph **LEE**, b. of Salisbury, Mar. 12, 1771, by Rev. Robert Cambel	2	45
Lucy A., m. George W. **HUTCHINSON**, b. of Salisbury, July 7, 1847, by Rev. W.H. Ferris	3	101
BRIGHAM, Bethiah, w. Jabez, d. Apr. 3, 1769, in the 66th y. of her age	2	48
BRINKERHOOF, Eve*, Mrs., of Woodbury, m. Rev. Jonathan **LEE**, of Salisbury, Nov. 22, 1762, by Rev. John Graham, in Woodbury *("Love" in Rudd's book)	1	250
BRINSMADE, BRINSMAID, Anna, m. Nath[anie]ll **GREEN**, b. of Salisbury, Feb. 11, 1773, by Rev. Jonathan Lee	2	45
Charles Wesley, s. John, Jr. & Francis, b. Sept. 24, 1809	3	49
Charlott, d. John & Mercy, b. Dec. 20, 1767	2	12
David, s. John & Mercy, b. Apr. 30, 1773	2	12
Huldah, m. John **LYMAN**, b. of Salisbury, Dec. 3, 1786, by Rev. Jonathan Lee	2	43
John, s. John & Marcy, b. Feb. 3, 1766	1	114
Julia, d. John, of Salisbury, m. Charles **SWIFT**, of Hoboken, N.J., Mar. 19, 1836, at Hillsdale, N.Y., b. Rev. Mr. Stillman	3	151
Mary, w. John, d. July 6, 1806, ae 66	3	166
Mary, d. John, Jr. & Frances, b. May 29, 1808	3	49
Noah, s. John & Mercy, b. May 24, 1770	2	12
Noah, m. Mary **SELLECK**, Nov. 10, 1805, by Rev. Cor[neliu]s Brewer, of Poughkeepsie	3	113
BRINTON, [see also **BRITTON**], Caroline, d. Preston H. & Caroline, b. June 4, 1827	3	77
Edward, s. Joseph & Naomi, b. Oct. 9, 1802	3	58
Harley, s. Joseph & Naomi, b. July 19, 1805	3	58
Harriet, d. Joseph & Naomi, b. Dec. 7, 1798	3	58
Joseph, d. Apr. 16, 1811, ae 44	3	167
Joseph A., s. Joseph & Naomi, b. Sept. 12, 1801	3	58
Mary, d. Joseph & Naomi, b. May 31, 1800	3	58
Nathaniel, s. Joseph & Naomi, b. June 14, 1810	3	58
Orineel R., s. Joseph & Naomi, b. Dec. 23, 1808	3	58
Permena, s. Joseph & Naomi, b. June 10, 1804	3	58
Preston Harrison, s. Ebenezer & Sally, b. May 7, 1807	3	56
Samuel, s. Joseph & Naomi, b. May 26, 1811	3	58
William, s. Joseph & Naomi, b. June 30, 1807	3	58
BRISTOL, [see under **BRITTAL**]		
BRITTAL, BRISTOL, John *, s. Claudius & Alathea, b. Nov. 8, 1766 *("John **BRITTAL**" in Rudd's book)	1	220
John, s. Claudias & Alathea, b. Nov. 8, 1766	2	28
Margaret, d. Claudias & Alathea, b. Nov. 12, 1769	2	28
Ruth*, Claudius & Alathea, b. Sept. 25, 1760 *("Ruth **BRITTAL**" in Rudd's book)	1	220
[**BRITTON**], **BRITON**, Fanny, m. Andrew **WINTERS**, Dec. 31, 1824, by Rev. John Lovejoy, of the M.E. Ch.	3	121
BROWN, Abigail, of New Marlborough, m. Ezra **SELLECK**, Jr., of Salisbury, Nov. 14, 1786, at New Marlborough, by Rev. Mr.		

	Vol.	Page
BROWN, (cont.)		
Storer, of Sandisfield	2	43
Abigail, d. Samuel & Jemimah, b. Nov. 19, 1805, in Norfolk	3	59
Caroline, d. Samuel & Jemimah, b. Apr. 25, 1809	3	59
Edmund, s. Sam[ue]ll & Jemimah, b. Aug. 20, 1811	3	59
Eli, of Stonington, m. Lucy **MOORE**, of Salisbury, Nov. 6, 1797, by Samuel Lee, J.P.	3	110
Eliza, Mrs., of Pittsfield, m. Samuel **LEE**, of Salisbury, June 23, 1792, by Thomas Allen	3	111
Eliza, d. Sam[ue]l & Jemimah, b. Jan. 30, 1802, in Jericho, Vt.	3	59
Eliza, d. of Samuel, of Salisbury, m. Joshua N. **MOSES**, of Norfolk, May 15, 1823, by Job Norton, J.P.	3	119
Eliza, d. Stephen H. & Achash, b. Feb. 14, 1827	3	71
Elizabeth, had d. Louisa Anne, b. May 28, 1767	2	7
George, m. Lucy **BUNDY**, Nov. 16, 1826, by L.E. Lathrop	3	125
Harriet, d. Samuel & Jemimah, b. Feb. 25, 1815	3	59
Hiram, s. Eli & Lucy, b. Sept. 24, 1798	3	15
Joseph G., m. Maria C. **MILLS**, b. of Salisbury, Dec. 6, 1820, by Lavius Hyde	3	116
Laura E., m. Rufus **REED**, b. of Salisbury, Mar. 6, 1828, by Rev. Stephen Beach, of St. Johns Ch.	3	129
Loiza, d. Sam[ue]l & Jemima, b. Mar. 27, 1800, in Jericho, Vt.	3	59
Louisa Anne, d. Elizabeth, b. May 28, 1767	2	7
Lucyet, d. Samuel & Jemimah, b. Aug. 2, 1813	3	59
Mary Ann, d. Stephen H. & Achash, b. Apr. 2, 1822	3	71
Moore, s. Eli & Lucy, b. Dec. 27, 1802	3	15
Moore, m. Emma **LANGDON**, b. of Salisbury, Feb. 28, 1827, by Rev. Stephen Beach, of St. Johns Ch.	3	126
Nelson Moore, s. Moore & Emma, b. Feb. 13, 1828	3	77
Phebe Adaline, d. Ransom & Sally, b. Oct. 26, 1828	3	80
Raman, m. Sally **LANGDEN**, b. of Salisbury, Jan. 13, 1825, by Rev. Stephen Beach, of the St. Johns Ch.	3	122
Ransom, s. Eli & Lucy, b. July 12, 1800	3	15
Ransom Hoye, s. Ransom & Sally, b. Jan. 27, 1826	3	80
Sarah, d. Stephen H. & Achash, b. Jan. 18, 1825	3	71
Sibel, m. John **COLVER**, b. of Salisbury, Feb. 4, 1773, by James Landon, J.P.	2	45
Stephen Harlow, s. Sam[ue]l & Jemima, b. June 14, 1798, in Jericho, Vt.	3	59
William*, s. Clement & Nancy, b. Feb. 28, 1803 *(Perhaps "William Brown **CLEMENT**")	3	32
BROWNSON, Abigail, d. Amos & Dorcase, b. Nov. 20, 1758, in Woodbury	2	10
Amos, s. Amos & Dorcase, b. Sept. 7, 1767	2	10
Bethena, d. Amos & Dorcase, b. Aug. 10, 1760, in Woodbury	2	10
Ebenezer, s. Amos & Dorcase, b. Aug. 26, 1772	2	10
Elizabeth, d. Timothy & Abigail, d. Aug. 8, 1761, in the 18th y. of her age	1	237
Elizabeth, d. Timothy, Jr. & Hannah, b. Feb. 16, 1762	1	128
Gideon, m. Cornelia **WHITE**, b. of Salisbury, Apr. 16, 1761, by Rev. Jonathan Lee	1	249

SALISBURY VITAL RECORDS 161

	Vol.	Page
BROWNSON, (cont.)		
Isaac, s. Gideon & Cornelia, b. Mar. 22, 1762	1	128
Joel, s. Amos & Dorcase, b. May 12, 1762, in Woodbury	2	10
Timothy, s. Gideon & Cornelia, b. Sept. 3, 1763	1	128
BRYAN, [see also **BRYANT**], Esther, d. Lewis & Esther, b. Nov. 7, 1758	1	172
Lewis, m. Esther **CASE**, b. of Salisbury, Aug. 17, 1757, by Rev. Jonathan Lee	1	247
Sarah Ann, m. Dady **BUNDY**, b. of Salisbury, Oct. 21, 1823, by Rev. Charles Prentice, of Canaan	3	119
BRYANT, [see also **BRYAN**], Aldin, s. Samuel & Chloe, b. Sept. 15, 1809	3	62
Alexander, s. Alex[ande]r & Sarah, b. Nov. 27, 1787	3	23
Almon Church, s. Samuel & Chloe, b. May 3, 1815	3	62
Clarissa, d. Samuel & Chloe, b. July 17, 1820	3	62
Harriet, d. Alex[ande]r & Sarah, b. Aug. 15, 1792	3	23
Harry, s. Alex[ande]r & Sarah, b. Aug. 3, 1794	3	23
Hiram Levitt, s. Samuel & Chloe, b. May 7, 1818	3	62
Polly, d. Alex[ande]r & Sarah, b. Mar. 6, 1791	3	23
Samuel Platt, s. Samuel & Chloe, b. Feb. 28, 1813	3	62
BUELL, BUEL, Abigail, of Coventry, m. Joshua **PORTER**, of Salisbury, May 14, 1759, by Rev. Oliver Webb	1	248
Abigail, d. Nathaniel & Hannah, b. July 29, 1768	2	15
Deborah, m. Azariah **NEWCOMB**, May 4, 1743	LR1	356-7
Deborah, d. May 16, 1778, ae 83	2	49
Eliphalet, of Salisbury, m. Sarah **REED**, of Sharon, Dec. 7, 1752, by Rev. Jonathan Lee	1	224
Elisha, of Marlbrough, m. Almyra **CANFIELD**, of Salisbury, Dec. 14, 1823, by David L. Perry	3	120
Hannah, d. Nathaniel & Hannah, b. Aug. 25, 1765	1	135
Hannah, of Salisbury, m. John **ELDREDGE**, of Mansfield, Nov. 28, 1782, by Rev. Jonathan Lee	2	42
Hannah, wid. Col. Nath[anie]l, d. Nov. 28, 1812, ae 74	3	167
Nathaniel, s. Eliphalet & Sarah, b. Dec. 12, 1753	1	198
Nathaniell, m. Hannah **LEE**, b. of Salisbury, Apr. 23, 1761, by Rev. Jonathan Lee	1	249
Nath[anie]ll, Col., d. Nov. 27, 1808, in the 74th y. of his age	3	167
Sally, d. Nathaniell & Hannah, b. Apr. 20, 1771	2	15
Sarah, d. Eliphalet & Sarah, b. Oct. 8, 1857* *(Probably intended for "1757")	1	198
Simon, s. Eliphalet & Sarah, b. Jan. 9, 1760	1	198
Simon, d. May 8, 1760	1	229
BUNCE, Mary Ann, of Salisbury, m. Sherman **JACQUA**, of Canaan, Oct. 27, 1834, by Leonard E. Lathrop	3	147
BUNDY, Dady, m. Sarah Ann **BRYAN**, b. of Salisbury, Oct. 21, 1823, by Rev. Charles Prentice, of Canaan	3	119
George, s. Hiram & Lucy, b. Jan. 25, 1831	3	80
Hiram, m. Lucy **MOORE**, b. of Salisbury, Feb. 1, 1829, by Rev. Stephen Beach, of St. Johns Ch.	3	133
Lucy, m. George **BROWN**, Nov. 16, 1826, by L.E. Lathrop	3	125
Rachel, m. Milton **PRATT**, b. of Salisbury, Nov. 29, 1838, by		

	Vol.	Page
BUNDY, (cont.)		
Adam Reid	3	157
BUNN, Hopestill, m. Noah **LYMAN**, b. of Salisbury, May 12, 1784, at Canaan, by Rev. Daniel Ferrand	2	43
BURBANK, John, s. Timothy & Esther, b. Mar. 19, 1752	1	221
Mary, d. Timothy & Esther, b. Mar. 3, 1750	1	221
BURCHARD, ----------, d. June 21, 1777	2	49
BURCK, Sebrina P., of Salisbury, m. Albert G. **SMITH**, of Sharon, May 27, 1828, by Rev. Stephen Beach, of St. Johns Ch.	3	130
BURGESS, Mary Loisa, d. Daniel R., b. Jan. 24, 1843	3	88
[BURNETT], [see under **BERNET**]		
BURR, Elizabeth, w. Oliver, d. Feb. 21, 1775, in the 25th y. of her age	2	49
William, s. Oliver & Elizabeth, b. Feb. 6, 1775	2	35
BURRELL, BURRALL, BURREL, Charles, m. Almira **NEVITT**, b. of Salisbury, Mar. 31, 1841, by Rev. Adam Reid	3	160
George B., m. Malinda **MARTIN**, b. of Salisbury, Nov. 8, 1847, by Rev. Adam Reed	3	102
William M., of Canaan, m. Abigail **STODDARD**, of Salisbury, Nov. 6, 1803, by Rev. Joseph W. Crossman	3	112
William P., of Canaan, m. Harriet A. **HOLLEY**, of Salisbury, [May] 9, [1831], by L.E. Lathrop	3	139
BURROUGHS, William, m. Bede **BINGHAM**, b. of Salisbury, Apr. 16, 1799, by Samuel Lee, J.P.	3	110
BURTON, Elizabeth, d. Simeon & Mary, b. July 13, 1742	LR1	353
Mary, of Salisbury, m. Stephen **BABCOCK**, of Stonington, Mar. 20, 1831, by Rev. Stephen Beach, of St. Johns Ch.	3	138
BUSH, Lewis, s. Joseph & Deborah, b. Nov. 23, 1776	2	33
Nancy, d. Joseph & Deborah, b. Mar. 15, 1779	2	33
Sarah Ann, of New York City, m. George **WOOSTER**, of Salisbury, Nov. 29, 1845, by Rev. D.W. Clark	3	97
BUSHNELL, BUSHNALL, BUSHELL, Albert, m. Ann **LEE**, b. of Salisbury, [Jan.]1, [1828], by L.E. Lathrop	3	128
Amelia, d. Samuel & Esther, b. Sept. 20, 1787	2	14
Barnett, s. Samuel, Jr. & Esther, b. Aug. 1, 1773, in Saybrook	2	14
Bille, s. Samuell, Jr. & Esther, b. June 30, 1775	2	14
Charles, s. Hannah, b. Dec. 18, 1776	3	11
Charles, s. Samuell, Jr. & Esther, b. Apr. 20, 1782	2	14
Charles, s. Albert & Ann L., b. Sept. 25, 1828	3	84
Charles D., s. Herman B. & Emeline J., b. June 7, 1834	3	87
Daphna, m. Joseph A. **HUBBARD**, Feb. 9, 1823, by Martin Strong, J.P.	3	118
Eliza, d. Jeremiah & Lucy, b. June 20, 1800	3	31
Eliza, m. Thomas Bidwell **PEET**, b. of Salisbury, Sept. 30, 1821, by Lavius Hyde	3	115
Enoch, s. Samuell, Jr. & Esther, b. Aug. 16, 1771, in Saybrook	2	14
Frederick, s. Samuell, Jr. & Esther, b. Apr. 2, 1785	2	14
Hannah, had s. James, b. Dec. 20, 1775 & Charles, b. Dec. 18, 1776	3	11
Harmon Butler, s. Jeremiah & Lucy, b. Sept. 17, 1807	3	31
Herman Butler, of Salisbury, m. Emeline Jane **DUTCHER**, of Canaan, Sept. 23, 1832, by Rev. Stephen Beach, of		

	Vol.	Page
BUSHNELL, BUSHNALL, BUSHELL, (cont.)		
St. Johns Ch.	3	141
Hester, d. Samuel, Jr. & Esther, b. Mar. 26, 1768, in Saybrook	2	14
Hester, m. Asa **EDDY**, b. of Salisbury, Jan. 12, 1786, by Peter Bishop, J.P.	2	43
James, s. Hannah, b. Dec. 20, 1775	3	11
Jerusha, m. Robert Walker **LEE**, b. of Salisbury, Oct. 29, 1786, by Rev. Jonathan Lee	2	43
Luther, s. Samuell, Jr. & Esther, b. July 6, 1780	2	14
Polly, d. Samuell, Jr. & Esther, b. June 1, 1778	2	14
Samuell, s. Samuell, Jr. & Esther, b. Dec. 16, 1769, in Saybrook	2	14
Samuel, s. Jeremiah & Lucy, b. May 21, 1796	3	31
Samuel, m. Sally **JACOBS**, Nov. 27, 1822, by Charles Printice	3	117
William, s. Jeremiah & Lucy, b. July 20, 1798	3	31
BUTLER, Ebenezer W., of Clinton, N.Y., m. Julia **HOLMES**, of Salisbury, Aug. 11, 1836, by Rev. Oliver V. Amerman, of M.E. Ch.	3	152
Hannah, d. Thomas & Jane, b. Aug. 18, 1772	2	31
John, m. Cloe **NORTON**, b. of Salisbury, May 9, 1769, by John Hutchinson, J.P.	2	44
John, s. Thomas & Jane, b. Aug. 28, 1774	2	31
Mehetabel, m. Moses **COATS**, Feb. 16, 1768, by Aaron Lyman, J.P., of Wallingford, Witnesses Comfort Butler & Mary Butler	3	109
Molley, d. Thomas & Jane, b. Nov. 20, 1770	2	31
Sarah, d. Thomas & Jane, b. May 15, 1776	2	31
Thomas, m. Jane **WHITE**, b. of Salisbury, June 1, 1769, by John Hutchinson, J.P.	2	44
BUTTON, Sarah, late of Norwich, m. Ebenezer **JEWELL**, Nov. 11, 1781, at Norwich, by Jonathan Brewster, J.P.	2	41
CABLE, Curtius R., of New Milford, m. Janette **COFFING**, of Salisbury, Jan. 20, 1829, by L.E. Lathrop	3	133
CADY, Adeline, d. Nath[anie]l & Delia, b. Feb. 21, 1824	3	70
Almon, s. Nath[anie]l & Delia, b. Dec. 15, 1821	3	70
Jennett, of Salisbury, m. Matthew **GILLETTE**, of New Hartford, July 8, 1828, by Charles Prentice	3	130
Nathaniel Benedict, s. Nathaniel & Delia, b. Jan. 7, 1818	3	70
Orpha, d. Nathaniel & Delia, b. Mar. 23, 1820	3	70
CALKINS, CALKIN, Jeremiah, of Sharon, m. Sarah **LAMB**, of Salisbury, Sept. 16, 1839, by Rev. Thomas Bainbridge	3	158
Moses, m. Thankfull **STEVENS**, b. of Salisbury, Dec. 7, 1780, by Rev. Jonathan Lee	2	41
Nelle, d. Elisha & Dorcas, b. June 6, 1789	2	21
William, s. Elisha & Dorcas, b. Nov. 25, 1786, in North East Precinct, Dutchess Co., N.Y.	2	21
CAMMARON, John, m. Prudence **BREWSTER**, b. of Salisbury, Jan. 25, 1769, by Rev. Jonathan Lee	2	44
CAMP, Abiel, of Salisbury, m. Mary **BOTCHFORD**, of Darby, Dec. 5, 1750, by Rev. Mr. Humphrey	1	223
Abial, s. Abial & Mary, b. Aug. 3, 1754	1	180
Abiel, s. Abiel & Mary, d. Sept. 7, 1757	1	228

CAMP, (cont.)

	Vol.	Page
Abigail, d. Luke & Rachel, b. Apr. 11, 1771	2	17
Abigail, m. Jedediah **STARK**, b. of Salisbury, Jan. 15, 1792, at Canaan, by Rev. Daniel Farrand	3	108
Almira, d. Benajah & Anna, b. Jan. 5, 1812	3	71
Ann, m. Charles **CHAPIN**, b. of Salisbury, Aug. 13, 1751, by Rev. Jonathan Lee	1	223
Ann, d. Joel & Zerviah, b. Dec. 24, 1759	1	186
Ann, m. Samuel **CHURCHILL**, b. of Salisbury, July 9, 1781, by Abial Camp, J.P.	2	41
Benajah, s. Joel & Zerviah, b. Feb. 5, 1780	2	23
Benajah, s. Benajah & Anna, b. Jan. 5, 1807	3	71
Benajah, Jr., s. Benajah & Anna, b. Apr. 9, 1816	3	71
Benajah, m. Thankfull **WHITNEY**, b. of Salisbury, Nov. 22, 1841, by J. Shaw	3	161
Betsey, d. Hezekiah, Jr. & Hannah, b. Jan. 8, 1790	3	1
Betsey, m. Jesse **SMITH**, Nov. 7, 1793. Witnesses Thomas Camp & Sabina Camp	3	109
Betty, d. John & Hannah, b. Nov. 20, 1775	2	34
Daniel, s. Luke & Rachel, b. Jan. 3, 1778	2	17
David, twin with James, s. Luke & Rachel, b. Aug. 28, 1775	2	17
David, s. Luke & Rachel, d. Aug. 28, 1775, ae about 5 hours old	2	49
Electa, d. Luke & Rachel, b. Feb. 9, 1773	2	17
Eunice, d. Joel & Zerviah, b. Feb. 19, 1776	2	23
Hannah, d. John & Hannah, b. Jan. 16, 1774	2	34
Harriet, d. Benajah & Anna, b. Oct. 3, 1808	3	71
Harriet, of Salisbury, m. Jason **DeFOREST**, of New Marlborough, June 20, 1833, by L.E. Lathrop	3	143
Hezekiah, Jr., of Salisbury, m. Sarah **LOTHROP***, of Ammete, Nov. 21, 1752, by Rev. Mr. Woodbridge *("**NORTHROP**" in Rudd's book)	1	240
Hezekiah, s. Hezekiah, Jr. & Sarah, b. July 21, 1755	1	184
Hezekiah, s. Hezekiah, Jr. & Sarah, d. Sept. 13, 1757	1	228
Hezekiah, s. Luke & Rachal, b. Jan. 26, 1767	1	156
Hezekiah, Jr., d. Sept. 29, 1774, in the 51st y. of his age	2	49
Hezekiah, of Salisbury, m. Hannah **MARSH**, of Canaan, Mar. 29, 1789, by Elisha Baker, J.P.	3	108
Hezekiah, Dea., d. Nov. 24, 1791, in the 92nd y. of his age	3	164
James, twin with David, s. Luke & Rachel, b. Aug. 28, 1775	2	17
Joel, of Salisbury, m. Zerruiah **BINGHAM**, of Windham, Mar. 9, 1757, by Jedediah Elderkin, in Windham	1	245
Joel & Zerviah, had d. [ ], b. Mar. 9, 1762; d. same day, also s. [ ], b. July 5, 1766; d. same day	1	186
Joel, s. Joel & Zerviah, b. Apr. 21, 1778	2	23
John, m. Hannah **JEWELL**, b. of Salisbury, Jan. 23, 1772, by Rev. Jonathan Lee	2	46
John, s. John & Hannah, b. Feb. 27, 1780	2	34
John, d. Sept. 16, 1784, in the 37th y. of his age	2	50
Joshua Stanton, s. Luke, Jr. & Elizabeth, b. Oct. 16, 1786	2	35
Lois, d. Luke & Rachel, b. Dec. 5, 1768	2	17
Lucy, d. Joel & Zerviah, b. Oct. 3, 1769	2	23

SALISBURY VITAL RECORDS

	Vol.	Page
CAMP, (cont.)		
Luke, s. Luke & Rachel, b. July 23, 1764	1	156
Luke, Jr., m. Elizabeth **STANTON**, b. of Salisbury, Feb. 2, 1786, by Rev. Jonathan Lee	2	43
Lydia, d. Luke & Rachel, b. Sept. 28, 1760	1	156
Mary, d. Joel & Zerviah, b. June 21, 1767	1	186
Mary Ann, d. Benajah & Anna, b. July 28, 1819	3	71
Nabby, d. Luke & Elizabeth, b. Dec. 17, 1788	2	35
Phebe, d. Joel & Zerviah, b. Nov. 1, 1772	2	23
Phebe Caroline, d. Benajah & Anna, b. Feb. 17, 1814	3	71
Rachel, d. Luke & Rachel, b. Aug. 30, 1762	1	156
Rachel, m. Benjamin **HOWES**, b. of Salisbury, on or about July 8, 1784, by Rev. Jonathan Lee. Witnesses Mylo Lee & Ruth Lee	3	108
Rachel, d. Luke & Elizabeth, b. Nov. 3, 1791	2	35
Rebecca, of New Milford, m. John **WHITTLESEY**, of Salisbury, Feb. 19, [1817], by Rev. Andrew Elliot, of New Milford	3	114
Ruth, d. Hezekiah, Jr. &Sarah, b. Dec. 29, 1760	1	184
Ruth, m. Mylo **LEE**, b. of Salisbury, May 23, 1782, by Rev. Jonathan Lee	2	42
Sabina, d. John & Hannah, b. Feb. 21, 1778	2	34
Sarah, d. Hezekiah, Jr. & Sarah, b. Oct. 28, 1753	1	184
Sarah, d. Hezekiah, Jr. & Sarah, d. Sept. 18, 1757	1	228
Sarah, d. Hezekiah, Jr. & Sarah, b. Aug. 8, 1758	1	184
Sarah, wid. Hez[ekiah], Jr., d. Sept. 6, 1785, in the 66th y. of her age	2	50
Sarah, Jr., d. Jan. 19, 1786, in the 27th y. of her age	2	50
William, s. Hezekiah, Jr. & Hannah, b. Nov. 12, 1792	3	1
William Henry, s. Benajah & Anna, b. Feb. 22, 1822	3	71
Zeruah, d. Joel & Zerviah, b. Feb. 22, 1758	1	186
CANE, W[illia]m, m. Dorcas E. **CROWELL**, Mar. 12, 1837, by Charles Printice	3	154
CANFIELD, CAMFIELD, Almyra, of Marlborough, m. Elisha **BUELL**, of Marlborough, Dec. 14, 1823, by David L. Perry	3	120
Asenath, m. Daniel **BREWSTER**, b. of Salisbury, Oct. 2, 1811, by Charles Printice	3	114
Caroline E., of Salisbury, m. Uriah H. **MINOR**, of Canaan, Sept. 9, 1843, by Rev. Stephen G. Stebbins	3	163
Edward, s. Joseph, Jr. & Abigail, b. Aug. 5, 1796	3	10
Ezekiel, s. Jonathan & Sarah, b. Mar. 18, 1767	2	21
Harmon, twin with Horace, s. Joseph, Jr. & Abigail, b. Oct. 9, 1791	3	10
Herman, of Warren, O., m. Anna A. **CHITTENDEN**, of Salisbury, Sept. 27, 1843, by Rev. Adam Reid	3	163
Horace, twin with Harmon, s. Joseph, Jr. & Abigail, b. Oct. 9, 1791	3	10
Jonathan, m. Sarah **WOODWORTH**, b. of Salisbury, Dec. 2, 1764, by Caleb Smith, J.P.	2	44
Jonathan, s. Jonathan & Sarah, b. Nov. 6, 1765	2	21
Joseph, Jr., d. Sept. 24, 1803, ae 36	3	166
Lee, s. Joseph, Jr. & Abigail, b. July 12, 1788	2	16

	Vol.	Page
CANFIELD, CAMFIELD, (cont.)		
Maria, of Salisbury, m. Julius **BENEDICT**, of Canaan, Jan. 5, 1846, by Rev. Albert Nash	3	98
Phebe, d. Joseph & Rachel, b. Aug. 7, 1766	2	26
Samuel, s. Jonathan & Sarah, b. Apr. 20, 1770	2	28
William, s. Joseph, Jr. & Abigail, b. May 1, 1799	3	10
CARNEY, Andrew, s. Andrew & Elizabeth, b. Nov. 5, 1789	3	31
Charity, d. Andrew & Elizabeth, b. Apr. 3, 1786	3	31
Elizabeth, d. Andrew & Elizabeth, b. Apr. 22, 1788	3	31
Lydia, d. Andrew & Elizabeth, b. Apr. 25, 1783	3	31
Mary, d. Andrew & Elizabeth, b. July 30, 1781	3	31
CARTER, Anna Emeline, d. Thomas & Anna, b. Aug. 14, 1804	3	39
Benoni, d. Apr. 11, 1812, ae 67	3	167
Caroline Herrick, d. Thomas & Anna, b. May 2, 1802	3	39
Lucius, s. Benoni & Hannah, b. Dec. 29, 1811	3	47
Thomas, m. Anna **JOSLIN**, b. of Salisbury, Apr. 13, 1800, by Samuel Lee, J.P.	3	112
CARY, [see also **CORY**], Abigail, m. William **PATESON**, b. of Salisbury, Apr. 11, 1757, by James Landon, J.P.	1	245
Hannah, had d. Mary **PORTER**, b. Sept. 13, 1759	1	189
Lockwood, m. Hannah **VAN VALKENBURY**, May 3, 1835, by Leonard E. Lathrop	3	148
Mary **PORTER**, d. Hannah, b. Sept. 13, 1759	1	189
Seth, m. Hannah **HOUSE**, b. of Salisbury, Feb. 28, 1750/1, by Rev. Jonathan Lee	1	223
CASE, Abigail, d. Seth & Elizabeth, d. Sept. 27, 1754	1	227
Esther, m. Lewis **BRYAN**, b. of Salisbury, Aug. 17, 1757, by Rev. Jonathan Lee	1	247
Ezekiel, s. Seth & Elizabeth, b. Apr. 19, 1760	1	219
Ichabod, s. Seth, d. Sept. 27, 1754	1	227
Lemuel, s. Seth & Elizabeth, b. Nov. 22, 1757	1	219
Seth, m. Elizabeth **COPLEY**, b. of Salisbury, Aug. 17, 1749, by Rev. Jonathan Lee	1	223
Seth, s. Seth & Elizabeth, b. Dec. 29, 1751	1	219
CASTEL, Mary, of Sheffield, m. Simeon **STRONG**, of Salisbury, Apr. 1, 1756, by Rev. Jonathan Hubbart	1	248
CATLIN, John, s. Wait & Peggy, b. Sept. 10, 1786	2	13
CAUL, [see under **COLE**]		
CHADWICK, David T., m. Chloe **LYMAN**, Sept. 10, 1833, by L.E. Lathrop	3	143
CHAMBERLAIN, Elizabeth, m. Tho[ma]s **BIRD**, b. of Salisbury, Feb. 14, 1776, by Rev. Jonathan Lee	2	41
Joel, of Lebanon, m. Mary **EVARTS**, of Salisbury, Feb. 25, 1783, by Rev. Jonathan Lee	2	42
Mary, d. Joel & Mercy, b. Aug. 22, 1784	2	39
William, m. Lucinda **PHILLO**, Jan. 18, 1824, by David L. Perry	3	120
CHAMPION, Sibbil, d. Daniel & Esther, b. July 18, 1756	1	107
CHAPIN, Aaron, s. Charles, Jr. & Theodosia, b. Feb. 27, 1779	2	12
Abiel, m. Harriet A. **STERLING**, June 28, 1815, by [ ]. Witnesses Andrew Chapin & Maria F. Chapin	3	115
Abigail, d. Charles & Ann, b. July 30, 1774	2	10

	Vol.	Page
CHAPIN, (cont.)		
Andrew, s. Phinehas & Love, b. Apr. 12, 1795	2	40
Abigail, m. Alexander **LAMB**, Aug. 9, 1795, by Adonijah Strong, J.P.	3	110
Abigail, d. David & Abigail, b. Jan. 24, 1811	3	35
Andrew, m. Maria **FARNUM**, May 20, 1819, by Rev. Lavius Hyde. Witness Newman Holley	3	115
Ann, d. Charles & Ann, b. Aug. 17, 1754	1	178
Anne, w. Charles, d. Mar. 11, 1758	1	228
Azariah, s. Charles, Jr. & Theodosia, b. Dec. 20, 1785; d. Dec. 22, 1785	2	12
Caroline Elenor, d. Luther & Hannah, b. Feb. 8, 1801	3	29
Charles, m. Ann **CAMP**, b. of Salisbury, Aug. 13, 1751, by Rev. Jonathan Lee	1	223
Charles, s. Charles & Ann, b. June 26, 1752	1	178
Charles, Jr., m. Theodosia **FERRE**, b. of Salisbury, Apr. 11, 1776, by Rev. Jonathan Lee	2	47
Charlotte J., of Marlborough, m. Robert **SPENCER**, of Colebrook, Sept. 8, 1838, by Rev. Thomas Bainbridge	3	156
Chloe, d. Charles & Ann, b. Apr. 19, 1772	2	10
Chloe, m. Daniel **REED**, b. of Salisbury, Dec. 23, 1798, by Rev. Joseph W. Crossman	3	111
Clarissa, d. Aaron & Martha, b. Apr. 7, 1798	3	25
Daniel, s. Charles & Anna, b. Feb. 2, 1761	1	178
Daniel, m. Parthenia **WHEELER**, b. of Salisbury, Oct. 26, 1783, by Rev. Jonathan Lee	2	42
David, s. Charles, Jr. & Theodosia, b. Apr. 24, 1781	2	12
David, of Salisbury, m. Abigail **SPARKS**, of Sheffield, Mar. 23, 1806, by Joseph W. Crossman	3	113
Edward, s. Andrew & Maria F., b. Jan. 1, 1821	3	66
Elisha Sterling, s. Abiel & Harriet, b. Mar. 24, 1818	3	66
Elizabeth, wid., m. John **JEWELL**, Jan. 21, 1801, by Samuel Lee, J.P.	3	114
Elizabeth, d. Phineas & Lucinda, b. Oct. 27, 1826	3	52
Esther, d. Reuben & Rebeckah, b. June 28, 1758	1	107
Eunice, d. Reuben & Sarah, b. Jan. 2, 1774	2	17
Eunice, d. Charles, Jr. & Theodosia, b. Oct. 21, 1784; d. Dec. 4, 1784	2	12
Frederick Martin, s. Phineas, Jr. & Lucinda, b. Mar. 4, 1814	3	52
Graham Hurd, s. Phinehas & Love, b. Feb. 10, 1799	2	40
Heman, s. Charles & Ann, b. Aug. 6, 1776	2	10
Henry, s. Phinehas & Love, b. Aug. 22, 1800	2	40
Henry, s. Abiel & Harriet, b. Jan. 25, 1817	3	66
Huldah, d. Charles & Ann, b. Apr. 7, 1778; d. Apr. 18, 1778	2	10
Jerusha, d. John & Elizabeth, b. Apr. 19, 1792	3	23
John, s. Reuben & Sarah, b. Dec. 20, 1766	1	107
Lament, d. Reuben & Rebeckah, b. Feb. 28, 1762	1	107
Love, d. Phinehas & Love, b. Sept. 3, 1784	2	40
Love, d. Phineas & Sarah, d. Aug. 10, 1793, in the 9th y. of her age	2	50
Love, d. Phineas, Jr. & Lucinda, b. May 9, 1810	3	52

	Vol.	Page
CHAPIN, (cont.)		
Love, m. Moses **WELLS**, Jr., b. of Salisbury, Dec. 1, 1829, by L.E. Lathrop	3	135
Lucinda Martin, d. Phineas, Jr. & Lucinda, b. Nov. 15, 1815, in Galen, N.Y.	3	52
Lucy, d. Charles & Ann, b. Jan. 23, 1768	2	10
Luther, s. Charles & Ann, b. May 26, 1779	2	10
Luther, m. Hannah **EVEREST**, b. of Salisbury, May 1, 1798, by Joseph W. Crossman	3	111
Maria Farnum, d. Phineas & Lucinda, b. Dec. 15, 1829	3	52
Martin Charles, s. David & Abigail, b. Mar. 21, 1809	3	35
Mary, d. Phinehas & Love, b. Nov. 25, 1791	2	40
Mary, d. Phineas & Lucinda, b. Sept. 8, 1817	3	52
Minerva, d. Luther & Hannah, b. Feb. 13, 1799	3	29
Minerva, d. Aaron & Martha, b. Sept. 12, 1799	3	25
Moses, s. Charles, Jr. & Theodosia, b. June 7, 1777	2	12
Olive, d. Reuben & Sarah, b. Oct. 8, 1775	2	17
Olive, d. Charles, Jr. & Theodosia, b. Mar. 12, 1783	2	12
Oliver, s. Charles & Anne, b. Mar. 29, 1766	1	130
Phebe, d. Charles & Ann, b. Apr. 22, 1770	2	10
Phinehas, s. Charles & Ann, b. Feb. 16, 1757	1	178
Phinehas, of Salisbury, m. Love **HURD**, of Woodbury, May 14, 1783, by Rev. Mr. Benedict, of Woodbury	2	42
Phinehas, s. Phinehas & Love, b. Mar. 7, 1789	2	40
Phineas, Jr., m. Lucinda **MARTIN**, b. of Salisbury, Mar. 1, 1809, by Rev. Joseph W. Crossman	3	113
Polly, d. John & Elizabeth, b. Feb. 4, 1796	3	23
Rebeckah, d. Reubin & Rebeckah, b. Aug. 17, 1747 O.S., at Summers	1	107
Rebeckah, w. Reubin, d. Mar. 31, 1762	1	238
Reuben, had d. [ ], d. Dec. 12, 1773, in the 16th y. of her age	2	49
Reuben, s. John & Elizabeth, b. Apr. 27, 1788	3	23
Reuben, s. John & Elizabeth, d. Oct. 29, 1791, in the 4th y. of his age	3	164
Reuben, d. June 1, 1793, ae 74	3	164
Rhoda, d. Charles & Anne, b. June 21, 1764	1	130
Ruth, d. Charles & Anne, b. July 29, 1762	1	130
Ruth Ann, d. Phineas, Jr. & Lucinda, b. Mar. 16, 1812	3	52
Samuel, d. Reuben & Rebecca, d. May 28, 1777, in the 16th y. of his age	2	50
Sarah, d. Reuben & Sarah, b. Oct. 26, 1768	2	17
Sarah, w. Reuben, d. June 5, 1784, in the 51st y. of her age	2	50
Theodore, s. Phineas & Lucinda, b. July 6, 1821	3	52
Theodosia, d. Charles, Jr. & Theodosia, b. Apr. 7, 1795	2	12
Theodosia, d. Aaron & Martha, b. May 18, 1801	3	35
CHAPMAN, Allen, m. Almira **BRASIA**, b. of Salisbury, Jan. 8, 1840, by Thomas Bainbridge	3	159
Asenath, m. Henry **DAUCHY**, b. of Salisbury, Apr. 28, 1833, by Rev. Stephen Beach, of St. Johns Ch.	3	143
Ersula, m. Henry E. **JOHNSON**, b. of Salisbury, Dec. 25, 1835, by Rev. Lucius M. Purdy, of St Johns Ch.	3	151

	Vol.	Page
CHAPMAN, (cont.)		
Joseph, s. Obadiah & Elizabeth, b. Mar. 2, 1776	2	37
Levi, s. Silas & Lois, b. Jan. 28, 1794	2	21
Mary, m. William **REED**, b. of Salisbury, Mar. 29, 1827, by Charles Printice	3	127
Milton, s. Reuben, Jr. & Phebe, b. Sept. 4, 1790	3	2
Newton, m. Salome **DAUCHY**, b. of Salisbury, Sept. 29, 1833, by Rev. L.M. Purdy, of St. Johns Ch.	3	143
Obediah, m. Elizabeth **NORTHRUP**, b. of Salisbury, Mar. 9, 1775, by Rev. Jonathan Lee	2	46
Phebe, d. Silas & Lois, b. Nov. 18, 1792	2	21
Reuben, d. Jan. 20, 1799, ae 66	3	164
Sarah, of Amenia, m. Jonathan **KELSEY**, of Salisbury, June 13, 1770, by Rev. Mr. Smith	2	45
Sidney, m. Elizabeth **COUL**, b. of Salisbury, Feb. 5, 1840, by Rev. Thomas Bainbridge	3	159
CHASE, Benjamin, s. Job & Rachel, b. Aug. 24, 1812	3	56
Tytus, s. Job & Rachel, b. Feb. 15, 1808	3	56
CHATFIELD, Benjamin, m. Luretia **DOUD**, Nov. 10, 1770, in Saybrook, by Rev. Stephen Holmes	2	47
Jesse, m. Freelove **WOODWORTH**, b. of Salisbury, Oct. 18, 1756, by Rev. Jonathan Lee	1	244
Mary, d. Phillip & Marcy, b. June 6, 1755	1	197
Mary, d. Stephen & Naomi, b. July 16, 1774	2	13
Stephen, had [ ], d. Jan. 2, 1782, ae 29	2	49
CHIPMAN, Abigail, d. John & Sarah, b. July 20, 1749	1	203
Abigail, d. John & Sarah, b. July 20, 1749	1	216
Abigail, d. Amos & Sarah, b. May 4, 1757	1	218
Abigail, m. Gamaleel **PAINTER**, Aug. 20, 1767, by Rev. Jonathan Lee	2	44
Abigail, d. Jonathan & Katharine, b. Sept. 19, 1767	2	12
Abigail, of Sunderland, m. Simeon **LYMAN**, of Salisbury, Sept. 19, 1774, by Rev. Mr. Dewey, of [Great] Barrington	2	46
Ammi, s. Amos & Sarah, b. Feb. 12, 1764	1	144
Amos, of Salisbury, m. Sarah **DAGGIT**, of Lebanon, Oct. 18, 1749, by Joseph Clark, J.P.	1	222
Amos, s. Amos & Sarah, b. Dec. 21, 1751	1	218
Barnabus Lathrop, s. Amos & Sarah, b. Nov. 5, 1762	1	218
Daniel, s. Jonathan & Katharine, b. Sept. 10, 1759	2	12
Daniel, s. Jonathan & Katharine, d. Oct. 8, 1759	2	48
Daniel, s. Samuel & Hannah, b. Oct. 22, 1765	1	131
Darius, s. Samuel & Hannah, b. Aug. 17, 1756	1	213
Eunice, d. Amos & Sarah, b. Apr. 8, 1753	1	218
Jesse, s. Amos & Sarah, b. Feb. 28, 1755	1	218
John, s. John & Sarah, b. Oct. 12, 1745	1	204
John & Sarah, had s. [ ], s. b. Aug. 12, 1747	1	204
John, d. Sept. 3, 1754, in the 38th y. of his age	1	243
John, of Salisbury, m. Olive **DOUGLASS**, of Canaan, May 13, 1767, by Rev. Daniel Farrand	2	44
John, m. Sarah **WASHBURN**, b. of Salisbury, Nov. 5, 1772, by Rev. Jonathan Lee	2	45

	Vol.	Page
CHIPMAN, (cont.)		
Jonathan, of Salisbury, m. Katharine **REED**, of Stanford, Oct. 5, 1756, by Rev. Mr. Mather	1	245
Jonathan, s. Jonathan & Katharine, b. Oct. 12, 1757	1	190
Jonathan, s. Jonathan & Katharine, b. Oct. 12, 1757	2	12
Joseph, s. Jonathan & Katharine, b. Aug. 5, 1761	2	12
Katharine, d. Jonathan & Katharine, b. Dec. 16, 1763	2	12
Laura, d. John & Sarah, b. Oct. 23, 1783	2	15
Lemuel, s. Samuel & Hannah, b. July 25, 1754	1	213
Mary, d. John & Sarah, b. Apr. 17, 1752	1	203
Mary, m. Aaron **SWEETLAND**, b. of Salisbury, Oct. 21, 1779, by Rev. James Nichols	2	41
Mary, m. Aaron **SWEETLAND**, b. of Salisbury, Oct. 21, 1779, by Rev. Jonathan Lee	2	42
Nathaniell, s. Samuel & Hanah, b. Nov. 27, 1752	1	213
Olive, d. John & Olive, b. Jan. 20, 1768	2	15
Olive, w. John, d. Jan. 30, 1768	2	48
Samuel, s. Samuel & Hannah, b. Oct. 8, 1750	1	213
Samuel & Hanah, had d. [ ], b. Oct. 28, 1758	1	213
Samuel, s. Samuel & Hannah, b. Dec. 10, 1763	1	131
Sarah, d. Amos & Sarah, b. Aug. 23, 1750	1	218
Sarah, m. Samuel **KEEP**, b. of Salisbury, Dec. 25, 1755, by Rev. Jonathan Lee	1	244
Sarah, d. John & Sarah, b. July 30, 1773	2	15
Siras, s. Samuel & Hannah, b. Dec. 3, 1761	1	131
Thomas, Dea., d. Aug. 5, 1752, in the 65th y. of his age	1	226
Thomas, s. Jonathan & Katharine, b. Apr. 12, 1766	2	12
Thomas, s. Jonathan & Katharine, d. Aug. 23, 1766	1	230
Thomas, s. Jonathan & Katharine, d. Aug. 23, 1766	2	48
Thomas, m. Mary **SABIN**, b. of Salisbury, Apr. 28, 1768, by Rev. Jonathan Lee	2	44
Thomas, d. Mar. 28, 1795, in the 83rd y. of his age	3	164
CHITTENDEN, Abigail, d. Timothy & Rebekah, b. Mar. 23, 1766	1	166
Abigail, m. Isaac **EVEREST**, b. of Salisbury, Feb. 15, 1787, by Rev. Jonathan Lee	2	43
Anna A., of Salisbury, m. Herman **CANFIELD**, of Warren, O., Sept. 27, 1843, by Rev. Adam Reid	3	163
Barton, s. Thomas & Elizabeth, b. Mar. 12, 1766	1	150
Belah, s. Bethuel & Deborah, b. Dec. 2, 1767	2	8
Bethuel, m. Deborah **STRONG**, b. of Salisbury, Dec. 16, 1762, by Rev. Jonathan Lee	1	250
Bethuel, s. Bethuel & Deborah, b. Dec. 6, 1772	2	8
B[e]ulah, d. Thomas & Elizabeth, b. May 23, 1763	1	150
Chloe, d. Bethuel & Deborah, b. Sept. 14, 1769	2	8
Clarinda, of Canaan, m. Oliver **JEWELL**, Jr., of Salisbury, Mar. 3, 1788, by Elisha Baker, J.P.	2	50
Ebenezer, s. Bethuel & Deborah, b. Dec. 5, 1763	1	149
Ebenezer, s. Bethuel & Deborah, d. Feb. 26, 1772, in the 9th y. of his age	2	48
Electe, d. Col. Thomas & Elizabeth, b. July 27, 1773	2	15
Elizabeth, d. Thomas & Elizabeth, b. Feb. 17, 1761	1	217

	Vol.	Page
CHITTENDEN, (cont.)		
Giles, s. Maj. Thomas & Elizabeth, b. July 30, 1768	2	15
Grace, m. Ezra **HOLMES**, Nov. 10, 1791, by Samuel Lee, J.P.	3	108
Hanah, d. Thomas & Elizabeth, b. July 13, 1756	1	217
Julette, d. Timothy, Jr. & Anna, b. July 7, 1784	2	23
Luther, s. Bethuel & Deborah, b. Sept. 30, 1765	1	149
Mabel, d. Thomas & Elizabeth, b. Oct. 7, 1750	1	217
Mary, d. Thomas & Elizabeth, b. Sept. 18, 1758	1	217
Mary, d. Timothy & Rebeckah, b. Jan. 22, 1773	2	14
Mary R., m. Chauncey **REED**, Jr., b. of Salisbury, [ ], 1839, by Rev. A. Reid	3	157
More, s. Timothy & Rebeckah, b. May 17, 1768	2	14
More, s. Timothy, Jr. & Anna, b. May 20, 1786	2	23
More, s. Capt. Timothy & Rebekah, d. Dec. 1, 1772, in the 5th y. of his age	2	48
Nancy, m. Oliver **STEVENS**, Aug. 23, 1780, by Rev. Jonathan Lee	2	41
Noah, s. Thomas & Elizabeth, b. Sept. 26, 1753	1	217
Olive, d. Timothy & Rebeckah, b. Feb. 24, 1770	2	14
Rebeckah, d. Timothy & Rebekah, b. Oct. 17, 1763	1	166
Roswell, s. Bethuel & Deborah, b. July 15, 1771	2	8
Roswell, s. Bethuel & Deborah, d. Feb. 16, 1772	2	48
Samuel, s. Timothy & Rebeckah, b. Jan. 23, 1772	2	14
Samuel, s. Timothy & Rebeckah, d. Feb. 16, 1772	2	48˙
Samuel, s. Timothy, Jr. & Anna, b. Apr. 1, 1791	2	23
Timothy, s. Timothy & Rebeckah, b. Mar. 5, 1759	1	166
Timothy, Jr., of Salisbury, m. Anna **PECK**, of Lyme, Nov. 7, 1782, by Rev. Daniel Miner, of Lyme	2	42
Timothy, s. Timothy, Jr. & Anna, b. Dec. 28, 1793	2	23
Timothy, m. Elizabeth O. **LEE**, [Nov.] 1, 1837, by Adam Reid	3	154
Truman, s. Col. Thomas & Elizabeth, b. Sept. 10, 1770	2	15
CHURCH, Albert, s. Samuel & Cynthia, b. Dec. 16, 1807	3	53
Caroline, d. Samuel & Cynthia, b. Jan. 6, 1810	3	53
Caroline E., m. George W. **HOLLEY**, b. of Salisbury, Aug. 26, 1833, in St. Johns Ch., by Rev. Lucius M. Purdy	3	144
Dorcas, w. Nath[anie]l, d. Apr. 27, 1799, ae 28	3	164
Elizabeth, of Sheffield, m. John **SELWIN***, of Salisbury, Mar. 21, 1769, by John Hutchinson, J.P. *("**WELDIN**" in Rudd's)	2	44
Ensign, s. Nathaniell & Lois, b. July 2, 1782	2	8
Frederick, s. Nathaniel & Ruth, b. Feb. 2, 1804	3	41
John, s. Nath[anie]ll & Dorcas, b. Feb. 28, 1797	3	16
Lois, w. Nathaniel, d. Feb. 19, 1785, in the 22nd y. of her age	2	50
Lois D., m. Samuell C. **SCOVILLE**, b. of Salisbury, Oct. 28, 1828, by Arnold Scholfield, Elder	3	132
Lois E., of Salisbury, m. Benjamin W. **STONE**, of Hudson, N.Y., Sept. 16, 1840, by Rev. S. Tonkin Carpenter	3	160
Lois Ensign, d. Samuel & Cynthia, b. Nov. 11, 1812	3	53
Liman, s. Nath[anie]ll & Dorcas, b. June 24, 1794	3	16
Nathaniel, s. Nathaniel & Ruth, b. Sept. 7, 1801	3	41
Oliver, m. Ruth **TOUSLEY**, b. of Salisbury, Sept. 19, 1771, by Rev. Jonathan Lee	2	45

	Vol.	Page
CHURCH, (cont.)		
Phebe, d. Tho[ma]s & Phebe, b. Mar. 24, 1800	3	35
Phebe, m. William **MORGAN**, b. of Salisbury, May 18, 1806, by Rev. Joseph W. Crossman	3	112
Ruth Amanda, of Salisbury, m. John Rogers **WARD**, of Sheffield, Mass., Dec. 1, 1835, by Rev. B. Griffen	3	151
Sally, d. Tho[ma]s & Phebe, b. Apr. 24, 1798; d. Jan. 13, 1800	3	35
Sally, d. Tho[ma]s & Phebe, b. Mar. 19, 1802	3	35
Sally, of Salisbury, m. Hiram **TAYLOR**, of Newtown, Dec. 6, 1824, by Rev. Stephen Beach, of St. John's Ch.	3	120
Sally, of Salisbury, m. Hiram **TAYLOR**, of Newtown, Dec. 10, 1824, by Rev. Stephen Beach, of St. Johns Ch.	3	123
Samuel, s. Nathaniell & Lois, b. Feb. 4, 1785	2	8
Samuel Peter, s. Samuel & Cynthia, b. Nov. 14, 1821	3	53
Thomas, m. Phebe **HOLMES**, Mar. 12, [1797], by Samuel Lee, J.P.	3	110
Thomas, d. Mar. 2, 1803, in the 33rd y. of his age	3	165
CHURCHILL, CHURCHEL, Augustus, s. Benjamin & Elizabeth, b. Sept. 1, 1797	2	29
Benjamin, d. Apr. 20, 1804, ae 58	3	166
Betsey, d. Benjamin & Elizabeth, b. Sept. 3, 1784	2	29
Charles, s. Benjamin & Elizabeth, b. July 26, 1793	2	29
Clarissa, d. Benjamin & Elizabeth, b. Mar. 18, 1788	2	29
Clarissa, d. Benjamin & Elizabeth, d. Apr. 8, 1804, ae 17	3	166
Ebenezer, s. Benjamin & Elizabeth, b. July 25, 1786	2	29
Elisha, s. Benjamin & Elizabeth, b. Sept. 12, 1782, in Chatham	2	29
Philo, s. Samuel & Ann, b. Feb. 23, 1782	2	9
Sally, d. Benjamin & Elizabeth, b. July 19, 1799	2	29
Samuel, m. Ann **CAMP**, b. of Salisbury, July 9, 1781, by Abial Camp, J.P.	2	41
Sophia, d. Benjamin & Elizabeth, b. June 5, 1791	2	29
CINNAMON, Hiram Leonard, s. Peter & Elizabeth, b. Mar. 14, 1812	3	51
Solomon, s. Peter & Elizabeth, b. Mar. 15, 1810	3	51
CLAGHORN, Andrew Ring, s. James & Elizabeth, d. Dec. 16, 1755, in the 7th y. of his age	1	227
Syntha*, d. James, Jr. & Ann, b. May 30, 1767 *("Cynthia")	1	119
Elenor, d. James, Jr. & Ann, b. July 27, 1763	1	119
Eleazer, s. James, Jr. & Ann, b. Aug. 8, 1770	2	20
Elizabeth, d. James & Elizabeth, d. Oct. 12, 1757, in the 12th y. of her age	1	228
Elizabeth, w. James, d. Nov. 11, 1768	2	48
Eunice, d. James, Jr. & Ann, b. Oct. 2, 1772	2	20
James, Jr. & Ann, had s. [ ], s.b. Apr. 1, 1766	1	119
James, s. James, Jr. & Ann, b. Mar. 11, 1769	2	20
James, s. James & Ann, d. July 13, 1771, in the 3rd y. of his age	2	48
John, s. James, Jr. & Ann, b. Dec. 2, 1764	1	119
Lucy, d. James, Jr. & Ann, b. May 5, 1776, in Rutland	2	20
Ruth, d. Sarah, b. Apr. 1, 1764	1	151
Sarah, had d. Ruth, b. Apr. 1, 1764	1	151
Sarah, had d. Silva, b. Apr. 7, 1766	1	151
Silva, d. Sarah, b. Apr. 7, 1766	1	151

	Vol.	Page
CLAGHORN, (cont.)		
Teressa, d. James, Jr. & Ann, b. Sept. 8, 1774, in Rutland	2	20
CLARK, David, of Bristol, Vt., m. Mary Electa **WOLCOTT**, of Salisbury, Sept. 14, 1825, by Rev. David Miller, of the M.E. Ch.	3	122
Delia Maria, d. Nehemiah & Polly, b. Dec. 25, 1810	3	60
Delia Maria, m. Deloss **DeLONG**, b. of Salisbury, Mar. 7, 1833, by Rev. Stephen Beach, of St. Johns Ch.	3	142
Horace, of Armenia, Dutchess Cty., N.Y., m. Mercy W. **SMITH**, of Salisbury, May 26, 1830, by Rev. Fitch Reed, of Sharon	3	136
Lucretia, m. Andrew **KENNEY**, b. of Salisbury, Mar. 23, 1834, by Eliphalet Whittlesey, J.P.	3	146
Nelson, of Sheffield, Mass. & Ann Maria **LANDON**, of Salisbury, Mar. 25, 1847, by D.W. Clark	3	100
Sally, m. Meritt S. **JONES**, May 8, 1836, by Rev. A. Bushnell	3	152
Sarah, m. Jonathan **JACOBS**, b. of Salisbury, Apr. 20, 1768, by Rev. Jonathan Lee	2	44
CLEMENT, William Brown*, s. Brown & Nancy, b. Feb. 28, 1803 *(Perhaps "William **BROWN**, s. Clement **BROWN**")	3	32
CLEVELAND, Jason, s. Jacob & Charity, b. May 18, 1780	2	15
John, of Genessee, N.Y., m. Mary S. **SMITH**, of Salisbury, [July] 1, 1829, by L.E. Lathrop	3	134
Philo, s. Jacob & Charity, b. June 27, 1772	2	15
Simon, s. Simon & Elizabeth, b. Feb. 13, 1757	1	197
CLINE, Joshua, m. Clarissa **WOODBECK**, b. of Salisbury, Nov. 17, 1833, by David L. Perry	3	145
COAL, [see under **COLE**]		
COATS, Betsey, d. Moses & Mehitable, b. Apr. 26, 1775	3	26
Esther, d. Moses & Mehetable, b. Aug. 3, 1782	3	26
Joseph, s. Moses & Mehitable, b. May 3, 1771	3	26
Lois, d. Moses & Mehitable, b. Nov. 29, 1779	3	26
Lucy, d. Moses & Mehitable, b. May 6, 1769	3	26
Moses, m. Mehetabel **BUTLER**, Feb. 16, 1768, by Aaron Lyman, J.P., of Wallingford. Witnesses Comfort Butler & Mary Butler	3	109
Moses, s. Moses & Mehitable, b. Feb. 17, 1785	3	26
Sally, d. Moses & Mehitable, b. Nov. 28, 1777	3	26
Salmon, s. Moses & Mehitable, b. Feb. 11, 1773	3	26
COBIN, [see also **COBURN**], John, s. John & Abigail, b. Apr. 2, 1765	1	136
COBURN, [see also **COBIN**], Adin W., of Windsor, "Mission K.", m. Hannah M. **SPENCER**, of Salisbury, Oct. 28, 1845, by Rev. Adam Reed	3	97
COFFING, COFFIN, Charles, [s. John C. & Jerusha], b. Apr. 4, 1812	3	55
Churchill, [s. John C. & Maria], b. Nov. 13, 1813	3	55
Clarinda, d. Isaac & Sarah, d. Aug. 29, 1786, ae 13	3	164
Clarissa, [d. John C. & Jerusha], b. June 16, 1808	3	55
Clarissa, m. William E. **BOSTWICK**, May 1, 1834, by Leonard E. Lathrop	3	146
George, [s. John C. & Maria], b. May 14, 1822	3	55
Janette, [d. John C. & Jerusha], b. Sept. 11, 1806	3	55
Janette, of Salisbury, m. Curtis R. **CABLE**, of New Milford,		

	Vol.	Page
COFFING, COFFIN, (cont.)		
Jan. 20, 1829, by L.E. Lathrop	3	133
Jerusha, d. June 30, 1812	3	55
John, [s. John C. & Jerusha], b. Feb. 3, 1811	3	55
John H., m. Rebecca F. **BOSTWICK**, b. of Salisbury, Feb. 27, 1833, by L.E. Lathrop	3	142
Joshua B., [s. John C. & Maria], b. May 31, 1815	3	55
Marcia, [d. John C. & Maria], b. Jan. 3, 1817	3	55
Marcia, m. Alexander H. **HOLLEY**, Sept. 10, 1835, by Leonard E. Lathrop	3	150
Maria, [d. John C. & Maria], b. July 19, 1819	3	55
Mary Maria B., d. George & Fanny W., b. Apr. 4, 1847	3	90
[COGGESHALL], COGSEL, [see also **COGSWELL**], Abigail, d. Peter & Abigail, b. Sept. 3, 1764	1	164
Eli, s. Peter & Abigail, b. Aug. 23, 1757	1	179
Peter, m. Abigail **LEE**, b. of Salisbury, May 26, 1754, by Rev. Jonathan Lee	1	241
Rebeckah, d. Peter & Abigail, b. Feb. 18, 1755	1	179
Salmon, s. Peter & Abigail, b. Dec. 27, 1760	1	179
COGGSWELL, [see also **COGGESHALL**], William J., of Jamaica, L.I., m. Anna C. **STERLING**, of Salisbury, June 12, 1839, by Rev. Adam Reid	3	157
COIT, Elizabeth, of Sheffield, m. Ezekiel **LANDON**, of Salisbury, Nov. 15, 1770, by J. Hutchinson, J.P.	2	45
Ruth, of Sheffield, m. Elias **REED**, Jr., of Salisbury, July 23, 1772, by Rev. Jonathan Lee	2	45
COLE, COAL, COOL, COOLE, COUL, [see also **COWLES**], Choice*, m. Samuel **SKINNER**, b. of Salisbury, Mar. 20, 1760, by John Waters, J.P., at Colchester *("Chloe" in Rud's book)	1	248
Elizabeth, m. Sidney **CHAPMAN**, b. of Salisbury, Feb. 5, 1840, by Rev. Thomas Bainbridge	3	159
Gideon, s. Philip & Persis, b. Sept. 16, 1760	1	167
Hyman Jacob, s. Philip & Parsis, b. Aug. 21, 1762	1	167
Isaac, s. Philip & Parsis, b. Feb. 3, 1759	1	167
Jacob, m. Matilda **DELLAMETER**, Apr. 5, 1844, by Roger Averill, J.P.	3	163
Josiah, s. Philip & Persis, b. Dec. 17, 1773	2	15
Lemuel, s. Philip & Parsis, b. Sept. 3, 1766	1	167
Philip, m. Judeth **WHITE**, Aug. 31, 1748, by Rev. Jonathan Lee	1	222
Philip, s. Philip & Persis, b. Dec. 22, 1756	1	167
Philip, s. Philip & Persis, d. Mar. 28, 1761, in the 5th y. of his age	1	236
Philip, s. Philip & Parsis, b. Jan. 16, 1765	1	167
Philip, s. Philip & Persis, d. Jan. 2, 1770, in the 5th y. of his age	2	48
Philip, d. Oct. 16, 1774	2	49
Samuel, s. Philip & Persis, b. Mar. 29, 1768	2	15
Samuel, of Salisbury, m. Anne **DARLING**, of Dover, Sept. 7, 1777, by John Hutchinson, J.P.	2	47
Samuel P., of Sharon, m. Eliza Jane **DECKER**, of Salisbury, July 3, 1841, by Rev. Jac[ob] Shaw	3	161
Sarah, d. Philip & Persis, b. Apr. 1, 1770	2	15

	Vol.	Page
COLE, COAL, COOL, COOLE, COUL, (cont.)		
Sarah, d. Philip & Persis, d. Aug. 24, 1770, in the 5th month of her age	2	48
COLLAR, Clarissa, d. Joseph & Clarissa, b. Sept. 6, 1810	3	52
Lyman, s. Joseph & Clarissa, b. Feb. 12, 1809	3	52
COLLINS, Annis, m. Jacob **WHITE,** b. of Salisbury, Apr. 5, 1773, by John Hutchinson, J.P.	2	45
Asa, s. John & Phenix, b. Apr. 5, 1771	2	31
Henry, s. John & Phenix, b. Aug. 19, 1773	2	31
Phenix, d. John & Phenix, b. Oct. 9, 1777	2	31
COLTON*, Hephzibah, m. John **HIGLEY,** b. of Salisbury, Nov. 6, 1755, by Rev. Jonathan Lee *("**COTTON**" in Rudd's book)	1	243
COLVER, Ephraim, m. Elizabeth **SMITH,** b. of Salisbury, June 12, 1745	LR1	356-7
Hannah, w. Ephraim, d. Jan. 20, 1744/5	LR1	350
Joel, m. Sibel **BROWN,** b. of Salisbury, Feb. 4, 1773, by James Landon, J.P.	2	45
COMEAGIN, COMEAGAIN, Abigail, d. [Jonathan & Susanna], b. Jan. 27, 1791	3	27
Clary, d. Jonathan & Susanna, b. Dec. 27, 1796	3	27
George, of Oxford, s. Jon[a]th[an] & Susanna b. Dec. 27, 1799	3	27
John, s. Jonathan & Susanna, b. Aug. 6, 1798	3	27
Jonathan, s. Jonathan & Susanna, b. Dec. 24, 1801	3	27
Mary, d. Jonathan & Susanna, b. Mar. 15, 1804	3	27
Ruby, d. Jonathan & Susanna, b. Oct. 19, 1795	3	27
CONE, William, of Norfolk, m. Lucy **ENSIGN,** of Salisbury, May 9, 1844, by Henry Goodwin	3	96
CONKLIN, Abigail, d. Thomas & Anna, b. Feb. 25, 1772	2	17
Anna, d. Thomas & Anna, b. Oct. 3, 1773	2	17
Betsey, d. Tho[ma]s & Anna, b. Jan. 29, 1784	3	14
Caroline, m. Milton **BRADLEY,** Jr., b. of Salisbury, Oct. 3, 1841, by J. Shaw	3	161
Claracy, d. Mabel **PARSONS,** b. Apr. 25, 1768	2	13
Eli, s. Tho[ma]s & Anna, b. June 6, 1793	3	14
Elizabeth D., of Salisbury, m. William F. **WHITING,** of Colebrook, Nov. 28, 1833, by Leonard E. Lathrop	3	145
Esther, d. Thomas & Anna, b. July 14, 1776	2	17
Isaac, s. Tho[ma]s & Anna, b. Apr. 17, 1782	3	14
Isaac N., m. Harriet **GREEN,** Nov. 7, 1832, by L.E. Lathrop	3	141
Jeremiah, s. Thomas & Anna, b. Nov. 8, 1789	3	14
Mary, d. Thomas & Anna, b. Aug. 19, 1775	2	17
Mary Adeline, d. Isaac & Harriet, b. Dec. 30, 1804	3	7
Orre, d. Tho[ma]s & Anna, b. Feb. 7, 1788	3	14
Sally, d. Tho[ma]s & Anna, b. Apr. 15, 1786	3	14
Thomas, s. Tho[ma]s & Anna, b. May 7, 1780	3	14
CONNER, Daniel, s. Daniel & Sarah, b. Mar. 3, 1756, in Oblong	1	152
John, s. Daniel & Sarah, b. June 13, 1758, in Oblong	1	152
COOK, Abigail, m. Benajah **WILLIAMS,** Aug. 10, 1758, by William Willer, J.P.	1	250
Cloe, d. Ezekiel & Hannah, b. Oct. 31, 1794	3	3

	Vol.	Page
COOK, (cont.)		
Ezekiel, m. Hannah **CRANE**, b. of Salisbury, Sept. 25, 1783, by Rev. Jonathan Lee	2	42
Hannah, d. Ezekiel & Hannah, b. May 27, 1785	3	3
Henry W., m. Eliza Ann **BATES**, Jan. 12, 1835, b. of Salisbury, by Rev. Julius Field	3	148
John, s. Ezekiel & Hannah, b. Sept. 8, 1791	3	3
Lois, d. Ezekiel & Hannah, b. May 5, 1788	3	3
COOPER, Sally, of Salisbury, m. Mervin **JUDD**, of Watertown, Jan. 3, 1822, by Lavius Hyde	3	116
COPLEY, Elizabeth, m. Seth **CASE**, b. of Salisbury, Aug. 17, 1749, by Rev. Jonathan Lee	1	223
CORNWALL, Eliza, m. Lewis **MOORE**, b. of Salisbury, Mar. 18, 1827, by Rev. Stephen Beach, of St. Johns Ch.	3	126
CORPE, Joseph, s. William & Bethsheba, b. Sept. 16, 1758	1	190
Phebe, d. William & Bethsheba, b. Dec. 22, 1756	1	190
William, m. Bethsheba **FULLER**, b. of Salisbury, Apr. 11, 1755, by David Whitney, J.P.	1	246
CORY, [see also **CARY**], Benjamin, m. Mehetable **HE[A]TH**, b. of Salisbury, Aug. 17, 1769, by Elisha Baker, J.P.	2	45
Benjamin, s. Benjamin & Mahitable, b. Sept. 12, 1771	2	26
Elizabeth, d. Benjamin & Mahitable, b. May 17, 1777, in New York State	2	26
Isaac, s. Benjamin & Mahitable, b. June 12, 1779	2	26
Job, s. Benjamin & Mahitable, b. June 24, 1773	2	26
Levina, d. Benjamin & Mahitable, b. Mar. 12, 1770	2	26
Samuel, s. Benjamin & Mahitable, b. Dec. 18, 1783	2	26
Silva, d. Benjamin & Mahitable, b. Feb. 13, 1782	2	26
William, s. Benjamin & Mahitable, b. July 23, 1786	2	26
COTTER, James P., of West Meriden, m. Mary R. **GAY**, Oct. 6, 1847, by Rev. G. Huntington Nicholls. Int. Pub.	3	101
COTTON*, Hephzibah, m. John **HIGLEY**, b. of Salisbury, Nov. 6, 1755, by Rev. Jonathan Lee *("**COLTON**" in Arnold Copy)	1	243
COWDARY, Benjamin Franklin, s. Jonathan & Mary, b. May 25, 1790, in New Marlbrough	3	5
Newton, s. Jonathan & Mary, b. Mar. 2, 1792	3	5
COWLES, [see also **COLE**], William, of Sharon, m. Vesta **TUPPER**, of Salisbury, Nov. 20, 1825, by L.E. Lathrop	3	123
CRANE, Anne, m. Selleck **ADAMS**, b. of Salisbury, Jan. 1, 1789, by Adonijah Strong, J.P.	2	50
Betsey, d. Ezra & Sarah, b. Oct. 10, 1796	3	9
Elizabeth, m. Nathaniell **JEWELL**, b. of Salisbury, Jan. 1, 1789, by Adonijah Strong, J.P.	2	50
Emmeline, m. George W. **TOMPKINS**, Sept. 23, 1832, by L.E. Lathrop	3	141
Hannah, m. Ezekiel **COOK**, b. of Salisbury, Sept. 25, 1783, by Rev. Jonathan Lee	2	42
Hiram, s. Ezra & Sarah, b. June 8, 1793	3	9
Mary, m. Joseph **JEWELL**, b. of Salisbury, Feb. 23, 1775, by Rev. Jonathan Lee	2	46

SALISBURY VITAL RECORDS 177

	Vol.	Page
CRANE, (cont.)		
Polly, d. Martin & Rachel, b. Oct. 21, 1788	2	30
Polly, d. Ezra & Sarah, b. Oct. 13, 1794	3	9
CRISSEY, Nancy, d. Stoddard & Sarah Ann, b. May 1, 1800, in Reading	3	57
Samuel Beers, s. Stoddard & Sarah, Ann, b. Apr. 21, 1813	3	57
William Stoddard, s. Stoddard & Sarah Ann, b. Apr. 21, 1811	3	57
CROSBY, Thomas, of Goshen, m. Maria **TOWSLEY**, of Salisbury, July 2, 1834, by Rev. Julius Field	3	149
CROSSMAN, Bishop Strong, s. Rev. Joseph Warren & Lucy, b. Apr. 9, 1799	3	29
Egbert, s. Joseph W. & Lucy, b. July 8, 1806	3	29
Jacob D., m. Polly **BOTSFORD**, Mar. 23, 1834, by Leonard E. Lathrop	3	146
John Newton, s. Rev. Joseph W. & Lucy, b. Apr. 11, 1803	3	29
Joseph, s. Rev. Joseph Warren & Lucy, b. Dec. 4, 1811	3	29
Joseph Warren, Rev., of Salisbury, m. Lucy **STRONG**, of Coventry, Jan. 14, 1798, in Coventry, by Rev. Abiel Abbot, of Coventry	3	111
Joseph Warren, Rev., d. Dec. 13, 1812, in the 37th y. of his age and the 16th y. of his ministry	3	168
Lucy Warren, d. Joseph W. & Lucy, b. July 17, 1809	3	29
William H., of Canaan, m. Mary Ann **WINTWORTH**, of Salisbury, [ ] 18, [ ], by Leonard E. Lathrop	3	150
CROWELL, Dorcas E., m. W[illia]m **CANE**, Mar. 12, 1837, by Charles Printice	3	154
CURTIS, CURTISS, Almira, m. Ezra **STONE**, b. of Salisbury, July 21, 1830, by Rev. Stephen Beach, of St. Johns Ch.	3	137
Burdsey, m. Jane A. **WINSHIP**, b. of Sterling, Nov. 19, 1840, by Rev. Adam Reid	3	160
Laura Ann, m. Ezra **STONE**, b. of Salisbury, July 21, 1830*, by Rev. Stephen Beach, of St. Johns Ch. Witness Birdsey Curtiss *("1839"?)	3	159
CUTLER, Eben[eze]r, m. Josepha **BACON**, Aug. 24, 1794, by Samuel Lee, J.P.	3	109
Elijah Tisdale, s. Ebenezer & Jerusha, b. Dec. 14, 1795	3	13
Lucinda Wright, d. Eben[eze]r & Jerusha, b. June 13, 1800	3	13
Ruth Adams, d. Eben[eze]r & Jerusha, b. Apr. 2, 1798	3	13
DAGGIT, Sarah, of Lebanon, m. Amos **CHIPMAN**, of Salisbury, Oct. 18, 1749, by Joseph Clark, J.P.	1	222
DAKIN, Orville, of North East N.Y., m. Augusta **SMITH**, of Salisbury, May 9, 1827, by Leonard E. Lathrop	3	127
DARLING, Anne, of Dover, m. Samuel **COLE**, of Salisbury, Sept. 7, 1777, by John Hutchinson, J.P.	2	47
DARROW, George A., m. Ann Cornelia **HARRISON**, Oct. 17, 1836, by Leonard E. Lathrop	3	153
Mary, m. James **LANDON**, b. of Salisbury, Oct. 10, 1838, by Rev. Adam Reid	3	156
Susan, m. Daniel **TYLER**, Nov. 27, 1828, by L.E. Lathrop	3	132
DAUCHY, Betsey, d. Jeremiah & Sarah, b. Apr. 25, 1788	2	17
Billy, s. Jeremiah & Sarah, b. May 15, 1789	2	17

	Vol.	Page
DAUCHY, (cont.)		
Edwin, s. Jeremiah & Sarah, b. Sept. 8, 1800	3	18
Elizabeth, w. Jeremiah, d. Aug. 16, 1786	2	50
Emeline, d. Jeremiah & Sarah, b. Apr. 13, 1804	3	18
Frederick Augustus, s. Jeremiah & Sarah, b. July 29, 1807	3	18
Henry, s. Jeremiah & Sarah, b. May 25, 1802	3	18
Henry, m. Asenath **CHAPMAN**, b. of Salisbury, Apr. 28, 1833, by Rev. Stephen Beach, of St. Johns Ch.	3	143
Herman, s. Jeremiah & Sarah, b. Mar. 5, 1793	2	17
Jeremiah, s. Nathan & Mary, b. May 20, 1777	2	39
Jeremiah, m. Elizabeth **SELLECK**, b. of Salisbury, Oct. 3, 1780, by Rev. Jonathan Lee	2	41
Jeremiah, m. Sarah **HULL**, June or July 12, 1787, by Rev. Jonathan Lee. Witnesses James Folliet & Ezra Selleck	2	50
Lucy, d. Jeremiah & Elizabeth, b. Dec. 12, 1782, in Ridgefield	2	17
Luther, s. Jeremiah & Elizabeth, b. Jan. 11, 1781	2	17
Mary, d. Nathan & Mary, b. Apr. 2, 1775	2	39
Nathan, s. Nathan & Mary, b. May 16, 1773	2	39
Nathan & Mary, had d. [ ], d. May 31, 1773	2	49
Polly, d. Jeremiah & Sarah, b. July 4, 1797	3	18
Sally, d. Jeremiah & Sarah, b. Jan. 30, 1795	3	18
Salome, m. Newton **CHAPMAN**, b. of Salisbury, Sept. 29, 1833, by Rev. L.M. Purdy, of St. Johns Ch.	3	143
Samuel, s. Nathan & Mary, b. July 1, 1769, in Ridgefield	2	39
Sarah, d. Nathan & Mary, b. Apr. 27, 1771	2	39
Susan, d. Jeremiah & Sarah, b. Nov. 3, 1791	2	17
DAVIS, Eunice, d. Jacobus & Eunice, b. July 18, 1781; d. July 23, 1783	2	32
Lucy, d. Jacobus & Eunice, b. Jan. 1, 1779	2	32
Samuel, s. Jacobus & Eunice, b. Feb. 6, 1784	2	32
DAY, Thomas, Jr., of Salisbury, m. Hannah E. **NOXAN**, of Florida, N.Y., [Sept.] 15, [1830], by L.E. Lathrop	3	137
DEAN, Amasa, s. Seth & Sarah, b. Feb. 8, 1769	2	20
Anne, d. Seth & Sarah, b. Nov. 8, 1754, in Salisbury	1	170
Benoni, s. John & Thankfull, b. July 24, 1754	1	201
Benoni, s. John & Thankfull, d. July 26, 1754	1	226
Gaius, s. Ens. John & Thankfull, b. Sept. 26, 1755	1	201
Hannah*, of Hebron, m. Elihu **MACKALL**, of Salisbury, Jan. 28, 1777, by Rev. Mr. Brockway *("Hannah **DUNK**" in Rudd's book)	2	47
James, Jr., of Whitestown, Oneida Cty., N.Y., m. Cornelia Esther **NORTON**, of Salisbury, Feb. 9, 1818, by Rev. Charles Printice. Witness Lot Norton	3	115
Jesse, s. Seth & Sarah, b. Sept. 3, 1766, in Canaan	2	20
Joel, s. Seth & Sarah, b. Oct. 3, 1759	1	170
John, Ens., of Salisbury, m. Thankfull **ASHLEY**, of Sheffield, Nov. 6, 1753, by Rev. Jonathan Lee	1	241
Lydia, d. Seth & Sarah, b. Jan. 21, 1762	1	170
Mary, d. John & Sarah, b. Jan. 13, 1751/2	1	201
Nathaniel, of Salisbury, m. Hannah **WOODS**, of New Milford, Jan. 1, 1751, by Paul Welch, J.P.	1	241
Phebe, d. Joel & Mary, b. Nov. 6, 1785	2	17

	Vol.	Page
DEAN, (cont.)		
Reuben, s. Seth & Sarah, b. Feb. 22, 1752, in York Gov.	1	170
Ruth, d. Seth & Sarah, b. Aug. 28, 1750, in York Gov.	1	170
Sarah, w. John, d. Jan. 15, 1751/2	1	255
Sarah, d. Seth & Sarah, b. July 28, 1757	1	170
Sarah, m. Harmon **WHITE**, b. of Salisbury, Aug. 7, 1775, by John Hutchinson, J.P.	2	46
Seth, s. Joel & Mary, b. July 11, 1783	2	17
Uriah, s. John & Rachel, b. Dec. 16, 1761	1	129
William, s. John & Sarah, b. Jan. 13, 1751/2	1	201
DECKER, Ambrose, m. Almira **ALTHOUSE**, Nov. 9, 1846, by Rev. Jonathan Lee	3	99
Eliza Jane, of Salisbury, m. Samuel P. **COLE**, of Sharon, July 3, 1841, by Rev. Jac[ob] Shaw	3	161
Goodeth, of the Co. of Ulster, m. Peter **WHITE**, of Salisbury, Nov. 3, 1749, by Rev. William Manches, of Kingston, Witness Isaac White	1	223
Jno, m. Harriet **ALTHOUSE**, Nov. 21, 1847, by W.H. Ferris	3	103
Martin*, m. Phebe **BARBER**, Nov. 11, 1848, by W.H. Ferris *(Arnold Copy has "Martin **DUCKER**")	3	103
DeFOREST, Jason, of New Marlborough, m. Harriet **CAMP**, of Salisbury, June 20, 1833, by L.E. Lathrop	3	143
DELIS, Claudias, Jr., d. Nov. 3, 1760, in the 32nd y. of his age	1	236
Ruth, d. Dec. 1, 1760	1	236
DELLAMETER, Matilda, m. Jacob **COUL**, Apr. 5, 1844, by Roger Averill, J.P.	3	163
DeLONG, Deloss, m. Delia Maria **CLARK**, b. of Salisbury, Mar. 7, 1833, by Rev. Stephen Beach, of St. Johns Ch.	3	142
DEMING, DEMMING, Catharine C., m. Charles E. **RUSSELL**, b. of Salisbury, May 31, 1829, by Eliphalet Whittlesey, J.P.	3	145
Julia, of Salisbury, m. John **DOTEN**, of Sheffield, Oct. 12, 1828, by Leonard E. Lathrop	3	131
Lorinda Maria, of Salisbury, m. Jesse **BARTHOLOMEW**, of Sheffield, Mass., Sept. 15, 1841, by Rev. Adam Reid	3	161
Sally, of Salisbury, m. James **MEAD**, of Mt. Washington, Mass., Nov. 28, 1822, by Eliphalet Whittlesey, J.P.	3	117
William, of Newpaltz, Ulster Cty., N.Y., m. Sally Ann **ROZELL**, of Salisbury, Nov. 14, 1830, by Rev. Aaron Pearce	3	137
DERBY, Lois, d. Phineas & Sarah, b. June 21, 1784	2	16
DEWEY, Samuel O., of Becket, Mass., m. Betsey A. **STANTON**, of Salisbury, Dec. 5, 1844, by Rev. C.V. Amerman	3	96
DEWING, Alexander, s. Michael & Ruth, b. Oct. 20, 1794	3	15
Andrew, s. Michael & Ruth, b. July 19, 1792	3	15
Sally Maria, d. Michael & Ruth, b. July 19, 1797	3	15
DEWITT, James, m. Harriet E. **WRIGHT**, b. of Salisbury, Sept. 11, 1844, by Rev. C.V. Amerman	3	96
DEXTER, Frederick, s. Willoby & Sally, b. May 7, 1808	3	44
Henry Edward, s. Willoby & Sally, b. July 26, 1806	3	44
Olivia M., of Salisbury, m. Henry G. **SHOOK**, of Wawasing, N.Y., Sept. 3, 1838, by Rev. Adam Reid	3	155
DIBBLE, Ebenezer, of Salisbury, m. Eunice **GILLETT**, of Sharon,		

	Vol.	Page
DIBBLE, (cont.)		
May 26, 1774, by Rev. Cotton Mather Smith	2	46
Polle, d. Ebenezer & Eunice, b. Feb. 3, 1775	2	35
DIKEMAN, Elizabeth, d. John T. & Sarah, b. Nov. 6, 1808	3	47
Elsa, d. John T. & Sarah, b. Jan. 9, 1807	3	47
DIMMICK, DIMMECK, Augustus, s. Solomon & Electa, b. Apr. 10, 1790	2	28
Elizabeth, d. Solomon & Electa, b. Jan. 27, 1784	2	28
Mary, d. Solomon & Elizabeth, b. Dec. 20, 1770	2	28
Polly, d. Solomon & Electa, b. Feb. 8, 1793	2	28
Solomon, m. Elizabeth **BEEBE**, b. of Salisbury, Apr. 5, 1770, by Rev. Jonathan Lee	2	45
Solomon, m. Electa **HALL***, b. of Salisbury, Jan. 18, 1781, by Rev. Jonathan Lee *("HULL" in Rudd's book)	2	41
Solomon, s. Solomon & Electa, b. Apr. 20, 1787	2	28
William Beebe, s. Solomon & Electa, b. Jan. 1, 1782	2	28
DODGE, George C., m. Mary **JEWELL**, b. of Salisbury, Mar. 16, 1842, by Rev. Adam Reid	3	162
George Chittenden, s. James B. & Julia, b. Dec. 25, 1815	3	45
Harriet A., m. Jared S. **HARRISON**, [Jan.] 2, 1827, by Leonard E. Lathrop	3	126
Harriet Abby, d. James B. & Julia, b. Apr. 17, 1808	3	45
Henry C., s. George C. & Mary, b. Jan. 13, 1844	3	90
Julia A., m. John H. **HUBBARD**, b. of Salisbury, May 2, 1830, by Leonard E. Lathrop	3	136
Julia Ann, d. James B. & Julia, b. May 4, 1806	3	45
DONOLDS, DONOLD, David, m. Lucina **MEIGS**, b. of Salisbury, Aug. 29, 1793, by Rev. Joshua Knapp, Jr., Witnesses Matilda Rockwell & Esther Donolds	3	109
Electa, d. David & Lucena, b. Mar. 2, 1794	3	14
Frederick, s. David & Lucena, b. Apr. 18, 1796	3	14
Pamelia, d. Samuell & Mary, b. Mar. 13, 1785	2	22
Rebecca, d. Samuel & Mary, b. Mar. 7, 1783	2	22
Samuel, m. Mary **WATEROUS**, b. of Salisbury, Oct. 14, 1779, by Rev. Jonathan Lee	2	41
DOOLITTLE, Betsey, of S⁻¹' bury, m. Henry **JACKSON**, of Ripley, N.Y., Sept. 19, 1834, by Leonard E. Lathrop	3	147
DOTEN, John, of Sheffield, m. Julia **DEMMING**, of Salisbury, Oct. 12, 1828, by Leonard E. Lathrop	3	131
DOUGLASS, Olive, of Canaan, m. John **CHIPMAN**, of Salisbury, May 13, 1767, by Rev. Daniel Farrand	2	44
[DOWD], DOUD, Bettey, d. Peleg & Merab, b. Sept. 5, 1777	2	21
James, s. Samuel & Lydia, b. Aug. 26, 1770	2	27
Lucretia, m. Benjamin **CHATFIELD**, Nov. 10, 1770, in Saybrook, by Rev. Stephen Holmes	2	47
Sene, d. Peleg & Merab, b. Apr. 4, 1773	2	21
Zina, s. Peleg & Merab, b. July 14, 1775	2	21
DRAKE, Abia, of Sheffield, m. John **WELDON**, of Salisbury, Jan. 24, 1775, by John Hutchinson, J.P.	2	46
DREW, Hannah, m. Frederic **BINGHAM**, b. of Salisbury, June 6, 1769, by Rev. Jonathan Lee	2	44

	Vol.	Page

DUNHAM, Rebeckah, of Sheffield, m. Selleck* **WOODWORTH**, of
   Salisbury, Dec. 30, 1773, by John Hutchinson, J.P.
   *("Selah" in Rudd's book) — 2 — 45

DUNK*, Hannah, of Hebron, m. Elihu **MACKALL**, of Salisbury, Jan.
   28, 1777, by Rev. Mr. Brockway *(Arnold Copy has
   "**DEAN**") — 2 — 47

DUTCHER, DUCHER, Abraham, s. Henry & Elenor, b. Oct. 27, 1743 — LR1 — 350
   Arconche, m. William **WHITNEY**, b. of Canaan, June 4, 1747,
   by Rev. Elisha Webster, of Canaan — 1 — 222
   Caroline M., of Canaan, m. Frederic A. **STERLING**, of Salisbury,
   June 23, 1825, by L.E. Lathrop. Int. Pub. — 3 — 122
   Catharine, d. Ruluff & Catharine, b. Dec. 4, 1746 — 1 — 196
   Catharine, d. Gabriel & Elizabeth, b. Sept. 18, 1749 — 1 — 200
   Catharine, d. Gabriel & Christian, b. July 2, 1774 — 2 — 32
   Christian, d. John & Christian, b. Mar. 1, 1755 — 1 — 178
   Christian, w. John, d. May 1, 1755, in the 39th y. of her age — 1 — 243
   Cristeen*, d. Ruluff & Catharine, b. Jan. 23, 1748 *("Christine") — 1 — 196
   Cornelius, s. John & Christian, b. Mar. 20, 1753 — 1 — 178
   Cornelius, s. John, d. Mar. 22, 1754 — 1 — 243
   David, s. Henry & Elenor, b. Apr. 21, 1741 — LR1 — 351
   Dereck, s. Henry & Eleanor, b. Aug. 4, 1734 — LR1 — 351
   Eleanor, d. Ruluff & Polly, b. Apr. 18, 1782 — 2 — 40
   Elizabeth, m. Joshua W. **STANTON**, b. of Salisbury, Oct. 27,
   1813, by Rev. Charles Printice, of South Canaan — 3 — 114
   Emeline Jane, of Canaan, m. Herman Butler **BUSHNELL**, of
   Salisbury, Sept. 23, 1832, by Rev. Stephen Beach, of St.
   Johns Ch. — 3 — 141
   Gabriel, s. John & Christian, b. June 16, 1747 — 1 — 178
   Hannah, d. John & Christian, b. Mar. 25, 1749 — 1 — 178
   Hannah, m. Ezekiel **FULLER**, b. of Salisbury, Mar. 1, 1771, by
   John Hutchinson, J.P. — 2 — 45
   Harry, s. Lawrence & Eunice, b. May 21, 1812 — 3 — 55
   Jacimitia*, d. Henry & Eleanor, b. Sept. 15, 1736 *(Arnold Copy
   has "Yacimitia") — LR1 — 351
   Janaca, d. Henry & Elenor, b. Aug. 3, 1746 — LR1 — 350
   Jane, d. Cornelius & Abigail, b. Apr. 30, 1741 — LR1 — 351
   Jane, d. John & Christian, b. Feb. 19, 1743 — 1 — 178
   Jane, d. Ruluff & Catharine, b. Dec. 31, 1743 — 1 — 196
   Jane*, wid., d. July 26, 1749 *(Written "Jane **DUTCHES**") — 1 — 243
   John, s. John & Christian, b. June 2, 1745 — 1 — 178
   John, Jr., m. Lois **WASHBURN**, Jan. 11, 1770, by John
   Hutchinson, J.P. — 2 — 44
   John, s. John, Jr. & Lowis, b. Apr. 8, 1773 — 2 — 34
   John, s. Gabriel & Christian, b. Mar. 12, 1778 — 2 — 32
   Joshua, s. Gabriel & Christian, b. Dec. 16, 1770 — 2 — 32
   Lawrence, s. Gabriel & Christian, b. Aug. [   ], 1776 — 2 — 32
   Lydia, d. John, Jr. & Lowis, b. Apr. 16, 1777 — 2 — 34
   Magdelena, d. Ruluff & Catharine, b. Sept. 1, 1741 — LR1 — 352
   Margaret, d. Cornelius & Abigail, b. Sept. 26, 1734 — LR1 — 351
   Margaret, of Salisbury, m. Alexander **BAULDWIN**, of Canaan,
   Mar. 31, 1755, by Rev. Jonathan Lee — 1 — 247

	Vol.	Page
DUTCHER, DUCHER, (cont.)		
Martin*, m. Phebe **BARBER**, Nov. 11, 1848, by W.H. Ferris *(Written "Martin **DUCKER**")	3	103
Mary, d. Gabriel & Christian, b. Oct. 19, 1769	2	32
Mary C., m. Lewis **MILLS**, of Kent, Apr. 7, 1836, by Leonard E. Lathrop	3	151
Mary C., m. Lewis **MILLS**, of Kent, Apr. 7, 1836, by Leonard E. Lathrop	3	152
Mathew, s. Henry & Eleanor, b. Mar. 2, 1739	LR1	351
Patience, d. John, Jr. & Lowis, b. Dec. 22, 1770, in Oblong	2	34
Phebe, d. John, Jr. & Lowis, b. Oct. 8, 1774	2	34
Ruluff, s. Cornelius & Abigail, b. Sept. 5, 1737	LR1	351
Ruluff, s. John & Christian, b. Sept. 15, 1741	1	178
Ruluff, s. Ruluff & Catharine, b. Aug. 2, 1751	1	196
Samuel A., of Canaan, m. Caroline E. **RUSSEL**, of Salisbury, Mar. 11, 1847, by Rev. G. Huntington Nicholls. Int. Pub.	3	101
Sarah, d. Gabriel & Christian, b. Oct. 17, 1772	2	32
William, s. Ruluff & Polly, b. Apr. 14, 1784	2	40
Yacimitia*, d. Henry & Eleanor, b. Sept. 15, 1736 *("Jacimitia" in Rudd's book)	LR1	351
DUTCHES, [see under **DUTCHER**]		
EATON, John, m. Martha **McURE**, b. of Salisbury, Apr. 11, 1771, by John Hutchinson, J.P.	2	45
EDDY, Abner, s. Zachariah & Mary, b. Feb. 20, 1747/8	1	207
Abner, s. Asa & Elizabeth, b. Apr. 4, 1772	2	8
Asa, m. Anne **EVARTS**, b. of Salisbury, Nov. 7, 1749, by Rev. Jonathan Lee	1	242
Asa, m. Hester **BUSHELL**, b. of Salisbury, Jan. 12, 1786, by Peter Bishop, J.P.	2	43
Asa, s. Asa & Hester, b. Dec. 21, 1787	2	16
Daniel, s. Zachariah & Marcy, b. Feb. 28, 1741/2	LR1	352
Ebenezer, s. Asa & Elizabeth, b. July 10, 1780	2	8
Elizabeth, w. Asa, d. Mar. 14, 1790, in the 52nd y. of her age	2	50
Hester, d. Asa & Hester, b. July 2, 1786	2	16
Hester, d. Asa, Jr. & Hester, d. May 9, 1788	2	50
John Wilks, a. Asa & Elizabeth, b. Apr. 16, 1767, in Preston	2	8
Josiah, s. Asa & Anne, b. Mar. 9, 1755	1	216
Newbury, 2nd, s. Zachariah & Mercy, b. Jan. 2, 1743/4	LR1	352
Phebe, d. Asa & Sarah, b. Nov. 19, 1791	2	8
Rufus, s. Asa & Elizabeth, b. May 22, 1778	2	8
Rufus, of Salisbury, m. Clarissa **BAYMONT**, of Sheffield, June 27, 1802, by Rev. Joseph W. Crossman	3	111
Sally, d. Asa & Elizabeth, b. Apr. 2, 1775	2	8
EDGERTON, Lucy, d. Nathaniell & Eunice, b. June 10, 1782	2	12
Nathaniel, s. Nathaniell & Eunice, b. Mar. 16, 1778	2	12
Phebe, d. Nathaniell & Eunice, b. June 26, 1788	2	12
Samuel, s. Nathaniell & Eunice, b. [ ]	2	12
Sarah, d. Daniel & Mary, b. Jan. 3, 1780	2	21
EDMISTER, Mary, d. William & Sarah, b. Apr. 8, 1761	1	163
EDMONDS, Benton, of Sheffield, Mass., m. Minerva **MORGAN**, of Salisbury, Jan. 2, 1844, by Rev. C.V. Amerman	3	96

SALISBURY VITAL RECORDS 183

	Vol.	Page
EDWARDS, Cornelia, d. Erastus & Maria, b. Mar. 9, 1823	3	80
George, of Salisbury, m. [Elisabeth]* **BAWLDIN**, of Oblong, Jan. 18, 1758, by Rev. Jonathan Lee *(Supplied from Rudd's)	1	247
EGGLESTON, EAGLESTON, Benjamin, of North East Dutchess, N.Y., m. Elizabeth **MILLS**, of Salisbury, Mar. 21, 1838, by Adam Reid	3	154
Patience, of Salisbury, m. Joseph **FULLER**, of Salisbury, Apr. 5, 1753, by Rev. Jonathan Lee	1	240
ELDREDGE, ELDRIDGE, ELDRED, ELDREG, Abigail, d. John & Lydia, b. June 25, 1770	2	11
Abigail, d. John, 2nd & Hannah, b. Oct. 12, 1797	2	37
Betsey, d. John & Lydia, b. Aug. 18, 1775	2	11
Charles, s. John & Lydia, b. Dec. 26, 1782	2	11
Chester, s. John, 2nd & Hannah, b. Sept. 12, 1788	2	37
Cornelia M., of Salisbury, m. Robert **LITTLE**, of Sheffield, Mass., Jan. 10, 1843, by Rev. Adam Reid	3	162
Edmond, s. John, 2nd & Hannah, b. Apr. 5, 1801	2	37
Electe, d. John & Lydia, b. July 22, 1765	1	135
Elisabeth, d. Erastus & Maria, b. Feb. 21, 1819	3	80
Gurdon, s. John, 2nd & Hannah, b. Sept. 24, 1790	2	37
Gurdon, s. John, 2nd & Hannah, d. Nov. 5, 1792, in the 3rd y. of his age	3	164
Hannah, d. John, 2nd & Hannah, b. Apr. 17, 1795	2	37
Hannah, d. John & Hannah, d. Nov. 20, 1810, ae 16	3	167
Hannah, w. John, d. Oct. 25, 1811, ae 47	3	167
Hezekiah, m. Dorcas **PALMER**, b. of Salisbury, Nov. 28, 1800, by Joseph W. Crossman	3	111
John, of Mansfield, m. Hannah **BUELL**, of Salisbury, Nov. 28, 1782, by Rev. Jonathan Lee	2	42
John, m. wid. Sally **EVEREST**, b. of Salisbury, Mar. 15, 1813, by Rev. Charles Printice, of Canaan,	3	114
Julia, w. Chester & d. Abraham **NOTT**, d. Dec. 2, 1815, ae 25, in Sharon	3	168
Lydia, d. John & Lydia, b. Dec. 16, 1767	2	11
Mary Meneda, d. Chester & Julia, b. Feb. 18, 1810	3	51
Nathaniel Buell, s. John, 2nd & Hannah, b. Dec. 25, 1785	2	37
Niran, s. John, 2nd & Hannah, b. July 11, 1793	2	37
Orson B., m. Laura Ann **BRASIE**, b. of Salisbury, Dec. 31, 1834, by Leonard E. Lathrop	3	147
Polly, d. John & Lydia, b. Aug. 2, 1779	2	11
Sally, d. John, 2nd & Hannah, b. July 11, 1783	2	37
Sary, m. Joseph **BIRD**, b. of Salisbury, May 11, 1752, by Rev. Jonathan Lee	1	224
Sarah, d. John & Lydia, b. July 3, 1773	2	11
ELLIOT, Sarah, m. Elisha **STERLING**, b. of Salisbury, [Dec.] 8, 1830, by Leonard E. Lathrop	3	137
ELWELL, Thomas, m. Flora **BATES**, Jan. 29, 1834, by Leonard E. Lathrop	3	146
ELY, Anna, m. Stephen **MASON**, Jan. 12, 1800, by [ ]. Witnesses Simeon Granger & Simeon Granger, Jr.	3	111

	Vol.	Page
ELY, (cont.)		
Augustus, s. Richard & Eustatia, b. Apr. 10, 1786	3	7
Betsey, d. Richard & Eustatia, b. Feb. 7, 1782	3	7
Henry, s. Richard & Eustatia, b. May 3, 1788	3	7
Irene, d. Richard & Eustatia, b. Aug. 19, 1792	3	7
Richard, s. Richard & Eustatia, b. Feb. 9, 1784	3	7
William, s. Richard & Eustatia, b. June 6, 1790	3	7
EMERSON, Andrew Surdam, s. Nathaniel & Mary, b. Aug. [ ], 1786	2	33
Esther, d. Nathaniel & Mary, b. June 25, 1789	2	33
Nath[anie]ll, m. Mary [ ], Sept. 1, 1785, by Elisha Baker, J.P.	2	50
ENSIGN, Charles, s. John & Rhoda, b. Dec. 7, 1788	3	5
Emily, m. Samuel S. **BOTSFORD**, b. of Salisbury, Mar. 27, 1829, by L.E. Lathrop	3	133
John Ely, of Canaan, m. Laura Ann **GOODWIN**, of Salisbury, [1839 (?)], by Rev. Charles T. Printice	3	158
Love Lee, d. John & Rhoda, b. Oct. 21, 1795	3	5
Lucy, of Salisbury, m. William **CONE**, of Norfolk, May 9, 1844, by Henry Goodwin	3	96
Mary Ann, d. John, Jr. & Susanna, b. Aug. 14, 1804	3	17
Polly M., of Salisbury, m. Chauncey G. **LAKE**, of Sharon, Oct. 14, 1845, by Rev. Albert Nash	3	98
Susannah, d. John & Rhoda, b. Feb. 14, 1791	3	5
ERWIN, William, Dr., of Kent, m. Love **SMITH**, of Salisbury, Nov. 13, [1832], by L.E. Lathrop	3	142
ESBEEK*, Katharine, of Nobletown, m. Abraham **VOSBURGH**, of Salisbury, Aug. 16, 1768, by Rev. Jonathan Lee *("WEDBACK" in Rudd's)	2	44
[**EVANS**], **EVENS**, Asenath, d. William & Abigail, b. Apr. 15, 1784	2	16
EVARTS, EVERTS, Abner, s. Nathaniell & Esther, b. Aug. 24, 1757	1	200
Ambros, s. Silvanus & Elisheba, b. Nov. 27, 1759	1	185
Anne, m. Asa **EDDY**, b. of Salisbury, Nov. 7, 1749, by Rev. Jonathan Lee	1	242
Anne, d. John, Jr. & Anna, b. Feb. 16, 1763	1	161
Aranthus, s. Daniel & Molly, b. May 24, 1782	2	22
Asenath, d. Stephen & Elizabeth, b. Sept. 14, 1794	3	2
Betsey, d. Eber & Hannah, b. Sept. 27, 1778	2	16
Betsey, d. Nathaniell, Jr. & Mary, b. Aug. 5, 1785	2	30
Betsey, d. Nathaniel & Mary, d. May 14, 1804, in the 19th y. of her age	3	166
Charity, Mrs., m. John **RUSSELL**, Nov. 8, 1787, by Philip Spencer, J.P.	3	109
Charles, s. John & Submit, b. July 13, 1751	1	197
Charles, s. Daniel & Molly, b. Sept. 18, 1783	2	22
Clementina, d. Stephen & Elizabeth, b. July 7, 1793	3	2
Daniel, m. Hertry **VANDUZEN**, b. of Salisbury, Sept. 9, 1767, by Daniel Castle, J.P.	2	44
David, s. Nathaniell, Jr. & Mary, b. Aug. 29, 1780	2	30
Deborah, d. Luther & Deborah, d. Oct. 12, 1770, in the 3rd y. of her age	2	48

	Vol.	Page
EVARTS, EVERTS, (cont.)		
Dorothy, d. Luther & Deborah, b. Apr. 16, 1768	2	16
Ebenezer, s. Elijah & Mary, b. Sept. 21, 1745, in Guilford	1	200
Eber, s. Nathaniell & Esther, b. Dec. 7, 1752	1	200
Electe, d. Silvanus & Elisheba, b. May 29, 1768	2	27
Electa, of Salisbury, m. Jesse **FORD**, Jr., of New Canaan, N.Y., Jan. 16, 1823, by Rev. Coles Carpenter	3	118
Eli, s. Silvanus & Elisheba, b. July 13, 1752	1	185
Eli, m. Jem[i]ma **TURNER**, b. of Salisbury, Apr. 5, 1781, by Rev. Jonathan Lee	2	41
Elijah, s. Elijah & Mary, b. Feb. 9, 1743, in Guilford	1	200
Elijah, d. Dec. 8, 1754	1	243
Elijah, s. Samuel & Sarah, b. May 26, 1777	2	38
Elisheba, d. Silvanus & Elisheba, b. Feb. 21, 1762	1	128
Elizabeth, d. Stephen & Elizabeth, b. Feb. 12, 1782	2	14
Esther, d. Nathaniell & Esther, b. July 2, 1750	1	200
Esther, d. Nathaniell, Jr. & Mary, b. Mar. 22, 1794	2	30
Esther, wid. Capt. Nath[anie]l, d. Apr. 21, 1797, in the 77th y. of her age	3	164
Eunice, m. Lathrop **HOLMES**, b. of Salisbury, Sept. 11, 1796, by John Whittlesey, J.P.	3	110
Hannah, d. Nathaniell, Jr. & Mary, b. Dec. 28, 1775	2	30
Hertry, d. Daniel & Hertry, b. Feb. 7, 1769	2	22
Herty, w. Daniel, d. Feb. 11, 1769	2	48
Joel, of Salisbury, m. Mary Ann **AUSTIN**, of Sheffield, Feb. 15, 1786, in Dutchess Co., N.Y., by Uriah Lawrence, J.P	2	43
Joel, s. Joel & Mary Ann, b. Dec. 24, 1786	2	38
Leenora, d. Stephen & Elizabeth, b. Apr. 1, 1784	2	14
Linus, s. Silvanus & Elisheba, b. Feb. 16, 1770	2	27
Loes, d. Amos & Marcy, b. Nov. 19, 1754	1	183
Luther, m. Deborah **NEWCOMB**, b. of Salisbury, Aug. 13, 1767, by Joshua Porter, J.P.	2	44
Luther, s. Luther & Sarah, b. Mar. 6, 1771	2	16
Martin, s. John & Submit, b. June 27, 1756	1	197
Martin, s. Gilbert & Rebekah, b. Oct. 7, 1765	1	162
Mary, d. Amos & Marcy, b. Oct. 29, 1747, in Guilford	1	183
Mary, d. Nathaniell, Jr. & Mary, b. Sept. 22, 1771	2	30
Mary, of Salisbury, m. Joel **CHAMBERLAIN**, of Lebanon, Feb. 25, 1783, by Rev. Jonathan Lee	2	42
Miles, s. Amos & Marcy, b. Oct. 13, 1750, in Guilford	1	183
Mindwell, d. Amos & Marcy, b. Sept. 15, 1753	1	183
Nancy, d. Nathaniel, Jr. & Mary, b. July 25, 1783	2	30
Nancy, m. John **McKEAN**, Sept. 25, 1797, by Rev. Amos Fowler, of 1st Ch. of Christ, in Guilford	3	110
Nathaniell, s. Nathaniell & Esther, b. June 6, 1748, in Guilford	1	200
Nath[anie]ll, m. Mary **MOORE**, b. of Salisbury, Dec. 12, 1770, by Rev. Jonathan Lee	2	45
Nathaniel, d. June 2, 1791, ae 73	2	50
Oliver, of Castleton, m. Nancy **LANDON**, of Salisbury, Feb. 22, 1776, by James Landon, J.P.	2	46
Orre, d. Nathaniell, Jr. & Mary, b. July 29, 1787	2	30

	Vol.	Page
EVARTS, EVERTS, (cont.)		
Peter P., m. Tryphenia **BERNET**, Dec. 28, 1834, by Rev. Julius Field	3	148
Phebe, d. Nathaniell, Jr. & Mary, b. Dec. 21, 1791	2	30
Renasda* Melville, s. Stephen & Elizabeth, b. Oct. 15, 1788		
*("Renaldo" in Rudd's book)	2	14
Rosanna, m. Gershom **WOODWORTH**, b. of Salisbury, Nov. 24, 1749, by [ ]	1	222
Roswell, s. Eli & Jemima, b. Apr. 2, 1782	2	35
Roswell, s. Eli & Jemima, d. June 17, 1782	2	50
Rozel, s. Silvanus & Elisheba, b. July 13, 1755	1	185
Rozel, s. Silvanus & Elizaheba, d. Feb. 1, 1762, in the 7th y. of his age	1	238
Rozel, s. Silvanus & Elisheba, b. Nov. 5, 1765	1	128
Samuel, of Salisbury, m. Sarah **FULLER**, of Sharon, Sept. 18, 1776, by James Landon, J.P.	2	47
Samuel, s. Samuel & Sarah, b. Sept. 20, 1780	2	38
Sarah, d. Amos & Marcy, b. Mar. 14, 1757	1	183
Sarah, d. John & Submit, b. Feb. 21, 1761	1	152
Sarah, d. Silvanus & Elisheba, b. Apr. 1, 1764	1	128
Sarah, d. Nathaniell, Jr. & Mary, b. Apr. 30, 1778	2	30
Serafina, d. Stephen & Elizabeth, b. May 10, 1791	2	14
Serafina, d. Stephen & Elizabeth, b. May [ ], 1793	2	14
Silas, s. Nathaniell & Esther, b. May 27, 1755	1	200
Silas, s. Nathaniell, Jr. & Mary, b. Oct. 1, 1773	2	30
Solomon, s. John, Jr. & Anne, b. Oct. 11, 1761	1	161
Sophia, d. Stephen & Elizabeth, b. Mar. 29, 1786	2	14
Stephen, s. John & Submit, b. Sept. 6, 1758	1	197
Stephen, s. John, Jr. & Anne, b. Mar. 20, 1760	1	161
Submit, d. John & Submit, b. Nov. 29, 1753	1	197
Submit, d. Luther & Deborah, b. May 26, 1769	2	16
Sibel, d. Nathaniell & Esther, b. Dec. [ ], 1759	1	200
Timothy, s. Silvanus & Elisheba, b. Sept. 25, 1749	1	185
EVEREST, Adoniran, m. Sally **HIMAN**, Nov. [, 1824 (?)], by Rev. L.E. Lathrop, of Cong. Ch.	3	120
Alma, d. Isaac & Abigail, b. Apr. 16, 1790	2	40
Almira, d. Isaac & Abigail, b. Feb. 18, 1788	2	40
Amanda Maria, d. Jehiel & Sally, b. Aug. 25, 1799	2	11
Amelia, d. Jehiel & Sally, b. Apr. 6, 1792	2	11
Amelia, m. Andrew **JEWELL**, b. of Salisbury, Apr. 8, 1835, by Leonard E. Lathrop	3	148
Anne, m. Daniel **GRINNELL**, Jr., b. of Salisbury, Feb. 20, 1777, by John Hutchinson	2	47
Benjamin, s. Benjamin & Hester, b. Jan. 7, 1751/2	1	205
Benjamin, of Salisbury, m. Betsey **AXTILL**, May 31, 1786, by Rev. Jonathan Lee	2	43
Benjamin, d. Feb. 14, 1796, in the 43rd y. of his age	2	50
Betsey, d. Elisha, Jr. & Susannah, b. June 1, 1784	2	24
Betsey, d. Benjamin & Betsey, b. Feb. 5, 1791	2	36
Damaris, d. David & Margaret, b. May 12, 1755	1	203
David, of Salisbury, m. Margaret **FERRIE**, of Sheffield, July 11,		

SALISBURY VITAL RECORDS 187

	Vol.	Page
EVEREST, (cont.)		
1754, by Rev. Jonathan Hubbart	1	242
David, s. David & Margaret, b. July 19, 1756	1	203
David, m. Lois **JACKSON**, b. of Salisbury, June 18, 1761, by John Hutchinson, J.P.	1	249
David & Lois, had d. [ ], d. Aug. 30, 1779, in the 4th y. of her age	2	49
David, s. Jared, Jr. & Hannah, b. Dec. 27, 1791	2	27
Edward Norman, s. Adoniram & Sally, b. Mar. 5, 1829	3	62
Electa, d. Benjamin & Betsey, b. June 6, 1795	2	36
Eliza, d. Jehiel & Sally, b. Feb. 3, 1797	2	11
Ethan, s. David & Lois, b. Dec. 28, 1763	1	126
Fidelia, d. James & Mary, b. Dec. 10, 1805	3	37
Hannah, d. David & Lois, b. Mar. 22, 1771	2	14
Hannah, m. Luther **CHAPIN**, b. of Salisbury, May 1, 1798, by Joseph W. Crossman	3	111
Hester, d. Benjamin & Hester, d. Mar. 23, 1758, in the 13th y. of her age	1	228
Hester, d. Benjamin & Hester, b. Jan. 8, 1760	1	205
Hiram, s. Jehiel & Sally, b. Jan. 4, 1786	2	11
Isaac, s. David & Lois, b. June 7, 1765	1	126
Isaac, m. Abigail **CHITTENDEN**, b. of Salisbury, Feb. 15, 1787, by Rev. Jonathan Lee	2	43
James, s. Elisha, Jr. & Susannah, b. Jan. 8, 1779	2	24
James Benjamin, s. Adoniram & Sally, b. July 26, 1827, in Canaan	3	62
Jared, Jr., m. Hannah **SELLECK**, b. of Salisbury, Nov. 22, 1786, by Rev. Jonathan Lee	2	43
Jared, d. July 22, 1792, in the 63rd y. of his age	2	50
Jared, s. Jared, Jr. & Hannah, b. Dec. 7, 1795	2	27
Jehiel, s. David & Lois, b. Aug. 28, 1762	1	126
Jehiel, m. Sally **MOORE**, b. of Salisbury, Jan. 6, 1785, by Rev. Jonathan Lee	2	43
Jehiel, Capt., d. Mar. 14, 1812, ae 49	3	167
Joseph, s. Benjamin & Betsey, b. Mar. 12, 1793	2	36
Joseph, s. Benjamin & Hester, b. [ ]	1	205
Libete*, d. David & Lois, b. July 5, 1774 *("Liberte" in Rudd's)	2	14
Lois, d. David & Lois, b. Dec. 22, 1769	2	14
Lois, m. John **MOORE**, Jr., Jan. 25, 1791, by Samuel Lee, J.P.	2	50
Luther, s. Benjamin & Bettey, b. Mar. 4, 1787	2	36
Margaret, d. David & Margaret, b. June 26, 1758	1	203
Margaret, w. David, d. Apr. 19, 1760, in the 39th y. of her age	1	229
Margaret, d. David & Margaret, d. Sept. 11, 1776	2	49
Marvin, s. Benjamin & Betsey, b. Nov. 18, 1788	2	36
Mary, wid. Jared, d. Jan. 15, 1796	2	50
Mary, of Salisbury, m. Henry **JACKSON**, of New Milford, Jan. 8, 1822, by Lavius Hyde	3	116
Mercy, d. Jared, Jr. & Hannah, b. Mar. 2, 1790	2	27
Mylo, s. Elisha, Jr. & Susannah, b. Dec. 6, 1782	2	24
Noah, s. David & Lois, b. Dec. 24, 1766	1	126
Olive, d. David & Lois, b. May 26, 1778	2	14

	Vol.	Page
EVEREST, (cont.)		
Olive, d. David & Lois, d. Aug. 19, 1779, in the 2nd y. of her age	2	49
Olive Jackson, d. Jehiel & Sally, b. Dec. 30, 1801	2	11
Olivia, d. Jared, Jr. & Hannah, b. July 8, 1788	2	27
Phebe, d. David & Lois, b. Aug. 12, 1776	2	14
Phebe, d. Jehiel & Sally, b. Oct. 24, 1787	2	11
Polly, d. Elisha, Jr. & Susannah, b. Jan. 26, 1787	2	24
Polly, d. Jehiel & Sally, b. Dec. 8, 1789	2	11
Polly, d. Jared, Jr. & Hannah, b. Nov. 10, 1793	2	27
Rebeckah Marsh, d. Erthan & Sylvia, b. Oct. 6, 1789	2	33
Rhoda, d. David & Lois, b. Jan. 25, 1773	2	14
Rhoda, d. Benjamin & Hester, b. [ ]	1	205
Sally, d. Elisha, Jr. & Susannah, b. Oct. 22, 1780	2	24
Sally, d. Jared, Jr. & Hannah, b. Feb. 10, 1798	2	27
Sally, wid., m. John **ELDREDGE**, b. of Salisbury, Mar. 15, 1813, by Rev. Charles Printice, of Canaan	3	114
Samuel, s. David & Lowis, b. Apr. 2, 1768	2	14
Sarah Ann, d. Jehiel & Sally, b. Nov. 15, 1794	2	11
Solomon, s. David & Margaret, b. Apr. 11, 1760	1	203
Sylvester, s. David & Lois, b. May 23, 1781	2	14
FALLOWS*, Rachel, of Sheffield, m. John **HOLMES**, Jr., of Salisbury, Jan. 21, 1750/1, by Rev. Jonathan Lee *("FELLOWS" in Rudd's)	1	222
FARNUM, FARNAM, Bazaleel, d. Jan. 26, 1776, in the 53rd y. of his age	2	49
Elizabeth*, m. Peter **MASON**, b. of Salisbury, Mar. 24, 1774, by Rev. Jonathan Lee *("Elisheba" in Rudd's book)	2	45
Freelove, d. Philip & Hannah, b. Apr. 13, 1787	2	7
Horace, s. Philip & Hannah, b. July 8, 1789	2	7
John, s. Bezaleel & Phebe, b. Dec. 1, 1762	1	119
Lorra, d. Peter & Silvia, b. Aug. 14, 1792	3	6
Maria, d. Peter & Silvia, b. July 10, 1799	3	6
Maria, m. Andrew **CHAPIN**, May 20, 1819, by Rev. Lavius Hyde. Witness Newman Holley	3	115
Meriam, of Salisbury, m. Abijah **HUTCHINSON**, of Lebanon, Feb. 27, 1783, by Abiel Camp, J.P.	2	42
Osmond Peter, s. Peter & Silvia, b. July 4, 1796	3	6
Peter Kirtland, s. Peter & Silvia, b. Aug. 21, 1804	3	6
Phebe, m. Hezekiah **HUTCHINSON**, b. of Salisbury, Jan. 4, 1776, by John Hutchinson, J.P.	2	46
Philip, s. Philip & Hannah, b. Aug. 15, 1791	2	7
FELLOWS*, Rachel, of Sheffield, m. John **HOLMES**, Jr., of Salisbury, Jan. 21, 1750/1, by Rev. Jonathan Lee *(Arnold Copy has "**FALLOWS**")	1	222
[**FERGUSON**], [see under **FORGASON**]		
FERRIE, [see under **FERRY**]		
FERRIS, James, s. William & Jane, b. Nov. 17, 1795	3	26
John, s. William & Jane, b. Dec. 14, 1797	3	26
William, s. William & Jane, b. Apr. 6, 1794	3	26
[**FERRY**], **FERRE, FERRIE**, Margaret, of Sheffield, m. David **EVEREST**, of Salisbury, July 11, 1754, by Rev. Jonathan		

	Vol.	Page
[FERRY], FERRE, FERRIE, (cont.)		
Hubbart	1	242
Theodosia, m. Charles **CHAPIN**, Jr., b. of Salisbury, Apr. 11, 1776, by Rev. Jonathan Lee	2	47
FISH, George H., of Whitehall, N.Y., m. Caroline **WHITTLESEY**, of Salisbury, Feb. 21, 1831, by Leonard E. Lathrop	3	138
Myron H., m. Fanny S. **LEE**, b. of Salisbury, Aug. 25, 1845, by Rev. Adam Reed	3	97
FITCH, Abiggail, d. Bille & Phebe, b. June 16, 1757, in Sheffield	1	185
Abigail, d. Jonathan & Anne, b. Oct. 13, 1764	1	123
Abigail, d. Joseph & Jemima, b. Dec. 11, 1770	2	16
Amanda, d. Elias & Rachel, b. Apr. 5, 1814	3	64
Anna, d. Bille & Phebe, b. Mar. 27, 1753	1	185
Anna, d. Joseph & Jemima, b. Sept. 23, 1783	2	16
Asa, s. Joshua, Jr. & Rebecca*, b. Oct. 20, 1778 *("Reba" in Rudd's)	2	33
Bette, d. Jonathan & Ann, b. July 25, 1771	2	25
Bille, m. Phebe **ROBARTS**, b. of Salisbury, Nov. 21, 1753, by Rev. Jonathan Lee	1	241
Charlotte, d. Joshua & Rebecca*, b. Apr. 5, 1774 *("Reba")	2	33
Charlotte, d. Joshua & Reba, d. Feb. 1, 1795, in the 21st y. of her age	2	50
David, s. Jonathan & Ann, b. May 8, 1769	2	25
Ebenezer, s. Ebenezer & Chloe, b. Mar. 15, 1766	1	119
Eben[eze]r, m. Hannah **WAY**, b. of Salisbury, May 19, 1768, by Rev. Jonathan Lee	2	44
Ebenezer, m. Sarah **TRUMBLE**, May 30, 1771, by Rev. Jonathan Lee	2	45
Ebenezer, s. Elijah & Temperance, b. Oct. 7, 1787	3	6
Elias, s. Joshua, Jr. & Rebecca, b. Oct. 12, 1783	2	33
Elias, s. Elias & Rachel, b. Dec. 5, 1816	3	64
Elizabeth, m. Hezekiah C. **LEE**, Jan. 15, 1807, by Joseph W. Crossman	3	113
Ephraim, s. Jonathan & Anne, b. Aug. 7, 1754, at Norwich	1	123
Ezra, s. Jonathan & Ann, b. Dec. 12, 1773	2	25
Fanny Bushnell, d. Elias & Rachel, b. Dec. 27, 1801	3	64
Hannah, of Coventry, m. Nathaniell **WINSLOW**, of Salisbury, Apr. 9, 1753, by [ ]. Witnesses Noah Porter & Rebekah Porter	1	240
Hannah, d. Joseph & Jemima, b. Oct. 3, 1768	2	16
Hannah, d. Ebenezer & Hannah, b. Apr. 7, 1771	2	22
Hannah, w. Ebenezer, d. Apr. 12, 1771, in the 38th y. of her age	2	49
Henrietta Maria, d. Richard & Lucinda, b. Jan. 14, 1802	3	37
Henry, s. Joshua, Jr. & Rebecca*, b. May 18, 1788 *("Reba")	2	33
Henry, s. Elias & Rachel, b. Oct. 17, 1810	3	64
Hezekiah, d. Dec. 24, 1797, in the 61st y. of his age	3	165
Jabez, s. James & Abiael, b. Aug. 11, 1738	1	199
James, s. James & Abiael, b. Mar. 17, 1747	1	199
James, s. Jonathan & Anne, b. July 8, 1762	1	123
James, s. Joseph & Jemima, b. July 22, 1787	2	16
Jamima, d. Joseph Trumble & Jamima, b. Jan. 8, 1765	1	141

	Vol.	Page
FITCH, (cont.)		
John, s. James & Abiael, b. Nov. 18, 1745	1	199
John, s. Joseph & Jemima, b. Jan. 30, 1775	2	16
John, s. Sarah, b. Jan. 15, 1782	2	24
Jonathan, s. Jonathan & Anne, b. Aug. 19, 1756	1	123
Joseph, s. James & Abiael, b.Oct. 17, 1749	1	199
Joshua, Jr., of Salisbury, m. Rebe **ROOD**, of Sheffield, Dec. 23, 1773, by John Hutchinson, J.P.	2	45
Joshua, s. Jonathan & Ann, b. May 23, 1777	2	25
Joshua, Sr., d. June 7, 1790, in the 87th y. of his age	2	50
Joshua, d. Apr. 29, 1792, ae 46 y.	2	50
Luzetta, d. David & Sally, b. May 2, 1798	3	19
Lydia, d. Joseph Trumble & Jamima, b. Dec. 11, 1766	1	141
Lydia, d. Joseph & Jemima, b. Mar. 6, 1777	2	16
Mary, d. Joshua & Rebecca, b. Sept. 7, 1776	2	33
Maxon*, s. Jonathan & Anne, b. May 30, 1761; d. July 22, 1761 *("Mason" in Rudd's book)	1	123
Nathaniell, s. James & Abiael, b. Aug. 7, 1752	1	199
Nathaniell, s. Jonathan & Ann, b. Feb. 15, 1767	2	25
Parnel, d. Joshua, Jr. & Rebecca, b. Dec. 5, 1780	2	33
Parnel, d. Elias & Rachel, b. June 29, 1812	3	64
Rachel, d. James & Abiael, b. July 7, 1736	1	199
Rachel, d. Joseph & Jemima, b. Jan. 25, 1773	2	16
Rebecca, d. Elias & Rachel, b. Aug. 30, 1808	3	64
Sally, d. Joseph & Jemima, b. Aug. 9, 1785	2	16
Sally, d. Elijah & Temperance, b. Mar. 7, 1789	3	6
Samuel, s. Bille & Phebe, b. May 26, 1754	1	185
Sanford, s. Ebenezer & Hannah, b. Aug. 12, 1769	2	22
Sarah, d. Ebenezer & Sarah, b. Oct. 20, 1774	2	22
Sarah, had s. John, b. Jan. 15, 1782	2	24
Sybel, d. James & Abiael, b. Sept. 13, 1743	1	199
Sibel, d. Joseph Trumble & Jamima, b. Nov. 13, 1762	1	141
Silvia, d. Elijah & Temperance, b. Apr. 8, 1792	3	6
Zoroaster, s. Jonathan & Anne, b. Feb. 23, 1759	1	123
FLETCHER, Bette, d. Ebenezer, Jr. & Olive, b. July 26, 1763	1	118
Cotton, of Salisbury, m. Thankfull **BARTLETT**, of Guilford, Sept. 9, 1756, by Rev. Jonathan Lee	1	245
Ebenezer, d. Oct. 3, 1771, in the 73rd y. of his age	2	48
Ebenezer, s. Ebenezer & Olive, b. July 18, 1772	2	27
John, s. Ebenezer, Jr. & Olive, b. Aug. 19, 1768	1	118
Jonathan Lee, s. John & Betsey, b. May 30, 1797	3	24
Lydiah, d. Ebenezer, Jr. & Olive, b. Aug. 4, 1770	2	27
Molle, d. Cotton & Thankfull, b. June 29, 1757	1	174
Olive, d. Ebenezer & Olive, b. Oct. 24, 1774	2	27
Osmond Ensign, s. John & Betsey, b. Apr. 28, 1804	3	34
Parmelia, d. Ebenezer & Olive, b. Sept. 19, 1777	2	27
Polly, d. Ebenezer & Olive, b. Sept. 25, 1780	2	27
Samuel, s. Cotton & Thankfull, b. Oct. 17, 1758	1	174
Silva, d. Ebenezer, Jr. & Olive, b. Feb. 15, 1766	1	118
FLINT, Charles B., m. Julia **KELSEY**, b. of Salisbury, June 26, 1828, by John Colver	3	130

	Vol.	Page
FLINT, (cont.)		
Joanna, d. Nathaniel, of Tolland & Joanna, b. Mar. 3, 1755, in Salisbury	1	212
FOLLIET, FOLIET, Dolly, d. James & Mary, b. Sept. 9, 1794	3	9
James, m. Mary **WHEELER**, Aug. 30, 1787, by Rev. Jonathan Lee. Witnesses Jeremiah Dauchy & Oliver Jewell, Jr.	2	50
Jesse, s. James & Mary, b. Aug. 16, 1798	3	9
John Wheeler, s. James & Mary, b. June 15, 1788	2	20
Polly, d. James & Mary, b. Sept. 8, 1790	3	9
Polly, d. James & Mary, b. Sept. 8, 1790	2	20
FORD, Jesse, Jr., of New Canaan, N.Y., m. Electa **EVERTS**, of Salisbury, Jan. 16, 1823, by Rev. Coles Carpenter	3	118
Willis, of Plymouth, m. Eliza **KELSEY**, of Salisbury, Dec. 18, 1828, by Rev. Noah Bigelow	3	132
FORGASON, Abigail, d. Daniel & Hannah, b. Oct. 20, 1763	2	29
Daniel, m. Hannah **JACKSON**, b. of Salisbury, Jan. 15, 1758, by James Landon, J.P.	2	45
Daniel, s. Daniel & Hannah, b. Mar. 26, 1769	2	29
Hannah, d. Daniel & Hannah, b. Oct. 23, 1761	2	29
Mary, d. Daniel & Hannah, b. Nov. 27, 1765	2	29
Rachel, d. Daniel & Hannah, b. May 20, 1767	2	29
Sarah, d. Daniel & Hannah, b. June 5, 1758	2	29
FOSTER, Albert, m. Clarissa **MAXAM**, Nov. 28, 1822, by Rev. Coles Carpenter	3	118
Caroline, m. William **JONES**, b. of Salisbury, Oct. 5, 1842, by Rev. Adam Reid	3	162
Hannah, m. William W. **SAUNDERS**, b. of Salisbury, Aug. 3, 1828, by Rev. Noah Bigelow	3	134
Loiza J., of Salisbury, m. Jonathan P. **McNEIL**, of Sheffield, Mass., Mar. 23, 1842, by Rev. Adam Reid	3	162
Theron Eugene, s. John & Laura S., b. Mar. 19, 1841	3	89
FOWLER, Hannah, w. Mark, d. Mar. 13, 1749, in the 24th y. of her age	1	225
FOX, Luna, m. Thomas **REED**, b. of Salisbury, Feb. 13, 1814, at Cornwall, by Rev. Nathaniel Swift, of Warren	3	114
FRAME, John, m. Roxanna **JACOBS**, b. of Salisbury, Sept. 2, 1773, by John Hutchinson, J.P.	2	45
John, his w. [ ], d. Nov. 4, 1776, in the 38th y. of her age	2	49
Lydia, d. John & Reliance, b. July 3, 1774	2	31
FREEMAN, [see also **TREMAIN**], Rhoda, m. Henry J. **TUCKER**, b. of Salisbury, July 5, 1846, by Roger Averill, J.P.	3	98
FRINCH, [see under **FRINK**]		
FRINK, FRINCH, Abigail, m. William **ROBERTS**, b. of Salisbury, Nov. 21, 1752, by Rev. Jonathan Lee	1	244
Cynthia J., of Salisbury, m. Curtis **MORRIS**, of New Milford, Sept. 2, 1827, by Leonard E. Lathrop	3	127
Cynthia Jane, d. Andrew & Esther, b. Oct. 1, 1791, in Sheffield	3	4
David, of Mt. Washington, m. Charlotte **LYONS**, of Salisbury, Aug. 9, 1832, by Rev. Stephen Beach, of St. Johns Ch.	3	140
Edmund William, s. Andrew & Esther, b. Apr. 28, 1798	3	4
Esther Fanna, d. Andrew & Esther, b. Feb. 3, 1795	3	4

	Vol.	Page
FRINK, FRINCH, (cont.)		
Frederick Parks, s. Andrew & Esther, b. May 3, [ ]	3	4
Mary Elizabeth, d. Edmund W. & Hannah T., b. Aug. 20, 1833	3	86
Sally Maria, d. Andrew & Esther, b. Mar. 11, 1790	3	4
FRISBIE, Daniel, of Norfolk, m. Maritta **HUBBARD**, of Salisbury, May 14, 1844, by Rev. Adam Reid	3	163
FROST, John, s. Abijah & Eunice, b. Feb. 2, 1770	2	27
FULLER, Abigail, w. Ezekiel, d. Nov. 14, 1763	1	238
Abigail, d. Ezekiel & Hannah, b. July 29, 1776	2	38
Amos, Jr., of Salisbury, m. Rachel **FULLER**, of Kent, Sept. 30, 1767, by Daniel Lee, J.P.	2	44
Amos, s. Amos, Jr. & Rachel, b. Feb. 29, 1772	2	20
Anne, d. Eleazer & Anne, b. June 17, 1773	2	28
Anne, w. Amos, d. Sept. 21, 1774, in the 24th y. of her age	2	49
Archibal, s. Ezekiel & Hannah, b. Sept. 29, 1796	2	38
Bethsheba, m. William **CORPE**, b. of Salisbury, Apr. 11, 1755, by David Whitney, J.P. *("Bathsheba")	1	246
Bathsheba, d. Ezekiel & Hannah, b. Nov. 25, 1789	2	38
Benjamin, s. Eleazer & Anne, b. Jan. 20, 1782	2	28
Cille, d. Eleazer & Hannah, b. Apr. 20, 1789	2	28
Eber, s. Joseph & Patience, b. Feb. 15, 1759	1	180
Eleazer, of Salisbury, m. Anna **LARABEE**, of Dutchess Co., Feb. 27, 1770, by James Landon, J.P.	2	45
Eleazer, s. Eleazer & Anne, b. Oct. 29, 1770	2	28
Ezekiel, m. Hannah **DUTCHER**, b. of Salisbury, Mar. 1, 1771, by John Hutchinson, J.P.	2	45
Ezekiel, s. Ezekiel & Hannah, b. Feb. 19, 1774	2	38
Faith, d. Ezekiel & Hannah, b. May 2, 1779	2	38
Hannah, d. Eleazer & Anne, b. Oct. 3, 1779	2	28
Hannah, d. Ezekiel & Hannah, b. Apr. 10, 1781	2	38
Isaiah, d. Sept. 18, 1760, in the 19th y. of his age	1	236
Isaiah, s. James & Abiah, b. Sept. 6, 1765	1	123
Isaiah, s. Eleazer & Anne, b. Oct. 9, 1776	2	28
John, s. Eleazer & Anne, b. Apr. 2, 1778	2	28
John, s. Ezekiel & Hannah, b. Apr. 4, 1785	2	38
Joseph, of Salisbury, m. Patience **EAGLESTON**, of Salisbury, Apr. 5, 1753, by Rev. Jonathan Lee	1	240
Joseph, s. Joseph & Patience, b. Jan. 19, 1755	1	180
Judeth, m. Willett **LARREBEE**, b. of Salisbury, Jan. 25, 1773, by James Landon, J.P.	2	46
Laure, d. Ezekiel & Hannah, b. Aug. 18, 1787	2	38
Luther, s. Jeremiah & Bethiah, b. Sept. 28, 1753	1	179
Luther, s. Jeremiah & Bethiah, b. Sept. 28, 1753	1	213
Lydia, d. Jeremiah & Bethiah, b. Dec. 28, 1755	1	179
Mary, d. Ezekiel & Abigail, b. Feb. [ ], 1761; d. July 1, 1761	1	118
Mary, d. Ezekiel & Abigail, b. Apr. 19, 1762	1	118
Mary, d. Amos, Jr. & Rachel, b. July 1, 1768	2	20
Matthew, s. Ezekiel & Hannah, b. Oct. 27, 1771	2	38
Mehetable, m. Gershom **MATTOON**, b. of Salisbury, Jan. 17, 1771, by J. Hutchinson, J.P.	2	45
Nathaniel, s. Amos & Rachel, b. Aug. 7, 1776	2	20

	Vol.	Page
FULLER, (cont.)		
Olive, d. Ezekiel & Hannah, b. Mar. 9, 1783	2	38
Oliver, s. Eleazer & Hannah, b. Oct. 10, 1786	2	28
Patience, d. Joseph & Patience, b. Jan. 21, 1761	1	180
Patience, had s. William, b. Aug. 7, 1781	2	11
Phebe, d. Eleazer & Hannah, b. Nov. 22, 1783	2	28
Prescilla, d. Eleazer & Hannah, b. Sept. 17, 1791	2	28
Rachel, of Kent, m. Amos **FULLER**, Jr., of Salisbury, Sept. 30, 1767, by Daniel Lee, J.P.	2	44
Rachel, d. Amos & Rachel, b. Aug. 1, 1774	2	20
Rebecca, of Salisbury, m. John **TORREY**, of Bethany, Penn., [Sept.] 28, 1830, by L.E. Lathrop	3	137
Rhoda, d. Amos, Jr. & Rachel, b. May 14, 1770	2	20
Ruth, d. Ephraim & Hannah, b. Mar. 25, 1782	2	50
Sarah, of Sharon, m. Samuel **EVARTS**, of Salisbury, Sept. 18, 1776, by James Landon, J.P.	2	47
Sibbel, d. Joseph & Patience, b. Dec. 16, 1756	1	180
William, s. Patience, b. Aug. 7, 1781	2	11
FULLERTON, Stewart M.G., of Colebrook, m. Amand[a] **ALEXANDER**, of Sheffield, Sept. 20, 1838, by Rev. Thomas Bainbridge	3	156
FURLONG, Angeline, d. John & Anna, b. Aug. 20, 1806	3	6
Artimisia, d. John & Anna, b. July 13, 1810	3	6
Aurilla, d. John & Anna, b. Nov. 24, 1807	3	6
Hiram Austin, s. John & Anna, b. Sept. 20, 1804	3	6
Maria Louisa, d. Benajah & Rhoda, b. Aug. 1, 1811	3	50
Norman Galusha, s. Benajah & Rhoda, b. Sept. 15, 1809	3	50
Orville Porter, s. Benajah & Rhoda, b. Sept. 17, 1813	3	50
GAGER, George W., m. Amelia S. **LOVERIDGE**, Dec. 9, 1840, by Rev. J. Tankin Carpenter	3	160
GALUSHA, Anna, of Salisbury, m. Ebenezer **WRIGHT**, of Mansfield, Feb. 24, 1788, by Elisha Fitch, J.P.	2	43
Desea, d. Jacob & Desea, b. Dec. 31, 1771	2	33
Desire, w. David, d. Sept. 28, 1775, in the 43rd y. of her age	2	49
Elias, s. Jacob & Desea, b. Sept. 9, 1775	2	33
Jacob, of Salisbury, m. Abigail **PORTER**, of Norwich, Feb. 25, 1776, at Norwich, by Joel Benedict	2	47
Lydia, m. Asa **HUTCHINSON**, b. of Salisbury, Oct. 19, 1786, by Rev. Jonathan Lee	2	43
Sarah, d. Jacob & Desea, b. June 30, 1774	2	33
Sarah, m. John Flavel **BACON**, Sept. 13, 1795, by Samuel Lee, J.P.	3	109
Susannah, d. Elias & Susannah, b. Oct. 25, 1797	3	12
GARFIELD, Elisha, of Tyringham, m. Roxanna Cecelia **PRATT**, of Salisbury, [June] 21, [1828], by Leonard E. Lathrop	3	130
GASTON, Phebe, d. Alexander & Mary, b. Apr. 22, 1765	1	157
GATES, Clarissa, d. James & Mary, b. Oct. 22, 1782	2	35
Clarissa, d. James & Mary, d. Dec. 1, 1782	2	50
Mary, d. James & Mary, b. June 1, 1781	2	35
GAY, Abigail, d. Henry S. & Mary, b. June 13, 1824	3	76
Edward F., m. Clarissa **LEE**, June [ ], [1824?], by Rev. L.E.		

	Vol.	Page
GAY, (cont.)		
Lathrop, of Cong. Ch.	3	120
Eloiza, m. Jarvis **JONES**, b. of Salisbury, Jan. 7, 1840, by Adam Reid	3	159
Henry S., m. Sophia **MOORE**, b. of Salisbury, Apr. 26, 1839, by Rev. Adam Reid	3	157
Maria H., of Salisbury, m. Franklin **PARSONS**, of Sharon, Oct. 10, 1838, by Rev. Adam Reid	3	155
Mary, d. Henry S. & Mary, b. July 24, 1827	3	76
Mary R., m. James P. **COTTER**, of West Meriden, Oct. 6, 1847, by Rev. G. Huntington Nicholls. Int. Pub.	3	101
Mylo Lee, s. Edward F. & Clarissa, b. June 20, 1825	3	76
Stephen Reed, s. Henry S. & Mary, b. Aug. 29, 1822	3	76
GIFFORD, Weston, of Falmouth, d. Jan. 19, 1756, ae about 22 y. at the house of Samuel Bellows. He was a soldier in Samuel Bellows' Company	1	243
GILLETT, GILLET, GELLET, GILLITT, GILLETTE, Abigail, d. John & Abigail, b. Apr. 9, 1764	1	173
Alice, d. Nathan & Hannah, b. Dec. 12, 1772	2	13
Annis, d. Isaac* & Deborah, b. Dec. 31, 1772 *("Jacob")	2	13
Caroline, m. Lyman **JUDD**, b. of Canaan, June 15, 1835, by Leonard E. Lathrop	3	149
Elijah, s. Nathan & Hannah, b. Mar. 23, 1775	2	13
Elizabeth, d. Nathan & Hannah, b. Mar. 25, 1768	2	13
Eunice, of Sharon, m. Ebenezer **DIBBLE**, of Salisbury, May 26, 1774, by Rev. Cotton Mather Smith	2	46
Hannah, d. Nathan & Hannah, b. Jan. 26, 1770	2	13
Irena, d. John & Abigail, b. June 29, 1760	1	173
Jacob, s. Nathaniell & Marcy, b. Mar. 19, 1749	1	213
Jacob, of Salisbury, m. Deborah **MUNROW**, of Sharon, Dec. 31, 1769, by Rev. Mr. Smith	2	44
John, of Salisbury, m. Abigail **HOUGH**, of Canaan, Nov. 14, 1754, by John Beebe, J.P.	1	242
John, s. John & Abigail, b. Feb. 20, 1768	2	11
Jonathan, d. Sept. 4, 1754	1	243
Jonathan, s. John & Abigail, b. Mar. 23, 1762	1	173
Joseph, s. Nathaniell & Marcy, b. Dec. 5, 1745; d. May 28, 1746	1	225
Joseph, s. Isaac* & Deborah, b. Dec. 19, 1770 *("Jacob")	2	13
Mary, d. John & Abigail, b. Sept. 29, 1755	1	173
Matthew, of New Hartford, m. Jennett **CADY**, of Salisbury, July 8, 1828, by Charles Prentice	3	130
Mercy, d. Nathan & Hannah, b. May 28, 1766	1	141
Nathan, s. Nathaniel & Mercy, b. Feb. 28, 1742/3	LR1	352
Nathaniell, s. John & Abigail, b. May 30, 1758, in Sharon	1	173
Ruth, d. Nathan & Hannah, b. May 28, 1779	2	13
Samuel, s. Elijah & Mary, b. Jan. 29, 1746/7, in Guilford	1	200
Temperance, d. Nathan & Hannah, b. Mar. 5, 1777	2	13
Tharris*, d. Isaac* & Deborah, b. Dec. 15, 1774 *("Tharzy, d. of John" in Rudd's book)	2	13
Thomas, a "bastard child", b. [ ], at the house of Hyman Jacob Bozrough; d. Sept. 20, 1772, in the 7th m. of his age	2	48

	Vol.	Page
GOODRICH, Harriet, twin with Horace, d. David & Abia, b. June 29, 1798	3	30
Horace, twin with Harriet, s. David & Abia, b. June 29, 1798	3	30
Mary*, of Sheffield, m. Prince **WINSLOW**, of Salisbury, June 21, 1763, by Rev. Jonathan Hubbart *("Sarah" in Arnold Copy)	1	251
Sarah*, of Sheffield, m. Prince **WINSLOW**, of Salisbury, June 21, 1763, by Rev. Jonathan Hubbart *"Mary" in Rudd's book)	1	251
Sarah, of Sharon, m. David **BISSELL**, of Salisbury, Feb. 14, 1767, by Rev. Cotton M. Smith	2	44
Walstein, m. Caroline **TIBBELLS**, Oct. 3, 1822, by David L. Perry	3	117
GOODSELL, Morris, of Kent, m. Olivia **ABELL**, of Salisbury, Oct. 14, 1835, by Leonard E. Lathrop	3	150
GOODWIN, Laura Ann, of Salisbury, m. John Ely **ENSIGN**, of Canaan, [, 1839?], by Rev. Charles T. Printice	3	158
Sarah, w. Samuel, d. Mar. 29, 1757	1	255
Submit, d. Samuel & Sarah, b. Mar. 24, 1757	1	191
Zebad*, s. Samuel & Sarah, b. Feb. 27, 1755 *("Zebade" in Rudd's)	1	196
GOULD, Asa, s. Benoni & Sarah, b. Mar. 7, 1756	1	193
Jonathan, s. Benoni & Sarah, b. Apr. 13, 1752	1	193
Martha, w. Job, d. Nov. 17, 1771, in the 24th y. of her age	2	48
GRAHAM, Moses L., m. Maria J. **BENTON**, June 19, 1845, by Rev. Jonathan Lee	3	97
GRANDY, Abigail, d. Robert & Bethiah, b. Aug. 16, 1758	1	110
Elizabeth, d. Robert & Bethiah, b. Apr. 19, 1760	1	110
GRANGER, Edward, s. Simeon & Phebe, b. Apr. 3, 1808	3	59
Erastus, s. Tho[ma]s & Jemima, b. May 26, 1796	3	26
Hannah, d. Tho[ma]s & Jemima, b. Nov. 20, 1793, in Sandisfield	3	26
Lemuel, s. Tho[ma]s & Jemima, b. Aug. 13, 1791, in Bethleham, Mass.	3	26
Mary Ann, d. Simeon & Phebe, b. Sept. 19, 1811	3	59
Renssalear, s. Simeon & Phebe, b. June 3, 1802	3	59
GRANNIS, Desire, m. Victory S. **TOUSLEY**, b. of Salisbury, Jan. 27, 1780, by Rev. Jonathan Lee	2	41
GRANT, Ambrose, m. Jannet **BARRETT**, b. of Salisbury, Nov. 22, 1838, by Rev. Thomas Bainbridge	3	156
GREEN, Cornelia, d. Isaac & Achsah, b. Dec. [ ], 1805	3	23
Cornelia E., m. Horace **LANDEN**, b. of Salisbury, Sept. 21, 1825, by L.E. Lathrop	3	122
Electa, d. Nathaniel & Anna, b. Mar. 4, 1779	2	33
Elizabeth*, m. Eliphaz **BREWSTER**, b. of Salisbury, Feb. 15, 1770, by J. Hutchinson, J.P. *("Elizabeth **GRAVES**"?)	2	44
Harriet, m. Isaac N. **CONKLIN**, Nov. 7, 1832, by L.E. Lathrop	3	141
Henry, m. Lucinda **MOORE**, b. of Salisbury, Sept. 1, 1833, by L.E. Lathrop	3	143
Isaac, s. Nathaniel & Anna, b. Jan. 29, 1776	2	33
Isaac, m. Achsah **SPENCER**, b. of Salisbury, Sept. 28, 1800, by Joseph W. Crossman	3	111
Ja[me]s, of Covington, N.Y., m. Mary **HOLMES**, of Salisbury,		

	Vol.	Page
GREEN, (cont.)		
May 5, 1830, by Rev. Stephen Beach, of St. Johns Ch.	3	136
Nancy, d. Nathaniel & Anna, b. Dec. 7, 1773	2	33
Nauncey, d. Nath[anie]ll & Ann, d. Dec. 11, 1773, same day of birth	2	48
Nath[anie]ll, m. Anna **BRINSMAID**, b. of Salisbury, Feb. 11, 1773, by Rev. Jonathan Lee	2	45
Osmond Spencer, s. Isaac & Achsah, b. Feb. 8, 1802	3	23
Sally, d. Nathaniel & Anna, b. Aug. 25, 1785	2	33
Statira, m. Ward **SWIFT**, Nov. 7, 1832, by L.E. Lathrop	3	141
GRIDLEY, Abigail, m. James **BIRD**, Aug. 23, 1750, by Rev. Mr. Barnum, of Kensington	1	244
Mary, d. Noah & Mary, b. Mar. 2, 1764	1	145
Samuel, of Berlin, m. Lucy **HANCHET**, of Salisbury, Oct. 2, 1799, by Lot Norton, J.P.	3	111
GRIFFAN*, Jerusha, m. Asa **LANDON**, b. of Salisbury, Oct. 20, 1757, by Rev. Jonathan Lee *("**GRIFFACE**" in Rudd's book)	1	247
GRINNELL, GRENNELL, GRINNEL, GRENNALL, [see also **GRINOLD**], Chapman, s. Peabody & Charity, b. Mar. 15, 1772	2	35
Charlotte, d. Daniell & Anna, b. Oct. 6, 1782	3	12
Chauncey, s. Samuel & Rebecca, b. [ ]	3	7
Daniel, Jr., m. Anne **EVEREST**, b. of Salisbury, Feb. 20, 1777, by John Hutchinson	2	47
Daniel, s. Daniell & Anna, b. Jan. 10, 1789	3	12
Elizabeth, d. Michael & Susannah, b. Mar. 5, 1782	2	7
Emma, m. Nathan **PECK**, Jr., b. of Salisbury, Mar. 29, 1831, by Leonard E. Lathrop	3	138
Ezra, s. Daniel & Anna, b. Aug. 6, 1785	3	12
Heman, s. Daniell & Anna, b. May 18, 1797	3	12
James, s. Peabody & Charity, b. Sept. 13, 1779	2	35
Lucretia, d. Samuel & Rebecca, b. Mar. 29, 1792	3	7
Nancy, d. Daniel & Anna, b. Dec. 6, 1777	3	12
Peabody, s. Peabody & Charity, b. July 21, 1774	2	35
Polly, d. Daniell & Anna, b. Feb. 27, 1780	3	12
Roxana, d. Daniell & Anna, b. Aug. 3, 1799	3	12
Rufus, s. Michael & Susannah, b. May 2, 1778	2	7
Samuell, m. Rebecca **WOODWORTH**, b. of Salisbury, Nov. 22, 1785, by Rev. Jonathan Lee	2	43
Sarah, d. Michael & Susannah, b. Apr. 2, 1780	2	7
Silvester, s. Peabody & Charity, b. Apr. 29, 1781	2	35
Tabithy, d. Peabody & Charity, b. July 21, 1776	2	35
William, s. Daniell & Anna, b. June 16, 1792	3	12
GRINOLD, [see also **GRINNELL & GRISWOLD**], James, Capt., d. June 25, 1816, in the 38th y. of his age	3	168
GRISWOLD, [see also **GRINOLD**], George, s. John & Elizabeth, b. May 8, 1761	1	131
Lucy, d. John & Elizabeth, b. Apr. [ ], 1760	1	131
GROAB, Lydia S., m. Charles **LYMAN**, b. of Salisbury, Nov. 30, 1843, by Rev. C.V. Amerman	3	96

	Vol.	Page
GROAT, Samuel D., of Mt. Washington, Mass., m. Mary **HARRIS**, of Salisbury, Oct. 12, 1825, by Eliphalet Whittlesey, J.P.	3	123
Sarah, m. William **HARRIS**, Dec. 19, [1827], by L.E. Lathrop	3	128
GROW, Harriet, d. Lora, b. Apr. 25, 1802	3	16
Lora, had d. Harriet, Apr. 25, 1802	3	16
GUNON, Michael, m. Caroline Maria **WATTON**, b. of Salisbury, Apr. 17, 1825, by Rev. Stephen Beach, of St. John's Ch.	3	121
HADSELL, Luke, of New Marlborough, Mass., m. Love **WHEELER**, of Salisbury, Oct. 10, 1833, by Eliphalet Whittlesey, J.P.	3	145
HAIGHT, **HAIT**, J.A., m. Thankfull M. **PAGE**, of Salisbury, June 15, 1834, by Leonard E. Lathrop	3	146
Richard M., of Edinburgh, Portage Cty., O., m. Sarah **AVERILL**, of Salisbury, Sept. 1, 1840, by Rev. Adam Reid	3	159
HALE, Abigail, m. Adonijah **STRONG**, b. of Salisbury, Mar. 8, 1770, by Rev. Jonathan Lee	2	44
HALL, [see also **HULL**], Amos, s. Silas & Eunice, b. Oct. 22, 1778	2	36
Benoni, s. David & Mary, b. Jan. 19, 1791	2	18
Daniel*, m. Rebeckah **KELSEY**, b. of Salisbury, Nov. 5, 1774, by Rev. Jonathan Lee *("Daniel **HULL**" in Rudd's book)	2	46
Darius*, s. Jonathan & Susanah, b. Jan. 8, 1777 *("Darius **HULL**" in Rudd's book)	2	9
Edward, s. Leonard & Sally, b. Feb. 15, 1807	3	41
Electa*, m. Solomon **DIMMICK**, b. of Salisbury, Jan. 18, 1781, by Rev. Jonathan Lee *("Electa **HULL**" in Rudd's book)	2	41
Heman*, s. Jonathan & Susannah, b. July 10, 1769 *("Heman **HULL**" in Rudd's book)	2	9
John & Silance, had twin s. [ ] with Lydia, st.b., Sept. 14, 1763	1	151
John F.*, s. Daniel & Rebeckah, b. July 26, 1775 *("John F. **HULL**" in Rudd's book)	2	8
Leonard, s. Silas & Eunice, b. Mar. 5, 1781	2	36
Leonard, m. Sally **LANDON**, b. of Salisbury, Sept. 1, 1805, by Rev. Joseph W. Crossman	3	112
Lot*, s. Jonathan & Susanah, b. June 6, 1775 *("Lot **HULL**" in Rudd's book)	2	9
Lydia, [twin with ----------], d. John & Silance, b. Sept. 14, 1763	1	151
Lydia, d. Silas L. & Eunice, b. Oct. 25, 1776	2	36
Salome*, d. Jonathan & Susannah, b. Feb. 27, 1771 *("Salome **HULL**" in Rudd's book)	2	9
Samuel*, s. Jonathan & Susanah, b. Aug. 22, 1772 *("Samuel **HULL**" in Rudd's book)	2	9
Sarah*, d. Jonathan & Susannah, b. Jan. 6, 1768 *("Sarah **HULL**" in Rudd's book)	2	9
Silas, s. Silas & Eunice, b. Apr. 20, 1783	2	36
Silas Leonard, m. Eunice **TITUS**, Apr. 4, 1774, by Uriah Lawrence, J.P.	2	47
William, m. Mary **HARRIS**, b. of Salisbury, [Oct.] 11, [1832], by L.E. Lathrop	3	141
HAMLIN, Barnabus, s. David & Silence, b. Apr. 5, 1780	3	1
Bethuel, s. David & Silence, b. May 14, 1782	3	1

	Vol.	Page
HAMLIN, (cont.)		
Caroline, of Salisbury, m. Mark **ROSSETER**, of Great Barrington, Mass., Jan. 14, 1828, by Leonard E. Lathrop	3	129
David, s. David & Silence, b. Aug. 7, 1774	2	33
Elezer, s. David & Silence, b. July 6, 1772	2	33
Elezer, Dea., d. Oct. 3, 1771, in the 76th y. of his age	2	48
Eunice, d. David & Silence, b. Aug. 22, 1778	3	1
Hulda, d. David & Silence, b. Apr. 13, 1768, on "Philipses Pattent"	2	33
Lovinia, d. David & Silence, b. June 20, 1789	3	1
Myron, m. Mary Ann **NEWELL**, b. of Salisbury, June 15, 1829, by L.E. Lathrop	3	134
Reuben, s. David & Silence, b. May 4, 1770	2	33
HANCHETT, HANCHET, Amos, of Salisbury, m. Hannah **HAWLEY**, of Sharon, Jan. 1, 1761, by Rev. Jonathan Lee	1	249
Amos, s. Amos & Hannah, b. Mar. 31, 1773	2	20
Asenath, d. Ebenezer, Jr. & Phebe, b. Dec. 31, 1768	2	25
Beulah, d. Ebenezer & Phebe, b. Oct. 2, 1774	2	25
Dan, s. Simeon & Mary, b. May 25, 1783	2	10
Daniel, s. Amos & Hannah, b. Sept. 14, 1775	2	20
Ebenezer, s. Ebenezer & Sarah, b. Feb. 7, 1747/8	1	206
Ebenezer, Jr., of Salisbury, m. Phebe **HOLLY**, of Sharon, Dec. 31, 1767, by Rev. Jonathan Lee	2	44
Enos, s. Ebenezer, Jr. & Phebe, b. Nov. 9, 1772	2	25
Ephraim, s. Simeon & Mary, b. Jan. 7, 1778, in Oblong	2	10
Hanna, d. Ebenezer & Sarah, b. May 27, 1750	1	206
Hannah, m. Zebulon **WALKER**, b. of Salisbury, June 7, 1773, by Rev. Jonathan Lee	2	45
Hannah, d. Amos & Hannah, b. Mar. 5, 1778	2	20
Isaac, s. Simeon & Mary, b. Jan. 19, 1782; d. June 29, 1782	2	10
John, s. Amos & Hannah, b. Aug. 28, 1764	1	110
Jonah, s. Ebenezer & Sarah, b. Jan. 30, 1758	1	186
Joseph, of Salisbury, m. Mrs. Sarah **THOMSON**, of Goshen, Sept. 28, 1759, by Rev. Stephen Heaton	1	222
Lucy, d. Ebenezer & Sarah, b. Aug. 18, 1745, in Canaan	1	206
Lucy, of Salisbury, m. Samuel **GRIDLEY**, of Berlin, Oct. 2, 1799, by Lot Norton, J.P.	3	111
Lydiah, d. Amos & Sarah, b. Mar. 5, 1771	2	20
Mary, of Sheffield, m. John **LANSON***, Jr., of Salisbury, Dec. 23, 1762, by John Beebe, J.P. *("**LANDON**" in Rudd's book)	1	251
Reuben, s. Amos & Hannah, b. Mar. 6, 1769	2	20
Ruth, d. Ebenezer & Sarah, b. July 3, 1755	1	206
Ruth, d. Ebenezer & Sarah, d. Nov. 6, 1759	1	237
Ruth, d. Amos & Hannah, b. Nov. 29, 1761	1	110
Sarah, m. Nath[anie]ll **TUPPER**, b. of Salisbury, Jan. 1, 1766, by Rev. Jonathan Lee	2	44
Sarah, d. Simeon & Mary, b. Mar. 25, 1775	2	10
Sarah, d. Simeon & Mary, b. Mar. 25, 1775	2	37
Silas, s. Amos & Hannah, b. June 20, 1780	2	20
Simeon, s. Ebenezer & Sarah, b. Feb. 4, 1753	1	206
Simeon, of Salisbury, m. Mary **RAIMENTON**, of Sheffield,		

SALISBURY VITAL RECORDS 199

	Vol.	Page
HANCHETT, HANCHET, (cont.)		
Aug. 15, 1774, by Rev. Mr. Gay	2	47
Simeon, s. Simeon & Mary, b. Dec. 25, 1779	2	10
Zilpha, d. Ebenezer, Jr. & Phebe, b. Dec. 1, 1770	2	25
HANKS, Polly, of Salisbury, m. Isaac **VOSBURGH**, of Sheffield, Dec. 22, 1799, by John Whittlesey, J.P.	3	104
HANMER, [see under **HARMER**]		
HARMER*, Benjamin, s. Joseph & Sibel, b. July 24, 1762 *("**HANMER**" in Rudd's book)	1	125
Lanson*, s. Joseph & Sibel, b. Sept. 19, 1765 *("Lanson **HANMER**" in Rudd's book)	1	125
HARRIS, HARRISS, Celesta E., of Salisbury, m. Albert C. **JONES**, of Poughkeepsie, N.Y., Oct. 28, 1846, in St. Johns Church, by Rev. G. Huntington Nicholls. Int. Pub.	3	99
Clarissa M., of Salisbury, m. Thomas M. **AUSTIN**, of Erie, Penn., Sept. 14, 1842, by Rev. Adam Reid	3	162
Eleanor, of Salisbury, m. Calvin **SPARKS**, of Sheffield, Dec. 21, 1831, by L.E. Lathrop	3	139
James Harvey, s. John, 3rd & Elizabeth, b. Nov. 3, 1795	3	5
John, s. John, 3rd & Elizabeth, b. Sept. 7, 1798	3	5
Maria, d. James & Love, b. Nov. 26, 1811	3	55
Mary, of Salisbury, m. Samuel D. **GROAT**, of Mt. Washington, Mass., Oct. 12, 1825, by Eliphalet Whittlesey, J.P.	3	123
Mary, m. William **HALL**, b. of Salisbury, [Oct.] 11, [1832], by L.E. Lathrop	3	141
Mary Ann, d. James & Love, b. Jan. 19, 1810	3	55
Mary Ann, m. Charles **ROSS**, b. of Salisbury, Nov. 26, 1838, by Rev. Thomas Bainbridge	3	156
Orra, of Salisbury, m. Lucius **HOLCOMB**, of Johnston, O., Mar. 15, 1837, by Rev. Oliver V. Amerman	3	154
Sarah M., m. Edwin **SORNBERGER**, [Sept.] 20, [1832], by L.E. Lathrop	3	141
William, m. Sarah **GROAT**, Dec. 19, [1827], by L.E. Lathrop	3	128
HARRISON, Alexander S., m. Marian E. **BISSELL**, b. of Salisbury, Sept. 28, 1842, by Rev. Adam Reid	3	162
Ann Cornelia, m. George A. **DARROW**, Oct. 17, 1836, by Leonard E. Lathrop	3	153
Beulah, m. Samuel **LEE**, 2nd, b. of Salisbury, July 20, 1806, by Samuel Lee, J.P.	3	112
Caroline B., m. Samuel H. **ALLEE** (?)*, of Pleasant Valley, N.Y., [ ] 20, [1834?], by Leonard E. Lathrop *(Perhaps "**ADEE**")	3	149
Hannah S., of Salisbury, m. James **ORR**, of Sharon, June 2, 1846, by G.S. Brownell	3	98
Jared S., m. Harriet A. **DODGE**, [Jan.] 2, 1827, by Leonard E. Lathrop	3	126
Mary H., of Salisbury, m. William T. **INGERSOLL**, of Amenia, N.Y., Jan. 1, 1839, by Adam Reid	3	157
HARTWELL, Nathaniel, of North East, m. Susan **REED**, of Salisbury, Dec. 26, 1822, by Charles Prentice	3	118
HASKINS, Henry, of Richmond, Mass., m. Sarah H. **WHITEHEAD**,		

	Vol.	Page
HASKINS, (cont.)		
of Salisbury, Apr. 9, 1846, by Rev. D.W. Clark	3	101
HAWLEY, Hannah, of Sharon, m. Amos **HANCHET**, of Salisbury, Jan. 1, 1761, by Rev. Jonathan Lee	1	249
HAYWARD, Jonas, s. John & Elizabeth, b. Nov. 6, 1758	1	169
HEATH, HETH, Abigail, d. Josiah & Marcy, b. Jan. 21, 1753	1	188
Abigail, d. Josiah & Marcy, d. Oct. 26, 1753	1	228
Elizabeth, d. Josiah & Marcy, b. May 13, 1761	1	116
Hannah, d. Josiah & Marcy, b. Sept. 3, 1744	1	201
Jonathan, s. Josiah & Mercy, d. on or about Apr. [ ], 1760	1	229
Josiah, s. Josiah & Marcy, b. Dec. 5, 1748	1	201
Levina, d. Josiah & Marcy, b. Mar. 26, 1749	1	201
Louis, d. Josiah & Mercy, b. Mar. 22, 1751	1	201
Lois, m. Amasa **HOLCOM[B]**, b. of Salisbury, Oct. 27, 1768, by John Hutchinson, J.P.	2	44
Lucy, d. Josiah & Marcy, b. Mar. 20, 1742	1	201
Mary*, d. Josiah & Marcy, b. July 21, 1755 *("Molly" in Rudd's)	1	116
Mehetabel, d. Josiah & Marcy, b. Dec. 30, 1745	1	201
Mehetable, m. Benjamin **CORY**, b. of Salisbury, Aug. 17, 1769, by Elisha Baker, J.P.	2	45
Mercy, w. Joshua, d. Oct. 28, 1763	1	229
Molle, d. Josiah & Marcey, b. July 21, 1755	1	188
Nathaniel, s. Josiah & Marcy, b. June 19, 1743	1	201
Obadiah, s. Josiah & Marcy, b. Sept. 30, 1757	1	188
Obediah, twin with Jonathan, s. Josiah & Mercy, d. on or about Apr. [ ], 1760	1	229
HEATON, HEATTON, David, s. Benjamin & Mary, of Sharon, b. July 3, 1775	2	10
Sarah, of Ridgefield, m. John **REED**, of Salisbury, Sept. 27, 1757, by Rev. Mr. Ingersoll	1	246
HENMAN, [see under **HINMAN**]		
HENSDILL, [see under **HINSDALE**]		
HERRICK, Jacob, s. Wait & Elizabeth, b. Dec. 24, 1749	1	221
HERVEY, Sally, of Amenia, m. Mylo **SELLECK**, of Salisbury, Oct. 21, 1812, by Isaac Atherton. Witnesses William Sheldon & Abraham Sheldon	3	114
HICOCK, Polly, of Sheffield, m. Lot **NORTON**, Jr., of Salisbury, May 8, 1791, by Rev. Daniel Farrand, of Canaan	3	108
HIDE, [see under **HYDE**]		
HIGGINS, [see also **HUGGINS**], Almirah Lucy*, d. Zadock & Thankfull, b. July 23, 1778 *("Almirah Lucy **HUGGINS**" in Rudd's)	2	35
James*, s. Zadock & Thankfull, b. Jan. 19, 1776 *("James **HUGGINS**" in Rudd's book)	2	35
Melicent*, d. Zadock & Thankfull, b. Aug. 13, 1780 *("Melicent **HUGGINS**" in Rudd's book)	2	35
Zenas*, s.Zadock & Thankfull, b. Dec. 9, 1774 *("Zenas **HUGGINS**" in Rudd's book)	2	35
HIGLEY, Anne, d. Josiah & Hephzibah, b. Oct. 1, 1760	1	176
Charity, d. Josiah, of Oblong & Hephzibah, b. Sept. 13, 1756	1	176

	Vol.	Page
HIGLEY, (cont.)		
John, m. Hephzibah **COLTON***, b. of Salisbury, Nov. 6, 1755, by Rev. Jonathan Lee *("**COTTON**" in Rudd's book)	1	243
HILL, James N., of Canaan, m. Caroline **SURDAM**, of Salisbury, Nov. 10, 1844, by Rev. C.V. Amerman	3	96
HIMAN, [see also **HINMAN**], Sally, m. Adoniram **EVEREST**, Nov. [, 1824?], by Rev. L.E. Lathrop, of Cong. Ch.	3	120
HINE, Alexander, of Waterford, m. Jance C. **PECK**, of Salisbury, Jan. 19, 1835, by Leonard E. Lathrop	3	148
Betsey, of Salisbury, m. Albert **ALLING**, of Sharon, Mar. 12, 1840, by Rev. Thomas Bainbridge	3	159
HINMAN, HENMAN, [see also **HIMAN**], Benjamin, m. Christian **SURDAM**, b. of Salisbury, Nov. 26, 1789, by Rev. Daniell Farrand, of Canaan	3	109
Hiram, s. Benj[ami]n & Christian, b. Apr. 8, 1797	3	16
John Hiram, s. Hiram & Catharine, b. Jan. 16, 1821	3	64
Laura, d. Benjamin & Christian, d. Feb. 1, 1792, ae 6 m.	3	164
Mary, d. Benjamin & Christian, b. June 23, 1794	3	16
Rulandus B., of Binghampton, N.Y., m. Mariette **SELLECK**, of Salisbury, Apr. 30, 1832, by Rev. Stephen Beach, of St. Johns Ch.	3	140
Ziporah, of Lainsborough, m. John **McNIELE**, of Salisbury, Oct. 24, 1769, by Rev. Mr. Collins	2	44
[**HINSDALE**], **HINSDILL**, Amanda, d. Moses & Ruth, b. Jan. 15, 1787	2	27
Betsey, d. Moses & Ruth, b. June 10, 1782	2	27
Betse, d. Moses & Ruth, d. Sept. 26, 1785, in the 4th y. of her age	2	50
Moses, m. Ruth **LORD**, b. of Salisbury, Sept. 16, 1779, by Elisha Baker, J.P.	2	41
Moses, s. Moses & Ruth, b. June 14, 1780	2	27
Moses, s. Moses & Ruth, d. Aug. 6, 1783, in the 4th y. of his age	2	50
Olivia, d. Moses & Ruth, b. Sept. 19, 1784	2	27
Truman, s. Moses & Ruth, b. Oct. 10, 1789	2	27
HODGEKER, Rachel, of New Haven, m. Moses **READ**, of Salisbury, Feb. 19, 1754, by Rev. Jonathan Lee. Witnesses Josiah Lounsbury & Martha Lounsbury	1	242
HOGABOOM, Jane, of Canaan, m. Miles **BRADLEY**, Oct. 17, 1770, by John Hutchinson, J.P.	2	45
HOGAN, Herman, s. James & Hannah, b. Feb. 23, 1793	3	13
John, s. James & Hannah, b. Nov. 22, 1790	3	13
HOLCOMB, HOLCOM, Amasa, m. Lois **HE[A]TH**, b. of Salisbury, Oct. 27, 1768, by John Hutchinson, J.P.	2	44
Eben T., m. Sophia T. **WILLIAMS**, b. of Salisbury, [Nov.] 22, 1835, by Leonard E. Lathrop	3	150
Eunice, w. Amasa, d. Dec. 8, 1767, in the 22nd y. of her age	2	48
Lucius, of Johnston, O., m. Orra **HARRIS**, of Salisbury, Mar. 15, 1837, by Rev. Oliver V. Amerman	3	154
Lucy, m. Joseph **NORTHROP**, Jr., Oct. 3, 1793, by Samuel Lee, J.P.	3	108
Sarah, d. Amasa & Eunice, b. May 25, 1765	2	7
William, s. Amasa & Eunice, b. Apr. 5, 1767	2	7

BARBOUR COLLECTION

	Vol.	Page
HOLLEY, HOLLY, Abigail, m. David **LORD**, Jr., Apr. 27, 1769, by Rev. Jonathan Lee	2	44
Abigail, d. Samuel & Abigail, b. June 3, 1776	2	24
Abigail, w. Samuel, d. Feb. 27, 1782, in the 30th y. of her age	2	50
Alexander H., m. Marcia **COFFING**, Sept. 10, 1835, by Leonard E. Lathrop	3	150
Alexander Hamilton, s. John M. & Sally, b. Aug. 12, 1804	3	48
Anne, d. Samuel & Abigail, b. Nov. 20, 1769	2	24
Caroline, d. Stephen & Lucy, b. Oct. 7, 1785	2	15
Caroline, d. Luther & Sarah, b. May 2, 1800	3	34
Caroline, of Salisbury, m. Thomas T. **WHITTLESEY**, of Danbury, Nov. 29, 1826, by L.E. Lathrop	3	125
Charlotte, d. Stephen & Lucy, b. May 9, 1781, in Canaan	2	15
Daniel, s. Stephen & Patience, b. Apr. 2, 1763	1	116
Diadama, d. Stephen & Mary, b. Sept. 13, 1774	2	15
Edward Nichols, s. Edward O. & Betsey, b. Jan. 16, 1804	3	36
Edward O., see Orville Luther **HOLLEY**	2	39
Edward Oramel, s. Luther & Sarah, b. Feb. 5, 1783	2	39
Francis Newman, s. Newman & Sally, b. May 13, 1807	3	49
Frederick, s. Newman & Sally, b. Feb. 6, 1818	3	49
George W., s. John M. & Sally, b. Feb. 17, 1810	3	48
George W., m. Caroline E. **CHURCH**, b. of Salisbury, Aug. 26, 1833, in St. Johns Ch., by Rev. Lucius M. Purdy	3	144
Hannah, d. Stephen & Patience, b. May 13, 1768	2	14
Hannah, d. John M. & Sally, b. Apr. 8, 1808	3	48
Harriet A., of Salisbury, m. William P. **BURRALL**, of Canaan, [May] 9, [1831], by L.E. Lathrop	3	139
Henry, s. Newman & Sally, b. May 22, 1811	3	49
Horace, s. Luther & Sarah, b. Feb. 13, 1781	2	39
John M., m. Sally **PORTER**, b. of Salisbury, Mar. 9, 1800, by Rev. Joseph W. Crossman	3	113
John Milton, s. John M. & Sally, b. Nov. 10, 1802	3	48
John Milton, see Milton **HOLLEY**	2	39
Josiah, s. Stephen & Patience, b. Jan. 26, 1767	1	116
Levi, s. Stephen & Patience, b. Jan. 15, 1770	2	25
Luther, s. Edward O. & Betsey, b. Apr. 3, 1806	3	36
Maria, d. John Milton & Sally, b. Feb. 19, 1800	3	48
Mary, d. Newman & Sally, b. Feb. 14, 1809	3	49
Mary, d. Newton & Sally, d. July 15, 1812, ae 3 y. 6 m.	3	168
Mary, d. Newman & Sally, b. Mar. 11, 1816	3	49
Mary, of Salisbury, m. F[rederic]k **MILES**, of Goshen, Sept. [ ], 1842, by Rev. S.T. Carpenter	3	162
Mary A., of Salisbury, m. Moses **LYMAN**, of Goshen, May 6, 1834, by Leonard E. Lathrop	3	146
Mary Ann, d. John M. & Sally, b. Apr. 18, 1806	3	48
Mary Ann, d. John M., d. Dec. 20, 1812, ae 6 y. 8 m. 2 d.	3	167
Mary Ann, d. John M. & Sally, b. May 30, 1813	3	60
Mary S., of Salisbury, m. Edwin B. **WILLIAMS**, of New York, June 29, 1847, by Adam Reed	3	101
Milton, s. Luther & Sarah, b. Sept. 7, 1777. "From the 7th of Sept. 1799, the said Milton by consent of his father assumed		

	Vol.	Page
HOLLEY, HOLLY, (cont.)		
the name of John Milton **HOLLEY**."	2	39
Myron, s. Luther & Sarah, b. Apr. 29, 1779	2	39
Newman, s. Luther & Sarah, b. Apr. 17, 1785	2	39
Newman, m. Sally **STILES**, b. of Salisbury, Nov. 17, 1805, by Rev. Joseph W. Crossman	3	112
Orville Luther, s. Luther & Sarah, b. May 19, 1791. "on Feb. 6, 1804, changed his name to Edward O. **HOLLEY**. His parents consenting."	2	39
Phebe, w. Stephen, d. Mar. 1, 1760	1	238
Phebe, of Sharon, m. Ebenezer **HANCHET**, Jr., of Salisbury, Dec. 31, 1767, by Rev. Jonathan Lee	2	44
Ransom, s. Newman & Sally, b. Aug. 8, 1813	3	49
Sally, w. John M., d. Feb. 24, 1816, ae 37 y. 5 m. 14 d.	3	168
Sally P., of Salisbury, m. Samuel S. **ROBINS**, of Canaan, [May 9, 1831], by L.E. Lathrop	3	139
Sally Porter, d. John M. & Sally, b. Sept. 10, 1811	3	48
Samuel, s. Stephen & Patience, b. Oct. 12, 1765	1	116
Samuel, m. Abigail **LEE**, b. of Salisbury, Feb. 21, 1769, by John Hutchinson, J.P.	2	44
Samuel, s. Samuel & Abigail, b. Sept. 22, 1778	2	24
Samuell, of Salisbury, m. Rebecca **TAYLOR**, of Winchester, Jan. 30, 1783, at Winchester, by Rev. Joshua Knapp	2	42
Sarah, d. Stephen, d. June 1, 1763, in the 13th y. of her age	1	238
Sarah, d. Stephen & Patience, b. July 15, 1764	1	116
HOLLISTER, HOLLESTER, Charles, s. Julius & Thankfull, b. Nov. 13, 1811; d. Dec. 4, 1812	3	51
Charles A., m. Maria N. **PIERCE**, b. of Salisbury, Oct. 1, 1839, by Rev. Adam Reid	3	158
Charles Augustus, s. Julius & Thankfull, b. Nov. 22, 1813	3	51
Clarissa, d. Horace & Sarah, b. June 2, 1820	3	78
Clarissa Lucretia, d. Horace & Artemisia, b. Oct. 26, 1832	3	78
Cinthia, d. Isaac, Jr. & Cinthia, b. Apr. 3, 1814; d. Apr. 21, 1814	3	31
Electa, d. Isaac, Jr. & Cynthia, b. Sept. [ ], 1819	3	31
Elizabeth Metcalf, d. Horace & Sarah, b. May 28, 1828	3	78
Horace, s. Horace & Sarah, b. June 3, 1826	3	78
Horace Hutchinson, s. Noah & Olive, b. Sept. 8, 1811	3	54
Isaac, Jr., m. Cynthia **KINGSBURY**, b. of Salisbury, Feb. 19, 1812, by Rev. Joseph W. Crossman	3	114
Julius, m. Thankfull **SPENCER**, b. of Salisbury, Nov. 29, 1810, by Rev. Joseph W. Crossman	3	114
Lee, s. Horace & Sarah, b. Jan. 2, 1823	3	78
Martin Galusha, s. Noah & Olive, b. Mar. 1, 1815	3	54
Noah, m. Olive **HUTCHINSON**, b. of Salisbury, Nov. 22, 1810, by Rev. Joseph W. Crossman	3	113
Richard, m. Phebe **REED**, b. of Salisbury, Dec. 24, 1822, by Charles Prentice	3	118
Sally Betsey, d. Isaac, Jr. & Cynthia, b. Feb. 3, 1813	3	31
Sarah, d. Horace & Sarah, b. Oct. 14, 1824	3	78
Walter, s. Noah & Olive, b. Mar. 15, 1813	3	54
William Davis, s. Isaac, Jr. & Cynthia, b. Mar. 24, 1815	3	31

	Vol.	Page
HOLMES, HOLMS, Alpheas, m. Ada **HURLBUTT**, b. of Salisbury, Nov. 8, 1769, by J. Hutchinson, J.P.	2	44
Asa, s. John, Jr. & Rachel, b. Mar. 2, 1754	1	181
Betsey, d. George & Betsey, b. May 3, 1793	3	14
Byram, s. James, 3rd & Lucy, b. Nov. 7, 1781	2	37
Eber, s. Ezra & Grace, b. July 7, 1792	2	34
Edwin, s. Jehoshaphat & Martha, b. July 27, 1797	3	9
Ezra, s. James & Sarah, b. Mar. 1, 1764	1	128
Ezra, m. Grace **CHITTENDEN**, Nov. 10, 1791, by Samuel Lee, J.P.	3	108
Frederick Augustus, s. Jehoshaphat & Martha, b. July 17, 1795	3	9
George, s. James & Sarah, b. July 12, 1766	2	17
George, m. Betsey **BALL**, Oct. 16, 1788, by Philip Spencer. Witnesses Thomas Mix & Lucy Mix	3	108
Harriet, d. Joshua & Mary, b. Sept. 3, 1797	3	6
Harriet, m. William S. **MORGAN**, b. of Salisbury, Sept. 25, 1839, by Rev. Tho[ma]s Bainbridge	3	158
Horace, s. Joshua & Mary, b. Sept. 11, 1804	3	6
James, m. Sarah **JEWELL**, b. of Salisbury, Apr. 1, 1755, by Rev. Jonathan Lee	1	242
James, s. James & Sarah, b. Feb. 14, 1758	1	128
James, s. James & Sarah, b. June 26, 1770	2	17
James, m. Sarah **STODDARD**, b. of Salisbury, Feb.* 29, 1772, by James Landon, J.P. *("Jan." in Rudd's book)	2	45
James, 3rd, of Salisbury, m. Lucy **BARBER**, of Torrington, June 21, 1780, by Rev. Mr. Marvin, of Torrington	2	41
James, s. Joshua & Mary, b. Oct. 6, 1801	3	6
John, Jr., of Salisbury, m. Rachel **FALLOWS***, of Sheffield, Jan. 21, 1750/1, by Rev. Jonathan Lee *("**FELLOWS**" in Rudd's book)	1	222
John, s. James & Sarah, b. Dec. 6, 1772	2	17
John, d. Sept. 19, 1785, in the 85th y. of his age	2	50
John, m. Mrs. Rachel **BOTSFORD**, Oct. 5, 1796, by Samuel Lee, J.P.	3	111
Joshua, s. Joshua & Mary, b. May 15, 1811	3	6
Julia, of Salisbury, m. Ebenezer W. **BUTLER**, of Clinton, N.Y., Aug. 11, 1836, by Rev. Oliver V. Amerman, of M.E. Ch.	3	152
Lathrop, m. Eunice **EVARTS**, b. of Salisbury, Sept. 11, 1796, by John Whittlesey, J.P.	3	110
Levi, s. James, 3rd & Lucy, b. Dec. 31, 1783	2	37
Lucy, d. James, 3rd & Lucy, b. Dec. 19, 1787	2	37
Manson Jarvis, s. Jehoshaphat & Martha, b. Nov. 1, 1793	3	9
Mary, w. Capt. John, d. Mar. 13, 1761, in the 58th y. of her age	1	237
Mary, d. James & Sarah, b. May 10, 1768	2	17
Mary, w. John, d. Aug. 28, 1785, in the 70th y. of her age	2	50
Mary, d. Joshua & Mary, b. Dec. 25, 1808	3	6
Mary, of Salisbury, m. Ja[me]s **GREEN**, of Covington, N.Y., May 5, 1830, by Rev. Stephen Beach, of St. Johns Ch.	3	136
Minerva, d. John & Rachel, b. Apr. 7, 1799	3	24
Minerva, of Salisbury, m. Samuel A. **BIGELOW**, of Norfolk, Sept. 16, 1823, by Rev. Charles Printice, of Canaan,	3	119

	Vol.	Page
HOLMES, HOLMS, (cont.)		
Myron, s. John & Rachel, b. Feb. 15, 1801	3	24
Phebe, d. James & Sarah, b. Sept. 19, 1776	2	17
Phebe, m. Thomas **CHURCH**, Mar. 12, [1797], by Samuel Lee, J.P.	3	110
Polly, d. Joshua & Mary, b. Dec. 6, 1795	3	6
Sarah, d. James & Sarah, b. Mar. 16, 1756	1	128
Sarah, d. James & Sarah, b. Mar. 16, 1756	1	206
Seth, s. James & Sarah, b. Nov. 30, 1761	1	128
Sophia Evarts, twin with Stephen Northrup, d. Lathrop & Eunice, b. Sept. 9, 1797	3	25
Stephen Northrup, twin with Sophia Evarts, s. Lathrop & Eunice, b. Sept. 9, 1797	3	25
HOPKINS, Benjamin G., of Cornwall, m. Mary B. **STANTON**, of Salisbury, Sept. 6, 1831, by L.E. Lathrop	3	140
HOSFORD, John L., of Canaan, m. Henrietta M. **STRONG**, of Salisbury, Sept. 27, 1829, by Rev. Stephen Beach, of St. Johns Ch.	3	134
HOSKINS, HOSKIN, Amos, s. Daniel & Sarah, b. July 8, 1768	2	19
An[n]a, d. Daniel & Sarah, b. Nov. 2, 1769	2	19
Daniel, s Daniel & Sarah, b. July 31, 1766	1	115
Dorcase, d. Micah & Abigail, b. May 22, 1762; d. Jan. 5, 1766	1	132
Lucy, d. Daniel & Sarah, b. Oct. 2, 1772	2	19
Nancy, d. Daniel & Sarah, b. Feb. 16, 1776	2	19
Noah, s. Asa & Sarah, b. July 31, 1784	2	15
Rachel, d. Daniel & Sarah, b. Apr. 14, 1774	2	19
Roswel, s. Micah & Abigail, b. Dec. 14, 1766	1	132
Silas, s. Benoni & Mehettabel, b. May 8, 1767	1	191
HOTCHKISS, Miles, of Cheshire, m. Sarah **BEARD**, of Sharon, Jan. 31, 1841, by Rev. Andrew M. Smith, of North East, N.Y.	3	160
HOUGH, Abigail, of Canaan, m. John **GILLET**, of Salisbury, Nov. 14, 1754, by John Beebe, J.P.	1	242
HOUSE, Hannah, m. Seth **CARY**, b. of Salisbury, Feb. 28, 1750/1, by Rev. Jonathan Lee	1	223
HOUSON, John, m. Anna Eliza **BALLOU**, b. of Salisbury, May 28, 1848, by Rev. Jonathan Lee	3	103
HOWES, HOWS, Benjamin, m. Rachel **CAMP**, b. of Salisbury, on or about July 8, 1784, by Rev. Jonathan Lee. Witnesses Mylo Lee & Ruth Lee	3	108
Benjamin, s. Benjamin & Rachel, b. Apr. 6, 1787	2	25
Electa, d. Benjamin & Rachel, b. Feb. 11, 1795	2	25
Martha, d. Benjamin & Rachel, b. July 29, 1789	2	25
William, s. Benjamin & Rachel, b. Apr. 24, 1785	2	25
HUBBARD, Charles Kirby, s. Horace K. & Sophia W., b. Jan. 17, 1822	3	79
Henry, s. Horace K. & Sophia W., b. Oct. 20, 1823	3	79
Jane, d. Horace K. & Sophia W., b. Apr. 27, 1828	3	79
John H., m. Julia A. **DODGE**, b. of Salisbury, May 2, 1830, by Leonard E. Lathrop	3	136
Joseph A., m. Daphna **BUSHNELL**, Feb. 9, 1823, by Martin Strong, J.P.	3	118
Lavinia, of Salisbury, m. James **WELCH**, M.D., of		

	Vol.	Page
HUBBARD, (cont.)		
Sandisfield, [May 18, 1831], by L.E. Lathrop	3	139
Maritta, of Salisbury, m. Daniel **FRISBIE**, of Norfolk, May 14, 1844, by Rev. Adam Reid	3	163
Mary Ann, m. Lewis **JUDD**, b. of Salisbury, Sept. 17, 1834, by Leonard E. Lathrop	3	147
Mary S., of Salisbury, m. Hiram **PULVER**, of Amenia, N.Y., Mar. 9, 1846, by Rev. Jonathan Lee	3	97
Mary Sophia, d. Horace K. & Sophia W., b. Feb. 14, 1826	3	79
Milton, m. Mary **RUSSELL**, b. of Salisbury, Oct. 23, 1828, by Leonard E. Lathrop	3	132
Sarah, of Salisbury, m. Samuel **HUMPHREY**, of Oswell, Rutland Cty., Vt., Dec. 27, 1825, by Eliphalet Whittlesey, J.P.	3	123
Sarah L., of Salisbury, m. Freeman P. **STODDARD**, of Sharon, July 2, [1839], by Adam Reid	3	159
Sarah Lewis, d. Horace K. & Sophia W., b. Feb. 2, 1820	3	79
HUBET, Patty, m. Luther **LANDON**, b. of Salisbury, May 16, 1809, by Rev. Joseph W. Crossman	3	113
HUGGINS, [see also **HIGGINS**], Almirah Lucy*, d. Zadock & Thankfull, b. July 23, 1778 *(Arnold Copy has "Almirah Lucy **HIGGINS**")	2	35
James*, s. Zadock & Thankfull, b. Jan. 19, 1776 *(Arnold Copy has "James **HIGGINS**")	2	35
Melicent, d. Zadock & Thankfull, b. Aug. 13, 1780 *(Arnold Copy has "Melicent **HIGGINS**")	2	35
Zadock, of Salisbury, m. Thankfull **HUTCHINSON**, of Sharon, Apr. 7, 1774, by Rev. Cotton Mather Smith	2	46
Zadoc & Thankfull, had s. [ ], d. Jan. 19, 1775	2	49
Zenas*, s. Zadock & Thankfull, b. Dec. 9, 1774 *(Arnold Copy has "Zenas **HIGGINS**")	2	35
Zenas, s. Zadock & Thankfull, d. Jan. 19, 1775	2	49
HULL, [see also **HALL**], Cloe, d. Jonathan & Susanna, b. July 5, 1758; d. Sept. 1, 1758	1	177
Daniel, s. Daniel & Susanah, b. Nov. 6, 1757	1	129
Daniel*, m. Rebeckah **KELSEY**, b. of Salisbury, Nov. 5, 1774, by Rev. Jonathan Lee *(Arnold Copy has "Daniel **HALL**")	2	46
Darius*, s. Jonathan & Susanah, b. Jan. 8, 1777 *(Arnold Copy has "Darius **HALL**")	2	9
Electa*, m. Solomon **DIMMICK**, b. of Salisbury, Jan. 18, 1781, by Rev. Jonathan Lee *(Arnold Copy has "Electa **HALL**")	2	41
Giles, m. Electe **BIRD**, b. of Salisbury, Mar. 16, 1775, by John Hutchinson, J.P.	2	46
Harriet, d. Henry & Rebecca, b. Nov. 20, 1785	2	35
Heman*, s. Jonathan & Susannah, b. July 10, 1769 *(Arnold Copy has "Heman **HALL**")	2	9
Herman, m. Polly **STANTON**, Sept. 19, 1790, by Samuel Lee, J.P.	3	108
Jehiel, d. Sept. 2, 1759	1	229
John F.*, s. Daniel & Rebeckah, b. July 26, 1775 *(Arnold Copy has "John F. **HALL**")	2	8
Jonathan, s. Jonathan & Susanna, b. Nov. 19, 1761	1	177

SALISBURY VITAL RECORDS 207

	Vol.	Page
HULL, (cont.)		
Lemuel Sheldon, s. Jonathan & Susannah, b. Mar. 31, 1765	1	177
Leverett*, see Leverett KULL		
Lot*, s. Jonathan & Susannah, b. June 6, 1775 *(Arnold Copy has "Lot HALL")	2	9
Mabel, d. Daniel & Susanah, b. Oct. 22, 1762	1	129
Moore Bird, s. Giles & Electa, b. Dec. 7, 1776	2	36
Moses, s. Daniel & Susanah, b. Oct. 24, 1760	1	129
Rachel, d. Jonathan & Susanna, b. May 27, 1759	1	177
Salome*, d. Jonathan & Susannah, b. Feb. 27, 1771 *(Arnold Copy has "Salome HALL")	2	9
Samuel*, s. Jonathan & Susan[n]ah, b. Aug. 22, 1772 *(Arnold Copy has "Samuel HALL")	2	9
Sarah*, d. Jonathan & Susannah, b. Jan. 6, 1768 *(Arnold Copy has "Sarah HALL")	2	9
Sarah, m. Jeremiah DAUCHY, June or July 12, 1787, by Rev. Jonathan Lee. Witnesses James Folliet & Ezra Selleck	2	50
Susannah, d. Daniel & Susannah, b. July 16, 1764	1	129
Susannah, w. Daniel, d. Mar. 9, 1774, in the 52nd y. of her age	2	49
William, s. Jonathan & Susanah, b. Oct. 10, 1763	1	177
HUMPHREY, Asahel, m. Victoria LYMAN, b. of Salisbury, Nov. 25, 1841, by Rev. Adam Reid	3	161
Griswold, m. Olive JONES, b. of Salisbury, Nov. 3, 1841, by Rev. Adam Reid	3	161
Keziah, of Salisbury, m. Ebenezer MAXFIELD, of Nelson, O., Apr. 22, 1822, by Lavius Hyde	3	116
Samuel, of Oswell, Rutland Cty., Vt., m. Sarah HUBBARD, of Salisbury, Dec. 27, 1825, by Eliphalet Whittlesey, J.P.	3	123
HUNT, John, of Canaan, m. Mary WILLIAMS, of Salisbury, Mar. 11, 1829, by Rev. Noah Bigelow. Int. Pub.	3	80a
John, of Canaan, m. Mary WILLIAMS, of Salisbury, Mar. 11, 1829, by Noah Bigelow. Int. Pub.	3	104
John, of Canaan, m. Mary WILLIAMS, of Salisbury, Mar. 11, 1829, by Rev. Noah Bigelow. Int. Pub.	3	133
Minerva L., of Canaan, m. Albert BRADLEY, of Torrington, Sept. 21, 1828, by Rev. Stephen Beach, of St. Johns Ch.	3	131
HURD, Eunice, m. Gideon SMITH, b. of Salisbury, Oct. 26, 1794, by Samuel Lee, J.P.	3	109
Love, of Woodbury, m. Phinehas CHAPIN, of Salisbury, May 14, 1783, by Rev. Mr. Benedict, of Woodbury	2	42
HURLBUTT, Ada, m. Alpheas HOLMES, b. of Salisbury, Nov. 8, 1769, by J. Hutchinson, J.P.	2	44
HUTCHINSON, Abijah, of Lebanon, m. Meriam FARNUM, of Salisbury, Feb. 27, 1783, by Abiel Camp, J.P.	2	42
Allice, d. John & Temperance, b. Feb. 12, 1749/50; d. Feb. 19, 1749/50	1	208
Alice, d. Daniel & Esther, b. Nov. 13, 1783	2	14
Alma, d. Asa & Lydia, b. May 1, 1797	3	5
Alma, d. Myron & Mary, b. July 21, 1829	3	81
Amos, s. Hezekiah & Phebe, b. Dec. 24, 1782	2	38
Asa, s. John & Temperance, b. June 12, 1753	1	208

	Vol.	Page

HUTCHINSON, (cont.)

	Vol.	Page
Asa, m. Lydia **GALUSHA**, b. of Salisbury, Oct. 19, 1786, by Rev. Jonathan Lee	2	43
Asa, m. Mary **ADAM**, b. of Salisbury, Apr. 17, 1804, by Rev. Joseph W. Crossman	3	112
Asa, of Salisbury, m. Hannah **MARTIN**, of Tyringham, May 10, 1807, by Rev. Joseph W. Crossman	3	112
Caroline, d. Myron & Mary, b. Dec. 14, 1831	3	81
Daniel, s. John & Temperance, b. Feb. 10, 1759	1	208
Daniel, of Salisbury, m. Esther **BABCOCK**, of Canaan, July 18, 1782, at Canaan, by Rev. Daniel Farrand	2	42
Elijah, s. Asa & Lydia, b. Dec. 2, 1790	2	31
Elijah, s. Asa & Lydia, d. Oct. 4, 1804, in the 14th y. of his age	3	165
George W., m. Lucy A. **BRIGGS**, b. of Salisbury, July 7, 1847, by Rev. W.H. Ferris	3	101
Graham Herd, s. Myron & Mary, b. Apr. 9, 1834	3	81
Hannah, d. John & Temperance, b. Dec. 9, 1745; d. Mar. 12, 1746/7	LR1	355
Hannah, w. Asa, d. July 31, 1832, in the 72nd y. of her age	3	168
Hephzibah, d. John & Temperance, b. Feb. 28, 1743/4; d. Jan. 2, 1746/7	LR1	353
Hephzabah, wid., d. Oct. 26, 1777, ae 93 y. 10 m. [ ] d.	2	49
Hezekiah, m. Phebe **FARNUM**, b. of Salisbury, Jan. 4, 1776, by John Hutchinson, J.P.	2	46
Horace, s. Asa & Lydia, b. July 3, 1787	2	31
James, s. John & Temperance, b. June 23, 1751	1	208
James, s. Asa & Lydia, b. Jan. 20, 1795	2	31
John, s. John & Temperance, d. Oct. 19, 1760, in the 19th y. of his age, a soldier at the Jarman Flatts, on his return from Oswego	1	231
John, d. Apr. 26, 1780, in the 69th y. of his age	2	49
Lemuel, s. Thomas, Jr. & Abigail, b. May 15, 1771	2	18
Luke, s. Thomas, Jr. & Abigail, b. Jan. 10, 1769	2	18
Lydia, d. Asa & Lydia, b. Jan. 4, 1799	3	5
Lydia, w. Asa, d. Aug. 11, 1802, in the 41st y. of her age	3	165
Marcia Maria, d. Myron & Mary, b. Dec. 10, 1827	3	81
Mary, d. John & Temperance, b. Oct. 14, 1760	1	208
Mary, m. Elisha **PARMELEE**, Oct. 27, 1782, by Amzi Lewis, V.D.M.	2	42
Mary, d. Asa & Lydia, b. Oct. 11, 1792	2	31
Mary, w. Asa, d. Oct. 24, 1805, in the 38th y. of her age	3	166
Mary, of Salisbury, m. Epaphras **LYMAN**, of Andover, O., Oct. 6, 1826, by L.E. Lathrop	3	124
Melinda, daughter-in-law of Asa & d. of Noah & Hannah **MARTIN**, late of Tyringham, d. Mar. 16, 1809, ae 75	3	166
Myron, s. Asa & Lydia, b. July 26, 1802	3	5
Myron, m. Mary **SMITH**, b. of Salisbury, [Jan.] 4, 1827, by Leonard E. Lathrop	3	126
Olive, d. Hezekiah & Phebe, b. May 28, 1781	2	38
Olive, d. Asa & Lydia, b. Feb. 27, 1789	2	31
Olive, m. Noah **HOLLISTER**, b. of Salisbury, Nov. 22, 1810, by		

	Vol.	Page
HUTCHINSON, (cont.)		
Rev. Joseph W. Crossman	3	113
Phebe, d. Hezekiah & Phebe, b. Nov. 16, 1785	2	38
Polly, d. Hezekiah & Phebe, b. Nov. 1, 1778	2	38
Sarah, d. Daniel & Esther, b. June 3, 1786	2	14
Temperance, d. June 14, 1781, in the 66th y. of her age	2	49
Thankfull, of Sharon, m. Zadock **HUGGINS**, of Salisbury, Apr. 7, 1774, by Rev. Cotton Mather Smith	2	46
Thomas, s. John & Temperance, b. Mar. 31, 1748	1	208
Thomas, d. Feb. 27, 1787, in the 74th y. of his age	2	50
Timothy, s. Hezekiah & Phebe, b. Apr. 29, 1777	2	38
----------, d. Feb. 27, 1778, in the 27th y. of his age	2	49
[HYDE], HIDE, Joshua, s. Joshua & Esther, b. Mar. 26, 1773	2	30
INGERSOLL, William T., of Amenia, N.Y., m. Mary H. **HARRISON**, of Salisbury, Jan. 1, 1839, by Adam Reid	3	157
ISBELL, ISBEL, Asenath, d. Noah & Jerusha, b. Dec. 13, 1767	1	156
Eli, s. Noah & Jerusha, b. Sept. 27, 1760	1	156
Hannah, d. Noah & Jerusha, b. Mar. 5, 1763	1	156
Nathan, s. Noah & Jerusha, b. July 30, 1765	1	156
IVES, Betsey, d. David & Elizabeth, b. July 24, 1775, in Hoosick	2	20
David, s. David & Elizabeth, b. June 22, 1781	2	20
James, s. David & Elizabeth, b. July 17, 1779	2	20
Jared, s. David & Elizabeth, b. May 15, 1777, in Hoosick	2	20
JACKSON, Hannah, m. Daniel **FORGASON**, b. of Salisbury, Jan. 15, 1758, by James Landon, J.P.	2	45
Henry, of New Milford, m. Mary **EVEREST**, of Salisbury, Jan. 8, 1822, by Lavius Hyde	3	116
Henry, of Ripley, N.Y., m. Betsey **DOOLITTLE**, of Salisbury, Sept. 19, 1834, by Leonard E. Lathrop	3	147
Lois, m. David **EVEREST**, b. of Salisbury, June 18, 1761, by John Hutchinson, J.P.	1	249
JACOBS, Adonijah, s. David & Mary, b. Mar. 27, 1751	1	202
Adonijah, of Salisbury, m. Elizabeth **LOOMIS**, of Lebanon, Jan. 24, 1772, by Uriah Lawrence, J.P.	2	45
Archillus, s. David & Ruth, b. Feb. 12, 1767	1	107
Benajah & Elizabeth, had twin d. [ ], s.b. July 5, 1773	2	48
Charlotte, d. Samuel & Polly, b. Nov. 5, 1795	3	30
David, d. Nov. 3, 1758	1	231
David, m. Ruth **TUPPER**, Jr., b. of Salisbury, Aug. 31, 1763, by John Hutchinson, J.P.	1	251
Dyer, s. Zuriel & Rhoda, b. Jan. 26, 1773; d. May 22, 1775	2	36
Eliakim, s. David & Ruth, b. Nov. 14, 1765* *("March 20, 1764" in Rudd's book)	1	107
Hannah, d. Zuriel & Rhoda, b. May 5, 1769	2	36
Isaac H., m. Huldah **BARNS**, b. of Salisbury, Feb. 10, 1822, by Lavius Hyde	3	116
John Hollenbeck, s. Hyman & Lucretia, b. Oct. 20, 1812	3	56
Jonathan, m. Sarah **CLARK**, b. of Salisbury, Apr. 20, 1768, by Rev. Jonathan Lee	2	44
Jonathan, s. Rosannah, b. Apr. 5, 1769	2	31
Jonathan, s. Benjamin*, d. Mar. 2, 1775, in the 6th y. of his		

	Vol.	Page
JACOBS, (cont.)		
age *("Rosanna" in Rudd's book)	2	49
Joseph, s. Zuriel & Rhoda, b. Oct. 5, 1775	2	36
Joshua F., m. Lavenia **WOODIN**, b. of Salisbury, Apr. 6, 1831, by Rev. Stephen Beach, of St. Johns Ch.	3	138
Joshua Fitch, s. Samuel & Polly, b. Oct. 16, 1798	3	30
Levi, s. Jonathan & Sarah, b. Feb. 15, 1771	2	9
Lucretia, w. Hinman, d. Sept. 11, 1821, in the 51st y. of her age	3	168
Lydia, d. Adonijah & Eunice, b. May 5, 1773	2	33
Mary, d. Zuriel & Rhoda, b. Oct. 28, 1765	1	144
Mary, d. Jonathan & Sarah, b. May 7, 1769	2	9
Olive, d. Zuriel & Rhoda, b. June 29, 1767; d. Apr. 10, 1775, in the 8th y. of her age	2	36
Olive, d. Jonathan & Sarah, b. Dec. 21, 1777	2	9
Phebe, d. Zuriel & Rhoda, b. Mar. 17, 1764	1	144
Rhoda, d. Zuriel & Rhoda, b. Apr. 30, 1761	1	144
Rosannah, had s. Jonathan, b. Apr. 5, 1769	2	31
Roxanna, m. John **FRAME**, b. of Salisbury, Sept. 2, 1773, by John Hutchinson, J.P.	2	45
Sally, m. Samuel **BUSHNELL**, Nov. 27, 1822, by Charles Printice	3	117
Sarah, d. Zuriel & Rhoda, b. Feb. 1, 1763	1	144
Sarah, d. Jonathan & Sarah, b. Feb. 21, 1775	2	9
Theresa*, d. Zuriel & Rhoda, b. Jan. 28, 1771, in Sharon *("Therzy" in Rudd's book)	2	36
[**JACQUES**], **JAQUA, JACQUA**, Asahel, s. Aaron & Rebekah, b. Apr. 9, 1752	1	196
Bephnon*, m. Thomas **TUPPER**, b. of Salisbury, Sept. 20, 1768, by John Hutchinson, J.P. *(Salisbury printed records "Pertenia")	2	44
Betsey, m. William **TUPPER**, b. of Salisbury, July 13, 1775, by Rev. Jonathan Lee	2	47
Betty, d. Aaron & Rebeckah, b. Sept. 11, 1759	1	196
Hannah, d. Aaron & Rebeckah, b. Aug. 8, 1747	1	196
Parthena, d. Aaron & Rebeckah, b. Aug. 17, 1749	1	196
Pertenia, see Bephnon **JOQUA**	2	44
Rebecca, d. Aaron & Rebecca, b. Oct. 8, 1761	1	196
Sherman, of Canaan, m. Mary Ann **BUNCE**, of Salisbury, Oct. 27, 1834, by Leonard E. Lathrop	3	147
Simon, s. Aaron & Rebekah, b. June 11, 1754	1	196
JESTEN*, Mary, m. Elijah **SKINNER**, b. of Salisbury, Dec. 30, 1756, by Rev. Daniel Farrin, of Canaan, *("**JOSLEN**" in Rudd's book)	1	245
JEWELL, JEWEL, [see also **JEWIT**], Aaron, s. Nathaniell, Jr. & Rachel, b. Feb. 28, 1764	1	152
Abi, d. Joshua & Mary, b. July 6, 1745, in Cornwall	1	182
Abi, d. Ebenezer & Ann, b. Apr. 18, 1771	2	21
Abi, d. Joshua, Jr. & Lucy, b. Nov. 18, 1784	2	21
Abigail, d. Nathaniell, Jr. & Rachel, b. May 26, 1773	2	22
Amy, d. Oliver & Ame, b. Dec. 17, 1790	2	25
Amy, w. Oliver, d. Oct. 5, 1791, in the 45th y. of her age	2	50

	Vol.	Page
JEWELL, JEWEL, (cont.)		
Andrew, s. Oliver & Ame, b. Sept. 19, 1779	2	25
Andrew, s. Oliver & Ame, b. Aug. 30, 1788	2	25
Andrew, m. Amelia **EVEREST**, b. of Salisbury, Apr. 8, 1835, by Leonard E. Lathrop	3	148
Ann, m. James **WATEROUS**, b. of Salisbury, Nov. 6, 1766, by Rev. Jonathan Lee	2	44
Anna, d. Joseph & Mary, b. May 25, 1787	2	31
Anne, d. Joshua & Mary, b. May 25, 1747, in Cornwall	1	182
Anne, d. Ebenezer & Ann, b. Sept. 29, 1765	1	174
Bette, d. David & Christian, b. Sept. 29, 1751	1	214
Bettey, d. Jonathan & Bettey, b. Mar. 30, 1772	2	7
Bettey, m. David **SPAFFORD**, b. of Salisbury, Jan. 22, 1778, by Rev. Jonathan Lee	2	41
Caroline, d. Andrew & Eliza, b. Sept. 2, 1826	3	70
Caroline, m. James W. **PARKS**, b. of Salisbury, Dec. 2, 1846, by Rev. Adam Reed	3	100
Clarinda, d. Oliver, Jr. & Clarinda, b. Oct. 31, 1789	2	18
Cyrene, d. Rachel, b. Feb. 2, 1783	2	23
Cyrus, s. Oliver & Ame, b. Dec. 25, 1781	2	25
Darius, s. Oliver & Ame, b. May 31, 1784	2	25
Darius, s. Oliver & Ann, d. Apr. 21, 1801, ae 17	3	164
David, s. Nathaniell, Jr. & Rachel, b. Feb. 24, 1771	2	22
David, s. Oliver & Phebe, b. Jan. 29, 1772	2	25
Dorcas, d. Ebenezer & Ann, b. Aug. 2, 1767	1	174
Ebenezer, m. Ann **NORTON**, b. of Salisbury, July 28, 1757, by Rev. Jonathan Lee	1	246
Ebenezer, s. Ebenezer & Ann, b. Dec. 14, 1759	1	174
Ebenezer, m. Sarah **BUTTON**, late of Norwich, Nov. 11, 1781, at Norwich, by Jonathan Brewster, J.P.	2	41
Ebenezer, s. Joseph & Mary, b. Feb. 8, 1789	2	31
Elias, s. Joseph & Mary, b. June 22, 1791	2	31
Eliphalet, s. Joshua & Mary, b. Nov. 22, 1736, in Plainfield	1	182
Eliphalet*, of Salisbury, m. Abigail **WHITNEY**, of Canaan, Sept. 20, 1757, by Rev. Daniel Ferris *(Arnold Copy has "Eliphalet **TRUMBLE**")	1	246
Eliphalet, s. Oliver & Phebe, b. Sept. 2, 1769	2	25
Eliza, d. Andrew & Eliza, b. Sept. 14, 1822	3	70
Elizabeth, d. Joseph & Mary, b. Dec. 16, 1784	2	31
Emily, d. Andrew & Eliza, b. Sept. 23, 1824	3	70
Ephraim, s. Joseph & Mary, b. Feb. 12, 1776; d. Feb. 21, 1776	2	31
Esther, d. Ebenezer & Ann, b. Sept. 5, 1761	1	174
Ezra, s. Oliver & Ame, b. Jan. 27, 1786	2	25
Frederick, s. Andrew & Eliza, b. Oct. 2, 1830	3	70
Hannah, d. Oliver & Phebe, b. Nov. 11, 1761	1	111
Hannah, m. John **CAMP**, b. of Salisbury, Jan. 23, 1772, by Rev. Jonathan Lee	2	46
Hannah, d. Ebenezer & Ann, b. July 12, 1773	2	21
Hannah, d. Joseph & Mary, b. May 27, 1777	2	31
Heman, s. Oliver, Jr. & Clarinda, b. June 30, 1788	2	18
Henry C., m. Mary Ann **RUSSELL**, Oct. 1, 1833, by L.E. Lathrop	3	144

JEWELL, JEWEL, (cont.)

	Vol.	Page
Jesse, s. David & Christian, b. Feb. 15, 1754	1	214
Joel, s. Joseph & Mary, b. Mar. 1, 1782	2	31
John, s. Nathaniell & Rachel, b. Jan. 18, 1769	2	22
John, s. Oliver & Ame, b. Nov. 2, 1777	2	25
John, m. wid. Elizabeth **CHAPIN**, Jan. 21, 1801, by Samuel Lee, J.P.	3	114
Jonathan, s. David & Christian, b. June 2, 1749	1	214
Jonathan, s. Oliver & Phebe, b. June 30, 1764	1	111
Joseph, m. Mary **CRANE**, b. of Salisbury, Feb. 23, 1775, by Rev. Jonathan Lee	2	46
Joseph, s. Joseph & Mary, b. Oct. 7, 1780	2	31
Joshua, s. Joshua & Mary, b. May 14, 1741, in Cornwall	1	182
Joshua, s. Oliver & Phebe, b. Dec. 26, 1775	2	25
Joshua, Jr., of Salisbury, m. Lucy **MURPHEY**, late of Susqueehannah, Mar. 25, 1779, by Rev. Jonathan Lee	2	41
Joshua, Ens., d. Oct. 19, 1789, ae 76	2	50
Lucy, d. Nathaniel, Jr. & Rachel, b. Apr. 5, 1761	1	152
Lucy, d. Joshua, Jr. & Lucy, b. June 28, 1780	2	21
Lucy, wid., of Salisbury, m. David **SMITH**, of Wyoming, Feb. 8, 1789, by Samuel Lee, J.P.	2	43
Marcus, s. Oliver, Jr. & Clarinda, b. Sept. 6, 1792	2	18
Maria, d. Andrew & Eliza, b. Oct. 4, 1828	3	70
Mary, d. Joshua & Mary, b. July 12, 1743, in Cornwall	1	182
Mary, d. Joshua, Jr. & Lucy, b. Apr. 2, 1782	2	21
Mary, wid. Ens. Joshua, d. Apr. 4, 1801, ae 85	3	164
Mary, d. Andrew & Eliza, b. Nov. 23, 1820	3	70
Mary, m. George C. **DODGE**, b. of Salisbury, Mar. 16, 1842, by Rev. Adam Reid	3	162
Minerva, m. Walhan **PECK**, Jan. 24, 1826, by L.E. Lathrop	3	124
Myron, s. Oliver, Jr. & Clarinda, b. May 17, 1794	2	18
Nathaniell, s. Nathaniell & Rachel, b. Sept. 17, 1762	1	152
Nathaniell, m. Elizabeth **CRANE**, b. of Salisbury, Jan. 1, 1789, by Adonijah Strong, J.P.	2	50
Oliver, s. Joshua & Mary, b. Mar. 14, 1739, in Plainfield	1	182
Oliver, s. Oliver & Phebe, b. July 7, 1766	1	111
Oliver, of Salisbury, m. Amey **STEVENS**, of Canaan, Feb. 23, 1777, by Elisha Baker, J.P.	2	47
Oliver, Jr., of Salisbury, m. Clarinda **CHITTENDEN**, of Canaan, Mar. 3, 1788, by Elisha Baker, J.P.	2	50
Oliver, m. Mary E. **WATTON**, b. of Salisbury, Oct. 6, 1841, by Rev. Adam Reid	3	161
Olivia, s. Andrew & Eliza, b. Sept. 2, 1819	3	70
Phebe, w. Oliver, d. Dec. 27, 1775, in the 35th y. of her age	2	49
Polly, d. Joseph & Mary, b. May 5, 1779	2	31
Polly, d. Ebenezer & Sarah, b. Nov. 21, 1783	2	9
Rachel, d. Nathaniell, Jr. & Rachel, b. July 1, 1766	1	152
Rachel, had d. Cyrene, b. Feb. 2, 1783	2	23
Reuben, s. Ebenezer & Ann, b. May 22, 1769	2	21
Sally, d. Nathaniell & Rachel, b. Sept. 30, 1784; d. Jan. 16, 1785	2	22
Sally, d. Oliver, Jr. & Clarinda, b. Dec. 24, 1790	2	18

	Vol.	Page
JEWELL, JEWEL, (cont.)		
Samuel, s. Nathaniell & Rachel, b. Aug. 14, 1781	2	22
Sarah, d. Joshua & Mary, b. Aug. 19, 1734, in Plainfield	1	182
Sarah, m. James **HOLMS**, b. of Salisbury, Apr. 1, 1755, by Rev. Jonathan Lee	1	242
Sarah, d. Ebenezer & Ann, b. May 21, 1758	1	174
Sarah, d. Nathaniell & Rachel, b. May 16, 1779	2	22
Sarah, d. Nathaniell & Rachel, b. May 16, 1779; d. May 20, 1782	2	22
Sarah, m. James **RENNOLDS**, b. of Salisbury, June 6, 1783, by Rev. Jonathan Lee. Witnesses Oliver Jewell, Jr., & George Holmes	3	108
Solomon, s. Nathaniell, Jr. & Rachel, b. Dec. 12, 1775	2	22
Thankfull, d. Ebenezer & Ann, b. Dec. 1, 1763	1	174
JEWIT, [see also **JEWELL**], John, of Sharon, m. Julia Ann **STEVENS**, of Salisbury, Apr. 15, 1832, by Rev. Stephen Beach, of St. Johns Ch.	3	140
JOHNS, Daniel Jabez, s. Daniel & Ruth, b. Mar. 18, 1797, at Alford	3	16
JOHNSON, [see also **JOHNSTON**], Abigail, of New Milford, m. John **WHITTLESEY**, Jr., of Salisbury, May 24, 1792, by Rev. Jeremiah Day, of New Preston	3	109
Daniel, s. John & Sibel, b. July 13, 1773	2	14
Daniel, m. Mary S. **BARNETT**, b. of Salisbury, May 2, 1841, by Rev. J. Shaw	3	161
Henry E., m. Ersula **CHAPMAN**, b. of Salisbury, Dec. 25, 1835, by Rev. Lucius M. Purdy, of St. Johns Ch.	3	151
Herman, s. Daniel & Molly, b. Oct. 27, 1789	3	7
James, s. James & Lydia, b. June 28, 1786	2	39
Newton, s. Archaball & Rebecka, b. Sept. 12, 1791	3	8
Sarah, d. James & Lydia, b. Dec. 17, 1781	2	39
Walter, s. James & Lydia, b. Oct. 15, 1780	2	39
Walter, m. Betsey **LANDON**, b. of Salisbury, Jan. 6, 1803, by Adonijah Strong, J.P.	3	112
JOHNSTON, [see also **JOHNSON**], Lydia, w. Capt. James, d. Feb. 25, 1804, ae 48	3	165
JONES, Abijah, m. Sarah **KNIGHT**, b. of Salisbury, May 23, 1776, by John Hutchinson, J.P.	2	47
Adaline, m. Noadiah **WARNER**, b. of Salisbury, Sept. 13, 1836, by Rev. Oliver V. Amerman, of M.E. Ch.	3	152
Albert C., of Poughkeepsie, N.Y., m. Celesta E. **HARRIS**, of Salisbury, Oct. 28, 1846, in St. Johns Church, by Rev. G. Huntington Nicholls. Int. Pub.	3	99
Almon Thomas, s. Benjamin & Sally, b. May 29, 1814	3	63
Amasa, s. Zipporah, b. Dec. 25, 1782	3	28
Edmund Storer, twin with Edwin Lines, s. Benjamin & Sally, b. Apr. 27, 1807, in Sheffield	3	63
Edwin Lines, twin with Edmund Storer, s. Benjamin & Sally, b. Apr. 27, 1807, in Sheffield	3	63
Esther Mariah, d. Benjamin & Sally, b. Dec. 10, 1798, in Sheffield	3	63
Hamilton Benjamin, s. Benjamin & Sally, b. July 29, 1804, in Sheffield	3	63
Hamilton J., m. Eady **WENTWORTH**, b. of Salisbury, Nov. 5,		

	Vol.	Page
JONES, (cont.)		
1838, by Rev. Thomas Bainbridge	3	156
Hannah Eliza, d. Benjamin & Sally, b. Sept. 9, 1809, in Sheffield	3	63
Jarvis, m. Eloiza **GAY**, b. of Salisbury, Jan. 7, 1840, by Adam Reid	3	159
John Wood, s. Benjamin & Sally, b. Sept. 7, 1811, in Sheffield	3	63
Meritt S., m. Sally **CLARK**, May 8, 1836, by Rev. A. Bushnell	3	152
Olive, m. Griswold **HUMPHREY**, b. of Salisbury, Nov. 3, 1841, by Rev. Adam Reid	3	161
Orr, s. Zipporah, b. June 23, 1789	3	28
Sally Sophronia, d. Benj[ami]n & Sally, b. Aug. 1, 1800, in Sheffield	3	63
Sally Sophronia, m. Ira **ADAMS**, b. of Salisbury, Apr. 27, 1823, by Rev. Charles Prentice, of Canaan	3	119
William, m. Caroline **FOSTER**, b. of Salisbury, Oct. 5, 1842, by Rev. Adam Reid	3	162
William, m. Jane Matilda **STODDARD**, b. of Salisbury, Oct. 16, 1846, by D.W. Clark	3	100
Zipporah, had s. Amasa, b. Dec. 25, 1782 & s. Orr, b. June 23, 1789	3	28
JOSLIN, JOCELYN, Anna, d. Darius & Sibel, b. Aug. 24, 1780, in Tyringham, Mass.	3	28
Anna, m. Thomas **CARTER**, b. of Salisbury, Apr. 13, 1800, by Samuel Lee, J.P.	3	112
Darius, s. Elias H. & Electa, b. June 13, 1832	3	79
Dolly, d. Darius & Sibel, b. Mar. 3, 1793, in Tyringham, Mass.	3	28
Elias Herrick, see Elias Tennent **JOSLIN**	3	28
Elias Tennent*, s. Darius & Sibel, b. Mar. 6, 1788, in Tyringham, Mass. *(On Apr. 17, 1813, name changed to "Elias Herrick")	3	28
Ellen Elizabeth, d. Elias H. & Electa, b. Dec. 22, 1828	3	79
Fanny, d. Darius & Sibel, b. Aug. 30, 1796	3	28
Harriet, of Salisbury, m. Samuel J. **TOWNSEND**, of Tyringham, May 7, 1843, by Rev. Adam Reid	3	163
Harriet Hollister, d. Elias H. & Electa, b. Sept. 13, 1818	3	79
Mary*, m. Elijah **SKINNER**, b. of Salisbury, Dec. 30, 1756, by Rev. Daniel Farrin, of Canaan *(Arnold Copy has " Mary **JESTEN**")	1	245
Polly, d. Darius & Sibel, b. Dec. 1, 1789, in Tyringham, Mass.	3	28
Sibel, d. Darius & Sibel, b. Apr. 14, 1782, in Tyringham, Mass.	3	28
JUDD, Lewis, m. Mary Ann **HUBBARD**, b. of Salisbury, Sept. 17, 1834, by Leonard E. Lathrop	3	147
Lyman, m. Caroline **GILLITT**, b. of Canaan, June 15, 1835, by Leonard E. Lathrop	3	149
Mervin, of Watertown, m. Sally **COOPER**, of Salisbury, Jan. 3, 1822, by Lavius Hyde	3	116
KEEP, Elizabeth, d. Jabez & Phebe, b. Mar. 22, 1769	2	21
Eunice, d. Samuel & Sarah, b. Aug. 30, 1756	1	176
Hannah, m. Moses **SHELDON**, Jr., b. of Salisbury, Jan. 10, 1782, by Rev. Jonathan Lee	2	41
Hannah, m. Moses **SHELDON**, Jr., b. of Salisbury, Jan. 10, 1782,		

	Vol.	Page
KEEP, (cont.)		
by Rev. Jonathan Lee	2	42
Luke, s. Jabez & Phebe, b. Mar. 25, 1771	2	21
Phebe, d. Jabez & Phebe, b. June 7, 1766	1	118
Samuel, m. Sarah **CHIPMAN**, b. of Salisbury, Dec. 25, 1755, by Rev. Jonathan Lee	1	244
Sarah, d. Jabez & Phebe, b. Aug. 29, 1763	1	118
Solomon, s. Jabez & Phebe, b. May 2, 1765	1	230
KELLOGG, Augustus, s. Truman & Abi, b. Aug. 6, 1790	2	7
James E., of Sheffield, Mass., m. Jennette **WARNER**, of Salisbury, Oct. 28, 1846, by Rev. J. Button Beach, of Sheffield	3	99
John, Capt., formerly of Sandisfield, d. Dec. 28, [ ], ae 80	3	166
Orson, s. Truman & Abi, b. Aug. 27, 1792, in Warrinborough, N.Y.	3	20
Truman, m. Abi **BINGHAM**, Dec. 3, 1789, by Rev. Daniel Farrand. Witnesses Benajah [ ] & Eunice [ ]	2	50
Truman, s. Truman & Abi, b. Oct. 15, 1795	3	20
KELSEY, Eliza, of Salisbury, m. Willis **FORD**, of Plymouth, Dec. 18, 1828, by Rev. Noah Bigelow	3	132
Hannah, of Salisbury, m. Phillip **ROCKERFELLER**, of Ancronn, N.Y., July 4, 1841, by Jac[ob] Shaw	3	161
Harriet, m. Alexander **BELCHER**, b. of Salisbury, July 3, 1823, by Senica Petter, J.P.	3	119
Horace S., m. Mary Ann **REED**, b. of Salisbury, Jan. 28, 1838, by Rev. O.V. Amerman	3	155
Jonathan, of Salisbury, m. Sarah **CHAPMAN**, of Amenia, June 13, 1770, by Rev. Mr. Smith	2	45
Julia, m. Charles B. **FLINT**, b. of Salisbury, June 26, 1828, by John Colver	3	130
Rebeckah, m. Daniel **HALL***, b. of Salisbury, Nov. 5, 1774, by Rev. Jonathan Lee *("HULL" in Rudd's book)	2	46
Sarah, d. Jonathan & Sarah, b. June 28, 1771	2	32
KENNEY, Andrew, m. Lucretia **CLARK**, b. of Salisbury, Mar. 23, 1834, by Eliphalet Whittlesey, J.P.	3	146
KENT, Darkis, d. Seth & Lois, b. Dec. 21, 1756	1	176
KETCHAM, Joseph, m. Phebe **MOORE**, b. of Salisbury, July 3, 1777, by Rev. Jonathan Lee	2	47
KEYES, Asa, s. Daniel & Mary, b. Jan. 14, 1785	2	30
Daniel, of Sheffield, m. Mary **THOMPSON**, of Salisbury, Oct. 14, 1784, by Rev. Jonathan Lee	2	42
Mary M., m. Peter **McARTHUR**, b. of Salisbury, Jan. 7, 1838, by Rev. O.V. Amerman	3	155
Sally, d. Stephen & Elisabeth, b. June 7, 1782	2	8
KIDDER, Daniel P., Rev., of Rochester, m. Cynthia H. **BISSELL**, of Salisbury, Nov. 9, 1836, by Rev. O.V. Amerman	3	153
KILMAN, KILLMAN, [see also **KILMER**], Charles, m. Angeline **WHITNEY**, b. of Salisbury, Sept. 29, 1836, by Rev. Oliver V. Amerman, of M.E. Ch.	3	153
Charles, m. Mary Ann **LANDON**, b. of Salisbury, Jan. 14, 1838, by Rev. O.V. Amerman	3	155

	Vol.	Page
KILMER, [see also **KILMAN**], Maria, m. Frederick **BARNETT**, b. of Salisbury, Feb. 21, 1847, by D.W. Clark	3	100
KING, Eli, s. Eli & Chloe, b. Jan. 10, 1789	2	26
Mehetable Hewit, d. John & Charlotte, b. July 7, 1804	3	65
Menila, d. Seth & Levinia, b. Apr. 14, 1799	3	32
Sally, d. Seth & Levinia, b. Apr. 25, 1788, in Foxborough, Mass.	3	32
Seth, s. Seth & Levinia, b. Apr. 6, 1794	3	32
Zarder*, s. Eli & Chloe, b. Dec. 27, 1786 *("Zardis" in Rudd's)	2	26
KINGSBURY, Cynthia, m. Isaac **HOLLISTER**, Jr., b. of Salisbury, Feb. 19, 1812, by Rev. Joseph W. Crossman	3	114
Delight, m. Luther **MOORE**, b. of Salisbury, Apr. 25, 1799, by Rev. Joseph W. Crossman	3	110
Sarah, m. James **SHELDON**, Jan. 8, 1797, at the house of Joseph Kingsbury, in Bethleham, by Rev. Mr. Avery. Witnesses Jabez Kingsbury & Denison Kingsbury	3	109
KINNON, Rebeckah J.*, m. Moore **BIRD**, b. of Salisbury, Nov. 9, 1752, by Rev. Jonathan Lee *("Rebeckah **SKINNER**" in Rudd's)	1	240
KNAPP, KNAP, Anne, d. Moses & Margaret, b. Nov. 28, 1765, at Woodbury	2	26
Calvin, s. Moses & Margaret, b. Apr. 18, 1770	2	26
Chauncy, s. Jabez & Mary, b. June 16, 1784	2	8
Eben Kasson, s. Moses & Margaret, b. Oct. 6, 1763, at Woodbury	2	26
Esther, d. Moses & Margaret, b. Dec. 26, 1761, at Woodbury	2	26
Henry, s. Jabez & Mary, b. Feb. 23, 1782	2	8
Jabez, s. Jabez & Mary, b. Oct. 14, 1792	2	9
Jemima, d. Jabez & Mary, b. Apr. 6, 1776	2	8
Johanna, d. Jabez & Mary, b. May 14, 1778	2	8
Joshua, s. Jabez & Mary, b. Mar. 25, 1769	2	8
Katharine, d. Jabez & Mary, b. Oct. 9, 1772	2	8
Mary, d. Jabez & Mary, b. Oct. 11, 1774	2	8
Moses, s. Jabez & Mary, b. Jan. 21, 1771	2	8
Phebe, d. Jabez & Mary, b. Mar. 28, 1780	2	8
Ruluff, s. Jabez & Mary, b. Dec. 21, 1767	2	8
Sarah, d. Jabez & Mary, b. May 11, 1789	2	8
Tamson, d. Moses & Margaret, b. Jan. 3, 1768	2	26
KNICKERBOCKER, KNICHOCKER, Abraham, s. John & Jemima, b. Apr. 12, 1733	1	194
Althea, d. Solomon & Anne, b. Feb. 2, 1785	2	30
Cornelius, s. Isaac & Hannah, b. May 9, 1774	2	9
Daniel, s. Solomon & Anne, b. Aug. 7, 1777	2	30
Elizabeth, d. Lawrence & Katharine, b. Mar. 16, 1764	1	109
Hannah, d. Isaac & Hannah, b. Jan. 20, 1783	2	9
Harmon, s. John & Jamima. b. Jan. 13, 1741/2	1	194
Isaac, s. John & Jamima, b. June 17, 1750	1	194
James, s. Solomon & Anne, b. May 19, 1787. Certified by Jemima Knickerbocker & Benjamin Marble	2	30
Jane, d. John & Jamima, b. Aug. 6, 1747	1	194
Jeremiah, s. Isaac & Hannah, b. Apr. 1, 1776	2	9
John, s. Harmon & Thankfull, b. Sept. 15, 1766	1	163
John, s. Lawrence & Katharine, b. Nov. 19, 1766, in New		

	Vol.	Page
KNICKERBOCKER, KNICHOCKER, (cont.)		
Canaan		
Lawrence, s. John & Jemima, b. Sept. 1*, 1739 *("Sept. 7" in	2	34
Rudd's book)	1	194
Maroche, of Dutchess Co., m. Ruluff **WHITE**, of Salisbury, May		
24, 1748, by Aaron P. Hetch, J.P. Witness Peter White	1	223
Mary, d. John & Jamima, b. Dec. 18, 1744	1	194
Molly, d. Abraham & Jerusha, b. Oct. 21, 1762	1	121
Reuben Murry, s. Isaac & Hannah, b. Aug. 9, 1781	2	9
Salmon, s. Lawrence & Katharine, b. Feb. 28, 1773	2	34
Samuel, s. Lawrence & Katharine, b. Jan. 12, 1762	1	109
Sarah, d. John & Jamima, b. Mar. 11, 1752	1	194
Solomon, s. John & Jamima, b. Oct. 12, 1754	1	194
Walter, s. Solomon & Anne, b. Aug. 7, 1782	2	30
William, s. Solomon & Anne, b. Aug. 4, 1780	2	30
KNIGHT, Deborah, of Sharon, m. Joel **THOMPSON**, of Salisbury,		
Jan. 4, 1781, by Rev. Jonathan Lee	2	41
Sarah, m. Abijah **JONES**, b. of Salisbury, May 23, 1776, by John		
Hutchinson, J.P	2	47
KULL*, Leverett, of Augusta, N.Y., m. Julia **SCOVILLE**, of		
Salisbury, May 16, 1827, by L.E. Lathrop *("**HULL**"?)	3	127
LAKE, Chauncey G., of Sharon, m. Polly M. **ENSIGN**, of Salisbury,		
Oct. 14, 1845, by Rev. Albert Nash	3	98
LAMB, Abi, d. Isaac & Elizabeth, b. Feb. 27, 1755	1	218
Alexander, m. Abigail **CHAPIN**, Aug. 9, 1795, by Adonijah		
Strong, J.P.	3	110
Charles Alexander, s. Alexander & Abigail, b. Aug. 21, 1815	3	27
Chloe, d. Alexander & Abigail, b. Feb. 6, 1798	3	27
Gideon, 5th, s. Thomas, b. Feb. 20, 1740/1	LR1	354
Hannah, d. Isaac & Elizabeth, b. Feb. 21, 1753	1	218
Isaac, 4th, s. Thomas, b. Feb. 1, 1738/9	LR1	354
John, s. Isaac & Elizabeth, b. May 19, 1757	1	218
Lavinia, d. Alex[ande]r & Abigail, b. Apr. 14, 1796	3	27
Luke, 2nd, s. Thomas, b. July 17, 1734	LR1	353
Sarah, of Salisbury, m. Jeremiah **CALKINS**, of Sharon, Sept. 16,		
1839, by Rev. Thomas Bainbridge	3	158
LANDON, [see under **LANGDON**]		
LANE, Charity, d. Jedediah & Phebe, b. July 25, 1774	2	7
Elisha, s. Samuel & Abigail, b. Jan. 7, 1762	1	120
Elisha & Charity, had d. [ ], b. Oct. 17, 1783	2	15
Jedediah, s. Jedidiah & Phebe, b. Dec. 10, 1769, in Killingworth	2	7
John, s. Jedediah & Phebe, b. June 7, 1772	2	7
Love, d. Elisha & Charity, b. Jan. 12, 1782	2	15
Lydia, d. Samuel & Abigail, b. Dec. 3, 1759, at Killingworth	1	120
Nabbe, d. Samuel & Abigail, b. Aug. 28, 1764	1	120
Phebe, d. Jedediah & Phebe, b. Jan. 23, 1765, in Killingworth	2	7
Roger, s. Jedediah & Phebe, b. Nov. 3, 1767, in Killingworth	2	7
Samuel, s. Samuel & Abigail, b. Oct. 9, 1757, at Killingworth	1	120
LANGDON, LANDEN, LANDON, LANGDEN, Abigail, w.		
Ambrose, d. Feb. 24, 1768, in the 25th y. of her age	2	38
Abigail, d. James, Jr. & Mary, b. Oct. 20, 1773	2	13

LANGDON, LANDEN, LANDON, LANGDEN, (cont.)

	Vol.	Page
Abigail, d. Asa & Jerusha, b. Sept. 20, 1775	2	16
Abigail, of Salisbury, m. Egbert **OWEN**, of North East, Oct. 21, 1839, by Rev. Tho[ma]s Bainbridge	3	158
Alice, d. Thomas & Hannah, b. Oct. 22, 1764	1	138
Alice, d. Thomas & Hannah, d. Jan. 3, 1765	1	239
Allen, s. James, Jr. & Sarah, b. June 27, 1795	3	3
Ambrose, s. Ambrose & Abigail, b. Feb. 5, 1768	2	14
Ann Maria, of Salisbury, m. Nelson **CLARK**, of Sheffield, Mass., Mar. 25, 1847, by D.W. Clark	3	100
Anne, d. Ezekiel & Azuba, b. Jan. 20, 1768	2	12
Asa, m. Jerusha **GRIFFAN***, b. of Salisbury, Oct. 20, 1757, by Rev. Jonathan Lee *("**GRIFFACE**" in Rudd's book)	1	247
Asa, s. Asa & Jerusha, b. Apr. 13, 1766	1	151
Asa & Jerusha, had d. [ ], d. Sept. 15, 1776	2	49
Ashbel, s. James, Jr. & Mary, b. Aug. 7, 1763	1	187
Azubah, w. Ezekiel, d. Feb. 3, 1770	2	48
Azuba, d. Elisha & Alice, b. Apr. 28, 1792	3	2
Betsey, m. Walter **JOHNSON**, b. of Salisbury, Jan. 6, 1803, by Adonijah Strong, J.P.	3	112
Bingham, s. Elisha & Alice, b. Aug. 9, 1794	3	2
Bingham, s. Elisha & Alice, d. Sept. 29, 1796, ae 2	3	164
Catey, d. Rufus & Sally, b. Sept. 6, 1795	3	13
Catharine, d. Luther & Patty, b. Dec. 28, 1816	3	43
Charles, s. George & Ruth, b. Oct. 2, 1799	3	19
Chloe, d. Rufus & Sally, b. Mar. 10, 1782	2	39
Concurrance, d. Thomas & Hannah, b. Jan. 28, 1770	2	12
Cynthia, d. James, Jr. & Sarah, b. Feb. 3, 1804	3	3
David, s. John & Katharine, b. July 4, 1763	1	112
David, s. John & Katharine, b. July 4, 1763	1	113
David, s. James, Jr. & Mary, b. Nov. 4, 1767	2	13
David M., m. Harriet **WHITMORE**, b. of Salisbury, Mar. 15, 1827, by Rev. Phinehas Cook, of the M.E. Ch.	3	126
Edgar, s. David & Johannah, b. May 27, 1802	3	43
Edmund, m. Sally D. **LOW**, May 1, 1826, by L.E. Lathrop	3	124
Electe, d. Asa & Jerusha, b. Aug. 9, 1770	2	16
Electa, d. John, 3rd & Loisa, b. July 24, 1801	3	15
Elisha, s. Ezekiel & Azubah, b. June 3, 1766	1	108
Elisha, m. Alice **BINGHAM**, b. of Salisbury, Apr. 16, 1789, by Adonijah Strong, J.P.	2	50
Elizabeth, d. John & Katharine, b. Sept. 27, 1756	1	198
Elizabeth, d. Ezekiel & Elizabeth, b. June 22, 1772	2	12
Elizabeth, d. James, Jr. & Mary, b. Dec. 19, 1775	2	13
Elizabeth, w. Ezekiel, d. Oct. 14, 1785, in the 39th y. of her age	2	50
Emma, m. Moore **BROWN**, b. of Salisbury, Feb. 28, 1827, by Rev. Stephen Beach, of St. Johns Ch.	3	126
Erastus, s. James, Jr. & Mary, b. Sept. 9, 1760	1	187
Esther, d. James, 3rd & Freelove, b. May 31, 1767, in Canaan	2	34
Ezekiel, s. Ezekiel & Azubah, b. Jan. 9, 1765	1	108
Ezekiel, of Salisbury, m. Elizabeth **COIT**, of Sheffield, Nov. 15, 1770, by J. Hutchinson, J.P.	2	45

	Vol.	Page
LANGDON, LANDEN, LANDON, LANGDEN, (cont.)		
Ezra, s. Asa & Jerusha, b. Feb. 22, 1773	2	16
Ezra, s. Asa & Jerusha, d. Sept. 11, 1776, in the 4th y. of his age	2	49
Frederick, s. David & Johannah, b. Oct. 1, 1797	3	43
Frederick C., m. Laura E. **BIDWELL**, b. of Salisbury, Mar. 3, 1846, by Roger Averill, J.P.	3	98
George, s. John & Catharine, b. June 23, 1749	1	207
Giles, s. Ezekiel & Elizabeth, b. May 11, 1774	2	12
Hannah, d. John & Katharine, b. Apr. 29, 1761	1	112
Hannah, d. John & Katharine, b. Apr. 29, 1761	1	113
Hannah, d. Asa & Jarusha, b. Jan. 6, 1764	1	151
Hannah, d. Thomas & Hannah, b. Mar. 17, 1772	2	12
Heman, s. Asa & Jerusha, b. July 15, 1768	2	16
Heman, s. John, 3rd & Louisa, b. May 4, 1789	2	15
Herman, s. Ezekiel & Sarah, b. Jan. 23, 1797	3	9
Horace, s. Ezekiel & Abi, b. Jan. 2, 1793	3	9
Horace, m. Cornelia E. **GREEN**, b. of Salisbury, Sept. 21, 1825, by L.E. Lathrop	3	122
Hulda, d. Thomas & Hannah, b. Feb. 5, 1768	2	12
James, s. John & Katharine, b. Sept. 28, 1744	LR1	354
James, Jr., m. Mary **REED**, b. of Salisbury, Nov. 18, 1756, by James Landon, J.P.	1	247
James, s. James, Jr. & Mary, b. Jan. 12, 1759	1	187
James, s. James, 3rd & Freelove, b. Apr. 2, 1770, in Canaan	2	34
James, m. Mary **DARROW**, b. of Salisbury, Oct. 10, 1838, by Rev. Adam Reid	3	156
James Hubell, s. Thomas & Hannah, b. Jan. 25, 1774	2	12
Jerusha, d. James, Jr. & Sarah, b. Nov. 15, 1805	3	3
Joel, s. James, Jr. & Mary, b. July 22, 1771	2	13
John, m. Katheren **WHITE**, Nov. 5, 1741	LR1	356-7
John, s. John & Katharine, b. July 28, 1742	LR1	351
John, Jr.*, of Salisbury, m. Mary **HANCHET**, of Sheffield, Dec. 23, 1762, by John Beebe, J.P. *(Arnold Copy has "John **LANSON**, Jr.")	1	251
John, s. Ezekiel & Azubah, b. July 7, 1763	1	108
John, s. Ambrose & Abigail, b. Sept. 13, 1765	1	151
John, his w. [ ], d. July 24, 1784, in the 39th y. of her age	2	49
John, 3rd, m. Louisa **BINGHAM**, b. of Salisbury, Nov. 17, 1785, by Rev. Jonathan Lee	2	43
John, s. Rufus & Sally, b. Mar. 7, 1798	3	13
John Hulet, s. Luther & Patty, b. Mar. 22, 1810	3	43
John Reed, s. James, Jr. & Mary, b. Apr. 13, 1780	2	13
Katharine, d. John & Katharine, b. May 4, 1754	1	207
Katharine, d. John & Mary, b. Apr. 14, 1765	1	116
Lois, d. Asa & Jerusha, b. May 20, 1759	1	170
Lois, m. James **SELLECK**, b. of Salisbury, Jan. 17, 1783, by Rev. Jonathan Lee	2	42
Loisa, d. John, 3rd & Loisa, b. Nov. 19, 1795	3	15
Lucretia, d. Rufus & Sally, b. June 11, 1780	2	39
Luther, s. James & Sarah, b. Sept. 16, 1752	1	180
Luther, m. Mary **SHELDON**, b. of Salisbury, Sept. 23, 1773, by		

LANGDON, LANDEN, LANDON, LANGDEN, (cont.)

	Vol.	Page
John Hutchinson, J.P.	2	45
Luther, s. Ezekiel & Elizabeth, b. Oct. 25, 1781	2	12
Luther, s. Rufus & Sally, b. Feb. 2, 1787	2	39
Luther, s. John, 3rd & Loisa, b. Apr. 30, 1793	3	15
Luther, m. Patty **HUBET**, b. of Salisbury, May 16, 1809, by Rev. Joseph W. Crossman	3	113
Lutia Electa, m. Harvey **SELLECK**, b. of Salisbury, Dec. 20, 1826, by Rev. Stephen Beach, of St. Johns Ch.	3	125
Lydia, d. John, Jr. & Mary, b. Feb. 15, 1763	1	116
Lydia, d. James, Jr. & Mary, b. Aug. 25, 1769	2	13
Malissa, d. John, 3rd & Loisa, b. July 17, 1798	3	15
Manda, d. Ezekiel & Elizabeth, b. Apr. 12, 1776	2	12
Martha, d. Luther & Patty, b. Mar. 5, 1821	3	43
Martin Strong, s. David & Johannah, b. Mar. 5, 1800	3	43
Mary, d. John & Katharine, b. Feb. 27, 1747	LR1	350
Mary, d. James, Jr. & Mary, b. July 18, 1757	1	187
Mary, w. Daniel, d. Nov. 21, 1771, in the 22nd y. of her age	2	48
Mary, d. Luther & Patty, b. Sept. 23, 1818	3	43
Mary, w. James, d. [ ], in the 40th y. of her age	2	50
Mary Ann, m. Charles **KILMAN**, b. of Salisbury, Jan. 14, 1838, by Rev. O.V. Amerman	3	155
Mary Emeline, d. David & Johannah, b. Jan. 8, 1805	3	43
Matthew, s. James, Jr. & Mary, b. Oct. 18, 1765	1	187
Miles, twin with Samuel, s. Samuel & Mary, b. Nov. 12, 1771	2	30
Milton, s. James, Jr. & Mary, b. May 30, 1762	1	187
Milton, s. James, Jr. & Mary, d. Sept. 29, 1762	1	238
Milton, s. Rufus & Sally, b. Jan. 13, 1785	2	39
Mylo, s. Rufus & Sally, b. Apr. 14, 1793	3	13
Nance, d. James & Sarah, b. Jan. 18, 1755	1	180
Nancy, of Salisbury, m. Oliver **EVERTS**, of Castleton, Feb. 22, 1776, by James Landon, J.P.	2	46
Noah, s. Elisha & Alice, b. May 10, 1790	3	2
Norman, s. Luther & Patty, b. Mar. 26, 1813; d. Aug. 3, 1818	3	43
Norman, s. Luther & Patty, b. Oct. 29, 1824	3	43
Oliver, s. Ezekiel & Elizabeth, b. Aug. 22, 1784	2	12
Orreante, d. John & Catharine, b. Feb. 7, 1751/2	1	207
Rebeckah, d. Samuel & Mary, b. Apr. 9, 1774	2	30
Reuben, s. Samuel & Mary, b. Jan. 11, 1776	2	30
Rufus, s. John & Katharine, b. Feb. 4, 1759	1	198
Rufus, s. Luther & Patty, b. May 3, 1815	3	43
Sally, d. Rufus & Sally, b. Mar. 5, 1791	2	39
Sally, d. Samuel & Polly, b. Aug. 7, 1797	3	14
Sally, m. Leonard **HALL**, b. of Salisbury, Sept. 1, 1805, by Rev. Joseph W. Crossman	3	112
Sally, d. Luther & Patty, b. Nov. 26, 1811	3	43
Sally, m. Raman **BROWN**, b. of Salisbury, Jan. 13, 1825, by Rev. Stephen Beach, of St. Johns Ch.	3	122
Samuel, twin with Miles, s. Samuel & Mary, b. Nov. 12, 1771	2	30
Samuel, m. Sarah **SPRAGUE**, of Sharon, May 12, 1773, by Rev. Cotton M. Smith	2	46

	Vol.	Page
LANGDON, LANDEN, LANDON, LANGDEN, (cont.)		
Sarah, d. Asa & Jerusha, b. Oct. 1, 1761	1	170
Sarah, d. Ezekiel & Azubah, b. Nov. 17, 1761	1	108
Sarah, d. John, 3rd & Louisa, b. Mar. 2, 1787	2	15
Seneca, s. George & Ruth, b. Nov. 14, 1790	3	19
Silas, s. John, 3rd & Louisa, b. Apr. 1, 1791	2	15
Susanna, d. James, Jr. & Sarah, b. May 31, 1799	3	3
Thomas, s. Thomas & Hannah, b. May 27, 1766	1	138
William, s. Ezekiel & Elizabeth, b. Jan. 13, 1779	2	12
William, m. Phebe **BERRY**, b. of Salisbury, Feb. 18, 1828, by Rev. Stephen Beach, of St. Johns Ch.	3	129
Zerah, s. Thomas & Hannah, b. Dec. 27, 1775	2	12
LANSON*, John, Jr., of Salisbury, m. Mary **HANCHET**, of Sheffield, Dec. 23, 1762, by John Beebe, J.P. *("**LANDON**" in Rudd's book)	1	251
[LARRABEE], LARREBEE, LARABEE, Anna, of Dutchess Co., m. Eleazer **FULLER**, of Salisbury, Feb. 27, 1770, by James Landon, J.P.	2	45
Judeth, d. Willett & Judeth, b. Dec. 4, 1775	2	35
Thomas, s. Willet & Judith, b. Aug. 28, 1773	2	35
Willett, m. Judeth **FULLER**, b. of Salisbury, Jan. 25, 1773, by James Landon, J.P.	2	46
LATSON, Mary Ann, m. Ichabod **MAXFIELD**, July 17, 1831, by Philander Wheeler, J.P.	3	139
LAW, Samuell, m. Meriam **MUNGER**, b. of Salisbury, July 13, 1769, by J. Hutchinson, J.P.	2	44
LEACH, Abby, m. William **MOORE**, b. of Salisbury, Apr. 28, 1839, by Rev. Thomas Bainbridge	3	158
Elijah, m. Annis **BIRD**, b. of Salisbury, Nov. 16, 1841, by J. Shaw	3	161
LEE, Abigail, d. Joseph, Jr. & Mary, b. Sept. 30, 1751	1	195
Abigail, m. Peter **COGSEL**, b. of Salisbury, May 26, 1754, by Rev. Jonathan Lee	1	241
Abigail, m. Samuel **HOLLEY**, b. of Salisbury, Feb. 21, 1769, by John Hutchinson, J.P.	2	44
Ann, d. Hezekiah C. & Elizabeth, b. Mar. 11, 1808	3	48
Ann, m. Albert **BUSHNELL**, b. of Salisbury, [Jan.] 1, [1828], by L.E. Lathrop	3	128
Charles Alfred, s. Samuel & Elizabeth, b. Mar. 3, 1801	3	12
Chauncey, s. Rev. Jonathan & Love, b. Nov. 9, 1763	1	148
Cloa, d. Jonathan & Elizabeth, b. Sept. 20, 1751	1	209
Cloe, d. Rev. Jonathan & Elizabeth, d. Nov. 26, 1752	1	226
Clarissa, m. Edward F. **GAY**, June [ ], [1824?], by Rev. L.E. Lathrop, of Cong. Ch.	3	120
Daniel, s. Samuel & Elizabeth, b. Sept. 30, 1802; d. Mar. 24, 1803	3	12
Daniel, s. Samuel & Elizabeth, d. Mar. 24, 1803, in the 6th m. of his age	3	165
Elisha, s. Rev. Jonathan & Elizabeth, b. Feb. 13, 1757	1	148
Elisha, s. Mylo & Ruth, b. Aug. 29, 1794	2	35
Elisha, s. Elisha & Almira S., b. Apr. 26, 1827	3	83
Elizabeth, d. Jonathan & Elizabeth, b. Sept. 4, 1747	1	209

	Vol.	Page
LEE, (cont.)		
Elizabeth, w. Rev. Jonathan, d. Feb. 22, 1762	1	238
Elizabeth, d. Samuel & Elizabeth, b. Nov. 5, 1796	3	12
Elizabeth O., m. Timothy **CHITTENDEN**, [Nov.] 1, 1837, by Adam Reid	3	154
Fanny S., m. Myron H. **FISH**, b. of Salisbury, Aug. 25, 1845, by Rev. Adam Reed	3	97
Fanny Scoville, d. Elisha & Almira S., b. Aug. 11, 1823	3	83
George Henry, s. Hezekiah C. & Elizabeth, b. Feb. 19, 1812	3	48
Graham, s. Elisha & Almira S., b. Jan. 22, 1821	3	83
Hannah, m. Nathaniell **BUELL**, b. of Salisbury, Apr. 23, 1761, by Rev. Jonathan Lee	1	249
Hannah, w. Samuel, d. July 23, 1790, in the [ ] y. of her age	3	164
Hannah, d. Samuel & Elizabeth, b. Aug. 6, 1794	3	12
Harriet Maria, of Salisbury, m. William James **SMITH**, of Harbor Creek, Penn., Aug. 6, 1843, by Rev. Jonathan Lee	3	163
Henry, s. Elisha & Almira S., b. Mar. 3, 1822	3	83
Hezekiah C., m. Elizabeth **FITCH**, Jan. 15, 1807, by Joseph W. Crossman	3	113
Hezekiah Camp, s. Mylo & Ruth, b. June 20, 1783	2	35
Hezekiah Fitch, s. Heze[kia]h C. & Elizabeth, b. Jan. 23, 1814	3	48
Jane, d. Hezekiah C. & Elizabeth, b. Nov. 19, 1809	3	48
Jane, m. Silas **WELLS**, Sept. 30, 1833, by L.E. Lathrop	3	144
John, s. Joseph & Mary, b. Oct. 18, 1747	LR1	350
John, s. Joseph, Jr. & Mary, b. Oct. 18, 1747	1	195
Jonathan, s. Jonathan & Elizabeth, b. Oct. 26, 1745	1	209
Jonathan, m. Mrs. Elizabeth **METCALF**, Oct. 26, 1745*, by Rev. Solomon Williams, of Lebanon *(Typed corrections in original state "**LEE**, Jonathan, m. Elizabeth **METCALF**, Oct. 26, 1745... (same date as birth of son Jonathan!) Should be Sept. 3, 1744 for mar. (cf. Dexter's Yale Annals I:716 &c." and "Error noted by Prof. Elmer I. Shepard of Williamstown, Mass. 3(?)/28/46")	1	240
Jonathan, Rev., of Salisbury, m. Mrs. Eve* **BRINKERHOOF**, of Woodbury, Nov. 22, 1762, by Rev. John Graham *("Love" in Rudd's book)	1	250
Jonathan, s. Mylo & Ruth, b. July 19, 1786	2	35
Jonathan, Rev., d. Oct. 8, 1788, in the 71st y. of his age and in the 45th y. of his ministry	2	50
Jonathan, Rev., of Otus, m. Mary **STRONG**, of Salisbury, Nov. 20, 1827, by Leonard E. Lathrop	3	128
Joseph, s. Joseph, Jr. & Mary, b. Aug. 9, 1755	1	195
Joseph, d. Aug. 18, 1764	1	239
Joseph, m. Abigail **BRIG[G]S**, b. of Salisbury, Mar. 12, 1771, by Rev. Robert Cambel	2	45
Judah, s. Samuel & Elizabeth, b. Dec. 2, 1810	3	46
Julia, d. Elisha & Almira S., b. May 3, 1825	3	83
Lois*, d. Rev. Jonathan & Lois, b. Dec. 5, 1767 *("Love" in Rudd's book)	2	10
Love, d. Robert Walker & Jerusha, b. July 24, 1789	2	38
Mary, d. Joseph, Jr. & Mary, b. May 3, 1743, in Reading	1	195

SALISBURY VITAL RECORDS 223

	Vol.	Page
LEE, (cont.)		
Mary, d. Feb. 1, 1769, in the 71st y. of her age	2	48
Mary, w. Joseph, d. Feb. 2, 1771, in the 53rd y. of her age	2	48
Mary, d. Samuel & Elizabeth, b. Mar. 22, 1808	3	46
Mary, m. Caleb B. **TICKNOR**, b. of Salisbury, Jan. 21, 1830, by L.E. Lathrop	3	136
Moses Allen, s. Samuel & Elizabeth, b. Mar. 2, 1806	3	46
Mylo, s. Jonathan & Elizabeth, b. June 27, 1760	1	209
Mylo, m. Ruth **CAMP**, b. of Salisbury, May 23, 1782, by Rev. Jonathan Lee	2	42
Mylo, s. Mylo & Ruth, b. July 2, 1789	2	35
Mylo, s. Elisha & Almira S., b. Nov. 12, 1828	3	83
Noah, s. Noah, of Norwalk, decd., & Elizabeth, b. Oct. 7, 1743, in Norwalk	1	221
Rhoda, d. Rev. Jonathan & Elizabeth, b. Feb. 26, 1753	1	209
Robert Walker, s. Rev. Jonathan & Love, b. Apr. 4, 1765	1	148
Robert Walker, m. Jerusha **BUSHNELL**, b. of Salisbury, Oct. 29, 1786, by Rev. Jonathan Lee	2	43
Robert Walker, s. Robert Walker & Jerusha, b. Sept. 30, 1787	2	38
Ruth A., d. Elisha & Almira, b. June 8, 1836	3	83
Salome, d. Jonathan & Elizabeth, b. Dec. 15, 1754	1	209
Samuell, s. Jonathan & Elizabeth, b. Sept. 27, 1749	1	209
Samuel, 2nd, m. Hannah **MOORE**, b. of Salisbury, Feb. 12, 1774, by Rev. Jonathan Lee	2	45
Samuel, 3rd, m. Mary **BINGHAM**, Jr., b. of Salisbury, Sept. 29, 1774, by Rev. Jonathan Lee	2	46
Samuel, of Salisbury, m. Mrs. Eliza **BROWN**, of Pittsfield, June 23, 1792, by Thomas Allen	3	111
Samuel, 2nd, m. Beulah **HARRISON**, b. of Salisbury, July 20, 1806, by Samuel Lee, J.P.	3	112
Samuel Brown, s. Samuel & Elizabeth, b. Nov. 15, 1798	3	12
Sarah, d. Mylo & Ruth, b. June 21, 1791	2	35
Sarah, d. Elisha & Almira, b. Mar. 7, 1831	3	83
Solomon, s. Samuel, 3rd & Mary, b. Sept. 11, 1775	2	37
William, s. Joseph, Jr. & Mary, b. Mar. 2, 1758	1	195
William, s. Joseph, Jr. & Mary, d. Mar. 3, 1758	1	228
William Graham, s. Robert Walker & Jerusha, b. Nov. 30, 1791	2	38
William Henry, s. Samuel & Elizabeth, b. May 21, 1793	3	12
LINCOLN, Eunice, m. Myron **SABINS**, Jan. 29, 1829, by Charles Prentice	3	133
George W., m. Jane Maria **BABCOCK**, Oct. 3, 1833, by L.E. Lathrop	3	144
LITTLE, Robert, of Sheffield, Mass., m. Cornelia M. **ELDRED**, of Salisbury, Jan. 10, 1843, by Rev. Adam Reid	3	162
LOCKWOOD, George M., m. Emma Jane **REED**, b. of Salisbury, Aug. 27, 1846, by Harley Goodwin	3	98
LOOMIS, Augustus, s. Phineas, b. May 29, 1794	3	17
Betsey, d. Phineas, b. Sept. 22, 1792	3	17
Eleazer, s. Hezekiah & Hephzibah, b. Dec. 17, 1748	1	220
Elizabeth, m. Isaac **WILLIAMS**, b. of Salisbury, Mar. 12, 1750, by Rev. Jonathan Lee	1	224

	Vol.	Page
LOOMIS, (cont.)		
Elizabeth, of Lebanon, m. Adonijah **JACOBS**, of Salisbury, Jan. 24, 1772, by Uriah Lawrence, J.P.	2	45
Hephzibah, d. Hezekiah, Jr. & Sarah, b. Mar. 22, 1751	1	212
Hephzibah, d. Hezekiah, Jr. & Sarah, d. Oct. 30, 1753, in the 7th y. of her age	1	228
Hephzibah, d. Hezekiah, Jr. & Sarah, b. Dec. 30, 1758	1	164
Hezekiah, Jr., of Salisbury, m. Sarah **PETTIT**, of Sharon, Nov. [ ], 1749, by John Searle	1	241
Hezekiah, Jr. & Sarah, had d. [ ]s.b. Dec. 14, 1752	1	212
Hezekiah, s. Hezekiah, Jr. & Sarah, b. Aug. 25, 1754; d. Aug. 29, 1754	1	212
Hezekiah, s. Hezekiah, Jr. & Sarah, b. Dec. 11, 1755	1	211
Hezekiah, Jr., of Salisbury, d. Nov. 24*, 1760 *("Nov. 26" in Rudd's book)	1	236
Phinehas, of Salisbury, m. Hannah **WILLIAMS**, of Sheffield, Mass., Feb. 14, 1829, by Eliphalet Whittlesey, J.P.	3	133
Sarah, d. Hezekiah, Jr. & Sarah, b. Dec. 14, 1749	1	212
LORD, Anna, d. Elijah & Mehetabel, b. May 4, 1789	2	34
Charles, s. Joel & Jerusha, b. [ ], 1785	2	39
Daniel, s. David & Lydia, b. Mar. 4, 1751	1	179
David, s. David & Lydia, b. July 4, 1744	1	179
David, Jr., m. Abigail **HOLLEY**, Apr. 27, 1769, by Rev. Jonathan Lee	2	44
David, d. Mar. 9, 1785, ae 66	2	50
Elijah, s. David & Lydia, b. Oct. 4, 1765	1	152
Elisha, s. David & Lydia, b. Nov. 17, 1758	1	179
Elizabeth, d. David & Lydia, b. Feb. 6, 1749	1	179
Hannah, d. David & Lydia, b. June 12, 1763	1	152
Harley, s. Joel & Jerusha, b. Jan. 25, 1792	2	39
Jerusha, d. Joel & Jerusha, b. Jan. 11, 1790	2	39
Joel, s. David & Lydia, b. Mar. 12, 1754, O.S.	1	179
Lorain, d. David & Lydia, b. Sept. 25, 1769	2	24
Lydia, d. David & Lydia, b. July 15, 1746	1	179
Lydia, w. David, d. Dec. 10, 1784, in the 56th y. of her age	2	50
Mary, d. David & Lydia, b. Feb. 27, 1761	1	152
Mary, d. David & Lydia, d. June 9, 1783, in the 23rd y. of her age	2	50
Noah, s. David, Jr. & Abigail, b. Nov. 4, 1772	2	26
Noah, s. David, Jr. & Abigail, d. Sept. 28, 1773, in the 11th y. of his age	2	48
Olivia, d. Joel & Jerusha, b. Jan. 14, 1782	2	39
Olivia, d. Joel & Jerusha, d. Oct. 7, 1784, ae 3	2	50
Phebe, d. David, Jr. & Abigail, b. Jan. 30, 1770	2	26
Phebe, d. David, Jr. & Abigail, d. Feb. 5, 1772, in the 3rd y. of her age	2	48
Ruth, d. David & Lydia, b. Nov. 23, 1756	1	179
Ruth, m. Moses **HENSDILL**, b. of Salisbury, Sept. 16, 1779, by Elisha Baker, J.P.	2	41
Salle, d. David, Jr. & Abigail, b. May 10, 1771	2	26
LOTHROP*, Sarah, of Ammete, m. Hezekiah **CAMP**, Jr., of Salisbury, Nov. 21, 1752, by Rev. Mr. Woodbridge		

SALISBURY VITAL RECORDS 225

	Vol.	Page
LOTHROP*, (cont.)		
*(**NORTHROP**" in Rudd's)	1	240
LOTTZ, Hertman, s. John Hertman & Martha, b. Apr. 9, 1789	2	19
John Hertman, m. Martha **TOUSLEY**, June 26, 1788, by		
Adonijah Strong, J.P.	2	50
Julia, d. John Hertman & Martha, b. Oct. 9, 1798	2	19
Sarah, d. John Hertman & Martha, b. June 25, 1791	2	19
[**LOUNSBURY**], **LOUNSBEARY, LOUNESBEARY**, Mary, d.		
Josiah & Martha, b. Mar. 31, 1753	1	192
Rachel, d. Josiah & Martha, b. Sept. 3, 1755	1	192
LOVELAND, Eliza Ann, m. William **BISSELL**, b. of Salisbury, Mar.		
8, 1822, by David L. Perry	3	117
Harriet, of Salisbury, m. David **WEST**, of North East, N.Y., Jan.		
3, 1827, by Rev. Stephen Beach, of St. Johns Ch.	3	125
LOVERIDGE, Amelia S., m. George W. **GAGER**, Dec. 9, 1840, by		
Rev. J. Tankin Carpenter	3	160
LOW, Sally D., m. Edmund **LANDEN**, May 1, 1826, by L.E. Lathrop	3	124
LUSHER, Samuel, m. Emily **REED**, b. of Salisbury, Mar. 22, 1842, by		
Rev. Andrew M. Smith, of North East, N.Y.	3	162
LYMAN, Abby, of Salisbury, m. Ashbell **WARREN**, of Bolton, Oct. 2,		
1825, by Leonard E. Lathrop	3	122
Abby, of Salisbury, m. Ashbell **WARNER**, of Bolton, Oct. 2,		
1825, by L.E. Lathrop	3	123
Abigail, d. David & Flavia, b. Nov. 24, 1800	3	17
Bernice, d. Simeon, Jr. & Joanna, b. July 30, 1788	2	19
Caleb, s. Noah & Hopestill, b. Feb. 5, 1788	2	14
Calvin, s. David & Flavia, b. May 16, 1803	3	17
Charles, m. Lydia S. **GROAB**, b. of Salisbury, Nov. 30, 1843, by		
Rev. C.V. Amerman	3	96
Chloe, d. Simeon & Elizabeth, b. June 18, 1764	1	121
Chloe, m. David T. **CHADWICK**, Sept. 10, 1833, by L.E.		
Lathrop	3	143
David, Jr., s. David & Flavia, b. Aug. 23, 18[ ]	3	17
Eliza, d. David & Flavia, b. Sept. 11, 1805	3	17
Elizabeth, d. Simeon & Elizabeth, b. Feb. 10, 1751	1	208
Elizabeth, w. Simeon, d. June 14, 1773, in the 42nd y. of her age	2	49
Epaphras, of Andover, O., m. Mary **HUTCHINSON**, of		
Salisbury, Oct. 6, 1826, by L.E. Lathrop	3	124
Hannah, d. Simeon & Elizabeth, b. Oct. 5, 1749	1	208
Hannah, d. Simeon, Jr. & Joanna, b. Aug. 29, 1781	2	19
Isaac, s. Simeon & Elizabeth, b. Apr. 3, 1766	1	121
Isaac, s. Simeon, Jr. & Joanna, b. July 6, 1783	2	19
John, s. Simeon & Elizabeth, b. Mar. 4, 1760	1	208
John, m. Huldah **BRINSMAID**, b. of Salisbury, Dec. 3, 1786, by		
Rev. Jonathan Lee	2	43
Levi, s. David & Flavia, b. July 22, 1798	3	17
Moses, of Goshen, m. Mary A. **HOLLEY**, of Salisbury, May 6,		
1834, by Leonard E. Lathrop	3	146
Noah, s. Simeon & Elizabeth, b. Mar. 28, 1756	1	208
Noah, s. Simeon & Elizabeth, d. Sept. 26, 1757	1	229
Noah, s. Simeon & Elizabeth, b. Mar. 10, 1758	1	208

	Vol.	Page
LYMAN, (cont.)		
Noah, m. Hopestill **BUNN**, b. of Salisbury, May 12, 1784, at Canaan, by Rev. Daniel Ferrand	2	43
Olive, d. Simeon & Elizabeth, b. May 16, 1762	1	121
Olive, m. Nathaniel **TREMAIN**, b. of Salisbury, Dec. 7, 1780, by Rev. Jonathan Lee	2	41
Sally, d. David & Flavia, b. Apr. 9, 1793	3	17
Samuel, s. David & Flavia, b. Aug. 18, 1794	3	17
Simeon, m. Elizabeth **BEEBE**, Jan. 5, 1748/9, by Rev. Jonathan Lee	1	222
Simeon, s. Simeon & Elizabeth, b. Jan. 7, 1754	1	208
Simeon, of Salisbury, m. Abigail **CHIPMAN**, of Sunderland, Sept. 19, 1774, by Rev. Mr. Dewey, of [Great] Barrington	2	46
Simeon, Jr., of Salisbury, m. Joanna **PARMER**, of Sheffield, Dec. 7, 1780, by Rev. Jonathan Lee	2	41
Simeon, d. Aug. 29, 1800, in the 83rd y. of his age	3	165
Simeon, of Sharon, m. Betsey **STRONG**, of Salisbury, Mar. 15, 1822, by David L. Perry	3	117
Stephen, s. Noah & Hopestill, b. Jan. 31, 1785	2	14
Timothy, s. Simeon, Jr. & Joanna, b. Aug. 7, 1787; d. Aug. 12, 1787	2	19
Victoria, m. Asahel **HUMPHREY**, b. of Salisbury, Nov. 25, 1841, by Rev. Adam Reid	3	161
LYONS, Charlotte, of Salisbury, m. David **FRINK**, of Mt. Washington, Aug. 9, 1832, by Rev. Stephen Beach, of St. Johns Ch.	3	140
Mary A., m. William **PRESTON**, Jan. 16, 1848, by W.H. Ferris	3	103
McARTHUR, Caroline, m. Seymour **VAN DUZEN**, b. of Salisbury, Nov. 28, 1833, by Leonard E. Lathrop	3	145
Peter, m. Mary M. **KEYES**, b. of Salisbury, Jan. 7, 1838, by Rev. O.V. Amerman	3	155
Polly, m. Newton J. **REED**, b. of Salisbury, Dec. 29, 1838, by Rev. Thomas Bainbridge	3	158
McCARTY, George, s. George & Mary, b. Feb. 8, 1774	2	22
Thomas, s. George & Mary, b. Aug. 16, 1775	2	22
McCUE, Ann, m. William **O'ROUKE**, [Nov.] 29, 1835, by Leonard E. Lathrop	3	150
McELROY, McCLROY, Charles, m. Caroline **MOORE**, b. of Salisbury, Oct. 30, 1827, by Rev. Stephen Beach, of St. Johns Ch.	3	128
Jane N., of Salisbury, m. W[illia]m **WRIGHT**, 3rd, of Mt. Washington, Mass., Apr. 11, 1847, by D.W. Clark	3	100
McINTYRE, MACINTIRE, Bette, d. Stephen & Abiah, b. May 17, 1774	2	32
Caroline, m. Frederic F. **MOORE**, b. of Salisbury, Apr. 11, 1827, by Rev. Stephen Beach, of St. Johns Ch.	3	127
Heman, s. Stephen & Abiah, b. June 19, 1772	2	32
Stephen, m. Abiah **TOUSLEY**, b. of Salisbury, Nov. 23, 1769, by Rev. Jonathan Lee	2	44
MACKALL, Elihu, of Salisbury, m. Hannah **DEAN***, of Hebron, Jan. 28, 1777, by Rev. Mr. Brockway *("DUNK" in Rudd's		

	Vol.	Page
MACKALL, (cont.)		
book)	2	47
Polly, d. Samuel & Lydia, b. June 23, 1775	2	7
McKEAN, John, m. Nancy **EVARTS**, Sept. 25, 1797, by Rev. Amos Fowler, of 1st ch. of Christ, in Guilford	3	110
Noyse Evarts, s. John & Nancy, b. Mar. 10, 1799	3	29
McNEIL, McNEILE, McNIELE, Archibald, s. John & Ziporah, b. Aug. 14, 1771	2	30
John, of Salisbury, m. Ziporah **HENMAN**, of Lainsborough, Oct. 24, 1769, by Rev. Mr. Collins	2	44
Jonathan P., of Sheffield, Mass., m. Loiza J. **FOSTER**, of Salisbury, Mar. 23, 1842, by Rev. Adam Reid	3	162
McURE, Martha, m. John **EATON**, b. of Salisbury, Apr. 11, 1771, by John Hutchinson, J.P.	2	45
MALTBY, Aden, s. Noah & Hulda, b. Feb. 16, 1773	2	31
Frederick, s. Noah & Hulda, b. Dec. 4, 1776	2	31
Hulda, d. Noah & Hulda, b. Aug. 25, 1771	2	31
Noah, s. Noah & Hulda, b. Nov. 20, 1774	2	31
MANSFIELD, Caroline C., of Salisbury, m. Sheldon A. **PARSONS**, of Norfolk, Oct. 19, 1842, by Rev. Adam Reid	3	162
MARKHAM, Asher, s. Israel & Penelope, b. July 20, 1767, at Lawisons Pattent	2	22
Dan, s. Israel & Penelope, b. Aug. 31, 1765, at Lawnson's Pattent	2	22
Darius, s. Israel & Penelope, b. Apr. 10, 1769	2	22
MARSH, Elizabeth, d. George & Katharine, b. Aug. 29, 1761	2	20
George, s. George & Katharine, b. Mar. 26, 1765	2	20
Hannah, of Canaan, m. Hezekiah **CAMP**, of Salisbury, Mar. 29, 1789, by Elisha Baker, J.P.	3	108
Jeremiah, s. George & Katharine, b. Nov. 21, 1767	2	20
Rebeckah, d. George & Katharine, b. Oct. 21, 1759, at Litchfield	2	20
Sarah, d. Eliphalet & Sarah, b. May 31, 1765	1	153
Silva, d. George & Katharine, b. Feb. 7, 1763	2	20
Susanah, d. George & Katharine, b. Mar. 3, 1769	2	20
MARSHALL, Mary, had d. Olive, b. May 23, 1786	2	22
Olive, d. Mary, b. May 23, 1786	2	22
MARTIN, Adaline Stanley, d. Noah S. & Olive E., b. Feb. 12, 1825	3	73
Amanda Maria, d. Noah & Olive E., b. Jan. 30, 1822	3	73
Hannah, of Tyringham, m. Asa **HUTCHINSON**, of Salisbury, May 10, 1807, by Rev. Joseph W. Crossman	3	112
Harriet, d. Noah S. & Olive E., b. Mar. 2, 1827	3	73
Lucinda, m. Phineas **CHAPIN**, Jr., b. of Salisbury, Mar. 1, 1809, by Rev. Joseph W. Crossman	3	113
Melinda, d. Noah & Hannah, late of Tyringham & daughter-in-law of Asa Hutchinson, d. Mar. 16, 1809, ae 75	3	166
Melinda, d. Noah S. & Olive E., b. Sept. 2, 1823	3	73
Malinda, m. George B. **BURREL**, b. of Salisbury, Nov. 8, 1847, by Rev. Adam Reed	3	102
MASON, Cyrus, s. Peter & Elisheba, b. May 24, 1791	2	23
Darius, s. Peter & Elisheba, b. Jan. 7, 1777	2	23
Elisheba, d. Peter & Elisheba, b. Nov. 9, 1784	2	23
Levi, s. Peter & Elisheba, b. July 1, 1782	2	23

	Vol.	Page
MASON, (cont.)		
Levi, m. Fanny **SUYDAM**, b. of Salisbury, July 4, 1837, by Rev. O.V. Amerman	3	154
Meriam, d. Peter & Elisheba, b. July 8, 1795	2	23
Merick Ely, s. Stephen & Anna, b. Nov. 16, 1801	3	36
Peter, m. Elizabeth* **FARNUM**, b. of Salisbury, Mar. 24, 1774, by Rev. Jonathan Lee *("Elisheba" in Rudd's book)	2	45
Peter, s. Peter & Elisheba, b. Oct. 16, 1786	2	23
Peter Lewis, s. Stephen & Ann, b. Feb. 14, 1803	3	36
Polly, d. Peter & Elisheba, b. Aug. 23, 1793	2	23
Sarah M., of Salisbury, m. Ambrose **WARD**, of Newtown, Oct. 14, 1828, by Leonard E. Lathrop	3	131
Stephen, s. Peter & Elisheba, b. Mar. 5, 1779	2	23
Stephen, m. Anna **ELY**, Jan. 12, 1800, by [ ]. Witnesses Simeon Granger & Simeon Granger, Jr.	3	111
Silvester, s. Peter & Elisheba, b. Oct. 13, 1774	2	23
Silvester, s. Peter & Elisheba, b. Apr. 27, 1789	2	23
MATTOON, Amasa Curtiss, s. Curtiss & Anna, b. July 27, 1806	3	53
Christopher, s. Gershom & Mehittable, b. Apr. 17, 1773	2	32
Curtiss Alexander, s. Curtiss & Anna, b. Sept. 16, 1814	3	53
Edwin, s. Curtiss & Anna, b. Aug. 12, 1808; d. Nov. 30, 1809	3	53
Edwin, s. Curtiss & Anna, b. Sept. 17, 1810	3	53
Electa, d. Curtiss & Anna, b. Sept. 10, 1812	3	53
Gershom, m. Mehetable **FULLER**, b. of Salisbury, Jan. 17, 1771, by J. Hutchinson, J.P.	2	45
Jonathan*, s. Gershom & Mehittable, b. Sept. 19, 1771 *("John" in Rudd's book)	2	32
MAXAM, MAXAN, Clarissa, m. Albert **FOSTER**, Nov. 28, 1822, by Rev. Coles Carpenter	3	118
Lucy, of Salisbury, m. Harvey **PARTRIDGE**, of Canaan, Mar. 15, 1826, by Rev. David Miller, of the M.E. Ch.	3	124
MAXFIELD, Ebenezer, of Nelson, O., m. Keziah **HUMPHREY**, of Salisbury, Apr. 22, 1822, by Lavius Hyde	3	116
Ichabod, m. Mary Ann **LATSON**, July 17, 1831, by Philander Wheeler, J.P.	3	139
MAXWELL, Samuel, of Stamford, N.Y., m. Jane **TURNER**, of Salisbury, Aug. 31, 1828, by Lot Norton, J.P.	3	131
MAY, Calvin, s. Lemuel & Huldah, b. Dec. 21, 1796	3	1
Huldah, twin with Lemuel, d. Lemuel & Huldah, b. Sept. 2, 1793, in Weathersfield *(Perhaps "1795")	3	1
Lamuel, twin with Huldah, s. Lemuel & Huldah, b. Sept. 2, 1793, in Weathersfield *(Perhaps "1795")	3	1
MEAD, Charles, s. Silas & Eunice, b. June 4, 1810	3	40
Eliza, d. Silas & Eunice, b. July 12, 1807	3	40
James, of Mt. Washington, Mass., m. Sally **DEMING**, of Salisbury, Nov. 28, 1822, by Eliphalet Whittlesey, J.P.	3	117
Olive Chapin, d. Silas & Eunice, b. Apr. 19, 1803	3	40
MEIGS, Julius, s. Janna & Rebeckah, b. Dec. 1, 1771	2	17
Lusina, d. Janno, Jr. & Rebekah, b. Mar. 8, 1765, in Wallingford	1	147
Lucina, m. David **DONOLDS**, b. of Salisbury, Aug. 29, 1793, by Rev. Joshua Knapp, Jr. Witnesses Matilda Rockwell &		

SALISBURY VITAL RECORDS 229

	Vol.	Page
MEIGS, (cont.)		
Esther Donolds	3	109
Lurania, d. Janna & Rebecca, b. Jan. 21, 1768	2	17
Polly Maria, d. Whiting & Charlotte, b. Mar. 11, 1802	3	38
Rebekah, d. Janna & Rebecca, b. Mar. 23, 1770	2	17
Whiting, s. Janna & Rebecca, b. Sept. 21, 1775	2	17
MERCHANT, Hiland K., m. Lavinia **WOODING**, b. of Salisbury, Sept. 15, 1839, by Rev. Thomas Bainbridge	3	158
MERRICK*, Esther, of Farmington, m. Lot **NORTON**, of Salisbury, Dec. 2, 1756, by Rev. Timothy Pitkin *("**MERRELLE**" in Rudd's book)	1	246
METCALF, Elizabeth, Mrs., m. Jonathan **LEE**, Oct. 26, 1745, by Rev. Solomon Williams, of Lebanon	1	240
MILES, [see also **MILLS**], F[rederic]k, of Goshen, m. Mary **HOLLEY**, of Salisbury, Sept. [ ], 1842, by Rev. S.T. Carpenter	3	162
Levina, d. Stephen & Abigail, b. June 22, 1788	2	32
Sarah, of Cornwall, m. Abraham **REED**, of Salisbury, Jan. 22, 1785, by Rev. Daniel Farrand, of Canaan. Witnesses Isaac Reed & Hephzibah Smith	2	42
Stephen, s. Stephen & Abigail, b. Nov. 23, 1792	2	32
Susannah, d. Stephen & Abigail, b. June 16, 1785	2	32
MILLARD, Marilla, d. Oliver & Sarah, b. Feb. 7, 1767	1	155
MILLER, Albert Needham, s. Daniel H. & Isabella, b. Dec. 22, 1805	3	46
Catharine, m. John **TEETER**, b. of Salisbury, May 9, 1847, by Rev. Jonathan Lee	3	100
Daniel Addison Saunders Hawkins, s. Daniel H. & Isabella, b. Aug. 30, 1804	3	46
MILLS, [see also **MILES**], Elizabeth, of Salisbury, m. Benjamin **EGGLESTON**, of North East, Dutchess, N.Y., Mar. 21, 1838, by Adam Reid	3	154
Lewis, of Kent, m. Mary C. **DUTCHER**, Apr. 7, 1836, by Leonard E. Lathrop	3	151
Lewis, of Kent, m. Mary C. **DUTCHER**, Apr. 7, 1836, by Leonard E. Lathrop	3	152
Maria C., m. Joseph G. **BROWN**, b. of Salisbury, Dec. 6, 1820, by Lavius Hyde	3	116
MINARD, Betsey, d. Joshua & Phebe, b. Dec. 28, 1798	3	11
Herman, m. Mary **VOSBURGH**, b. of Salisbury, Aug. 25, 1830, by L.E. Lathrop	3	136
James, s. Joshua & Phebe, b. July 21, 1795	3	11
Joshua, s. Joshua & Phebe, b. Mar. 29, 1797	3	11
Nathan, s. Joshua & Phebe, b. Apr. 9, 1791	3	11
Phebe, d. Joshua & Phebe, b. Oct. 20, 1793	3	11
MINOR, David Willey, s. Asa & Lois, b. Sept. 3, 1782	3	13
Henry, s. Asa & Lois, b. Aug. 14, 1789	3	13
Jerusha, d. Asa & Lois, b. Jan. 10, 1787	3	13
Laura, d. Asa & Lois, b. Sept. 27, 1784	3	13
Uriah H., of Canaan, m. Caroline E. **CANFIELD**, of Salisbury, Sept. 9, 1843, by Rev. Stephen G. Stebbins	3	163
MIX, Hester Ann, d. William & Sybel, b. Oct. 21, 1816	3	41
Love, d. Thomas & Lucy, b. Oct. 11, 1790	3	1

	Vol.	Page
MIX, (cont.)		
Pamelia Angeline, d. William & Sybel, b. Nov. 9, 1814	3	41
Phebe, d. Thomas & Lucy, b. Feb. 10, 1793	3	1
Phebe Caroline, d. William & Sibel, b. Sept. 24, 1812	3	41
Thomas Newton, s. Thomas & Lucy, b. Feb. 20, 1795	3	1
Thomas Newton, s. William & Sibel, b. Aug. 15, 1808	3	41
Wesley Dela F., d. W[illia]m & Sybel, b. Feb. 24, 1819	3	41
William, s. Thomas & Lucy, b. Jan. 30, 1789	3	1
William, m. Sebil **WRIGHT**, b. of Salisbury, Aug. 6, 1807, by Rev. Joseph W. Crossman	3	113
William Newman, s. William & Sibel, b. Dec. 30, 1810	3	41
MOER, [see under **MOORE**]		
[MONROE], MUNROW, Deborah, of Sharon, m. Jacob **GILLETT**, of Salisbury, Dec. 31, 1769, by Rev. Mr. Smith	2	44
MONTGOMERY, Hugh, m. Betsey **TOUSLEY**, b. of Salisbury, Mar. 8, 1785, by Rev. Jonathan Lee	2	42
MOORE, MOER, Abigail, m. Philip **SPENCER**, b. of Salisbury, Sept. 25, 1751, by Rev. Jonathan Lee	1	224
Alanson, s. Jonathan, Jr. & Anna, b. Sept. 22, 1766	2	14
Albert, s. Silas & Marvel, b. May 12, 1799	3	36
Almirah Hannah, d. William & Katharine, b. Apr. 14, 1805	3	22
Amos, s. Amos & Alta, b. Nov. 10, 1808	3	11
Anna, of Nine Partners, m. Ephraim **WOODWORTH**, of Salisbury, Aug. 15, 1754, by Samuel Hutchinson, J.P. Witnesses Jesse Chatfield & Sarah Chatfield	1	241
Arson, see Audson **MOORE**	2	14
Audson*, s. Jonathan, Jr. & Anna, b. Sept. 13, 1769 *("Arson" overwritten)	2	14
Betsey, d. Calvin & Abigail, b. Sept. 20, 1805	3	33
Bingham, s. John & Lois, b. June 29, 1807	3	10
Calvin, s. John & Mary, b. May 16, 1773	2	13
Calvin & Abigail, had d. [ ], b. Aug. 17, 1809	3	33
Caroline, m. Charles **McELROY**, b. of Salisbury, Oct. 30, 1827, by Rev. Stephen Beach, of St. Johns Ch.	3	128
Caroline Precilla, d. William & Katharine, b. June 7, 1807	3	22
Charles, s. Calvin & Abigail, b. Sept. 5, 1801	3	33
Chloe, d. Samuel, Jr. & Hannah, b. June 18, 1766	1	146
Chloe, d. Sam[uel], Jr. & Hannah, d. Sept. 1, 1787, in the 22nd y. of her age	2	50
Clarissa, d. Amos & Alta, b. May 23, 1793	3	11
Cornelia, d. Amos & Alta, b. Mar. 15, 1806	3	11
Sintha, d. Jonathan, Jr. & Anna, b. Apr. 24, 1768 ("Cynthia")	2	14
Daniel, s. Samuel, Jr. & Hannah, b. Mar. 2, 1764	1	146
Daniel, m. Electa **TUPPER**, b. of Salisbury, Oct. 22, 1789, by Adonijah Strong, J.P.	2	50
David, s. Capt. Samuel & Rachel, b. Sept. 2, 1758	1	211
David, s. John & Mary, b. June 24, 1777	2	13
Edward, s. John, Jr. & Lois, b. Nov. 27, 1803	3	10
Elden, s. William & Katharine, b. Mar. 22, 1803	3	22
Elden, s. William & Katharine, d. June 10, 1810, ae 8	3	167
Electa, d. Lewis & Eliza, b. Jan. 19, 1831	3	72

	Vol.	Page

MOORE, MOER, (cont.)

	Vol.	Page
Elijah, s. Jonathan & Abigail, b. Apr. 13, 1752	1	206
Eliza A., m. Arthur **SCHOLFIELD**, b. of Salisbury, Nov. 29, 1838, by Rev. Thomas Bainbridge	3	157
Elizabeth*, d. Apr. 24, 1752 *(Written over "Elijah"?)	1	225
Frederic F., m. Caroline **McINTYRE**, b. of Salisbury, Apr. 11, 1827, by Rev. Stephen Beach, of St. Johns Ch.	3	127
Frederick Jay, s. Calvin & Abigail, b. July 21, 1799	3	33
Frederick Walter, s. Frederick J. & Caroline, b. Mar. 2, 1834	3	87
George, s. John & Mary, b. Sept. 11, 1769	2	13
Hannah, d. Samuel & Rachel, b. Nov. 15, 1751	1	211
Hannah, d. Samuel, Jr. & Hannah, b. July 23, 1772	2	13
Hannah, m. Samuel **LEE**, 2nd, b. of Salisbury, Feb. 12, 1774, by Rev. Jonathan Lee	2	45
Hannah, w. Samuel, d. Oct. 10, 1805, in the 65th y. of her age	3	166
Hannah, d. Luther & Delight, b. Mar. 21, 1812	3	37
Harry, s. John & Mary, b. Sept. 15, 1786	2	13
James, [twin with Nancy], s. John & Mary, b. Mar. 19, 1780; d. same day	2	13
James, s. John, Jr. & Lois, b. Mar. 13, 1793	3	10
Jehiel, s. Jonathan & Abigail, b. Nov. 13*, 1747 *("Nov. 19" in Rudd's book)	1	206
Jehiel, s. Jonathan & Abigail, d. June 15, 1750, in the 3rd y. of his age	1	206
John, m. Mary **BINGHAM**, b. of Salisbury, Dec. 15, 1762, by Rev. Jonathan Lee	1	250
John, s. John & Mary, b. May 31, 1766	1	116
John, Jr., m. Lois **EVEREST**, Jan. 25, 1791, by Samuel Lee, J.P.	2	50
John, d. May 6, 1802, in the 63rd y. of his age	3	165
John, s. John & Lois, b. Mar. 2, 1811	3	10
Jonathan, s. Jonathan, Jr. & Anna, b. Sept. 26, 1758	1	155
Jonathan, s. Jonathan, Jr. & Anna, d. Aug. 26, 1759	1	236
Jonathan, s. Jonathan, Jr. & Anna, b. Nov. 6, 1759	1	155
Jonathan, s. Jonathan, Jr. & Anna, d. Jan. 21, 1761	1	236
Jonathan, d. Sept. 8, 1770, in the 94th y. of his age	2	48
Joshua Whitney, s. John & Lois, b. May 28, 1793	3	10
Julia Ann, d. Luther & Delight, b. Jan. 28, 1801	3	37
Julia Ann, of Salisbury, m. Dr. Uriah **TURNER**, of New Marlborough, Jan. 7, 1823, by Pitkin Cowles	3	118
Justes, s. Simon & Abigail, b. Dec. 22, 1754, in Oblong	1	169
Levina, d. Simon & Abigail, b. Feb. 23, 1758	1	169
Lewis, s. Samuel, Jr. & Hannah, b. Apr. 12, 1771	2	13
Lewis, s. Daniel & Priscilla*, b. Nov. 26, 1789 *("Electa" written over. See Salisbury printed records. Priscilla d. before birth of Lewis)	2	40
Lewis, s. William & Katharine, b. Apr. 18, 1801	3	22
Lewis, m. Eliza **CORNWALL**, b. of Salisbury, Mar. 18, 1827, by Rev. Stephen Beach, of St. Johns Ch.	3	126
Lois, d. John & Lois, b. Dec. 1, 1805; d. Dec. 2, 1805	3	10
Lucinda, d. William & Katharine, b. Sept. 19, 1811	3	22
Lucinda, m. Henry **GREEN**, b. of Salisbury, Sept. 1, 1833, by		

	Vol.	Page
MOORE, MOER, (cont.)		
L.E. Lathrop	3	143
Lucy, d. Samuel, Jr. & Hannah, b. Oct. 13*, 1774 *("Oct. 18" in Rudd's book)	2	13
Lucy, d. Nathan & Juliana, b. Jan. 14, 1797	3	24
Lucy, of Salisbury, m. Eli **BROWN**, of Stonington, Nov. 6, 1797, by Samuel Lee, J.P.	3	110
Lucy, d. Luther & Delight, b. Dec. 19, 1809	3	37
Lucy, m. Hiram **BUNDY**, b. of Salisbury, Feb. 1, 1829, by Rev. Stephen Beach, of St. Johns Ch.	3	133
Lucy Brown, d. William & Katharine, b. Nov. 11, 1809	3	22
Luther, s. John & Mary, b. June 27, 1771	2	13
Luther, m. Delight **KINGSBURY**, b. of Salisbury, Apr. 25, 1799, by Rev. Joseph W. Crossman	3	110
Luther Lorain, s. Luther & Delight, b. July 10, 1814	3	37
Maria, d. Lewis & Eliza, b. Aug. 1, 1829	3	72
Martha, d. John & Mary, b. Dec. 23, 1767	2	13
Martha, m. Samuel **STODDARD**, b. of Salisbury, July 6, 1785, by Rev. Jonathan Lee	2	43
Martha Emeline, d. Luther & Delight, b. Sept. 27, 1807	3	37
Mary, d. Samuell & Rachel, b. Jan. 28, 1748/9	1	211
Mary, d. Jonathan, Jr. & Anna, b. June 3, 1762	1	155
Mary, m. Nath[anie]ll **EVARTS**, b. of Salisbury, Dec. 12, 1770, by Rev. Jonathan Lee	2	45
Mary Ann, d. Calvin & Abigail, b. Oct. 10, 1803	3	33
Mary Ann, m. Wolcott **TURNER**, Dec. 6, 1826, by L.E. Lathrop	3	125
Mary Catharine, d. W[illia]m & Katharine, b. June 9, 1816	3	22
Molley, d. John & Mary, b. Sept. 14, 1763	1	116
Myron, s. Luther & Delight, b. Apr. 17, 1803	3	37
Nancy, [twin with James], d. John & Mary, b. Mar. 19, 1780, d. same day	2	13
Nathan, s. Samuel, Jr. & Hannah, b. July 10, 1765	1	146
Orlo, s. William & Katharine, b. Dec. 13, 1798	3	22
Orville, s. Calvin & Abigail, b. Nov. 20, 1797	3	33
Patty, d. John, Jr. & Lois, b. Oct. 21, 1794	3	10
Phebe, d. Capt. Samuel & Rachel, b. Jan. 17, 1756	1	211
Phebe, d. John & Mary, b. June 5, 1775	2	13
Phebe, m. Joseph **KETCHAM**, b. of Salisbury, July 3, 1777, by Rev. Jonathan Lee	2	47
Phebe Ruggles, d. Luther & Delight, b. Aug. 14, 1805	3	37
Polly, d. John, Jr. & Lois, b. Nov. 21, 1791	3	10
Polly, m. John **URE**, b. of Salisbury, Oct. 19, 1785, by Rev. Jonathan Lee	2	43
Polly, d. Amos & Alta, b. Dec. 19, 1816	3	11
Polly, m. David R. **PAINTER**(?), May 15, 1827, by L.E. Lathrop	3	127
Priscilla, d. Daniel & Priscilla, b. Jan. 3, 1788	2	40
Prescilla, w. Daniel, d. Feb. 3, 1788, in the 28th y. of her age	2	50
Rachel, m. Solomon **BINGHAM**, b. of Salisbury, June 4, 1761, by Rev. Jonathan Lee	1	249
Rachel, wid. Capt. Samuel, d. Sept. 19, 1798, in the 82nd y. of his age	3	164

SALISBURY VITAL RECORDS 233

	Vol.	Page
MOORE, MOER, (cont.)		
Rhoda, d. John, Jr. & Lois, b. Mar. 31, 1797	3	10
Richard, s. John & Mary, b. Jan. 7, 1782	2	13
Roderick, s. Jonathan, Jr. & Anna, b. Feb. 9, 1761	1	155
Rodger, s. Rodger & Meriam, b. Sept. 24, 1765	1	134
Ruth, d. Jonathan, Jr. & Anna, b. Oct. 3, 1764	1	155
Sally, m. Jehiel **EVEREST**, b. of Salisbury, Jan. 6, 1785, by Rev. Jonathan Lee	2	43
Samuel, Jr., of Salisbury, m. Hannah **BEEBE**, of Canaan, Mar. 7, 1763, by Rev. Daniel Farrand, of Canaan	1	251
Samuel, s. Samuel, Jr. & Hannah, b. Dec. 18, 1767	2	13
Samuel, Capt., d. Jan. 5, 1796, in the 81st y. of his age	3	164
Samuel, of Salisbury, m. Mrs. Mary **VIBBERT**, of New York, June 28, 1807, by Rev. Joseph W. Crossman	3	113
Sarah, d. Samuell & Rachel, b. Apr. 11, 1746	LR1	351
Sarah, d. John & Mary, b. Dec. 23, 1764	1	116
Sidney White, s. Calvin & Abigail, b. Dec. 4, 1811	3	33
Silas, s. Capt. Samuel & Rachel, b. Sept. 9, 1762	1	211
Silas, m. Marvel **BREWSTER**, b. of Salisbury, June 24, 1798, by Samuel Lee, J.P.	3	110
Silas Brewster, s. Silas & Marvel, b. Oct. 21, 1808	3	36
Solomon Everitt, s. John, Jr. & Lois, b. Feb. 8, 1802	3	10
Sophia, d. John, Jr. & Lois, b. Nov. 2, 1798	3	10
Sophia, m. Henry S. **GAY**, b. of Salisbury, Apr. 26, 1839, by Rev. Adam Reid	3	157
Susanah, d. Rodger & Meriam, b. Dec. 20, 1763	1	134
Susanah, d. Rodger & Meriam, b. Dec. 20, 1763	1	145
Sylvester Everitt, s. John, Jr. & Lois, b. Dec. 22, 1800; d. Jan. 24, 1801	3	10
Walter, s. Calvin & Abigail, b. Jan. 12, 1814	3	37
William, s. Samuel, Jr. & Hannah, b. Jan. 27, 1769	2	19
William, s. Samuel, Jr. & Hannah, b. Feb.*, 27, 1769 *(Salisbury printed records give date as "Jan. 27")	2	13
William, m. Abby **LEACH**, b. of Salisbury, Apr. 28, 1839, by Rev. Thomas Bainbridge	3	158
William Eldon, s. William & Katharine, b. July 30, 1814	3	22
----------or, d. Calvin & Abigail, b. Mar. 17, 1807	3	33
MORGAN, Anna, d. Joshua & Anna, b. Sept. [ ], 1781	2	9
Ira, s. Joshua & Anna, b. May 8, 1785	2	8
Joshua, s. Joshua & Anna, b. July 3, 1779	2	9
Minerva, of Salisbury, m. Benton **EDMONDS**, of Sheffield, Mass., Jan. 2, 1844, by Rev. C.V. Amerman	3	96
Sally, d. Joshua & Anna, b. July 18, 1783	2	8
Samuel & Hannah, had s. [ ], d. May 24, 1779, in the 9th y. of his age	2	49
William, m. Phebe **CHURCH**, b. of Salisbury, May 18, 1806, by Rev. Joseph W. Crossman	3	112
William S., m. Harriet **HOLMES**, b. of Salisbury, Sept. 25, 1839, by Rev. Tho[ma]s Bainbridge	3	158
William Seymour, s. William & Phebe, b. Sept. 5, 1807	3	29
MORHOUS, Andrew, s. Andrew & Phebe, b. Nov. 6, 1750	1	219

	Vol.	Page
MORRIS, Curtis, of New Milford, m. Cynthia J. **FRINK**, of Salisbury, Sept. 2, 1827, by Leonard E. Lathrop	3	127
Daniel, s. Daniel & Elizabeth, b. [ ], 1754	1	197
Lowes, s. Daniel & Elizabeth, b. Mar. 11, 1756	1	197
Sarah, d. David & Elizabeth, b. Sept. 14, 1758	1	197
MORRISON, Mary Ann, m. Pliney N. **PERRY**, b. of Salisbury, Jan. 19, 1830, by Rev. Noah Bigelow. Int. Pub.	3	135
MOSES, Joshua N., of Norfolk, m. Eliza **BROWN**, d. Samuel, of Salisbury, May 15, 1823, by Job Norton, J.P.	3	119
MOULTON, Daniel, s. Daniel & Sarah, b. Feb. 22, 1769	2	22
Hannah, d. Samuel & Sarah, b. Apr. 10, 1771	2	22
Heman*, s. Samuel & Sarah, b. Apr. 23, 1773, in Castletown *(Arnold Copy has " Thomas")	2	22
John, s. Samuel & Sarah, b. Dec. 18, 1766	1	137
Thomas*, s. Samuel & Sarah, b. Apr. 23, 1773, in Castletown *("Heman" in Rudd's book with a note that the entry is crossed out)	2	22
Trueman, s. Samuel & Sarah, b. Feb. 10, 1765	1	137
MUNGER, Bille, m. Hanna **SIKES**, b. of Salisbury, Apr. 15, 1752, by Rev. Jonathan Lee	1	224
Billy, s. Billy & Hanna, b. Dec. 16, 1754	1	217
Hannah, d. Billy & Hannah, b. June 28, 1757	1	217
Lucy, d. Billy & Hannah, b. Feb. 4, 1769	2	21
Mary, d. Billy & Hannah, b. Oct. 29, 1759	1	217
Mary, d. Billy & Hannah, b. Feb. 8, 1762	1	128
Meriam, d. Billy & Hanna, b. Mar. 18, 1753, in Oblong	1	217
Meriam, m. Samuell **LAW**, b. of Salisbury, July 13, 1769, by J. Hutchinson, J.P.	2	44
Salome, d. Billy & Hannah, b. Oct. 15, 1766	2	21
Silvanus, s. Billy & Hannah, b. July 3, 1764	1	128
Silvanus, s. Billy & Hannah, b. July 3, 1764	2	21
MURGETHROYD, MURGITHROYD, John B., late of Claverick, m. Amelia **SMITH**, of Salisbury, Nov. 13, 1810, by Rev. Joseph W. Crossman	3	114
John Walker, s. John B. & Amelia, b. Aug. 12, 1813	3	56
Mary, d. John B. & Amelia, b. Oct. 14, 1811	3	56
[MURPHY], MURPHEY, George, s. John & Lucy, b. Sept. 30, 1776, at Deleware	2	21
John, s. John & Lucy, b. Feb. 19, 1775, at Susquehannah	2	21
Lucy, late of Susqueehannah, m. Joshua **JEWELL**, Jr., of Salisbury, Mar. 25, 1779, by Rev. Jonathan Lee	2	41
Sarah, d. John & Lucy, b. Aug. 19, 1776, at Susquehannah	2	21
NABB*,Calestia, d. James & Mercy, b. Mar. 20, 1780 *("**NOBLE**" in Rudd's book)	2	40
Dianthe*, d. James & Mercy, b. Nov. 19, 1782 *("Dianthe **NOBLE**" in Rudd's book)	2	40
Warham*, s. James & Mercy, b. Jan. 5, 1778, in Westfield *("Warham **NOBLE**" in Rudd's book)	2	40
NEVITT, Almira, m. Charles **BURRALL**, b. of Salisbury, Mar. 31, 1841, by Rev. Adam Reid	3	160
NEWCOMB, Azariah, m. Deborah **BUELL**, May 4, 1743	LR1	356-7

	Vol.	Page
NEWCOMB, (cont.)		
Azariah, m. Rebecca **BRADLEY**, b. of Salisbury, Jan. 17, 1782, by Rev. Jonathan Lee	2	41
Azariah, m. Rebekah **BRADLEY**, b. of Salisbury, Jan. 17, 1782, by Rev. Jonathan Lee	2	42
Buell, s. Azariah & Deborah, b. Mar. 28, 1744; d. Sept. 22, 1746	LR1	354
Deborah, d. Cyrenius & Sarah, b. May 24, 1745	LR1	355
Deborah, m. Luther **EVARTS**, b. of Salisbury, Aug. 13, 1767, by Joshua Porter, J.P.	2	44
Deborah, wid., d. Dec. 29, 1784, in the 60th y. of her age	2	50
Judeth, d. Azariah & Deborah, b. Sept. 22, 1745	LR1	355
NEWELL, Mary Ann, m. Myron **HAMLIN**, b. of Salisbury, June 15, 1829, by L.E. Lathrop	3	134
Sally, m. Thomas **STILES**, b. of Salisbury, Nov. 26, 1829, by Rev. Stephen Beach, of St. Johns Ch.	3	135
NICHOLS, Betsey, d. Philo & Rhoda, b. Sept. 2, 1784	2	20
Caleb Bemont, s. Dan[ie]ll & Deborah, b. Sept. 30, 1811	3	33
Caroline Zerviah, d. Dan[ie]ll & Deborah, b. Sept. 7, 1808	3	33
Cynthia, d. Philo & Rhoda, b. Mar. 9, 1788	2	20
Daniel, s. Caleb & Deborah, b. Nov. 1, 1771, in New Town	2	22
Daniel P., of Danbury, m. Matilda **ARERILL**, of Salisbury, June 9, 1846, by G.S. Brownell	3	98
Deborah, d. Caleb & Deborah, b. Sept. 23, 1775	2	22
Hannah, d. John & Abigail, b. Aug. 20, 1757	1	189
Hiram, s. Joshua & Abia, b. Nov. 20, 1798	3	24
James, s. Joshua & Alice, d. Dec. 25, 1799, ae 4	3	164
John, Jr., m. Abigail **BARET**, b. of Salisbury, May 24, 1756, by Rev. Jonathan Lee. Witnesses Phineas Adams & Dorothy Cobb	1	243
Mary Ensign, d. Dan[ie]ll & Deborah, b. Nov. 17, 1799	3	33
Philo, s. Caleb & Deborah, b. Nov. 3, 1762, in New Town	2	22
Polly, d. Caleb & Deborah, b. Nov. 2, 1766, in New Town	2	22
NICKERSON, Rebeckah, m. George **BALIS**, Jan. 5, 1791, by Lot Norton, J.P.	JC	152
NOBLE*, Calestia, d. James & Mercy, b. Mar. 20, 1780 *(Arnold Copy has "**NABB**")	2	40
Dianthe*, d. James & Mercy, b. Nov. 19, 1782 *(Arnold Copy has "**NABB**")	2	40
Warham*, s. James & Mercy, b. Jan. 5, 1778, in Westfield *(Arnold Copy has "Warham **NABB**")	2	40
NODINE, Chloe, of Salisbury, m. Benjamin **BENSON**, of Sharon, Dec. 5, 1847, by Rev. Jonathan Lee	3	102
NOKES, Anna, of Nobletown, m. Solomon **TYLER**, of Salisbury, Apr. 27, 1786, by Rev. Jonathan Lee	2	43
NORTHROP, NORTHRUP, Abi, d. Joseph, Jr. & Mary, b. Feb. 13, 1767	1	149
Abi, d. Abner & Jerusha, b. Jan. 14, 1810	3	41
Abigail, d. Joseph, Jr. & Mary, b. Feb. 19, 1771	2	7
Abigail, m. Levi **WEED**, b. of Salisbury, May 9, 1799, by Rev. Joseph W. Crossman	3	110
Abner, s. Joseph, [Jr.] & Mary, b. Nov. 27, 1777	2	7
Anna, m. Abijah **ROOD**, b. of Salisbury, Aug. 22, 1763, by John Hutchinson, J.P.	1	251

	Vol.	Page
NORTHROP, NORTHRUP, (cont.)		
Anna, d. Samuel & Phebe, b. Aug. 12, 1770	2	27
Caroline Elizabeth, d. Stephen & Rhoda, b. Dec. 13, 1821	3	68
Charles, of Mt. Ross, N.Y., m. Betsey **WHITMAN**, of Salisbury, Nov. 7, 1827, by Rev. Phinehas Cook, of the M.E. Ch.	3	128
Daniel Bradley, s. Joseph, Jr. & Lucy, b. Nov. 11, 1799	3	19
Elizabeth, d. Joseph & Allen, b. Dec. 4, 1756, in Ridgefield	1	126
Elizabeth, m. Obediah **CHAPMAN**, b. of Salisbury, Mar. 9, 1775, by Rev. Jonathan Lee	2	46
Eunice, d. Joseph & Allen, b. May 3, 1755, in Ridgefield	1	126
Eunice, d. Joseph, Jr. & Mary, b. Mar. 9, 1773	2	7
Hannah, d. Joseph, Jr. & Mary, b. Oct. 2, 1775	2	7
Heman, s. Joseph, Jr. & Lucy, b. Aug. 31, 1795	3	19
Ira, s. Nathaniell & Sarah, b. Nov. 8, 1776	2	38
Jeremiah, s. Joseph & Allen, b. Jan. 8, 1759, in Ridgefield	1	126
Jeremiah, s. Joseph & Allen, d. Sept. 29, 1762, in the 4th y. of his age	1	238
Jeremiah, s. Samuel & Phebe, b. Feb. 12, 1765	1	111
John Gibbs, s. Abner & Jerusha, b. Feb. 6, 1805	3	41
Joseph, s. Joseph, Jr. & Mary, b. Mar. 25, 1769	2	7
Joseph, Jr., m. Lucy **HOLCOMB**, Oct. 3, 1793, by Samuel Lee, J.P.	3	108
Joseph Kellogg, s. Stephen & Rhoda, b. Oct. 14, 1807, in Bethel, Co. of Sullivan, N.Y.	3	62
Lucy, d. Joseph, Jr. & Lucy, b. Apr. 20, 1798	3	19
Mary, d. Joseph, Jr. & Mary, b. Feb. 17, 1765	1	149
Nancy Maria, d. Stephen & Rhoda, b. Mar. 19, 1816	3	62
Phebe, d. Samuel & Phebe, b. Feb. 19, 1766	1	111
Sarah*, of Ammete, m. Hezekiah **CAMP**, Jr., of Salisbury, Nov. 21, 1752, by Rev. Mr. Woodbridge *(Arnold Copy has " Sarah **LOTHROP**")	1	240
Stephen, s. Joseph, Jr. & Mary, b. Sept. 26, 1780	2	7
Stephen, m. Rhoda **VOSBURGH**, Feb. 8, 1803, by Ephraim Judson. Witnesses Polly Grenold & Diadama Vosbough	3	115
NORTON, [see also **ORTON**], Abigail, d. Samuell & Sarah, b. Apr. 13, 1756	1	133
Ann, m. Ebenezer **JEWELL**, b. of Salisbury, July 28, 1757, by Rev. Jonathan Lee	1	246
Arthur, s. Lot, Jr. & Martha, b. May 20, 1832	3	81
Chloe, d. Samuel & Sarah, b. Aug. 10, 1752, in Salisbury	1	133
Cloe, m. John **BUTLER**, b. of Salisbury, May 9, 1769, by John Hutchinson, J.P.	2	44
Cornelia Dean, d. Lot, Jr. & Martha, b. Nov. 17, 1827	3	81
Cornelia Esther, of Salisbury, m. James **DEAN**, Jr., of Whitetown, Oneida Cty., N.Y., Feb. 9, 1818, by Rev. Charles Printice. Witness Lot Norton	3	115
Eliphalet Whittlesey, s. Lot, Jr. & Martha W., b. Sept. 18, 1830,	3	81
Esther, d. Lot & Esther, b. June 22, 1759	1	165
Esther, m. John Pope **WALTON**, Jan. 1, 1792, by Rev. Daniel Farrand, of Canaan	3	108
Esther, d. Lot & wid. of John **WALTON**, d. Oct. 19, 1809, ae 51	3	167
Esther Cornelia, d. Lot, Jr. & Polly, b. Oct. 18, 1792	3	8
Gulielma Maria, d. Lot, Jr. & Mary, b. Sept. 9, 1795	3	8

SALISBURY VITAL RECORDS 237

	Vol.	Page
NORTON, (cont.)		
Gulielmo Maria, d. Lot, Jr. & Mary, d. Mar. 8, 1806, at East Guilford, ae 10 y. 6 m.	3	166
Harriet Emeline, d. Lott, Jr. & Polly, b. Aug. 9, 1807	3	8
Henry Sidney, s. Lot, Jr. & Polly, b. Nov. 12, 1800	3	8
Henry Sidney, s. Henry S. & Lucy M., b. Aug. 19, 1832	3	8
Henry Sidney, s. Henry S. & Lucy M., d. Feb. 22, 1834	3	168
Huldah, d. Samuel & Sarah, b. June 2, 1761	1	133
Huldah, d. Samuel & Sarah, d. Feb. 20, 1765	1	239
Huldah, d. Samuel & Sarah, b. June 9, 1765	1	133
Ishi, s. Samuel & Sarah, b. Oct. 27, 1757	1	133
Ishi, s. Samuel & Sarah, d. July 18, 1762	1	239
Ishi, s. Samuel & Sarah, b. Nov. 5, 1763	1	133
Ishi, s. Samuel & Sarah, d. May 24, 1766	1	239
Jonathan Todd, s. Henry S. & Lucy M., b. May 26, 1824	3	8
Lois, d. Samuel & Sarah, b. Oct. 9, 1767	2	13
Lot, of Salisbury, m. Esther **MERRICK***, of Farmington, Dec. 2, 1756, by Rev. Timothy Pitkin *("**MERRELLE**" in Rudd's book)	1	246
Lot & Esther, had s. [ ], b. Mar. 24, 1761; d. same day	1	165
Lot, s. Lot & Esther, b. Apr. 17, 1769	2	24
Lot, his w. [ ], d. Nov. 10, 1778, in the 49th y. of her age	2	49
Lot, Jr., of Salisbury, m. Polly **HICOCK**, of Sheffield, May 8, 1791, by Rev. Daniel Farrand, of Canaan	3	108
Lot, had negro Candace, d. Lyndia, b. May 2, 1795	3	22
Lot, Jr. & Polly, had d. [ ], b. Sept. 26, 1797; d Oct. 20, 1797	3	8
Lott, s. Lott, Jr. & Mary, b. Jan. 15, 1803	3	8
Lot, d. Apr. 16, 1810, ae 77	3	167
Lot, m. Martha **WHITTLESEY**, Sept. 6, 1826, by Leonard E. Lathrop	3	124
Lucy Matilda, d. Henry S. & Lucy M., b. May 31, 1826	3	8
Martha Strong, d. Lot, Jr. & Martha, b. Jan. 12, 1836	3	81
Miriam Carolina, d. Lot, Jr. & Polly, b. Oct. 12, 1798	3	8
Miriam Caroline, d. Lot, Jr. & Polly, d. Jan. 6, 1802, ae 4	3	155
Sally Maria, d. Lott, Jr. & Polly, b. Feb. 4, 1805	3	8
Samuel, s. Samuel & Sarah, b. Oct. 16, 1748, in Guilford	1	133
Sarah, d. Samuell & Sarah, b. Sept. 23, 1750, in Guilford	1	133
Sarah, d. Lot & Esther, b. Apr. 26, 1766	1	165
Sarah, d. Lot, Jr. & Martha, b. Feb. 10, 1840	3	81
Thomas Lot, s. Lot, Jr. & Martha W., b. Aug. 11, 1842	3	81
NOTT, Abraham Pratt, s. Abraham & Abigail, b. Jan. 15, 1802	3	34
Harriet Abigail, d. Abraham & Abigail, b. Apr. 21, 1805	3	34
Harriet Abigail, m. William Duncan **BLACK**, b. of Salisbury, Dec. 11, 1823, by Lot Norton, J.P.	3	120
Hiram Goodwin, s. Abraham & Abigail, b. Apr. 8, 1788, in Canaan	3	34
Julia, d. Abraham & Abigail, b. May 23, 1790, in Canaan	3	34
Julia, d. Abraham & w. of Chester **ELDREDGE**, d. Dec. 2, 1815, ae 25, in Sharon	3	168
NOXAN, Hannah E., of Florida, N.Y., m. Thomas **DAY**, Jr., of Salisbury, [Sept.] 15, [1830], by L.E. Lathrop	3	137
ODELL, Charles R., m. Mary P. **ODELL**, b. of Salisbury, Oct. 15, 1846,		

	Vol.	Page
ODELL, (cont.)		
by Rev. Harley Goodwin	3	99
Charles R., m. Mary P. **ODELL**, b. of Salisbury, Oct. 15, 1846, by		
Rev. Harley Goodwin	3	169
Mary P., m. Charles R. **ODELL**, b. of Salisbury, Oct. 15, 1846, by		
Rev. Harley Goodwin	3	99
Mary P., m. Charles R. **ODELL**, b. of Salisbury, Oct. 15, 1846, by		
Rev. Harley Goodwin	3	169
[OLMSTEAD], [see under **UMSTEAD**]		
[O'ROURKE], **O'ROUKE**, William, m. Ann **McCUE**, [Nov.] 29, 1835,		
by Leonard E. Lathrop	3	150
ORR, James, of Sharon, m. Hannah S. **HARRISON**, of Salisbury, June 2,		
1846, by G.S. Brownell	3	98
ORTON, [see also **NORTON**], Anne, of Great Barrington, m. Silas		
BINGHAM, late of Salisbury, now of Great Barrington, Feb.		
28, 1773, by John Hutchinson, J.P.	2	45
OWEN, Aaron, s. John, 2nd & Johannah, b. Oct. 23, 1776	2	22
Abel, s. Lernerd & Mary, b. Feb. 26, 1772	2	9
Abigail, d. Lernerd & Mary, b. May 26, 1766	2	9
Abigail, d. Lenerd & Mary, b. July 18, 1766	1	113
Alathea, d. John & Deborah, b. Oct. 17, 1762	1	125
Amasa, s. Jonathan & Patience, b. Feb. 10, 1753	1	210
Ambrose, s. Elijah & Alice, b. Dec. 25, 1770	2	29
Ann, d. David & Margret, b. Apr. 14, 1747	1	204
Ann, d. Elijah & Olive, b. Aug. 27, 1765	1	188
Asenath, d. John & Deborah, b. July 12, 1764	1	125
Asenath, d. John & Deborah, b. July 12, 1764	1	138
Charles, s. Lernerd, Jr. & Kesiah, b. June 28, 1775, in Salisbury	2	9
Charlotte, d. Eliphalet & Eunice, b. Nov. 17, 1773	2	9
Chauncey Lee, s. Lernerd, Jr. & Kesiah, b. Oct. 23, 1782	2	9
Chloe, d. John & Deborah, b. Aug. 12, 1766	1	125
Cynthia, d. James & Joanna, b. Sept. 27, 1771	2	7
Daniel, s. David & Margret, b. Aug. 20, 1753	1	204
Daniel, s. Lernerd & Mary, b. Feb. 14, 1768	2	9
David, s. David & Margaret, b. Nov. 13, 1756	1	191
Deidamia, d. Eliphalet & Eunice, b. Mar. 2, 1763	1	155
Ebenezer, s. John, 2nd & Johannah, b. May 16, 1769	2	22
Egbert, of North East, m. Abigail **LANDON**, of Salisbury, Oct. 21,		
1839, by Rev. Tho[ma]s Bainbridge	3	158
Electe, d. Elijah & Olive, b. Jan. 3, 1762	1	188
Elijah, s. Elijah & Patience, b. Jan. 28, 1755; d. same day	1	243
Elijah, m. Olive **BEMAN**, b. of Salisbury, Nov. 10, 1756, by James		
Landon, J.P.	1	244
Elijah, s. Elijah & Olive, b. Apr. 27, 1759	1	188
Elisha, s. Elijah & Olive, b. Oct. 5, 1760	1	188
Elizabeth, d. John, 1st & Deborah, b. Aug. 6, 1768	2	19
Esther, d. Elijah & Olive, b. Aug. 22, 1763	1	188
Ethan, s. John, 2nd & Johannah, b. June 10, 1774	2	22
Eunice, d. Lernerd & Experience, b. Nov. 31 [sic], 1754	1	219
Eunice, had d. Matte*, June 11, 1770 *("Molle" in Rudd's book)	2	9
Experience, w. Lernerd, d. May 1, 1756, in the 24th y. of her age	1	227

SALISBURY VITAL RECORDS 239

	Vol.	Page
OWEN, (cont.)		
Gideon, s. Eliphalet & Eunice, b. June 23, 1765	1	155
Herman*, s. John, 2nd & Johannah, b. Dec. 8, 1779 *("Heman" in Rudd's book)	2	22
Hulda, d. Elijah & Patience, b. Jan. 28, 1755; d. same day	1	209
Irene, m. Asa **BLOGGET**, b. of Salisbury, Dec. 7, 1750, by Rev. Jonathan Lee	1	223
Irene, d. Eliphalet & Eunice, b. Dec. 1, 1760	1	155
James, s. James & Johana, b. Apr. 1, 1765	1	145
Jemima, d. Joshua & Hanna, b. Sept. 19, 1754	1	175
Johannah, d. James & Joanna, b. Sept. 13, 1769	2	7
John, m. Deborah **WILLIAMS**, Mar. 4, 1762, by Rev. Jonathan Lee	1	250
John, 2nd, of Salisbury, m. Johanna **PHELPS**, of Win[d]sor, May 31, 1768, by Rev. Mr. Russell	2	44
John, s. John, 2nd & Johannah, b. Dec. 23, 1771	2	22
Jonathan, 2nd, s. [Jonathan & Patience], b. Mar. 18, 1742/3	LR1	355
Joseph, s. Jonathan & Patience, b. Feb. 20, 1750/1	1	210
Joseph, d. Sept. 9, 1758, in the 74th y. of his age	1	231
Julius, s. Elijah & Olive, b. Apr. 23, 1769	1	188
Lenerd, s. Lernerd & Experience, b. Apr. 20, 1756	1	219
Lenerd, m. Mary **STANNARD**, b. of Salisbury, Apr. 28, 1757, by Rev. Jonathan Lee	1	246
Loes, d. Elijah & Olive, b. Feb. 28, 1767	1	188
Lusina, d. Lenerd & Mary, b. Oct. 18, 1764	1	113
Lydia, m. Thomas **TUTTLE**, b. of Salisbury, Feb. 1, 1753, by Rev. Jonathan Lee	1	240
Margaret, d. Joshua & Hannah, b. Aug. 4, 1759	1	175
Martha, m. Claudias **BEGROUGH**, b. of Salisbury, Mar. 19, 1760, by Rev. Jonathan Lee	1	249
Mary, d. [Jonathan & Patience], b. Apr. 16, 1745	LR1	355
Mary, d. Lernerd & Mary, b. June 20, 1759	1	219
Matte*, d. Eunice, b. June 11, 1770 *("Molle" in Rudd's book)	2	9
Meriam, d. Joshua & Hannah, b. Nov. 8, 1763	1	175
Molle*, d. Eunice, b. June 11, 1770 *(Arnold Copy has " Matte")	2	9
Naomi, d. Elijah & Patience, b. Feb. 19, 1750	1	209
Naomi, d. Elijah & Patience, b. Mar. 3, 1751	1	209
Naomi, of Salisbury, m. Modecai **SOAPER**, of Nine Partners, Apr. 4, 1770, by Rev. Jonathan Lee	2	41
Oliver, s. Jonathan & Patience, b. Sept. 24, 1748	1	210
Patience, d. Elijah & Patience, b. Mar. 14, 1756; d. Mar. 18, 1756	1	209
Patience, w. Elijah, d. Mar. 19, 1756	1	227
Patience, d. Elijah & Olive, b. Feb. 2, 1758	1	188
Pegge, d. James & Joanna, b. Aug. 16, 1767	2	7
Phebe, d. Elijah & Patience, b. Mar. 1, 1753	1	209
Rebekah, d. David & Margret, b. May 30, 1751	1	197
Rhoda, d. Eliphalet & Eunice, b. June 3, 1771	2	9
Rosel, s. Samuel & Lowis, b. Dec. 2, 1763	2	18
Ruth, d. Joshua & Hannah, b. May 13, 1756	1	175
Sabre, d. Lernerd & Mary, b. Dec. 26, 1757	1	219
Samuel, s. Samuel & Lowes, b. July 8, 1767	2	9
Sary, d. Elijah & Patience, b. July 18, 1748, in Lebanon	1	209

	Vol.	Page

OWEN, (cont.)
    Sarah, m. Heber **ALLEN**, b. of Salisbury, Mar. 17, 1768, by Rev. Jonathan Lee — 2, 44
    Sarah, m. Elijah **SMITH**, b. of Salisbury, Jan. 2, 1771, by Rev. Jonathan Lee — 2, 45
    Sarah, of Sheffield, m. Elisha **TYLER**, of Salisbury, Oct. 31, 1782, at Sheffield, Mass., by Lemuel Bernard, J.P. — 2, 42
    Sibel, d. Lenerd & Mary, b. Sept. 1, 1761 — 1, 113
    Thadeus, s. Lenerd & Mary, b. Jan. 27, 1763 — 1, 113
    Thomas, s. David & Margaret, b. Feb. 27, 1748/9 — 1, 204
    William, s. Jonathan & Patience, b. Apr. 7, 1741 — LR1, 355

PAGE, Electa, w. Asa & d. of Daniel **BRADLEY**, d. Mar. 13, 1807, ae 22 — 3, 166
    Eliza Ann, d. Asa & Lotty, b. Nov. 25, 1808 — 3, 6
    James Downs, s. Asa & Lotty, b. Nov. 7, 1818 — 3, 6
    Jane, d. Asa & Lotty, b. Mar. 12, 1813 — 3, 6
    Laura, d. Asa & Lotty, b. Jan. 1, 1811 — 3, 6
    Lotty Landon, d. Asa & Lotty, b. July 5, 1816 — 3, 6
    Mary Rebekah, d. Asa & Electa, b. Apr. 16, 1806 — 3, 6
    Thankfull M., m. J.A. **HAIGHT**, June 15, 1834, by Leonard E. Lathrop — 3, 146

PAINIER (?), [see under **PAINTER**]

PAINTER (?), David R., m. Molly **MOORE**, May 15, 1827, by L.E. Lathrop — 3, 127
    Edward Moore, s. David R. & Polly, b. Aug. 20, 1828 — 3, 82
    Gamaleel, m. Abigail **CHIPMAN**, Aug. 20, 1767, by Rev. Jonathan Lee — 2, 44
    Hannah Sophia, d. David R. & Polly, b. Sept. 1, 1829 — 3, 82
    Joseph, s. Gamaleel & Abigail, b. Oct. 22, 1770 — 2, 21
    Samuel, s. Gamaleel & Abigail, b. May 3, 1772 — 2, 21

PALMER, PARMER, Charles Kellogg, s. Archer & Anna Mariah, b. Jan. 22, 1804 — 3, 35
    Dorcas, m. Hezekiah **ELDREDGE**, b. of Salisbury, Nov. 28, 1800, by Joseph W. Crossman — 3, 111
    James Albert, s. Daniel & Peggy, b. Oct. 6, 1794 — 3, 16
    Joanna, of Sheffield, m. Simeon **LYMAN**, Jr., of Salisbury, Dec. 7, 1780, by Rev. Jonathan Lee — 2, 41
    Nina Mariah, d. Archer & Anna Mariah, b. Apr. 11, 1805 — 3, 35

PALMETER, Philomela, d. William & Lorana, b. Oct. 2, 1789 — 2, 17

PARKER, Philip Spencer, s. Medad & Tryphena, b. Sept. 7, 1776 — 2, 10
    Ralph, s. Medad & Tryphena, b. Sept. 17, 1772 — 2, 10
    Tryphena, d. Medad & Tryphena, b. Sept. 14, 1774 — 2, 10

PARKS, Alma C., of Salisbury, m. Thomas **WARNER**, of Sheffield, Mar. 28, 1844, by Rev. Adam Reid — 3, 163
    Esther, d. James & Mary, b. May 25, 1771 — 2, 19
    James W., m. Caroline **JEWELL**, b. of Salisbury, Dec. 2, 1846, by Rev. Adam Reed — 3, 100
    John, s. James & Mary, b. Jan. 27, 1769 — 2, 19
    Polly, d. James & Mary, b. Jan. 16, 1772 — 2, 19
    William, s. James & Mary, d. May 22, 1802, ae 23 — 3, 166

PARMELEE, Elisha, m. Mary **HUTCHINSON**, Oct. 27, 1782, by Amzi Lewis, V.D.M. — 2, 42

SALISBURY VITAL RECORDS 241

	Vol.	Page
PARSONS, Claracy **CONKLIN**, d. Mabel, b. Apr. 25, 1768	2	13
Franklin, of Sharon, m. Maria H. **GAY**, of Salisbury, Oct. 10, 1838, by Rev. Adam Reid	3	155
Mabel, had d. Claracy **CONKLIN**, b. Apr. 25, 1768	2	13
Sheldon A., of Norfolk, m. Caroline C. **MANSFIELD**, of Salisbury, Oct. 19, 1842, by Rev. Adam Reid	3	162
PARTRIDGE, Harvey, of Canaan, m. Lucy **MAXAN**, of Salisbury, Mar. 15, 1826, by Rev. David Miller, of the M.E. Ch.	3	124
PATTERSON, PATESON, Cordelia, m. George W. **SMITH**, b. of Salisbury, June 14, 1846, by D.W. Clark	3	98
Daniel, s. William & Abigail, b. Jan. 5, 1758	1	189
William, m. Abigail **CARY**, b. of Salisbury, Apr. 11, 1757, by James Landon, J.P.	1	245
PEASE, Susanna, m. Elijah **STANTON**, Jan. 20, 1816, by Edward Bagley, J.P.	3	114
PECK, Abigail, twin with Mahitable, d. Isaac & Ruth, b. June 14, 1754	1	181
Anna, of Lyme, m. Timothy **CHITTENDEN**, Jr., of Salisbury, Nov. 7, 1782, by Rev. Daniel Miner, of Lyme	2	42
Ensign, of Salisbury, m. Mary Ann **BARD**, of Sharon, Sept. 29, 1836, by Rev. Oliver V. Amerman, of M.E. Ch.	3	153
Isaac, m. Betty **WHITE**, b. of Salisbury, Nov. 10, 1768, by John Hutchinson, J.P.	2	44
Jance C., of Salisbury, m. Alexander **HINE**, of Waterford, Jan. 19, 1835, by Leonard E. Lathrop	3	148
Katharine, d. Isaac & Elizabeth, b. Apr. 7, 1769	2	25
Lowrain*, d. Isaac & Ruth, b. May 23, 1756 *("Lorrain")	1	181
Lorranee, m. Joshua **WHITE**, b. of Salisbury, Sept. 8, 1776, by John Hutchinson, J.P.	2	47
Mary Polly, m. Asa **SPENCER**, b. of Salisbury, July 10, 1774, by Rev. Jonathan Lee	2	46
Mahitable, twin with Abigail, d. Isaac & Ruth, b. June 14, 1754	1	181
Nathan, Jr., m. Emma **GRENNELL**, b. of Salisbury, Mar. 29, 1831, by Leonard E. Lathrop	3	138
Sarah, m. Isaac **WHITE**, Jr., b. of Salisbury, May 14, 1770, by John Hutchinson, J.P.	2	45
Walhan, m. Minerva **JEWELL**, Jan. 24, 1826, by L.E. Lathrop	3	124
PEET, Abijah C., m. Betsey **BOTSFORD**, Dec. 8, 1822, by Samuel Church, J.P.	3	117
Abiram, Dr., d. Apr. 8, 1812, in the 40th y. of his age	3	168
Abiram Lewis, s. Abiram & Lois, b. Mar. 15, 1808	3	68
Ann, m. Sheldon **WELLING**, b. of Salisbury, Aug. 16, 1820, by Lavius Hyde	3	115
Francis Augusta, d. Abiram & Lois, b. Aug. 27, 1810	3	68
Frederic Plumb, s. Abiram & Lois, b. June 9, 1812	3	68
George W., of Canaan, m. Mary **ADAMS**, of Salisbury, Feb. 29, 1848, by Rev. Adam Reed	3	103
Jasper William, s. Abiram & Lois, b. May 26, 1800	3	68
Jeremiah Bushnell, s. Thomas B. & Eliza, b. July 10, 1822	3	69
Lucy Stoddard, d. W[illia]m W. & Lucy, b. Aug. 4, 1833	3	87
Mary Montague, d. Abiram & Lois, b. Feb. 26, 1803	3	68
Silence Leavitt, d. Abijah C. & Silence, b. Apr. 16, 1813	3	61

	Vol.	Page
PEET, (cont.)		
Silence S., m. Norton J. **BARD**, Sept. 6, 1836, by Leonard E. Lathrop	3	152
Thomas Bidwell, m. Eliza **BUSHNELL**, b. of Salisbury, Sept. 30, 1821, by Lavius Hyde	3	115
PERKINS, Amariah J., of Brookfield, m. Julia A. **SMITH**, of Salisbury, Sept. 8, 1845, by Rev. Adam Reed	3	97
PERRY, Alanson, s. Amos & Cynthia, b. Mar. 25, 1792	3	4
Anna Maria, of Salisbury, m. Jeremiah **ROOT**, of Canaan, Feb. 17, 1841, by Rev. J. Shaw	3	161
Harry, s. Amos & Cynthia, b. Sept. 16, 1788	3	4
James, s. Amos & Cynthia, b. May 11, 1790	3	4
Pliney N., m. Mary Ann **MORRISON**, b. of Salisbury, Jan. 19, 1830, by Rev. Noah Bigelow. Int. Pub.	3	135
PERS, Sarah, of Stratford, m. Thomas **REED**, Jr., of Norwalk, Apr. 7, 1763, by Moses Mather, V.D.M.	1	251
PERSONS, Mabel, m. Daniel **RENNOLLS**, Sept. 1, 1771, by John Hutchinson, J.P.	2	45
PETTEE, Aaron Everitt, s. Joseph & Joanna, b. Sept. 9, 1807	3	9
Eliza J., m. Robert **BOSTWICK**, b. of Salisbury, June 2, 1835, by Leonard E. Lathrop	3	149
Eunice E., m. Junius L. **STERLING**, b. of Salisbury, May 28, 1839, by Rev. Adam Reed	3	157
Eunice Everitt, d. Joseph & Joanna, b. Aug. 3, 1817	3	9
Joseph, s. Joseph & Joanna, b. Mar. 14, 1809	3	9
Joseph, Jr., m. Mary **PIERCE**, b. of Salisbury, [Jan.] 24, [1835], by Leonard E. Lathrop	3	148
Mary, d. Joseph & Joanna, b. Mar. 24, 1811	3	9
Stephen, s. Joseph & Joanna, b. May 30, 1814; d. Dec. 8, 1814	3	9
Stephen, s. Joseph & Joanna, d. Dec. 8, 1814, ae 7 m.	3	168
William Jenkins, s. Joseph & Joanna, b. Sept. 21, 1819	3	9
PETTIBONE, Julia A., of Salisbury, m. Ralph W. **SHEPHERD**, of Herkimer, N.Y., Oct. 27, 1840, by Rev. Adam Reid	3	160
PETTIT, Sarah, of Sharon, m. Hezekiah **LOOMIS**, Jr., of Salisbury, Nov. [ ], 1749, by John Searle	1	241
PEW*, William, m. Olive **VANDUSEN**, b. of Salisbury, Jan. 20, 1763, by John Hutchinson, J.P. *("**READ**" in Arnold Copy)	1	250
PHELPS, Daniel, s. Daniel & Eunice, b. Oct. 29, 1745, in Anchrom, on Levingtons Manor, Prov. of N.Y.	1	210
Ely, s. Daniel & Eunice, b. Nov. 14, 1751	1	210
Jabez, s. Daniel & Eunice, b. Nov. 18, 1743, in Sheffield	1	210
Johanna, of Win[d]sor, m. John **OWEN**, 2nd, of Salisbury, May 31, 1768, by Rev. Mr. Russell	2	44
Pyna, d. Daniel & Eunice, b. Oct. 8, 1749	1	210
Sarah, d. Daniel & Eunice, b. Sept. 12, 1747	1	210
PHILIPS, Sarah, m. Lawrence **WHITE**, b. of Salisbury, Apr. 1, 1773, by John Hutchinson, J.P.	2	45
PHILLO, Lucinda, m. William **CHAMBERLAIN**, Jan. 18, 1824, by David L. Perry	3	120
PHINNEY, Cornelia, of Salisbury, m. William **WINEGAR**, of Armenia, June 4, 1833, by L.E. Lathrop	3	143
PIERCE, Emela, d. Joseph & Lois, b. Mar. 31, 1814	3	61

	Vol.	Page
PIERCE, (cont.)		
James, m. Abigail **SCRIBNER**, Nov. 15, 1798, by William Bronson, J.P.	3	110
Joel B., m. Lydia **SWIFT**, b. of Salisbury, Feb. 27, [1825], by L.E. Lathrop	3	121
John, s. James & Abigail, b. July 3, 1802	3	34
John Hillard, s. James, 2nd & Polly, b. Oct. 23, 1809; d. Oct. 5, 1810	3	45
Maria N., m. Charles A. **HOLLISTER**, b. of Salisbury, Oct. 1, 1839, by Rev. Adam Reid	3	158
Mary, of Litchfield, m. Adonijah **STRONG**, of Salisbury, June 28, 1774, at Litchfield, by Andrew Adams, J.P.	2	46
Mary, d. James, 2nd & Polly, b. Feb. 21, 1807	3	45
Mary, m. Joseph **PETTEE**, Jr., b. of Salisbury, [Jan.] 24, [1835], by Leonard E. Lathrop	3	148
Nancy Maria, d. James, 2nd & Polly, b. Feb. 20, 1811	3	45
Sally, m. John **WALLING**, b. of Salisbury, Nov. 24, 1803, by Rev. Joseph W. Crossman. Witnesses Seth Tuttle & Ruth Tuttle	3	112
Sally Mariah, d. James & Abigail, b. May 30, 1808	3	34
Samuel, s. James, 2nd & Polly, b. Aug. 13, 1813	3	45
Stephen, s. James & Abigail, b. Oct. 11, 1804	3	34
PINKERTON, Polly, d. William & Cloe, b. Feb. 14, 1778	2	15
William, s. William & Cloe, b. Feb. 15, 1776, in New York State	2	15
PLUMB, Walter, of Bloomfield, m. Diantha **WEBB**, of Otis, Nov. 12, 1839, by Rev. Thomas Bainbridge	3	158
POLLARD, Emeline, of Salisbury, m. Ja[me]s N. **RACE**, of Claverack, N.Y., July 4, 1847, by Rev. W.H. Ferris	3	101
POMPELLY, POMPELY, Harriet, d. John & Hannah, b. Nov. 10, 1791	3	11
Herman, s. John & Hannah, b. Aug. 1, 1795	3	11
Jerusha, d. John & Hannah, b. [ ], 1778, in New York State, d. Nov. 22, 1793	3	11
Mary, d. John & Hannah, b. June 17, 1788	3	11
PORTER, Abigail, d. Nathaniell & Abigail, b. Jan. 12, 1750, in Woodbury	1	184
Abigail, d. Joshua & Abigail, b. Oct. 20, 1762	1	156
Abigail, of Norwich, m. Jacob **GALUSHA**, of Salisbury, Feb. 25, 1776, at Norwich, by Joel Benedict	2	47
Abigail, d. Nicholas & Rachel, b. June 12, 1782	2	32
Augustus, s. Joshua & Abigail, b. Jan. 18, 1769	2	7
Augusta, d. Joshua, Jr. & Hannah, b. Mar. 19, 1784	2	13
Daniel, s. Nicholas & Rachel, b. Apr. 17, 1775	2	32
David, s. Nathaniell & Abigail, b. Dec. 4, 1763	1	184
Dyer, s. Nicholas & Rachel, b. Jan. 15, 1788	2	32
Elizabeth, d. Nicholos & Rachel, b. Feb. 13, 1772	2	32
Esther, d. Nathaniell & Abigail, b. July 11, 1759	1	184
Eunice, d. Joshua & Abigail, b. Sept. 10, 1765	1	156
Frederick Augustus, s. Joshua, Jr. & Hannah, b. Aug. 6, 1789	2	13
George Griswold, s. Nicholas & Rachel, b. Jan. 1, 1792	2	32
James, s. Nicholas & Rachel, b. May 8, 1785	2	32
Joanna, d. Nathaniell & Abigail, b. Dec. 10, 1756	1	184
Joseph, s. Nathaniell & Abigail, b. Aug. 16, 1761	1	184
Joshua, of Salisbury, m. Abigail **BUEL**, of Coventry, May 14, 1759,		

	Vol.	Page
PORTER, (cont.)		
by Rev. Oliver Webb	1	248
Joshua, s. Joshua & Abigail, b. May 1, 1760	1	156
Lucy, d. Nathaniell & Abigail, b. Dec. 24, 1766	1	110
Mary, d. Nathaniell & Abigail, b. Mar. 12, 1752	1	184
Mary, d. Hannah **CARY**, b. Sept. 13, 1759	1	189
Minerva, d. Joshua, Jr. & Hannah, b. Sept. 26, 1787	2	13
Nathaniell, s. Nathaniell & Abigail, b. Aug. 26, 1754	1	184
Peter Buell, s. Joshua & Abigail, b. Aug. 14, 1773	2	7
Rebeckah, mother of Ens. Benjamin **SMALLEY**, d. Aug. 31, 1753, in the 78th y. of her age	1	226
Sally, d. Joshua & Abigail, b. Sept. 10, 1778	2	7
Sally, m. John M. **HOLLEY**, b. of Salisbury, Mar. 9, 1800, by Rev. Joseph W. Crossman	3	113
Stephen, s. Nicholas & Rachel, b. Sept. 30, 1779	2	32
Silvia*, d. Nicholas & Rachel, b. Feb. 6, 1790 *("Sylvia")	2	32
POST, Jane, of Sheffield, m. Richard **BECKWITH**, of Bavaria, N.Y., Oct. 11, 1841, by Rev. Adam Reid	3	161
PRATT, Asa D., of Sherbourne, Mass., m. Bridget B. **BABCOCK**, of Salisbury, Nov. 27, 1834, by Leonard E. Lathrop	3	147
Daniel, s. Schuyler & Olive, b. Mar. 9, 1823	3	69
Harrison, s. Schuyler & Olive, b. Dec. 24, 1826	3	69
Henry, s. Schuyler & Olive, b. Jan. 11, 1825	3	69
Louisa, d. Schuyler & Olive, b. May 4, 1833	3	69
Mary, d. Schuyler & Olive, b. Dec. 21, 1820	3	69
May G., of Salisbury, m. Lemuel J. Townsend, of Tyringham, Mass., Apr. 22, 1840, by Rev. Adam Reid	3	159
Milton, m. Rachel **BUNDY**, of Salisbury, Nov. 29, 1838, by Adam Reid	3	157
Olive, d. Schuyler & Olive, b. Apr. 6, 1831	3	69
Roxanna Cecelia, of Salisbury, m. Elisha **GARFIELD**, of Tyringham, [June] 21, [1828], by Leonard E. Lathrop	3	130
PRESTON, William, m. Mary A. **LYONS**, Jan. 16, 1848, by W.H. Ferris	3	103
PRIME, Dea, d. Benjamin & Mary, b. Jan. 3, 1787	2	16
Ebenezer Young, s. Benjamin & Mary, b. Dec. 7, 1781	2	16
Isaac Miller, s. Benjamin & Mary, b. July 13, 1783	2	16
James Hector, s. Benjamin & Mary, b. July 13, 1785	2	16
PRINCE, Abigail, of Salisbury, m. Simeon **BOSWORTH**, of Sandisfield, Dec. 16, 1838, by Rev. Thomas Bainbridge	3	157
Joel B., m. Lydia **SWIFT**, b. of Salisbury, Feb. 27, [1825], by L.E. Lathrop	3	121
PULVER, Hiram, of Amenia, N.Y., m. Mary S. **HUBBARD**, of Salisbury, Mar. 9, 1846, by Rev. Jonathan Lee	3	97
RACE, Fidelia, m. John T. **BIRCH**, b. of Salisbury, Mar. 12, 1828, by Rev. Stephen Beach, of St. Johns Ch.	3	129
Ja[me]s N., of Claverack, N.Y., m. Emeline **POLLARD**, of Salisbury, July 4, 1847, by Rev. W.H. Ferris	3	101
RAIMENTON, Mary, of Sheffield, m. Simeon **HANCHETT**, of Salisbury, Aug. 15, 1774, by Rev. Mr. Gay	2	47
RAY, Asa, s. Patrick & Sarah, b. May 9, 1778	2	23
Billy, s. Patrick & Sarah, b. Dec. 9, 1771	2	23

	Vol.	Page
RAY, (cont.)		
Hannah, d. Patrick & Sarah, b. Oct. 16, 1775	2	23
James, s. Patrick & Sarah, b. Aug. 29, 1769	2	23
READ, REED, [see also **RUDD**], Abigail, d. Elias & Mary, b. Jan. 15, 1754	1	219
Abigail, d. Elias & Mary, b. Jan. 15, 1754	1	132
Abigail, d. Moses & Rachel, d. May 10, 1758, ae 1 d.	1	229
Abigail, m. Ezra **SHELDON**, b. of Salisbury, July 4, 1776, by Rev. Jonathan Lee	2	47
Abraham, s. Moses & Rachel, b. Mar. 30, 1762	1	215
Abraham, of Salisbury, m. Sarah **MILES**, of Cornwall, Jan. 22, 1785, by Rev. Daniel Farrand, of Canaan. Witnesses Isaac Reed & Hephzibah Smith	2	42
Anna, d. Moses & Rachel, b. Sept. 25, 1754	1	215
Anne, d. Peter & Thankfull, b. Apr. 18, 1765	1	168
Benjamin, m. Hannah M. **WALKER**, Oct. 10, 1827, by Leonard E. Lathrop	3	128
Charles G., m. Samantha E. **BIRD**, b. of Salisbury, Dec. 25, 1822, by Charles Prentice	3	118
Chauncey, [twin with Henry Josiah], s. Chauncey & Lavinia, b. Mar. 14, 1813	3	84
Chauncey, Jr., m. Mary R. **CHITTENDEN**, b. of Salisbury, [ ], 1839, by Rev. A. Reid	3	157
Clooe, d. Moses & Rachel, b. May 3, 1756	1	215
Chloe, w. Daniel, d. Apr. 23, 1813, ae 41	3	168
Daniel, s. Elias & Mary, b. May 22, 1756	1	219
Daniel, s. Elias & Mary, b. May 24, 1756	1	132
Daniel, s. Thomas & Sarah, b. Jan. 8, 1764	1	147
Daniel, m. Chloe **CHAPIN**, b. of Salisbury, Dec. 23, 1798, by Rev. Joseph W. Crossman	3	111
Desire, d. Elias & Mary, b. Sept. 28, 1743, in Stanford	1	132
Desia, m. Andrew **BARTON**, b. of Salisbury, Dec. 11, 1760, by James Landon, J.P.	1	248
Desire, d. Peter & Thankfull, b. July 12, 1775	2	22
Ebenezer, s. Peter & Thankfull, b. Nov. 21, 1760	1	168
Electa, d. Elias, Jr. & Ruth, b. Feb. 4, 1776	2	10
Eli, s. Peter & Thankfull, b. Mar. 27, 1773	2	22
Eli, s. Daniel & Chloe, b. Oct. 16, 1799	3	35
Elias, s. Elias & Mary, b. Apr. 28, 1749, in Stanford	1	132
Elias, Jr., of Salisbury, m. Ruth **COIT**, of Sheffield, July 23, 1772, by Rev. Jonathan Lee	2	45
Emily, m. Samuel **LUSHER**, b. of Salisbury, Mar. 22, 1842, by Rev. Andrew M. Smith, of North East, N.Y.	3	162
Emma Jane, m. George M. **LOCKWOOD**, b. of Salisbury, Aug. 27, 1846, by Harley Goodwin	3	98
Henry Josiah, [twin with Chauncey], s. Chauncey & Lavinia, b. Mar. 14, 1813	3	84
Isaac, s. Peter & Thankfull, b. Mar. 7, 1759	1	168
Isaac, s. Peter & Thankfull, d. Aug. 30, 1760, in the 2nd y. of his age	1	236
Isaac, s. Moses & Rachel, b. July 15, 1764	2	19
Isaac, s. Peter & Thankfull, b. Feb. 12, 1767	1	168

READ, REED, (cont.)

	Vol.	Page
Ithiel, b. Apr. 26, 1728, in Stanford	1	197
Jacob, s. Moses & Lucy, b. May 19, 1769	2	20
Jacob, s. Moses & Lucy, d. May 19, 1769	2	48
James E., of Darien, m. Phebe A. **SURDAM**, of Salisbury, June 1, 1840, by Rev. Tho[ma]s Bainbridge	3	159
Jane Eliza, d. Chauncey & Lavinia, b. June 16, 1817	3	84
Jillen*, d. Peter & Thankfull, b. Apr. 11, 1769 *("Gillen" in Rudd's book)	2	22
Job Spencer, s. Chauncey & Lavina, b. Dec. 15, 1809	3	84
Joel, s. Elias & Mary, b. Oct. 24, 1751, in Stanford	1	132
John, of Salisbury, m. Sarah **HEATON**, of Ridgefield, Sept. 27, 1757, by Rev. Mr. Ingersoll	1	246
John, s. Elias & Mary, b. Jan. 21, 1764	1	132
John, s. Moses & Rachel, b. July 22, 1768	2	19
John, s. Moses & Ruth*, d. July 22, 1768 *("Lucy"?)	2	48
Katharine, of Stanford, m. Jonathan **CHIPMAN**, of Salisbury, Oct. 5, 1756, by Rev. Mr. Mather	1	245
Lewis, s. Moses & Lucy, b. Jan. 12, 1774	2	20
Lucy, d. Moses & Lucy, b. Jan. 13, 1777	2	20
Martha, d. Elias & Mary, b. Nov. 24, 1745, in Stanford; d. Feb. 4, 1746	1	132
Martha, d. Elias & Mary, b. Nov. 9, 1746, in Stanford	1	132
Mary, d. Elias & Mary, b. Dec. 12, 1740, in Stanford	1	132
Mary, m. James **LANDON**, Jr., b. of Salisbury, Nov. 18, 1756, by James Landon, J.P.	1	247
Mary, d. Thomas & Sarah, b. Aug. 19, 1768	2	16
Mary, w. Elias, d. Feb. 9, 1787, in the 65th y. of her age	2	50
Mary Ann, m. Horace S. **KELSEY**, b. of Salisbury, Jan. 28, 1838, by Rev. O.V. Amerman	3	155
Mehettabel*, m. Bartholomew **BARRET**, b. of Salisbury, Mar. 6, 1755, by Rev. Jonathan Lee *("Mehettabel **ROOD**" in Rudd's)	1	242
Molly, d. Elias, Jr. & Ruth, b. Jan. 12, 1770	2	10
Moses, of Salisbury, m. Rachel **HODGEKER**, of New Haven, Feb. 19, 1754, by Rev. Jonathan Lee. Witnesses, Josiah Lounsbury & Martha Lounsbury	1	242
Moses & Lydia, had s. [ ], st.b. June 28, 1765	1	239
Moses, m. Lucy **TURNER**, b. of Salisbury, Sept. 22, 1767, by James Landon, J.P.	2	44
Moses, s. Moses & Lucy, b. Jan. 30, 1772	2	20
Myron C., of Auburn, N.Y., m. Sally Maria **STRONG**, of Salisbury, Oct. 16, 1828, by Leonard E. Lathrop	3	131
Nancy M., m. George W. **BLACKESLEY**, June 22, 1845, by Rev. D.W. Clark	3	97
Nathan, s. Elias & Mary, b. May 28, 1758; d. Nov. 2, 1764	1	132
Newton J., m. Polly **McARTHUR**, b. of Salisbury, Dec. 29, 1838, by Rev. Thomas Bainbridge	3	158
Orville Lord, s. Aaron & Lydia, b. July 9, 1802	3	37
Phebe, d. Daniel & Chloe, b. July 15, 1801	3	35
Phebe, m. Richard **HOLLISTER**, b. of Salisbury, Dec. 24, 1822, by		

	Vol.	Page
READ, REED, (cont.)		
Charles Prentice	3	118
Philander, s. Peter & Thankfull, b. Jan. 16, 1771	2	22
Polly, d. Stephen & Abigail, b. Apr. 4, 1795	3	20
Rachel, d. Moses & Rachel, b. Nov. 15, 1759	1	215
Rachel, w. Moses, d. Jan. 17, 1767	2	48
Rachel Lavinia, d. Chauncey & Lavinia, b. Apr. 27, 1823	3	84
Rufus, m. Laura E. **BROWN**, b. of Salisbury, Mar. 6, 1828, by Rev. Stephen Beach, of St. Johns Ch.	3	129
Ruth, d. Elias, Jr. & Ruth, b. Nov. 11, 1773	2	10
Sally, d. Abraham & Sarah, b. Mar. 10, 1785	2	18
Sally Ann, of Salisbury, m. Henry **WOODWORTH**, of North East, N.Y., Jan. 12, 1842, by Rev. Adam Reid	3	162
Sarah, of Sharon, m. Eliphalet **BUELL**, of Salisbury, Dec. 7, 1752, by Rev. Jonathan Lee	1	224
Sarah, d. John, Jr. & Sarah, b. Sept. 10, 1758	1	161
Sarah, w. John, Jr., d. Jan. 20, 1783, in the 48th y. of her age	2	50
Stephen, s. Elias & Mary, b. Oct. 7, 1761	1	132
Susan, of Salisbury, m. Nathaniel **HARTWELL**, of North East, Dec. 26, 1822, by Charles Prentice	3	118
Thankfull, d. Peter & Thankfull, b. June 17, 1763	1	168
Theron, s. Chauncey & Lavinia, b. Mar. 19, 1815	3	84
Thomas, Jr., of Norwalk, m. Sarah **PERS**, of Stratford, Apr. 7, 1763, by Moses Mather, V.D.M.	1	251
Thomas, s. Thomas & Sarah, b. May 1, 1775	2	16
Thomas, d. Jan. 23, 1801, ae 71	3	164
Thomas, m. Luna **FOX**, b. of Salisbury, Feb. 13, 1814, by Rev. Nathaniel Swift, of Warren, at Cornwall	3	114
William*, m. Olive **VANDUSEN**, b. of Salisbury, Jan. 20, 1763, by John Hutchinson, J.P. *("William **PEW**" in Rudd's book)	1	250
William, m. Mary **CHAPMAN**, b. of Salisbury, Mar. 29, 1827, by Charles Printice	3	127
William, of Canaan, m. Eunice M. **BOTSFORD**, of Salisbury, Jan. 2, 1832, by L.E. Lathrop	3	139
Zanthy, s. Ebenezer & Polly, b. Aug. 14, 1784	2	21
REYNOLDS, RENNOLDS, RENNOLLS, RENALLS, Amey, twin with Phebe, d. James & Sarah, b. Mar. 12, 1786	2	24
Anne, d. James & Sarah, d. Nov. 5, 1789, in the 4th y. of her age	2	50
Betsey, m. Noah **SELLECK**, Mar. 18, 1799, by Elijah Wood	3	110
Daniel, m. Mabel **PERSONS**, Sept. 1, 1771, by John Hutchinson, J.P.	2	45
James, m. Sarah **JEWELL**, b. of Salisbury, June 6, 1783, by Rev. Jonathan Lee. Witnesses Oliver Jewell, Jr. & George Holmes	3	108
Lydia, d. John & Rachel, b. June 26, 1790	2	28
Phebe, twin with Amey, d. James & Sarah, b. Mar. 12, 1786	2	24
Prudence, of Oblong, m. Stephen **BENTON**, of Salisbury, May 4, 1759, by Rev. Jonathan Lee	1	248
Walter, s. John & Rachel, b. Jan. [ ], 1787	2	28
Walter, s. John & Bethiah, d. Feb. 27, 1791, ae 2 y.	2	50
RICHARDSON, Leonard, m. Lucy Ann **BARNUM**, Apr. 16, 1832, by Rev. Stephen Beach, of St. Johns Ch.	3	140

	Vol.	Page
RICHMOND, Julia Ann, m. Edwin J. **STRONG**, b. of Salisbury, May 20, 1829, by Rev. Stephen Beach, of St. Johns Ch.	3	134
ROBBINS, ROBINS, Lucy B., of Salisbury, m. Philip **BEACH**, of Litchfield, Sept. 29, 1847, by Rev. Adam Reed	3	102
Samuel S., of Canaan, m. Sally P. **HOLLEY**, of Salisbury, [May 9, 1831], by L.E. Lathrop	3	139
ROBERTS, ROBARTS, ROBBARTS, Esther, d. William & Abigail, b. Feb. 20, 1760	1	184
Mary, d. William & Abigail, b. June 24, 1756	1	184
Phebe, m. Bille **FITCH**, b. of Salisbury, Nov. 21, 1753, by Rev. Jonathan Lee	1	241
Rozel, s. William & Abigail, b. July 20, 1758	1	184
Sarah, m. Josiah **STODDARD**, Nov. 7, 1743	LR1	356-7
William, m. Abigail **FRINK**, b. of Salisbury, Nov. 21, 1752, by Rev. Jonathan Lee	1	244
William, s. Willaim & Abigail, b. Sept. 3, 1753	1	184
ROCKERFELLER, Phillip, of Ancronn, N.Y., m. Hannah **KELSEY**, of Salisbury, July 4, 1841, by Jac[ob] Shaw	3	161
ROCKWELL, Lucy, d. Jonah & Lucy, b. Feb. 15, 1762	1	150
Mary Ann, d. Dr. Samuel & Hannah, b. June 2, 1800	3	34
Rosewell, s. Jonah & Lucy, b. Apr. 23, 1763	1	150
ROE, Heman, s. Phinehas & Mary, b. July 3, 1779	2	16
ROOD, [see also **REED**], Abijah, m. Anna **NORTHROP**, b. of Salisbury, Aug. 22, 1763, by John Hutchinson, J.P.	1	251
Allen Hare*, s. Abijah & Anna, b. June 4, 1767 *("Haze" in Rudd's book)	1	141
Allen Haze, s. Abijah & Anna, b. Jan. 10, 1771	2	28
Azariah, s. Azariah & Desire, b. Jan. 20, 1758	1	178
David, s. Azariah & Desiah, b. May 29, 1755	1	178
Eli, s. Abijah & Anna, b. Aug. 9, 1765	1	141
Jeremiah, s. Abijah & Anna, b. Feb. 11, 1764	1	141
Mehettabel*, m. Bartholomew **BARRET**, b. of Salisbury, Mar. 6, 1755, by Rev. Jonathan Lee *("Mehettabel **REED**" in Arnold Copy)	1	242
Olive, d. Moses & Lydia, b. Feb. 27, 1764	1	150
Rebe, of Sheffield, m. Joshua **FITCH**, Jr., of Salisbury, Dec. 23, 1773, by John Hutchinson, J.P.	2	45
Silas, s. Azariah & Desire, b. Sept. 9, 1759	1	163
ROOT, Jeremiah, of Canaan, m. Anna Maria **PERRY**, of Salisbury, Feb. 17, 1841, by Rev. J. Shaw	3	161
ROSE, Martha, m. Eliphalet **WHITTLESEY**, Apr. 12, 1804, by Joseph W. Crossman	3	112
ROSS, Charles, m. Mary Ann **HARRISS**, b. of Salisbury, Nov. 26, 1838, by Rev. Thomas Bainbridge	3	156
ROSSETER, Elizabeth M., m. Weston **THORP**, b. of Salisbury, Jan. 1, 1844, by Rev. C.V. Amerman	3	96
Mark, of Great Barrington, Mass., m. Caroline **HAMLEN**, of Salisbury, Jan. 14, 1828, by Leonard E. Lathrop	3	129
ROWLEY, ROWLEE, Cloe, d. Simeon & Jane, b. June 12, 1755, in Kent	1	171
Deborah, d. Simeon & Jane, b. Sept. 10, 1762	2	14
Hiel, s. Simeon & Jane, b. Mar. 29, 1757, in Oblong	1	171

	Vol.	Page
ROZELL, Sally Ann, of Salisbury, m. William DEMING, of Newpaltz, Ulster Cty., N.Y., Nov. 14, 1830, by Rev. Aaron Pearce	3	137
RUGG, Abigail, d. Nicholas & Hephzabah, b. Feb. 18, 1800	3	5
RUSSELL, RUSSEL, Caroline E., of Salisbury, m. Samuel A. DUTCHER, of Canaan, Mar. 11, 1847, by Rev. G. Huntington Nicholls. Int. Pub.	3	101
Catharine Cornelia, d. John & Charity, b. Apr. 3, 1807	3	16
Charity, d. John & Charity, b. Dec. 3, 1799	3	16
Charles E., m. Catharine C. DEMING, b. of Salisbury, May 31, 1829, by Eliphalet Whittlesey, J.P.	3	145
Charles Evarts, s. John & Charity, b. Oct. 25, 1807 [sic]	3	16
Elijah, m. Jemima VANDUSEN, b. of Salisbury, Dec. 17, 1755, by Rev. Jonathan Lee. Witnesses Ruluff Dutcher, Samuel Russell & Lawrence Van Dusen	1	244
Fatina, d. John & Charity, b. Jan. 19, 1795	3	16
John, m. Mrs. Charity EVARTS, Nov. 8, 1787, by Philip Spencer, J.P.	3	109
John, s. John & Charity, b. May 25, 1789	3	16
Mary, m. Milton HUBBARD, b. of Salisbury, Oct. 23, 1828, by Leonard E. Lathrop	3	132
Mary Ann, m. Henry C. JEWELL, Oct. 1, 1833, by L.E. Lathrop	3	144
Mehetabel, d. Elijah & Jamima, b. May 15, 1756	1	202
Olive V., of Salisbury, m. Sidney B. WEBB, of Hamilton, Madison Cty., N.Y., [ ], by Rev. Lucius M. Brady, of St. Johns Ch.	3	146
Olive Vandusen, d. John & Charity, b. Aug. 14, 1804	3	16
Polly, d. John & Charity, b. Oct. 9, 1791	3	16
Reuben, s. John & Charity, b. Feb. 22, 1793	3	16
Rhoda, d. Elijah & Jamima, b. Oct. 7, 1758	1	202
Solomon, s. John & Charity, b. Jan. 23, 1797	3	16
Thomas Jefferson, s. John & Charity, b. Apr. 30, 1801	3	16
William Pew, s. John & Charity, b. Mar. 29, 1788	2	40
RUSTIN, Hiram, s. William & Olive, b. June 5, 1807	3	51
SABIN, SABINS, Mary, m. Thomas CHIPMAN, b. of Salisbury, Apr. 28, 1768, by Rev. Jonathan Lee	2	44
Myron, m. Eunice LINCOLN, Jan. 29, 1829, by Charles Prentice	3	133
SAGE, Julia M., m. Seth WALTON, b. of Salisbury, Feb. 25, 1847, by Rev. Adam Reed	3	100
St. JOHN, Jemima, of Sharon, m. Isaac BENTON, of Salisbury, Oct. 30, 1755, by Rev. Cotton Mather Smith	1	243
SANFORD, Richard, s. Ira & Mahola, b. Oct. 4, 1799, in Roxbury	3	39
Sarah, d. Ira & Mahala, b. Mar. 9, 1803	3	39
SARDAM, [see also SURDAM], Delia, m. William SARDAM, Jr., b. of Salisbury, Apr. 6, 1831, by Leonard E. Lathrop	3	138
Phebe A., of Salisbury, m. James E. REED, of Darien, June 1, 1840, by Rev. Tho[ma]s Bainbridge	3	159
William, Jr., m. Delia SARDAM, b. of Salisbury, Apr. 6, 1831, by Leonard E. Lathrop	3	138
SAUNDERS, Caroline, m. Samuel BLODGET, b. of Salisbury, Dec. 9, 1824, by Rev. David Miller, of the M.E. Ch.	3	121
Henriette, m. William B. SNYDER, Dec. 4, 1845, by D.W. Clark	3	97
Horrace, s. William Thomas & Hannah, b. Feb. 17, 1796	3	18

	Vol.	Page
SAUNDERS, (cont.)		
Sophia Matilda, m. Harry **VOSBURGH**, b. of Salisbury, Nov. 29, 1832, by Rev. Thomas Sparks	3	142
Walter, s. William Thomas & Hannah, b. Apr. 11, 1794	3	18
William W., m. Hannah **FOSTER**, b. of Salisbury, Aug. 3, 1828, by Rev. Noah Bigelow	3	134
SAWYER, Selina Emma, d. Thomas J. & Sophia, b. Mar. 26, 1835	3	88
SCOFIELD, SCHOLFIELD, [see also **SCOVILLE**], Arthur, m. Eliza A. MOORE, b. of Salisbury, Nov. 29, 1838, by Rev. Thomas Bainbridge	3	157
Jared Harrison, s. Stephen & Asenath, b. Jan. 9, 1803	3	38
Mary Emmy, d. Stephen & Asenath, b. Sept. 8, 1799	3	38
Olive Margaret, d. Stephen & Asenath, b. Feb. 9, 1801	3	38
SCOVILLE, SCOVEL, [see also **SCOFIELD**], Almira, d. Jonathan & Sally, b. Feb. 26, 1797	3	38
Betsey, d. Jonathan & Sally, b. Sept. 23, 1789	3	38
David, s. Jonathan & Sally, b. Sept. 11, 1794	3	38
Deborah, m. Timothy **TORNER**, b. of Salisbury, Mar. 10, 1774, by John Hutchinson, J.P.	2	45
Emelia, d. Jonathan & Sally, b. May 17, 1799	3	38
Fanny, d. Jonathan & Sally, b. Oct. 29, 1791	3	38
Julia, of Salisbury, m. Leverett **KULL***, of Augusta, N.Y., May 16, 1827, by L.E. Lathrop *("HULL"?)	3	127
Julian, d. Jonathan & Sally, b. Feb. 1, 1802	3	38
Sally, d. Jonathan & Sally, b. Mar. 14, 1785	3	38
Samuell C., m. Lois D. **CHURCH**, b. of Salisbury, Oct. 28, 1828, by Arnold Scholfield, Elder	3	132
SCRIBNER, Abigail, m. James **PIERCE**, Nov. 15, 1798, by William Bronson, J.P.	3	110
SEARL, Isaac, s. Isaac & Hannah, b. Sept. 2, 1757	1	166
Isaac, s. Isaac & Hannah, d. Apr. [ ], 1759	1	231
Isaac, s. Isaac & Hannah, d. May 8, 1759	1	229
Jacob, s. Isaac & Hannah, b. Feb. 15, 1759	1	166
SEELEY, Lucius G., m. Wealthy W. **BARDON**, b. of Salisbury, Jan. 29, 1838, by Rev. O.V. Amerman	3	155
SELDEN, SELDIN, Caleb, s. Jesse & Ruth, b. Mar. 12, 1772	2	19
David, s. Jesse & Ruth, b. July 30, 1765	2	19
Jonathan, s. Jesse & Ruth, b. Aug. 21, 1770	2	19
SELLECK, Albert, s. Samuel & Olive, b. June 29, 1802	3	25
Betsey, d. Ezra, Jr. & Abigail, b. Dec. 30, 1787	2	27
Charles, s. Mylo & Sally, b. Aug. 8, 1813	3	59
Columbus, s. Levi & Olive, b. Nov. 22, 1805	3	43
Daniel, s. Bethel & Ruth, b. May 15, 1758	1	115
Deborah, d. Ezra & Mary, b. Dec. 13, 1765	2	29
Elizabeth, m. Jeremiah **DAUCHY**, b. of Salisbury, Oct. 3, 1780, by Rev. Jonathan Lee	2	41
Ezra, s. Ezra & Mary, b. Aug. 10, 1760, in Stamford	2	29
Ezra, Jr., of Salisbury, m. Abigail **BROWN**, of New Marlborough, Nov. 14, 1786, at New Marlborough, by Rev. Mr. Storer, of Sandisfield	2	43
Hannah, d. Ezra & Mary, b. Oct. 22, 1763	2	29

	Vol.	Page
SELLECK, (cont.)		
Hannah, m. Jared **EVEREST**, Jr., b. of Salisbury, Nov. 22, 1786, by Rev. Jonathan Lee	2	43
Harmon, s. Samuel & Olive, b. May 4, 1800	3	25
Harriet, d. Ezra, Jr. & Abigail, b. Sept. 11, 1793	2	27
Harriette, d. Samuel & Olive, b. July 3, 1812	3	25
Harvey, m. Lutia Electa **LANDON**, b. of Salisbury, Dec. 20, 1826, by Rev. Stephen Beach, of St. Johns Ch.	3	125
Hervey, s. Samuel & Olive, b. Feb. 17, 1805	3	25
James, s. Ezra & Mary, b. Feb. 19, 1761, in Stamford	2	29
James, m. Lois **LANDON**, b. of Salisbury, Jan. 17, 1783, by Rev. Jonathan Lee	2	42
James Hervey, s. James Hervey & Minervy, b. Aug. 8, 1819	3	67
Kibbon*, s. Bethel & Ruth, b. Sept. 25, 1769 *("Kilbun" in Rudd's book)	1	115
Levi, s. Ezra & Mary, b. Jan. 3, 1768	2	29
Mariette, of Salisbury, m. Rulandus B. **HINMAN**, of Binghampton, N.Y., Apr. 30, 1832, by Rev. Stephen Beach, of St. Johns Ch.	3	140
Martha, d. Bethel & Ruth, b. Dec. 13, 1755	1	115
Mary, m. Noah **BRINSMAID**, Nov. 10, 1805, by Rev. Cor[neliu]s Brewer, of Poughkeepsie	3	113
Mary Ann, d. [James Hervey & Minervy], b. Sept. 16, 1821	3	67
Mercy, d. Ezra & Mary, b. June 10, 1772	2	29
Milo*, s. Bethel & Ruth, b. Apr. 1, 1776 *(Arnold Copy has "Riley")	1	115
Milton, s. Ezra, Jr. & Abigail, b. Aug. 23, 1791	2	27
Molly, d. Behtel & Ruth, b. Apr. 19, 1762	1	115
Mylo, of Salisbury, m. Sally **HERVEY**, of Amenia, Oct. 21, 1812, by Isaac Atherton. Witnesses William Sheldon & Abraham Sheldon	3	114
Noah, s. Ezra & Mary, b. Aug. 15, 1774	2	29
Noah, m. Betsey **REYNOLDS**, Mar. 18, 1799, by Elijah Wood	3	110
Noah, m. Electa **SPARKS**, b. of Salisbury, Oct. 31, 1813, by Enos Hopkins, J.P.	3	114
Phebe, d. Ezra & Mary, b. Sept. 21, 1777	2	29
Phebe, m. Calvin **ACKLEY**, b. of Salisbury, Dec. 24, 1795, by Samuel Lee, J.P.	3	109
Phebe R., m. Lorenzo **TUPPER**, b. of Salisbury, Mar. 24, 1844, by Rev. C.V. Amerman	3	96
Phebe Riley, d. Sam[ue]ll & Olive, b. Jan. 11, 1817	3	25
Polly, d. Ezra, Jr. & Abigail, b. Dec. 2, 1789	2	27
Rebeckah, d. Bethel & Ruth, b. June 28, 1772, in Salisbury	1	115
Rhoda, m. Isaac **BIRD**, b. of Salisbury, Feb. 28, 1782, by Rev. Jonathan Lee	2	42
Riley*, s. Bethel & Ruth, b. Apr. 1, 1776 *("Milo" in Rudd's)	1	115
Ruth, d. Bethel & Ruth, b. Nov. 10, 1753, at Stamford	1	115
Ruth, w. Bethuel, d. Apr. 30, 1790, in the 58th y. of her age	2	50
Sally Ann, d. Samuel & Olive, b. Feb. 4, 1810	3	25
Salome, d. Ezra & Mary, b. Nov. 15, 1770	2	29
Semantha, d. Samuel & Olive, b. Oct. 4, 1797	3	25
Samuel, s. Bethel & Ruth, b. Aug. 24, 1767	1	115

	Vol.	Page
SELLECK, (cont.)		
Sarah, d. Bethel & Ruth, b. June 26, 1764	1	115
Seymore, s. Bethel & Ruth, b. Mar. 2, 1760	1	115
SELWIN*, John, of Salisbury, m. Elizabeth **CHURCH**, of Sheffield, Mar. 21, 1769, by John Hutchinson, J.P. *("**WELDIN**" in Rudd's)	2	44
SERRINS, Chloe, had d. Jenny, b. Feb. 29, 1792 & d. Samantha, b. Mar. 11, 1794	2	18
Jenny, d. Chloe, b. Feb. 29, 1792	2	18
Samantha, d. Chloe, b. Mar. 11, 1794	2	18
[**SEWARD**], **SEAWARD, SEYWARD**, Caleb, s. Daniel & Martha, b. Feb. 12, 1760	1	162
Hezekiah, s. Ashur & Lydia, b. Mar. 31, 1760	1	162
SEXTON, Jonathan, s. Jonathan & Anna, b. Oct. 26, 1776, at Sheffield	2	29
SEYMORE, Mary, of Hartford, m. Hyman Jacob **BOGROUGH**, of Salisbury, May 30, 1773, by Rev. Jonathan Lee	2	45
SHARP, Betsey, d. Truman & Zipporah, b. July 24, 1794	3	28
John, s. Truman & Zipporah, b. Oct. 11, 1792	3	28
SHELDON, Abigail, d. Ezra & Abigail, b. Feb. 8, 1779	2	36
Betsey, d. James & Sarah, b. May 4, 1799; d. Sept. 25, 1800	3	44
Caroline, d. Moses, Jr. & Hannah, b. July 30, 1802	2	39
Elias, s. Ezra & Abigail, b. June 1, 1793	2	36
Elisha, s. Elisha & Sarah, b. June 8, 1766	2	8
Elizabeth, d. Elisha & Sarah, b. Feb. 8, 1762	1	159
Elizabeth, w. Moses, d. May 19, 1782, in the 59th y. of her age	2	50
Elizabeth, d. Ezra & Abigail, b. Dec. 13, 1782	2	36
Elizabeth, d. Moses, Jr. & Hannah, b. June 14, 1793	2	39
Esther, d. Moses, Jr. & Hannah, b. Sept. 15, 1782	2	39
Esther, d. James & Sarah, b. Feb. 6, 1801	3	44
Ezra, m. Abigail **REED**, b. of Salisbury, July 4, 1776, by Rev. Jonathan Lee	2	47
George, s. Elisha & Sarah, b. Sept. 13, 1767	2	8
Hiram, s. James & Sarah, b. Jan. 18, 1805	3	44
James, s. Ezra & Abigail, b. Feb. 6, 1777	2	36
James, s. Moses, Jr. & Hannah, d. Nov. 9, 1785, ae 5 m.	2	50
James, m. Sarah **KINGSBURY**, Jan. 8, 1797, at the house of Joseph Kingsbury, in Bethleham, by Rev. Mr. Avery. Witnesses Jabez Kingsbury & Denison Kingsbury	3	109
Joel Reed, s. Ezra & Abigail, b. Aug. 24, 1795	2	36
Kerlista, d. Ezra & Abigail, b. Oct. 15, 1790	2	36
Laura, d. Ezra & Abigail, b. Sept. 13, 1787	2	36
Maria, d. Moses, Jr. & Hannah, b. Dec. 4, 1795	2	39
Mary, d. Elisha & Sarah, b. July 4, 1763	1	159
Mary, m. Luther **LANDON**, b. of Salisbury, Sept. 23, 1773, by John Hutchinson, J.P.	2	45
Mary, d. Elisha, Jr. & Elizabeth, b. May 6, 1787	2	34
Mary Caroline, d. James & Sarah, b. Aug. 7, 1807; d. Mar. 3, 1808	3	44
Moses, Jr., m. Hannah **KEEP**, b. of Salisbury, Jan. 10, 1782, by Rev. Jonathan Lee	2	41
Moses, Jr., m. Hannah **KEEP**, b. of Salisbury, Jan. 10, 1782, by Rev. Jonathan Lee	2	42
Moses, d. Jan. 12, 1808, in the 92nd y. of his age	3	166

	Vol.	Page
SHELDON, (cont.)		
Olive, d. Moses, Jr. & Hannah, b. Nov. 1, 1790	2	39
Oscar Painter, s. Moses, Jr. & Hannah, b. Mar. 3, 1800	2	39
Polly, d. Ezra & Abigail, b. Nov. 15, 1780	2	36
Ruhama, of Anesand, m. Alexander **SMITH**, of Salisbury, Oct. 9, 1836, by Rev. Oliver V. Amerman, of the M.E. Ch.	3	153
Sally, d. Ezra & Abigail, b. Mar. 14, 1785	2	36
Sally Abigail, d. Elias & Senelda Adams, b. June 22, 1817	3	64
Samuel, s. Moses, Jr. & Hannah, b. Aug. 3, 1784	2	39
Samuel, s. Moses, Jr. & Hannah, b. Aug. 1, 1786	2	39
Samuel Bellows, s. Elisha & Sarah, b. Apr. 26, 1760	1	159
Sarah, d. Elisha & Sarah, b. July 26, 1770	2	8
Sarah Bellowes, d. George & Joanna, b. Jan. 18, 1788	2	34
Walter, s. Moses, Jr. & Hannah, b. Sept. 16, 1788	2	39
William, s. James & Sarah, b. Nov. 18, 1797; d. Sept. 25, 1800	3	44
William Ormon, s. James & Sarah, b. Nov. 29, 1802	3	44
SHEPHERD, Ralph W., of Herkimer, N.Y., m. Julia A. **PETTIBONE**, of Salisbury, Oct. 27, 1840, by Rev. Adam Reid	3	160
SHERMAN, James, s. John Lee & Elizabeth, b. Mar. 19, 1764	1	143
John, s. John Lee & Elizabeth, b. Nov. 17, 1765	1	143
John Lee, m. Elizabeth **WATEROUS**, b. of Salisbury, Mar. 31, 1763, by John Hutchinson, J.P.	1	251
Levi, s. John Lee & Elizabeth, b. Dec. 18, 1767	1	143
SHERWOOD, John W., m. Clarissa J. **SHOOK**, b. of Salisbury, Nov. 26, 1841, by J. Shaw	3	161
SHIPPING, Polly, d. William & Rhoda, b. Nov. 16, 1781	2	8
SHOOK, Clarissa J., m. John W. **SHERWOOD**, b. of Salisbury, Nov. 26, 1841, by J. Shaw	3	161
Cornelia, m. John **WILLIAMS**, b. of Salisbury, Feb. 13, 1848, by Rev. Jonathan Lee. Int. Pub.	3	102
Henry G., of Wawasing, N.Y., m. Olivia M. **DEXTER**, of Salisbury, Sept. 3, 1838, by Rev. Adam Reid	3	155
SHULTZ, Benjamin, of Rhinebeck, N.Y., m. Julia Esther **STANTON**, Oct. 3, 1833, by Eliphalet Whittlesey, J.P.	3	144
SIKES, Hanna, m. Bille **MUNGER**, b. of Salisbury, Apr. 15, 1752, by Rev. Jonathan Lee	1	224
SILVERNAIL, Maria, of Salisbury, m. Theodore **WOODWORTH**, of Ellenville, N.Y., Oct. 20, 1838, by Rev. Thomas Bainbridge	3	156
SKINNER, Asenath, d. Elijah & Mary, b. Jan. 19, 1764	1	171
Chloe, d. Samuel & Chloe, b. Dec. 4, 1760	1	154
Sintha*, d. Samuel & Chloe, b. Apr. 13, 1765 *("Cynthia")	1	154
Daniel, s. John & Elizabeth, b. Dec. 1, 1773	2	26
Elijah, m. Mary **JESTEN***, b. of Salisbury, Dec. 30, 1756, by Rev. Daniel Farrin, of Canaan *("**JOSLEN**" in Rudd's book)	1	245
Elijah, s. Elijah & Mary, b. Mar. 24, 1758	1	171
Elizabeth, d. John & Elizabeth, b. Nov. 7, 1775	2	26
Erastus, s. John & Elizabeth, b. Apr. 14, 1772	2	26
Esther, d. Samuel & Chloe, b. Sept. 15, 1770	2	33
James, s. John & Elizabeth, b. Nov. 29, 1777	2	26
John, s. John & Elizabeth, b. Dec. 19, 1769	2	26
Mary, d. Elijah & Mary, b. June 17, 1759	1	171

	Vol.	Page
SKINNER, (cont.)		
Milo, s. John & Elizabeth, b. May 23, 1770	2	26
Moore Bird, s. Samuel & Chloe, b. Sept. 2, 1772	2	33
Nathaniel, Jr., d. May 12, 1750	1	225
Nathaniel, s. John & Elizabeth, b. June 24, 1767	2	26
Nathaniel, s. John & Elizabeth, d. July 4, 1767	2	48
Nathaniel, s. Samuel & Chloe, b. Jan. 22, 1768	2	11
Rebeckah*, m. Moore **BIRD**, b. of Salisbury, Nov. 9, 1752, by Rev. Jonathan Lee *(Arnold Copy has "Rebeckah J. **KINNON**")	1	240
Rebeckah, d. Elijah & Mary, b. May 11, 1762	1	171
Samuel, m. Choice* **COLE**, b. of Salisbury, Mar. 20, 1760, by John Waters, J.P., at Colchester *("Chloe" in Rudd's book)	1	248
Samuel, s. Samuel & Chloe, b. June 28, 1762	1	154
Sarah, d. John & Elizabeth, b. Jan. 23, 1781	2	26
Solomon, s. Elijah & Mary, b. Oct. 14, 1760	1	171
Zalmon, s. Samuell & Hannah, b. Jan. 31, 1777	2	11
SMALLEY, Ama, d. Benjamin, Jr. & Martha, d. Jan. 1, 1754, in the 1st y. of her age	1	226
Anah, d. Benjamin & Martha, b. July 29, 1757	1	214
Asa, s. Benjamin & Martha, b. Oct. 6, 1754	1	214
Benjamin, Ens., d. Aug. 30, 1754	1	226
Imri, s. Benjamin & Martha, b. Sept. 16, 1761	1	214
Zerah, s. Benjamin & Martha, b. Mar. 19, 1759	1	214
SMITH, Abigail, d. John & Phebe, b. Mar. 1, 1768	2	26
Albert G., of Sharon, m. Sebrina P. **BURCK**, of Salisbury, May 27, 1828, by Rev. Stephen Beach, of St. Johns Ch.	3	130
Alexander, of Salisbury, m. Ruhama **SHELDON**, of Anesand, Oct. 9, 1836, by Rev. Oliver V. Amerman, of M.E. Ch.	3	153
Amelia, d. Jacob & Mary, b. Jan. 31, 1788	2	40
Amelia, of Salisbury, m. John B. **MURGITHROYD**, late of Claverick, Nov. 13, 1810, by Rev. Joseph W. Crossman	3	114
Augusta, d. Gideon, Jr. & Eunice, b. Feb. 25, 1804	3	20
Augusta, of Salisbury, m. Orville **DAKIN**, of North East, N.Y., May 9, 1827, by Leonard E. Lathrop	3	127
Betsey, d. Elijah & Sarah, b. July 18, 1783	2	11
Caroline Matilda, d. Matthew & Clarissa, b. Oct. 19, 1829	3	85
Charity, d. Gideon & Allen, b. Aug. 8, 1764; d. Aug. 18, 1764	1	154
Cyrenius, s. Nathaniel & Keziah, b. Jan. 16, 1743/4	LR1	353
Daniel, s. Samuel, b. Sept. 26, 1807	3	44
David, of Wyoming, m. wid. Lucy **JEWELL**, of Salisbury, Feb. 8, 1789, by Samuel Lee, J.P.	2	43
Ebenezer, s. Elijah & Sarah, b. Feb. 11, 1789	3	28
Edward, m. Susan **TURNER**, b. of Salisbury, [Jan.] 4, 1832, by L.E. Lathrop	3	139
Elijah, m. Sarah **OWEN**, b. of Salisbury, Jan. 2, 1771, by Rev. Jonathan Lee	2	45
Elijah, s. Elijah & Sarah, b. June 7, 1781	2	11
Eliza Ann, d. Matthew & Clarissa, b. June 7, 1824	3	85
Elizabeth, m. Ephraim **COLVER**, b. of Salisbury, June 12, 1745, by [ ]	LR1	356-7
Ephraim, s. Elijah & Sarah, b. Oct. 3, 1777	2	11

	Vol.	Page
SMITH, (cont.)		
Esther, d. Jacob & Mary, b. Feb. 1, 1785	2	40
Esther, d. Elijah & Sarah, b. Nov. 22, 1790	3	28
Eunice, w. Dea. Gideon, Jr., d. Nov. 2, 1805, ae 30	3	166
Eunice, d. Gideon, Jr. & Dolly, b. Feb. 12, 1811	3	20
Eunice, of Salisbury, m. Sheldon **WHITTLESEY**, of New Preston, Dec. 13, 1837, by Adam Reid	3	154
Ezekiel, s. Gideon & Allen, b. Aug. 14, 1766	1	154
Fanny, d. Gideon, Jr. & Dolly, b. Feb. 12, 1814	3	20
George W., m. Cordelia **PATTERSON**, b. of Salisbury, June 14, 1846, by D.W. Clark	3	98
Gideon, s. Gideon & Allen, b. May 10, 1762	1	154
Gideon, s. Gideon & Mehittabel, b. Dec. 22, 1774, in Addams	2	39
Gideon, m. Eunice **HURD**, b. of Salisbury, Oct. 26, 1794, by Samuel Lee, J.P.	3	109
Grover, s. Caleb & Rhoda, b. June 2, 1754	1	207
Hannah, m. Seth **AUSTIN**, b. of Salisbury, Apr. 26, 1770, by Rev. Jonathan Lee	2	45
Hannah, of New Fairfield, m. Abner **WOODIN**, of Salisbury, June 10, 1777, by Rev. Mr. Bradford	2	41
Harriet, d. Matthew & Clarissa, b. Jan. 15, 1831	3	85
Harriet, d. Thaddeus & Hannah, b. [ ], in Durham, N.Y.	3	14
Heman*, s. Elijah & Sarah, b. Sept. 30, 1779 *(Arnold Copy has "Thomas **SMITH**, b. Apr. 30")	2	11
Henry, s. Samuel, b. June 30, 1803	3	44
Henry, s. Gideon, Jr. & Dolly, b. June 8, 1812	3	20
Hephzabah, d. John & Phebe, b. May 15, 1770	2	26
Horace, s. Gideon, Jr. & Eunice, b. July 31, 1795	3	20
Ira, s. Thaddeus & Hannah, b. Aug. [ ], 1795, at Durham, N.Y.	3	14
Jacob, s. Jacob & Mary, b. Dec. 16, 1782	2	40
Jared, d. Mar. 12, 1813, in the 72nd y. of his age	3	167
Jesse, s. Gideon & Mehittabel, b. May 26, 1771, in Addams	2	39
Jesse, m. Betsey **CAMP**, Nov. 7, 1793. Witnesses Thomas Camp & Sabina Camp	3	109
John M., m. Rebecca **BATES**, b. of Salisbury, Nov. 3, 1830, by Rev. Aaron Pearce	3	137
John Wesley, s. Matthew & Clarissa, b. Dec. 14, 1816	3	85
Judith, d. Caleb & Rhode, b. Jan. 6, 1751/2	1	207
Julia A., of Salisbury, m. Amariah J. **PERKINS**, of Brookfield, Sept. 8, 1845, by Rev. Adam Reed	3	97
Julia Ett, d. Matthew & Clarissa, b. Oct. 3, 1826	3	85
Love, d. Gideon, Jr. & Eunice, b. Aug. 9, 1805	3	20
Love, of Salisbury, m. Dr. William **ERWIN**, of Kent, Nov. 13, [1832], by L.E. Lathrop	3	142
Luther, s. Elijah & Sarah, b. Apr. 7, 1787	3	28
Luther, twin with Lucy, s. Jacob & Mary, b. Nov. 13, 1790	2	40
Maria, d. Matthew & Clarissa, b. Feb. 11, 1822	3	85
Marie, d. Thaddeus & Hannah, b. [ ], 1797, in Durham, N.Y.	3	14
Mary, m. Joel **THOMPSON**, b. of Salisbury, June 20, 1759, by Rev. Jonathan Lee	2	45
Mary, d. Jacob & Mary, b. Sept. 22, 1780	2	40

	Vol.	Page
SMITH, (cont.)		
Mary, d. Gideon, Jr. & Eunice, b. Apr. 2, 1802	3	20
Mary, d. Thaddeus & Hannah, b. Feb. [ ], 1805	3	14
Mary, d. Matthew & Clarissa, b. July 1, 1818	3	85
Mary, m. Myron **HUTCHINSON**, b. of Salisbury, [Jan.] 4, 1827, by Leonard E. Lathrop	3	126
Mary S., of Salisbury, m. John **CLEVELAND**, of Genessee, N.Y., [July] 1, 1829, by L.E. Lathrop	3	134
Malissa A., m. David S. **WING**, Dec. 17, 1834, by Rev. Richard Wymond	3	149
Mercy W., of Salisbury, m. Horace **CLARK**, of Armenia, Dutchess Cty., N.Y., May 26, 1830, by Rev. Fitch Reed, of Sharon	3	136
Molly, d. Elijah & Sarah, b. June 15, 1773	2	11
Newcomb, s. Nathaniel & Kezia, b. Feb. 28, 1741/2	LR1	351
Phebe, d. John & Phebe, b. Feb. 10, 1766	2	26
Phebe, w. John, d. May 24, 1770	2	48
Polly, d. Elijah & Sarah, b. Apr. 29, 1785	2	11
Priscilla, d. Nathaniel & Kezia, b. Jan. 24, 1745/6	LR1	355
Rebeckah, d. Caleb & Rhode, b. Feb. 17, 1749/50	1	207
Reubin, s. Caleb & Rhoda, b. Feb. 2, 1747/8	1	207
Rhoda, d. Caleb & Rhoda, b. Sept. 28, 1743	LR1	352
Rhoda, d. Gideon & Mehittabel, b. May 26, 1764, in Litchfield	2	39
Rhoda, d. Jacob & Mary, b. Mar. 22, 1793	2	40
Sally, d. John & Phebe, b. May 11, 1764, in Saybrook	2	26
Sally, d. Elijah & Sarah, b. Sept. 25, 1775	2	11
Sally, d. Gideon, Jr. & Eunice, b. Mar. 4, 1799	3	20
Sally, d. Dea. Gideon, Jr. & Eunice, d. Jan. 3, 1804, in the 5th y. of her age	3	165
Sally, d. Gideon, Jr. & Dolly, b. Sept. 20, 1816	3	20
Sarah, d. Gideon & Mehittabel, b. June 14, 1767, in Addams	2	39
Solomon, of Monroe, Orange Cty., N.Y., m. Anna **WELDON**, of Sheffield, Mass., Nov. 6, 1821, by Eliphalet Whittlesey, J.P.	3	116
Susanah, d. Gideon & Allen, b. July 10, 1760	1	154
Thankfull, of Sheffield, m. James **WELDIN**, of Salisbury, Aug. 11, 1767, by John Ashley, J.P.	2	44
Thomas*, s. Elijah & Sarah, b. Apr. 30, 1779 *("Heman b. Sept. 30" in Rudd's book)	2	11
William, s. Elijah & Sarah, b. Nov. 30, 1793	3	28
William, m. Zilpha **TOWSLEY**, Apr. 1, 1836, by Leonard E. Lathrop	3	151
William, m. Zilpha **TOWSLEY**, Apr. 1, 1836, by Leonard E. Lathrop	3	152
William Fletcher, s. Matthew & Clarissa, b. Mar. 11, 1820	3	85
William James, of Harbor Creek, Penn., m. Harriet Maria **LEE**, of Salisbury, Aug. 6, 1843, by Rev. Jonathan Lee	3	163
William Sidney, m. Abigail Lorilla **WOLCOTT**, b. of Salisbury, Nov. 9, 1830, by Aaron Pearce	3	138
Zeruiah, m. Christopher **WINTER**, b. of Salisbury, Oct. 22, 1767, by Rev. Jonathan Lee	2	44
SNYDER, William B., m. Henriette **SAUNDERS**, Dec. 4, 1845, by D.W. Clark	3	97

SALISBURY VITAL RECORDS

	Vol.	Page
SOAPER, Elijah, s. Mordecai & Naomi, b. May 20, 1773, in Ryeport	2	38
Elizabeth, d. Mordecai & Naomi, b. Oct. 16, 1770	2	38
Mo[r]decai, of Nine Partners, m. Naomi **OWEN**, of Salisbury, Apr. 4, 1770, by Rev. Jonathan Lee	2	41
Ruth, d. Merdecai & Naomi, b. Aug. 16, 1778	2	38
William, s. Mordecai & Naomi, b. Oct. 12, 1775, in Poultney	2	38
SORNBERGER, Edwin, m. Sarah M. **HARRIS**, [Sept.] 20, [1832], by L.E. Lathrop	3	141
SPAFFORD, Adah, d. Jonathan & Christian, b. Sept. 21, 1771	2	11
Adah, d. Jonathan & Christian, d. Jan. 2, 1772	2	48
Betty, d. David & Betsey, b. Aug. 23, 1779	2	21
David, m. Bettey **JEWELL**, b. of Salisbury, Jan. 22, 1778, by Rev. Jonathan Lee	2	41
David, s. David & Betty, b. Oct. 31, 1781	2	21
Hannah, d. Jacob & Rebekah, b. Feb. 16, 1765	1	113
Isaac*, s. Jonathan & Christian, b. Sept. 25, 1769 *("Jacob" in Rudd's book)	2	11
Jacob*, s. Jonathan & Christian, b. Sept. 25, 1769 *(Arnold Copy has "Isaac")	2	11
Job*, s. Jacob & Rebekah, b. Jan. 29, 1759 *(Arnold Copy has "Jos")	1	192
Jonathan, s. Jonathan & Christian, b. June 28, 1775	2	11
Jos*, s. Jacob & Rebekah, b. Jan. 29, 1759 *("Job" in Rudd's)	1	192
Mary, d. Jacob & Rebekah, b. Jan. 24, 1763	1	113
Mary, m. Solomon **STANTON**, b. of Salisbury, May 25, 1781, by Abial Camp, J.P.	2	42
Phebe, d. Jonathan & Christian, b. Sept. 23*, 1780 *("Sept. 28" in Rudd's book)	2	11
Rebekah, d. Jacob & Rebekah, b. Jan. 23, 1755	1	192
Rebekah, w. Jacob, d. Feb. 16, 1769, in the 43rd y. of her age	2	48
Sanabey*, s. Jonathan & Christian, b. Oct. 14, 1772 *("Smalley" in Rudd's book)	2	11
Sarah, d. Jonathan & Christian, b. Nov. 11, 1767	2	11
Smalley*, s. Jonathan & Christian, b. Oct. 14, 1772 *(Arnold Copy has "Sanabey")	2	11
Solomon, s. Jacob & Rebekah, b. Sept. 21, 1756	1	192
Temperance, d. Jacob & Rebeckah, b. May 1, 1761	1	113
Thomas, s. Jonathan & Christian, b. Mar. 22, 1778	2	11
SPARKS, Abigail, of Sheffield, m. David **CHAPIN**, of Salisbury, Mar. 23, 1806, by Joseph W. Crossman	3	113
Calvin, of Sheffield, m. Eleanor **HARRIS**, of Salisbury, Dec. 21, 1831, by L.E. Lathrop	3	139
Electa, m. Noah **SELLECK**, b. of Salisbury, Oct. 31, 1813, by Enos Hopkins, J.P.	3	114
SPENCER, Abigail, d. Phillip & Abigail, b. May 8, 1752	1	183
Abner Peck, s. Asa & Mary, b. Apr. 17, 1786	2	17
Achsah, d. Eliphaz & Statira, b. Apr. 13, 1778, in East Haddam	3	3
Achsah, m. Isaac **GREEN**, b. of Salisbury, Sept. 28, 1800, by Joseph W. Crossman	3	111
Alexander, s. Philip & Abigail, b. June 16, 1769, in Oblong	2	25

	Vol.	Page
SPENCER, (cont.)		
Ambrose, s. Philip & Abigail, b. Dec. 13, 1765	1	183
Asa, m. Mary Polly **PECK**, b. of Salisbury, July 10, 1774, by Rev. Jonathan Lee	2	46
Betsey, d. Asa & Mary, b. July 31, 1777	2	17
Deidamia, d. Philip & Abigail, b. June 27, 1759	1	183
Deidamia, of Oblong, N.Y., m. William **WHEELER**, of Salisbury, Jan. 6, 1780, by Rev. Jonathan Lee	2	41
Gordon, s. Eliphaz & Statira, b. Mar. 26, 1781, in East Haddam; d. Feb. 24, 1788	3	3
Gordon, s. Eliphaz & Statira, b. Apr. 29, 1789	3	3
Hannah, d. Job & Hannah, b. Mar. 23, 1815	3	15
Hannah, w. Job, d. Apr. 5, 1815, ae 44	3	168
Hannah M., of Salisbury, m. Adin W. **COBURH**, of Windsor, "Mission K," Oct. 28, 1845, by Rev. Adam Reed	3	97
James, s. Asa & Mary, b. Apr. 26, 1780	2	17
Job, m. Elizabeth **BINGHAM**, July 17, 1822, by Lavius Hyde	3	117
Job Brewster, s. Job & Hannah, b. Jan. 17, 1723	3	15
Laura, d. Asa & Mary, b. May 18, 1788	2	17
Lovina, d. Eliphaz & Statira, b. Oct. 5, 1785; d. Aug. 18, 1786	3	3
Lovina, d. Job, Jr. & Rachel, b. July 21, 1786	3	15
Olivia, d. Asa & Mary, b. June 23, 1784	2	17
Philip, m. Abigail **MOER**, b. of Salisbury, Sept. 25, 1751, by Rev. Jonathan Lee	1	224
Philip, s. Philip & Abigail, b. Sept. 26, 1763	1	183
Polly, d. Asa & Mary, b. Apr. 15, 1782	2	17
Robert, of Colebrook, m. Charlotte J. **CHAPIN**, of Marlborough, Sept. 8, 1838, by Rev. Thomas Bainbridge	3	156
Sally, d. Job, Jr. & Rachel, b. Aug. 13, 1788	3	15
Sally, d. Job, Jr. & Rachel, d. Nov. 1, 1795, in the 9th y. of her age	3	164
Sally, d. Job & Hannah, b. Nov. 21, 1813	3	15
Statira, d. Eliphaz & Statira, b. Mar. 29, 1791	3	3
Thankfull, d. Job, Jr. & Rachel, b. Jan. 27, 1791	3	15
Thankfull, m. Julius **HOLLISTER**, b. of Salisbury, Nov. 29, 1810, by Rev. Joseph W. Crossman	3	114
Tryphene, d. William, of Sheffield, d. Sept. 21, 1754, in the 18th y. of her age	1	226
Tryphena, d. Philip & Abigail, b. May 1, 1755	1	183
SPINK, Polly, d. Job & Marcy, b. Feb. 4, 1787	2	12
SPRAGUE, Hannah, d. John, Jr. & Sarah, d. Mar. 25, 1753	1	226
Hulda, m. Joseph **BIRD**, Jr., b. of Salisbury, May 23, 1753, by Rev. Jonathan Lee	1	240
Sarah, of Sharon, m. Samuel **LANDON**, May 12, 1773, by Rev. Cotton M. Smith	2	46
SPURR, Catharine, of Sheffield, m. Jacob **VOSBROUGH**, of Salisbury, Apr. [ ], 1776, by Rev. Mr. Keep	2	47
STANNARD, Mary, m. Lenerd **OWEN**, b. of Salisbury, Apr. 28, 1757, by Rev. Jonathan Lee	1	246
STANTON, Abigail, twin with Joshua, s. Joshua & Abigail, b. Feb. 19, 1770	2	27
Betsey, d. Elijah & Jemima, b. Jan. 6, 1776	2	23

	Vol.	Page
STANTON, (cont.)		
Betsey, d. Elijah & Jemima, d. July 30, 1790, in the 15th y. of her age	2	50
Betsey, d. John & Silvia, b. May 16, 1796	3	12
Betsey A., of Salisbury, m. Samuel O. **DEWEY**, of Becket, Mass., Dec. 5, 1844, by Rev. C.V. Amerman	3	96
Caleb Nichols, s. Joshua W. & Eliza, b. June 11, 1820	3	63
Cynthia Harriet, d. Joshua W. & Eliza, b. Apr. 14, 1827	3	63
David, s. Elijah & Jemima, b. Jan. 2, 1783	2	23
David Beach, s. Joshua W. & Eliza D., b. June 10, 1815	3	63
Elijah, of Salisbury, m. Jemima **BEECH**, of Sheffield, Oct. 1, 1772, by John Hutchinson, J.P.	2	45
Elijah, s. Elijah & Jemima, b. Feb. 28, 1778	2	23
Elijah, s. Elijah & Jemima, d. Oct. 23, 1779, ae 25	2	50
Elijah, s. Solomon & Mary, b. Nov. 13, 1781	2	35
Elijah, s. Richard Pierce & Julia, b. Aug. 2, 1808	3	47
Elijah, m. Susanna **PEASE**, Jan. 20, 1816, by Edward Bagley, J.P.	3	114
Elizabeth, d. Joshua & Abigail, b. Aug. 6, 1766	1	136
Elizabeth, m. Luke **CAMP**, Jr., b. of Salisbury, Feb. 2, 1786, by Rev. Jonathan Lee	2	43
Esther, d. Elijah & Jemima, b. May 2, 1784	2	23
George Munrow, s. Joshua W. & Eliza D., b. Oct. 22, 1832	3	63
Harriet, d. Elijah & Jemima, b. Oct. 26, 1790	2	23
Harriet, d. John & Silvia, b. Mar. 29, 1798	3	12
Harriet, m. Jacob **VOSBURGH**, Jr., b. of Salisbury, Nov. 15, 1807, by Rev. Joseph W. Crossman	3	113
Henrietta, d. Joshua W. & Eliza, b. Feb. 2, 1823	3	63
Jane Bennett, d. Joshua W. & Eliza, b. Mar. 5, 1825	3	63
John Gardiner, s. Joshua W. & Eliza, b. July 16, 1830	3	63
Joshua, twin with Abigail, s. Joshua & Abigail, b. Feb. 19, 1770	2	27
Joshua W., m. Elizabeth **DUTCHER**, b. of Salisbury, Oct. 27, 1813, by Rev. Charles Printice, of South Canaan	3	114
Julia Esther, m. Benjamin **SHULTZ**, of Rhinebeck, N.Y., Oct. 3, 1833, by Eliphalet Whittlesey, J.P.	3	144
Mary, d. Elijah, b. Apr. 8, 1755	1	175
Mary B., of Salisbury, m. Benjamin G. **HOPKINS**, of Cornwall, Sept. 6, 1831, by L.E. Lathrop	3	140
Polly, d. Elijah & Jemima, b. Nov. 26, 1773	2	23
Polly, m. Herman **HULL**, Sept. 19, 1790, by Samuel Lee, J.P.	3	108
Polly, d. John & Silvia, b. Dec. 28, 1793	3	12
Richard Pierce, s. Elijah & Jemima, b. Jan. 24, 1788	2	23
Sally, d. Joshua & Abigail, b. Feb. 17, 1778	2	27
Sally, d. Elijah & Jemima, b. May 2, 1780	2	23
Solomon, m. Mary **SPAFFORD**, b. of Salisbury, May 25, 1781, by Abial Camp, J.P.	2	42
Waite Dyer, d. John & Silvia, b. Oct. 24, 1800	3	12
W[illia]m Henry, s. Joshua W. & Eliza, b. Mar. 20, 1818	3	63
STARK, Jedediah, m. Abigail **CAMP**, b. of Salisbury, Jan. 15, 1792, at Canaan, by Rev. Daniel Farrand	3	108
STERLING, Anna C., of Salisbury, m. William J. **COGGSWELL**, of Jamaica, L.I., June 12, 1839, by Rev. Adam Reid	3	157
Elisha, had negro Guy **CARLOS**, b. about Jan. 6, 1792	3	21

	Vol.	Page
STERLING, (cont.)		
Elisha, had negroes Mary **JONES**, b. Dec. 2, 1809 & Jane **JONES**, b. Jan. 28, 1812	3	21
Elisha, m. Sarah **ELLIOT**, b. of Salisbury, [Dec.] 8, 1830, by Leonard E. Lathrop	3	137
Elisha Thomas, s. Elisha & Alma, b. July 15, 1806	3	21
Frederic A., of Salisbury, m. Caroline M. **DUTCHER**, of Canaan, June 23, 1825, by L.E. Lathrop. Int. Pub.	3	122
Frederick Augustus, s. Elisha & Alma, b. Mar. 18, 1796	3	21
Harriet A., m. Abiel **CHAPIN**, June 28, 1815, by [ ]. Witnesses Andrew Chapin & Maria F. Chapin	3	115
Henry Dudley, s. Elisha & Alma, b. Jan. 12, 1811	3	21
John Montgomery, s. Elisha & Alma, b. Feb. 24, 1800	3	21
Junius L., m. Eunice E. **PETTEE**, b. of Salisbury, May 28, 1839, by Rev. Adam Reed	3	157
Theodore Beebe, s. Elisha & Alma, b. July 18, 1808	3	21
STEVENS, STEEVENS, Aden, s. Ebenezer & Lucy, b. June 7, 1768	2	24
Amey, of Canaan, m. Oliver **JEWELL**, of Salisbury, Feb. 23, 1777, by Elisha Baker, J.P.	2	47
Bulah, d. Ebenezer & Lucy, b. Aug. 7, 1753	1	193
Ebenezer, s. Ebenezer & Lucy, b. June 29, 1755	1	193
Frederick, s. Ebenezer & Lucy, b. July 6, 1757	1	193
Frederick, s. Adin & Abigail, b. July 3, 1794	3	18
Joel, s. Ebenezer & Lucy, b. Mar. 27, 1765	2	24
Julia Ann, of Salisbury, m. John **JEWIT**, of Sharon, Apr. 15, 1832, by Rev. Stephen Beach, of St. Johns Ch.	3	140
Lucy, m. Zerah **BEECH**, b. of Salisbury, Nov. 27, 1768, by Rev. Jonathan Lee	2	44
Lydia, d. Ebenezer & Lucy, b. Aug. 15, 1762	2	24
Mindwell, d. Ebenezer & Lucy, b. May 9, 1761	2	24
Oliver, m. Nancy **CHITTENDEN**, Aug. 23, 1780, by Rev. Jonathan Lee	2	41
Polly, d. Adin & Abigail, b. Jan. 23, 1793	3	18
Rebeckah, of Killingworth, m. Heldrick **BARRETT**, of Salisbury, Nov. 29, 1763, by John Hutchinson, J.P.	1	251
Thankfull, d. Ebenezer & Lucy, b. Apr. 2, 1759	1	193
Thankfull, m. Moses **CALKINS**, b. of Salisbury, Dec. 7, 1780, by Rev. Jonathan Lee	2	41
STILES, Benjamin, s. Francis & Sarah, b. July 22, 1784	3	24
Francis, d. Apr. 5, 1796, ae 48	3	164
Judson, of Derby (late of Salisbury), d. Nov. 11, 1795, ae about 33 y.	3	164
Ramon, s. Francis & Sarah, b. Dec. 29, 1790	3	24
Sally, d. Francis & Sarah, b. Apr. 17, 1786	3	24
Sally, m. Newman **HOLLY**, b. of Salisbury, Nov. 17, 1805, by Rev. Joseph W. Crossman	3	112
Thomas, s Francis & Sarah, b. Feb. 21, 1789	3	24
Thomas, m. Sally **NEWELL**, b. of Salisbury, Nov. 26, 1829, by Rev. Stephen Beach, of St. Johns Ch.	3	135
Thomas Augustine, s. Thomas & Sarah A., b. Aug. 22, 1831, at Mt. Higa, Salisbury	3	75
STILL, Elizabeth, had s. John, b. June 16, 1774	2	28

	Vol.	Page
STILL, (cont.)		
Eunice, d. David & Elizabeth, b. Aug. 12, 1770	2	28
John, s. Elizabeth, b. June 16, 1774	2	28
STOCK, James Landon, s. Jedediah & Abigail, b. Oct. 12, 1792	3	1
STODDARD, Abigail, d. Luther & Mary, b. Sept. 30, 1783	2	32
Abigail, w. Maj. Luther, d. July 8, 1784, in the 22nd y. of her age	2	50
Abigail, of Salisbury, m. William M. **BURRELL**, of Canaan, Nov. 6, 1803, by Rev. Joseph W. Crossman	3	112
Derias, s. Josiah & Sarah, b. May 17, 1754	1	204
Freeman P., of Sharon, m. Sarah L. **HUBBARD**, of Salisbury, July 2, [1839], by Adam Reid	3	159
Hammond, of Cornwall, m. Sall Ann **WHEELER**, of Salisbury, June 5, 1838, by Rev. Adam Reid	3	155
Herman, s. Samuel & Martha, b. Oct. 13, 1786	2	9
James, s. Josiah & Sarah, b. Oct. 18, 1749	1	204
James*, s. Luther & Mary, b. Sept. 15, 1772 *("James Grovner **STODDARD**" in Rudd's book)	2	32
Jane Matilda, m. William **JONES**, b. of Salisbury, Oct. 16, 1846, by D.W. Clark	3	100
Josiah, m. Sarah **ROBBARTS**, Nov. 7, 1743	LR1	356-7
Josiah, s. Josiah & Sarah, b. Dec. 2, 1747	1	204
Josiah, s. John & Mary, b. Nov. 25, 1784	2	24
Josiah, s. Samuel & Martha, b. Nov. 3, 1785; d. Nov. 5, [1785]	2	9
Luther, s. Josiah & Sarah, b. Mar. 31, 1746	LR1	355
Luther, m. Mary **WHEELER**, Dec. 19, 1771, by James Landon, J.P.	2	45
Lydia, d. Josiah & Sarah, b. Aug. 7, 1744	LR1	350
Mary, d. Josiah & Sarah, b. Aug. 5, 1762	1	159
Olive, d. Josiah & Sarah, b. Aug. 26, 1756	1	204
Prudence, d. Ens. Josiah & Sarah, b. Oct. 15, 1758	1	204
Prudence, d. Ens. Josiah, d. Nov. 23, 1758	1	231
Richard Montgomery, s. Luther & Mary, b. May 15, 1775	2	32
Samuel, s. Josiah & Sarah, b. Nov. 23, 1759	1	159
Samuel, m. Martha **MOORE**, b. of Salisbury, July 6, 1785, by Rev. Jonathan Lee	2	43
Sarah, d. Josiah & Sarah, b. Feb. 14, 1752	1	204
Sarah, m. James **HOLMES**, b. of Salisbury, Feb*. 29, 1772, by James Landon, J.P. *("Jan." in Rudd's book)	2	45
STONE, Ann Maria, d. Oramil & Polly, b. Mar. 25, 1829	3	66
Benjamin W., Rev., of Hudson, N.Y., m. Lois E. **CHURCH**, of Salisbury, Sept. 16, 1840, by Rev. S. Tonkin Carpenter	3	160
Ezra, m. Almira **CURTISS**, b. of Salisbury, July 21, 1830, by Rev. Stephen Beach, of St. Johns Ch.	3	137
Ezra, m. Laura Ann **CURTIS**, b. of Salisbury, July 21, 1830*, by Rev. Stephen Beach, of St. Johns Ch. Witness Birdsey Curtiss *("1839" (?))	3	159
Harmon, s. Oramil & Polly, b. Jan. 23, 1827	3	66
Thankfull, d. Oramil & Polly, b. Apr. 4, 1825	3	66
STRONG, Abigail, w. Adonijah, d. Sept. 5, 1772, in the 29th y. of her age	2	48
Adonijah, m. Abigail **HALE**, b. of Salisbury, Mar. 8, 1770, by Rev. Jonathan Lee	2	44
Adonijah, of Salisbury, m. Mary **PIERCE**, of Litchfield, June 28,		

	Vol.	Page
STRONG, (cont.)		
1774, at Litchfield, by Andrew Adams, J.P.	2	46
Adonijah, of Salisbury, m. Abigail **BATES**, of Hanover, Morris Cty., N.J., July 28, 1777, by Rev. Joseph Grover	2	47
Adonijah, s. Martin & Sally, b. Oct. 8, 1800	3	42
Asa, s. John & Agnis, b. Aug. 11, 1760	1	157
Betsey, of Salisbury, m. Simon **LYMAN**, of Sharon, Mar. 15, 1822, by David L. Perry	3	117
Deborah, d. Elisha & Disea, b. Apr. 13, 1760	1	181
Deborah, m. Bethuel **CHITTENDEN**, b. of Salisbury, Dec. 16, 1762, by Rev. Jonathan Lee	1	250
Disea, d. Elisha & Disea, b. Mar. 22, 1754	1	181
Edwin J., m. Julia Ann **RICHMOND**, b. of Salisbury, May 20, 1829, by Rev. Stephen Beach, of St. Johns Ch.	3	134
Ephraim, s. Elisha & Disea, b. Jan. 9, 1758	1	181
Frances, s. Simeon & Mary, b. Jan. 11, 1764	2	23
Henrietta M., of Salisbury, m. John L. **HOSFORD**, of Canaan, Sept. 27, 1829, by Rev. Stephen Beach, of St. Johns Ch.	3	134
Henry Pierce, s. Adonijah & Abigail, b. Feb. 23, 1785; bp. by Rev. Mr. Lee	2	30
Isaac, s. Elisha & Desiah, b. Jan. 28, 1765	1	176
Jared, s. Enoch & Sarah, b. July 24, 1760	1	114
Johannah, d. Simeon & Mary, b. Jan. 18, 1762	2	23
John Bates, s. Adonijah & Abigail, b. Oct. 4, 1780; bp. by Rev. Mr. Smith	2	30
Jonathan, s. Simeon & Mary, b. July 18, 1769	2	23
Josiah, s. Adonijah & Abigail, b. May 10, 1771	2	30
Josiah, s. Adonijah & Abigail, d. Jan. 9, 1772	2	48
Josiah Hale, s. Adonijah & Mary, b. Mar. 1, 1775	2	30
Lucy, of Coventry, m. Rev. Joseph Warren **CROSSMAN**, of Salisbury, Jan. 14, 1798, in Coventry, by Rev. Abiel Abbot, of Coventry	3	111
Lydia, w. Noah, d. Dec. 23, 1757	1	228
Lydia, m. Samuel **BENTON**, b. of Salisbury, Dec. 17, 1760, by James Landon, J.P.	1	248
Martin, s. Simeon & Mary, b. Nov. 16, 1760	2	23
Martin, s. Adonijah & Abigail, b. Dec. 7, 1778; bp. May [ ], 1779, by Rev. Mr. Benedict	2	30
Martin, m. Sally **THOMSON**, b. of Salisbury, Oct. 2, 1799, by Adonijah Strong, J.P.	3	112
Mary, d. John & Agnis, b. July 28, 1764	1	157
Mary, w. Adonijah, d. Sept. 24, 1775, in the 22nd y. of her age	2	49
Mary, d. Adonijah & Abigail, b. Oct. 19, 1787; bp. by Rev. Mr. Lee	2	30
Mary, of Salisbury, m. Rev. Jonathan **LEE**, of Otus, Nov. 20, 1827, by Leonard E. Lathrop	3	128
Molly, d. Simeon & Mary, b. Mar. 20, 1766	2	23
Noah, s. Elisha & Disea, b. July 19, 1752	1	181
Noah, d. June 23, 1771, at Crown Point, in the 69th y. of his age	2	48
Olive, d. Elisha & Desiah, b. Sept. 6, 1767	1	176
Phinehas, s. Simeon & Mary, b. Dec. 2, 1758	2	23
Reuben, s. Elisha & Desiah, b. Nov. 2, 1762	1	176

	Vol.	Page

STRONG, (cont.)

	Vol.	Page
Sally Maria, d. Martin & Sally, b. June 1, 1805	3	42
Sally Maria, of Salisbury, m. Myron C. **REED**, of Auburn, N.Y., Oct. 16, 1828, by Leonard E. Lathrop	3	131
Samuel, s. John & Agnis, b. July 19, 1762	1	157
Sarah, d. Simeon & Mary, b. Feb. 27, 1757	2	23
Sarah, d. Enoch & Sarah, b. Jan. 27, 1758, at Coventry	1	114
Sarah Pardee, d. Adonijah & Abigail, b. Mar. 15, 1791; bp. by Rev. Cotton M. Smith	2	30
Simeon, of Salisbury, m. Mary **CASTEL**, of Sheffield, Apr. 1, 1756, by Rev. Jonathan Hubbart	1	248
Theron Rudd, s. Martin & Sally, b. Nov. 7, 1802	3	42
William Lightburn, s. Adonijah & Abigail, b. Oct. 18, 1782	2	30

SURDAM, SIRDAM, SUYDAM, [see also **SARDAM**]

	Vol.	Page
Abigail, d. Peter & Elizabeth, b. July 1, 1756	1	220
Andrew, m. Margret **WHITE**, b. of Salisbury, Aug. 4, 1751, by Rev. Jonathan Lee	1	224
Andrew, s. Solomon & Lovisa, b. May 17, 1796	3	19
Andros, s. Peter & Elizabeth, b. July 10, 1758	1	220
Caroline, of Salisbury, m. James N. **HILL**, of Canaan, Nov. 10, 1844, by Rev. C.V. Amerman	3	96
Charity, d. Joshua & Charity, b. Dec. 2, 1772	2	12
Christian, d. Tunis, 1st & Jane, b. Aug. 27, 1765	2	17
Christian, m. Benjamin **HENMAN**, b. of Salisbury, Nov. 26, 1789, by Rev. Daniell Farrand, of Canaan	3	109
Christopher, s. Joshua & Charity, b. Oct. 12, 1773	2	12
Daniel, s. Tunis, 1st & Jane, b. June 7, 1776	3	16
Edmond, m. Maria **WOODWORTH**, b. of Salisbury, Nov. 10, 1844, by Rev. C.V. Amerman	3	96
Edward William, s. Daniel & Letty, b. Apr. 14, 1807	3	32
Elener, d. Peter & Elizabeth, b. Feb. 4, 1748/9	1	220
Elenor, d. Tunis & Jane, b. Apr. 4, 1763	1	129
Eliza, d. Daniel & Letty, b. Oct. 20, 1799	3	32
Fanny, m. Levi **MASON**, b. of Salisbury, July 4, 1837, by Rev. O.V. Amerman	3	154
Hannah, d. Peter & Elizabeth, b. Jan. 25, 1750/1	1	220
Hannah, d. Joshua & Charity, b. Feb. 16, 1767	2	12
Hannah, d. Tunis, 1st & Jane, b. July 9, 1768	2	17
Hannah, m. Jacob **BAGROUGH**, b. of Salisbury, Mar. 30, 1769, by Rev. Jonathan Lee	2	44
Hannah, d. Tunis, 2nd & Abigail, b. Feb. 28, 1774	2	8
Henry, s. Henry & Silvia, b. Oct. 18, 1787	3	12
Jane, d. Samuel & Jane, b. Aug. 8, 1762	1	167
Jane, d. Joshua & Charity, b. Oct. 21, 1769	2	12
Jane, d. Samuel & Jane, d. Apr. 14, 1766, in the 4th y. of her age	1	239
Jane, d. Tunis, 1st & Jane, b. Jan. 18, 1774	3	16
Jane, d. Daniel & Letty, b. Nov. 8, 1804	3	32
Jerusha, d. Daniel & Letty, b. Oct. 8, 1802	3	32
John, s. Tunis, 2nd & Abigail, b. Mar. 17, 1767	2	8
John, s. Tunis, 1st & Jane, b. Dec. 8, 1782	3	16
Joshua, m. Charity **WHITNEY**, b. of Salisbury, Oct. 15, 1766, by		

	Vol.	Page
SURDAM, SIRDAM, SUYDAM, (cont.)		
David Whitney, J.P.	2	44
Lawrence, s. Peter & Elizabeth, b. Oct. 1, 1749	1	220
Letty, d. Daniel & Letty, b. Aug. 1, 1809	3	32
Lydia, d. Tunis, 1st & Jane, b. Feb. 1, 1771	3	16
Margaret, mother of Samuel, d. Oct. 10, 1750, in the 79th y. of her age	1	231
Margret, d. Samuell & Jane, b. Dec. 16, 1757	1	167
Martha Emilia, d. Daniel & Letty, b. Aug. 1, 1811	3	32
Mary, twin with Sarah, d. Tunis, 2nd & Abigail, b. Nov. 26, 1776	2	8
Mary, d. Solomon & Lovisa, b. July 17, 1794	3	19
Mary, d. Solomon & Lovinia, d. Sept. 23, 1796, in the 3rd y. of her age	3	164
Noah, s. Joshua & Charity, b. Mar. 17, 1776	2	12
Peter, of Salisbury, m. Elizabeth **YOUNGLOVE**, of Sheffield, Oct. 5, 1748, by Rev. Jonathan Hobart	1	224
Peter, s. Tunis & Jane, b. Dec. 7, 1761	1	129
Polly, d. Charles, b. Sept. 10, 1781	2	12
Polly, d. Solomon & Lovisa, b. June 11, 1798	3	19
Sally, d. Tunis, 1st & Jane, b. Jan. 14, 1779	3	16
Samuel & Jane, had d. [ ], b. Feb. 8, 1748; d. 17th of same month	1	167
Samuell & Jane, had s. [ ], b. Jan. 26, 1749; d. in 3 wks. & had d. [ ], b. Oct. 10, 1755; d. Nov. 15, 1755	1	167
Samuel, s. Peter & Elizabeth, b. Dec. 18, 1752	1	220
Samuel, s. Samuel & Jane, b. Mar. 18, 1761	1	167
Sarah, twin with Mary, d. Tunis, 2nd & Abigail, b. Nov. 26, 1776	2	8
Susannah, d. Tunis, 2nd & Abigail, b. June 17, 1766	2	8
Silvester*, s. Henry & Silvia, b. Apr. 2, 1790 *("Sylvester")	3	12
Tunis, s. Peter & Elizabeth, b. Dec. 18, 1754	1	220
SURRINER, Catharine, m. Jeremiah **THOMAS**, Oct. 27, 1833, by Philander Wheeler, J.P.	3	145
SWEETLAND, SWETLAND, Aaron, m. Mary **CHIPMAN**, b. of Salisbury, Oct. 21, 1779, by Rev. James Nichols	2	41
Aaron, m. Mary **CHIPMAN**, b. of Salisbury, Oct. 21, 1779, by Rev. Jonathan Lee	2	42
William, s. Aaron & Mary, b. Apr. 19, 1782	2	38
SWIFT, Abigail, d. Jabez & Lucy, b. May 31, 1770	2	16
Amos Bird, s. Jabez & Lucy, b. Dec. 25, 1772	2	16
Betsey, d. Jabez & Lucy, b. July 16, 1774	2	16
Charles, of Hoboken, N.J., m. Julia **BRINSMADE**, d. of John, of Salisbury, Mar. 19, 1836, at Hillsdale, N.Y., by Rev. Mr. Stillman	3	151
Lucy, d. Jabez & Lucy, b. Oct. 26, 1765	1	134
Lucy, d. Jabez & Lucy, d. Apr. 7, 1766	1	230
Lucy, d. Jabez & Lucy, b. Sept. 6, 1768	2	16
Lydia, m. Joel B. **PRINCE**, b. of Salisbury, Feb. 27, [1825], by L.E. Lathrop	3	121
Lydia, m. Joel B. **PIERCE**, b. of Salisbury, Feb. 27, [1825], by L.E. Lathrop	3	121
Ward, m. Statira **GREEN**, Nov. 7, 1832, by L.E. Lathrop	3	141

SALISBURY VITAL RECORDS 265

	Vol.	Page
[SYKES], [see under **SIKES**]		
TAYEE (?), [see also **TAYLOR & TEETER**], Sally, of Salisbury, m. Chester **THORP**, of Sheffield, Mar. 23, 1826, by Rev. David Miller, of the M.E. Ch.	3	124
TAYLOR, Eunice, d. Jesse & Meriam, of New Marlborough, d. Nov. 1, 1785, in the 23rd y. of her age	2	50
Harriet, d. Elijah & Phebe, b. Feb. 23, 1789	2	35
Hiram, of Newtown, m. Sally **CHURCH**, of Salisbury, Dec. 6, 1824, by Rev. Stephen Beach, of St. Johns Ch.	3	120
Hiram, of Newtown, m. Sally **CHURCH**, of Salisbury, Dec. 10, 1824, by Rev. Stephen Beach, of St. Johns Ch.	3	123
Rebecca, of Winchester, m. Samuell **HOLLEY**, of Salisbury, Jan. 30, 1783, at Winchester, by Rev. Joshua Knapp	2	42
TEETER, [see also **TAYEE**], John, m. Catharine **MILLER**, b. of Salisbury, May 9, 1847, by Rev. Jonathan Lee	3	100
TERRY, John, d. Nov. 25, 1760, in the 35th y. of his age	1	236
THARE, Joseph, s. Oliver & Mindwell, b. May 31, 1754	1	198
THOMAS, Jeremiah, m. Catharine **SURRINER**, Oct. 27, 1833, by Philander Wheeler, J.P.	3	145
THOMPSON, THOMSON, Asenath, d. Joel & Mary, b. Apr. 30, 1769	2	27
James, s. Joel & Mary, b. Sept. 5, 1771	2	27
Joel, m. Mary **SMITH**, b. of Salisbury, June 20, 1759, by Rev. Jonathan Lee	2	45
Joel, s. Joel & Mary, b. Mar. 20, 1760	2	27
Joel, of Salisbury, m. Deborah **KNIGHT**, of Sharon, Jan. 4, 1781, by Rev. Jonathan Lee	2	41
Mary, d. Joel & Mary, b. Jan. 28, 1763	2	27
Mary, w. Joel, d. Dec. 7, 1773, in the 30th y. of her age	2	50
Mary, of Salisbury, m. Daniel **KEYES**, of Sheffield, Oct. 14, 1784, by Rev. Jonathan Lee	2	42
Olive, d. James & Lucretia, b. Oct. 2, 1792	3	8
Phebe, d. Joel & Mary, b. Nov. 26, 1773	2	27
Polly, d. James & Lucretia, b. May 15, 1791	3	8
Rachel, d. Joel & Mary, b. June 15, 1767	2	27
Saba, d. Joel & Mary, b. Apr. 21, 1765	2	27
Sabra, m. Ruluff **BIGNALL**, b. of Salisbury, Aog. 20, 1786, by [ ]	2	43
Sally, m. Martin **STRONG**, b. of Salisbury, Oct. 2, 1799, by Adonijah Strong, J.P.	3	112
Sarah, Mrs., of Goshen, m. Joseph **HANCHET**, of Salisbury, Sept. 28, 1759, by Rev. Stephen Heaton	1	222
THORNTON, Daniel, m. Electa **WENTWORTH**, b. of Salisbury, Oct. 23, 1828, by Rev. Noah Bigelow. Int. Pub. Oct. 19, 1828, in M.E. Ch.	3	132
Ezra, s. Ezra & Ruth, b. Oct. 13, 1759	1	140
Ezra, s. Ezra & Sarah, b. May 2, 1789	2	24
Henry, s. Ezra & Sarah, b. Mar. 29, 1787	2	24
Ira, s. Ezra & Sarah, b. Oct. 6, 1784	2	24
John, s. Ezra & Ruth, b. Sept. 6, 1761	1	140
John, s. Ezra & Sarah, b. Sept. 6, 1782, in Livingstone Manor	2	24
Michael, s. Ezra & Ruth, b. Nov. 15, 1763	1	140

	Vol.	Page
THORNTON, (cont.)		
Phebe, m. Solomon **WOODWORTH,** Oct. 18, 1770, by Rev. Jonathan Lee	2	45
Ruth, d. Ezra & Ruth, b. Nov. 19, 1768	2	29
Sally, d. Ezra & Sarah, b. May 7, 1792	2	24
THORP, Chester, of Sheffield, m. Sally **TAYEE** (?), of Salisbury, Mar. 23, 1826, by Rev. David Miller, of the M.E. Ch.	3	124
Hercules, m. Esther J. **BRASSIE,** Mar. 20, 1848, by W.H. Ferris	3	103
Weston, m. Elizabeth M. **ROSSETER,** b. of Salisbury, Jan. 1, 1844, by Rev. C.V. Amerman	3	96
THURBER, Polly, m. William **BACON,** May 15, 1796, by Samuel Lee, J.P.	3	109
TIBBELLS, Caroline, m. Walstein **GOODRICH,** Oct. 3, 1822, by David L. Perry	3	117
Halsey, m. Julia **ABELS,** Oct. 16, 1822, by David L. Perry	3	117
TICKNOR, Benajah, m. Bethiah **BINGHAM,** b. of Salisbury, Feb. 9, 1786, by Rev. Jonathan Lee	2	43
Benajah, s. Benajah & Bethiah, b. May 22, 1788, in Jerecho, Vt.	3	4
Caleb B., m. Mary **LEE,** b. of Salisbury, Jan. 21, 1830, by L.E. Lathrop	3	136
Harmon, s. Benajah & Bethiah, b. Mar. 17, 1792	3	4
Hiram, s. Benajah & Bethiah, b. Mar. 21, 1801; d. Apr. 3, following	3	4
Lois C., d. Robert & Sophia B. **BALL,** & adopted d. of Benajah & Grace **TICKNOR,** m. Donald J. **WARNER,** b. of Salisbury, Nov. 16, 1847, by Rev. G. Huntington Nicholls. Int. Pub.	3	102
Luther, s. Benajah & Bethiah, b. Mar. 9, 1790, in Jericho, Vt.	3	4
Mary, of Sharon, m. Christopher **WHITNEY,** of Salisbury, Dec. 1, 1774, by Rev. Daniel Farrand	2	46
Myram, s. Benajah & Bethiah, b. Feb. 12, 1798	3	4
Norman, s. Benajah & Bethiah, b. Mar. 17, 1796	3	4
Sarah, m. Jesse **BOSTWICK,** b. of Salisbury, July 25, 1762, by Rev. Jonathan Lee	1	250
Sophia Bingham, d. Benajah & Berthiah, b. June 12, 1802	3	4
TILER, [see under **TYLER**]		
TITUS, Eunice, m. Silas Leonard **HALL,** Apr. 4, 1774, by Uriah Lawrence, J.P.	2	47
Sarah, d. Levi & Eunice, b. Apr. 11, 1773	2	16
TOMPKINS, George W., m. Emmeline **CRANE,** Sept. 23, 1832, by L.E. Lathrop	3	141
TOMS, Stephen, s. Robert & Sarah, b. Aug. 4, 1759	1	171
TORNER, [see under **TURNER**]		
TORRANCE, Molly, d. Robert & Lucy, b. Apr. 21, 1766	1	137
Olive, d. Robert & Lucy, b. Jan. 27, 1765	1	137
Olive, d. Robart & Lucy, d. Aug. 4, 1767, in the 3rd y. of her age	1	231
Olive, d. Robert & Lucy, b. Feb. 7, 1768	2	9
Rhoda, d. Robert & Lucy, b. Apr. 7, 1770	2	9
Robert, s. Robert & Lucy, b. Apr. 13, 1772	2	9
Stiles, s. Robert & Lucy, b. June 1, 1774	2	9
TORREY, John, of Bethany, Penn., m. Rebecca **FULLER,** of Salisbury, [Sept.] 28, 1830, by L.E. Lathrop	3	137
TOUSLEY, TOWSLEY, Abiah, d. Samuel & Agnes, b. July 24, 1748	1	206

	Vol.	Page
TOUSLEY, TOWSLEY, (cont.)		
Abiah, m. Stephen **MACINTIRE**, b. of Salisbury, Nov. 23, 1769, by Rev. Jonathan Lee	2	44
Ann, w. Samuel, d. Sept. 27, 1788, in the 40th y. of her age	2	50
Anna, d. Victory Sikes & Anne, b. Apr. 23, 1782	2	28
Anne, d. Samuell, Jr. & Anne, b. Mar. 16, 1766	1	109
Annis, d. Samuel & Agnis, b. Mar. 5, 1760	1	158
Annis, d. Samuel & Agnis, b. Mar. 5, 1760	1	163
Ariel, s. Samuell & Agnis, b. Mar. 25, 1762; d. June 4, 1762	1	158
Ariel, s. Samuel & Agnis, b. Mar. 25, 1762	1	163
Ariel, s. Samuel & Agnes, d. June 4, 1762	1	239
Ariel, s. Samuel & Agnis, b. Aug. 30, 1764	1	163
Betsey, m. Hugh **MONTGOMERY**, b. of Salisbury, Mar. 8, 1785, by Rev. Jonathan Lee	2	42
Charles, s. Samuel & Agnis, b. Oct. 23, 1767	2	7
Clooe, d. Matthew & Martha, b. May 22, 1752	1	193
Eli, s. Samuell, Jr. & Ann, b. Jan. 23, 1777	2	15
Elizabeth, d. Matthew & Martha, b. May 6, 1760	1	193
Heman, s. Samuell, Jr. & Ann, b. July 18, 1768	2	15
Herman*, s. Samuel & Ann, d. Aug. 30, 1771 *("Heman")	2	48
Hulda, s. Matthew & Martha, b. Apr. 25, 1757	1	193
Job, s. Samuel & Agnis, b. Mar. 26, 1758	1	208
Johannah, d. Samuel, Jr. & Ann, b. Jan. 22, 1774	2	15
Jonah, s. Victory Sikes & Anna, b. Dec. 20, 1780	2	28
Jonah, s. Victory S. & Desire, b. Aug. [ ], 1784; d. Jan. 9, 1785	2	28
Julia, d. Samuell & Ann, b. Sept. 7, 1784	2	15
Lot, s. Samuel & Agnis, b. Mar. 5, 1756	1	208
Lot, s. Victory Sikes & Anna, b. July 10, 1776	2	28
Lot, s. Samuell & Ann, b. Sept. 3, 1786	2	15
Lucy, d. Samuell & Ann, b. Jan. 5, 1782	2	15
Maria, of Salisbury, m. Thomas **CROSBY**, of Goshen, July 2, 1834, by Rev. Julius Field	3	149
Martha, d. Matthew & Martha, b. June 24, 1764	1	193
Martha, m. John Hertman **LOTTZ**, June 26, 1788, by Adonijah Strong, J.P.	2	50
Mary, d. Matthew & Martha, b. Nov. 4, 1754	1	193
Matthew, m. Martha **WRIGHT**, b. of Salisbury, Sept. 12, 1750, by Rev. Jonathan Lee	1	222
Munson Matthew, s. Reuben & Mary, b. Mar. 16, 1814	3	57
Phebe*, d. Samuel, Jr. & Ann, b. July 3, 1772 *("Philo son" in Rudd's book)	2	15
Philo, s. Samuel & Ann, d. Sept. 6, 1773	2	48
Reuben, s. Matthew & Martha, b. May 15, 1767	1	193
Robert, s. Mathew & Martha, b. Aug. 6, 1773	2	29
Robert Stansfield, s. Reuben & Mary, b. Oct. 1, 1810	3	57
Roswell, s. Victory Sikes & Anna, b. Dec. 24, 1772	2	28
Ruth, m. Oliver **CHURCH**, b. of Salisbury, Sept. 19, 1771, by Rev. Jonathan Lee	2	45
Sally, d. Mathew & Martha, b. Feb. 27, 1771	2	29
Sally Ann, d. Reuben & Mary, b. Mar. 17, 1809	3	57
Samuel, s. Samuel & Agnes, b. Dec. 25, 1744	LR1	354

	Vol.	Page

TOUSLEY, TOWSLEY, (cont.)
    Samuel, s. Samuel, Jr. & Ann, b. July 18, 1770 — 2, 15
    Sarah, had d. Sarah, b. Mar. 30, 1746 — LR1, 351
    Sarah, d. Sarah, b. Mar. 30, 1746 — LR1, 351
    Sikes, s. Victory Sikes & Anna, b. May 26, 1774 — 2, 28
    Silvanus, s. Samuell & Agnes, b. July 17, 1752 — 1, 206
    Silvanus, s. Samuel & Agnis, d. Mar. 5, 1754 — 1, 226
    Silvanus, s. Samuell & Agnes, b. Apr. 16, 1754 — 1, 206
    Silvanus, s. Victory Sikes & Anna, b. May 10, 1779 — 2, 28
    Silvanus Chauncey, s. Samuell & Ann, b. [   ], 1779 — 2, 15
    Victory, s. Victory Sikes & Desire, b. Sept. 12, 1785 — 2, 28
    Victory S., m. Desire **GRANNIS**, b. of Salisbury, Jan. 27, 1780, by Rev. Jonathan Lee — 2, 41
    Victory Siks, s. Samuel & Agnes, b. Nov. 14, 1751 — 1, 206
    Victory Sikes, m. Anna **BENTON**, b. of Salisbury, Feb. 3, 1773, by Rev. Mr. Hall — 2, 45
    Victory, Sikes, d. May 18, 1779, ae 23 — 2, 49
    William, s. Samuell & Ann, b. [   ] — 2, 15
    William Clark, s. Reuben & Mary, b. June 14, 1812 — 3, 57
    Zilpha, m. William **SMITH**, Apr. 1, 1836, by Leonard E. Lathrop — 3, 151
    Zilpha, m. William **SMITH**, Apr. 1, 1836, by Leonard E. Lathrop — 3, 152

TOWNSEND, Lemuel J., of Tyringham, Mass., m. May G. **PRATT**, of Salisbury, Apr. 22, 1840, by Rev. Adam Reid — 3, 159
    Samuel J., of Tyringham, m. Harriet **JOCELYN**, of Salisbury, May 7, 1843, by Rev. Adam Reid — 3, 163

TOZER, Hulda, d. John & Mary, b. Jan. 3, 1750/1 — 1, 198
    John, m. Mary **BABCOCK**, b. of Salisbury, Sept. 16, 1750, by Rev. Jonathan Lee — 1, 223
    Mary, d. John & Mary, b. Sept. 23, 1752 — 1, 198

TRACY, Abigail, of Richmond, m. Pain **TURNER**, of Salisbury, Aug. 17, 1777, by John Hutchinson, J.P. — 2, 47

TREMAIN, [see also **FREEMAN**], Calvin, s. Nathaniell & Olive, b. Mar. 19, 1791 — 2, 19
    Calvin*, s. Lieut. Nath[anie]l & Olive, d. Aug. 11, 1792, in the 2nd y. of his age   *(Written "**FREEMAN**") — 3, 164
    Cloe, d. Nathaniell & Olive, b. June 13, 1787 — 2, 19
    Chloe, d. Nathaniell & Olive, b. Mar. 3, 1793 — 2, 19
    Isaac, s. Nathaniell & Olive, b. Dec. 28, 1781 — 2, 19
    Levi, s. Nathaniell & Olive, b. June 13, 1783 — 2, 19
    Lorelia*, of Westfield, d. Aug. 12, 1783, in the 18th y. of her age *("Lucretia" in Rudd's book) — 2, 50
    Nathaniel, m. Olive **LYMAN**, b. of Salisbury, Dec. 7, 1780, by Rev. Jonathan Lee — 2, 41
    Nathaniel, s. Nathaniell & Olive, b. Feb. 23, 1789 — 2, 19
    William, s. Nathaniell & Olive, b. Feb. 23, 1785 — 2, 19

TRIPP, John D., of Pine Plains, N.Y., m. Jeanette **VAN DEUZEN**, of Salisbury, Sept. 1, 1835, by Rev. Lucius M. Purdy, of St. Johns Ch. — 3, 150

TRUMBLE, Eldad, s. Ebenezer & Rachel, b. Nov. 3, 1751 — 1, 195
    Eliphalet*, of Salisbury, m. Abigail **WHITNEY**, of Canaan, Sept. 20, 1757, by Rev. Daniel Ferris   *("Eliphalet **JEWELL**" in

SALISBURY VITAL RECORDS 269

	Vol.	Page
TRUMBLE, (cont.)		
Rudd's book)	1	246
Eunice, twin with Jonathan, d. William & Mary, b. Nov. 26, 1762	1	177
Jonathan, twin with Eunice, s. William & Mary, b. Nov. 26, 1762	1	177
Mary, d. William & Mary, b. May 22, 1756	1	177
Mary, d. William & Rachel, b. July 25, 1779	2	34
Ruth Sarah*, d. Sarah, b. Jan. 13, 1769 *("Rocksanah" in Rudd's)	2	14
Sarah, had d. Ruth Sarah, b. Jan. 13, 1769	2	14
Sarah, m. Ebenezer **FITCH**, May 30, 1771, by Rev. Jonathan Lee	2	45
Solomon, s. William & Mary, b. Mar. 3, 1754	1	203
TUCKER, Henry J., m. Rhoda **FREEMAN**, b. of Salisbury, July 5, 1846, by Roger Averill, J.P.	3	98
TUPPER, Absolom, s. Thomas & Ruth, b. July 11, 1759	1	164
Absolom, s. Thomas & Ruth, d. May 3, 1760	1	237
Absolom, s. Thomas & Ruth, b. Apr. 22, 1761	1	164
Archelos, 2nd, s. Thomas & Ruth, b. Oct. 3, 1752	1	202
Archelaus, s. Tho[ma]s & Parthenia, b. June 22, 1784	2	40
Benjamin, s. Thomas & Ruth, b. Feb. 27, 1749	1	202
Charles, s. Thomas & Ruth, b. Mar. 30, 1743	1	202
Chauncey, s. Thomas & Parthenia, b. Aug. 18, 1779	2	40
Claracy*, d. Charles & Hannah,b. Mar. 27, 1768 *("Clarney" in Rudd's book)	2	15
Darius, s. Thomas & Ruth, b. June 15, 1754	1	202
Electa, d. Thomas & Parthenia, b. Feb. 21, 1769	2	40
Electa, m. Daniel **MOORE**, b. of Salisbury, Oct. 22, 1789, by Adonijah Strong, J.P.	2	50
Elizabeth, d. William & Bettey, b. Nov. 20, 1777	2	31
Hazel, d. Charles & Hannah, b. Dec. 26, 1765	2	15
Jerusha, d. Thomas & Ruth, b. Mar. 21, 1741	1	202
Johanner, d. Thomas & Ruth, b. Mar. 19, 1756	1	202
Lorenzo, m. Phebe R. **SELLECK**, b. of Salisbury, Mar. 24, 1844, by C.V. Amerman	3	96
Lydia, d. Thomas & Ruth, b. Oct. 26, 1750	1	202
Lydia, d. Thomas & Ruth, d. Nov. 1, 1759	1	237
Lydia, d. Charles & Hannah, b. May 26, 1764	2	15
Lydia, d. Charles & Hannah, d. July 23, 1764	2	48
Marcy, twin with Ruth, d. Thomas & Ruth, b. Dec. 4, 1745	1	202
Nath[anie]ll, m. Sarah **HANCHET**, b. of Salisbury, Jan. 1, 1766, by Rev. Jonathan Lee	2	44
Philander, d. Thomas & Parthenia, b. July 4, 1775; d. Sept. 1, 1776	2	40
Philander, d. William & Bettey, b. May 19, 1780	2	31
Philainda, d. Thomas & Parthenia, b. Oct. 23, 1781	2	40
Ruth, twin with Marcy, d. Thomas & Ruth, b. Dec. 4, 1745	1	202
Ruth, Jr., m. David **JACOBS**, b. of Salisbury, Aug. 31, 1763, by John Hutchinson, J.P.	1	251
Samuel, s. Nathaniell & Sarah, b. Nov. 4, 1766	2	14
Sarah, d. Thomas & Parthenia, b. Dec. 5, 1773; d. Aug. 27, 1776	2	40
Sarah, d. Thomas & Parthenia, b. June 4, 1777	2	40
Thomas, s. Thomas & Ruth, b. Nov. 16, 1747	1	202
Thomas, d. May 13, 1761	1	237
Thomas, m. Bephnon* **JOQUA***, b. of Salisbury, Sept. 20, 1768, by		

	Vol.	Page
TUPPER, (cont.)		
John Hutchinson, J.P. *(Salisbury printed records "Pertenia JAQUA")	2	44
Thomas, s. Thomas & Parthenia, b. Apr. 20, 1771	2	40
Vesta, of Salisbury, m. William **COWLES**, of Sharon, Nov. 20, 1825, by L.E. Lathrop	3	123
William, m. Betsey* **JAQUA**, b. of Salisbury, July 13, 1775, by Rev. Jonathan Lee *("Bella" in Rudd's book)	2	47
William, s. William & Bettey, b. Feb. 19, 1776	2	31
Zillah, d. William & Bettey, b. May 29, 1784	2	31
Zuriel, s. Thomas & Ruth, b. Mar. 21, 1758	1	202
TURNER, TORNER, Abel, s. Samuel & Mary, b. Aug. 22, 1756	1	216
Anne, d. Samuel & Mary, b. Oct. 10, 1762	1	216
Edward, s. Samuel & Mary, b. Dec. 16, 1752	1	216
Hains, s. Pain & Abigail, b. Aug. 24, 1778	2	9
Jane, of Salisbury, m. Samuel **MAXWELL**, of Stamford, N.Y., Aug. 31, 1828, by Lot Norton, J.P.	3	131
Jam[i]ma, m. Eli **EVARTS**, b. of Salisbury, Apr. 5, 1781, by Rev. Jonathan Lee	2	41
Lucy, m. Moses **REED**, b. of Salisbury, Sept. 22, 1767, by James Landon, J.P.	2	44
Mary, d. Samuel & Mary, b. Oct. 16, 1769	2	25
Mary, d. Jonathan & Mary, b. Mar. 27, 1774	2	16
Mercy, d. Jonathan & Mary, b. Oct. 29, 1772, at New London	2	16
Miles, s. Samuel & Mary, b. June 8, 1760	1	216
Nathaniel Wolcott, s. Wolcott & Mary Ann, b. Sept. 23, 1827	3	82
Pain, of Salisbury, m. Abigail **TRACY**, of Richmond, Aug. 17, 1777, by John Hutchinson, J.P.	2	47
Rebeckah, m. Artemus **BLOGGET**, b. of Salisbury, Aug. 4, 1774, by Elder Dakins	2	46
Roswell, s. Reuben & Sarah, b. Mar. 17, 1766	1	150
Samuel, s. Samuel & Mary, b. Jan. 18, 1749/50	1	216
Steven, s. Jonathan & Mary, b. Aug. 30, 1775	2	16
Susan, m. Edward **SMITH**, b. of Salisbury, [Jan.] 4, 1832, by L.E. Lathrop	3	139
Timothy, m. Deborah **SCOVEL**, b. of Salisbury, Mar. 10, 1774, by John Hutchinson, J.P.	2	45
Uriah, Dr., of New Marlborough, m. Julia Ann **MOORE**, of Salisbury, Jan. 7, 1823, by Pitkin Cowles	3	118
William, d. Oct. 13, 1752, in the 95th y. of his age	1	226
Wolcott, m. Mary Ann **MOORE**, Dec. 6, 1826, by L.E. Lathrop	3	125
TUTTLE, Chandler, s. Thomas & Lydia, b. Sept. 19, 1763	1	117
Eliza, d. Seth & Ruth, b. Apr. 21, 1804; d. Apr. 14, 1805	3	40
Jesse, s. Thomas & Lydia, b. Aug. 24, 1759	1	221
John, s. Thomas & Lydia, b. July 5, 1766	1	117
John William, s. Seth & Ruth, b. Sept. 12, 1802	3	40
Lydia, d. Thomas & Lydia, b. July 18, 1753	1	221
Martha, d. Thomas & Lydia, b. Dec. 6, 1761	1	221
Othniel, s. Thomas & Lydia, b. Sept. 26, 1769	2	24
Solomon, s. Thomas & Lydia, b. Sept. 3, 1757	1	221
Thomas, m. Lydia **OWEN**, b. of Salisbury, Feb. 1, 1753, by Rev.		

	Vol.	Page
TUTTLE, (cont.)		
Jonathan Lee	1	240
Thomas, s. Thomas & Lydia, b. May 5, 1755	1	221
TUTTLETON, Levinie, d. Dec. 19, 1758, in the 19th y. of her age	1	231
TYLER, TILER, Abia, s. Solomon & Anna, b. Dec. 17, 1790	2	14
Charlotte, d. Elisha & Sarah, b. Aug. 24, 1783	2	32
Daniel, m. Susan **DARROW**, Nov. 27, 1828, by L.E. Lathrop	3	132
Ebenezer, d. July 1, 1782, in the 66th y. of his age	2	50
Elisha, s. Ebenezer & Sarah, b. Feb. 5, 1759	1	180
Elisha, of Salisbury, m. Sarah **OWEN**, of Sheffield, Oct. 31, 1782, at Sheffield, Mass., by Lemuel Bernard, J.P.	2	42
Joel, s. Ebenezer & Sarah, b. July 28, 1762	1	123
Joel, s. Ebenezer & Sarah, d. Nov. 3, 1764	1	239
Joel, s. Ebenezer, Jr. & Mary, b. May 16, 1771	2	29
Olive, d. Solomon & Anna, b. Nov. 23, 1787	2	14
Sally, d. Solomon & Anna, b. Aug. 13, 1799	2	14
Sarah, d. Ebenezer & Sarah, b. May 25, 1756	1	180
Sarah, d. Feb. 27, 1769, in the 84th y. of her age	2	48
Solomon, of Salisbury, m. Anna **NOKES**, of Nobletown, Apr. 27, 1786, by Rev. Jonathan Lee	2	43
UMSTEAD, Levi, s. John & Katharine, b. Dec. 29, 1795	3	22
Nancy, d. John & Katharine, b. Sept. 15, 1800	3	22
Polly, d. John & Katharine, b. Nov. 10, 1798	3	22
URE, John, m. Polly **MO[O]RE**, b. of Salisbury, Oct. 19, 1785, by Rev. Jonathan Lee	2	43
VALLENS, Elizabeth, m. Lawrence **WHITE**, b. of Salisbury, June 17, 1755, by James Landon, J.P.	1	242
VANDUSEN, VANDUZEN, VANDEUSDEN, VAN DEUZEN,		
Abraham, s. James & Katharine, b. Feb. 18, 1741	1	212
Abraham, s. Hartman & Marget, b. Jan. 16, 1741/2	1	212
Abraham, s. Hendrick & Nelche, b. Sept. 9, 1742	LR1	350
Abraham, d. Apr. 16, 1746	LR1	350
Arconchee, d. Hendrick & Welchee, b. Apr. 3, 1740	LR1	356-7
Desia, d. Lawrence & Content, b. Jan. 10, 1772	2	25
Henry, s. Lawrence & Content, b. Dec. 7, 1764	1	146
Henry, s. Abraham & Sarah, b. Jan. 28, 1771	2	11
Heretray, d. Hendrick & Nelche, b. July 30, 1747	LR1	350
Hertry, m. Daniel **EVARTS**, b. of Salisbury, Sept. 9, 1767, by Daniel Castle, J.P.	2	44
Hertry, d. Abraham & Sarah, b. Apr. 11, 1775	2	11
Horatio G., m. Jane **VANDUZEN**, b. of Salisbury, Oct. 11, 1829, by Rev. Stephen Beach, of St. Johns Ch.	3	135
Horatio Gates, s. Abraham & Sarah, b. June 27, 1777	2	11
Jane, m. Horatio G. **VANDUZEN**, b. of Salisbury, Oct. 11, 1829, by Rev. Stephen Beach, of St. Johns Ch.	3	135
Jeanette, of Salisbury, m. John D. **TRIPP**, of Pine Plains, N.Y., Sept. 1, 1835, by Rev. Lucius M. Purdy, of St. Johns Ch.	3	150
Jemima, m. Elijah **RUSSELL**, b. of Salisbury, Dec. 17, 1755, by Rev. Jonathan Lee. Witnesses Ruluff Dutcher, Samuel Russell & Lawrence VanDusen	1	244
John, s. Hartman & Margret, b. May 15, 1740	1	212

	Vol.	Page
VANDUSEN, VANDUZEN, VANDEUSDEN, VAN DEUZEN, (cont.)		
John, s. Abraham & Sarah, b. Nov. 8, 1765	1	144
John, s. Lawrence & Content, b. Apr. 30, 1769	2	25
Lawrence, s. Hendrick & Neeche, b. Nov. 15, 1738	LR1	350
Lawrence, m. Content **WILLIAMS**, of Great Barrington, Aug. 26, 1762, by John Hutchinson, J.P.	1	250
Lawrence, d. Nov. 20, 1772	2	48
Lawrence & Content, had d. [ ], d. Jan. 7, 1776, in the 14th y. of his age	2	49
Molley, d. Lawrence & Content, b. Nov. 11, 1762	1	146
Nelle, d. Abraham & Sarah, b. May 20, 1767	2	11
Olive, m. William **READ***, b. of Salisbury, Jan. 20, 1763, by John Hutchinson, J.P. *("**PEW**" in Rudd's book)	1	250
Samuel, s. Abraham & Sarah, b. Mar. 5, 1773	2	11
Sarah, d. James & Katharine, b. June 11, 1743	1	212
Sarah, d. Lawrence & Content, b. Feb. 25, 1768	2	25
Sarah, d. Abraham & Sarah, b. Apr. 23, 1769	2	11
Seymour, m. Caroline **McARTHUR**, b. of Salisbury, Nov. 28, 1833, by Leonard E. Lathrop	3	145
Yockamenchee, d. Hendrick & Nelche, b. Mar. 26, 1736	LR1	350
Yonake, d. Hartman & Margret, b. Apr. 28, 1748	1	212
VAN KEAVEN, Benjamin J., of Pleasant Valley, m. Mary Ann **BARNUM**, of Salisbury, Feb. 13, 1833, by Leonard E. Lathrop	3	142
VAN VALKENBURY, Hannah, m. Lockwood **CARY**, May 3, 1835, by Leonard E. Lathrop	3	148
VIBBERT, Mary, Mrs., of New York, m. Samuel **MOORE**, of Salisbury, June 28, 1807, by Rev. Joseph W. Crossman	3	113
VOSBURGH, VOSBROUGH, VOSBURG, Abraham, of Salisbury, m. Katharine **ESBEEK***, of Nobletown, Aug. 16, 1768, by Rev. Jonathan Lee *("**WEDBACK**" in Rudd's book)	2	44
Andrew Richard, s. Richard & Almira, b. Jan. 20, 1817	3	65
Catharine, twin with Nicholas, d. Jacob & Catharine, b. Feb. 17, 1786	2	36
Catharine, d. Jacob & Catharine, b. Mar. 15, 1794	2	38
Christian, d. Jacob & Catharine, b. Apr. 28, 1781	2	36
Derrick, s. Jacob & Esther, b. July 11, 1747	1	205
Derick, s. Jacob & Catharine, b. June 28, 1790	2	38
Emeline, d. Isaac & Mary, b. Nov. 16, 1826	3	45
Esther Anne, d. Jacob & Catharine, b. June 12, 1779	2	36
Frederick Jay, s. Jacob & Harriet, b. Jan. 14, 1817	3	47
George Lewis, s. Richard & Almira, b. Feb. 6, 1814	3	65
Graham Wheeler, s. Isaac & Mary, b. Oct. 13, 1815	3	45
Harry, m. Sophia Matilda **SAUNDERS**, b. of Salisbury, Nov. 29, 1832, by Rev. Thomas Sparks	3	142
Isaac, s. Jacob & Catharine, b. Mar. 11, 1788	2	38
Isaac, of Sheffield, m. Polly **HANKS**, of Salisbury, Dec. 22, 1799, by John Whittlesey, J.P.	3	104
Isaac, m. Mary **WHEELER**, b. of Salisbury, Oct. 4, 1807, by Rev. Jacob W. Crossman	3	113
Jacob, s. Jacob & Esther, b. Feb. 15, 1744/5	LR1	355
Jacob, of Salisbury, m. Catharine **SPURR**, of Sheffield, Apr. [ ], 1776, by Rev. Mr. Keep	2	47

	Vol.	Page
VOSBURGH, VOSBROUGH, VOSBURG, (cont.)		
Jacob, s. Jacob & Catharine, b. Oct. 10, 1783	2	36
Jacob, Jr., m. Harriet **STANTON**, b. of Salisbury, Nov. 15, 1807, by Rev. Joseph W. Crossman	3	113
Jacob, d. May 12, 1810, ae 67	3	167
John, s. Abraham & Sally, b. Feb. 25, 1798	3	20
Julia Ann, d. Jacob & Harriet, b. May 23, 1813	3	47
Mary, m. Herman **MINARD**, b. of Salisbury, Aug. 25, 1830, by L.E. Lathrop	3	136
Mary Ann, d. Isaac & Mary, b. Mar. 19, 1809	3	45
Myron Parker, s. Jacob & Harriet, b. Aug. 16, 1815; d. Apr. 5, 1816	3	47
Nicholas, twin with Catharine, s. Jacob & Catharine, b. Feb. 17, 1786	2	36
Nicholas, s. Jacob & Catharine, b. Nov. 1, 1795	2	38
Norman Beach, s. Jacob & Catharine, b. June 2, 1811	3	47
Olive Catharine, d. Isaac & Mary, b. Aug. 20, 1812	3	45
Rhoda, m. Stephen **NORTHROP**, Feb. 8, 1803, by Ephraim Judson. Witnesses Polly Grenold & Diadama Vosbough	3	115
Sally Maria, d. Jacob, Jr. & Harriet, b. Oct. 23, 1808	3	47
Sarah, d. Jacob & Katharine, b. June 27, 1777	2	11
Sarah, d. Jacob & Catharine, b. June 27, 1777	2	36
WAITE*, Oreonche, d. William & Mry, d. Apr. 28, 1767 *(Arnold Copy has "**WHITE**")	2	48
WALKER, Alice, of Salisbury, m. John **ADAMS**, of Sandisfield, Mass., Nov. 5, 1833, by Leonard E. Lathrop	3	145
Hannah M., m. Benjamin **REED**, Oct. 10, 1827, by Leonard E. Lathrop	3	128
Zebulon, m. Hannah **HANCHET**, b. of Salisbury, June 7, 1773, by Rev. Jonathan Lee	2	45
WALLING, James, s. John & Sally, b. Sept. 3, 1804	3	40
John, m. Sally **PIERCE**, b. of Salisbury, Nov. 24, 1803, by Rev. Joseph W. Crossman. Witnesses Seth Tuttle & Ruth Tuttle	3	112
WALTON, Esther, wid. John & d. Lot **NORTON**, d. Oct. 19, 1809, ae 51	3	167
Frederic Augustus, s. Dr. W[illia]m & Mary, b. Mar. 18, 1794	2	40
John Pope, m. Esther **NORTON**, Jan. 1, 1792, by Rev. Daniel Farrand, of Canaan	3	108
Lucius C., of Lyons, Mich., m. Mary V. **WHITTLESEY**, of Salisbury, Feb. 21, 1844, by Rev. Adam Reid	3	163
Polly, d. William & Mary, b. Sept. 1, 1787	2	40
Seth, m. Julia M. **SAGE**, b. of Salisbury, Feb. 25, 1847, by Rev. Adam **REED**	3	100
William, s. William, Jr. & Mary, b. Sept. 1, 1785; d. Oct. 27, 1786	2	40
William, Dr., d. Apr. 14, 1787, in the 52nd y. of his age	2	50
William Henry, s. Dr. W[illia]m & Mary, b. Sept. 10, 1791	2	40
WARD, Ambrose, of Newtown, m. Sarah M. **MASON**, of Salisbury, Oct. 14, 1828, by Leonard E. Lathrop	3	131
John Rogers, of Sheffield, Mass., m. Ruth Amanda **CHURCH**, of Salisbury, Dec. 1, 1835, by Rev. B. Griffen	3	151
WARDEN, [see also **WERDEN**], Caroline, m. Harry **WARDEN**, b. of Salisbury, Nov. 8, 1844, by Rev. C.V. Amerman	3	96
Harry, m. Caroline **WARDEN**, b. of Salisbury, Nov. 8, 1844, by Rev. C.V. Amerman	3	96

	Vol.	Page
WARDWELL, Sarah A., of Salisbury, m. George **WOOD**, of North East, Oct. 6, 1844, by Rev. C.V. Amerman	3	96
WARN, WARNE, [see also **WARNER**], Francis, s. Robert & Sarah, b. Jan. 29, 1746, in the Manor of Levington	1	207
Jacob, s. Robert & Sarah, b. Sept. 31 [sic], 1744	LR1	354
John, s. Robert & Sarah, b. Feb. 28, 1742	LR1	351
Mary, d. Robart & Sarah, b. July 28, 1749	1	207
Richard, s. Robert & Sarah, b. Nov. 22, 1740	LR1	351
Robart, of Salisbury, m. Catharine **BENNET**, of the Co. of Albany, Dec. 30, 1751, by Rev. Jonathan Lee	1	224
Samuel, s. Robart & Catharine, b. Nov. 3, 1752	1	207
Samuel, s. Robert & Catharine, b. Dec. 3, 1752	1	207
Sarah, d. Robert & Sarah, b. Jan. 29, 1746, in the Manor of Levington	1	207
Sarah, w. Robart, d. Aug. 8, 1749	1	225
William, s. Robart & Catharine, b. Aug. 3, 1754, in Taugheonick	1	207
WARNER, [see also **WARN**], Ashbell, of Bolton, m. Abby **LYMAN**, of Salisbury, Oct. 2, 1825, by L.E. Lathrop	3	123
Donald J., m. Lois C. **TICKNOR**, d. Robert & Sophia B. **BALL** & adopted d. of Benejah & Grace **TICKNOR**, b. of Salisbury, Nov. 16, 1847, by Rev. G. Huntington Nicholls. Int. Pub.	3	102
Electa Harriet, d. Daniel, Jr. & Judeth, b. Apr. 18, 1801	3	39
Jennette, of Salisbury, m. James E. **KELLOGG**, of Sheffield, Mass., Oct. 28, 1846, by Rev. J. Button Beach, of Sheffield	3	99
Judeth Maria, d. Daniel, Jr. & Judeth, b. July 21, 1803	3	39
Noadiah, m. Adaline **JONES**, b. of Salisbury, Sept. 13, 1836, by Rev. Oliver V. Amerman, of M.E. Ch.	3	152
Thomas, of Sheffield, m. Alma C. **PARKS**, of Salisbury, Mar. 28, 1844, by Rev. Adam Reid	3	163
WARREN, Ashbell, of Bolton, m. Abby **LYMAN**, of Salisbury, Oct. 2, 1825, by Leonard E. Lathrop	3	122
WASHBURN, Deborah, d. Abisha & Hannah, b. Nov. 10, 1771, in Ankrom	2	32
Lois, m. John **DUTCHER**, Jr., Jan. 11, 1770, by John Hutchinson, J.P.	2	44
Mary, d. Abisha & Hannah, b. Oct. 25, 1763	1	143
Olive, d. Abisha & Hannah, b. Jan. 16, 1766	1	143
Rebeckah, d. Abisha & Hannah, b. Feb. 7, 1769	2	19
Sarah, m. John **CHIPMAN**, b. of Salisbury, Nov. 5, 1772, by Rev. Jonathan Lee	2	45
WATERMAN, Anna, d. David & Anna, b. Jan. 30, 1776, in Ulster Co., N.Y.	3	11
Betsey, d. David & Anna, b. Mar. 6, 1778, in Kent	3	11
David, s. David & Anna, b. July 1, 1793	3	11
Edgar Conklin, s. David & Anna, b. May 2, 1796	3	11
Harriet, d. David & Anna, b. Sept. 13, 1782, in Kent	3	11
Polly, d. David & Anna, b. May 16, 1791	3	11
Thomas, s. David & Anna, b. Jan. 22, 1787, in Kent	3	11
William Melnor, s. David & Anna, b. May 20, 1798	3	11
WATROUS, WATEROUS, WATEROUSE, Ann, d. James & Ann, b. Jan. 2, 1775	2	10
Clarendy, d. Samuel & Mary, b. Mar. 15, 1763, in Kilinworth	2	34

	Vol.	Page
WATROUS, WATEROUS, WATEROUSE, (cont.)		
Dyer, s. Joseph & Abigail, b. Nov. 5, 1762	1	110
Edward, s. Samuel & Mary, b. Mar. 22, 1775	2	34
Eleazer, s. Abe & Phebe, b. Apr. 5, 1782	2	7
Elizabeth, m. John Lee **SHERMAN**, b. of Salisbury, Mar. 31, 1763, by John Hutchinson, J.P.	1	251
Esther, s. James & Anne, b. July 29, 1779	2	13
Harry Stevens, s. Josiah & Martha, b. Feb. 20, 1783	2	11
Hephzabah, m. Asa **WHITNEY**, b. of Salisbury, Oct. 23, 1776, by Rev. Jonathan Lee	2	47
James, m. Ann JEWELL, b. of Salisbury, Nov. 6, 1766, by Rev. Jonathan Lee	2	44
James, s. James & Anne, b. July 23, 1782	2	13
Joseph, s. James & Ann, b. July 7, 1767	2	10
Josiah, s. Samuel & Mary, b. May 25, 1768, in Killingworth	2	34
Mary, d. Samuel & Mary, b. [ ], 1760, in Branford	2	34
Mary, m. Samuel **DONOLD**, b. of Salisbury, Oct. 14, 1779, by Rev. Jonathan Lee	2	41
Olivia, d. Josiah & Martha, b. Feb. 27, 1780	2	11
Rebekah, d. Samuel & Mary, b. Mar. 18, 1765, in Killingworth	2	34
Samuel, s. Samuel & Mary, b. June 25, 1758, in Branford	2	34
Sarah, d. Samuel & Mary, b. July 25, 1772	2	34
Submit, d. James & Ann, b. Aug. 7, 1772	2	10
Submit, d. James & Anne, b. Apr. 22, 1777	2	13
Submit, d. James & Anne, d. Dec. 20, 1778	2	50
William, s. James & Ann, b. July 22, 1770	2	10
WATTON, Caroline Maria, m. Michael **GUNON**, b. of Salisbury, Apr. 17, 1825, by Rev. Stephen Beach, of St. Johns Ch.	3	121
Mary E., m. Oliver **JEWELL**, b. of Salisbury, Oct. 6, 1841, by Rev. Adam Reid	3	161
WAY, Hannah, m. Eben[eze]r **FITCH**, b. of Salisbury, May 19, 1768, by Rev. Jonathan Lee	2	44
Maria, d. Abner & Sally, b. Mar. 10, 1805	3	32
WEAVER, George Edward, s. Samuel & Hannah, b. Oct. 11, 1812	3	54
Harvey, s. Samuel & Hannah, b. June 1, 1824	3	54
Horace, s. Samuel & Hannah, b. May 11, 1819	3	54
Julius, twin with William, s. Samuel & Hannah, b. Oct. 11, 1810	3	54
Mary, d. Samuel & Hannah, b. Jan. 14, 1815	3	54
Mary, of Salisbury, m. Alonzo R. **BISHOP**, of Winsted, Oct. 10, 1833, by L.E. Lathrop	3	144
Norman, s. Samuel & Hannah, b. Dec. 22, 1816	3	54
William, twin with Julius, s. Samuel & Hannah, b. Oct. 12, 1810	3	54
WEBB, WIBB, Arta, d. Isaac & Abigail, b. Aug. 22, 1787	2	33
Caroline Elizabeth, d. John & Elizabeth, b. Mar. 29, 1800	3	30
Diantha, of Otis, m. Walter **PLUMB**, of Bloomfield, Nov. 12, 1839, by Rev. Thomas Bainbridge	3	158
James, s. Isaac & Abigail, b. Jan. 29, 1790	2	33
John Freeman, s. John & Elizabeth, b. Mar. 21, 1798	3	30
Maria Louisa, d. John & Elizabeth, b. Dec. 15, 1796	3	30
Reynold, s. Isaac & Abigail, b. Aug. 24, 1785	2	33
Sidney B., of Hamilton, Madison Cty., N.Y., m. Olive V. **RUSSELL**,		

	Vol.	Page
WEBB, WIBB, (cont.)		
of Salisbury, [ ], by Rev. Lucius M. Brady, of St. Johns Ch.	3	146
WEDBACK*, Katharine, of Nobletown, m. Abraham, **VOSBURGH**, of Salisbury, Aug. 16, 1768, by Rev. Jonathan Lee *(Arnold Copy has "**ESBEEK**")	2	44
WEED, Abi, d. Levi & Dolly, b. Oct. 22, 1800	3	20
Dolley, d. Levi & Dolley, b. May 16, 1798	3	20
Dolly, w. Levi, d. Aug. 26, 1798, ae 21	3	164
Elizabeth, d. Eben[eze]r & Salome, b. May 18, 1793	3	12
James, s. Ebenezer & Salome, b. Mar. 10, 1792	3	12
Levi, m. Abigail **NORTHROP**, b. of Salisbury, May 9, 1799, by Rev. Joseph W. Crossman	3	110
Lewis, m. Dolly **BINGHAM**, June 4, 1797, by Samuel Lee, J.P.	3	110
Susanna, w. Belding, d. Dec. 15, 1802, in the 46th y. of her age	3	165
WELCH, Elizabeth, d. Samuell & Hannah, b. Sept. 2, 1739	LR1	354
Hiram Castle, s. Marvin & Betsey, b. Mar. 28, 1811	3	33
James, M.D., of Sandisfield, m. Lavinia **HUBBARD**, of Salisbury, [May 18, 1831], by L.E. Lathrop	3	139
Sally Sophia, d. Marvin & Betsey, b. Aug. 28, 1809	3	33
Samuel, s. Samuel & Hannah, b. Dec. 31, 1743/4	LR1	352
Samuel, s. Samuel & Hannah, b. Jan. 26, 1747	LR1	350
WELDON, WELDIN, WELDING, Abiah, d. Elijah & Ruth, b. Jan. 2, 1786	2	37
Abigail, d. Jesse & Ruth, b. Jan. 21, 1758, at Glastonbury	1	120
Abigail Maria, d. Mylo & Abigail, b. Feb. 18, 1809	3	46
Abraham, s. John & Elizabeth, b. July 5, 1757	1	211
Abraham, s. Elijah & Ruth, b. Dec. 24, 1778	2	37
Anna, of Sheffield, Mass., m. Solomon **SMITH**, of Monroe, Orange Cty., N.Y., Nov. 6, 1821, by Eliphalet Whittlesey, J.P.	3	116
Betsey, d. Abraham & Sarah, b. July 22, 1798	2	9
David, s. Jesse & Ruth, b. July 30, 1765	2	23
Elijah, s. John & Elizabeth, b. July 5, 1753	1	211
Elijah, of Salisbury, m. Ruth **WESSCOOT**, of Stanford*, Apr. 5, 1775, by Rev. Mr. Mills *("Bedford" in Rudd's book)	2	47
Elizabeth, d. John & Elizabeth, b. Dec. 2, 1747	1	211
Elizabeth, w. John, d. July 27, 1768	2	48
Elizabeth, d. Elijah & Ruth, b. Dec. 19, 1780	2	37
Hannah, d. Anthony & Elizabeth, b. Mar. 7, 1741	LR1	352
Isaac, s. John & Elizabeth, b. Apr. 7, 1760	1	108
Jacob, s. Abraham & Sarah, b. Oct. 4, 1784	2	9
James, s. John & Elizabeth, b. Apr. 7, 1745	LR1	355
James, of Salisbury, m. Thankfull **SMITH**, of Sheffield, Aug. 11, 1767, by John Ashley, J.P.	2	44
James, s. James & Thankfull, b. July 21, 1768	2	21
Jerusha, d. Jesse & Ruth, b. Aug. 11, 1760	1	120
John, s. John & Elizabeth, b. Feb. 15, 1749/50	1	211
John*, of Salisbury, m. Elizabeth **CHURCH**, of Sheffield, Mar. 21, 1769, by John Hutchinson, J.P. *(Arnold Copy has "John **SELWIN**")	2	44
John, of Salisbury, m. Abia **DRAKE**, of Sheffield, Jan. 24, 1775, by		

	Vol.	Page
WELDON, WELDIN, WELDING, (cont.)		
John Hutchinson, J.P.	2	46
John, d. Oct. 18, 1800, in the 97th y. of his age	3	167
Loana*, [twin with Lois], d. Jesse & Ruth, b. Oct. 5, 1763		
*("Loara" in Rudd's book)	1	120
Lois, [twin with Loana], d. Jesse & Ruth, b. Oct. 5, 1763	1	120
Mary, d. Anthony & Elizabeth, b. Feb. 13, 1743	LR1	353
Mary, d. John & Elizabeth, b. May 4, 1768	2	21
Merian*, d. Jesse & Ruth, b. June 7, 1762 *("Meriam" in Rudd's)	1	120
Mylo, s. Elijah & Ruth, b. Feb. 17, 1783	2	37
Naomi, d. Mylo & Abigail, b. Nov. 30, 1804	3	46
Peter Larabee, s. Abraham & Sarah, b. Oct. 29, 1786, in Quermans Patten	2	9
Polly, d. Abraham & Sarah, b. Aug. 8, 1789	2	9
Rachel, d. Elijah & Ruth, b. Mar. 26, 1777	2	37
Ruth, d. Jesse & Ruth, b. Nov. 27, 1773	2	23
Ruth, w. Elijah, d. Aug. 2, 1786, in the 30th y. of her age	2	50
Sally, d. Abraham & Sarah, b. July 15, 1793	2	9
Warren, s. Abraham & Sarah, b. Sept. 21, 1791	2	9
William, s. John & Elizabeth, b. Jan. 12, 1766	2	21
WELLING, Sheldon, m. Ann **PEET**, b. of Salisbury, Aug. 16, 1820, by Lavius Hyde	3	115
WELLS, Edward, s. Moses, Jr. & Love, b. Mar. 4, 1834	3	83
Frederick, s. Moses, Jr. & Love, b. Oct. 10, 1830	3	83
George Miles, s. Miles & Eliza, b. Mar. 24, 1825	3	51
Jane Eliza, d. Miles & Eliza, b. Jan. 22, 1827	3	51
Miles Doolittle, s. Moses & Ruth, b. Nov. 23, 1801	3	36
Moses, Jr., m. Love **CHAPIN**, b. of Salisbury, Dec. 1, 1829, by L.E. Lathrop	3	135
Moses Kellogg, s. Moses & Ruth, b. Aug. 2, 1803	3	36
Silas, m. Jane **LEE**, Sept. 30, 1833, by L.E. Lathrop	3	144
WENTWORTH, WINTWORTH, Eady, m. Hamilton J. **JONES**, b. of Salisbury, Nov. 5, 1838, by Rev. Thomas Bainbridge	3	156
Electa, m. Daniel **THORNTON**, b. of Salisbury, Oct. 23, 1828, by Rev. Noah Bigelow. Int. Pub. Oct. 19, 1828, in M.E. Ch.	3	132
Mary Ann, of Salisbury, m. William H. **CROSSMAN**, of Canaan, [ ], 18, [ ], by Leonard E. Lathrop	3	150
WERDEN, [see also **WARDEN**], William, m. Lucy B. **WHITTLESEY**, b. of Salisbury, [ ], by Rev. Adam Reed	3	101
WESSCOOT, Ruth, of Stanford*, m. Elijah **WELDON**, of Salisbury, Apr. 5, 1775, by Rev. Mr. Mills *("Bedford")	2	47
WEST, David, of North East, N.Y., m. Harriet **LOVELAND**, of Salisbury, Jan. 3, 1827, by Rev. Stephen Beach, of St. Johns Ch.	3	125
Sarah, d. Christopher & Amy, b. Dec. 29, 1752, in York Gov.	1	170
Submit, d. Christopher & Amy, b. Apr. 29, 1757, in York Gov.	1	170
[WETHERELL], WITHERELL, William B., m. Mary **BOSWORTH**, b. of Salisbury, Sept. 22, 1839, by Rev. Thomas Bainbridge	3	158
WHEELER, Deodamia, d. William & Deodamia, b. Dec. 3, 1780	2	20
Dorothy, wid. John, d. June 9, 1812	3	167
Freeman, s. John H. & Catharine, b. Sept. 25, 1803	3	33
George, s. Isaac & Catharine, b. Apr. 16, 1812	3	57

	Vol.	Page
WHEELER, (cont.)		
Hiram, s. John H. & Christeen, b. Mar. 12, 1802	3	33
Horace, s. John H. & Christeen, b. July 2, 1800	3	33
Horace, of Montecello, N.Y., m. Olive **BENEDICT**, of Salisbury, Apr. 24, 1825, by Rev. Stephen Beach	3	121
John, d. Dec. 24, 1811	3	167
Josiah, s. Josiah & Eunice, b. Jan. 22, 1779	2	18
Love, of Salisbury, m. Luke **HADSELL**, of New Marlborough, Mass., Oct. 10, 1833, by Eliphalet Whittlesey, J.P.	3	145
Mary, d. John & Mary, b. Nov. 25, 1762	1	122
Mary, m. Luther **STODDARD**, Dec. 19, 1771, by James Landon, J.P.	2	45
Mary, m. James **FOLIET**, Aug. 30, 1787, by Rev. Jonathan Lee. Witnesses Jeremiah Dauchy & Oliver Jewell, Jr.	2	50
Mary, m. Isaac **VOSBURGH**, b. of Salisbury, Oct. 4, 1807, by Rev. Jacob W. Crossman	3	113
Parthenia, m. Daniel **CHAPIN**, b. of Salisbury, Oct. 26, 1783, by Rev. Jonathan Lee	2	42
Sall Ann, of Salisbury, m. Hammond **STODDARD**, of Cornwall, June 5, 1838, by Rev. Adam Reid	3	155
Susanna, w. John, d. Nov. 21, 1791	2	50
Tama, d. John & Mary, b. Mar. 2, 1765	1	122
William, of Salisbury, m. Deidamia **SPENCER**, of Oblong, N.Y., Jan. 6, 1780, by Rev. Jonathan Lee	2	41
W[illia]m, Dr., d. Jan. 13, 1781	2	49
WHEELOCK, Rodolphus, see Ralph **BINGHAM**	1	255
WHIPPLE, Franklin Andrew, s. Perley & Mary A., b. May 13, 1821	3	73
Paul Edwards, s. Perley & Mary A., b. Apr. 24, 1826	3	73
WHITE, Aaron, s. William & Elizabeth, b. Dec. 8, 1759	1	192
Aaron, s. William & Elizabeth, d. Dec. 16, 1759	1	231
Abigail, d. Isaac, Jr. & Sarah, b. Jan. 31, 1776	2	32
Almira, d. Samuel, 2nd & Olive, b. Mar. 10, 1793	3	30
Arconche, d. William & Mary, b. Nov. 3, 1755	1	200
Arconche, see also Oreonche		
Benjamin, s. Ruluff & Mary, b. Oct. 24, 1757 N.S.	1	203
Benjamin, s. Ruluff & Mary, d. Apr. 14, 1760	1	236
Benjamin, s. Isaac, Jr. & Sarah, b. Feb. 23, 1774	2	32
Betty, m. Isaac **PECK**, b. of Salisbury, Nov. 10, 1768, by John Hutchinson, J.P.	2	44
Bette, d. William & Ruth, b. July 8, 1771	2	9
Beulah, d. Jacob & Anne, b. Oct. 11, 1776	2	12
Calvin, s. Jacob & Anne, b. Sept. 18, 1781	2	12
Catharin, d. Isaac & Magdelen, b. Apr. 25, 1749	1	214
Catharine, w. Benjamin, d. Oct. 18, 1750	1	225
Catharine, d. Peter & Goodeth, b. Sept. 22, 1752	1	192
Catharine, d. Ruluff & Mary, b. Mar. 25, 1766	1	169
Catharine, d. Herman & Sarah, b. Oct. 11, 1775	2	35
Chauncey, s. Jacob & Anna, b. May 15, 1774	2	12
Chester, s. Samuell & Olive, b. Aug. 21, 1795	3	30
Chritian*, d. Ruluff & Maracha, b. Dec. 1, 1749 *("Christeen" in Rudd's book)	1	203
Clarissa, d. Jacob & Anne, b. May 10, 1779	2	12

SALISBURY VITAL RECORDS

	Vol.	Page
WHITE, (cont.)		
Cornelia, d. Isaac & Magdelena, b. Oct. 24, 1742	LR1	352
Cornelia, m. Gideon **BROWNSON**, b. of Salisbury, Apr. 16, 1761, by Rev. Jonathan Lee	1	249
Cornelia, d. Isaac & Sarah, b. Feb. 11, 1771	2	32
David, s. William, tailor & Elizabeth, b. Nov. 11, 1757	1	192
Eliza, d. Benjamin & Betsey, b. Nov. 11, 1794	3	25
Elizabeth, d. Isaac & Magdeline, b. Feb. 3, 1750/1	1	214
Elizabeth, d. William & Elizabeth, b. Apr. 17, 1765	1	192
Elizabeth, d. William, 1st & Elizabeth, d. Jan. 20, 1766	1	239
Elizabeth, w. Lawrence, d. Feb. 2, 1771	2	48
Elizabeth, d. Isaac, Jr. & Sarah, b. July 14, 1779	2	32
George, s. Lawrence & Elizabeth, b. Apr. 24, 1759	1	182
George, s. Lawrence & Elizabeth, b. Apr. 26, 1759	2	29
George, s. Samuel & Ruth, b. Apr. 18, 1783	2	15
Goodeth*, m. Philip **COOLE**, Aug. 31, 1748, by Rev. Jonathan Lee *(Arnold Copy has "Judeth")	1	222
Hannah, d. William & Elizabeth, b. Jan. 8, 1761	1	192
Hannah, m. Richard **BICKNAL**, Apr. 16, 1761, by John Hutchinson, J.P.	1	248
Hannah, d. William & Ruth, b. Aug. 14, 1767	2	9
Harmon, m. Sarah **DEAN**, b. of Salisbury, Aug. 7, 1775, by John Hutchinson, J.P.	2	46
Herman, s. Isaac & Magdeline, b. Feb. 5, 1753	1	214
Herman*, s. Herman & Sarah, b. Aug. 30, 1780 *(Arnold Copy has "Simeon")	2	35
Hiram, s. Herman & Sarah, b. Dec. 29, 1791	2	35
Horace, s. Jacob & Anne, b. May 4, 1784	2	12
Isaac, s. Isaac & Magdelena, b. Dec. 4, 1746	LR1	355
Isaac, Jr., m. Sarah **PECK**, b. of Salisbury, May 14, 1770, by John Hutchinson, J.P.	2	45
Isaac, s. Herman & Sarah, b. Feb. 2, 1789	2	35
Jacob, m. Annis **COLLINS**, b. of Salisbury, Apr. 5, 1773, by John Hutchinson, J.P.	2	45
James, s. William & Elizabeth, b. Dec. 29, 1755	1	192
James, s. William & Elizabeth, d. June 19, 1757	1	228
Jane, d. Ruluff & Maracha, b. Aug. 27, 1752 O.S.	1	203
Jane, m. Thomas **BUTLER**, b. of Salisbury, June 1, 1769, by John Hutchinson, J.P.	2	44
Jesse, s. Herman & Sarah, b. July 17, 1785	2	35
John, s. Isaac & Magdelene, b. May 12, 1745	LR1	355
John, s. Herman & Sarah, b. June 2, 1783	2	35
Joshua, s. Ruluff & Maracha, b. Feb. 20, 1754 N.S.	1	203
Joshua, d. Nov. 4, 1765, in the 68th y. of his age	1	239
Joshua, m. Lorranee **PECK**, b. of Salisbury, Sept. 8, 1776, by John Hutchinson, J.P.	2	47
Joshua, s. Joshua & Lorain, b. Mar. 9, 1778	2	31
Judeth*, m. Philip **COOLE**, Aug. 31, 1748, by Rev. Jonathan Lee *(Rudd's book has "Goodeth")	1	222
Katheren, m. John **LANDON**, Nov. 5, 1741	LR1	356-7
Lawrence, m. Elizabeth **VALLENS**, b. of Salisbury, June 17, 1755,		

	Vol.	Page
WHITE, (cont.)		
by James Landon, J.P.	1	242
Lawrence, s. Ruluff & Mary, b. Aug. 11, 1759	1	169
Lawrence, m. Sarah **PHILIPS**, b. of Salisbury, Apr. 1, 1773, John Hutchinson, J.P.	2	45
Lucy, d. Benjamin & Betsey, b. Mar. 12, 1796	3	25
Lucy, d. [Benjamin & Betsey], d. Sept. 19, 1797	3	25
Lydia, d. William & Elizabeth, b. May 17, 1768	2	15
Margret, m. Andrew **SIRDAM**, b. of Salisbury, Aug. 4, 1751, by Rev. Jonathan Lee	1	224
Maria D., of Danbury, m. Roger **AVERILL**, of Salisbury, Oct. 16, 1844, in Danbury, m. (by?) Rev. Rollin S. Stone, of the Cong. Ch.	3	97
Mary, w. William, d. Sept. 24, 1766	2	48
Mary, d. Lawrence & Elizabeth, b. Jan. 27, 1767	2	29
Mary, d. Joshua & Lorain, b. Nov. 13, 1776	2	31
Olive, d. Sam[ue]ll, 2nd & Olive, b. Sept. 5, 1797	3	30
Oliver, s. Lawrence & Elizabeth, b. July 27, 1764	2	29
Oreonche*, d. William & Mary, d. Apr. 28, 1767 *(C. Randall says "Oreonche **WAITE**")	2	48
Oreonche, see also Arconche		
Peter, of Salisbury, m. Goodeth **DECKER**, of the Co. of Ulster, Nov. 3, 1749, by Rev. William Manches, of Kingston. Witness Isaac White	1	223
Phebe, d. William, tailor & Elizabeth, b. Dec. 11, 1766; d. Jan. 1, 1767	1	145
Polly, d. Samuel & Ruth, b. Feb. 18, 1791	2	15
Polly, d. Luther & Sarah, b. June 17, 1795	3	17
Rhoda, d. Lawrence & Elizabeth, b. Jan. 7, 1762	1	182
Rhoda, d. Lawrence & Elizabeth, b. Jan. 8, 1762	2	29
Ruluff, of Salisbury, m. Maroche **KNICKERBOCKER**, of Dutchess Co., May 24, 1748, by Aaron P. Hetch, J.P. Witness Peter White	1	223
Ruluff, s. Ruluff & Mary, b. Mar. 20, 1762	1	169
Samuel, s. Lawrence & Elizabeth, b. July 13, 1756	1	182
Samuel, s. William & Ruth, b. Oct. 18, 1769	2	9
Samuel, s. Samuell & Ruth, b. Jan. 4, 1785	2	15
Sarah, d. Ruluff & Mary, b. Oct. 22, 1755	1	203
Sarah, d. Lawrence & Elizabeth, b. June 22, 1769	2	29
Sarah, d. Lawrence & Elizabeth, d. Mar. 7, 1771	2	48
Sarah, d. Herman & Sarah, b. Sept. 10, 1777	2	35
Sarah, d. Isaac, Jr. & Sarah, b. Aug. 5, 1781	2	32
Simeon*, s. Herman & Sarah, b. Aug. 30, 1780 *("Herman" in Rudd's book)	2	35
Solomon, s. William & Elizabeth, b. Mar. 26, 1763	1	192
Solomon, s. Samuel & Ruth, b. Apr. [ ], 1788	2	15
Sophronia, d. Samuel, 2nd & Olive, b. Oct. 26, 1791	3	30
Ward Walton, s. Benjamin & Betsey, b. Sept. 19, 1799	3	25
Wealthy, d. Benj[ami]n & Betsey, b. Feb. 15, 1798	3	25
William, d. Jan. 5, 1750/1, in the 85th y. of his age	1	225
William, s. William & Ruth, b. Nov. 30, 1761	2	9

	Vol.	Page
WHITE, (cont.)		
William, of Salisbury, m. Ruth **ASHMOND**, of Canaan, Dec. 28, 1766, by John Beebe, J.P.	2	44
WHITEHEAD, Betsey Clarissa, d. Justus & Harriet E., b. June 25, 1820	3	75
Ja[me]s Alonzo, s. Justus & Harriet Electa, b. July 28, 1822	3	75
Rufus Justus, s. Justus & Harriet E., b. Sept. 2, 1818	3	75
Sarah H., of Salisbury, m. Henry **HASKINS**, of Richmond, Mass., Apr. 9, 1846, by Rev. D.W. Clark	3	101
Sarah Harriet, d. Justus & Harriet E., b. Oct. 13, 1824	3	75
WHITING, Anna, d. William & Sarah, b. Apr. 8, 1780	2	7
Mary, d. William & Sarah, b. Oct. 21, 1775	2	7
William F., of Colebrook, m. Elizabeth D. **CONKLING**, of Salisbury, Nov. 28, 1833, by Leonard E. Lathrop	3	145
WHITMAN, Betsey, of Salisbury, m. Charles **NORTHRUP**, of Mt. Ross, N.Y., Nov. 7, 1827, by Rev. Phinehas Cook, of the M.E. Ch.	3	128
WHITMORE, Betsey, d. Samuel & Deliverance, b. May 7, 1776	3	5
Harriet, d. Samuel & Deliverance, b. Oct. 25, 1783	3	5
Harriet, m. David M. **LANGDON**, b. of Salisbury, Mar. 15, 1827, by Rev. Phinehas Cook, of the M.E. Ch.	3	126
Nathaniel, s. Samuel & Deliverance, b. July 2, 1786	3	5
Polly, d. Samuel & Deliverance, b. Jan. 9, 1779	3	5
Samuel, s. Samuel & Deliverance, b. Apr. 9, 1772	3	5
WHITNEY, Abigail, of Canaan, m. Eliphalet **TRUMBLE***, of Salisbury, Sept. 20, 1757, by Rev. Daniel Ferris *(**"JEWELL"** in Rudd's)	1	246
Angeline, m. Charles **KILLMAN**, b. of Salisbury, Sept. 29, 1836, by Rev. Oliver V. Amerman, of M.E. Ch.	3	153
Appleton, s. Asa & Hephzabah, b. Jan. 4, 1779	2	18
Asa, m. Hephzabah **WATEROUS**, b. of Salisbury, Oct. 23, 1776, by Rev. Jonathan Lee	2	47
Billa, s. Christopher & Mary, b. May 12, 1775	2	35
Charity, m. Joshua **SIRDAM**, b. of Salisbury, Oct. 15, 1766, by David Whitney, J.P.	2	44
Christopher, s. William & Arconche, b. Sept. 28, 1751	1	195
Christopher, of Salisbury, m. Mary **TICKNOR**, of Sharon, Dec. 1, 1774, by Rev. Daniel Farrand	2	46
Cornelius, s. William & Arconche, b. Dec. 31, 1753	1	195
George Washington, s. Asa & Hephzabah, b. Sept. 1, 1777	2	18
George Washington, see also Washington **WHITNEY**		
Hentry, d. William & Arconcha, b. Aug. 4, 1748, in Canaan *("Heretry" in Rudd's book)	1	220
James, s. Asa & Hephzabah, b. Jan. 19, 1782	2	18
Jane, d. William & Jane, b. May 22, 1766	2	10
John, s. William & Jane, b. Oct. 5, 1757	2	10
Joshua, of Salisbury, m. Ann **ASHLEY**, of Sheffield, Jan. 9, 1770, by John Ashley, J.P.	2	44
Mary, d. William & Arconcha, b. Aug. 24, 1750; d. [ ]	1	220
Mary, d. William & Jane, b. Oct. 1, 1759	2	10
Milton, s. Asa & Hephzabah, b. Apr. 7, 1786	2	18
Noah Ashley, s. Joshua & Anna, b. Dec. 26, 1770	2	28
Olive, d. Christopher & Mary, b. Mar. 18, 1780	2	35

	Vol.	Page

WHITNEY, (cont.)

	Vol.	Page
Ruluff, s. Christopher & Mary, b. June 25, 1777	2	35
Solomon, s. William & Jane, b. Mar. 11*, 1763 *("Mar. 1" in Rudd's)	2	10
Thankfull, m. Benajah **CAMP**, b. of Salisbury, Nov. 22, 1841, by J. Shaw	3	161
Washington*, s. Asa & Hephzabah, d. Dec. 12, 1777 *("George Washington" in Rudd's book)	2	49
Washington, see also George Washington **WHITNEY**		
William, m. Arconche **DUTCHER**, b. of Canaan, June 4, 1747, by Rev. Elisha Webster, of Canaan	1	222
WHITTLESEY, Caroline, d. Eliphalet & Martha, b. Mar. 24, 1805	3	42
Caroline, d. Eliphalet & Martha, d. Mar. 17, 1807, ae 1 y. 11 m. 24 d.	3	166
Caroline, d. Eliphalet & Martha, b. Dec. 7, 1809	3	42
Caroline, of Salisbury, m. George H. **FISH**, of Whitehall, N.Y., Feb. 21, 1831, by Leonard E. Lathrop	3	138
Charles, s. Eliphalet & Martha, b. Oct.1, 1819	3	72
Eliphalet, m. Martha **ROSE**, Apr. 12, 1804, by Joseph W. Crossman	3	112
Eliphalet, Jr., s. Eliphalet & Martha, b. Apr. 2, 1815	3	42
Eliphalet, Jr., s. Eliphalet & Martha, d. Sept. 10, 1815, ae 5 m. 8 d.	3	168
Eliphalet, Jr., s. Eliphalet & Martha, b. July 13, 1816	3	42
Elisha, s. Eliphalet & Martha, b. Nov. 13, 1821	3	72
George, s. Eliphalet & Martha, b. Oct. 9, 1825	3	72
John, Jr., of Salisbury, m. Abigail **JOHNSON**, of New Milford, May 24, 1792, by Rev. Jeremiah Day, of New Preston	3	109
John, d. Mar. 22, 1812, ae 71	3	167
John, s. Eliphalet & Martha, b. July 12, 1813	3	42
John, s. Eliphalet & Martha, d. May 9, 1815, ae 1 y. 9 m. 27 d.	3	168
John, of Salisbury, m. Rebecca **CAMP**, of New Milford, Feb. 19, [1817], by Rev. Andrew Elliot, of New Milford	3	114
John, s. Eliphalet & Martha, b. Mar. 15, 1818	3	42
John, s. Eliphalet & Martha, d. Oct. 6, 1820, ae 2 y. 6 m. 21 d.	3	168
Lucy B., m. William **WERDEN**, b. of Salisbury, [1847 (?)], by Rev. Adam Reed	3	101
Lucy Bishop, d. Eliphalet & Martha, b. May 6, 1823	3	72
Martha, d. Eliphalet & Martha, b. Sept. 25, 1806	3	42
Martha, m. Lot **NORTON**, Sept. 6, 1826, by Leonard E. Lathrop	3	124
Mary, w. John, d. Sept. 30, 1802, in the 58th y. of her age	3	165
Mary Abby, d. John & Abigail, b. Aug. 9, 1799	3	31
Mary V., of Salisbury, m. Lucius C. **WALTON**, of Lyons, Mich., Feb. 21, 1844, by Rev. Adam Reid	3	163
Philander, s. Eliphalet & Martha, b. Dec. 1, 1811	3	42
Sheldon, of New Preston, m. Eunice **SMITH**, of Salisbury, Dec. 13, 1837, by Rev. Adam Reid	3	154
Thomas T., of Danbury, m. Caroline **HOLLEY**, of Salisbury, Nov. 29, 1826, by L.E. Lathrop	3	125
Walter Rose, s. Eliphalet & Martha, b. Feb. 1, 1808	3	42
WILBER, Sylvanus A., of Hyde Park, N.Y., m. Loiza **BARNUM**, of Salisbury, Oct. 16, 1833, by Leonard E. Lathrop	3	144
[**WILCOX**], **WILCOCKS**, Heman, s. Stephen & Alice, b. Feb. 23, 1778	2	25
Stephen, m. Alice **BEEBE**, b. of Salisbury, June 25, 1777, by Rev.		

	Vol.	Page
[WILCOX], WILCOCKS, (cont.)		
Jonathan Lee	2	41
WILLARD, Esther, m. Daniel **BINGHAM,** Jr., b. of Salisbury, Jan. 12, 1775, by Rev. Jonathan Lee	2	46
WILLIAMS, Abigail, d. Benajah & Abigail, b. Mar. 16, 1761	1	127
Benajah, m. Abigail **COOK,** Aug. 10, 1758, by William Willer, J.P.	1	250
Content, of Great Barrington, m. Lawrence **VANDUSEN,** Aug. 26, 1762, by John Hutchinson, J.P.	1	250
Deborah, m. John **OWEN,** Mar. 4, 1762, by Rev. Jonathan Lee	1	250
Edwin B., of New York, m. Mary S. **HOLLEY,** of Salisbury, June 29, 1847, by Rev. Adam Reed	3	101
Electe, d. Benajah & Abigail, b. Feb. 28, 1763	1	127
Ephraim, s. Benajah & Abigail, b. Dec. 11, 1766	1	127
Eunice, d. Benajah & Abigail, b. Mar. 16, 1765	1	127
Hannah, d. Joseph & Hannah, b. Aug. 26, 1750, at Nine Partners	1	199
Hannah, of Sheffield, Mass., m. Phinehas **LOOMIS,** of Salisbury, Feb. 14, 1829, by Eliphalet Whittlesey, J.P.	3	133
Henry, b. Nov. 21, 1746, in Stonington	2	32
Hiram, s. Isaac & Elizabeth, b. June 14, 1757	1	194
Isaac, m. Elizabeth **LOOMIS,** b. of Salisbury, Mar. 12, 1750, by Rev. Jonathan Lee	1	224
Isaac, s. Isaac & Elizabeth, b. Feb. 6, 1753	1	194
Isaiah, s. Joseph & Hannah, b. Jan. 3, 1762	1	153
Israel, s. Joseph & Hannah, b. Sept. 19, 1757	1	199
Jabin, s. Joseph & Hannah, b. Nov. 12, 1753	1	199
John, m. Cornelia **SHOOK,** b. of Salisbury, Feb. 13, 1848, by Rev. Jonathan Lee. Int. Pub.	3	102
Joseph, s. Joseph & Hannah, b. Apr. 8, 1752	1	199
Martha, d. Joseph & Hannah, b. June 15, 1749, at Nine Partners	1	199
Mary, d. William & Lucretia, b. Dec. 16, 1805	3	34
Mary, of Salisbury, m. John **HUNT,** of Canaan, Mar. 11, 1829, by Rev. Noah Bigelow. Int. Pub.	3	80a
Mary, of Salisbury, m. John **HUNT,** of Canaan, Mar. 11, 1829, by Noah Bigelow. Int. Pub.	3	104
Mary, of Salisbury, m. John **HUNT,** of Canaan, Mar. 11, 1829, by Rev. Noah Bigelow. Int. Pub.	3	133
Pressilla, d. Joseph & Hannah, b. Sept. 27, 1759	1	153
Saline, d. Benajah & Abigail, b. Nov. 2, 1769	2	26
Solomon, s. Isaac & Elizabeth, b. Dec. 7, 1750	1	194
Sophia T., m. Eben T. **HOCOMB,** b. of Salisbury, [Nov.] 22, 1835, by Leonard E. Lathrop	3	150
William, of Stockbridge, m. May B. **AVERILL,** of Salisbury, July 5, 1843, by Rev. Adam Reid	3	163
WINEGAR, William, of Armenia, m. Cornelia **PHINNEY,** of Salisbury, June 4, 1833, by L.E. Lathrop	3	143
WING, David S., m. Malissa A. **SMITH,** Dec. 17, 1834, by Rev. Richard Wymond	3	149
WINSHIP, Jane A., m. Burdsey **CURTISS,** b. of Sterling, Nov. 19, 1840, by Rev. Adam Reid	3	160
WINSLOW, Bethiah, d. Nathaniell & Hannah, b. Dec. 31, 1759	1	221
Charity, d. Nathaniell & Hannah, b. Dec. 24, 1774	2	8

	Vol.	Page
WINSLOW, (cont.)		
Elizabeth, d. Samuel* & Elizabeth, b. Jan. 6, 1784 *("Lemuel" in Rudd's book)	2	21
Hanah, d. Nathaniell & Hanah, b. Feb. 14, 1757	1	221
Jared, s. Nathaniell & Hannah, b. June 9, 1771	2	8
John, s. Nathaniel & Hannah, b. May 4, 1767	1	136
Jonathan, s. Nathaniell & Hannah, b. June 7, 1769	2	8
Lemuel, s. Nathaniel & Hannah, b. Apr. 1, 1755	1	221
Lovina, d. Nathaniel & Hannah, b. May 3, 1765	1	136
Marcy, d. Nathaniell & Hannah, b. Mar. 16, 1763	1	221
Miriam, d. Prince & Sarah, b. Mar. 25, 1764	1	131
Nathaniell, of Salisbury, m. Hannah **FITCH**, of Coventry, Apr. 9, 1753, by [ ]. Witnesses Noah Porter & Rebekah Porter	1	240
Nathaniel, s. Nathaniell & Hannah, b. Apr. 9, 1761	1	136
Prince, of Salisbury, m. Sarah* **GOODRICH**, of Sheffield, June 21, 1763, by Rev. Jonathan Hubbart *("Mary" in Rudd's book)	1	251
Rhoda, d. Nathaniell & Hannah, b. May 7, 1777	2	8
WINTERS, WINTER, Andrew, m. Fanny **BRITON**, Dec. 31, 1824, by Rev. John Lovejoy of the M.E. Ch.	3	121
Christopher, m. Zeruiah **SMITH**, b. of Salisbury, Oct. 22, 1767, by Rev. Jonathan Lee	2	44
John, s. Christopher & Zerviah, b. Aug. 13, 1768	2	16
Mary A., of Salisbury, m. Orville A. **ANDREWS**, of Sheffield, Mass., Oct. 26, 1846, by Rev. Jonathan Lee	3	99
Zerviah, d. Christopher & Zerviah, b. June 12, 1770	2	16
WOLCOTT, Abiather Robbins, s. Abiather & Mary, b. May 1, 1801	3	2
Abiather Robbins, s. Abiather & Mary, b. May 1, 1801	3	27
Abigail Lorilla, m. William Sidney **SMITH**, b. of Salisbury, Nov. 9, 1830, by Aaron Pearce	3	138
Mary Electa, of Salisbury, m. David **CLARK**, of Bristol, Vt., Sept. 14, 1825, by Rev. David Miller, of the M.E. Ch.	3	122
Oliver Ellsworth, s. Abiather & Mary, b. Sept. 3, 1802	3	27
Oliver Ellsworth, s. Abiather & Mary, b. Sept. 8, 1802	3	2
Wells, Rev., m. Emily **BANCROFT**, b. of Salisbury, Oct. 11, 1832, by Rev. Thomas Sparks	3	141
William, s. Abiather & Mary, b. Sept. 10, 1810	3	2
William, s. Abiather & Mary, b. Sept. 10, 1810	3	27
WOOD, George, of North East, m. Sarah A. **WARDWELL**, of Salisbury, Oct. 6, 1844, by Rev. C.V. Amerman	3	96
WOODBECK, Clarissa, m. Joshua **CLINE**, b. of Salisbury, Nov. 17, 1833, by David L. Perry	3	145
WOODIN, WOODING, Abner, of Salisbury, m. Hannah **SMITH**, of New Fairfield, June 10, 1777, by Rev. Mr. Bradford	2	41
Lavenia, m. Joshua F. **JACOBS**, b. of Salisbury, Apr. 6, 1831, by Rev. Stephen Beach, of St. Johns Ch.	3	138
Lavinia, m. Hiland K. **MERCHANT**, b. of Salisbury, Sept. 15, 1839, by Rev. Thomas Bainbridge	3	158
WOODS, Hannah, of New Milford, m. Nathaniel **DEAN**, of Salisbury, Jan. 1, 1751, by Paul Welch, J.P.	1	241
WOODWORTH, Abigail, d. Cyrenius & Abigail, b. July 15, 1762	1	124
Abigail, d. Luke & Jane, b. July 3, 1793	3	2

SALISBURY VITAL RECORDS

	Vol.	Page
WOODWORTH, (cont.)		
Abner, s. Elisha & Anna, b. May 13, 1785	2	38
Amos, s. Caleb & Jane, b. May 4, 1741	LR1	353
Anna, d. Ephraim & Anna, b. Mar. 30, 1755; d. Apr. 12, 1755	1	211
Ariel, s. Elisha & Anna, b. Sept. 6, 1787, in Albany County, N.Y.	2	38
Caleb, s. Solomon & Phebe, b. Apr. 7, 1771	2	30
Caleb, s. Solomon & Phebe, d. Apr. 13, 1771	2	48
Clarissa, d. David & Hannah, b. Jan. 30, 1799	3	25
Cyrenius, s. Caleb & Jane, b. Nov. 15, 1736	LR1	353
Cyrenius, s. Cyrenius & Abigail, b. June 28, 1766	1	124
Darius, twin with Luther, s. Cyrenius & Abigail, b. Nov. 23, 1775	2	17
Deliverance, d. Caleb & Jane, b. Oct. 23, 1745	LR1	355
Dyre, s. Abner & Hannah, b. Oct. 20, 1757	1	173
Elisha, m. Anne **BRADLEY**, b. of Salisbury, Jan. 11, 1776, by Rev. Jonathan Lee	2	47
Elisha, s. Elisha & Anna, b. Aug. 16, 1781	2	38
Ephraim, s. Caleb & Jane, b. Sept. 22, 1732	LR1	353
Ephraim, of Salisbury, m. Anna **MOORE**, of Nine Partners, Aug. 15, 1754, by Samuel Hutchinson, J.P. Witnesses Jesse Chatfield & Sarah Chatfield	1	241
Ephraim, s. Ephraim & Anna, b. Mar. 2, 1756	1	211
Erastus, s. Elisha & Anna, b. May 12, 1779	2	38
Freelove, d. Caleb & Jane, b. Nov. 1, 1738	LR1	353
Freelove, m. Jesse **CHATFIELD**, b. of Salisbury, Oct. 18, 1756, by Rev. Jonathan Lee	1	244
Gersham, s. Caleb & Jane, b. Sept. 16, 1728	LR1	353
Gershom, m. Rosanna **EVARTS**, b. of Salisbury, Nov. 24, 1749, by [ ]	1	222
Hannah, d. Abner & Hannah, b. June 18, 1754	1	173
Henry, of North East, N.Y., m. Sally Ann **REED**, of Salisbury, Jan. 12, 1842, by Rev. Adam Reid	3	162
James, s. Cyrenius & Abigail, b. Oct. 24, 1778	2	17
James, of Great Barrington, Mass., m. Ellen **BARTLETT**, of Salisbury, May 31, 1848, by Rev. Adam Smith	3	103
Jane, d. Caleb & Jane, b. Sept. 20, 1730	LR1	353
Jerusha, d. Ephraim & Anna, b. Apr. 17, 1758	1	211
Joel, s. Cyrenius & Abigail, b. June 3, 1783	2	17
Joseph, s. Abner & Hannah, b. Oct. 18, 1759	1	173
Josiah, s. Cyrenius & Abigail, b. Nov. 10, 1768	2	17
Luke, s. Cyrenius & Abigail, b. Aug. 10, 1771	2	17
Luther, twin with Darius, s. Cyrenius & Abigail, b. Nov. 23, 1775	2	17
Maria, m. Edmond **SURDAM**, b. of Salisbury, Nov. 10, 1844, by Rev. C.V. Amerman	3	96
Mary, m. Levi **BENTON**, b. of Salisbury, Oct. 30, 1769, by Rev. Mr. Lee	2	45
Polly, d. Elisha & Anna, b. Jan. 24, 1777	2	38
Rebecca, m. Samuell **GRINNELL**, b. of Salisbury, Nov. 22, 1785, by Rev. Jonathan Lee	2	43
Sally, d. Luke & Jane, b. July 31, 1791	3	2
Samuel, s. Cyrenius & Abigail, b. Aug. 20, 1763	1	124
Sarah, d. Caleb & Jane, b. Aug. 2, 1743	LR1	353

	Vol.	Page
WOODWORTH, (cont.)		
Sarah, d. Abner & Hannah, b. Oct. 18, 1759	1	173
Sarah, m. Jonathan **CAMFIELD**, b. of Salisbury, Dec. 2, 1764, by Caleb Smith, J.P.	2	44
Sarah, d. Elisha & Anna, b. July 16, 1783	2	38
Sarah, m. Theodore **WOODWORTH**, b. of Salisbury, Apr. 16, 1828, by Rev. Phinehas Cook	3	130
Selleck*, of Salisbury, m. Rebeckah **DUNHAM**, of Sheffield, Dec. 30, 1773, by John Hutchinson, J.P. *("Selah" in Rudd's book)	2	45
Solomon, s. Caleb & Jane, b. May 4, 1748	1	212
Solomon, m. Phebe **THORNTON**, Oct. 18, 1770, by Rev. Jonathan Lee	2	45
Theodore, m. Sarah **WOODWORTH**, b. of Salisbury, Apr. 16, 1828, by Rev. Phinehas Cook	3	130
Theodore, of Ellenville, N.Y., m. Maria **SILVERNAIL**, of Salisbury, Oct. 20, 1838, by Rev. Thomas Bainbridge	3	156
William, s. Caleb & Jane, b. Jan. 4, 1735	LR1	353
WOOSTER, George, of Salisbury, m. Sarah Ann **BUSH**, of New York City, Nov. 29, 1845, by Rev. D.W. Clark	3	97
WRIGHT, Albert, s. William & Ann, b. May 6, 1802	3	39
Charles, s. William & Ann, b. Feb. 14, 1795	3	39
Ebenezer, of Mansfield, m. Anna **GALUSHA**, of Salisbury, Feb. 24, 1788, by Elisha Fitch, J.P.	2	43
Edward, s. William & Ann, b. Jan. 23, 1799	3	39
Harriet E., m. James **DEWITT**, b. of Salisbury, Sept. 11, 1844, by Rev. C.V. Amerman	3	96
Henry, s. Ebenezer & Anna, b. May 25, 1791, in Mansfield	3	15
John Wilton, s. Ebenezer & Anna, b. Nov. 22, 1793	3	15
Lucinda, d. Ebenezer & Anna, b. Feb. 15, 1789, in Mansfield	3	15
Martha, m. Matthew **TOUSLEY**, b. of Salisbury, Sept. 12, 1750, by Rev. Jonathan Lee	1	222
Mary, d. Benjamin & Joanna, b. Aug. 8, 1757	1	187
Mary, d. William & Ann, b. Sept. [ ], 1800	3	39
Mehitable, of Salisbury, m. Lyman Y. **ANDREWS**, of Winchester, Aug. 24, 1840, by Rev. Jacob Shaw	3	160
Robert H., of Torrington, m. Katharine **BENNETT**, of Salisbury, Jan. 1, 1847, by Robert N. Fuller, J.P.	3	100
Samuel, d. May 15, 1772, in the 93rd y. of his age	2	48
Sebil, m. William **MIX**, b. of Salisbury, Aug. 6, 1807, by Rev. Joseph W. Crossman	3	113
William, s. William & Ann, b. Nov. 10, 1796	3	39
W[illia]m, 3rd, of Mt. Washington, Mass., m. Jane N. **McCLROY**, of Salisbury, Apr. 11, 1847, by D.W. Clark	3	100
YATES, Sarah, d. William & Prudence, b. Sept. 22, 1775	2	9
YOUNGLOVE, Elizabeth, of Sheffield, m. Peter **SIRDAM**, of Salisbury, Oct. 5, 1748, by Rev. Jonathan Hobbart	1	224
NO SURNAME		
Catharine, b. Dec. 8, 1816	3	80a
Henry, [b.] June 11, 1785	2	34
Martha, b. Mar. 5, 1821	3	80a
Mary, m. Nath[anie]ll **EMERSON**, Sept. 1, 1785, by Elisha		

	Vol.	Page
NO SURNAME (cont.)		
Baker, J.P.	2	50
Moses, b. Sept. 23, 1818	3	80a
Newman, d. Aug. 3, 1818, ae 5 [yrs.] 5 m.	3	80a
Newman, b. Oct. 29, 1824	3	80a
Rufus, b. May 3, 1815	3	80a

www.ingramcontent.com/pod-product-compliance
Lightning Source LLC
Chambersburg PA
CBHW071238230426
43668CB00011B/1485